D0446851

600	400	200 BCE	0 CE	300
Zarathustra and origins of Zoroastrranism Magi preserve *Gathas* Achaemenid dynasty (558–330) Cyrus the Achaemenid (558–530) Conquest of Babylonia by Cyrus (539) Cambyses (530–522) Darius (521–486) Persian Wars (500–479) Xerxes (486–465)	Alexander invades Persia (334) Battle of Guagamela (331) Alexander crowned Persian king (330) Seleucid dynasty (323) Parthian dynasty (247)	Mithradates (171–155) Seleucids defeated by Rome (83)	Jesus of Nazareth	Spread of Manichaeism
Confucius (Kong Fuzi) (551–479)—*Analects* Laozi (6th century)—*Daodejing*	Shang Yang (390–338)—The Book of Lord Shang Mencius (372–289) Zhuangzi (369–286)—Zhuangzi Xunzi (298–238) Han Feizi (280–233) Qin unification of China (221) Qin Shihuangdi (221–210) Former Han Dynasty (206 B.C.E.–9 C.E.) Liu Bang (206)	Spread of Buddhism to Central Asia Han Wudi (141–87) Imperial university (124) Defeat of Xiongnu Opening of silk roads Sima Qian (99) Spread of Buddhism to China	Wang Mang (9–23) Later Han dynasty (23–220) Invention of paper (100) Epidemic disease Yellow Turban rebellion (189)	Nomadic invasions of northern China Early spread of Buddhism in China
Siddhartha Gautama, the Buddha (563–483) Vardhamana Mahavira (540–468) Charvaka sect (6th century) Darius of Persia conquers Gandhara Persian influence	Alexander of Macedon enters India (327) Unification under Chandragupta Maurya (321) *Arthashastra* Ashoka (268–232) Spread of Buddhism	Mauryan dynasty ends (185)	*Mahabharata* and *Ramayana* in written form	Gupta dynasty (320–550) Samudra Gupta (335–375) Chandra Gupta II (375–415) Final form of *Bhagavad Gita* (400) Nalanda Buddhist monastery founded
Development of an alphabetic script for the Meroitic language Arrival of domesticated camels in north Africa	Port city of Rhapta links east Africa to Indian Ocean trade networks	Roman conquest of Egypt (31)	Decline of hieroglyphic writing Foundation of the Kingdom of Axum	Adoption of Christianity in the Kingdom of Axum Arrival of Malay seafarers in Madagascar
Foundation of Teotihuacan in Mesoamerica Decline of Lapita trade networks	Decline of Chavin cult in Andes	Expansion of Teotihuacan in Mesoamerica Emergence of cities in Andean South America Austronesians reach Tahiti and Marquesas Islands		Maya society in Mesoamerica (300–900) Mochica state in Andes (300–700) Austronesians reach Hawai'i
Sappho (600) Solon's reforms and rise of democracy (500s) Establishment of Roman republic (509) Battles of Marathon (490) and Salamis (480) Golden Age of Athens (400s) Pericles, Socrates, Plato, Aristotle Aeschylus, Sophocles, Euripides Peloponnesian War (431–404)	Greek conquest by Phillip II of Macedon (359–336) Conquests of Alexander of Macedon (336–323) Antigonid, Ptolemaic, and Seleucid dynasties Hellenistic age Epicurianism, Skepticism, Stoicism Punic Wars (264–146)	Reforms and assassinations of Gracchi brothers (133–121) Marius and Sulla (87–78) Julius Caesar (100–44) Battle of Actium (31) Octavian receives title of Augustus (27) Pax Romana	Paul of Tarsus and spread of Christianity Epidemic disease (165–180) Mani and spread of Manichaeism Diocletian (284–305)	Constantine (313) Edict of Milan Theodosius—Christianity as official religion (380) St. Augustine (354–430) Rome falls to Odovacer (476)

ENCOUNTERS IN WORLD HISTORY

*Sources and Themes from the Global Past,
Volume One: To 1500*

FIRST EDITION

THOMAS SANDERS
United States Naval Academy

SAMUEL H. NELSON
United States Naval Academy

STEPHEN MORILLO
Wabash College

NANCY ELLENBERGER
United States Naval Academy

Boston Burr Ridge, IL Dubuque, IA Madison, WI New York
San Francisco St. Louis Bangkok Bogotá Caracas Kuala Lumpur
Lisbon London Madrid Mexico City Milan Montreal New Delhi
Santiago Seoul Singapore Sydney Taipei Toronto

The McGraw·Hill Companies

Higher Education

ENCOUNTERS IN WORLD HISTORY: SOURCES AND THEMES FROM THE GLOBAL
PAST, VOLUME 1: TO 1500
Published by McGraw-Hill, an imprint of The McGraw-Hill Companies, Inc., 1221 Avenue of the
Americas, New York, NY 10020. Copyright © 2006. All rights reserved. No part of this publication
may be reproduced or distributed in any form or by any means, or stored in a database or retrieval
system, without the prior written consent of The McGraw-Hill Companies, Inc., including, but not
limited to, in any network or other electronic storage or transmission, or broadcast for distance
learning.

This book is printed on acid-free paper.

3 4 5 6 7 8 9 0 DOC/DOC 0 9 8 7

ISBN: 978-0-07-245101-6
MHID: 0-07-245101-7

Vice president and Editor-in-chief:
   Emily G. Barrosse
Publisher: Lyn Uhl
Sponsoring editor: Jon-David Hague
Marketing manager: Katherine Bates
Developmental editor: Kristen Millett
Project manager: Carey Eisner
Manuscript editor: Elaine Kehoe
Design manager: Kim Menning
Interior and cover design: Glenda King

Art editor: Ayelet Arbel
Photo editor: Alexandra Ambrose
Photo researcher: Judy Mason
Production supervisor: Randy Hurst
Composition: 10/12 Galliard by
   Thompson Type
Printing: 45# New Era Plus by R. R. Donnelley
Cover: The voyages of Marco Polo (from the
   Book of Wonders). 15th century manuscript.
   © Snark / Art Resource, NY

Credits: The credits section for this book begins on page 455 and is considered an extension of the
copyright page.

Library of Congress Cataloging-in-Publication Data
Encounters in world history : sources and themes from the global past / Thomas Sanders . . .
  [et al.].—1st ed.
    p. cm.
  Contents: v. 1. To 1500 — v. 2. From 1500.
  ISBN 0-07-245101-7 (softcover : v. 1) — ISBN 0-07-245103-3 (softcover : v. 2)
    1. History—Examinations, questions, etc.   2. World history.   3. World history—Sources.
  4. Historiography.   5. History—Philosophy.   I. Sanders, Thomas, 1951–

D21.E575 2005
907'.6—dc22   2005041590

The Internet addresses listed in the text were accurate at the time of publication. The inclusion of a
website does not indicate an endorsement by the authors or McGraw-Hill, and McGraw-Hill does not
guarantee the accuracy of the information presented at these sites.

http://www.mhhe.com

To Jolene, Brooke, Joseph, and Jose for their love and support,
and to my mentors, colleagues, and students
for all that they taught me.—TS

To my family.—SHN

To Lynne, Robin, Dione, and Raphael:
you can have the computer back now.
And to Velazquez, Vermeer, and Georgia,
missed but not forgotten.—SRM

ABOUT THE AUTHORS

THOMAS SANDERS received his doctorate in Russian history from Stanford University. He has taught at a variety of colleges and universities, including Stanford, Georgia Southern, the University of Dayton, Oberlin College, and since 1990 at the United States Naval Academy. His most recent book is a collaborative translation and commentary entitled *Against the Mountains: Qarakhi's Shining Swords and Tolstoy's Hadji Murat Depict Russian-Muslim Conflict in the Caucasus* (Routledge-Curzon, 2004). He has just begun a biography of the Soviet composer Vladimir Shainskii.

SAMUEL H. NELSON's interest in world cultures began during his service in the Peace Corps, when he taught secondary school in a small town in the Congo. Afterwards, he studied African history and anthropology at Stanford University, where he received his PhD. He joined the faculty of the United States Naval Academy in 1987 and created courses on African history, comparative world cultures, and illness and therapy. He has conducted fieldwork in central and southern Africa, and is the author of a history of the Congo basin and, more recently, articles on the HIV/AIDS epidemic in Africa.

STEPHEN MORILLO grew up in New Orleans, received his AB from Harvard and his DPhil from Oxford. He has taught at Loyola (New Orleans), the University of Georgia, and since 1989 at Wabash College, with a year at Hawai'i Pacific University as their NEH Distinguished Visiting Professor in 2003–04. He is the author of several books and numerous articles on various combinations of medieval, military, and global history.

NANCY ELLENBERGER received a BA in political science from Wellesley College, an MA in International Relations from the University of Chicago, and a PhD in British history from the University of Oregon. Her interest in global history grew out of this eclectic background and was reinforced by her teaching of the history of the British Empire at the United States Naval Academy, where she has been on the faculty since 1983. Her research interests center around the British social and political elites of the late-Victorian and Edwardian generation.

BRIEF CONTENTS

CONTENTS

❧

Preface   xxi

PART TWO

FOUNDATION CULTURES: 600 BCE TO 300 CE

PART THREE

THE TRADITIONAL WORLD: 300 CE TO 1100 CE

PART FOUR
TOWARD A GLOBAL WORLD: 1100 CE TO 1500 CE

PREFACE

❧❦❧

History is an encounter with the past, and the past is a history of encounters. This book is designed to introduce students to both of these sorts of encounters.

APPROACH

The past as a history of encounters is the organizing theme of this book. Each chapter consists of primary sources illustrating various encounters between and within civilizations and cultures. Some encounters involved one group of humans meeting another group of humans, and so encountering different ways of life, modes of thought, and ambitions. Some of these sorts of encounters produced violent confrontations: the meeting of settled farming-based societies with nomadic herding-based societies, or the encounter of industry-based imperial powers with nonindustrial peoples in the nineteenth century, often resulted in warfare. But many, as in the encounters different peoples had with practitioners of new religions, were peaceful, resulting in exchanges of ideas, goods, and populations. Sometimes such encounters produced both peaceful and violent outcomes. The variety of human encounters is one of the things that makes studying history so interesting.

Another sort of encounter this book presents is more abstract, involving not the meeting of separate groups of people, but the encounter of groups of people with their environment, and even more abstractly, the encounter of groups of people with the problems of living together in a functioning society. People encountered nature and their need to explain it; they encountered the conflict between the need for social order and the need for individual freedom and generated codes of behavior; and they encountered divisions in their society, whether based on gender, class, or other sorts of divisions.

We strove to put before the student substantive selections that present the historical evidence for cultural encounters as directly as possible, but in a context that makes the problems the sources address comprehensible. The problem of context and comprehension is a perennial issue in World Civilization courses; we believe the "encounter" format will be effective both in enriching students' understanding and in helping to provide unity and coherence to the ideas that instructors are trying to get across.

In presenting not a finished narrative of world history, but a selection of sources on which such a narrative could be based, this book shows students some of the evidence that historians use and invites them to interpret that evidence themselves and come to their own conclusions. In other words, it invites them to become historians and to join the constant work in progress that is history.

GENERAL ORGANIZATION AND PRIMARY SOURCES

While "encounters" serves as our overall conceptual device, the book is organized in a broadly chronological fashion, and each chapter is organized around a particular theme. In this way, we have been able to introduce general concepts such as authority, violence, gender, transcendent spirituality, and so on, concepts that are useful in the analysis of concrete historical situations from global human history. We hope by means of the encounters idea and the thematic elements integrated into the various chapters to participate productively in the current effort to present world civilization and history in an integrated and meaningful fashion. We aspire, as well, to assist instructors in providing students not merely with new information, but also with new ways of thinking about the human historical experience.

To provide instructors flexibility in their assignments, we have sought to incorporate a range of civilizations and to rely on as diverse a set of "texts"—including various nonwritten materials—as possible. The encounters themselves were chosen according to criteria of (1) cross-cultural interest or significance, (2) appropriateness to the chronological periods of world history, and (3) applicability to classroom instruction. It is our desire that instructors in all areas of specialization, research interest, and pedagogical approach find in our reader materials that suit their purposes and help them communicate their interpretations of world civilization to their students. To that end, the selections have been judiciously edited to be manageable for students, while retaining enough length to provide a fuller feel for the civilizations that produced these sources and allow students to formulate their own opinions.

We have tried to arrive at a useful mix of new materials and of "classic," well-established sources. In many cases, even when we have included well-known sources, we have used nontraditional selections or edited the material in novel ways consistent with the perspective of a given chapter's theme. The inclusion of both new materials and new approaches to traditional sources makes this book unique.

CHAPTER ORGANIZATION

Each chapter begins with a general introduction, providing students with the context and background required to appreciate the sources that follow. For example, we attempt to connect particular historical encounters with modern versions of the same sorts of encounters. Comparing how different societies have handled similar problems again shows the variety of human experience, but also offers lessons (if only, at times, in what not to do!). The possibility of learning from the past is another valuable outcome of studying history.

A set of general questions follows the chapter introduction, to orient readers and help them make connections among all of the sources in the chapter. Brief Introductions to each group of related sources outline the cultural and historical context in which the encounter occurred and, just as importantly, seek to locate the encounter conceptually for readers without telling them what to think or what they will discover in exploring the sources themselves. Similarly, a set of Questions to Consider precedes each group of sources, guiding students' reading without telling them what to think or burdening them with a theoretical apparatus. It is our intention that the dialogue established between the documents will (1) give the students a richer information source on which to base their judgments and (2) by focusing on perceptions and ways of "seeing" the other, allow for student assessments even in the absence of extensive background information on the specific cultures.

ACKNOWLEDGMENTS

Many people contributed to making this book both possible and better than it otherwise would have been. The authors would like to thank the following reviewers, who read the manuscript and offered helpful feedback:

Thomas Callahan
Rider University

Douglas B. Chambers
University of Southern Mississippi

Denise Z. Davidson
Georgia State University

Paul B. Goodwin, Jr.
University of Connecticut

Russell A. Hart
Hawai'i Pacific University

Scott W. Howlett
Saddleback College

Jonathan Judaken
University of Memphis

Eric C. Rust
Baylor University

William A. Wood
Point Loma Nazarene University

Sanders, Nelson, and Ellenberger would like to thank those Naval Academy colleagues who so generously shared their scholarly expertise and their teaching experience during many lunchtime teaching seminars and corridor chats. They note with particular gratitude the patient advice rendered by Larry Thompson, Dan Masterson, Mary DeCredico, David Peeler, Ernie Tucker, Maochun Yu, Brian VanDeMark, Lori Bogle, and Allison Mellis. In addition to his erudition and collegial assistance, Rich Abels put us in touch with Stephen Morillo. They also express their deep appreciation to Barbara Manvel of Nimitz Library, who chased down our obscure references and rare sources with unflagging energy and resourcefulness. Morillo thanks Wabash College, Hawai'i Pacific University, and the National Endowment for the Humanities for jointly funding the sabbatical year during which much of his work was accomplished; his colleagues, especially in the History Department and the Cultures and Traditions Program at Wabash, for suggestions and ongoing communal discussions about teaching primary sources (with special thanks to David Blix and Joe Day); and Judy Oswalt for valuable technical assistance. Finally, all the authors would like to express our appreciation to Lyn Uhl, who has been a patient, supportive, and knowledgeable editor throughout this long process, and to Kristen Mellitt and the rest of the McGraw-Hill staff, who skillfully picked up the project and steered it through the final shoals to completion.

Thomas Sanders
Samuel H. Nelson
Stephen Morillo
Nancy Ellenberger

PART ONE

EARLY HUMAN
SOCIETIES
TO 600 BCE

CHAPTER 1

Doing History

Using Evidence to Unlock the Human Past

INTRODUCTION

History is an encounter with the past, and the past is a history of encounters. This book is designed to introduce you to both of these sorts of encounters.

The past as a history of encounters is the organizing theme of this book. Each chapter presents sources that illustrate a certain type of encounter common to human history but that focus chronologically on a period of particular importance for that encounter. Some encounters involved one group of humans meeting another group of humans, and so encountering different ways of life, modes of thought, and ambitions. Some of these sorts of encounters produced violent confrontations: the meetings of settled farming-based societies with nomadic herding-based societies or the encounters of industrially based imperial powers with nonindustrial peoples in the nineteenth century often resulted in warfare. But many, as in the encounters different peoples had with practitioners of new religions, were peaceful, resulting in exchanges of ideas, goods, and populations. Sometimes such encounters produced both peaceful and violent outcomes. The variety of human encounters is one of the things that makes studying history so interesting.

Another sort of encounter this book presents is more abstract, involving not the meeting of separate groups of people but the encounter of groups of people with their environment and, even more abstractly, the encounter of groups of people with the problems of living together in a functioning society. People encountered nature and their need to explain it; they encountered the conflict between the need for social order and the need for individual freedom and generated codes of behavior; and they encountered divisions in their society, whether based on gender, class, or other sorts of divisions. In presenting historical instances of such encounters, we attempt in the chapter introductions to connect them with modern versions of the same sorts of encounters. Comparing how different societies have handled similar problems again shows the variety of human experience and also offers lessons (if only, at times, in what not to do!). The possibility of learning from the past is another of the things that makes studying history interesting.

Learning from or, more generally, encountering the past, however, raises several difficult problems. The first is the problem of evidence: How do we know about the past? What parts of it do we encounter? The second is the problem of interpretation: no piece of evidence, no source, speaks clearly and unambiguously for itself. Historians must extract meaning from the sources they have, and they often disagree with each other about what particular sources mean. Not all differing interpretations are contradictory, it should be noted. Different historians ask different questions of the sources, depending on their interests and the issues relevant to them in their own time and place. The encounter between different interpretations of the past can often produce a fuller, more complex understanding of the past than any single version could achieve.

In presenting to you not a finished narrative of world history but the selections of sources on which such a narrative could be based, this book shows you some of the evidence that historians use and invites you to interpret it yourself and come to your own conclusions. In other words, it invites you to become a historian and to join the constant work in progress that is history, a work fueled by historians' encounter with the evidence of the past and with each other.

Sources and Evidence

There are many different kinds of evidence about what happened in the past, and evidence and interpretations are inextricably linked together. Before we turn to the difficult evidence for early human history, let's think about the problem a bit more. Imagine that you return home one evening to an apartment you share with a roommate. You call out "Hello," but no one answers: evidence that your roommate is not there. You walk into the kitchen and discover a pile of freshly dirty dishes in the sink. More evidence—but of what? Physical evidence of this sort does not tell its own story; you must interpret it. Fairly clearly, your roommate had dinner. Careful examination of the dishes might tell you what was on the menu. Applying your knowledge of your roommate's habits, you conclude further that, because your roommate is not normally a slob about dishes, either her character has taken a turn for the worse or something came up suddenly. You lean toward the latter interpretation, but exactly what came up is still, with this sort of evidence, a mystery. You then notice that the dishwashing liquid is empty. You now lean to the interpretation that your roommate dashed out to the store for more and will return shortly. But then you find a note. It says "Amber called with tickets to the show!!! Had to run—back later!!!" As you had discussed this show with your roommate, you now know pretty clearly what happened (and are perhaps jealous).

You have, in short, been a historian of a tiny part of the recent past. You used physical evidence (the dishes) of the sort often uncovered by archaeologists. You used the evidence of patterns of human behavior (in this case, your roommate's habits) of the sort developed by anthropologists from the study of many different societies. And you used a piece of written evidence (the note) of the sort most

commonly used by historians. Any one gave you part of a picture; all three together gave you a pretty clear picture.

But note how much interpretation is built into your "reading" of each of these
kinds of evidence already and how delicate the "truth" of your reading is. The
empty dishwashing liquid already had temporarily led you astray and, without the
note, would have formed a perfectly reasonable piece of physical evidence for a
different interpretation. Your knowledge of your roommate has unthinkingly led
you to avoid any interpretation based on the note being a lie. And the references
in the note are clear to you: your mutual friend Amber and the nature of the show
are both known to you. How much these "built-in" interpretations help your
reading of the evidence becomes clearer if we change some aspects of the scenario.

What if you'd walked into a stranger's apartment and found the same set of
evidence? You might still get a fair idea of what happened, but you'd be less sure
of the details. What if the apartment were in a foreign country, so that the dishes,
the food, even the sink are different from what you expect? Maybe people in this
country don't wash dishes. Even worse, you can't read the note, because it's in a
foreign language. Unless you can find someone to translate it for you, it won't
help you much. What if you do find a translator and he tells you it says "Amber
yelled about papers for the display. Must exercise—back later." Not, in fact, an
unreasonable translation, but one that leads you wildly astray in interpreting the
scene. (And would "show" mean more to you than "display" if you had no idea
what the show was?) Now assume that much of the evidence has disappeared:
many of the dishes are gone, the food has dried up or been eaten by insects, the
dishwashing liquid has evaporated (or was it gone in the first place?), and half the
note has been torn off and lost. Can you figure out what happened?

Welcome to encountering the past as a historian. "The past is a foreign country," as the historian E. P. Hartley once said, "they do things differently there."
Much of the evidence has been lost. And the people of the past aren't going to return after the show to tell you whether you got it right. Clearly, there will be room
for different interpretations of the past, many (though not all) of them quite reasonable, and some of the perfectly reasonable ones completely contradictory.
Equally clearly, the more evidence and the more different kinds of evidence that
historians can examine for any particular part of the past, the better their interpretations of that part will be, for evidence does not determine interpretations, but it
does constrain them. This book presents you with a selection of evidence to examine directly.

Early Human History

This first chapter provides an introduction to the problems of evidence and interpretation through an examination of early human history. Because there are no
written sources for most of this period, it is sometimes referred to as "prehistory,"
on the assumption that history emerges with writing. But because any evidence
from and about the past (including oral accounts, which are valuable even when
writing is pervasive) is material for the historian, we see no reason to make the
"prehistory" distinction. The whole past is history.

The part of the past that includes humans, or at least human ancestors, dates to about 6 million years ago in Africa. According to genetic evidence, that was when humans and chimpanzees, our closest living relatives, diverged evolutionarily. The family tree of early hominids (human ancestors who are not counted in the genus *homo*, meaning "man" in Latin) is complicated and subject to continual debate and revision by paleoanthropologists (those who study the oldest human populations), but the broad outlines are agreed upon, so its details need not concern us here. Already marked by the binocular vision and opposable thumbs common to apes, ancestral hominids developed bipedalism (walking on two feet, leaving the hands free) before 4 million years ago. By perhaps 2.5 million years ago the early human species *homo habilis* (literally "handy man"), probably ancestral to modern humans, had learned to fashion and use simple stone tools. By roughly 1.9 million years ago early humans of the species *homo ergaster,* whose brains were about three-quarters the size of those of modern humans, were not only making stone tools but had mastered the use of fire. *Homo erectus* ("erect man"), a branch of these early humans, became the first hominids to move out of Africa, occupying the temperate and tropical zones of Asia starting around 1 million years ago.

Then, about 200,000 years ago, a separate group descended from *homo ergaster* emerged in east Africa as the modern human species *homo sapiens* ("wise man"). The evidence for this date comes from both genetics and comparative linguistics; the first *homo sapiens* fossils date only to 130,000 years ago. The oldest *homo sapiens* fossils outside of Africa were found in southwest Asia and date to 90,000 years ago. Almost as early is the first evidence of not only new sorts of tools but also the first new products that could have artistic or ritual significance. Certainly by the period starting 40,000 years ago, with some hints dating well before that, there was an explosion of technology and art, as well as a tremendous expansion of the geographic range of *homo sapiens* (and their close relatives *homo neanderthalis,* Neanderthal man) into areas never colonized by *homo erectus,* including subarctic and arctic climes and land masses such as Australia, separated from the Afro-Eurasian mainland by significant stretches of open water. By 14,000 years ago humans occupied all the major continents except Antarctica.

Up to this point, all humans had lived by hunting and gathering. By 10,000 years ago agriculture had appeared in a few areas; domestication of plants and animals would be repeated independently several times and spread from those various points of origin. Agriculture made possible permanent settlements, more complex societies, and the whole range of activities, inventions, and cultures that make up most of history since then.

We will look at physical evidence of various sorts from three important aspects of early human history, each of which tells us something about the deep roots of many human activities. First, the development of the human toolkit shows humans as increasingly effective manipulators of their environment, as well as giving some insight into the development of the capacities for self-conscious intelligence and symbolic communication that characterize humans as biological creatures. We examine some of the earliest stone tools, down through the increasingly sophisticated technologies that preceded the invention of agriculture and the emergence of the complex, literate societies that dominate the bulk of later history. Second, at the same time that the toolkit was suddenly expanding, art and evidence for ritual behavior appear, providing us with even more direct evidence for the thought processes, not just the activities, of early humans. Finally, from the end of this period, we present evidence of early permanent settlements in areas where agriculture joined the human toolkit, the development of trade between such settlements, and the ways in which art and ritual began to shape the constructed environments of human habitation. The "house" of evidence for early human history is particularly bare, including the fact that there are no "notes"— no writing of any kind—until the very end of this period, around 5,000 years ago. So the problems of interpreting this evidence highlight the challenges of the historian's craft with great clarity. Experts disagree about what much of the evidence means, so if you feel lost, or if you disagree with your classmates about some of it, that just shows that you're really doing history. Good luck, and have fun.

CHAPTER QUESTIONS

1. As you walk into the "house" of early humans represented by this whole chapter's worth of pictorial evidence, what seems strange to you? That is, what part of this is "foreign country"?

2. What part, on the other hand, seems familiar? That is, what are the points of connection between your own life (including your tools, art, and habitation, broadly defined) and those of early humans?

3. Is there a noticeable break in the evidence at which things become more familiar, or at least less strange? If so, when does this break occur, and what are its significant features?

4. What do these features say about what is "essentially human" about all people, if anything?

5. How difficult is it to answer such questions, or come to any firm conclusions at all, in the absence of written documentation? Are some nonwritten sources clearer than others in telling a story and inviting certain interpretations?

THE HUMAN TOOLKIT

The basic "tool" of all humans, and the one that makes use of all other tools possible, is the intelligence generated by a brain that is, as a percentage of body weight, unusually large. Sheer size does not necessarily equate to high intelligence; the ratio of brain weight to body weight and the complexity of the internal organization of the brain are more important. But what the fossil record illustrates is the growth in the size of human brains, much of which is very recent in evolutionary terms. What can we learn about the evolution of human intelligence and cognitive capabilities from this fossil record?

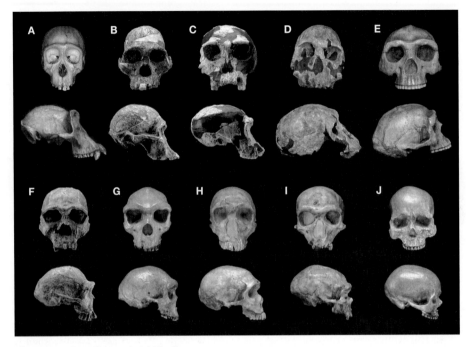

Figure 1.1 Fossil Hominid Skulls

Figure 1.1 shows the changes in skull shape that characterize human evolution. It understates the growth in size because the pictures are not all to the same scale—the later skulls are significantly larger than the earlier ones. The skulls belong to the following species, with the date of the particular fossil noted.

A. *Pan troglodytes,* a modern chimpanzee, our closest living relative.

B. *Australopithecus africanus,* 2.6 million years ago. *A. africanus* walked upright, used simple stone tools, and had a brain about one-third the size of a modern human brain.

C. *Homo habilis,* 1.8 million years ago. *Homo habilis* made and used a variety of simple stone tools and had a brain perhaps half the size of a modern human brain.

D. *Homo rudolfensis,* 1.8 million years ago. *H. rudolfensis* was similar to and contemporary with *H. habilis* and is the more likely ancestor of later human species.

E. *Homo erectus,* 1.75 million years ago. *Homo erectus* is the branch of *homo ergaster* (see next entry) that left Africa. With a brain about two-thirds the size of a modern human's, *Homo erectus* used a somewhat more complex set of stone tools than earlier species and mastered the use of fire.

F. *Homo ergaster* (early *H. erectus*), 1.75 million years ago. The variant of *Homo erectus,* slightly more similar to modern humans, that stayed in

Africa and invented a significant advance in the production of chipped stone tools known as Acheulean technology.

G. *Homo heidelbergensis,* "Rhodesia man," 300,000–125,000 years ago. Sometimes called archaic modern humans, Rhodesia man's brain was around three-quarters of the size of a modern human's. Ancestor, in Africa, of both Neanderthals and modern humans.

H. *Homo sapiens neanderthalensis,* 70,000 years ago.

I. *Homo sapiens neanderthalensis,* 60,000 years ago. Contrary to popular imagery, Neanderthals were not stupid hulking brutes but were a closely related variant of modern humans who shared some (but not all) of the technological and cultural advances of *Homo sapiens* before dying out about 30,000 years ago.

J. *Homo sapiens sapiens,* "Cro-Magnon man," 30,000 years ago. Our species that, starting at least 70,000 years ago, initiated a revolution in material and intellectual culture that continues to this day.

In examining this set of skulls, the growth of size is obvious. So is the change in shape, which is at least as significant for changes in the cognitive, or thinking, processes in human species. Look especially at two areas. The frontal lobes (at the front of the brain) are associated with complex abstract cognition, including many processes crucial to language use. The parietal lobe (on top toward the rear) is associated with technological, abstract, and computational thinking.

QUESTIONS TO CONSIDER

1. Where and when does growth occur in the size and shape of human brains?
2. Do changes seem to correlate with what we know of tool use and other cultural advances?
3. Many scientists now talk not of intelligence but of multiple intelligences, computational modules that evolved, separately at times, for things such as tool use, knowledge of plants and animals, social relations with other humans (including facial recognition), and different aspects of communication. Do the changes illustrated in Figure 1.1 seem to support this sort of theory?
4. Are any of your conclusions clear and firm? What other evidence would you want to correlate with fossils like these in order to learn more about the evolution of human cognitive abilities?

For most of the history of early humans, the basic toolkit consisted of simple stone tools, most often created by chipping part of a stone off with another stone to create a cutting or scraping edge, making a simple hand axe. Our next pictures are of these sorts of tools.

Figure 1.2 Hand axe from Africa, about 1,800,000 Years Ago

Figure 1.3 Hand axe from
France, about 250,000 Years Ago

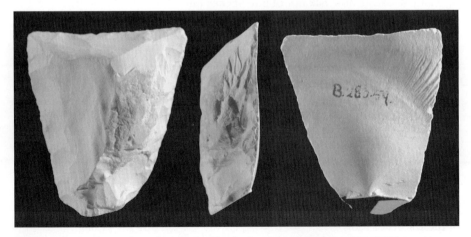

Figure 1.4 Hand axes from Northern Rhodesia, about 100,000 to 200,000 Years Ago

QUESTIONS TO CONSIDER

1. What sorts of tasks do the tools in Figures 1.2–1.4 look useful for? What do they tell you about the life of early human hunters and gatherers?
2. How much do the tools change over time? Why do you think the toolkit changed so little over such a long period? What does this tell you about the cognitive abilities of early humans?
3. If, as we noted about the evolution of multiple intelligences, toolmaking in *homo erectus* and *homo ergaster* was a separate cognitive ability from, say, language and social interaction, how might this account for the slow pace of technological change?

You can see where the rocks have been chipped to make edges and that there's a certain amount of skill involved in making any of these tools. But note also how little difference there is between the axe from almost 2 million years ago and the axe from 250,000 years ago. This is typical of the toolkits of *homo erectus* and *homo ergaster*—even the improvements made by the latter (reflected in the bottom two axes) are minor by modern standards of technological innovation. Further-more, tools from this period are always of one material, never of two combined (wooden spears were not fitted with stone spear points, bows and arrows did not exist yet), and, except for a broad variant from southeast Asia (where suitable stone was uncommon, leading to use of bamboo for some tools), *homo erectus* tools were not adapted to the peculiarities of particular locations.

Then, starting at least 70,000 years ago (probably earlier, but the evidence is scarce and sometimes contested), and certainly only in association with fossils of anatomically modern humans—*homo sapiens*—the human toolkit changes. The changes are particularly dramatic after 40,000 years ago in Europe, the beginning of what paleontologists call the Upper Paleolithic (or latest Old Stone Age) pe-riod, which coincides with the arrival of *homo sapiens* in Europe at the ultimate ex-pense of Neanderthals. Figures 1.5 and 1.6 illustrate the change.

In addition, we get our first evidence of constructed human habitations, such as mammoth bone huts in Russia. The foundations of one such hut, dating to roughly 20,000 years ago, are shown in Figure 1.7.

QUESTIONS TO CONSIDER

1. What do the tools in Figures 1.5 and 1.6 look useful for? What do these tools and habitations tell you about the lives of early modern humans?
2. How are the lives of early modern humans similar to the lives of earlier human species such as *homo erectus*? How are they different? Are the similarities or the differences more important?

Figure 1.5 Stone Blades
from Upper Paleolithic

3. What sort of change in human cognitive abilities had to happen for people to suddenly improve on a two-million-year-old toolkit so dramatically? Do the inventors of these tools seem fully human to you?

UPPER PALEOLITHIC STONE TOOLS AND HABITATION

The craftsmanship, the variety of sizes and shapes, and the efficiency of manufacture of these tools are clearly significantly advanced over the earlier hand axes. Figure 1.5 shows a number of stone blades—tools more than twice as long as they were wide, which provided more cutting surface and more efficient use of raw materials. Better stone tools facilitated the production of bone needles (the second object in Figure 1.6) and specialized hunting tools such as the barbed harpoon point (the fourth object) and, as the fifth object shows, the combining of materials to produce stone-pointed spears, arrows, and harpoons. Another new characteristic of Upper Paleolithic tools was that they were constructed from materials available only far from where the tools were made, indicating the early emergence of trade networks. These sophisticated tools in turn allowed the creation of sewn clothing and constructed shelters.

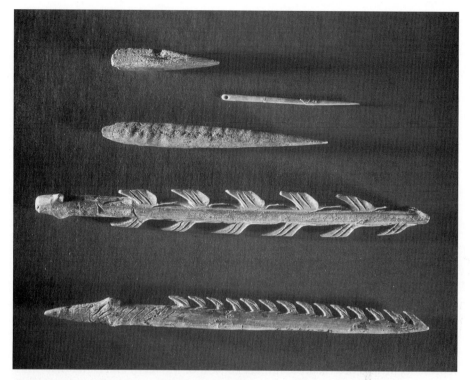

Figure 1.6 Stone Tools from Upper Paleolithic

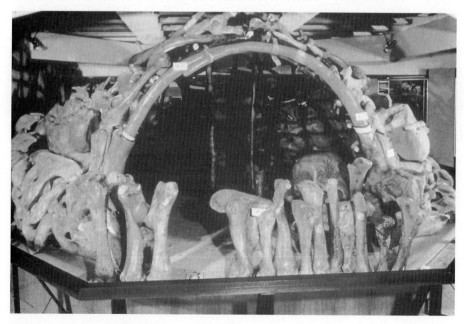

Figure 1.7 Habitation from Upper Paleolithic

The circular hut was constructed with a foundation of interlocked mammoth jaw bones supporting ribs and other bones. The mammoth hunters then covered this frame with mammoth hides stitched together and tied down at the foundations. Inside, they laid down mammoth-skin rugs and slept on furs from fox, wolf, and other animals. They made tools and decorative objects from the ivory tusks and ate the meat—sometimes this was all they ate. All this attests to the degree of specialization and adaptation to particular (and sometimes very harsh) environments *homo sapiens* could achieve using what was clearly a new level of cognitive ability. It also attests, sadly but impressively, to the hunting efficiency such specialization brought and the degree of impact humans could now have on their environment: mammoths, like many large animals in territories in which humans arrived suddenly—especially Australia and the Americas—were eventually hunted to extinction. In Australia and the Americas, such extinctions took only a few thousand years.

The Human Toolkit and the Human Encounter with Nature

The human toolkit introduces us to one of the first major encounters of human history, that between humans and their natural environment. Tools such as those shown in the figures, in addition to the taming of fire, were used for dealing with natural challenges, primarily the fundamental problem of finding sufficient food. But in this sense the human toolkit, at least up to 40,000 years ago (in Europe), represents little more than the human version of the teeth and claws that other predators employed to the same end.

And, indeed, the limited nature of the human toolkit, and even more the extremely slow rate at which it changed, raise a central question for the interpretation of such evidence: Was nature, especially the search for food, not in fact the primary challenge to their intelligence that early humans faced? That breakthroughs in the human toolkit and humans' encounter with nature are associated with a whole range of other developments in human culture and, by inference from this other evidence, in human cognitive capabilities suggests that a more challenging encounter than food gathering may have been driving the increase in human brain size that led to the emergence of the modern human species. It is to these developments and this second encounter that we now turn.

THE EMERGENCE OF ART AND RITUAL

If tools alone are not enough to give a sense of the modern mental capabilities of Stone Age *homo sapiens,* technology alone also cannot account for the efficiency of the hunting techniques of modern humans compared with those of their ancestors. Another sort of evidence that appears at the same time as the new and improved human toolkit, however, may offer further insight into both areas. That evidence is the emergence of art, personal decoration, and what at least looks like ritual, especially with regard to death, again starting at least 70,000 years ago but again showing up dramatically and regularly in Europe (whose prehistoric remains have been more extensively studied than elsewhere) from the beginning of the Upper Paleolithic period 40,000 years ago.

Some of that evidence can be seen in Figures 1.8–1.13.

The three pictures in Figures 1.8–1.10 come from the central French region of limestone hills riddled with caves. People used them during the last Ice Age 30,000 years ago for shelter and also as the site of the production of some of the most amazing artwork in history. The pictures of the horse and the bull are from the largest and most famous cave at Lascaux; the drawing of a mammoth is from a nearby cave at Rouffignac.

Figure 1.11 is a famous figurine, about 5 inches tall, known as the Venus of Willendorf, after the site in Germany where it was found.

At the top of Figure 1.12 are four carved ivory disks, perhaps used as decorations on spears. At the bottom is a carved ivory animal pendant designed to be strung together with numerous small beads on a necklace or bracelet. It still shows traces of red paint. The ivory comes from a mammoth tusk, and the objects were found in an excavation in Russia.

Figure 1.13 is a musical wind instrument similar to a flute or recorder, made from bird bone. It was discovered at a southern French site that dates to between 28,000 and 22,000 years ago.

Figure 1.14 shows an adult male buried at Sunghir in Russia 28,000 years ago.

Figure 1.8 Cave Art: Horse

Figure 1.9 Cave Art: Bull

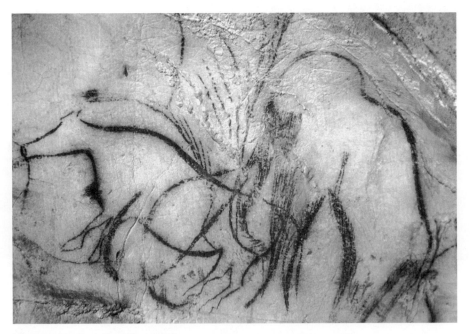

Figure 1.10 Cave Art: Mammoth

Figure 1.11 Venus of Willendorf

QUESTIONS TO CONSIDER

1. What characteristics of the artistic objects in Figures 1.8–1.13 and their contexts stand out to you?

2. What do they tell you about the lives of their makers? What does this evidence, added to the evidence of tools, add to your understanding of these early humans? Can you see more about social life, and if so, what do you see?

3. How do the lives of these people differ from the world of *homo erectus?* What are the similarities? Are the similarities or the differences more striking?

4. What does this evidence tell you about how these people viewed their world, what they believed about it, and what characteristics they attributed to it (as opposed to simply how they lived in it)?

5. What sort of changes in how early humans thought or how they related to each other could account for the sudden appearance of art and ritual and all they imply about belief systems in this period?

Figure 1.12 Ivory Carvings

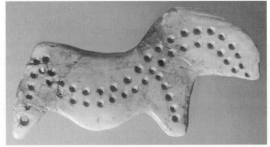

The cave art is quite varied. Different pictures are drawn, painted, or engraved—a full range of modern picture-making techniques—and the artistic quality of the representations of animals in motion is stunning. A range of technologies, including scaffolds, fat-burning lamps, and pigment making, supported the efforts of the artists.

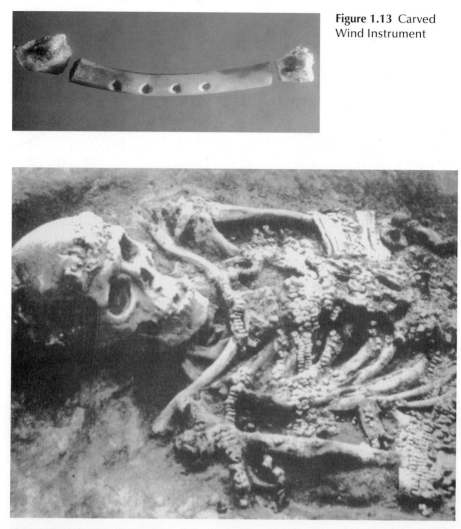

Figure 1.13 Carved Wind Instrument

Figure 1.14 Human Skeleton

The content of this art is always animals, people, or cryptic symbols; plants, landscapes, and so forth are never subjects. Many of the scenes are hunting scenes. This has led many interpreters to see in these drawings not just art for art's sake (if such a thing exists) but a visual aspect of hunting rituals, ranging from a form of previsualization of a successful hunt (something like the visualization of successful technique sometimes recommended by sports psychologists) to a ritual invocation of nature spirits for a successful hunt or a ritual propitiation of the spirits of animals already killed or about to be killed (suggested by the abstract symbols that sometimes accompany the animal and human figures). The focus on hunting to the exclusion of gathering has also led some to infer that the drawings relate to reinforcing gender roles (hunting was generally a male activity, gathering female).

Gender roles clearly influence the female figurine in Figure 1.11. The "Venus" designation of this small statue is now sometimes replaced simply with "woman," as it is not at all clear what the figurine "means" or was used for. It is, like the cave drawings of animals, a masterpiece of representational art: the artist depicts an obese (not pregnant) woman, forearms held over her breasts, vulva emphasized. She never had feet, and she lacks a face, though this may be interpreted as her head bent down onto her chest, better displaying her hair, which actually spirals down from the top of the head.

Seeing the figurine as a representation of a particular woman, however, is problematic on two counts. First, female figurines of this sort (as well as less obese ones, including clearly younger females) are common across a large part of Upper Paleolithic Europe. (Male figures are much less common.) Second, extremely obese people, male or female, cannot have been common among a population that made its living by hunting and gathering, so any real model for such figurines must have had some rare special status.

The most common interpretations focus on the prominent vulva, which shows traces of a red pigment that may have represented menstrual blood, the breasts, and the hair, emphasized at the expense of any facial features and important to sexual attraction for its odor-bearing qualities. They see in such figurines fertility amulets, perhaps designed to be carried in a hand (in which they fit very comfortably). An older line of interpretation that saw these figurines as representations of a universal "Mother Goddess" was based on no real evidence and has largely been abandoned, though its traces still remain in the sometime-designation "Venus."

The flute is an especially remarkable object. Music is not just a form of art or entertainment but a form of symbolic communication, like painting. Some anthropologists speculate about the role of music, in connection with rhythmic dancing, in training hunters to work together at a complex physical task requiring careful timing; others about the possible role of music in mating behavior; and others about the connection of musical and linguistic ability. Wherever the truth lies, music clearly attests to the changed cognitive and cultural capacities of early *homo sapiens*.

The context for the discovery of such objects of personal decoration or use is often burial sites. The earliest instances of intentional burial of the dead are contested, because it is difficult to tell accidental burial from an intentional act in many instances. Such questions complicate the evidence for Neanderthal burial practices, which may have been purely utilitarian (dead bodies would have attracted predators and scavengers, so they may have been buried without the burial taking on any symbolic or ritual significance). But obviously arranged graves, with burial objects associated with and on the corpse, began to become increasingly common around 40,000 years ago, always in association with *homo sapiens* remains.

The body of the man interred at Sunghir (Figure 1.14) was buried fully stretched out, which requires a larger hole to be dug than if the body is bent up. He wears the remains of a headdress decorated with mammoth-ivory beads, a tunic onto which were sewn thousands of ivory beads, and several ivory bracelets on his arms. Modern experiments in making ivory beads suggest that the decoration on this man took several thousand hours of labor to create—and he is less adorned than the corpses of two adolescents buried at the same site. With arranged burial accompanied by personal objects we have direct evidence for at least some level of ritual behavior in human populations.

Art, Ritual, and Humans' Encounter with Themselves

Art and ritual highlight even more the problem we posed at the end of the section on tools. They have no obvious and immediate utilitarian benefit in terms of subsistence, and yet humans began spending vast amounts of effort producing such things—think of the thousands of hours invested in making the ivory beads buried with the man at Sunghir. Why? And what does this tell us about what changed in the way humans thought? Complicating the question is the fact that, though art appears to have no immediate benefit to hunting, the efficiency of humans as hunters improved in step with their artistic ability.

Anthropologists agree that art and ritual play crucial roles in social relationships. What people wear, what they eat, how they decorate themselves and their surroundings send important signals about who they are, and so are fundamental in constructing people's social connections. They can signal hierarchy, power, relatedness, and so on. The appearance of art and ritual therefore says something important about the growing complexity of the human social environment (as opposed to the fairly constant challenge of their physical environment).

This in turn may tell us that the most important factor stimulating the rise in human brain size and cognitive ability starting millions of years ago was humans' interactions with each other in their social groups. In effect, a sort of "smartness competition" drove the evolution of intelligence, or at least of one set of intelligences relating to social interaction and communication, including "brain modules" for facial recognition, language, and "social smarts." If these particular cognitive abilities were at first not strongly connected to the ones humans were simultaneously developing for tool use and the understanding of nature, this could account for the long period during which tools changed little despite increases in brain size.

If the increasingly sophisticated mental tools humans had developed for understanding and dealing with each other—tools that included the ability to evaluate emotions and motivations, anticipate actions, deploy deception, and so forth—then became more strongly connected to the intelligences for nature and technology, it would have opened up new worlds for human analysis and exploitation. Perhaps, in effect, humans came to see the entire cosmos in the terms they'd previously reserved for each other: as a world imbued with emotions and motivations subject to negotiation, deception, and propitiation (appeasement). Ascribing human mental characteristics to animals could improve hunting efficiency by allowing hunters to anticipate prey reactions more effectively and even manipulate those reactions through better group hunting strategies. It might also have led people to see spirits in the animals they hunted and moved them to appeal artistically to those spirits. And if animals had spirits characterized by humanlike emotions and motivations, then why not also dead ancestors, trees, rocks, the weather, indeed the entire cosmos? The origins of not just art and ritual but religion may thus appear at the limits of the Upper Paleolithic age 40,000 years ago.

Above all, a rich linguistic toolkit, developed for social relationships but now applied to nature and technology, allowed people to develop and specialize their toolkits, as we've already seen, and to push the development of their social organizations further. By 10,000 years ago, the results of these processes put a few human groups, in specific natural environments, on the verge of a revolutionary change in their means of subsistence. It is to permanent settlements, expanding trade, and the invention of agriculture that we now turn.

SETTLEMENT, TRADE, AND AGRICULTURE

The efficiency of humans as hunters meant that a shift to agriculture was by no means inevitable: where game was abundant, hunting and gathering would have produced a better, more varied diet than agriculture with less effort. But efficient hunting in some areas had two opposed effects that resulted in agriculture making more sense. First, populations with steady access to abundant game and vegetation could have increased in absolute numbers and in density and could have established semipermanent or even fairly permanent camps, rather than moving all the time to follow the animals they hunted. Settling in one place would have encouraged the building of more permanent structures to live in and the creation of bulkier, less mobile, but more effective technologies for storing and processing food that had already been gathered. It also would have brought these populations (especially the females who did the gathering of plant-based food) into closer contact with and knowledge of the complete life cycles of food-producing plants. Finally, settlement would have both necessitated and facilitated trading for materials not available locally.

But the second effect of efficient hunting in some areas was an eventual decline in the number of game animals. At this point, with a significant investment already made in their habitations and associated possessions, populations in such areas faced two choices: abandoning their established life or exploiting the resources left to them more systematically. In areas that followed the second path, the result was the domestication of plants, deliberately planting and harvesting what had previously been simply gathered. In addition, it turned out that some animals could be captured and turned into breeding stock rather than being immediately slaughtered. Thus domestication of animals often (though not always) joined domestication of plants as the basis of an agricultural mode of production that could support larger and denser populations than even the most successful hunting and gathering could (though nutrition, especially in terms of protein, on a per-person basis may well have declined in agricultural compared with hunting societies). Agriculturally based populations also, at times, began to live in even more permanent and built-up settlements. We now turn to the evidence for this process.

Figure 1.15 is a fragment of a painted stone vessel. It dates from around 6000 BCE and comes from Syria, near the southeastern area of modern Turkey, where many experts believe the first of several independent inventions of agriculture occurred. Its fine workmanship means that this is not an everyday storage container.

Figure 1.15 Painted Stone Vessel

QUESTIONS TO CONSIDER

1. What might the vessel in Figure 1.15 have been used for?
2. Who might have owned it?

Representing a much more common sort of object is the set of pots in Figure 1.16, from a site in Greece occupied since Paleolithic times. These pots also date from about 6000 BCE, but in an area to which agriculture came somewhat later than Syria. Pots such as these, with many regional variations in shape,

Figure 1.16 Clay Pots

decorations, and even method of manufacture, were widely used for storing, cooking, and eating food, in many places even before agriculture was practiced in an area, but increasingly after the rise of agriculture.

QUESTIONS TO CONSIDER

1. What do the pots in Figure 1.16 tell you about how people lived in early agricultural communities? How would their lives have been different from the lives of hunter–gatherers?
2. What other technologies and social organizations are implied by the existence of pottery for everyday use?
3. Bearing in mind the significance of art discussed previously, why do you think people consistently decorated utilitarian objects such as these?

Many early agriculturalists lived in small villages whose social complexity was not much greater than in the semipermanent or permanent settlements of successful hunter–gatherers. Indeed, some very successful hunter–gatherers at sites with

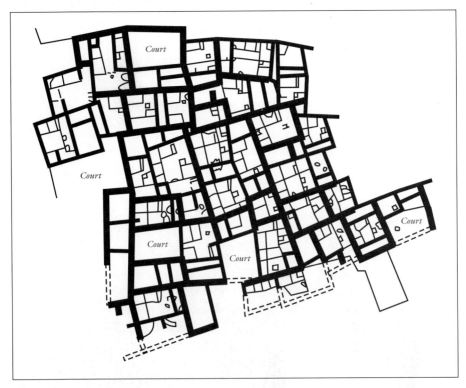

Figure 1.17 Map of Catal Höyük

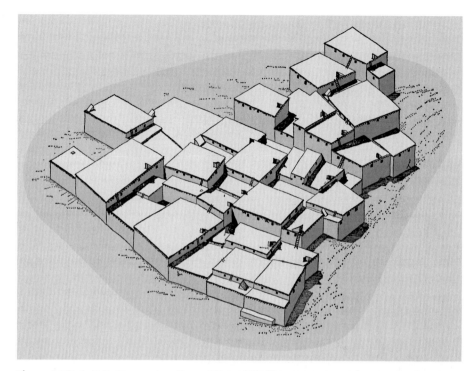

Figure 1.18 Artist's Reconstruction of Catal Höyük

rich naturally renewable resources, such as the Native Americans of the Pacific northwest who lived on salmon runs, developed more complex social structures than many simple village agriculturalists. But agriculture had the potential for supporting denser and larger populations than even the most successful hunter–gatherer sites could manage. One of the earliest permanent large settlements with characteristics that make it more than just a simple agricultural village is shown in plan in Figure 1.17, as discovered by archaeological excavation, and in Figure 1.18 as an artist's reconstruction of what the settlement may have looked like at its height.

The oldest excavated urban site in the world is at Catal Höyük on the Anatolian plateau in modern Turkey. The people of this settlement apparently made the transition to agriculture as long ago as 6500 BCE, taking advantage of the wild, large-seeded cereals, ancestors of domesticated wheat, that grew abundantly in the area. Catal Höyük also contains artwork, shrines dedicated to a religion that apparently focused on hunting (a good reminder of the mixed economies of early agricultural settlements and of the long transition from food gathering to food production), and evidence of such typically urban concerns as garbage disposal (buried under ash in the courtyards of the enclosed houses). Finally, the people of Catal Höyük exposed their dead to vultures outside the city and, after the bones were picked clean, stored them under their sleeping platforms.

QUESTIONS TO CONSIDER

1. Based on the plan and reconstruction (Figures 1.17 and 1.18), what were the lives of the inhabitants of Catal Höyük like? How did they differ from the lives of people in simpler villages and from the lives of hunter–gatherers?

2. What inferences or speculation has the artist made in creating a reconstruction from the ground plan discovered through excavation? Do any of them seem unreasonable to you?

3. What can we still not know about Catal Höyük from the archaeological evidence? Can we infer anything about how the city was governed from the evidence we have, for instance?

Note the density of settlement achieved in this settlement of close to 5,000 inhabitants. Agriculture made such density possible, but two other factors may have contributed as well. First, a set of buildings with substantial walls built into virtually a single block would have been easier to defend against raids on the settlement's stored surpluses and goods by nearby nomadic groups. Access to the houses was through openings in the roofs, and the "streets" of the settlements seem to have been its rooftops. Second, the residents developed a sophisticated economy. In addition to farming, herding, and hunting, they manufactured pottery and cloth, both of which they traded outside the settlement. They also conducted trade in obsidian, a black volcanic glass that can be made into very sharp cutting tools and that could be collected in abundance from a mountain near the settlement.

One of the pieces of speculation presented in the preceding description of Catal Höyük is the potential usefulness of its unified exterior walls for defense. They may have served this purpose, but there is no clear evidence of warfare or its associated technologies at this site. In fact, there is no undisputed evidence for warfare, defined as large-scale and organized killing of humans by other humans, in any of the evidence uncovered by archaeologists for human societies before about 8,000 years ago—that is, well after the beginnings of agriculture. There was undoubtedly interpersonal violence and aggression among and between human groups before then, but it seems from the evidence to have resembled the occasional murder or small-scale confrontation rather than organized and intentional combat, and even at that to have been very rare. This makes sense, as hunter–gatherer bands were small enough that they could not have survived much fatal internal feuding, and hunting population densities were low enough and game widely enough dispersed that moving to avoid conflict with neighboring groups would have made more sense than fighting for any particular piece of land.

But the permanent settlements and stored surpluses enabled by the rise of agriculture created at least some of the conditions necessary for the invention of warfare, and the evidence from our next site shows that by 3500–3000 BCE war was decisively affecting city planning in the Near East.

Figure 1.19 Walls of Jericho

Figure 1.19 shows part of the excavated wall of the ancient city of Jericho. (Its walls famously came tumbling down in the Bible; the archaeological evidence indicates that wall collapses happened a number of times, several of them from earthquakes.) The site had been occupied in Paleolithic times but had been abandoned periodically. The people who settled there around 3500 BCE built a wall around their hilltop settlement, and the site remained fortified after that. The original wall also had at least one tower built into it; others were added later, with the walls growing to several meters thick and over 10 meters high.

QUESTIONS TO CONSIDER

1. Examine Figure 1.19. Before the walled town, inhabitants of the site accumulated trash in and around their housing. After the wall, trash was dumped outside the wall and the streets kept clean. Why do you think this change occurred?

2. What other changes in people's lives, if any, are implied by the presence of walls around a settlement? Does a wall tell us anything more about political organization than we learned from Catal Höyük?

In addition to dense permanent settlements and stored surpluses of food and other forms of wealth, several other conditions had to arise before war entered the collection of human cultural inventions. The most important of these was probably the existence of more unified forms of leadership over more complex social organizations—essentially the rise of chiefdoms. The spread of metallurgy, especially the working of bronze, from which effective weapons could be made more easily than from stone, may also be associated with the rise of warfare. Finally, a sudden environmental change and resulting shortages of resources seem to be associated with the first evidence of organized warfare, which comes from northern Iraq around 6,000–7,000 years ago. Once invented, it spread very rapidly—it was, after all, a very successful new invention for at least one of the parties involved in the first wars—and has formed a major part of human history ever since. In addition, war undoubtedly further stimulated the rise of strong, centralized leadership.

The more complex social and political organizations that accompanied the spread of agriculture, metallurgy, and war necessitated better systems of recording, storing, and using information. Our next pieces of evidence show us the development of writing that met that need.

Figure 1.20 shows a set of impressed clay seals from the Indus Valley civilization of city-states that thrived between roughly 2500 BCE and 1500 BCE. These show various animals, including bulls, a rhinoceros, and an elephant. The figures are accompanied by brief inscriptions in a writing system that has yet to be deciphered. We have a note, in other words, but we cannot read it. The distribution of these seals tells us something of their use and meaning: they seem to have marked ownership (and perhaps content) of items of commerce, as they occur not just in the Indus Valley but in Mesopotamia and other areas connected to the Indus civilization by trade routes. Thus, despite the inscriptions being too short to decipher, the seals still tell us some things about this early complex society.

Figure 1.20 Indus Valley Clay Seals

Figure 1.21 Chinese
Oracle Bone
Ching-hua 2

QUESTIONS TO CONSIDER

1. Examine Figure 1.20. What does the mere presence of writing imply about the lives of the people of Indus Valley city-states?
2. What can you infer about this civilization from the animals they chose to depict on their seals?

Finally, we have an artifact from the Yellow River region of north China (Figure 1.21). It is what Chinese historians call an "oracle bone," and it dates from near the end of the Shang dynasty in China that lasted between about 1800 BCE and 1100 BCE. Oracle bones such as this one were bones, usually pieces of tortoise shell, that were heated in a fire until they cracked. A question about the future having been asked of the bone before it was heated, the patterns of cracks revealed an answer to the question to those who knew how to interpret them, this skill being one of the attributes of kingship. After the process of divining the future was completed, the question, the interpretation, and often some account of how the interpretation accorded with actual events were recorded on the bone itself in a set of characters that are the earliest lineal ancestors of modern Chinese writing—characters that can be read. The following is a translation of the inscription on one such bone.

[Preface:] Crack making on *gui-si* day, Que divined:

[Charge:] In the next ten days there will be no disaster.

[Prognostication:] The king, reading the cracks, said, "There will be no harm; there will perhaps be the coming of alarming news."

[Verification:] When it came to the fifth day, *ding-you,* there really was the coming of alarming news from the west. Zhi Guo, reporting, said, "The Du Fang [a border people] are besieging our eastern borders and have harmed two settlements." The Gong-fang [another people] also raided the fields of our western borders.

QUESTIONS TO CONSIDER

1. What concerns does the oracle bone in Figure 1.21 inscription illustrate?
2. What would you want to know from the archaeological evidence for the context of this bone and the society it comes from to interpret those concerns more accurately?

Settlement, Trade, Agriculture, and the Human Encounter with Complex Social Organization

The earliest evidence for systems of writing comes from the city-states of Mesopotamia; we present some of what they wrote as the first sources in chapter 2. What the evidence from archaeology and from the emerging technology of writing has begun to show us is the third major encounter in early human history: the encounter of humans with the challenges and opportunities presented by living in more complex and increasingly hierarchical societies. It is to the many and varied answers to these challenges and opportunities—or, put another way, to the many encounters that made up this one big encounter—that the rest of this book is devoted.

CHAPTER 2

Creation–Origin Myths and the Mythic Mode of Thought

INTRODUCTION

In contemporary American usage, *myth* and *mythic* have very restricted and generally very negative connotations. For us, a "myth" is a more or less conscious lie. A candidate for political office, for example, in a campaign speech will assert that "My opponent claims that he will launch all these new programs without raising taxes. That is just a myth." The implication is that his opponent is either too dense to see the real facts or, more likely, is knowingly attempting to deceive the voters. The way that the terms *myth* and *mythic* are used by cultural anthropologists and students of comparative religions is profoundly different from this common contemporary usage. For them, myths function for human social organizations in much the same way that binary languages operate within computers: they encode a particular structure of understanding and functioning in the world and predicate and shape all social processes. The social anthropologist Bronislaw Malinowski, for instance, defined myth as a tale

> told in satisfaction of deep religious wants, moral cravings, social . . . requirements. Myth fulfills in primitive culture an indispensable function: it expresses, enhances, and codifies belief; it safeguards and enforces morality; it . . . contains practical rules for the guidance of man. Myth is thus a vital ingredient of human civilization; it is not an idle tale, but a hard-worked active force; it is not an intellectual explanation or an artistic imagery, but a pragmatic charter of primitive faith and moral wisdom[,] . . . a statement of a primeval, greater, and more relevant reality, by which the present life, fates and activities of mankind are determined. . . .[1]

Myth, then, provides a substructure of values and justifies and privileges specific types of behavior. The themes of this chapter are the mythic mode of thought and the way that myths structure and define human life.

Virtually every human society has generated myths to fill this human need to explain. In American culture, the story of George Washington and the cherry tree affirms the legitimacy of the American constitutional system by showing that its main founding father was constitutionally incapable of telling an untruth. Similarly, the myth of the frontier operates as a kind of deep background behind much of American consciousness. The frontiersman ethos lies at the base of everything from our eagerness to "be our own boss" to the names of sport utility vehicles, which all conjure up images of the "rugged individualism" of a people who "tamed the wild frontier." Understood in this way, myth is not something that is the cultural property only of humans in "primitive" civilizations, who are trying to understand the mystifying and threatening power of nature in the only ways that their limited understanding of science allows for. Rather, myth informs every human culture, from the earliest human social organisms to our present-day developed societies. In fact, it has been said that "nothing is really important until it becomes a myth."

One of the most fundamental of human desires is to explain where the world and humans came from. Human societies have used a variety of mythic forms to achieve this purpose. Tales that explain where the cosmos or the world came from are called creation myths, and those that relate how humans came into being or how a particular people came into existence are called origin myths. In addition, there are heroic tales that acquire mythic stature. The documents in this chapter represent three creation and origin myths and one mythic epic from four distinctive cultural traditions—the Mesopotamian, Hindu, Jewish, and Mayan cultures. The readings were selected from the vast array of creation and origin myths produced by different human societies, because they provide explanations not merely of how things came into existence but also why they coalesced into the particular social order and way of life that they did. As such, they are rich with significance about how different cultural traditions conceived of the proper way for humans to interact with each other, with the divine, and with the natural world.

The first document presented here comes from *The Epic of Gilgamesh,* a tale with very deep roots in the culture of Mesopotamia and the ancient Middle East. The tale in the form that we have it was transcribed as part of a general royal order by the Assyrian king Assurbanipal (668–626 BCE) to collect and record all the ancient literature of Mesopotamia. Lost for centuries, the story was rediscovered by European archaeologists in the nineteenth century, although there are still lines and sections missing. It is thought that there was in the third millennium BCE a great king of Uruk named Gilgamesh, but the main character in this tale is pure epic hero—going on quests, slaying monsters, even spurning the affections of the goddess of love. This tale is valued, however, not only for its heroic scale but also for its tragic aspect. Through that tragic dimension, it helps to explain aspects of human life, and it was undoubtedly so popular and widespread in the ancient world because of its implicit lessons.

The second texts are products of the ancient Hindu culture in India. Hinduism is a very ancient and multifaceted religious system that evolved over the course of about three millennia, starting around 2500 BCE. Because of its diversity, Hinduism has many creation stories. Roughly in the middle of that three-thousand-year process of development, a series of religious works known as Vedas ("Wisdoms") were composed. The "Purusha Hymn" included here is from the Rig-Veda, the first of the Veda texts, and it portrays the creation of the universe, the gods, and the human social order. The second Hindu text excerpted here is a later representation of the creation process in slightly different terms. It is from the *Code of Manu* from the second to third centuries CE, and it restates and reaffirms the values and structures of the "Purusha Hymn."

Our third source is the best-known creation story in the Western world. It comes from the book of Genesis, which forms the first part of both the Jewish Torah and the Christian Bible. Indeed, in English the word *genesis* means "origin" or "creation." From Genesis we have excerpted the story it contains of creation and the tale of the expulsion of Adam and Eve from the Garden of Eden. In addition, as a counterpoint to the tales of divine anger and destructive floods in the other cultural traditions presented in this chapter, the tale of Noah and the Flood is also included.[2] The tales are saturated with explanations for the human condition and with prescriptions for human behavior. Although these are familiar stories in the Western canon, reconsideration of them in this comparative context should shed new light on them.

Finally, we leave the Old World and present one of the oldest tales of pre-Columbian native culture. Popol Vuh is the sacred text of the Quiche Maya peoples. Although it is a very ancient tale, the form that has come down to us was recorded by an unknown Mayan intellectual or priest in the 1500s. It was written down, then, after the Spanish Conquest so that the old beliefs would not be lost. This was undoubtedly inspired by the vigorous Christianization of the Americas pursued by the Spanish and by the onslaught that native cultures endured as a result of Spanish political, military, and economic domination. According to the worldview of the Maya and of Popol Vuh, spiritual forces are deeply embedded in the world, and proper knowledge of them is necessary for successful life. Both the point of view and the tone of Popol Vuh differ from those of the other texts and traditions represented here. It is perhaps the most profoundly and thoroughly mythical of the four cultures.

All of these creation and origin stories explain why humans are the way we are and why we have such and such relationship with the gods, with nature, and with each other. The selections in this chapter were chosen because—in the words of Mircea Eliade—they "narrate not only the origin of the World, of animals, of plants, and of man, but also the primordial events in consequence of which man became what he is today—mortal, sexed, organized in a society, obliged to work in order to live, and working in accordance with certain rules."[3] Because of the sophistication and complexity of modern life, the significance of myths and of the mythic mode of thought is misunderstood and underappreciated. The readings in this chapter allow us to explore the diverse ways that humans have understood the basic spiritual and social structure of the universe. In addition, they are designed to deepen our understanding of the mythic orientation to reality and to enhance our appreciation of the "mythic" as a fundamental part of human existence.

CHAPTER QUESTIONS

1. What is the relationship between humans and the divine (God or gods) presented in these different religious texts? How are hierarchies of the relative authority, power, and value of the divine and human portrayed here?

2. List the aspects of human social order and existence—such as different relations between humans, how humans came to live the types of lives they lead, our relationship with nature—that you can identify in these texts. What do you think of these mythic explanations? What significant themes emerge from your list?

3. Some of these stories include destruction tales, as well as creation narratives. Identify the different reasons that the God or gods destroyed life. What do these reasons tell you about the human relationship to nature and each other?

4. In general, what can we conclude about the values attributed to gods from the stories presented here? How does a society's view of the divine affect its understanding of the human and natural worlds?

5. What common answers to the mysteries of spiritual and social life are presented in these myths? Which mythic understandings are most similar to each other and which most distinctive? Are the ideas about religious and social values and about the mythic mode of understanding presented in these texts relevant to your life?

A CREATION MYTH FROM ANCIENT MESOPOTAMIA

The first selection in this chapter is from the oldest epic poem in history, *The Epic of Gilgamesh,* a heroic tale of ancient Mesopotamia that became one of the best-known stories of the ancient Middle East. Mesopotamia formed the heart of one of the early centers of agricultural civilization. By 3000 BCE great Sumerian city-states dominated Mesopotamia, and the city-states in turn were dominated by military leaders, who ruled as kings. Gilgamesh was one of these military leaders, a *lugal,* or big man, of the city of Uruk around 2700 BCE. Although based on an actual historical figure, the character of Gilgamesh in this story assumed mythic proportions. By 2000 BCE it had become the most widespread story of the ancient world. The tale was told across the territory stretching from the headwaters of the Persian Gulf to the coast of the eastern Mediterranean. It has been found recorded in many different sites and languages, showing that it enjoyed enduring and extensive popularity.

As befits an epic figure, Gilgamesh was involved in all kinds of heroic adventures with his friend Enkidu, a wild man sent by the gods as a rival capable of absorbing Gilgamesh's excess energy. Eventually, they become too great for their station in life and become a challenge to the gods, who kill Enkidu as punishment. Beset by grief and fearful that he too must die someday, Gilgamesh sets out to get answers from Ut-napishtim, a Noah-like character, who had earned immortality himself. Ultimately, Gilgamesh's quest for immortality fails.

Gilgamesh and his story touch on many issues that are frequently present in creation and origin myths: the relationship between man and the gods, the distinction between civilized life and the wilderness, and the all-too-human subject of mortality. The selections included here contain the introduction to Gilgamesh, the creation and taming of his friend–companion Enkidu, Enkidu's dream vision of death, advice to Gilgamesh on how to live life, the Flood story, and Gilgamesh's search for immortality. Although it is not a creation myth, *The Epic of Gilgamesh* nonetheless contains complex explanations to thorny questions about aspects of human existence. As such, it both provides an encoded set of values and serves as a point of comparison with the other readings in this chapter.

QUESTIONS TO CONSIDER

1. Describe the relationship between the people of Uruk and their king, Gilgamesh. Were they proud of him and their city? What did they pray to the gods for?

2. The three modes of human existence by the time of the Gilgamesh tale were hunter–gatherer, pastoral, and agricultural. Based on the description of Uruk and of the taming of Enkidu, how were these modes of existence viewed by the Mesopotamians?

3. How does the Flood story here compare with the famous Flood story from Genesis? Compare the reasons for the Flood and the gods' reaction afterward with Yahweh's behavior in Genesis.

4. Compare the visions of life presented by Siduri and Ut-napishtim. In your opinion, which of them offers a better way of approaching life and death? Why?

5. What do you think explains the popularity of the Gilgamesh tale? What are its heroic aspects? What parts might appeal to the common man? Does any part of the story appeal to you?

THE EPIC OF GILGAMESH

Of him who found out all things, I shall tell the land,
Of him who experienced everything, I shall teach the whole.
He searched lands everywhere.

Source: From *Myths from Mesopotamia: Creation, the Flood, Gilgamesh, and Others,* trans. Stephanie Dalley, 50–56, 88–89, 95–116, 118–19, 150–51. Copyright © 1989 Oxford University Press, Inc. Used by permission of Oxford University Press, Inc.

He who experienced the whole gained complete wisdom.
He found out what was secret and uncovered what was hidden,
He brought back a tale of times before the Flood.
He had journeyed far and wide, weary and at last resigned.
He engraved all toils on a memorial monument the whole of stone. . . .
The story of that man, Gilgamesh, who went through all kinds of sufferings.
He was superior to other kings, a warrior lord of great stature,
A hero born of Uruk, a goring wild bull.
He marches at the front as leader,
He goes behind, the support of his brothers,
A strong net, the protection of his men, . . .
Son of Lugalbanda,* Gilgamesh, perfect in strength,
Son of the lofty cow, the wild cow Ninsun.†
He is Gilgamesh, perfect in splendour,
Who opened up passes in the mountains, . . .
Who crossed the ocean, the broad seas, as far as the sunrise.
Who inspected the edges of the world, kept searching for eternal life,
Who reached Ut-napishtim the far-distant, by force. . . .
There is nobody among the kings of teeming humanity
Who can compare with him,
Who can say "I am king" beside Gilgamesh.
Gilgamesh was named from birth for fame.
Two-thirds of him was divine, and one-third mortal.

Belet-ili‡ designed the shape of his body,
Made his form perfect, . . .
In Uruk the Sheepfold he would walk about,
Show himself superior, his head held high like a wild bull.
He had no rival, . . .

The young men complain to the gods, because Gilgamesh keeps them out on
    military campaigns.
The young maidens complain, because he won't leave them alone.

The gods often heard their complaints. . . .
They called upon great Aruru:§
"You, Aruru, create someone for him, to match the ardour of his energies!
Let them be regular rivals, and let Uruk be allowed peace!"
When Aruru heard this, she pinched off a piece of clay, cast it out into open country.

---

*The hero of two early Sumerian epic poems. Gilgamesh is sometimes indicated to be his son.
†Lugalbanda's wife. Also, the cow goddess.
‡Goddess of fertility.
§A Babylonian mother goddess.

She created a primitive man, Enkidu the warrior: offspring of silence, sky-bolt of
   Ninurta.*
His whole body was shaggy with hair, he was furnished with tresses like a woman,
His locks of hair grew luxuriant like grain.
He knew neither people nor country; he was dressed as cattle are.
With gazelles he eats vegetation,
With cattle he quenches his thirst at the watering place
A hunter . . . saw him . . . beside the watering place and was dumbstruck to see him. . . .
The hunter went off to see . . . Gilgamesh:
"There was a young man who came from the mountain,
On the land he was strong, he was powerful.
His strength is very hard, like a sky-bolt of Anu.† . . .
I am too frightened to approach him.
He kept filling in the pits that I dug,
He kept pulling out the traps that I laid.
He kept helping cattle, wild beasts of open country, to escape my grasp.
He did not allow me to work in the open country."
Gilgamesh spoke to him, to the hunter,
"Go, hunter, lead forth the harlot Shamhat, . . .
He will see her and go close to her.
Then his cattle, who have grown up in open country with him, will become alien
   to him."
The hunter went; he led forth the harlot Shamhat with him, . . .
And he, Enkidu, . . . satisfied his need for water with wild beasts. . . .
"Here he is, Shamhat, bare your bosom, . . .
Do for him, the primitive man, as women do. . . ."
Shamhat did for him, the primitive man, as women do.
His love-making he lavished upon her. . . .
When he was sated with her charms,
He set his face towards the open country of his cattle.
The gazelles saw Enkidu and scattered,
The cattle of open country kept away from his body.
For Enkidu had stripped; his body was too clean.
His legs, which used to keep pace with his cattle, were at a standstill.
Enkidu had been diminished, he could not run as before.
Yet he had acquired judgement, had become wiser. . . .
The harlot spoke to him, . . . "You have become profound, Enkidu, you have become
   like a god.
Why should you roam open country with wild beasts?
Come, let me take you into Uruk the Sheepfold,
To . . . Gilgamesh. . . . "

---

*God of thunderstorms and the plow. In some stories, he was the hero of climactic battles for order,
and he is sometimes equated with Marduk.
†God of heaven and chief god of their pantheon.

[After this, Enkidu encounters Gilgamesh in Uruk. They become fast friends and companions in fantastic adventures. They slay the terrifying monster Humbaba, who guards the pine forest in the north. Ishtar, the goddess of sex, is smitten with Gilgamesh and offers to marry him. Knowing that Ishtar quickly tires of her husbands and then inflicts horrible punishments on them, Gilgamesh rejects her. Insulted, Ishtar gets her father, Anu, the chief of the gods, to send the Bull of Heaven against Gilgamesh and Enkidu. But the two heroes kill the Bull of Heaven and insult Ishtar with part of its carcass. The gods decide they have gone too far and one of them must die: Enkidu. Enkidu has a dream, which foreshadows his death and which provides a picture of what happens after death.]

Then Enkidu wept, for he was sick at heart. . . .
He spoke what was in his mind to his friend.
"Listen, again, my friend! I had a dream in the night.
The sky called out, the earth replied.
I was standing in between them.
There was a young man, whose face was obscured.
His face was like that of . . . [a] bird.
He had the paws of a lion, he had the claws of an eagle.
He seized me by my locks, using great force against me. . . .
Like a wild bull he trampled on me, . . .
I cried out: "Save me, my friend, don't desert me!"
But you were afraid, and did not help me. . . .
He seized me, drove me down to the dark house, . . .
To the house which those who enter cannot leave,
On the road where traveling is one way only.
To the house where those who stay are deprived of light,
Where dust is their food, and clay their bread.
They are clothed, like birds, with feathers,
And they see no light, and they dwell in darkness.

[As Enkidu sickens and dies, Gilgamesh mourns and fears his own death. He decides to visit Ut-napishtim, who is legendary for wisdom and has attained immortality, to find the answers. To reach Ut-napishtim Gilgamesh must undertake a dangerous journey to the land beyond the realm of the living. He has various encounters along the way, one of which is with an innkeeper, who is actually Siduri, the goddess of brewing and wisdom. She advises Gilgamesh.]

The alewife spoke to him, to Gilgamesh,
"Gilgamesh, where do you roam?
You will not find the eternal life you seek.
When the gods created mankind
They appointed death for mankind,
Kept eternal life in their own hands.
So, Gilgamesh, let your stomach be full,
Day and night enjoy yourself in every way,

Every day arrange for pleasures.
Day and night, dance and play,
Wear fresh clothes.
Keep your head washed, bathe in water,
Appreciate the child who holds your hand,
Let your wife enjoy herself in your lap.
This is the work . . . [of] the living.*

[Gilgamesh perseveres and with the help of Ur-shanabi, the ferryman, he finally reaches Ut-napishtim.]

Ut-napishtim spoke to him, to Gilgamesh,
"Why are your cheeks wasted, your face dejected,
Your heart so wretched, your appearance worn out,
And grief in your innermost being? . . ."
Gilgamesh spoke to him, to Ut-napishtim,
"How would my cheeks not be wasted, nor my face dejected,
Nor my heart wretched, nor my appearance worn out, . . .
Enkidu my friend was the hunted mule, wild ass of the mountain, leopard of open
    country.
We who met and scaled the mountain,
Seized the Bull of Heaven and slew it,
Demolished Humbaba who dwelt in the Pine Forest,
Killed lions in the passes of the mountains, . . .
Enkidu my friend whom I love so much, who experienced every hardship
    with me—
The fate of mortals conquered him! For six days and seven nights I wept over him, . . .
I was frightened. I am afraid of Death, and so I roam open country. . . .
The words of Enkidu my friend weigh upon me. . . .
How, O how could I stay silent, how, O how could I keep quiet?
My friend whom I love has turned to clay:
Enkidu my friend whom I love has turned to clay.
Am I not like him? Must I lie down too,
Never to rise, ever again?" . . .
Ut-napishtim spoke to him, to Gilgamesh,
"Why do you prolong grief, Gilgamesh?
Since the gods made you from the flesh of gods and mankind,
Since the gods made you like your father and mother,
Death is inevitable at some time, both for Gilgamesh and for a fool. . . .
Why have you exerted yourself? What have you achieved?
You have made yourself weary for lack of sleep,
You only fill your flesh with grief,
You only bring the distant days of reckoning closer.
Mankind's fame is cut down like reeds in a reed-bed.

---

*This section comes from the Old Babylonian Version.

A fine young man, a fine girl, . . .
Nobody sees Death,
Nobody sees the face of Death,
Nobody hears the voice of Death.
Savage Death just cuts mankind down.
Sometimes we build a house, sometimes we make a nest,
But then brothers divide it upon inheritance.
Sometimes there is hostility in the land,
But then the river rises and brings flood-water.
Dragonflies drift on the river,
Their faces look upon the face of the Sun,
But then suddenly there is nothing.
The sleeping and the dead are just like each other,
Death's picture cannot be drawn. . . .
The Anunnaki,* the great gods, . . . appointed death and life.
They did not mark out days for death,
But they did so for life."
Gilgamesh spoke to him, to Ut-napishtim the far-distant, . . .
"[Tell me] how you came to stand in the gods' assembly and sought eternal life?
Ut-napishtim spoke to him, to Gilgamesh,
"Let me reveal to you the secret of the gods. . . .
[T]he gods . . . decided [to] make a flood. . . .
Far-sighted Ea† swore the oath (of secrecy) with them,
So he repeated their speech to a reed hut,‡
"Reed hut, reed hut, brick wall, brick wall:
This is the message:
Man of Shuruppak, son of Ubara-Tutu,§
Dismantle your house, build a boat.
Leave possessions, search out living things.
Reject chattels** and save lives!
Put aboard the seed of all living things, into the boat.
The boat that you are to build
Shall have her dimensions in proportion,
Her width and length shall be in harmony,
Roof her like the Apsu."††
I realized and spoke to my master Ea,
"I have paid attention to the words that you spoke in this way,
My master, and I shall act upon them. . . .

---

*The first-born gods.

†God of fresh water, wisdom and magic; helper of mankind.

‡Ea uses the ploy of speaking to an inanimate object in a way that Ut-napishtim can overhear, in order to get around his oath that he would not reveal the coming Flood to humans.

§This is Ut-napishtim, son of Ubara-Tutu, king of the city of Shuruppak.

**Property.

††Apsu is the realm of fresh water under the earth, from which streams arise; the domain of Ea.

I loaded her with everything there was,
Loaded her with all the silver,
Loaded her with all the gold
Loaded her with all the seed of living things, all of them.
I put on board the boat all my kith and kin.
Put on board cattle from open country, wild beasts from open country, all kinds of
    craftsmen. . . .
That hour arrived; . . .
I saw the shape of the storm,
The storm was terrifying to see.
I went aboard the boat and closed the door. . . .
For six days and seven nights
The wind blew, flood and tempest overwhelmed the land;
When the seventh day arrived the tempest, flood and onslaught
Which had struggled like a woman in labour, blew themselves out.
The sea became calm, the wind grew quiet, the flood held back.
[S]ilence reigned, for all mankind had returned to clay. . . .
The boat had come to rest on Mount Nimush.* . . .
When the seventh day arrived,
I put out and released a dove.
The dove went; it came back,
For no perching place was visible to it; and it turned round.
I put out and released a swallow.
The swallow went; it came back,
For no perching place was visible to it, and it turned round.
I put out and released a raven.
The raven went, and saw the waters receding.
And it ate, preened, lifted its tail and did not turn round.
Then . . . I made a sacrifice, . . .
The gods smelt the pleasant fragrance and . . . gathered like flies over the
    sacrifice. . . .
Ellil† . . . was furious,
Filled with anger at the Igigi‡ gods. . . .
"No man should have lived through the destruction!" . . .
Ea made his voice heard and spoke,
He said to the warrior Ellil,
"You are the sage of the gods, warrior,
So how, O how, could you fail to consult, and impose the flood?
Punish the sinner for his sin, punish the criminal for his crime, . . .

*[As Gilgamesh prepares to go back to the land of the living, Ut-napishtim tells him a
secret that promises eternal life. Gilgamesh gets it, but loses it again.]*

---

*A high mountain in modern-day Iraq.

†Main god of the second generation of gods (Igigi); his realm was earth.

‡The second generation of gods. Compare with Anunnaki, the first-born gods.

"Gilgamesh, . . . let me tell you the secret of the gods.
There is a plant whose . . . thorn, like a rose's, will spike your hands.
If you yourself can win that plant, you will find rejuvenation."
When Gilgamesh heard this, he . . . tied heavy stones to his feet.
They dragged him down into the Apsu,*. . .
He took the plant himself: it spiked his hands.
He cut the heavy stones from his feet.
The sea threw him up on to its shore.
Gilgamesh spoke to him, to Ur-shanabi the boatman,
"Ur-shanabi, this plant is a plant to cure a crisis!
With it a man may win the breath of life. . . .
Its name shall be: 'An old man grows into a young man.'
I too shall eat it and turn into the young man that I once was." . . .
At thirty leagues they stopped for the night. . . .
A snake smelt the fragrance of the plant.
It came up silently and carried off the plant.
As it took it away, it shed its scaly skin.
Thereupon Gilgamesh sat down and wept.
His tears flowed over his cheeks. . . .
"For what purpose, Ur-shanabi, have my arms grown weary? . . .
I did not gain an advantage for myself,
I have given the advantage to the 'lion of the ground.'"[†]

HINDU CREATION MYTHS

The second set of texts derives from the Hindu religious tradition. Hinduism, which developed in the Indus Valley region between 2500 BCE and 800 CE, is an extremely diverse religion that evolved from a mixture of two religious systems. One was the belief system of the pastoral, horse-based Aryans, an Indo-European people who migrated into the Indus River valley beginning around 1500 BCE. The other was the religious system of the agricultural civilization that already existed in India at the time of the Aryan in-migration.

Hinduism and the Hindu religious texts contain more contradictory, or at the very least unreconciled, elements than is true of the texts of the main monotheistic religions (Judaism, Christianity, and Islam). An example of this is polytheism versus monotheism in Hinduism. Hindus worship literally thousands of

----

*A primordial body of water believed to be under the earth. Ea resided there.
†The snake. This story explains why snakes shed their skins.

gods. At the same time, a basic tenet of Hinduism is that the ultimate goal of all souls is *moksha*, which is release from ego-based attachment to the material world. One who achieves *moksha* unites with Brahman, which is translated variously as the One, the World Soul, and the Ultimate Reality. Hence, because all spirit is ultimately part of Brahman, Hinduism can also be thought of as a monotheistic religion.

Two other related elements of Hindu belief influence the nature of the texts presented here. They are reincarnation and the caste system. According to Hindu beliefs, all life forms are reincarnations of spirits from previous existence. The "first end of man" is *dharma*. Although *dharma* can be defined as the religious duties associated with one's social and family position, its essence is much more fundamental than that. The meaning of the root of *dharma* is "to sustain." So the fulfilling of the "first end of man" by living according to the demands of station in life serves to sustain the order of the world. In addition, if one properly fulfills one's *dharma*, then one achieves good *karma* and moves up in the next incarnation to a higher life form. If not, then one develops bad *karma* and moves down. All life represents the constant flow of spirits along the reincarnation path, having unification with Brahman as the ultimate goal. Connected with this understanding of life and belief in reincarnation is the Hindu caste system. Caste probably originated from linguistic, social, and ethnic differences between the Aryan intruders and the preexisting population of India. Eventually, the system of castes (*varna*) developed many subcastes, called *jatis*. Different obligations, privileges, and marriage and employment possibilities exist for members of different castes and subcastes.

An enormous body of religious writings has developed in Hinduism. The selections presented here come from only two parts of that religious literature. The first text is the "Purusha Hymn," and it comes from the first of the Vedas, the Rig-Veda. The Vedas (deriving from the word *veda*, or "wisdom") are the earliest religious works in Hinduism. They are considered by Hindus to be sacred utterings and were composed orally between 1200 and 400 BCE by the Aryans. The Vedas include hymns dedicated to gods and goddesses, as well as sacrificial, mystical, and philosophical texts. The passage included here is a creation story. It differs from the Judeo–Christian creation story from Genesis because of the cosmic continuity of the relationship between divinity and humanity that is characteristic of Hinduism, in which an individual human soul can achieve unity with Brahman in a way that is inconceivable to a Christian. The "Purusha Hymn" also explains the sacred origins of the caste system.

The second text is included here to help clarify the principles of the "Purusha Hymn." The two main sources of authority in Hinduism are the *Shruti*, or divine revelation, which includes the Vedas and the "Purusha Hymn." The other type of source is *Smriti*, or human traditions. The *Smriti* were believed to be based on and consistent with the *Shruti*, so they had the authority of divine revelation. One of the most important examples of *Smriti* is the *Code of Manu*, which dates from the second to third centuries CE. The *Code of Manu* came after a period of unrest and instability, and it seeks to reaffirm *dharma*.

QUESTIONS TO CONSIDER

1. Identify the different roles that Purusha plays in the creation of the universe. How does Purusha's part in creation differ from that of Yahweh in Genesis?

2. What aspects of the natural, spiritual, and social worlds were created by Purusha? How does the "Purusha Hymn" explain the origins of castes? How do the parts of Purusha used to create different castes correspond to the social role of each group? What is the significance both of this correspondence and of the organic unity of the social body that is created?

3. Religions frequently ask their followers to act in imitation of the God or gods. What might a Hindu do to act in imitation of Purusha? How might imitation of Purusha contribute to achieving *moksha*, or release?

4. Which of the two texts do you find to be clearer in the way it presents its ideas? Which of the texts is more rigid in the way it defines castes? What explanations can you come up with to explain the differences in these texts?

5. The caste system has been interpreted as a very rigid social ordering device. What can you find in these two texts that supports that point of view? How might a Hindu argue that, on the contrary, Hinduism provides for great social flexibility and mobility?

Hindu Gods and Spiritual Characters

Purusha—Embodied spirit of Man, the Male principle

Indra—King of the Gods

Agni—God of Fire

Vayu—God of Wind

Viraj—The Female counterpart to Purusha, the Female principle

Hindu Castes

brahmans   priests

rajanya   warrior or ruling class

vaishya   merchants and landowners

shudra   servants and landless farmers

PURUSHASUKTA (PURUSHA HYMN)

1 A thousand heads hath Purusha, a thousand eyes, a thousand feet. On every side pervading earth he fills a space ten fingers wide.

2 This Purusha is all that yet hath been and all that is to be; The Lord of Immortality which waxes greater still by food.

Source: Hinduism: The Rig Veda, trans. Ralph T. H. Griffith (New York: Book-of-the-Month Club, 1992 [1896]), 602–603, from Book X, Hymn XC.

3 So mighty is his greatness; yea, greater than this is Purusha. All creatures are one-fourth of him, three-fourths eternal life in heaven.

4 With three-fourths Purusha went up: one fourth of him again was here. Thence he strode out to every side over what eats not and what eats.

5 From him Viraj was born; again Purusha from Viraj was born. As soon as he was born he spread eastward and westward o'er the earth.

6 When Gods prepared the sacrifice with Purusha as their offering, its oil was spring, the holy gift was autumn; summer was the wood.

7 They balmed as victim on the grass Purusha born in earliest time. With him the Deities and all Sadhyas and Rsis* sacrificed.

8 From that great general sacrifice the dripping fat was gathered up. He formed the creatures of the air, and animals both wild and tame.

9 From that great general sacrifice Rcas† and Sama-hymns‡ were born: Therefrom were spells and charms produced; the Yajus§ had its birth from it.

10 From it were horses born, from it all cattle with two rows of teeth: From it were generated kine,** from it the goats and sheep were born.

11 When they divided Purusha how many portions did they make? What do they call his mouth, his arms? What do they call his thighs and feet?

12 The Brahman was his mouth, of both his arms was the Rajanya made. His thighs became the Vaisya, from his feet the Sudra was produced.

13 The Moon was gendered from his mind, and from his eye the Sun had birth; Indra and Agni from his mouth were born, and Vayu from his breath.

14 Forth from his navel came mid-air, the sky was fashioned from his head, Earth from his feet, and from his ear the regions. Thus they formed the worlds.

15 Seven fencing-sticks had he, thrice seven layers of fuel were prepared, when the Gods, offering sacrifice, bound, as their victim, Purusha.

16 Gods, sacrificing, sacrificed the victim, these were the earliest holy ordinances. The Mighty Ones attained the height of heaven, there where the Sadhyas, Gods of old, are dwelling.

CODE OF MANU

But in the beginning he assigned their several names, actions, and conditions to all (created beings), even according to the words of the Veda.

*Ancient celestial beings and saints.

†Hymns related to sacrifice from the Rig-Veda.

‡Hymns related to sacrifice from the Sama-Veda.

§Ritual portions of the Yajur-Veda.

**Cattle.

Source: The Law of Manu, in *The Sacred Books of the East,* vol. XXV, trans. G. Bühler (Oxford, UK: Clarendon Press, 1886), 12–14, 24.

He, the Lord, also created the class of the gods, who are endowed with life, and whose nature is action; and the subtile class of the Sadhyas,* and the eternal sacrifice.

But from fire, wind, and the sun he drew forth the threefold eternal Veda, called Rik, Yagus, and Saman,† for the due performance of the sacrifice.

Time and the divisions of time, the lunar mansions and the planets, the rivers, the oceans, the mountains, plains, and uneven ground,

Austerity, speech, pleasure, desire, and anger, this whole creation he likewise produced, as he desired to call these beings into existence. . . .

Whatever he assigned to each at the (first) creation, noxiousness or harmlessness, gentleness or ferocity, virtue or sin, truth or falsehood, that clung (afterwards) spontaneously to it.

As at the change of the seasons each season of its own accord assumes its distinctive marks, even so corporeal beings (resume in new births)‡ their (appointed) course of action.

But for the sake of the prosperity of the worlds, he created the Brahmana, the Kshatriya, the Vaishya, and the Shudra to proceed from his mouth, his arms, his thighs, and his feet. . . .

To Brahmanas he assigned teaching and studying (the Veda), sacrificing for their own benefit and for others, giving and accepting (of alms).

The Kshatriya he commanded to protect the people, to bestow gifts, to offer sacrifices, to study (the Veda), and to abstain from attaching himself to sensual pleasures;§

The Vaishya to tend cattle, to bestow gifts, to offer sacrifices, to study, to trade, to lend money, and to cultivate land.

One occupation only the lord prescribed to the Shudra, to serve meekly even these (other) three castes.

THE CREATION STORY OF THE JEWS

The third selection in this chapter encompasses some of the best-known religious passages of western civilization. The selections come from the beginning of the book of Genesis, which is the first chapter of both the Jewish Torah and the Christian Bible. These passages are included here both as a seminal text of three great religious traditions (Jewish, Christian, and Muslim) and as a point of comparison with other religious traditions. The portions of Genesis included here involve the creation of the universe and of life, as well as the expulsion from Eden and the story of the Flood.

---

*The "Gods of old."

†These are variant spellings of the Rcas, Sama, and Yajur Vedas.

‡That is, upon reincarnation.

§That is, to exercise self-discipline.

Christianity divides its books of revealed literature into the Old and New Testaments. The first five books of the Old Testament are called the Pentateuch, and the traditional Christian understanding of the Pentateuch is that it is the revealed word of God as written down by Moses. Many Christians still hold this belief. Many Biblical scholars, however, approach the material from a much different perspective. Beginning in the nineteenth century, scholars applied to the Bible the techniques of literary criticism that are commonly used on other texts. They have discerned different narrative strands in the Old Testament. The most prominent are the Elohim (E strand) or Jahweh (J strand), which identify texts depending on how God is referred to. These scholars have also called into question the early history of the Jews as it is presented in the Old Testament, the nature of their monotheism at various points in the evolution of Judaism, and the originality of many of the stories. According to this point of view, the material that makes up the Old Testament is a combination of different materials put together relatively late in the history of the Jews (by the time of the Babylonian Captivity in 586 BCE).

Of course, these are questions of enormous significance, especially concerning the authority of the biblical texts. At the same time, the texts themselves can be approached and assessed independent of the question of their origins. That is to say, they can be analyzed for the answers they provide about the origins of the universe and mankind, the nature of divinity, and man's key relationships with each other, with the divinity, and with the material world, regardless of whether one believes that they are the revealed word of God recorded directly by Moses or were produced out of a variety of different sources. Hence, the introductory passages of Genesis serve as an excellent touchstone against which to assess different visions and explanations of divinity and of the universe and the place of human and other life forms in it.

QUESTIONS TO CONSIDER

1. According to Genesis, what is the relationship between humans and the rest of creation? What does this tell us about the understanding of the relationship between humans and nature in this religious tradition?

2. What is the order and method of creation of Adam and Eve? What might this imply about the proper relationship between men and women, according to Genesis? How else does Eve figure in the Garden of Eden story, and how might it affect the way that women are viewed?

3. What are the consequences of Adam and Eve's "fall from grace" as a result of eating the forbidden fruit? List the aspects of human life that are explained by this story.

4. Why does God destroy all humans and other living things, except for Noah and those on the Ark? In your opinion, is God justified in unleashing this devastating Flood?

5. Based on the story of the expulsion from the Garden of Eden and the story of Noah and the Flood, what does God value most in humans? Does the thing most valued change between the two stories? In general, what can we tell about the nature of God from these Genesis stories?

THE BOOK OF GENESIS

In the beginning God created the heavens and the earth. The earth was without form and void, and darkness was upon the face of the deep; and the Spirit of God was moving over the face of the waters.

And God said, "Let there be light"; and there was light. And God saw that the light was good; and God separated the light from the darkness. God called the light Day, and the darkness he called Night. And there was evening and there was morning, one day. And God said, "Let there be a firmament in the midst of the waters, and let it separate the waters from the waters." And God made the firmament and separated the waters which were under the firmament from the waters which were above the firmament. And it was so. And God called the firmament Heaven. And there was evening and there was morning, a second day.

And God said, "Let the waters under the heavens be gathered together into one place, and let the dry land appear." And it was so. God called the dry land Earth, and the waters that were gathered together he called Seas. And God saw that it was good. And God said, "Let the earth put forth vegetation, plants yielding seed, and fruit trees bearing fruit in which is their seed, each according to its kind, upon the earth." And it was so. The earth brought forth vegetation, plants yielding seed according to their own kinds, and trees bearing fruit in which is their seed, each according to its kind. And God saw that it was good. And there was evening and there was morning, a third day.

And God said, "Let there be lights in the firmament of the heavens to separate the day from the night; and let them be for signs and for seasons and for days and years, and let them be lights in the firmament of the heavens to give light upon the earth." And it was so. And God made the two great lights, the greater light to rule the day, and the lesser light to rule the night; he made the stars also. And God set them in the firmament of the heavens to give light upon the earth, to rule over the day and over the night, and to separate the light from the darkness. And God saw that it was good. And there was evening and there was morning, a fourth day.

And God said, "Let the waters bring forth swarms of living creatures, and let birds fly above the earth across the firmament of the heavens." So God created the great sea monsters and every living creature that moves, with which the waters swarm, according to their kinds, and every winged bird according to its kind. And God saw that it was good. And God blessed them, saying, "Be fruitful and multiply and fill the

Source: The Holy Bible, Revised Standard Edition (New York: American Bible Society, 1952): Genesis 1; 2:1–9, 15–25; 3; 6:1–3, 5–8, 13–14, 22; 7:1–5, 11–12, 17, 22–24; 8:1, 4, 6–12, 18–22; 9:1, 9–13.

waters in the seas, and let birds multiply on the earth." And there was evening and there was morning, a fifth day.

And God said, "Let the earth bring forth living creatures according to their kinds: cattle and creeping things and beasts of the earth according to their kinds." And it was so. And God made the beasts of the earth according to their kinds and the cattle according to their kinds, and everything that creeps upon the ground according to its kind. And God saw that it was good.

Then God said, "Let us make man in our image, after our likeness; and let them have dominion over the fish of the sea, and over the birds of the air, and over the cattle, and over all the earth, and over every creeping thing that creeps upon the earth."

So God created man in his own image, in the image of God he created him; male and female he created them. And God blessed them, and God said to them, "Be fruitful and multiply, and fill the earth and subdue it; and have dominion over the fish of the sea and over the birds of the air and over every living thing that moves upon the earth." And God said, "Behold, I have given you every plant yielding seed which is upon the face of all the earth, and every tree with seed in its fruit; you shall have them for food. And to every beast of the earth, and to every bird of the air, and to everything that creeps on the earth, everything that has the breath of life, I have given every green plant for food." And it was so. And God saw everything that he had made, and behold, it was very good. And there was evening and there was morning, a sixth day.

Thus the heavens and the earth were finished, and all the host of them. And on the seventh day God finished his work which he had done, and he rested on the seventh day from all his work which he had done. So God blessed the seventh day and hallowed it, because on it God rested from all his work which he had done in creation.

These are the generations of the heavens and the earth when they were created.

In the day that the Lord God made the earth and the heavens, when no plant of the field was yet in the earth and no herb of the field had yet sprung up—for the Lord God had not caused it to rain upon the earth, and there was no man to till the ground; but a mist went up from the earth and watered the whole face of the ground—then the Lord God formed man of dust from the ground, and breathed into his nostrils the breath of life; and man became a living being. And the Lord God planted a garden in Eden, in the east; and there he put the man whom he had formed. And out of the ground the Lord God made to grow every tree that is pleasant to the sight and good for food, the tree of life also in the midst of the garden, and the tree of the knowledge of good and evil. . . .

The Lord God took the man and put him in the garden of Eden to till it and keep it. And the Lord God commanded the man, saying, "You may freely eat of every tree of the garden; but of the tree of the knowledge of good and evil you shall not eat, for in the day that you eat of it you shall die."

Then the Lord God said, "It is not good that the man should be alone; I will make him a helper fit for him." So out of the ground the Lord God formed every beast of the field and every bird of the air, and brought them to the man to see what he would call them; and whatever the man called every living creature, that was its name. The man gave names to all cattle, and to the birds of the air, and to every beast of the field; but for the man there was not found a helper fit for him. So the Lord God caused a deep sleep to fall upon the man, and while he slept took one of his ribs and closed up its place with flesh; and the rib which the Lord God had taken from the man he made into a woman and brought her to the man. Then the man said, "This at last is bone of my bones and flesh of my flesh; she shall be called Woman, because she was taken out of Man."

Therefore a man leaves his father and his mother and cleaves to his wife, and they become one flesh. And the man and his wife were both naked, and were not ashamed.

Now the serpent was more subtle than any other wild creature that the Lord God had made. He said to the woman, "Did God say, 'You shall not eat of any tree of the garden'?" And the woman said to the serpent, "We may eat of the fruit of the trees of the garden; but God said, 'You shall not eat of the fruit of the tree which is in the midst of the garden, neither shall you touch it, lest you die.'" But the serpent said to the woman, "You will not die. For God knows that when you eat of it your eyes will be opened, and you will be like God, knowing good and evil." So when the woman saw that the tree was good for food, and that it was a delight to the eyes, and that the tree was to be desired to make one wise, she took of its fruit and ate; and she also gave some to her husband, and he ate. Then the eyes of both were opened, and they knew that they were naked; and they sewed fig leaves together and made themselves aprons.

And they heard the sound of the Lord God walking in the garden in the cool of the day, and the man and his wife hid themselves from the presence of the Lord God among the trees of the garden. But the Lord God called to the man, and said to him, "Where are you?" And he said, "I heard the sound of thee in the garden, and I was afraid, because I was naked; and I hid myself." He said, "Who told you that you were naked? Have you eaten of the tree of which I commanded you not to eat?" The man said, "The woman whom thou gavest to be with me, she gave me fruit of the tree, and I ate." Then the Lord God said to the woman, "What is this that you have done?" The woman said, "The serpent beguiled me, and I ate." The Lord God said to the serpent, "Because you have done this, cursed are you above all cattle, and above all wild animals; upon your belly you shall go, and dust you shall eat all the days of your life. I will put enmity between you and the woman, and between your seed and her seed; he shall bruise your head, and you shall bruise his heel."

To the woman he said, "I will greatly multiply your pain in childbearing; in pain you shall bring forth children, yet your desire shall be for your husband, and he shall rule over you."

And to Adam he said, "Because you have listened to the voice of your wife, and have eaten of the tree of which I commanded you, 'You shall not eat of it,' cursed is the ground because of you; in toil you shall eat of it all the days of your life; thorns and thistles it shall bring forth to you; and you shall eat the plants of the field. In the sweat of your face you shall eat bread till you return to the ground, for out of it you were taken; you are dust, and to dust you shall return." The man called his wife's name Eve, because she was the mother of all living. And the Lord God made for Adam and for his wife garments of skins, and clothed them.

Then the Lord God said, "Behold, the man has become like one of us, knowing good and evil; and now, lest he put forth his hand and take also of the tree of life, and eat, and live for ever"—therefore the Lord God sent him forth from the garden of Eden, to till the ground from which he was taken. He drove out the man; and at the east of the garden of Eden he placed the cherubim, and a flaming sword which turned every way, to guard the way to the tree of life. . . .

When men began to multiply on the face of the ground, and daughters were born to them, the sons of God saw that the daughters of men were fair; and they took to wife such of them as they chose. Then the Lord said, "My spirit shall not abide in man for ever, for he is flesh, but his days shall be a hundred and twenty years." . . .

The Lord saw that the wickedness of man was great in the earth, and that every imagination of the thoughts of his heart was only evil continually. And the Lord was sorry that he had made man on the earth, and it grieved him to his heart. So the Lord said, "I will blot out man whom I have created from the face of the ground, man and beast and creeping things and birds of the air, for I am sorry that I have made them." But Noah found favor in the eyes of the Lord. . . .

And God said to Noah, "I have determined to make an end of all flesh; for the earth is filled with violence through them; behold, I will destroy them with the earth. Make yourself an ark of gopher wood. . . ." Noah did this; he did all that God commanded him.

Then the Lord said to Noah, "Go into the ark, you and all your household, for I have seen that you are righteous before me in this generation. Take with you seven pairs of all clean animals, the male and his mate; and a pair of the animals that are not clean, the male and his mate; and seven pairs of the birds of the air also, male and female, to keep their kind alive upon the face of all the earth. For in seven days I will send rain upon the earth forty days and forty nights; and every living thing that I have made I will blot out from the face of the ground." And Noah did all that the Lord had commanded him. . . .

[A]nd the windows of the heavens were opened. And rain fell upon the earth forty days and forty nights . . . ; and the waters increased, and bore up the ark, and it rose high above the earth. . . . [E]verything on the dry land in whose nostrils was the breath of life died. He blotted out every living thing that was upon the face of the ground, man and animals and creeping things and birds of the air; they were blotted out from the earth. Only Noah was left, and those that were with him in the ark. And the waters prevailed upon the earth a hundred and fifty days.

But God remembered Noah and all the beasts and all the cattle that were with him in the ark. And God made a wind blow over the earth, and the waters subsided. . . . [T]he ark came to rest upon the mountains of Ar'arat.

At the end of forty days Noah opened the window of the ark which he had made, and sent forth a raven; and it went to and fro until the waters were dried up from the earth. Then he sent forth a dove from him, to see if the waters had subsided from the face of the ground; but the dove found no place to set her foot, and she returned to him to the ark, for the waters were still on the face of the whole earth. So he put forth his hand and took her and brought her into the ark with him. He waited another seven days, and again he sent forth the dove out of the ark; and the dove came back to him in the evening, and lo, in her mouth a freshly plucked olive leaf; so Noah knew that the waters had subsided from the earth. Then he waited another seven days, and sent forth the dove; and she did not return to him any more. . . .

So Noah went forth, and his sons and his wife and his sons' wives with him. And every beast, every creeping thing, and every bird, everything that moves upon the earth, went forth by families out of the ark.

Then Noah built an altar to the Lord, and took of every clean animal and of every clean bird, and offered burnt offerings on the altar. And when the Lord smelled the pleasing odor, the Lord said in his heart, "I will never again curse the ground because of man, for the imagination of man's heart is evil from his youth; neither will I ever again destroy every living creature as I have done. While the earth remains, seedtime and harvest, cold and heat, summer and winter, day and night, shall not cease."

And God blessed Noah and his sons, and said to them, "Be fruitful and multiply, and fill the earth. . . . Behold, I establish my covenant with you and your descendants after you, and with every living creature that is with you, . . . that never again shall all flesh be cut off by the waters of a flood, and never again shall there be a flood to destroy the earth." And God said, "This is the sign of the covenant which I make between me and you and every living creature that is with you, for all future generations: I set my [rain]bow in the cloud, and it shall be a sign of the covenant between me and the earth."

THE CLASSICAL CREATION STORY OF MESOAMERICA

The final mythic structure included in this chapter comes from Mesoamerican civilization, in particular from the culture of the people known as Quiche Maya. The Classical Era of Mayan history runs from around 600 to 800 CE, and the Mayan cultural zone extended across parts of what is now southern Mexico, Guatemala, and Belize. Mayan civilization seems to have been influenced by the earlier Olmec culture, and it definitely influenced in its own turn the Aztec civilization encountered by the Spanish in 1519. Theirs was a maize-based economy with traditional social classes: rulers (believed to be gods or related to the gods), priests, nobility, and peasants.

What distinguishes Mayan civilization in particular was their intricate calendar computations and their sophisticated knowledge of astronomy (although parts of their system we might consider closer to astrology). The Mayan calendar year was based on eighteen "months" of twenty days each plus five intercalendrical days. Each day was identified with a specific symbol and character, which determined what one should do on that day. Because of this fixation on matters of time and calendars, the Mayans produced calendar computations of extraordinary precision. Their calendar year was 365.2420 days long, an infinitesimal 3/10000ths off from the actual length of a year and more accurate than the calendars used in Europe.[4]

Calendar computations based on their so-called Long Count system created a cycle that would not begin to repeat for 377,440 years![5] Of most immediate impact in terms of their daily lives and their religious beliefs were their twenty-day months and intercalendrical days. Each day was identified with a specific symbol and character, and each was a propitious or inauspicious day, a good or a bad day for certain types of activities. Hence, the Quiche assumed a deep structure of meaning and direction to the universe according to which one could and should organize one's life.

The foundation for this view of time is the sacred Mayan story known as the Popol Vuh, or the Council Book. It is of quite ancient vintage, although the version that we have was produced by a Mayan around 1560, that is, after the Spanish Conquest and the forced Christianization that accompanied it. It was discovered some two hundred years later by a priest and translated into Spanish. The extant copy of it is now in the Newberry Library in Chicago. Its anonymous recorder wanted to ensure that there was still "a place to see 'The Light That Came from Across the Sea,' . . . a place to see 'The Dawn of Life.'" The passages reproduced here present the Mayan view of creation, which the Popol Vuh calls "'the fourfold siding, fourfold cornering, measuring, fourfold staking, halving the cord, stretching the cord in the sky, on the earth, the four sides, the four corners,' as it is said, 'by the Maker, Modeler, mother–father of life, of humankind, giver of breath, giver of heart, bearer, upbringer in the light that lasts of those born in the light, begotten in the light; worrier, knower of everything, whatever there is: sky–earth, lake–sea.'"[6] The passages included here cover the gods' efforts at creating proper worshippers, a process that required some trial and error. Between the two passages included here there is a very long but still delightful narrative of the clever undertakings of two sets of twins. Their actions provide much of the material for a proper reading of the days. The passages presented here narrate and explain what was necessary to produce creatures capable of properly reading and observing the days.

QUESTIONS TO CONSIDER

1. Describe the process by which the gods created life. How does this story compare with the creation stories in Genesis and in the Hindu texts?

2. How does the destruction presented in Popol Vuh compare with the Flood stories from *Gilgamesh* and Genesis? Compare the motivation behind the destruction unleashed by Yahweh in Genesis and by the gods in Popol Vuh.

3. Compare the relationship between man and nature presented in Genesis with that implicit in Popol Vuh. Why was animals' flesh made food for others? Human possessions and domestic animals destroy the wood-carving people with the gods' approval. What does that imply about the justification for human use of the material and animals found in the world?

4. What does Popol Vuh tell us about proper human behavior? What about the relationship between men and women? What do you think of the explanations for human limitations given in Popol Vuh, Genesis, and the Gilgamesh story? In your opinion, are any of them more acceptable or convincing than others?

5. What can we discern about the nature of the divine (the gods) in the Mayan belief system from Popol Vuh? How does this compare with Yahweh's nature in Genesis and the behavior of the gods in *Gilgamesh* and in the Hindu texts?

POPOL VUH

Part One

This is the account, here it is:

Now it still ripples, now it still murmurs, ripples, it still sighs, still hums, and it is empty under the sky.

Here follow the first words, the first eloquence:

There is not yet one person, one animal, bird, fish, crab, tree, rock, hollow, canyon, meadow, forest. Only the sky alone is there; the face of the earth is not clear. Only the sea alone is pooled under all the sky; there is nothing whatever gathered together. It is at rest; not a single thing stirs. It is held back, kept at rest under the sky.

Whatever there is that might be is simply not there: only the pooled water, only the calm sea, only it alone is pooled.

Whatever might be is simply not there: only murmurs, ripples, in the dark, in the night. Only the Maker, Modeler alone, Sovereign Plumed Serpent, the Bearers, Begetters are in the water, a glittering light. They are there, they are enclosed in quetzal feathers, in blue-green.

Thus the name, "Plumed Serpent." They are great knowers, great thinkers in their very being.

And of course there is the sky, and there is also the Heart of Sky. This is the name of the god, as it is spoken.

And then came his word, he came here to the Sovereign Plumed Serpent, here in the blackness, in the early dawn. He spoke with the Sovereign Plumed Serpent, and they talked, then they thought, then they worried. They agreed with each other, they joined their words, their thoughts. Then it was clear, then they reached accord in the light, and then humanity was clear, when they conceived the growth, the generation of trees, of bushes, and the growth of life, of humankind, in the blackness, in the early dawn . . . .

So . . . Heart of Sky . . . came to the Sovereign Plumed Serpent, when the dawn of life was conceived: "How should it be sown, how should it dawn? Who is to be the provider, nurturer?"

"Let it be this way, think about it: this water should be removed, emptied out for the formation of the earth's own plate and platform, then comes the sowing, the dawning of the sky–earth. But there will be no high days and no bright praise for our work, our design, until the rise of the human work, the human design," they said.

And then the earth arose because of them, it was simply their word that brought it forth. For the forming of the earth they said "Earth." It arose suddenly, just like a cloud, like a mist, now forming, unfolding. Then the mountains were separated from the water, all at once the great mountains came forth. By their genius alone, by their cut-

Source: Reprinted with the permission of Simon & Schuster Adult Publishing Group from *Popol Vuh: The Definitive Edition of the Mayan Book of the Dawn of Life and the Glories of the Gods and Kings.* Trans. Dennis Tedlock, 72–85, 163–67. Copyright © 1985, 1996 by Dennis Tedlock.

ting edge alone they carried out the conception of the mountain-plain, whose face grew instant groves of cypress and pine.

And the Plumed Serpent was pleased with this: . . . .

And the earth was formed first, the mountain-plain. The channels of water were separated; their branches wound their ways among the mountains. The waters were divided when the Great mountains appeared.

Such was the formation of the earth when it was brought forth by the Heart of the Sky, Heart of Earth, as they are called, since they were the first to think of it. The sky was set apart, and the earth was set apart in the midst of the waters.

Such was their plan when they thought, when they worried about the completion of their work.

Now they planned the animals of the mountains, all the guardians of the forest, creatures of the mountains: the deer, birds, pumas, jaguars, serpents, rattlesnakes, yellow-bites,* guardians of the bushes.

A Bearer, Begetter speaks:

"Why this pointless humming? Why should there merely be rustling beneath the trees and bushes?"

"Indeed, they had better have guardians," the others replied. As soon as they thought it and said it, deer and birds came forth.

And then they gave out homes to the deer and the birds:

"You, the deer: sleep along the rivers, in the canyons. Be here in the meadows, in the thickets, in the forests, multiply yourselves. You will stand and walk on all fours," they were told.

So then they established the nests of the birds, small and great:

"You, precious birds: your nests, your houses are in the trees, in the bushes. Multiply there, scatter there, in the branches of trees, the branches of bushes," the deer and birds were told.

When this deed had been done, all of them had received a place to sleep and a place to stay. So it is that the nests of the animals are on the earth, given by the Bearer, Begetter. Now the arrangement of the deer and birds was complete.

And then the deer and birds were told by the Maker, Modeler, Bearer, Begetter:

"Talk, speak out. Don't moan, don't cry out. Please talk, each to each, within each kind, within each group," they were told—the deer, birds, puma, jaguar, serpent.

"Name now our names, praise us. We are your mother, we are your father. Speak now:

'Hurricane,

Newborn Thunderbolt, Raw Thunderbolt,

Heart of Sky, Heart of Earth,

Maker, Modeler,

Bearer, Begetter,'

---

*The poisonous snake known as fer-de-lance.

speak, pray to us, keep our days,"* they were told. But it didn't turn out that they spoke like people: they just squawked, they just chattered, they just howled. It wasn't apparent what language they spoke; each one gave a different cry. When the Maker, Modeler heard this:

"It hasn't turned out well, they haven't spoken," they said among themselves. "It hasn't turned out that our names have been named. Since we are their mason and sculptor, this will not do," the Bearers and Begetters said among themselves. So they told them:

"You will simply have to be transformed. Since it hasn't turned out well and you haven't spoken, we have changed our word:

"What you feed on, what you eat, the places where you sleep, the places where you stay, whatever is yours will remain in the canyons, the forests. Although it turned out that our days were not kept, nor did you pray to us, there may yet be strength in the keeper of days, the giver of praise whom we have yet to make. Just accept your service, just let your flesh be eaten.

"So be it, this must be your service," they were told when they were instructed—the animals, small and great, on the face of the earth.

And then they wanted to test their timing again, they wanted to experiment again, and they wanted to prepare for the keeping of days again. They had not heard their speech among the animals; it did not come to fruition and it was not complete.

And so their flesh was brought low: they served, they were eaten, they were killed—the animals on the face of the earth.

Again there comes an experiment with the human work, the human design, by the Maker, Modeler, Bearer, Begetter:

"It must simply be tried again. The time for the planting and dawning is nearing. For this we must make a provider and nurturer. How else can we be invoked and remembered on the face of the earth? We have already made our first try at our work and design, but it turned out that they didn't keep our days, nor did they glorify us.

"So now let's try to make a giver of praise, giver of respect, provider, nurturer," they said. . . . "There is yet to find, yet to discover how we are to model a person, construct a person again, a provider, nurturer, so that we are called upon and we are recognized: our recompense is in words. . . .

"It is well that there be your manikins, wood-carvings, talking, speaking, there on the face of the earth."

"So be it," they replied. The moment they spoke it was done: the manikins, wood-carvings, human in looks and human in speech.

This was the peopling of the face of the earth:

They came into being, they multiplied, they had daughters, they had sons, these manikins, wood-carvings. But there was nothing in their hearts and nothing in their minds, no memory of their mason and builder. They just went and walked wherever they wanted. Now they did not remember the Heart of Sky.

---

*That is, to prepare someone to keep track of and honor the sacred days of the calendar.

And so they fell, just an experiment and just a cutout for humankind. They were talking at first but their faces were dry. They were not yet developed in the legs and arms. They had no blood, no lymph. They had no sweat, no fat. Their complexions were dry, their faces were crusty. They flailed their legs and arms, their bodies were deformed.

And so they accomplished nothing before the Maker, Modeler who gave them birth, gave them heart. They became the first numerous people here on the face of the earth.

Again there comes a humiliation, destruction, and demolition. The manikins, wood-carvings were killed when the Heart of Sky devised a flood for them. A great flood was made; it came down on the heads of the manikins, wood-carvings. The man's body was carved from the wood of the coral tree by the Maker, Modeler. And as for the woman, the Maker, Modeler needed the pith of reeds for the woman's body. They were not competent,* nor did they speak before the builder and sculptor who made them and brought them forth, and so they were killed, done in by a flood:

There came a rain of resin from the sky.

There came the one named Gouger of Faces: he gouged out their eyeballs.

There came Sudden Bloodletter: he snapped off their heads.

There came Crunching Jaguar: he ate their flesh.

There came Tearing Jaguar: he tore them open.

They were pounded down to the bones and tendons, smashed and pulverized even to the bones. Their faces were smashed because they were incompetent before their mother and their father, the Heart of Sky, named Hurricane. The earth was blackened because of this; the black rainstorm began, rain all day and rain all night. Into their houses came the animals, small and great. Their faces were crushed by things of wood and stone. Everything spoke: their water jars, their tortilla griddles, their plates, their cooking pots, their dogs, their grinding stones, each and every thing crushed their faces. . . .

Now they run for it, helter-skelter.

They want to climb up on the houses, but they fall as the houses collapse.

They want to climb the trees; they're thrown off by the trees.

They want to get inside caves, but the caves slam shut in their faces.

Such was the scattering of the human work, the human design. The people were ground down, overthrown. The mouths and faces of all of them were destroyed and crushed. And it used to be said† that the monkeys in the forests today are a sign of this. They were left as a sign because wood alone was used for their flesh by the builder and sculptor.

So this is why monkeys look like people: they are a sign of a previous human work, human design—mere manikins, mere wood-carvings. . . .

---

*They could not offer prayer and praise to the gods nor keep track of the sacred days.

†Before the imposition of Christianity by the Spanish.

Part Four

And here is the beginning of the conception of HUMANS, and of the search for the ingredients of the human body. So they spoke, the Bearer, Begetter, the Makers, Modelers named Sovereign Plumed Serpent:

"The dawn has approached, preparations have been made, and the morning has come for the provider, nurturer, born in the light, begotten in the light. Morning has come for humankind, for the people of the face of the earth," they said. It all came together as they went on thinking in the darkness, in the night, as they searched and they sifted, they thought and they wondered.

And here their thoughts came out in clear light. They sought and discovered what was needed for human flesh. . . .

And these were the ingredients for the flesh of the human work, the human design, and the water was for the blood. It became human blood, and corn was also used by the Bearer, Begetter.

And so they were happy over the provisions of the good mountain, filled with sweet things, thick with yellow corn, white corn, and thick with . . . rich foods . . . [and all] the edible fruits were there: small staples, great staples, small plants, great plants. . . .

And then the yellow corn and white corn were ground, and . . . did the grinding nine times. Corn was used, along with the water she rinsed her hands with, for the creation of grease; it became human fat when it was worked by the Bearer, Begetter, Sovereign Plumed Serpent, as they are called.

After that, they put it into words:

the making, the modeling of our first mother–father,
with yellow corn, white corn alone for the flesh,
food alone for the human legs and arms,
for our first fathers, . . .

They were simply made and modeled, it is said: they had no mother and no father. We have named the men by themselves. No woman gave birth to them, nor were they begotten by the builder, sculptor, Bearer, Begetter. By sacrifice alone, by genius alone they were made, they were modeled by the Maker, Modeler, Bearer, Begetter, Sovereign Plumed Serpent. And when they came to fruition, they came out human:

They talked and they made words.
They looked and they listened.
They walked and they worked.

They were good people, handsome, with looks of the male kind. Thoughts came into existence and they gazed; their vision came all at once. Perfectly they saw, perfectly they knew everything under the sky, whenever they looked. The moment they turned around and looked around in the sky, on the earth, everything was seen without any obstruction. They didn't have to walk around before they could see what was under the sky; they just stayed where they were.

As they looked, their knowledge became intense. Their sight passed through trees, through rocks, through lakes, through seas, through mountains, through plains. Jaguar Quitze, Jaguar Night, Mahucutah, and True Jaguar were truly gifted people.

And then they were asked by the builder and mason:

"What do you know about your being? Don't you look, don't you listen? Isn't your speech good, and your walk? So you must look, to see out under the sky. Don't you see the mountain-plain clearly? So try it," they were told.

And then they saw everything under the sky perfectly. After that, they thanked the Maker, Modeler:

"Truly now
double thanks, triple thanks
that we've been formed, we've been given
our mouths, our faces,
we speak, we listen,
we wonder, we move,
our knowledge is good, we've understood
what is far and near,
and we've seen what is great and small
under the sky, on the earth.
Thanks to you we've been formed,
we've come to be made and modeled,
our grandmother, our grandfather,"
they said when they gave thanks for having been made and modeled. They understood everything perfectly, they sighted the four sides, the four corners in the sky, on the earth, and this didn't sound good to the builder and sculptor:

"What our works and designs have said is no good:

"'We have understood everything, great and small,' they say." And so the Bearer, Begetter took back their knowledge:

"What should we do with them now? Their vision should at least reach nearby, they should see at least a small part of the face of the earth, but what they're saying isn't good. Aren't they merely 'works' and 'designs' in their very names? Yet they'll become as great as gods, unless they procreate, proliferate at the sowing, the dawning, unless they increase."

"Let it be this way: now we'll take them apart just a little, that's what we need. What we've found out isn't good. Their deeds would become equal to ours, just because their knowledge reaches so far. They see everything," so said the Heart of Sky, Hurricane,
Newborn Thunderbolt, Raw Thunderbolt,
Sovereign Plumed Serpent,
Bearer, Begetter,
Xpiyacoc, Xmucane,
Maker, Modeler,
as they are called. And when they changed the nature of their works, their designs, it was enough that the eyes be marred by the Heart of Sky. They were blinded as the face of a mirror is breathed upon. Their eyes were weakened. Now it was only when they looked nearby that things were clear.

And such was the loss of means of understanding, along with the means of knowing everything, by the four humans. The root was implanted.

And such was the making, modeling of our first grandfather, our father, by the Heart of Sky, Heart of Earth.

And then their wives and women came into being. Again, the same gods thought of it. It was as if they were asleep when they received them, truly beautiful women were there. . . . With their women there they became wider awake. Right away they were happy at heart again, . . .

So these are . . . their wives, who became ladies of rank, giving birth to the people of the tribes, small and great.

And this is our root. We who are the Quiche people.

NOTES

1. B. Malinowski, *Myth in Primitive Psychology* (New York: W. W. Norton & Co., 1926, 19, 30.

2. There is a Hindu tale about Manu and the Flood, but it contains no moral implications or reflections on divine anger, and so it is not included in this chapter.

3. Mircea Eliade, *Myth and Reality* (New York: Harper Torchbooks, 1963), 11.

4. Miguel Leon-Portilla, *Time and Reality in the Thought of the Maya*, 2nd ed. (Norman, OK: University of Oklahoma Press, 1988), 11.

5. Ibid., p. 6.

6. *Popol Vuh: The Definitive Edition of the Mayan Book of the Dawn of Life and the Glories of the Gods and Kings*. Trans. Dennis Tedlock (New York: Simon and Schuster, 1985), 71–72.

CHAPTER 3

Kingship and Authority in the Ancient World

INTRODUCTION

In J. R. R. Tolkien's *The Lord of the Rings,* when Aragorn healed the victims of the evil Ringwraiths, he proved himself the true king, because it was said that "the hands of the king are the hands of the healer." Tolkien did not invent this idea. As an Oxford professor and expert in early English literature, he knew of the deeply rooted belief in medieval Western Europe that "the royal touch" had sacred powers, and he transplanted that idea to Middle Earth. In Europe, belief in the healing powers of the king was intimately connected with the idea that royal power acquired legitimacy because of divine approval. This conception of royal authority stemming from divine sanction was a part of most political cultures. From Israel and Mesopotamia to India and China, from Asia to Mesoamerica, royalty was viewed as "anointed." Although this idea of ruling by "divine right" contributed at times to despotism and abuse of power, it also established very real expectations and assumptions about the purposes of royal government. Moral limitations were placed on royal power, because each culture generated its own understanding of what constituted the legitimate exercise of power. The relationship between the legitimacy of royal authority in different cultures and the proper fulfillment of the moral requirements of those cultures—and, more generally, the character and functioning of authority in human cultures—are the themes of this chapter.

The readings in this chapter show that the elevated stature of one chosen and anointed by the heavens carried with it obligations and responsibilities that qualified and limited "despotic" power. In different cultures divinity was conceived of in different ways: in one culture as a monotheistic God, in another as a group of polytheistic gods, in a third as an impersonal power of Heaven. Similarly, the ruler was viewed in various ways: as a manifestation of the divine, as a quasi-divine figure, or merely as a divinely designated human. Despite these differences, royal authority—understood as the legitimate exercise of power, as opposed to illegitimate force or mere coercion—was nested in value systems that constrained and

61

compelled the emperor or king to live up to certain expectations. Failure to do so could and did lead to dethronement and death. More routinely, dynastic turmoil and foreign conquest were interpreted as resulting from inability or refusal to adhere to the ethical responsibilities of the office.

The issues raised here also allow us to consider the nature and working of authority in human social relations. A useful way to approach this subject might be to contrast "authority" with "power." Someone in a position of power—a parent, a teacher, a boss, a political figure—can wield that power, and within certain limits there is nothing that can be done legally to take that power away or diminish it. At the same time, the raw exercise of power by itself cannot lend legitimacy to an action. In fact, the arbitrary exercise of power actually diminishes legitimacy. The reason for this is that an action's legitimacy is a function of a social value system that the individual holder and exerciser of power can do little to affect or define. *Monarchy* literally means "one-person rule." But if authority is understood as power based on respect for and wielded in accordance with a moral value system, then it is easy to see that legitimate authority cannot be "monarchical" in the literal sense of the word. Rather, it can only be exercised in conjunction with the values of the society, and so its operation is mutually defined by the ruler and the ruled. If this is the case for royal authority, then it applies all the more to modern democratic political systems. Moreover, ethical limitations are also part of parental, educational, and other forms of authority. Hence the encounter between the structures of political authority and the society over which they rule retains its relevance to the present day.

An example of the effect of popular understanding of royal authority on other types of authority in the society is the idea of the monarch as literally or symbolically serving as the "father" of a nation or a people. By analogy, then, the behavior expected of him coincided with the ideal actions of the father in a human family. Conversely, the attributes of the ideal ruler were by extension applied to fathers in the society as a whole. The result invariably was a network of mutually reinforcing expectations, responsibilities, and ideals that served to define right action within the social and political order as a whole. This is a far cry from unlimited royal power, from one-person rule.

The first two readings come from Mesopotamia. The first document includes excerpts from one of the most famous legal documents in history, the Code of Hammurabi. Although Hammurabi's code dates from around 1750 BCE, it includes elements of previous law codes, and it was copied in turn in law codes issued after it. Most famous for its principle of *lex talionis,* or "an eye for an eye, a tooth for a tooth," Hammurabi's code also addresses the social and governmental purposes behind the law code, so it encodes an image of legitimate legal authority. The second document is from another empire in the same region a thousand years later. The Neo-Assyrian empire was noted for the ferocious violence that it used to establish and maintain power. Yet in the document "Advice to a Prince" presented here, we see the endurance of many of the ideals of legitimate authority incorporated in Hammurabi's code.

The second document comes from the Jewish and Christian traditions, and it represents the ideals of kingship in ancient Israel. The selections included here come from 1 Samuel. The Jewish interpretation of royal authority was distinctive in certain ways. An important undercurrent in the sacred literature up through Samuel was the idea that Israel did not need a king, because it received leadership and guidance directly from Yahweh. Although that principle was altered in Samuel, it continued to affect the way kingship and the legitimacy of the ruler were defined in the Jewish tradition.

Next, we turn to the Hindu culture of India and the way that political authority was comprehended there. The best and best-known representation of royal authority and legitimacy in Indian culture is their magnificent epic, *The Ramayana*. This tale existed as part of the oral tradition of India for centuries before it was written down, so it reflects deeply rooted and enduring Hindu values. Because the main character Rama is a physical incarnation of the Hindu god Vishnu, his behavior and values literally embody the Hindu ideal of kingship.

Finally, we include a foundation text of Chinese political culture. "The Mandate of Heaven," which comes from the *Shu Ching* (*The Book of History*), may have been edited by Confucius (551–479 BCE). Although it certainly reveals a Confucian understanding of the basis of legitimate political authority, "The Mandate of Heaven" also reflects earlier Chinese views of the encounter between political power and the society it governs. Because of its antiquity and because it remained a part of the political tradition of China for centuries, this text is of singular importance.

The traditions presented here, no matter how authoritarian, defined legitimate government as the fulfillment of binding social obligations. In examining the specific traditions, their distinctive characteristics, and the implications of both their social systems and their values, then, we will be, in effect, assessing the extent to which human social systems and the authority by which they are governed are ethical constructions. Thus the theme of this chapter is the exercise of legitimate political authority as a continuous encounter between leaders and the moral and religious values of their societies.

CHAPTER QUESTIONS

1. How is authority represented in these depictions? Is there a universal representation or set of characteristics for authority common to all the cultures?

2. How is authority limited? Later in European history there will be something known as "absolute monarchs." Based on what you've read here, is that a contradictory term?

3. In different societies the emperors or kings were thought of differently—human, semidivine, divine. Can you see any correlations between a society's understanding of the ruler's nature and the freedom from constraint that royal authority enjoyed?

4. Group together any readings that express similar ideas of the proper exercise of royal authority. What accounts for the similarities? Which tradition of political authority is most distinctive? Why?

5. Do the depictions of royal authority in these readings and the kinds of constraints that the climate of social expectations imposed compare at all to the way that authority operates in your world, in either private or public circumstances? How has your understanding of authority changed as a result of these readings?

KINGSHIP IN ANCIENT MESOPOTAMIA

The first two readings come from the Babylonian and Neo-Assyrian empires, respectively, and they represent the Mesopotamian royal tradition. Because of its geography, Mesopotamia was open to the movements of different peoples, and it was a multiethnic region from very early on in its history. Despite its ethnic diversity and the fact that it was unified under different kingdoms dominated by different peoples, there developed a common conception of the rights and responsibilities of the king. The king was thought to be a divinely designated individual. According to an ancient text known as the "Sumerian King List," "kingship was lowered from heaven." A document from the city-state of Lagash circa 2450 BCE describes the king as having a divine father and being nursed and given his span of years by a goddess.[1] Because *lugals* ("big men" or kings) were key to the organization and management of the early agriculture-based city-states, it is understandable that kings should have enjoyed such an elevated profile.

Central and fundamental to the Mesopotamian understanding of proper royal behavior were the two Akkadian words *andurarum* (freedom) and *misharum* (equity) that expressed the public idea of royal responsibilities in the general Mesopotamian cultural zone.[2] An important part of the process of providing freedom and equity was legal action by the monarch. A common New Year practice of kings was rectifying some of the uncertainties of life—for example, robbers attacking a trade caravan, wolves devastating a flock, or bad weather wiping out a crop. Kings acted to ensure that the individuals who suffered these catastrophes would not be punished for debt. More generally, legal codes such as Hammurabi's gave substance to these principles, so the law was seen as an agent for rectifying injustice and for ensuring those core principles of freedom and equity. This legal tradition views the law as a public entity, independent of and greater than any individual.

The first document in this section comprises the Prologue, Epilogue, and certain statutes from the famous Code of Hammurabi, a king of Babylon. The dates of the Babylonian Empire are given as 1894–1595 BCE, but Babylon was really a regional city-state until Hammurabi became king, and it began a slow decline after his death. Even under him, there was very little expansion until he had already reigned for thirty years. Then in a dramatically condensed period of time (1763–1755 BCE), he established control over most of Mesopotamia. His code is known from a beautiful dark stone stele over seven feet tall on which it is carved. Much of the code is made up of legal statutes based on the principle of *lex talionis,* or "an eye for an eye, a tooth for a tooth." Punishments differed according to social class, gender, and age (noble, commoner, slave, male and female, minor and adult). These laws served to affirm public, royal authority in a society still accustomed to private "justice" by means of vendetta and blood feuds. Because of their value as sources for social history and for the functioning of the law code, we have included representative selections of those laws. Those statutes are interesting sources for social history. Preceding and following them, we present the introduction and conclusion of the law code, including Hammurabi's self-representation and the public ideal of kingship.

QUESTIONS TO CONSIDER

1. What purposes does Hammurabi cite for issuing the law code? Who is it supposed to serve? Can you think of other purposes for law codes and other groups to serve?

2. Identify the terms that Hammurabi uses to describe himself. What does he compare himself to? What do those descriptive terms and comparisons have to do with the purpose of the law code?

3. From what source does Hammurabi derive his authority? Why does he think he was given that authority (i.e., what is he supposed to do with it)?

4. How do the specific statutes compare with Hammurabi's claims in the Prologue and Epilogue? In your opinion, do the statutes achieve what he claims? Are the statutes fair? Do you think they would be effective?

5. How do the Prologue, Epilogue, and statutes embody the twin Mesopotamian legal principles of *andurarum* (freedom) and *misharum* (equity)? How does equity differ from equality and how is that reflected in the statutes?

CODE OF HAMMURABI (circa 1750 BCE)

Prologue

When the lofty Anu,* king of the Anunnaki,† and Enlil,‡ lord of heaven and earth, who determines the destinies of the land, committed the rule of all mankind to Marduk§, the first-born son of Ea, and made him great among the Igigi;** when they

---

Source: J. M. Powis Smith, *The Origin and History of Hebrew Law* (Chicago: The University of Chicago Press, 1931), 181, 183, 186, 190–91, 198–99, 209–10, 218–20, 222.

*Father and king of the gods.

†Gods of the earth.

‡God of wind.

§Patron god of Babylon.

**Gods of the heavens.

pronounced the lofty name of Babylon, made it great among the quarters of the world and in its midst established for him an everlasting kingdom whose foundations were firm as heaven and earth—at that time Anu and Enlil named me, Hammurabi, the exalted prince, the worshiper of the gods, to cause righteousness to prevail in the land, to destroy the wicked and the evil, to prevent the strong from plundering the weak, to go forth like the sun over the black-headed race, to enlighten the land and to further the welfare of the people. Hammurabi, the shepherd named by Enlil am I, who increased plenty and abundance; who made everything complete. . . . The ancient seed of royalty, the powerful king, the sun of Babylon, who caused light to go forth over the lands of Sumer and Akkad; the king who caused the four quarters of the world to render obedience; the favorite of Innanna* am I. When Marduk sent me to rule the people and to bring help to the land, I established law and justice in the language of the land and promoted the welfare of the people.

Statutes

If a man accuse a man, and charge him with murder, but cannot convict him, the accuser shall be put to death. . . .

If a man practice brigandage and be captured, that man shall be put to death.

If the brigand be not captured, the man who has been robbed shall establish the amount of his loss before the god, and the city and the governor, in whose land or border the robbery was committed, shall compensate him for whatsoever was lost. . . .

If a man owe a debt and Adad† inundate the field or the flood carry the produce away, or, through lack of water, grain have not grown in the field, in that year he shall not make any return of grain to the creditor, he shall alter his contract-tablet and he need not pay the interest for that year. . . .

If a man neglect to strengthen his dike, and do not strengthen his dike, and a break be made in his dike and he let the water carry away the farmland, the man in whose dike the break has been made shall restore the grain which has been damaged.

If he be not able to restore the grain, they shall sell him and his goods, and the farmers whose grain the water has carried away shall divide [the results of the sale]. . . .

If a man give to another silver, gold, or anything else for safekeeping, whatever he gives he shall show to witnesses and he shall draw up contracts and then give it for safekeeping.

If a man give for safekeeping without witnesses or contracts, and at the place of deposits they dispute with him, that case has no penalty.

If a man give to another silver, gold, or anything else for safekeeping in the presence of witnesses and the latter dispute with him [or deny it], they shall call that man to account and he shall double whatever he has disputed and repay it.

If a man give anything of his for safekeeping and at the place of deposit either by burglary or by pillage his property along with the property of the owner of the house be carried off, the owner of the house who has been negligent and has lost whatever was

---

*The goddess of love; a different name for the goddess Ishtar in the Gilgamesh tale.

†Sumerian name of the god of rain and storms.

given to him on deposit shall make good [the loss] and restore [it] to the owner of the goods; the owner of the house may institute a search for what has been lost and take it from the thief.

If a man, nothing of whose has been carried off, say, "Something of mine has been carried off," alleging he sustained loss when nothing of his had been carried off, he shall declare his [alleged] loss in the presence of God, and he shall double and pay the amount for which he had made claim for his [alleged] loss. . . .

If a man take a wife and do not draw up a contract with her, that woman is not his wife.

If the wife of a man be taken in lying with another man, they shall bind them and throw them into the water. If the husband of the woman spare the life of his wife, the king shall spare the life of his . . . subject [the offending man]. . . .

If a man force the [betrothed] wife* of a man, who has not known a male and is living in her father's house, and lie in her bosom, and they take him, that man shall be put to death and that woman shall go free.

If a man accuse his wife and she have not been taken in lying with another man, she shall take an oath in the name of God and she shall return to her house.

If the finger have been pointed at the wife of a man because of another man, and she have not been taken in lying with another man, for her husband['s sake] she shall throw herself into the sacred river [i.e., she shall submit to the ordeal by water]. . . .

If the wife of a man bring about the death of her husband because of another man, they shall impale that woman. . . .

If a man, after [the death of] his father, lie in the bosom of his mother, they shall burn both of them. . . .

If a man strike his father, they shall cut off his hand.

If a man destroy the eye of another man, they shall destroy his eye.

If he breaks a man's bone, they shall break his bone.

If he destroy the eye of a common man or break a bone of a common man, he shall pay one mana of silver.

If he destroy the eye of a man's slave or break a bone of a man's slave, he shall pay one-half his price.

If a man knock out a tooth of a man of his own rank, they shall knock out his tooth.

If he knock out a tooth of a common man, he shall pay one-third mana of silver.

Epilogue

The righteous laws which Hammurabi the wise king established and by which he gave the land a firm support and a gracious rule. Hammurabi the perfect king am I. I was not careless nor was I neglectful of the black-headed people, whom Bel[†] presented to me and whose care Marduk gave to me. Regions of peace I spied out for

---

*Fiancée.

†Babylonian god of the earth.

them. With the powerful weapon which Zamama* and Innanna intrusted to me, with the breadth of vision which Ea allotted to me, with the might which Marduk gave me, I expelled the enemy north and south; I made an end of their raids; I promoted the welfare of the land; I made the peoples to rest in habitations of security; I permitted no one to molest them. The great gods have named me and I am the guardian shepherd whose scepter is righteous; my beneficent shadow is spread over the city. In my bosom I have carried the peoples of the land of Sumer and Akkad, under my protection I brought their brethren into security; with my wisdom I covered them; that the strong might not oppress the weak, and that they should give justice to the orphan and the widow, in Babylon, the city whose head Anu and Enlil raised aloft, in Esagila,[†] the temple whose foundations stand firm as heaven and earth, to pronounce judgements for the land, to render decisions for the land, to give justice to the oppressed, my weighty words I have written upon my monument, and in the presence of the image of me, king of righteousness, have I set it up.

The king who is preeminent among kings am I. My words are precious, my wisdom is unrivaled. By the command of Shamash,[‡] the great judge of heaven and earth, may I make righteousness to shine forth on the land; by the word of Marduk, my lord, may there be none to set aside my statutes; in Esagila which I love may my name be remembered with favor forever. Let any oppressed man who has a cause come before the image of me, the king of righteousness! Let him have read to him the writing on my monument! Let him give heed to my weighty words! And may my monument enlighten him as to his cause and may he understand his case! May it set his heart at ease. "Hammurabi indeed is a ruler who is like a real father to his people; he has given reverence to the word of Marduk, his lord; he has obtained Marduk's victory north and south; he has made glad the heart of Marduk, his lord; he has established prosperity for all time and has led the land aright," let him proclaim aloud and let him pray with his whole heart before Marduk, my lord, and Zarpanit,[§] my lady, and may the protecting deities, the gods who enter Esagila, the walls of Esagila, make his thoughts acceptable daily before Marduk, my lord, and Zarpanit, my lady! In the days to come, for all time, let the king who arises in the land observe the words of righteousness which I have written upon my monument! Let him not alter the judgements of the land which I have pronounced, the decisions of the country which I have rendered! Let him not efface my statutes! If that man have wisdom and be able to guide his land aright, let him give attention to the words which I have written upon my monument! And may this monument enlighten him as to procedure and administration, the judgements of the land which I have pronounced, and the decisions of the land which I have rendered! And let him guide aright the black-headed people! Let him pronounce their judgements and render their decisions! Let him root out the wicked and the evildoer from his land! Let him promote the welfare of his people!

---

*A warrior god associated with Marduk.

†The temple of Marduk.

‡The god of Justice.

§Marduk's consort.

Hammurabi, the king of righteousness, to whom Shamash has presented these laws am I. . . . If that man do not give heed to my words which I have written upon my monument, . . . as for that man, . . . may the great Anu, father of the gods, . . . take from him the glory of sovereignty, may he break his scepter and curse his fate! . . . May the great lords of heaven and earth, the Anunnaki in their totality . . . curse him with powerful curses and may they [i.e., the curses] come upon speedily!

KINGSHIP IN ANCIENT ASSYRIA

The period of Mesopotamian history from 934 to 610 BCE is known as the Neo-Assyrian era, because during this time period the Assyrian kingdom was restored and its power expanded to cover most of the Middle East. Our second Mesopotamian source dates from that era. Some sense of the ebb and flow of empires in that region and of its multiethnic nature can be gauged from the different eras, empires, and sources we have already referred to. The material we include here comes from the second period of Assyrian imperial glory, which reached its peak in the last century and a half of that era, from 745 to 610. In some ways, the Assyrians took elements of Mesopotamian kingship to an extreme. They believed in the active involvement of the gods in human affairs and that the preservation of order in the world called for strict application of the divinely established requirements. A leading scholar of the ancient Middle East gave as the subheading for a section on the Neo-Assyrian empire "Loyalty, Terror, Mercy, and Vengeance." This might be said to describe Neo-Assyrian imperial policy. A carving in one of the royal palaces depicts the great Assyrian king Assurbanipal in repose in a garden and drinking wine with his queen with the severed head of his defeated enemy, the King of Elam, hanging by its nose in the background.[3]

There is an unprecedented ferocity about Neo-Assyrian political culture, and yet, as the following reading demonstrates, the royal concern with public welfare remains present in the education and moral formation of princes. The following document was intended to teach princes how they should rule. In typical Assyrian style, it presents a sort of negative ideal for a ruler: If you do not do this, here is what will happen to you.

QUESTIONS TO CONSIDER

1. According to this "Advice," what are the most important things that a ruler must do? Whose interests does this "Advice" serve (the king, the nobles, the people)?

2. On the basis of the "Advice" presented here, devise a composite picture of an unsuccessful prince. Characterize the failings of this unsuccessful prince (for example, moral, political, religious, economic, and so on).

3. If the prince fails in his duty, who will punish him? Identify the actions against him that will occur if the prince fails to do his duty. Which involve moral punishments and which involve political rebellion?

4. How are *andurarum* (freedom) and *misharum* (equity) defended in this document? How does it compare with the Code of Hammurabi?

5. The American Declaration of Independence rejected British rule on both moral and political grounds. How do the abuses warned against here compare with those that the American Founding Fathers accused the British of?

ADVICE TO A PRINCE (circa 750 BCE)

If a king does not heed justice, his people will be thrown into chaos and his land will be devastated.

If he does not heed the justice of his land, Ea, king of destinies, will alter his destiny and he will not cease from hostilely pursuing him.

If he does not heed his nobles, his life will be cut short.

If he does not heed his adviser, his land will rebel against him.

If he heeds a rogue, the status quo in his land will change.

If he heeds a trick of Ea, the great gods in unison and in their just ways will not cease from prosecuting him.

If he improperly convicts a citizen of Sippar,* but acquits a foreigner, Shamash, judge of heaven and earth, will set up a foreign justice in his land, where the princes and judges will not heed justice.

If citizens of Nippur are brought to him for judgement, but he accepts a present† and improperly convicts them, Enlil, lord of the lands, will bring a foreign army against him to slaughter his army, whose prince and chief officers will roam his streets like fighting-cocks.

If he takes silver of the citizens of Babylon and adds it to his own coffers, or if he hears a lawsuit involving men of Babylon but treats it frivolously, Marduk, lord of Heaven and earth, will set his foes upon him, and will give his property and wealth to his enemy.

If he imposes a fine on the citizens of Nippur, Sippar or Babylon, or if he puts them in prison, the city where the fine was imposed will be completely overturned, and a foreign enemy will make his way into the prison in which they were put.

If he mobilized the whole of Sippar, Nippur and Babylon, and imposed forced labor on the people, exacting from them a corvée‡ at the herald's proclamation,

---

Source: W. G. Lambert, *Babylonian Wisdom Literature*, 113, 115. Copyright © 1967 Clarendon Press. Reprinted by permission of Eisenbrauns, Inc., Winona Lake, IN. Only one version of this text, which was on a tablet in the libraries of Assurbanipal, exists.

*Another ancient Mesopotamian city. Shamash, the god of Justice, was its patron.

†Takes a bribe.

‡Forced labor for some specified period of time.

Marduk, the sage of the gods, the prince, the counsellor, will turn his land over to his enemy so that the troops of his land will do forced labour for his enemy, for Anu, Enlil and Ea, the great gods, who dwell in heaven and earth, in their assembly affirmed the freedom of those people from such obligations.

If he gives the fodder of the citizens of Sippar, Nippur and Babylon to his own steeds, the steeds who eat the fodder will be led away to the enemy's yoke, and . . . mighty Erra,* who goes before his army, will shatter his front line and go at this enemy's side.

If he looses the yokes of their oxen, and puts them into other fields, . . . If he seizes their . . . stock of sheep, Addu,† canal supervisor of heaven and earth, will extirpate his pasturing animals by hunger and will amass offerings for Shamash.

If the adviser or chief officer of the king's presence denounces them‡ and so obtains bribes from them, at the command of Ea, king of the Apzu, the adviser or chief officer will die by the sword, their place will be covered over as a ruin, the wind will carry away their remains and their achievements will be given over to the storm wind.

If he declares their treaties void, or alters their inscribed treaty stele, sends them on a campaign or press-gangs them into hard labour, Nabu, scribe of Esagila, who organizes the whole of heaven and earth, who directs everything, who ordains kingship, will declare the treaties of his land void, and will decree hostility.

If either a shepherd or a temple overseer, or a chief officer of the king, who serves as a temple overseer of Sippar, Nippur or Babylon imposes forced labour on them§ in connection with the temples of the great gods, the great gods will quit their dwelling in their fury and will not enter their shrines.

KINGSHIP IN ISRAEL

Our second section is devoted to the kingship of ancient Israel as depicted in the Jewish Bible. The selection we include deals with the tribes' insistence on having a king against the objections of both the prophet/judge Samuel and what the work presents as the will of Yahweh himself. One tradition presented in the Jewish Bible up to I Samuel is that the real king of Israel was their god Yahweh, and that they did not need a mortal placeholder for him, because he made his wishes known to them via prophets and revelations. A second, opposing theme in the last chapters of Judges is that moral and political rot had set in during the period before the kingship was established. The ethical mess is summed up in the assertion that ends Judges, "In those days there was no king in Israel; every man did what was right in his own eyes."[4]

---

*God of war.

†God of storm and rain.

‡The people of Sippar, Nippur, and Babylon.

§The people of Sippar, Nippur, and Babylon.

In historical terms, the Jews had been a patriarchal people organized in a clan system (tribes), but the power and challenge of the Philistines over both resources and land contributed to the emergence of kingship in Israel. Historically, the Philistines had occupied the southern coastal regions, and the Jews had been centered in the inland highlands. There was not much trouble between them until both peoples had expanded enough to come into competition over resources and land. The Philistines had advantages over the Jews in both political organization and technology, at one point even capturing the Ark of the Covenant. To muster resources and manpower to meet the Philistine challenge, the Jews came to accept, and even demand, that a king be established.

Around 1000 BCE the Jews began the transition to a monarchical government. The basic story in 1 Samuel, although different versions appear in both 2 Samuel and 1 Chronicles,[5] is as follows: The Jews insist on a king; although Samuel and the Yahweh figure object, Yahweh accedes to this and designates Saul as leader. Saul demonstrates a certain effectiveness in fighting the Philistines, but, when the great Philistine champion Goliath comes forth and calls on the Jews to send out a challenger, none comes forth except for a young man slight of build and untested in terms of combat: David. Of course, David slays Goliath, but the fame that David garners from this also earns him Saul's envy and suspicion. Eventually, Saul proves his unworthiness for kingship, and he is defeated by the Philistines and killed, to be succeeded by the much more successful David, who had been anointed by Samuel. We learn little of Saul and much more about David, which accurately reflects their political and military achievements. Here our main concern is the picture of kingship that is presented, the form of election, and the responsibilities of a good ruler.

QUESTIONS TO CONSIDER

1. According to 1 Samuel, why do the Jews want a king? Why does this seem ungrateful to the Yahweh figure in these passages, and what kind of picture does the Yahweh figure draw of kingship? Is this an accurate picture of what royal governments, especially in that age, did?

2. Examine the reason that Saul had proven unworthy to be king and what made David pleasing to Yahweh. According to this material, what does the Yahweh figure value most in a king?

3. What reasons does Saul give that David is more fit than he to be king? According to this view, what should a Jewish king be like?

4. How does the role of kingship in Jewish society, according to 1 Samuel, differ from Mesopotamian kingship?

5. In your opinion, which system is closer to what legitimate government should be? Why?

1 SAMUEL

Samuel judged Israel all the days of his life. . . .

When Samuel became old, he made his sons judges over Israel. . . . Yet his sons did not walk in his ways, but turned aside after gain; they took bribes, and perverted justice.

Then all the elders of Israel gathered together and came to Samuel at Ramah and said to him, "Behold, you are old, and your sons do not walk in your ways; now appoint for us a king to govern us like all the nations." But the thing displeased Samuel when they said, "Give us a king to govern us." And Samuel prayed to the Lord. And the Lord said to Samuel, "Hearken to the voice of the people in all that they say to you; for they have not rejected you, but they have rejected me from being king over them. According to all the deeds which they have done to me, from the day I brought them up out of Egypt even to this day, forsaking me and serving other gods, so they are also doing to you. Now then, hearken to their voice; only, you shall solemnly warn them, and show them the ways of the king who shall reign over them."

So Samuel told all the words of the Lord to the people who were asking a king from him. He said, "These will be the ways of the king who will reign over you: he will take your sons and appoint them to his chariots and to be his horsemen; and to run before his chariots; and he will appoint for himself commanders of thousands and commanders of fifties, and some to plow his ground and to reap his harvest, and to make his implements of war and the equipment of his chariots. He will take your daughters to be perfumers and cooks and bakers. He will take the best of your fields and vineyards and olive orchards and give them to his servants. He will take the tenth of your grain and of your vineyards and give to his officers and to his servants. He will take your menservants and maidservants, and the best of your cattle and your asses, and put them to his work. He will take the tenth of your flocks, and you shall be his slaves. And in that day you will cry out because of your king, whom you have chosen for yourselves; but the Lord will not answer you in that day."

But the people refused to listen to the voice of Samuel; and they said, "No! but we will have a king over us, that we also may be like all the nations; and that our king may govern us and go out before us and fight our battles." And when Samuel had heard all the words of the people, he repeated them in the ears of the Lord. And the Lord said to Samuel, "Hearken to their voice, and make them a king." . . .

[Yahweh selects Saul to be king and has Samuel anoint him. The people have what they wanted, but Yahweh is displeased at their insistence on having a king, and Saul will eventually prove his unfitness for kingship. Yahweh says that he will give Saul victory, and then Saul must destroy all the livestock of the conquered people. Saul wins the victory, but together with the Jews he keeps the best livestock, arguing

---

Source: The Holy Bible, Revised Standard Edition (New York: American Bible Society, 1952), 1 Samuel 7:15; 8:1, 3–22; 13:1; 15:22–28; 16:4, 6–8, 10–13; 24:6–20.

to Samuel that the very best were sacrificed to Yahweh. For this Saul loses Yahweh's approval.]

And Samuel said, "Has the Lord as great delight in burnt offerings and sacrifices, as in obeying the voice of the Lord? Behold, to obey is better than sacrifice, and to hearken than the fat of rams. For rebellion is as the sin of divination, and stubbornness is as iniquity and idolatry. Because you have rejected the word of the Lord, he has also rejected you from being king."

And Saul said to Samuel, "I have sinned; for I have transgressed the commandment of the Lord, and your words, because I feared the people, and obeyed their voice. Now therefore, I pray, pardon my sin, and return with me, that I may worship the Lord." And Samuel said to Saul, "I will not return with you: for you have rejected the word of the Lord, and the Lord has rejected you from being king over Israel." As Samuel turned to go away, Saul laid hold upon the skirt of his robe, and it tore. And Samuel said to him, "The Lord has torn the kingdom of Israel from you this day, and has given it to a neighbor of yours, who is better than you. . . ."

[Yahweh directs Samuel to the place where Saul's successor will be, so that Samuel may anoint him.]

Samuel did what the Lord commanded, and came to Bethlehem. . . . When they came, he looked on Eliab and thought, "Surely the Lord's anointed is before him." But the Lord said to Samuel, "Do not look on his appearance or on the height of his stature, because I have rejected him; for the Lord sees not as man sees; man looks on the outward appearance, but the Lord looks on the heart." Then Jesse . . . made seven of his sons to pass before Samuel. And Samuel said to Jesse, "The Lord has not chosen these." And Samuel said to Jesse, "Are all your sons here?" And he said, "There remains yet the youngest, but behold, he is keeping the sheep." And Samuel said to Jesse, "Send and fetch him: for we will not sit down till he come here." And he sent, and brought him in. Now he was ruddy, and had beautiful eyes, and was handsome. And the Lord said, "Arise, anoint him; for this is he." Then Samuel took the horn of oil, and anointed him in the midst of his brothers: and the Spirit of the Lord came mightily upon David from that day forward. . . .

[The Philistine armies and their great champion Goliath challenge Saul to send out a champion to fight him. David was away when this challenge was issued, but he returns and accepts the challenge. David's faith gives him courage. Although the armor is too big and heavy for him, he goes into battle and fells Goliath with a stone from his slingshot, and then cuts off Goliath's head with the giant's own sword. The people now praise David, and Saul becomes jealous. He tries to get David killed in combat, to marry his daughter to him, and even throws a spear at him in anger. David flees, but Saul chases him to a remote spot. Though hidden, David is very close to Saul and cuts off the hem of his robe. But he could not harm the king, and he shows himself to Saul.]

He said to his men, "The Lord forbid that I should do this thing to my lord, the Lord's anointed, to put forth my hand against him, seeing he is the Lord's anointed."

So David persuaded his men with these words, and did not permit them to attack Saul. And Saul rose up and left the cave, and went upon his way.

Afterward David also arose, and went out of the cave, and called after Saul, saying, "My lord the king!" And when Saul looked behind him, David bowed with his face to the earth and did obeisance. And David said to Saul, "Why do you listen to the words of men who say, 'Behold, David seeks your hurt?' Lo, this day your eyes have seen how the Lord gave you today into my hand in the cave; and some bade me kill you, but I spared you. I said, 'I will not put forth my hand against my lord; for he is the Lord's anointed.' See, my father, see the skirt of your robe in my hand; for by the fact that I cut off the skirt of your robe, and did not kill you, you may know and see that there is no wrong or treason in my hands. I have not sinned against you, though you hunt my life to take it. May the Lord judge between me and you, may the Lord avenge me upon you; but my hand shall not be against you. As the proverb of the ancients says, 'Out of the wicked comes forth wickedness'; but my hand shall not be against you. After whom has the king of Israel come out? After whom do you pursue? After a dead dog! After a flea! May the Lord therefore be judge, and give sentence between me and you, and see to it, and plead my cause, and deliver me from your hand."

When David had finished speaking these words to Saul, Saul said, "Is this your voice, my son David?" And Saul lifted up his voice and wept. He said to David, "You are more righteous than I; for you have repaid me good, whereas I have repaid you evil. And you have declared this day how you have dealt well with me, in that you did not kill me when the Lord put me into your hands. For if a man finds his enemy, will he let him go away safe? So may the Lord reward you with good for what you have done to me this day. And now, behold, I know that you shall surely be king, and that the kingdom of Israel shall be established in your hand.

KINGSHIP IN INDIA

The Indian cultural and political traditions, to which we turn next, developed along far different lines than did those of Mesopotamia and the Jews. The model of kingship that will be presented here derives from the Hindu religious and cultural traditions. The main Hindu principle relating to kingship is *dharma*. In general, *dharma* means right actions necessary to sustain the moral, social, and political order. It encompasses the meanings of a whole range of duties and ethical obligations and ideals, such as duty, righteousness, virtue, justice, and morality. It also implies proper fulfillment of rituals.

The most important and best-known source in Hindu culture for the representation of ideal royal *dharma* is the great Indian epic, *The Ramayana*. It was probably originally composed somewhere around 400 BCE. Like *The Iliad*, *The Ramayana* was only recorded in written form hundreds of years after it had taken shape as a product of oral culture. Hence, we cannot know to what degree the modern form of it corresponds to the way it was told for any of the centuries before it was written down. Nonetheless, it is one of the great central tales of

Hinduism, and it is still a very popular story. Thus it embodies core values of Hindu culture. One of the most important Hindu feast days, the Festival of Lights, celebrates the triumph of good over evil and order over disorder, one example of which is from *The Ramayana*.

There is a fairy-tale quality about *The Ramayana* that distinguishes it both from the other sources in this section and from the other traditions. Rama is very much the ideal ruler in the Indian political culture. In the story, he is opposed by Ravana, who heads up a demon kingdom and who kidnaps Rama's wife, Sita. In the contrast between Rama and Ravana, we have the Indian representation of good and bad rulership. Although he does not know it, Rama is an incarnation of the god Vishnu. Unaware that he is a human form of a god, he undergoes various adventures and tests before he is finally crowned king. For our purposes, there are two parts of interest. The first is the scene in which Rama's human father, King Dasaratha, decides to step down from the throne and transfer power to his son. In this scene, we get a variety of indications, both direct and indirect, of what proper behavior for a king should be. The second is a brief description of Ravana, holding court in his palace. He is a photographic negative of Rama. His description shows what Hindu culture valued in rulers by sketching the traits of the worst sort of ruler by way of contrast.

QUESTIONS TO CONSIDER

1. According to his father, what are Rama's attributes that will make him an ideal king? Most of the focus of this passage is on Rama, but Dasaratha is a king too, of course. What ideals of royal behavior does he portray? Taken together, how do their attributes compare with the ideal traits of a Mesopotamian or Jewish king?

2. In the other traditions, we saw that there were certain obligations placed on the king both by the gods and by the people over whom the king ruled. Are there any such obligations expressed here?

3. What are the connections between the people and the kings (i.e., Dasaratha and Rama)? How do these compare with the linkages between monarch and people in the other readings in this section?

4. Identify Ravana's main features. Can you identify attributes of Rama that are the opposite of Ravana's traits? What does the negative image add to the ideal of kingship?

5. How does it change your perception of what this ideal means in Hindu culture to know that Rama is a manifestation of a god? Does this strengthen or weaken the obligations of human kings to act according to this model? How does it affect the representation of authority?

THE RAMAYANA

Ramayana

[One day Rama's father, King Dasaratha, realized that age had creeped up on him. He decided that it would be vanity to hold on to power any longer and that Rama was certainly capable of handling the responsibilities.]

In the loneliness of his chamber, Dasaratha told himself, "One must know when to cease, and not wait for death or dotage. While my faculties are intact, let me seek retirement and rest. There is no sense in continuing and repeating the same set of activities performed all these . . . years, as it seems to me now. Enough, I have done enough. I must now find the time to stand back and watch and lay aside the burdens of office."

He arrived at a drastic decision. He summoned his aide to the door, and told him to summon Sumanthra, his chief minister, immediately. "Send round an announcement for all our officers and public men, sages and wise men, and all our allies and kings and relations to gather at our hall of assembly. Let as many as possible arrive."

. . . Messengers were dispatched in all directions. The assembly hall filled up. Dasaratha ascended the steps to his seat and, after the routine ceremonials, gestured to all to resume their seats, and spoke: "I have performed my duties as King of this country long enough. Now I have an irresistible feeling that the burden must be shifted over to younger shoulders. What do you gentlemen think about it? Under the white umbrella of the royal state, apparently there has been no change—but actually the body under it is withering. I have lived and functioned long enough. If I still thought that I should continue thus endlessly, it would amount to avarice. The other day I realized that my signature on a document was hazy. My hand must have trembled without my knowing it. The time has come for me to sit back and rest—and anticipate the coming of grandchildren. If you will agree, I want to hand over the kingdom to Rama. He should be my successor, an embodiment of all perfection. He is perfect and will be a perfect ruler. He has compassion, a sense of justice, and courage, and he makes no distinction between human beings—old or young, prince or peasant; he has the same consideration for everyone. In courage, valour, and all the qualities—none to equal him. He will be your best protector from any hostile force, be it human or subhuman or superhuman. His asthras,* acquired from his master, . . . have never been known to miss their mark. . . . I hope I shall have your support in anointing him immediately as the Emperor of Kosala."

A joyous shout rang through the assembly. Dasaratha waited for it to subside and asked, "I note the zest with which you welcome my successor. Should I take it that you do so because you have been bearing with me silently for any reason all

Source: R. K. Narayan, *The Ramayana*, 35–38, 79. Copyright © 1977 Penguin Books. Used by permission of Penguin Putnam Group (USA) Inc.

*Any kind of weapon powered by a supernatural force.

these years, although I had thought I had dedicated my life fully to the welfare of my subjects?"

A spokesman arose and explained. "Do not mistake us, Your Majesty. It is our love for Rama that makes us so happy now. We have long looked forward to this moment. To see him ride the Royal Elephant in full paraphernalia through the streets of our capital is a vision of the future that we cherish, young and old alike, for we are lost in the splendour of Rama's personality. It is that anticipation that makes us applaud your proposal so unreservedly. It is not that we do not wish for the continuance of Your Majesty."

Dasaratha said, "I agree with you. I just wanted to know without a trace of doubt that you approve of my desire to make Rama your King. I desire that tomorrow when the *Pushya* star* is in combination with the moon, and the time is auspicious, Rama be crowned."

He summoned his minister and the priest. "Let everything, every little detail be ready for the ceremony of coronation tomorrow. Let there be widespread decorations and have all items ready at the coronation hall. Let the streets be washed, cleaned, and decorated. Let people feast and play and enjoy themselves unlimitedly. Let there be arrangements to serve a feast continuously in every corner of this capital. . . ."

He sent for Rama. He watched his arrival from his balcony, received him warmly, took him aside, and said, "Tomorrow, you will be crowned my successor. I need rest from work."

Rama accepted the proposal with a natural ease. Dasaratha continued. "You know everything, but still I feel it a duty to say a few words. You will have to pursue a policy of absolute justice under all circumstances. Humility and soft speech—there could be really no limit to these virtues. There can be no place in a king's heart for lust, anger, or meanness." He went on thus for some time and terminated the meeting. . . .

Ravana

Ravana, the supreme lord of this and other worlds, sat in his . . . hall, surrounded by a vast throng of courtiers and attendants. The kings of this earth whom he had reduced to vassaldom stood about with their hands upraised in an attitude of perpetual salutation, lest at any moment Ravana should turn in their direction and think that they were not sufficiently servile. Beauties gathered from all the worlds surrounded him, singing, dancing, ministering to his wants, ever ready to give him pleasure and service, with all their eyes fixed on him watching for his slightest sign of command. Every minute vast quantities of flowers were rained on him by his admirers. . . .

KINGSHIP IN CHINA

The material in this selection relates to the principle of imperial legitimacy in China, a component of Chinese political culture that endured into the twentieth century. China differed from the other cultural zones treated in this section in

---

*An Indian astrological or birth star.

that its moral values rested on an ethical system rather than on a dominant religious foundation. Or perhaps it is more accurate to say that ethics and religion were woven together indistinguishably, and as a result China lacked a separate, powerful priestly or ecclesiastical order. From very early on in Chinese cultural development there arose an idea that the cosmos is possessed of a divine order and that humans must live in concert with that order. The dominant answer that evolved as to how one should go about living in concert with the cosmic order is called *Confucianism*. Confucianism has been called "a world view, a social ethic, a political ideology, a scholarly tradition, and a way of life."[6] Though Confucius lived from 551 to 479 BCE, the body of literature on which Confucianism is founded includes both earlier literature and later commentaries and interpretations. Confucian philosophy was optimistic and maintained that humans could live in accord with the requirements of a depersonalized divine order (Heaven), if one lived the right life and maintained properly the five key relationships (king–subject, father–son, husband–wife, brother–brother, and friend–friend).

In terms of political theory, the same idea was maintained. That is, if the emperor lived and ruled properly, carried out the proper rituals and maintained the right order, then the kingdom would know peace and prosperity. Thus, in extreme cases, the absence of domestic peace and prosperity could be used to legitimize the overthrow or replacement of one dynasty by another. This aspect of Chinese political culture is known as the "Mandate of Heaven."

The earliest expression of the theory of the Mandate of Heaven appears in one of the so-called Five Classics, which make up part of the accepted body of works in the Confucian tradition. The selection that follows is from *Shu Jing*, or the *Book of History*. Confucius himself is supposed to have edited and written commentary for this book. The passage you will read is supposed to involve advice given to a young king of the Shang dynasty by Yi Yin. Yi Yin is explaining to the young monarch why the Shang dynasty had legitimately replaced the earlier Xia dynasty. In actual fact, this text was written after the overthrow of the Shang dynasty by the Zhou dynasty. Hence the text justifies the seizure of power by the Zhou dynasty (from the Shang) by showing that the Shang dynasty itself had initially come to power by a similar process and had been legitimized by the same principle—the Mandate of Heaven. Thus the ascent to power of the Zhou dynasty could only have occurred because of the loss of the Mandate by the Shang.

QUESTIONS TO CONSIDER

1. What evidence can you find of the Confucian emphasis on proper maintenance of relations? Can you identify instances of the Chinese tradition of the correct performance of rituals?
2. What are some examples of improper or immoral behavior that will lead to the disruption of the kingdom? What happens as a result of this improper behavior?

3. In some of the other texts we have read, there is an emphasis on a paternal relationship and also on justice. Do you see any signs of those in this text? If not, how do you explain their absence from this text? Do you think the Chinese were indifferent to these considerations?

4. In some of the texts you have already read, the rulers are at pains to show their concern and their intention to help and serve the people. Can you see anything in this text that reflects those same concerns?

5. How are authority and legitimate rule related in the Chinese tradition? How does the Chinese relationship between authority and legitimacy compare with the other traditions presented in this chapter?

THE INSTRUCTIONS OF YI (THE MANDATE OF HEAVEN)

In the twelfth month of the first year . . . , Yi Yin sacrificed to the former king* and presented the heir-king reverently before the shrine of his grandfather. All the princes from the domain of the nobles and the royal domain were present; all the officers also, each continuing to discharge his particular duties, were there to receive the orders of the chief minister. Yi Yin then clearly described the complete virtue of the Meritorious Ancestor for the instruction of the young king.

He said, "Oh! of old the former kings of Xia cultivated earnestly their virtue, and then there were no calamities from Heaven. The spirits of the hills and rivers alike were all in tranquility; and the birds and beasts, the fishes and tortoises, all enjoyed their existence according to their nature. But their descendant did not follow their example, and great Heaven sent down calamities, employing the agency of our ruler†— who was in possession of its favoring appointment. The attack on Xia may be traced to . . . [their] orgies . . . , but our rise began in Po.‡ Our king of Shang brilliantly displayed his sagely prowess; for oppression he substituted his generous gentleness; and the millions of the people gave him their hearts. Now your Majesty is entering on the inheritance of his virtue—all depends on how you commence your reign. To set up love, it is for you to love your relations; to set up respect, it is for you to respect your elders. The commencement is in the family and the state. . . .

Oh! the former king§ began with careful attention to the bonds that hold men together. He listened to expostulation, and did not seek to resist it; he conformed to the wisdom of the ancients; occupying the highest position, he displayed intelligence; occupying an inferior position, he displayed his loyalty; he allowed the good qualities of

---

Source: James Legge, trans., *The Sacred Books of China: The Texts of Confucianism,* in *The Sacred Books of the East,* ed. F. Max Mueller, 50 vols. (Oxford, UK: Clarendon Press, 1879–1910), vol. 3, pp. 92–95.

*That is, to the young king's recently deceased father.

†That is, the young king's grandfather and founder of the Shang dynasty.

‡The name of the home territory of the Shang dynasty.

§Again, the young king's grandfather.

the men whom he employed and did not seek that they should have every talent. . . . It was thus he arrived at the possession of the myriad regions. How painstaking was he in these things!

He extensively sought out wise men, who should be helpful to you, his descendant and heir. He laid down the punishments for officers, and warned those who were in authority, saying, "If you dare to have constant dancing in your palaces, and drunken singing in your chambers—that is called the fashion of sorcerers; if you dare to set your hearts on wealth and women, and abandon yourselves to wandering about or to the chase,*—that is called the fashion of extravagance; if you dare to despise sage words, to resist the loyal and upright, to put far from you the aged and virtuous, and to seek the company of precocious youth—that is called the fashion of disorder. Now if a high noble or officer be addicted to one of these three fashions with their ten evil ways, his family will surely come to ruin; if the prince of a country be so addicted, his state will surely come to ruin. The minister who does not try to correct such vices in the sovereign shall be punished with branding." These rules were minutely inculcated also in the son of officers and nobles in their lessons.

"Oh! do you, who now succeed to the throne, revere these warnings in your person. Think of them!—sacred counsels of vast importance, admirable words forcibly set forth! The ways of Heaven are not invariable: on the good-doer it sends down all blessings, and on the evil-doer it sends down all miseries. Do you but be virtuous, be it in small things or in large, and the myriad regions will have cause for rejoicing. If you be not virtuous, be it in large things or in small, it will bring the ruin of your ancestral temple."

NOTES

1. Amelie Kuhrt, *The Ancient Near East,* vol. 1 (New York: Routledge, 1998), 33.

2. See C. C. Lamberg-Karlovsky, "The Near Eastern 'Breakout' and the Mesopotamian Social Contract," in *The Breakout: The Origins of Civilization,* ed. M. Lamberg-Karlovsky (Cambridge, MA: Peabody Museum Monographs, 2000), 14–15, 20–21.

3. Amelie Kuhrt, *The Ancient Near East,* vol. 2 (London and New York: Routledge, 1998), 514, 517.

4. On Judges, see Howard Clark Lee, et al., *The Cambridge Companion to the Bible* (Cambridge, UK: Cambridge University Press, 1997), 118–19. The passage cited is from Judges 21:25.

5. See Cyrus H. Gordon and Gary A. Rendsburg, *The Bible and the Ancient Near East* (New York: W. W. Norton & Co., 1997 [1953]), 186–87. In 2 Samuel, a different hero named Elhanan kills Goliath. 1 Chronicles has Elhanan killing Goliath's brother.

6. Tu Wei-ming, "The Confucian Tradition in Chinese History," in *Heritage of China: Contemporary Perspectives on Chinese Civilization,* ed. P. S. Ropp (Berkeley, CA: University of California Press, 1990), 112.

---

*Hunting.

PART TWO

FOUNDATION CULTURES:
600 BCE TO 300 CE

CHAPTER 4

Individual Ethics and Social Responsibility

INTRODUCTION

The Corporate and Criminal Fraud Accountability Act of 2002, signed into law on July 30, 2002, by President George W. Bush, established strong protections for corporate whistleblowers. "Without protecting the whistleblowers, corporate reform efforts would have failed," said Kris Kolesnik, Executive Director of the National Whistleblower Center.[1]

Whistleblowers—employees who report illegal (but usually profitable) behavior on the part of their employers—face a modern version of an old dilemma: the potential conflict between individual actions and the harmonious workings of the larger social group of which the individual is a member (in the case of whistleblowers, the company they work for). Is it better to obey one's leaders without question, on the premise that unless everyone does their part loyally the society will fall apart? If no one questions authority, however, will the result be a mindlessly conformist society in which, for example, six million Jews could die because everyone was "only following orders"? Is it therefore better for each individual to do as he or she thinks best? Or will chaos and social breakdown result from a lack of agreed-on leadership and norms—how, after all, does one decide what is best? Is there a middle ground where individual ethical action can contribute to the harmonious functioning of society? As the director of the National Whistleblower Center points out, whistleblowers who are disruptive troublemakers from one perspective are from another perspective social reformers serving a higher cause.

There are no easy answers to these questions. They arise in any complex society, but they become particularly acute in times of crisis and transformation, when the need for reform may be greatest. Around 600 BCE, many of the most populous and complex societies of Eurasia seemed to face just such a time of crisis. A number of factors—including growing population, increased contact with other cultures, the spread of iron-working technology, and political disruptions often associated with nomadic incursions—brought instability to older systems of political organization and so brought the intellectual systems that legitimized those political organizations into question. Mythic worldviews based in sacrifice and obedience to angry gods, although not discarded, no longer provided adequate answers to the problems of social organization and individual ethical action within society.

In this context, there arose a remarkable range of thinkers, both secular and religious, who suggested answers to these problems within their own societies. A simple list of names from the first several centuries after 600 BCE suggests the importance of the theories developed during this period and their continuing impact: Confucius, Mencius, Lao Tzu, the Buddha, Zarathustra, Isaiah, Socrates, and Plato, to name only some of the most prominent. These thinkers produced systems of philosophy and religion of such power and intellectual coherence that they have formed the foundations of social and ethical theory in many parts of the world ever since. In this sense, these are the names of a classical age, an age of the creation of great traditions. This chapter explores some of these systems of philosophy and religion and the encounter between individual ethics and social responsibility within them.

But as the list of names suggests, societies tended to produce many different answers to such complex questions, and another set of encounters this chapter examines is the philosophical encounter of thinker against thinker. In every area, there were arguments, experiments, and, usually, an ultimate synthesis that began to emerge sometime around 200 BCE. Thus, as you read different sources from any one civilization, look not just for the points of disagreement between them, which will be fairly clear, but for their bases of agreement as well. Often this agreement will reside at the level of fundamental assumptions about the topic rather than in the details of what each source says, and it is the character of these fundamental assumptions that would come to characterize the synthesis, or the Great Tradition, and the intellectual nature of the civilization that produced it. For example, Pericles, in the funeral oration Thucydides records in his *History of the Peloponnesian Wars,* outlines a conception of citizenship in which civic duty is paramount. Sophocles, on the other hand, bases the tragedy of *Antigone* on the conflict between such civic duty and a higher duty to family and the gods. The disagreement is clear. The perhaps less obvious agreement is that the *polis,* the independent city-state, was the natural and proper realm of both individual action and social organization. The question for each, in other words, is the proper functioning of the *polis* and the limits of its power over individuals. Although Confucius and Lao Tzu deal with the same big issue—the relationship of individual ethical action and social order—their unstated assumptions, or the particular way they frame the question, are different. Figuring out what those assumptions are will reveal important intellectual and cultural characteristics about each civilization.

The encounter between philosophies also brought to the fore the issue of education, for individual thinkers gained influence only insofar as they gathered followers who spread the master's teachings, creating a school of thought. And education became a topic for many of these thinkers, as well as a practical issue, because depending on where one sees the balance between social order and individual action, one will see the function of education differently. Is the purpose of education to produce free thinkers, creative minds that will question authority and accepted ways of doing things? This is a dominant modern conception of the purpose of education, embodied in the liberal arts education offered at many colleges and universities. But it has by no means eclipsed another conception: that the purpose of education is to train people in a society's accepted principles and ways of doing things, thereby producing good citizens (or subjects) and social harmony. One need only look at the arguments about national history standards in the United States today to see both sides of this argument flourishing, with one side arguing that we need a common history to hold us together, the other side arguing that the myths and exclusiveness of the usually told common story contribute to oppression and prejudice.

We look at thinkers from four Great Traditions that emerged in this age. First, Confucius, Lao Tzu, and Han Fei Tzu are three of the wellsprings of the Chinese tradition. The first two lived near the end of the Chou dynasty (771 to 464 BCE); the last lived in the middle of the subsequent Warring States era of Chinese history (464 to 221 BCE). The later Chou era saw the breakdown of the political unity established in China by the Chou, as the regional princes who owed obedience to the Chou king increasingly followed their own paths, including fighting each other for prestige and honor. The shift to the Warring States was marked by an increase in the intensity of warfare and the gradual disappearance of many of the hundreds of small states of the Chou era. The centrality of warfare and conflict in Chinese life during these centuries, as well as the lack of political unity, proved intensely troublesome to many Chinese thinkers, some of whom looked back to the early Chou era as a sort of "Golden Age" of peace and harmony in the Chinese cultural world, others of whom looked for contemporary answers to these problems.

Next, we look at Thucydides and Sophocles, mentioned previously, from the Greek tradition. Frequent warfare also characterized the world of Classical Greece (650–350 BCE), but political disunity was taken as the norm in the Greek world, which was divided into numerous small *poleis* (singular *polis*), or city-states. Each *polis* was defended by groups of its own citizens, who also participated in the fractious and competitive politics of their city-state. This participation ranged from informal, in more narrowly ruled monarchical or aristocratic cities, to completely formal and empowered in democratic Athens. In this world, and especially in Athens, where broad participation in politics raised questions of social order with special intensity and where leadership in the war against the Persians broadened the importance of the issues, questions of individual ethics and social order were debated by politicians, philosophers, and makers of culture, including playwrights.

The Greeks and Chinese approached these issues from a basically secular perspective. This does not mean that religion had no importance in these societies. But religion in both places tended to serve purposes other than answering questions of individual ethical action within the context of social order. Religion was central, however, to the next two traditions we examine, rising in both places to the level of philosophical systems that functioned in the same way the secular traditions of China and Greece did. First, we have a classic statement of social responsibility from India in the *Bhagavad-Gita,* followed by the early teachings of the Buddha. Indian religion, in particular what would come to be known as the Hindu religion, developed over a long period after the Aryan invasions of the subcontinent around 1500 BCE. By the period 700–500 BCE, the major outlines of Brahminical Hinduism, a faith shaped by the teachings of the Brahmins, the priestly class, were moving from the realm of oral traditions to texts known as *Upanishads,* which means "to sit down before [a teacher]." The Upanishads' orientation toward a priest-dominated religion reflects the movement of Indian society from a warrior-dominated system in the wake of the invasions to a society in which the Brahmins occupied the highest position in what was becoming a caste system. *Caste* refers to hierarchical social divisions determined at birth—that is, a rigid class system with no mobility between castes. The four major castes, or *varna,* were the Brahmins; the Kshatriyas, or rulers and warriors; the Vaisyas, or laborers; and the Sudras, or slaves. The caste system and the cosmological[2] assumptions that underlay it came to dominate the intellectual landscape of India. It shaped both efforts to explain and justify social order and individual responsibility within it, which is the function of the *Bhagavad-Gita,* and efforts to escape the rigidity of the caste system, which characterizes early Buddhism.

Finally, we look at two statements of ethical theism from southwest Asia: the Persian tradition, stemming from the prophet Zarathustra, and the Hebrew tradition, as stated by the prophet Isaiah. Southwest Asia, perhaps the area of the world most open to external influences because of its position as a crossroads of Afro-Eurasian trade, migration, and invasion, had already witnessed by 600 BCE the rise and fall of many kingdoms and empires and the encounters of numerous peoples. Around 600, one of these peoples, the Persians of the Iranian plateau, inherited the imperial mission in the area and created the first of the great empires of this age. It was in the context of Persian conquest of and rule over many peoples and already venerable civilizations that both the Persians and the Hebrews developed remarkably similar (and probably cross-fertilized) religious views of the cosmos, history, and their peoples' place in the social order and ethical struggles of the universe.

Though their approaches differed widely, all of these traditions addressed the problems of social order and its interaction with individual ethical decision making and action. Hence these readings involve fundamental aspects of human existence: encounters between individual ethics and systems of social values, encounters between individual thinkers within the grand ethical traditions, and encounters between the ethical systems themselves. The answers that the thinkers of these traditions arrived at continue to have relevance today.

CHAPTER QUESTIONS

1. What are the crucial issues that bring individual ethics and social order into focus for these authors? That is, what problems face the societies of this age? Are they similar across Eurasia?

2. Considering these sources as a group, where does the balance seem to lie in classical societies between individually motivated action and social constraints? Is there variation among the sources? Which seems most individualistic and which most socially oriented?

3. What appears to be the basis for underlying agreement within each tradition? That is, what would the authors from each tradition agree on that distinguishes them from the authors of the other traditions?

4. What are the vested interests in these debates? That is, does the position of a source's author within the social hierarchy seem to influence where he draws the line between individual and society (or between stability and reform)? And does that line differ for different members of society as determined by class, gender, or occupation?

5. What would each author think about whistleblowers? Would they wish to reward or punish a whistleblower's "betrayal" of his or her employer? Which of these authors might be considered a whistleblower in his own society?

THE CHINESE TRADITION

Classical Chinese systems of thought arose during the last centuries of the Chou dynasty (771 to 464 BCE) and the period known as the Warring States (464 to 221 BCE). During this time the political unity established in north China by the first dynasty for which we have substantial information, the Shang, and continued by their Chou successors after 1050 BCE broke down, and China became a land of many small states that tended to engage in constant warfare with each other. Many Chinese thinkers responded to this disorder with programs for social and political reform. We shall look at the foundational texts for what proved, in the long run, to be the most influential of these many schools of thought: Confucianism, Taoism, and Legalism. Each addresses the problem of social order, individual responsibility, and the role of the state in maintaining the balance between the two, but each puts the emphasis on a different aspect of this set of factors. Although the three schools competed with and criticized each other, their different emphases meant that in many ways they proved complementary rather than mutually exclusive.

The Confucian Tradition

In the long run the most influential of Chinese philosophers was Kung Fu Tzu (Master Kung Fu), whose name was Latinized by the Jesuits in the seventeenth century to Confucius. Born in 551 BCE in the state of Lu, Confucius traveled widely, looking for a ruler who would heed his advice on good rulership and restoring the harmony to Chinese civilization. His prescriptions for reform looked back to the age of the founders of the Chou dynasty, King Wen and King Wu—and, indeed, even farther back to the semilegendary founders of the Shang dynasty—for models of leadership, correct individual behavior, and the foundations of social order. His program of reform was, therefore, like many such programs in the traditional world, backward looking, advocating a return to the virtues of an earlier Golden Age. But Confucius was no simple imitator of old ways. His teachings—collected by his students and eventually written down in several versions, one of which is *The Analects* as we have it—stress the importance of education and the malleability of human nature, and so offered openings for further interpretation. The nature of the *Analects* themselves—fragmentary, organized apparently haphazardly, but with an underlying coherence that invites further study and thought—contributed to the vitality of Confucian philosophy.

Confucius himself, however, found no real takers for his services among those in power during his lifetime. He died in 479 BCE, thinking that he had failed as a teacher and government advisor. It was only in later generations that his teachings became central to the Chinese tradition.

Key terms and concepts in *The Analects*

li: ritual, decorum, civility, rites, rules of propriety

ren: humanity, humaneness, human-heartedness, benevolence, goodness

te: virtue, moral force, power

tien ming: the biddings or mandate of Heaven, the will of Heaven

wen: culture, civilization, refinement

Confucius weaves these concepts together into a coherent account of social relationships and individual responsibility within them. As the list of terms shows, proper behavior—not just what we would call manners, but also ritual, rites, and the music that accompanied them—was central to Confucius's teaching.

QUESTIONS TO CONSIDER

1. What are the qualities of a Confucian "gentleman"? How does he differ from a "small man"?
2. What does Confucius mean by "humanity" or "being humane"? Why does he think that the wrong way to cultivate humanity is through chastisement, regulations, and law? What is the right way?
3. What are the foundations of social order for Confucius? What models of authority and obedience does he cite?
4. What sort of social order would be produced if everyone strictly followed his advice? What is the relationship for Confucius between individual behavior and social order? Would Confucian government benefit the common people, as he claims? How practical do you think his program of reform is?
5. Would Confucius encourage whistleblowers?

THE ANALECTS

Confucius

Book 1

1.1. The Master said, To learn and at due times to repeat what one has learned, is that not after all a pleasure? That friends should come to one from afar, is this not after all

---

Source: The translation is a version of *The Analects of Confucius,* trans. Arthur Waley, edited in part by David Blix of Wabash College. Copyright © 1989. Used by permission of Vintage Books, a division of Random House, Inc.

delightful? To remain unsoured even though one's merits are unrecognized by others, is that not after all what is expected of a gentleman?

1.2. Master Yu [a disciple of Confucius] said, Those who in private life behave well towards their parents and elder brothers, in public life seldom show a disposition to resist the authority of their superiors. And as for such men starting a revolution, no instance of it has ever occurred. It is upon the root that a gentleman works. When that is firmly planted, the Way* grows. And surely proper behavior towards parents and elder brothers is the root of humanity.

1.5. The Master said, A country of a thousand war-chariots cannot be administered unless the ruler attends strictly to business, punctually observes his promises, is economical in expenditure, shows affection towards his subjects in general, and uses the labor of the common people only at the proper times of year.

1.6. The Master said, A young man's duty is to behave well to his parents at home and to his elders abroad, to be cautious in giving promises and punctual in keeping them, to have kindly feelings towards everyone, but to associate with humane men. If, when all that is done, he has any energy to spare, then let him study the polite arts [*wen*].

Book 2

2.1. The Master said, He who rules by virtue [*te*] is like the pole-star, which remains in its place while all the lesser stars do homage to it.

2.2. The Master said, If out of the three hundred *Songs*† I had to take one phrase to cover all my teaching, I would say "Let there be no evil in your thoughts."

2.3. The Master said, Govern the people by regulations, keep order among them by chastisements, and they will flee from you, and lose all self-respect. Govern them by virtue, keep order among them by ritual, and they will keep their self-respect and come to you of their own accord.

2.4. The Master said, At fifteen I set my heart upon learning. At thirty, I had taken my stance. At forty, I no longer suffered from perplexities. At fifty, I knew what were the biddings of Heaven [*t'ien-ming*]. At sixty, I heard them with docile ear. At seventy, I could follow the dictates of my own heart; for what I desired no longer overstepped the boundaries of righteousness.

2.5. Meng Yi Tzu [a disciple] asked about the treatment of parents. The Master said, Never disobey! When Fan Ch'ih [another disciple] was driving his carriage for him, the Master said, Meng asked me about the treatment of parents and I said, Never disobey! Fan Ch'ih said, In what sense did you mean it? The Master said, While they are alive, serve them according to ritual. When they die, bury them according to ritual, and sacrifice to them according to ritual.

Tao, meaning "The Way," is the word used by virtually every Chinese school of thought to name its teachings as a whole. Thus, there is a Confucian Way, a Legalist Way, and so forth. But later Chinese and Western scholarship have also attached *Tao* specifically to the teachings of Taoism (see next source). This is not the sense used here; this is the Way of Confucius (or the Way of the Gentleman, as Confucius might have said).

†*The Book of Songs,* a collection of poems from Chou times taken as a canonical text by Confucius. As songs, they were connected with music and rites in the realm of Confucian proper behavior.

2.13. Tzu-kung [a disciple] asked about the true gentleman. The Master said, He does not preach what he practices till he has practiced what he preaches.

2.14. The Master said, A gentleman can see a question from all sides without bias. The small man is biased and can see a question only from one side.

2.15. The Master said, He who learns but does not think, is lost. He who thinks but does not learn is in great danger.

Book 3

3.3. The Master said, A man who is not humane, what can he have to do with ritual [li]? A man who is not humane, what can he have to do with music?

3.7. The Master said, Gentlemen never compete. You will say that in archery they do so. But even then they bow and make way for one another when they are going up to the archery-ground, when they are coming down, and at the subsequent drinking-bout. Thus even when competing, they still remain gentlemen.

Book 6

6.16. The Master said, When inborn qualities prevail over culture, you get the boorishness of the rustic. When culture prevails over inborn qualities, you get the pedantry of the scribe. Only when culture and inborn qualities are duly blended do you get the true gentleman.

Book 8

8.2. The Master said, Courtesy not bounded by the prescriptions of ritual becomes tiresome. Caution not bounded by the prescriptions of ritual becomes timidity, daring becomes turbulence, inflexibility becomes harshness. The Master said, When gentlemen deal generously with their own kin, the common people are incited to humanity. When old dependents are not discarded, the common people will not be fickle.

8.9. The Master said, The common people can be made to follow it; they cannot be made to understand it.

Book 13

13.3. Tzu-lu said, If the prince of Wei were waiting for you to come and serve in his government, what would be your first measure? The Master said, It would certainly be the rectification of names.* Tzu-lu said, Can I have heard you aright? Surely what you say has nothing to do with the matter. Why should names be rectified? The Master said, Tzu-lu! How boorish you are! With regard to things he does not understand, a gentleman should maintain an attitude of reserve. If names are not rectified, then what is said does not correspond to what is meant. If what is said does not correspond to what is meant, then what is to be done will not be accomplished. If what is to be

---

*"Rectification of names" is an important Confucian doctrine that advocated not just calling things by their proper names but also encouraging people to conform to the proper meaning of the "name" of their social position. Thus Confucius said: "Let the father be a father, let the son be a son." That is, let each rectify his behavior to match the ideal implied by the word, and let the word be used only of fathers and sons who act as true fathers and sons. The doctrine recognizes and attempts to shape the social power of language.

done cannot be accomplished, then ritual and music will not flourish. If ritual and music do not flourish, then punishments will go astray. If punishments go astray, then the common people will not know where to put hand and foot. Thus the gentleman gives to things only those names which can be used in speech, and says only what can be carried out in practice. A gentleman, in what he says, leaves nothing to mere chance.

Book 15

15.14. The Master said, To demand much from oneself and little from others is the way for a ruler to banish discontent.

15.20. The Master said, The demands that a gentleman makes are upon himself. Those that a small man makes are upon others.

15.21. The Master said, A gentleman is proud, but not quarrelsome, allies himself with individuals, but not with parties.

15.23. Tzu-kung asked, Is there any single saying that one can act upon all day and every day? The Master said, Perhaps the saying about consideration: "Never do to others what you would not like them to do to you."

15.29. The Master said, To have faults and to be making no effort to amend them is to have faults indeed!

15.31. The Master said, A gentleman, in his plans, thinks of the Way. He does not think how he is going to make a living. Even farming sometimes entails times of shortage; and even learning may incidentally lead to high pay. But a gentleman's anxieties concern the progress of the Way. He has no anxiety concerning poverty.

15.35. The Master said, When it comes to being humane, one need not avoid competing with one's teacher.

Book 17

17.2. The Master said, By nature men are pretty much alike; it is learning and practice that set them apart.

LAO TZU AND TAOISM

Little is known of Lao Tzu, the supposed author of the *Tao te ching*, or "Classic of the Way and its Virtue." He was (probably) an older contemporary of Confucius: legend has it he was visited several times by Confucius, to whom he once said: "Abandon your arrogant ways and countless desires, your suave demeanor and unbridled ambition, for they do not promote your welfare. That is all I have to say to you." Parts of the *Tao te ching* certainly seem to respond to Confucian teachings. Legend also has it that he was the Keeper of the Archives in Chou, where the last of the Chou kings still lived, before disappearing forever into the west in his old age, leaving behind only his small, enigmatic book on the Tao.

Tao (pronounced "dow") means "way." Confucius and Han Fei Tzu both also use this word, but with a very different meaning from Lao Tzu, and it is to

Lao Tzu's version of the Way that Chinese history has attached the term *Taoism.* Even more than *The Analects,* the *Tao te ching* is cryptic, poetically mysterious, and open to multiple interpretations (and indeed multiple translations, some of which don't even look like the same work!). In other words, don't look for a logical, linear argument here, but for images, suggestions, and definition by negation. The last may be taken as a metaphor for the Taoist concept of "action through inaction": by doing nothing (or saying what something is not), something (an idea of what something is) is accomplished.

The Tao is, like *The Analects,* partly a handbook for rulers, but it has been taken even more often as a guide to individual life and behavior, and indeed the individualism and emphasis on individual freedom and choice of the *Tao*'s teachings is one of the things that distinguishes it from Confucian thought. This emphasis leads to a clear opposition to ritual in the *Tao.* Read it both as a response and as a potential complement to Confucianism, for the two teachings are not mutually exclusive: One could in certain ways be both a Confucian and a Taoist.

QUESTIONS TO CONSIDER

1. What is the *Tao*? What qualities does Lao Tzu ascribe to it? What metaphors does he use to describe it?
2. A key term in the *Tao* is *wu-wei,* variously translated (loosely) as "inaction" or, more evocatively, "going with the flow." How is *wu-wei* a means to the managing of affairs?
3. What are the principles of social order for Lao Tzu? How do they emerge from the meaning of the *Tao*? What is the role of the individual in fostering social order?
4. Do you think Lao Tzu's Taoism would work as a form of government? As a basis for social order? As an individual lifestyle? Why or why not?
5. What would Lao Tzu think of whistleblowers?

TAO TE CHING

Lao Tzu

Book I: The Book of the Way

1. The Tao that can be told of is not the eternal Tao.
The name that can be named is not the eternal name.
The Nameless is the origin of Heaven and Earth.
The Named is the mother of all things.

Source: From *The Way of Lao Tzu, Tao te ching,* trans. Wing-tsit Ch'an. Copyright © 1963 Prentice-Hall. Reprinted by permission of Pearson Education, Inc., Upper Saddle River, NJ.

Therefore let there always be non-being so we may see their subtlety,
And let there always be being so we may see their outcome.
The two are the same.
But after they are produced, they have different names.
They both may be called deep and profound.
Deeper and more profound,
The door of all subtleties!

2. When the people of the world all know beauty as beauty,
There arises the recognition of ugliness.
When they all know the good as good,
There arises the recognition of evil.
Therefore:
Being and non-being produce each other.
Difficult and easy complete each other.
Long and short contrast each other.
High and low distinguish each other.
Sound and voice harmonize with each other.
Front and back follow each other.
Therefore the sage manages affairs without action [*wu-wei*],
And spreads doctrines without words.
All things arise, and he does not turn away from them.
He produces them, but does not take possession of them.
He acts, but does not rely on his own ability.
He accomplishes his task, but does not claim credit for it.
It is precisely because he does not claim credit that his accomplishment remains
    with him.

3. Do not exalt the worthy, so that the people shall not compete.
Do not value goods that are hard to get, so that the people shall not steal.
Do not display objects of desire, so that the people's hearts shall not be disturbed.
Therefore in the government of the sage,
He keeps their hearts vacuous,
Fills their bellies,
Weakens their ambitions,
And strengthens their bones.
He always causes his people to be without knowledge or desire,
And the crafty to be afraid to act.
By acting without action, all things will be in order.

5. Heaven and Earth are not humane [*ren*].
They regard all things as straw dogs.*
The sage is not humane.
He regards all people as straw dogs.

---

*Dogs made of straw were used for sacrifices in ancient China and then thrown away.

How Heaven and Earth are like a bellows!
While vacuous, it is never exhausted.
When active, it produces even more.
Much talk will of course come to a dead end.
It is better to keep to the center.

8. The best man is like water.
Water is good; it benefits all things and does not compete with them.
It dwells in lowly places that all disdain.
This is why it is so near to the Tao.
The best man in his dwelling loves the earth.
In his heart, he loves what is profound.
In his associations, he loves humanity.
In his words, he loves faithfulness.
In government, he loves order.
In handling affairs, he loves competence.
In his activities, he loves timeliness.

11. Thirty spokes are united around the hub to make a wheel,
But it is on its non-being that the utility of the carriage depends.
Clay is molded to form a utensil,
But it is on its non-being that the utility of the utensil depends.
Doors and windows are cut out to make a room,
But it is on its non-being that the utility of the room depends.
Therefore turn being into advantage, and turn non-being into utility.

17. The best rulers are those whose existence is merely known by the people.
The next best are those who are loved and praised.
The next are those who are feared.
And the next are those who are despised.
It is only when one does not have enough faith in others that others will have
   no faith in him.

18. When the great Tao declined,
The doctrines of humanity and righteousness arose.
When knowledge and wisdom appeared,
There emerged great hypocrisy.
When the six family relationships* are not in harmony,
There will be the advocacy of filial piety and deep love to children.
When a country is in disorder,
There will be praise of loyal ministers.

---

*Father–son, elder brother–younger brother, husband–wife; these family relationships were important to Confucian thought.

Book II: The Book of Virtue

48. The pursuit of learning is to increase day after day.
The pursuit of the Tao is to decrease day after day.
It is to decrease and further decrease until one reaches the point of taking no action.
No action is undertaken, and yet nothing is left undone.
An empire is often brought to order by having no activity.
If one likes to undertake activity, he is not qualified to govern the empire.

80. Let there be a small country with few people.
Let there be ten times and a hundred times as many utensils,
But let them not be used.
Let the people value their lives highly and not migrate far.
Even if there are ships and carriages, none will ride in them.
Even if there are armor and weapons, none will display them.
Let the people again knot cords and use them [in place of writing].
Let them relish their food, beautify their clothing, be content with their homes, and
     delight in their customs.
Though neighboring communities overlook one another, and the crowing of cocks
     and barking of dogs can be heard,
Yet the people there may grow old and die without ever visiting one another.

HAN FEI TZU AND LEGALISM

The third writer here differs from the first two in a number of ways. Han Fei Tzu
(Master Han Fei) was born a prince of the northern state of Han, one of the
successor states of the old state of Chou, and was thus of noble lineage. He lived
later—he was born around 280 BCE, near the end of the Warring States era.
And therefore the urgency of reform showed itself differently to Han Fei Tzu
than it had to Confucius or Lao Tzu: The state of Han's very existence was threatened during Han Fei Tzu's lifetime by the growing power of the state of Qin to
its west.

   Han Fei had been educated in Confucianism as a young man, but the condition of his own state led him to doubt and eventually reject these teachings as im-
practical and to focus instead on what could be done to strengthen the state. The
result of his concern was a long book, known now as the *Han Fei Tzu*, after its
author, that is the clearest statement of the school of thought known as Legalism,
or the Way of Law. Han Fei advocated strengthening agriculture and the army, reducing the influence of "enemies of the state" through the impartial application
of law, and ruling through an efficient administration. In terms of individual behavior and social order, Han Fei obviously gives primacy to social order and, indeed, subordinates even that to the needs of the state, which are the primary
concern in his writing. This formula arrives at very different answers to the problems posed in this chapter from those of Confucius and Lao Tzu.

Unfortunately, Han Fei's book, aimed at his own king, found no response there and came instead to the attention of the king of Qin. Han Fei met the Qin monarch on a diplomatic mission in 233 BCE and was at first kindly received. But he got caught up in court intrigues and was imprisoned and forced to drink poison. Shortly afterward the ruler of Qin, following some of Han Fei Tzu's advice, conquered Han, then went on to conquer and unite the rest of China by 221 BCE, becoming the First Emperor of China. Han Fei Tzu thus won an ironic victory in the battle of armies and philosophies that characterized the Warring States era. The victory proved short-lived in one way, as the harshness of Qin rule brought the new imperial dynasty down within twenty years. Legalism was discredited in the eyes of later Chinese scholars, mostly Confucian. But the structures of Chinese rule, laid down in the Warring States period by Legalist rulers, persisted beneath the cover of Confucian (and Taoist) philosophy.

QUESTIONS TO CONSIDER

1. Who are the "Five Vermin"? Why are these types of people enemies of a strong state, according to Han Fei Tzu? What are the "Two Handles" and how do they lead to an orderly society?
2. How does Han Fei Tzu propose to measure individual action? Is this a system of ethical decision making for individuals?
3. How does strict adherence to Law (including the use of strict punishments) lead to social order, according to Han Fei Tzu?
4. Does Legalism strike you as a workable system of government? Is it a useful guide to individual action and the creation of social order? What might the advantages and dangers of a strictly Legalist state be?
5. What would Han Fei Tzu think of whistleblowers?

THE FIVE VERMIN

Han Fei Tzu

An enlightened ruler will administer his state in such a way as to decrease the number of merchants, artisans, and other men who make their living by wandering from place to place, and will see to it that such men are looked down upon. In this way he lessens the number of people who abandon primary pursuits [i.e., agriculture] to take up secondary occupations. Nowadays, however, if a man can enlist the private pleading of someone at court, he can buy offices and titles. When offices and titles can be

Source: From *Han Fei Tzu,* trans. Burton Watson. Copyright © 1964 Columbia University Press. Reprinted with permission.

bought, you may be sure that merchants and artisans will not remain despised for long. And when wealth and money, no matter how dishonestly gotten, can buy what is in the market, you may be sure that the number of merchants will not remain small for long. When a man who sits back and collects taxes makes twice as much as the farmer, and enjoys greater honor than the plowman or the soldier, then public-spirited men will grow few, and merchants and tradesmen will increase in number.

These are the customs of a disordered state. Its scholars praise the ways of the former kings and imitate their humanity and righteousness. They put on a fair appearance and speak in elegant phrases, thus casting doubt upon the laws of the time and causing the ruler to be of two minds. Its speechmakers propound false schemes and borrow influence from abroad, furthering their private interests and forgetting the welfare of the state's altars of the soil and grain. Its swordsmen gather bands of followers about them and perform deeds of honor, making a fine name for themselves and violating the prohibitions of the five government bureaus. Those of its people who are worried about military service flock to the gates of private individuals and pour out their wealth in bribes to influential men who will plead for them. In this way they escape the hardship of battle. Its merchants and artisans spend their time making luxury goods, accumulating riches, waiting for the best time to sell, and exploiting the farmers.

These five groups are the vermin of the state. If the rulers do not wipe out such vermin, and in their place encourage men of integrity and public spirit, then they should not be surprised when they look about the area within the four seas, and see states perish and ruling houses wane and die.

On Having Standards

In our present age he who can put an end to private scheming and make men uphold the public law will see his people secure and his state well-ordered. He who can block selfish pursuits and enforce the public law will see his armies growing stronger and his enemies weakening. . . .

Now if able men are selected for promotion on the basis of reputation alone, then the officials will disregard the ruler and seek only the good will of their associates and subordinates. If appointments to office are controlled by cliques, then men will work only to establish profitable connections and will not try to achieve office by regular routes. In such cases, official posts will never be filled by able men, and the state will fall into disorder.

If rewards are handed out on the basis of good report alone, and punishments on the basis of slander, then men who covet rewards and fear punishment will abandon the public interest and pursue only private schemes, banding together to further each other's interests.

A truly enlightened ruler uses the law to select men for him; he does not choose them himself. He uses the law to weigh their merits; he does not attempt to judge them for himself. Hence men of true worth will not be able to hide their talents, nor spoilers to gloss over their faults. Men cannot advance on the basis of praise alone, nor be driven from court by slander. Then there will be a clear understanding of values between the ruler and his ministers, and the state can be easily governed. But only if the ruler makes use of law can he hope to achieve this.

The Two Handles

The enlightened ruler controls his ministers by means of two handles alone. The two handles are punishment and favor. What do I mean by punishment and favor? To inflict mutilation and death on men is called punishment; to bestow honor and reward is called favor. Those who act as ministers fear the penalties and hope to profit by the rewards. Hence, if the ruler wields his punishments and favors, the ministers will fear his sternness and flock to receive his benefits.

If the ruler of men wishes to put an end to evil-doing, then he must be careful to match up names and results, that is to say, words and deeds. The ministers come forward to present their proposals. The ruler assigns them tasks on the basis of their words, and then concentrates on demanding the accomplishment of the task. If the accomplishment fits the task, and the task fits the words, then he bestows reward. But if they do not match, he doles out punishment.

Hence, if one of the ministers comes forward with big words but produces only small accomplishments, the ruler punishes him—not because the accomplishments are small, but because they do not match the name that was given to the undertaking. Likewise, if one of the ministers comes forward with small words but produces great accomplishments, he too is punished—not because the ruler is displeased at great accomplishments, but because he considers the discrepancy in the name given to the undertaking to be a fault too serious to be outweighed by great accomplishments.

Hence an enlightened ruler, in handling his ministers, does not permit them to gain merit by overstepping their offices, or to speak words that do not tally with their actions. Those who overstep their offices are condemned to die. Those whose words and actions do not tally are punished. If the ministers are made to stick to their proper duties and speak only what is just, then they will be unable to band together in cliques to work for each other's benefit.

THE GREEK TRADITION

The Persian invasions of Greece in 490 and 480 BCE stimulated significant changes in the world of Classical Greece (c. 650–350 BCE). Athens, already one of the largest and most democratic of the many city-states into which Greece was divided, was the main beneficiary of these changes. Athens had gained glory and its citizens pride and confidence by defeating the first Persian invasion at Marathon in 490, and the Athenian navy proved decisive in repelling the second invasion at the Battle of Salamis in 480. Though the Spartan army contributed to the final defeat of the second Persian invasion the following year, Athens took the lead in constructing a coalition of states that carried a naval counteroffensive across the Aegean Sea. Using the revenues generated by the coalition and from a new silver mine, Athens built up its navy and turned the alliance into an empire.

Athenian naval power rested on the participation of the poorer classes of Athenian citizens as rowers in the oar-driven ships of the navy, and this military role was linked to the large role the mass of Athenian citizenry had in running the state. To us, Athenian democracy is an inspiring early example of a form of government common today, an example whose limitations on citizenship and voting rights seem less prominent than its inclusivity. But even in Classical Greece, never mind by the standards of the rest of the world in that age and in all times until at least the nineteenth century, Athens's experiment in mass participatory government was radical. Unlike the firm and centralized control exercised by monarchy, democracy raised serious questions about social order and cohesion and about the freedoms and duties of individual citizens.

It was in this heady atmosphere, combining self-confidence and prosperity with serious philosophical questions open to debate by large numbers of citizens, that Athens created a golden age of cultural output that encompassed virtually every arena of intellectual inquiry and that built on intellectual changes initiated earlier in other parts of the Greek world. We will look at two examples of this output, the historical writing of Thucydides and the drama of the playwright Sophocles. They give us two different perspectives on and ways of talking about the issues of individual ethical action and social order that were so central to this city's culture in the fifth century BCE.

Thucydides, *History of the Peloponnesian War*

The rise of Athenian power raised serious concerns in the other leading Greek city-state, Sparta, and by the 430s most of Greece had divided into two hostile coalitions led by these two cities. War broke out in 431. The Peloponnesian War (named for the Spartan-led Peloponnesian League that fought the Athenian alliance and empire) against monarchical, conservative Sparta challenged not just Athens's political power and leadership but its cultural self-identity.

We know the story of the war from the history written by Thucydides, an Athenian born around 460 to an upper-class family. A relative had served as a general in the Persian wars, and Thucydides was elected general in 424. But an unsuccessful campaign led to his being exiled for the duration of the war. Basing himself on family estates in Thrace, he traveled through Greece and devoted himself to writing a history of the great war. He died sometime after the end of the war (which Athens ultimately lost) in 404, his history unfinished.

We present here a speech Thucydides puts in the mouth of Pericles, the Athenian politician who set Athenian strategy for the early stages of the war and a man admired by Thucydides. Thucydides reports many speeches in the course of his history; in his own words, they are not transcriptions of the actual orations but reconstructions shaped by Thucydides according to what was "fitting" for the occasion. This does not mean that they are inaccurate, just that their truth is at a more general level than verbatim reporting. Pericles was speaking at the state funeral of some of the first Athenian casualties of the war; he took the occasion to defend the Athenian constitution and way of life, including its balance of personal freedom and social order. This is, in other words, an ideal statement of Athenian virtues.

QUESTIONS TO CONSIDER

1. What are the specific strengths of Athenian democracy, according to Pericles? How do they compare with the characteristics of Sparta—the "enemy" Pericles refers to a number of times in the oration and whose society and government he describes by implication and by contrast with the Athenian system?

2. How does Pericles reconcile the individual freedoms enjoyed by Athenian citizens with the need for social order and cohesion? What costs is he willing to concede as part of the Athenian system?

3. What limits on freedom are visible here? What, in particular, is the place of women in Athens according to the (meager) evidence in this speech?

4. How does the Athenian balance of freedom and order compare with those described by the Chinese authors? What basic assumptions about society and the state are different here from the ones in the Chinese texts?

5. What lessons for individual freedom and social order does Pericles' speech hold for modern democracies such as the United States? What would Pericles and the Athenians think of whistleblowers?

PERICLES' FUNERAL ORATION

Many of those who have spoken here in the past, have praised the institution of this speech at the close of our ceremony. It seemed to them a mark of honour to our soldiers who have fallen in war that a speech should be made over them. I do not agree. These men have shown themselves valiant in action, and it would be enough, I think, for their glories to be proclaimed in action, as you have just seen it done at this funeral organized by the state. . . . However, the fact is that this institution was set up and approved by our forefathers, and it is my duty to follow the tradition and do my best to meet the wishes and the expectations of every one of you. . . .

I have no wish to make a long speech on subjects familiar to you all: so I shall say nothing about the warlike deeds by which we acquired our power or the battles in which we or our fathers gallantly resisted our enemies, Greek or foreign. What I want to do is, in the first place, to discuss the spirit in which we faced our trials and also our constitution and the way of life which has made us great. After that I shall speak in praise of the dead, believing that this kind of speech is not inappropriate to the present occasion, and that this whole assembly, of citizens and foreigners, may listen to it with advantage.

Let me say that our system of government does not copy the institutions of our neighbours. It is more the case of our being a model to others, than of our imitating

Source: From Thucydides in *History of the Peloponnesian War,* trans. Rex Warner, 144–48, 151. Copyright © 1986 Penguin Books. Used by permission of Penguin Putnam Group (USA) Inc.

anyone else. Our constitution is called a democracy because power is in the hands not of a minority but of the whole people. When it is a question of settling private disputes, everyone is equal before the law; when it is a question of putting one person before another in positions of public responsibility, what counts is not membership of a particular class, but the actual ability which the man possesses. No one, so long as he has it in him to be of service to the state, is kept in political obscurity because of poverty. And, just as our political life is free and open, so is our day-to-day life in our relations with each other. We do not get into a state with our next-door neighbour if he enjoys himself in his own way, nor do we give him the kind of black looks which, though they do no real harm, still do hurt people's feelings. We are free and tolerant in our private lives; but in public affairs we keep to the law. This is because it commands our deep respect.

We give our obedience to those whom we put in positions of authority, and we obey the laws themselves, especially those which are for the protection of the oppressed, and those unwritten laws which it is an acknowledged shame to break.

And here is another point. When our work is over, we are in a position to enjoy all kinds of recreation for our spirits. There are various kinds of contests and sacrifices regularly throughout the year; in our own homes we find a beauty and a good taste which delight us every day and which drive away our cares. Then the greatness of our city brings it about that all the good things from all over the world flow in to us, so that to us it seems just as natural to enjoy foreign goods as our own local products.

Then there is a great difference between us and our opponents, in our attitude towards military security. Here are some examples: Our city is open to the world, and we have no periodical deportations in order to prevent people observing or finding out secrets which might be of military advantage to the enemy. This is because we rely, not on secret weapons, but on our own real courage and loyalty. There is a difference, too, in our educational systems. The Spartans, from their earliest boyhood, are submitted to the most laborious training in courage; we pass our lives without all those restrictions, and yet are just as ready to face the same danger, as they are. Here is a proof of this: When the Spartans invade our land, they do not come by themselves, but bring all their allies with them; whereas we, when we launch an attack abroad, do the job by ourselves, and, though fighting on foreign soil, do not often fail to defeat opponents who are fighting for their own hearths and homes. As a matter of fact none of our enemies has ever yet been confronted with our total strength, because we have to divide our attention between our navy and the many missions on which our troops are sent on land. Yet, if our enemies engage a detachment of our forces and defeat it, they give themselves credit for having thrown back our entire army; or, if they lose, they claim that they were beaten by us in full strength. There are certain advantages, I think, in our way of meeting danger voluntarily, with an easy mind, instead of with a laborious training, with natural rather than with state-induced courage. We do not have to spend our time practising to meet sufferings which are still in the future; and when they are actually upon us we show ourselves just as brave as these others who are always in strict training. This is one point in which, I think, our city deserves to be admired. There are also others:

Our love of what is beautiful does not lead to extravagance; our love of the things of the mind does not make us soft. We regard wealth as something to be properly used, rather than as something to boast about. As for poverty, no one need be ashamed to admit it: the real shame is in not taking practical measures to escape from it. Here each individual is interested not *only in* his own affairs but in the affairs of the state as well: even those who are mostly occupied with their own business are extremely well informed on general politics—this is a peculiarity of ours: we do not say that a man who takes no interest in politics is a man who minds his own business; we say that he has no business here at all. We Athenians, in our own persons, take our decisions on policy or submit them to proper discussions: for we do not think that there is an incompatibility between words and deeds; the worst thing is to rush into action before the consequences have been properly debated. . . .

Taking everything together then, I declare that our city is an education to Greece, and I declare that in my opinion each single one of our citizens, in all the manifold aspects of life, is able to show himself the rightful lord and owner of his own person, and do this, moreover, with exceptional grace and exceptional versatility. And to show that this is no empty boasting for the present occasion, but real tangible fact, you have only to consider the power which our city possesses and which has been won by those very qualities which I have mentioned. Athens, alone of the states we know, comes to her testing time in a greatness that surpasses what was imagined of her. In her case, and in her case alone, no invading enemy is ashamed at being defeated and no subject can complain of being governed by people unfit for their responsibilities. . . .

Perhaps I should say a word or two on the duties of women to those among you who are now widowed. I can say all I have to say in a short word of advice. Your great glory is not to be inferior to what God has made you, and the greatest glory of a woman is to be least talked about by men, whether they are praising you or criticizing you.

SOPHOCLES, *ANTIGONE*

Sophocles was born in 495 BCE, just outside of Athens, and died in 404 after a long and distinguished career as perhaps the greatest of the Athenian writers of tragedy. He wrote *Antigone* in 442, making it the earliest of his seven surviving plays (out of 120 that he wrote). Sophocles was interested above all in questions of individual psychology, and *Antigone* explores the conflict between the demands of the state and social order against the dictates of individual conscience and ethical choice through the tragedy of the lead character, Antigone.

It is interesting, however, that Sophocles pursues this theme through a female character—one of a number of strong female portrayals in his body of work—adding gender to an already complicated encounter of ideals. Questions of gender roles had, perhaps, special meaning in Athens, where increasing freedom and social responsibility for its male citizens was matched by a far more restricted and subordinate life for its women than was common in other Greek city-states. His work allows us a rare glimpse at the influence of conceptions of gender on questions of social order and individual ethics.

The play is set in the city of Thebes and involves the ill-fated family of Oedipus, the Theban ruler who killed his father and married his mother, producing four children by her: the twin sons Eteocles and Polynices and the sisters Ismene and Antigone. After discovering his horrible fate, Oedipus blinds himself and goes into exile. Eteocles takes the Theban throne, but Polynices contests his rule with an invading army. The two brothers kill each other, and rule of Thebes passes to their uncle Creon, who accords the loyal Theban Eteocles a state burial but decrees that the traitor Polynices's corpse should rot, unburied. Antigone sees this order not through the eyes of the state but as a violation of family relationships and the dictates of religion with regard to proper burial. She defies the order, and eventually dies as a result of her uncle's decision; this proves to have tragic consequences for Creon.

Sophocles therefore presents a conflict of principles with no winners (thus, a tragedy) and no easy answers to the clash between individual conscience and collective responsibility. The key statements of principle by the two central characters are contained in the excerpts that follow.

QUESTIONS TO CONSIDER

1. What principles does Creon appeal to in support of his position? What principles does Antigone appeal to? Are the two positions necessarily incompatible?
2. What are the implications of each position for individual ethical choice and social order?
3. How do you think Antigone's gender influences her position and Creon's reaction to it? What would Pericles say about this dispute?
4. What lessons would an Athenian audience of the sort implied in Pericles' speech have drawn from this tragedy? What comment does it offer on Athenian state and society?
5. What would Creon and Antigone think of whistleblowers? Would they agree?

ANTIGONE

Sophocles

Creon:

My countrymen, the ship of state is safe. The gods who rocked her, after a long, merciless pounding in the storm, have righted her once more. Out of the whole city I have called you here alone. Well I know, first, your undeviating respect for the throne and royal power of King Laius. Next, while Oedipus steered the land of Thebes, and even after he died, your loyalty was unshakable, you still stood by their children. Now

Source: Sophocles, *The Three Theban Plays*, 67–69, 72–74, 81–82. Copyright © 1982 Penguin Books. Used by permission of Penguin Putnam Group (USA) Inc.

then, since the two sons are dead—two blows of fate in the same day, cut down by each other's hands, both killers, both brothers stained with blood—as I am next in kin to the dead, I now possess the throne and all its powers.

Of course you cannot know a man completely, his character, his principles, sense of judgment, not till he's shown his colors, ruling the people, making laws. Experience, there's the test. As I see it, whoever assumes the task, the awesome task of setting the city's course, and refuses to adopt the soundest policies but fearing someone, keeps his lips locked tight, he's utterly worthless. So I rate him now, I always have. And whoever places a friend above the good of his own country, he is nothing: I have no use for him. Zeus is my witness, Zeus who sees all things, always—I could never stand by silent, watching destruction march against our city, putting safety to rout, nor could I ever make that man a friend of mine who menaces our country. Remember this: our country is our safety. Only while she voyages true on course can we establish friendships, truer than blood itself.

Such are my standards. They make our city great. Closely akin to them I have proclaimed, just now, the following decree to our people concerning the two sons of Oedipus. Eteocles, who died fighting for Thebes, excelling all in arms: he shall be buried, crowned with a hero's honors, the cups we pour to soak the earth and reach the famous dead. But as for his blood brother, Polynices, who returned from exile, home to his father-city and the gods of his race, consumed with one desire—to burn them roof to roots—who thirsted to drink his kinsmen's blood and sell the rest to slavery: that man—a proclamation has forbidden the city to dignify him with burial, mourn him at all. No, he must be left unburied, his corpse carrion for the birds and dogs to tear, an obscenity for the citizens to behold!

These are my principles. Never at my hands will the traitor be honored above the patriot. But whoever proves his loyalty to the state—I'll prize that man in death as well as life.

Leader of the Chorus:

If this is your pleasure, Creon, treating our city's enemies and our friend this way. . . . The power is yours, I suppose, to enforce it with the laws, both for the dead and all of us, the living.

[The burial of Polynices in contradiction of this order is revealed by a Guard to Creon, who at first suspects the Guard or someone else did this for money.]

Leader of the Chorus:

My king, ever since he began I've been debating in my mind, could this possibly be the work of the gods?

Creon:

Stop before you make me choke with anger—the gods! You, you're senile, must you be insane? You say—why it's intolerable—say the gods could have the slightest concern for that corpse? Tell me, was it for meritorious service they proceeded to bury him, prized him so? The hero who came to burn their temples ringed with pillars, their golden treasures—scorch their hallowed earth and fling their laws to the winds. Exactly when did you last see the gods celebrating traitors? Inconceivable!

No, from the first there were certain citizens who could hardly stand the spirit of my regime, grumbling against me in the dark, heads together, tossing wildly, never keeping their necks beneath the yoke, loyally submitting to their king. These are the instigators, I'm convinced—they've perverted my own guard, bribed them to do their work.

Money! Nothing worse in our lives, so current, rampant, so corrupting. Money— you demolish cities, root men from their homes, you train and twist good minds and set them on to the most atrocious schemes. No limit, you make them adept at every kind of outrage, every godless crime—money!

Everyone—the whole crew bribed to commit this crime, they've made one thing sure at least: sooner or later they will pay the price.

Wheeling on the sentry.

You—I swear to Zeus as I still believe in Zeus, if you don't find the man who buried that corpse, the very man, and produce him before my eyes, simple death won't be enough for you, not till we string you up alive and wring the immorality out of you. Then you can steal the rest of your days better informed about where to make a killing. You'll be learned, at last, it doesn't pay to itch for rewards from every hand that beckons. Filthy profits wreck most men, you'll see—they'll never save your life.

[Antigone is brought before Creon, having been caught in the act of reburying her brother, whose body had been exposed once again.]

Creon:

You, tell me briefly, no long speeches—were you aware a decree had forbidden this?

Antigone:

Well aware. How could I avoid it? It was public.

Creon:

And still you had the gall to break this law?

Antigone:

Of course I did. It wasn't Zeus, not in the least, who made this proclamation—not to me. Nor did that Justice, dwelling with the gods beneath the earth, ordain such laws for men. Nor did I think your edict had such force that you, a mere mortal, could override the gods, the great unwritten, unshakable traditions. They are alive, not just today or yesterday: they live forever, from the first of time, and no one knows when they first saw the light.

These laws—I was not about to break them, not out of fear of some man's wounded pride, and face the retribution of the gods. Die I must, I've known it all my life—how could I keep from knowing?—even without your death-sentence ringing in my ears. And if I am to die before my time I consider that a gain. Who on earth, alive in the midst of so much grief as I, could fail to find his death a rich reward? So for me, at least, to meet this doom of yours is precious little pain. But if I had allowed my own mother's son to rot, an unburied corpse—that would have been an agony! This is nothing. And if my present actions strike you as foolish, let's just say I've been accused of folly by a fool.

Leader:
Like father like daughter, passionate, wild . . . she hasn't learned to bend before adversity.

THE INDIAN TRADITION

The Indian religious tradition arose during the long period between the Aryan invasions of India around perhaps 1500 BCE and the emergence of the tradition from oral into written form beginning as early as 400 BCE, though some parts were recorded as late as 600 CE. The development of the ethical and philosophical thought that came to undergird both Hinduism and Buddhism in different forms responded in part to state disorder and warfare, as the Chinese and Greek thinkers did, but the greater challenge met by the development of this tradition seems to have been internally generated: the problem of elaborating and making workable the increasingly rigid and detailed caste system that defined Indian society. Caste, or class divisions defined by birth and admitting of no social mobility, may have developed from the invading Aryans' attempts to maintain an identity separate from their conquered subjects—*varna,* the Sanskrit word for class or caste, means "color," and it may reflect the difference between the lighter-skinned Aryans and the darker pre-Aryan populations. The four major classes were priests, warriors and kings, commoners (farmers and merchants), and servants or slaves; over many centuries following this age numerous subcastes, or *jati,* based on occupation and ranked within the four major classes, evolved. Each caste had its *dharma,* meaning caste-law or sacred duty, to perform.

In one sense it is incorrect to say that there was no social mobility in the caste system, however. For the other crucial part of the context for the emergence of the Hindu and Buddhist religious traditions was the universal Indian belief in *samsara,* or the cycle of reincarnation that all souls were trapped in ("trapped" because rebirth into the world of cares and illusions was a bad thing). What drove *samsara* was *karma,* or the theory of consequences of action (what is translated in the *Bhagavad-Gita* as "fruits of action"). Proper performance of one's *dharma* was reflected in one's *karma,* which in turn determined into what level of the caste system one was reborn (or if one was reborn as a human at all). Finally, only those at the very top of the system, priests and a few great warriors, had a chance for *moksha,* or release from the cycle, meaning that one's undying soul rejoined the universal soul, never to be reborn.

The philosophical and ethical thought of Hinduism and of the Buddha turned to the problems of existence implicit in this view of the cosmos and human life, giving the Indian consideration of individual ethical action and its implications for social order its particular form.

Indian Terms

varna   caste or class

jati   subcastes

dharma   caste-law, sacred duty, duties and responsibilities of each caste

samsara   cycle of reincarnation

karma   consequences or "fruits of action"

moksha   release from *samsara* or the cycle of reincarnation

yoga   discipline

The *Bhagavad-Gita*

The first source we read is probably the most famous and fundamental of all Hindu religious texts, the epic poem known as the *Bhagavad-Gita*.[3] The *Bhagavad-Gita* tells the story of Arjuna, one of the great warrior-kings fighting for the kingdom. The poem opens just as Arjuna is about to go into battle against his cousins and kinsmen from the opposing family line, which sets up the central moral problem of the story. For Arjuna's *dharma* (duty) as a warrior is to fight, but his *dharma* as a family member (and his emotions) tells him not to kill relatives. How to solve a conflict of *dharmas* is the point of the poem, and as such has application to any moral conflict of principles, not just Arjuna's particular dilemma. It is the fundamental Hindu text on the encounter of individual ethical decision making and social order.

Faced with this dilemma, Arjuna freezes in indecision before the battle. Fortunately for Arjuna, he has a charioteer named Krishna who is, in fact, the god Vishnu in disguise. Time stops, in effect, and Krishna holds a dialogue with Arjuna in which he explains why and how he must do his duty as a warrior. This involves his explaining first the fundamental nature of birth, death, and rebirth. Arjuna understands this but remains emotionally unconvinced. Krishna therefore explains the three *yogas*, or disciplines, by which one may attain the proper mental and emotional attitude toward one's *dharma*. The first is the yoga of action, or more accurately the yoga of proper attitude toward action. Achieving this attitude requires that one master the second yoga, the yoga of knowledge, by which one gains control over the illusions that beset the human mind. Achieving this sort of mind control in turn requires that one commit to the yoga of devotion, or complete faith in Vishnu. In the course of explaining the third yoga of devotion, Krishna reveals himself to Arjuna in all his universal, infinite, all-encompassing and awe-inspiring form as Vishnu; Arjuna is the only mortal ever accorded this honor aside from (indirectly) the visionary poet Sanjaya who hears the dialogue and tells us the story. It is this revelation that puts the emotional seal for Arjuna on the philosophical arguments Krishna makes.

QUESTIONS TO CONSIDER

1. What is it about the nature of death and rebirth that makes it acceptable for Arjuna to kill his relatives?
2. How do the three yogas explain how he is supposed to perform this action? In particular, what does "acting without desiring the fruits of action" mean here?
3. How are these yogas applicable to any individual's ethical decision-making process? What would "acting without desiring the fruits of action" mean in other situations? How is this related to release from the cycle of rebirth?
4. What is the relationship of individual ethical choice to social order presented in the *Gita*? Which side of the equation seems more important to you? What sort of society would result if everyone followed the advice of the *Gita*?
5. What would Krishna think of whistleblowers?

THE *BHAGAVAD-GITA*

The Dilemma

Arjuna
I see omens of chaos,
Krishna; I see no good
in killing my kinsmen
in battle.

Evil will haunt us if we kill them,
even though their bows are drawn to kill.

Honor forbids us to kill
our cousins. . . .

When the family is ruined,
the timeless laws of family duty
perish; and when duty is lost,
chaos overwhelms the family.

In overwhelming chaos, Krishna,
women of the family are corrupted;
and when women are corrupted,
disorder is born in society.

The sins of men who violate
the family create disorder in society
that undermines the constant laws
of caste and family duty.

Death and Rebirth

Lord Krishna
Why this cowardice
in time of crisis, Arjuna?
the cowardice is ignoble, shameful,
foreign to the ways of heaven.

You grieve for those beyond grief,
and you speak words of insight,
but learned men do not grieve
for the dead or the living.

Never have I not existed,
nor you, nor these kings;
and never in the future
shall we cease to exist.

Source: Selections from *The Bhagavad-Gita*, trans. Barbara Stoler Miller. Copyright © 1986. Used by permission of Bantam Books, a division of Random House, Inc.

Just as the embodied self
enters childhood, youth, and old age,
so does it enter another body. . . .

Arjuna, when a man knows the self
to be indestructible, enduring, unborn,
Unchanging, how does he kill
or cause anyone to kill?

Death is certain for anyone born,
and birth is certain for the dead;
since the cycle is inevitable,
you have no cause to grieve!

Look to your own duty;
do not tremble before it;
nothing is better for a warrior
than a battle of sacred duty.

The Yoga of Action

Lord Krishna
Understanding is defined in terms of
    philosophy;
now hear it in spiritual discipline.
Armed with this understanding,
    Arjuna,
you will escape the bondage of
    action.

Be intent on action,
not on the fruits of action;
avoid attraction to the fruits
and attachment to inaction!

Wise men disciplined by understanding
relinquish the fruit born of action;
freed from those bonds of rebirth,
they reach a place beyond decay.

A man cannot escape the force
of action by abstaining from actions;
he does not attain success
just by renunciation.

No one exists for even an instant
without performing an action. . . .

Always perform with detachment
any action you must do;
performing action with detachment,
one achieves supreme good.

These worlds would collapse
if I did not perform action;
I would create disorder in society,
living beings would be destroyed.

The Yoga of Knowledge

Lord Krishna
Without doubt, the mind
is unsteady and hard to hold,
but practice and dispassion
can restrain it, Arjuna.

The Yoga of Devotion

Lord Krishna
Without faith in sacred duty,
men fail to reach me, Arjuna;
they return to the cycle
of death and rebirth.

If he is devoted solely to me,
even a violent criminal
must be deemed a man of virtue,
for his resolve is right.

I am time grown old,
creating world destruction,
set in motion
to annihilate the worlds;
even without you,
all these warriors
arrayed in hostile ranks
will cease to exist.

Therefore, arise
and win glory!
Conquer your foes
and fulfill your kingship!
They are already
killed by me.
Be just my instrument,
the archer at my side!

Acting only for me, intent on me,
free from attachment,
hostile to no creature, Arjuna,
a man of devotion comes to me.

Action in sacrifice, charity,
and penance is to be performed,
not relinquished—for wise men,
they are acts of sanctity.

But even these actions
should be done by relinquishing to me
attachment and the fruit of action—
this is my decisive idea.

Conclusion

Lord Krishna
The actions of priests, warriors,
commoners, and servants
are apportioned by qualities
born of their intrinsic being.

Tranquility, control, penance,
purity, patience and honesty,
knowledge, judgment, and piety
are intrinsic to the action of a priest.

Heroism, fiery energy, resolve,
skill, refusal to retreat in battle,

charity, and majesty in conduct
are intrinsic to the action of a warrior.

Farming, herding cattle, and commerce
are intrinsic to the action of a
     commoner,
action that is essentially service
is intrinsic to the servant.

Each one achieves success
by focusing on his own action. . . .

Better to do one's own duty imperfectly
than to do another man's well;
doing action intrinsic to his being
a man avoids guilt.

Arjuna
Krishna, my delusion is destroyed,
and by your grace I have regained
     memory;
I stand here, my doubt dispelled,
ready to act on your words.

Sanjaya
Where Krishna is lord of discipline
and Arjuna is the archer,
there do fortune, victory, abundance,
and morality exist, so I think.

BUDDHISM

The Buddha was born Gautama Siddhartha, prince and heir to a small kingdom at the foot of the Himalayas in modern Nepal. But we know little else for certain about his life, for the sources all were written long after his death and reflect conflicting oral traditions. Though they agree that he lived to the age of eighty, different traditions place his birth as early as 624 BCE or as late as 448 BCE. The sources also agree on the outlines of his career: an early life of sheltered luxury, followed by a deeply disturbing encounter with the universal suffering caused by sickness, old age, and death and a quest to find the cause (and so alleviate) this suffering. Finding the answer neither in the teachings of Hindu priests nor in the practice for several years of extreme asceticism,[4] he finally sat under a bo tree and meditated until he achieved enlightenment and became the Buddha, or Enlightened One.

His answer to the problem of suffering is presented here, in a version of his first sermon, along with a lesson about what his teachings do not address and why such things are unimportant. Like the emerging Hindu tradition, Buddhism accepted the reality of *samsara* (cycle of reincarnation) as the central problem of human existence. But the Buddha rejected all divine beings—the universe is instead an uncreated infinity—as well as the restrictions of the caste system: the practice of Buddhism was open to anyone. Properly followed, they led to *nirvana,* which literally means "extinguishment," or the release of the soul from the cycle of rebirth and suffering.

The key concept in Buddhism is variously translated as "desire," "craving," or perhaps most appropriately simply "attachment." It is attachment—to health, loved ones or things, life itself—that causes suffering (a psychological state, not the same as pain, which is physical); attachment is a result of the illusion of the self. Because the universe is for Buddhism in constant flux, attachment to any impermanent constellation of causes and effects, such as a body or a self, constitutes attachment to an illusion. For the Buddha, nonattachment was therefore the key to understanding individual action and its relation to social order.

QUESTIONS TO CONSIDER

1. What is the cause of all suffering for the Buddha? How is suffering then eliminated? Do you agree with the Buddha's diagnosis? Do you agree with his prescription for dealing with the problem?
2. What are the components of the Eightfold Path? How do they reflect the Buddha's emphasis on a Middle Way, neither excessively ascetic nor overly indulgent, as the path to individual moral virtue?
3. What things are unimportant to the Buddha? Why are they unimportant to him? What implications for the relationship of right individual conduct to social order are contained in these views?
4. How does the path to Enlightenment presented here relate to the paths to right conduct and release from *samsara* in the *Bhagavad-Gita*? Is it an easier or a harder path? Who would Buddhism have appealed to in a caste-bound Hindu society?
5. What would the Buddha think of whistleblowers?

THE TEACHINGS OF THE BUDDHA

The Four Noble Truths

The world is full of suffering. Birth is suffering, old age is suffering, sickness and death are sufferings. To meet a man whom one hates is suffering. To be separated from a beloved one is suffering. To be vainly struggling to satisfy one's needs is suffering. In

Source: From *The Teachings of the Buddha,* 1980. Reprinted by permission of Numata Center for Buddhist Translation and Research.

fact, life that is not free from desire and passion is always involved with distress. This is called the Truth of Suffering.

The cause of human suffering is undoubtedly found in the thirsts of the physical body and in the illusions of worldly passion. If these thirsts and illusions are traced to their source, they are found to be rooted in the intense desires of physical instincts. Thus, desire, having a strong will-to-live as its basis, seeks that which it feels desirable, even if it is sometimes death. This is called the Truth of the Cause of Suffering.

If desire, which lies at the root of all human passion, can be removed, then passion will die out and all human suffering will be ended. This is called the Truth of the Cessation of Suffering.

In order to enter into a state where there is no desire and no suffering, one must follow a certain Path. The stages of this Noble Eightfold Path are: Right Understanding, Right Purpose, Right Speech, Right Behavior, Right Livelihood, Right Effort, Right Mindfulness, and Right Concentration. This is called the Truth of the Noble Path to the Cessation of the Cause of Suffering.

People should keep these Truths clearly in mind, for the world is filled with suffering, and if anyone wishes to escape from suffering, he must sever the ties of worldly passion, which is the sole cause of suffering. The way of life which is free from all worldly passion and suffering can only be known through Enlightenment, and Enlightenment can only be attained through the discipline of the Noble Eightfold Path.

The Search for Enlightenment

In the search for truth there are certain questions that are unimportant. Of what material is the universe constructed? Is the universe eternal? Are there limits or not to the universe? In what way is this human society put together? What is the ideal form of organization for human society? If a man were to postpone his searching and practicing for Enlightenment until such questions were solved, he would die before he found the path.

Suppose a man were pierced by a poisoned arrow, and his relatives and friends got together to call a surgeon to have the arrow pulled out and the wound treated.

If the wounded man objects, saying, "Wait a little. Before you pull it out, I want to know who shot this arrow. Was it a man or a woman? Was it someone of noble birth, or was it a peasant? What was the bow made of? Was it a big bow or a small bow that shot the arrow? Was it made of wood or bamboo? What was the bowstring made of? Was it made of fiber or of gut? Was the arrow made of rattan or of reed? What feathers were used? Before you extract the arrow, I want to know all about these things." Then what will happen?

Before all this information can be secured, no doubt the poison will have time to circulate all through the system and the man may die. The first duty is to remove the arrow, and its poison prevented from spreading.

When a fire of passion is endangering the world, the composition of the universe matters little. What is the ideal form for the human community is not so important to deal with.

The question of whether the universe has limits or is eternal can wait until some way is found to extinguish the fires of birth, old age, sickness, and death. In the presence of lamentation, sorrow, suffering, and pain, one should first search for a way to solve these problems and devote oneself to the practice of that way.

The Buddha's teaching teaches what is important to know and not what is unimportant. That is, it teaches people that they must learn what they should learn, remove what they should remove, train for what they should become enlightened about.

Therefore, people should first discern what is of the first importance, what problem should first be solved, what is the most pressing issue for them. To do all this, they must first undertake to train their minds; that is, they must first seek mind-control.

Those who seek the true path to Enlightenment must not expect an easy task or one made pleasant by offers of respect and honor and devotion. And further, they must not aim with a slight effort, at a trifling advance in calmness or knowledge or insight.

First of all, one should get clearly in mind the basic and essential nature of this world of life and death.

Human Life

There is an allegory that depicts human life. Once there was a man rowing a boat down a river. Someone on the shore warned him, "Stop rowing so gaily down the swift current. There are rapids ahead and a dangerous whirlpool, and there are crocodiles and demons lying in wait in rocky caverns. You will perish if you continue."

In this allegory, "the swift current" is a life of lust. "Rowing gaily" is giving rein to one's passion. "Rapids ahead" means the ensuing suffering and pain. "Whirlpool" means pleasure. "Crocodiles and demons" refers to the decay and death that follow a life of lust and indulgence. "Someone on the shore" who calls out is Buddha.

Everything is changeable, everything appears and disappears. There is no blissful peace until one passes beyond the agony of life and death.

SOUTHWEST ASIAN TRADITIONS

The Indian religious tradition, encompassing both early Hinduism and early Buddhism, infused the entire cosmos with spirituality, seeing gods, nature, and man as all part of the same web of being—indeed, the Buddhists did not even conceive of the universe as created but saw it as infinite in past and future. The two related religious traditions of southwest Asia that we examine next, by contrast, saw a fundamental separation in kind between a Creator and his Creation, the physical universe. But they connected the Creator to Creation through moral laws played out in a human history with a purpose and direction, whereas the very continuity of existence in the Indian tradition seems to have deemphasized the importance of mere human action (and thus history) in favor of metaphysical speculation or attention to the universal problem of suffering. The Persians and Hebrews, therefore, give us another religious take on the problem of individual ethics and social order, but one quite different from the Indian tradition.

Persia: Zarathustra, Sayings of the Prophet

Early Persian religion sprang from the same Indo-European roots as early Aryan-Indian religion. And despite the existence of a single prophet, or carrier of the word of god, in the history of the Persian religion, its development is just as difficult to trace in the historical sources as that of Hinduism is. The traditions of the religion that became known as Zoroastrianism[5] put the prophet's life in the half century just after 600 BCE, but the internal linguistic evidence of the earliest sayings of the prophet point to a much earlier date. Complicating the picture is the fact that most of the *Avesta,* the holy written text of Zoroastrianism, dates from after 224 CE. Thus the true role of Zarathustra in the creation of this religion is largely unknowable.

The religion's rise to prominence does fit squarely into the era of world history covered by this chapter, however, as it became the official religion of the Persian royalty under Darius the Great (r. 522–486 BCE). Much of the philosophical development of Zoroastrianism probably dates to the century before Darius, when the Persians began creating their empire. Following Zarathustra's lead, the multiplicity of gods in early Persian religion was pared down to one uncreated creator of the universe, *Ahura* (Lord) *Mazda.* His foe was another uncreated being, *Angra Mainyu* (Hostile Spirit, also known as The Liar), as ageless as Ahura Mazda but lesser in ultimate power, whose evil creations and machinations caused the pain and spiritual pollution in the universe. The story of the cosmos for Zoroastrians, therefore, came down to a struggle between good and evil that good was eventually destined to win but that demanded choice by individuals as to which side they would support. Individual ethical decision making was therefore tied to cosmic standards of right and wrong, as well as to proper social order, and individuals received appropriate eternal rewards and punishments according to the choices made. The ethical philosophy built into this religion may have encouraged good government; it also, however, created a special place for the Persians, the bearers of Zarathustra's Truth, in history, a special place that may well have helped the Persians maintain their separate cultural identity in the vast mix of peoples and cultures—some much older than the Persians—that made up the empire they ruled.

The uncreated nature of Angra Mainyu marks Zoroastrianism as a dualistic religion, and its dualistic view of the universe would later influence Christianity, as well as Islam and some strains of Judaism. But the dualism is also a bit misleading (as calling Christianity dualistic because of the existence of Satan would be), because the emphasis and the ultimate meaning of Zoroastrianism are focused on Ahura Mazda, the principle of good.[6] These views distinguish the Southwest Asian religious and ethical systems from those of China and India and provide a distinctive understanding of the relationship between individual ethical action and social responsibility.

QUESTIONS TO CONSIDER

1. What sorts of beliefs and behaviors does Ahura Mazda demand of his followers? What are the consequences of obedience or disobedience to Mazda's wishes?

2. How do the injunctions about individual choice and behavior connect to social order? What is the role of Mazda's act of creation in structuring the cosmos and society?

3. Ahura Mazda is presented as the single, universal creator. Yet there is no injunction to spread the faith (and in fact Persians were happy to let their subject peoples retain their native religious traditions). Why do you think this was the case? What is the role of the Persian people in the history of Mazda's universe?

4. Persians had a reputation for good government. What do you think the role of Zoroastrianism might have been in promoting good government over conquered peoples? What would be the advantages and disadvantages of a fully Zoroastrian society?

5. What would Zarathustra think of whistleblowers?

YASNAS

Zarathustra

Yasna 19

15. The evil one at once arose (to oppose Him), but He (Ahura) repelled that wicked one with His interdict, and with this repelling renunciation: Neither our minds are in harmony, nor our precepts, nor our comprehensions, nor our beliefs, nor our words, nor our actions, nor our consciences, nor our souls!

16. And this saying, uttered by Mazda, has three stages, or measures, and belongs to four classes (of men as its supporters), and to five chiefs (in the political world, without whom its efficiency is marred), and it has a conclusion ending with a gift. *(Question.)* How are its measures (constituted)? *(Answer.)* The good thought, the good word, and the good deed.

17. *(Question.)* With what classes of men? *(Answer.)* The priest, the charioteer (as the chief of warriors), the systematic tiller of the ground, and the artisan. These classes therefore accompany the religious man throughout his entire duty with the correct thought, the truthful word, and the righteous action. These are the classes and states in life which give attention to the rulers, and fulfill the (laws) of religion; (yea, they are the guides and companions of that religious man) through whose actions the settlements are furthered in righteousness.

18. *(Question.)* How are the chiefs (constituted)? *(Answer.)* They are the house-chief, the village-chief, and the tribe-chief, the chief of the province, and the Zarathushtra* as the fifth. That is, so far as those provinces are concerned which are different from, and outside of the Zarathushtrian regency, or domain. . . . *(Question.)* How are the chiefs of this one constituted? *(Answer.)* They (are) the house-chief, the village-chief, the tribe-chief, and the Zarathushtra as the fourth.

19. *(Question.)* What is the thought well thought? *(Answer.)* (It is that which the holy man thinks), the one who holds the holy thought to be before all other things. *(Question.)* What is the word well spoken? *(Answer.)* It is the Mathra Spenta, the bounteous

Source: Translated by L. H. Mills (From *Sacred Books of the East*, American Edition, 1898.)

*The priests of Zoroastrianism and the royal family that ruled in the name of Zoroastrianism.

word of reason. *(Question.)* What is the deed well done? *(Answer.)* It is that done with praises, and by the creatures who regard Righteousness as before all other things.

20. *(Question.)* Mazda made a proclamation, whom did He announce? *(Answer.)* Some one who was holy, and yet both heavenly and mundane. *(Question.)* What was His character, He who made this sacred enunciation? *(Answer.)* He who is the best (of all), the ruling one. *(Question.)* Of what character (did He proclaim him the coming one)? *(Answer.)* As holy and the best, a ruler who exercises no wanton or despotic power.

Yasna 30

1. Now I will proclaim to those who are willing to hear the things that the under-standing man should remember, for hymns unto Ahura and prayers to Good Thought; also the felicity that is with the heavenly lights, which those who think wisely shall behold through Right.

2. Hear with your ears the best things; look upon them with clear-seeing thought, for decision between the two Beliefs, each man for himself before the Great consumma-tion, bethinking you that it be accomplished to our pleasure.

3. Now the two primal Spirits, who reveal themselves in vision as Twins, are the Bet-ter and the Bad, in thought and word and action. And between these two the wise ones chose rightly, the foolish not so.

4. And when these two Spirits came together in the beginning, they created Life and Not-Life, and [decided] that at the end the Worst Existence shall be [allotted] to the followers of the Lie, but the Best Existence to him that follows Right.

5. Of these two Spirits he that followed the Lie chose doing the worst things; the holi-est Spirit chose Right, he that clothes himself with the massy heavens as a garment. So likewise they that are eager to please Ahura Mazda by dutiful actions.

6. Between these two the Daevas* also chose not rightly, for infatuation came upon them as they took counsel together, so that they chose the Worst Thought. Then they rushed together to Violence, that they might enfeeble the world of men.

7. And to him (i.e. mankind) came Dominion, and Good Mind, and Right and Piety gave continued life to their bodies and indestructibility, so that by Your retributions through (molten) metal he may gain the prize over the others.

8. So when there comes their punishment for their sins, then, O Mazda, at Your com-mand shall Good Thought establish the Dominion in the Consummation, for those who deliver the Lie, O Ahura, into the hands of Right.

9. So may we be those that make this world advance, O Mazda and you other Ahuras, come hither, bestowing (on us) admission into your company . . . , in order that (our) thought may gather together while reason is still shaky.

10. Then truly on the (world of) Lie shall come the destruction of delight; but they who get themselves good name shall be partakers in the promised reward in the fair abode of Good Thought, of Mazda, and of Right.

Source: Translation by C. Bartholomae, from I. J. S. Taraporewala, *The Divine Songs of Zarathushtra.*
*Spirits, originally lesser gods, who were reinterpreted by Zarathustra as demonic creations of Angra Mainyu.

11. If, O you mortals, you mark those commandments which Mazda has ordained—of happiness and pain, the long punishment for the follower of the [Wrong], and blessings for the followers of the Right—then hereafter shall it be well.

Yasna 31

11. When You, O Mazda, in the beginning created the Individual and the Individuality, through Your Spirit, and powers of understanding—when You made life clothed with the body, when (You made) actions and teachings, whereby one may exercise one's convictions at one's free-will;

12. Then lifts up his voice the false speaker or the true speaker, he that knows or he that knows not, (each) according to his own heart and mind. . . .

13. Whatever open or whatever secret (acts) may be visited with punishment, or whether a person for a little sin demands the highest punishment,—of all this . . . You are aware, observing it with Your flashing eye.

THE HEBREWS: SECOND ISAIAH

One of the peoples the Persians conquered were the Chaldeans, who in 586 BCE had themselves conquered the kingdom of Judah and its capital of Jerusalem. Judah was the remaining southern kingdom of the Hebrews, the larger kingdom of Israel to its north having fallen to the Assyrians a century and a half earlier. The Chaldeans destroyed Jerusalem and sent many of the Hebrew elites into exile in their capital at Babylon. But after Cyrus the Great, king of the Persians, destroyed the Chaldean Empire, he freed the Hebrews from what became known as the Babylonian Captivity in 538 BCE.

An otherwise unknown prophet of the time, named Isaiah, took the lead in interpreting these events from the perspective of earlier Hebrew history and faith. His reinterpretation (and the impression the Babylonian Captivity made on the Hebrew elite) proved central to the transformation of early Hebrew religion into the faith now called Judaism. The key shift seems to have been Isaiah's claiming for Yahweh, the exclusive god of the Hebrews, a much larger role as sole God in and creator of the universe, to whom the Hebrews stood in a special relationship. By incorporating Cyrus into the story of the Lord (as Yahweh was increasingly referred to) and his People, Isaiah made all of history part of his God's plan for the universe, with the Chosen People playing a special role in history. Such a conception not only explained the Babylonian Captivity but also contributed to helping the Hebrews (or Jews) maintain their separate cultural identity in the great mix of cultures and peoples that made up the empire of which they were only a small part. At the same time, Isaiah's interpretation put morality, or "righteousness," at the center of his story's (and history's) meaning.

Maintaining their group identity had been a common problem in Hebrew history, especially after this originally pastoral group had settled in Palestine and adopted the settled farming and monarchical ways of their neighbors. The tendency for the Hebrew population to drift away from the exclusive worship of Yahweh had given rise to a long string of prophets, or people bearing the word of God, whose role had been to call back the errant Hebrews to Yahweh. The prophets lay outside the power structure of the Hebrew kingdoms but had been essential to the cohesion of the Hebrews before they had kings and to their culture even after the kings arose, and they had already moved the faith, in the process of defending it, toward more universal and moral bases. An earlier great prophet of the eighth century BCE had also been named Isaiah, and the teachings of the Isaiah of the sixth century were appended to those of the first Isaiah in the Bible's book of Isaiah. We are therefore reading the words of the prophet known as Second Isaiah, who synthesized and advanced the development of Judaism so effectively that he was one of the last of the great prophetic line.

QUESTIONS TO CONSIDER

1. What beliefs and actions constitute "righteousness" for Isaiah? What are the consequences for those who do or do not follow the path of righteousness?
2. What is the relationship of individual righteousness to social order in Isaiah? How is this relationship complicated by the Jews' subject status in the Persian Empire? How does Isaiah explain the role of the Persians?
3. Like Ahura Mazda, Yahweh is presented here not as the particular god of the tribes of Hebrews but as the universal and only God, creator of the universe. What is the role of the Hebrews in the history of Yahweh's universe?
4. Given the similarities between Zoroastrianism and Judaism, what do you think the influences of Zoroastrianism were on Isaiah (or vice versa, in fact)? Can we know for sure? What aspects of southwest Asian historical context might account for the similarities?
5. How specific and practical are Isaiah's calls for reform? What would a fully Isaiahan society look like? What would its advantages and disadvantages be? What would Isaiah think of whistleblowers? Was he one himself?

THE BOOK OF ISAIAH

Isaiah 44

24: Thus says the LORD, your Redeemer, who formed you from the womb: "I am the LORD, who made all things, who stretched out the heavens alone, who spread out the earth—Who was with me?—

25: who frustrates the omens of liars, and makes fools of diviners; who turns wise men back, and makes their knowledge foolish;

Source: The Holy Bible, Revised Standard Edition (New York, 1952), 756–58, 769, 770–71.

26: who confirms the word of his servant, and performs the counsel of his messengers; who says of Jerusalem, 'She shall be inhabited,' and of the cities of Judah, 'They shall be built, and I will raise up their ruins';

27: who says to the deep, 'Be dry, I will dry up your rivers';

28: who says of Cyrus,* 'He is my shepherd, and he shall fulfil all my purpose'; saying of Jerusalem, 'She shall be built,' and of the temple, 'Your foundation shall be laid.'"

Isaiah 45

1: Thus says the LORD to his anointed, to Cyrus, whose right hand I have grasped, to subdue nations before him and ungird the loins of kings, to open doors before him that gates may not be closed:

2: "I will go before you and level the mountains, I will break in pieces the doors of bronze and cut asunder the bars of iron,

3: I will give you the treasures of darkness and the hoards in secret places, that you may know that it is I, the LORD, the God of Israel, who call you by your name.

4: For the sake of my servant Jacob, and Israel my chosen, I call you by your name, I surname you,† though you do not know me.

5: I am the LORD, and there is no other, besides me there is no God; I gird you, though you do not know me,

6: that men may know, from the rising of the sun and from the west, that there is none besides me; I am the LORD, and there is no other.

7: I form light and create darkness, I make weal and create woe, I am the LORD, who do all these things.

8: Shower, O heavens, from above, and let the skies rain down righteousness; let the earth open, that salvation may sprout forth, and let it cause righteousness to spring up also; I the LORD have created it.

9: Woe to him who strives with his Maker, an earthen vessel with the potter! Does the clay say to him who fashions it, 'What are you making?' or 'Your work has no handles'?

10: Woe to him who says to a father, 'What are you begetting?' or to a woman, 'With what are you in travail?'"

11: Thus says the LORD, the Holy One of Israel, and his Maker: "Will you question me about my children, or command me concerning the work of my hands?

12: I made the earth, and created man upon it; it was my hands that stretched out the heavens, and I commanded all their host.

13: I have aroused him in righteousness, and I will make straight all his ways; he shall build my city‡ and set my exiles free, not for price or reward," says the LORD of hosts.

14: Thus says the LORD: "The wealth of Egypt and the merchandise of Ethiopia, and the Sabe'ans, men of stature, shall come over to you and be yours, they shall follow

---

*The Persian king who liberated the Hebrews from Babylon.

†Cyrus the Great; the surname "the Great" is claimed here as a gift from Yahweh.

‡Jerusalem.

you; they shall come over in chains and bow down to you. They will make supplication to you, saying: 'God is with you only, and there is no other, no god besides him.'"

15: Truly, thou art a God who hidest thyself, O God of Israel, the Savior.*

16: All of them are put to shame and confounded, the makers of idols go in confusion together.

17: But Israel is saved by the LORD with everlasting salvation; you shall not be put to shame or confounded to all eternity.

18: For thus says the LORD, who created the heavens (he is God!), who formed the earth and made it (he established it; he did not create it a chaos, he formed it to be inhabited!): "I am the LORD, and there is no other.

19: I did not speak in secret, in a land of darkness; I did not say to the offspring of Jacob, 'Seek me in chaos.' I the LORD speak the truth, I declare what is right.

20: Assemble yourselves and come, draw near together, you survivors of the nations! They have no knowledge who carry about their wooden idols, and keep on praying to a god that cannot save."

Isaiah 56

1: Thus says the LORD: "Keep justice, and do righteousness, for soon my salvation will come, and my deliverance be revealed.

2: Blessed is the man who does this, and the son of man who holds it fast, who keeps the sabbath, not profaning it, and keeps his hand from doing any evil."

Isaiah 57, 1–2, 15–21

1: The righteous man perishes, and no one lays it to heart; devout men are taken away, while no one understands. For the righteous man is taken away from calamity,

2: he enters into peace; they rest in their beds who walk in their uprightness.

15: For thus says the high and lofty One who inhabits eternity, whose name is Holy: "I dwell in the high and holy place, and also with him who is of a contrite and humble spirit, to revive the spirit of the humble, and to revive the heart of the contrite.

16: For I will not contend for ever, nor will I always be angry; for from me proceeds the spirit, and I have made the breath of life.

17: Because of the iniquity of his covetousness I was angry, I smote him, I hid my face and was angry; but he went on backsliding in the way of his own heart.

18: I have seen his ways, but I will heal him; I will lead him and requite him with comfort, creating for his mourners the fruit of the lips.

19: Peace, peace, to the far and to the near, says the LORD; and I will heal him.

20: But the wicked are like the tossing sea; for it cannot rest, and its waters toss up mire and dirt.

21: There is no peace, says my God, for the wicked."

---

*Scholarly consensus is that Isaiah's use of "Savior" and references to "salvation" and "being saved" refer to earthly peace and prosperity, rather than any sort of eternal reward or punishment.

NOTES

1. Press release at http://www.whistleblowers.org.
2. The understanding of the nature of the universe and humans' place in it.
3. It occurs as a long interlude in an even longer epic poem called the *Mahabharata*, or story of the Great Bharata, legendary king of the state of Dhritarashtra, and of the family feuds of his descendants for control of the kingdom.
4. Self-denial, avoidance of worldly pleasures.
5. From Zoroaster, the Greek version of the name of the prophet Zarathustra, who first preached its basic tenets.
6. The following selections come from the *Yasnas*, or liturgical texts, of the *Avesta*, which contain some of the *Gathas*, or sayings of the Prophet.

CHAPTER 5

Empires, War, and Order

INTRODUCTION

"If you wanna end war 'n stuff you gotta sing loud."

So said Arlo Guthrie in his anti–Vietnam War song "Alice's Restaurant." Because of television coverage and the nature of U.S. war aims—ambiguous and lacking broad public support—Vietnam brought much of the U.S. population into an encounter both with a people, the Vietnamese, whose aspirations and style of warfare seemed foreign to American traditions, and with modern warfare itself. The resulting protests and civic unrest came as a shock to many, whose image of warfare and the U.S. role in the world had been formed thirty or so years earlier in World War II. That had been a "good war," fought against a set of foes universally agreed to be evil and fought for the preservation of freedom and democracy. The encounters of World War II, with enemies who could be beaten and then remade in our own image and with warfare that, however terrible in cost, had a moral purpose, went much better for the United States than the encounters in Vietnam, which left deep scars on an America seen by many as an oppressive imperialist power and on a Vietnam that lost over a million people. This chapter explores encounters of ancient societies with each other in warfare, encounters that raised issues sometimes very similar to those the United States faced in its twentieth-century wars.

The range of questions raised by encounters with others through warfare and with warfare itself can be divided into questions about individuals and questions about states. Why do individuals go to war? In some cases, because they are compelled, either by mechanisms of state control (conscription) or by the demands of their social position. We saw an example of the latter in the previous chapter: Arjuna, the hero of the *Bhagavad-Gita*, has a moral duty to fight arising from his social role as a warrior, a role he was born into. As his dilemma demonstrates, or as the antiwar, draft-protesting sentiments of "Alice's Restaurant" show in a dif-

124

ferent context, such compulsion need not be accepted unhesitatingly: *Should* individuals go to war is a different question from the question of *why* they do. An individual's moral stance toward war can differ from his state or society's dominant view. But in some cases, individuals go to war willingly. It may be that they do so simply to make a living as a mercenary or out of sheer bloodthirstiness. But it may be that they have personal reasons—defending their homes and families, fighting for a religious or political cause, winning glory—that may also coincide with or support their state's reasons for going to war and that may or may not count as moral, depending on their culture.

Why do states go to war? Like individuals, they may be compelled, either by alliance commitments or by the threat of force. Or they may go to war in defense of their freedom and state interests. But states in the traditional world often went to war for honor, glory, or on the whim of a despotic ruler. As with individuals, the question of whether states *should* go to war is different from the question of *why* they do. And once at war, both individuals and states face the problem of what sorts of behaviors are allowable in war. Almost all warfare has been constrained in some way by cultural conventions and moral rules, putting some wartime behavior off limits to the participants. Some forms of warfare, as between certain Polynesian tribes, were highly ritualized and involved very little killing. In the absence of such rituals and rules, any possible benefits of warfare tend to be exceeded by the costs, right up to and including total mutual destruction by both sides in a conflict. One need not even imagine the global devastation of a full-scale nuclear exchange between the United States and the old Soviet Union to see this. The people of Easter Island, Polynesians and builders of impressive monumental stone heads, virtually wiped each other out hundreds of years ago in a fit of unrestrained warfare. But rules are often broken, and cultures tend not to agree on what the rules are, which is the reason warfare across cultures often seems so much more brutal and unconstrained than intracultural warfare.

And even in intracultural warfare, the realities of war on the ground are mostly brutal. War brings injury, death, destruction, and dislocation directly to portions of the populations involved. In fragile, agriculturally based societies, the indirect effects of war could be even worse. Destruction of crops brought famine and often drove independent farmers into dependence on rich landlords or off the land completely. Armies also acted as carriers of disease by bringing epidemics in their wake or by confining large numbers of people with inadequate food and water in a besieged city, thus fostering the outbreak of diseases. Such indirect consequences were likely to strike women and children especially hard, and women in all ages have been victims of rapes perpetrated by invading armies (and even by the armies supposedly defending them). It is these realities, of course, that make for the deep moral dilemmas created by war, for if warfare involved nothing but glory for winners and shame for losers, it would have no more moral resonance than a big football game.

In the period of world history starting around 200 BCE, following the age of the rise of the great traditions discussed in chapter 4, a number of great empires arose in the areas of the great traditions, drawing on and sometimes synthesizing those emerging traditions to help govern the lands they ruled. The creation of these empires inevitably involved the use of military force. Force could unite a set of states that shared a common set of cultural traditions, as in the creation of the Chinese Empire. It could bring foreign peoples under the rule of a conquering society and defend the resulting empire against rebellions by the conquered, as with the creation and defense of the Roman Empire. The creation of the Mauryan Empire in India shared features of both of these models: There were common cultural (especially religious) elements uniting much of the Indian subcontinent, but differences in language, geography, and climate tended to make different areas of India fairly foreign to each other in other ways. Greek warfare produced only the short-lived Athenian Empire within the Greek world, but Greek attitudes toward war informed the approaches to war of both of the imperial powers who subsequently came to control Greece: the Macedon of Alexander the Great and then Rome. Alexander's warfare also brought down the empire of the Persians, earning him a lasting reputation for evil in the Zoroastrian tradition. In all these cases, imperial civilizations faced the same encounters the United States later did in World War II and Vietnam: encounters with other peoples through warfare, and encounters with warfare itself—its purpose, meaning, and moral justification. The preceding questions exercised thinkers in different civilizations, who came to sometimes very different conclusions.

We examine first the classic writing on warfare from the Chinese tradition, Sun Tzu's *The Art of Warfare,* as well as accounts of warfare by the father of Chinese history writing, Sima Qian. As we saw in the last chapter, during the last centuries of the Chou dynasty (771 to 464 BCE) and the period known as the Warring States (464 to 221 BCE), the political unity of China broke down, and China became a land of many small states that tended to engage in constant warfare with each other. Warfare before 464 BCE was mostly an aristocratic affair, fought between chariot armies for honor and symbolic precedence, not conquest. But in the Warring States period, some rulers raised the stakes of warfare, aiming at the conquest of their enemies and the incorporation of enemy territory into their own. The number of states steadily declined, and the survivors grew in size and military power. Eventually, the ruler of the western state of Qin defeated his five remaining rivals and unified China under his autocratic rule. The warfare of the Warring States period called into being increasingly larger armies of disciplined infantry who drove aristocratic forces from the field and engaged in sieges of the walled cities, whence control of states emanated. Such armies in turn required the creation of complex bureaucratic administrations that could raise and support large forces and the formulation of policies and procedures to make effective use of such forces. Whereas philosophers such as Confucius and Han Fei Tzu debated broader questions of governance in this world, Sun Tzu became the most successful and widely read of the writers who focused on the use of military force in this context. Sima Qian describes this new style of warfare and its consequences.

The Greek tradition gives us a set of poems about civic militarism and its alternatives, the first by the Spartan Tyrtaeus, the second by Archilochus of Paros. Warfare was endemic among the Greek *poleis* (city-states, singular *polis*) of the Classical period (650 to 350 BCE). Such wars were at first small, brief affairs between neighboring city-states and involved conflict over disputed agricultural territory separating the combatants. But more than simple economic motivation was at stake. Communal pride became tied to defense of the *polis'* territory, and communal effort by the city's land-owning farmers, serving as citizen soldiers, went into defending the city's land and honor. Tyrtaeus's poem reflects this sort of warfare. The Persian Wars, starting in 490 BCE, however, stimulated alliance systems and larger, more prolonged warfare that resulted in the creation by Athens of a naval-based empire that collapsed in the Peloponnesian Wars against a Spartan coalition. In these longer, more drawn-out wars, mercenaries came to play a larger role in the fighting; Archilochus's poem gives us a glimpse of the way a mercenary's values differed from those of citizen soldiers.

We will see Roman warfare both from the point of view of its grand imperial results, in the *Res Gestae* of Augustus Caesar, and in terms of how it dealt with rebellion in a section from Josephus's *Jewish Wars*. Between 300 BCE and the early years of the first century CE, the Roman Republic built an empire out of a long series of wars against foreign enemies. Its army was at first composed, like those of Greek *poleis,* of citizen soldiers serving in infantry units called legions. It underwent a transformation as wars took longer and the theaters of conflict moved farther from the heartland of the Italian peninsula. Long-serving professionals, often poor and landless when they joined, replaced the land-owning militia. Their loyalty came to focus, therefore, less on the Roman state, to which their ties were more tenuous than those of the farmer-soldiers had been, and more on the generals whose success earned them plunder and land as pensions. Those generals then fought a series of civil wars that brought the republic to an end. Though he never used the title, Augustus was the first emperor of Rome, and his successors maintained the empire against foreign threats and against revolts such as that of the Jews in 70 CE, about which Josephus writes, and attempted with varying success to keep the loyalty of the army focused on the person of the emperor.

Finally, the Indian tradition gives us a very different take on the results of war from the Rock and Pillar Edicts of Emperor Asoka. Indian warfare before 330 BCE or so resembled Chinese warfare under the early Chou: aristocratic, somewhat ritualized, and based on tribute rather than on conquest of territory. But the incursion of Alexander the Great into northwest India in 324 BCE stimulated at least some Indian rulers to think along more Alexandrian lines. One of these princes, Chandragupta Maurya, initiated the conquests that would form the Mauryan Empire, India's largest pre-Muslim polity. His grandson Asoka continued the expansion of the empire, using the large professional army backed by a complex bureaucracy that his grandfather and father had built. But bloodiness and misery caused by the conquest of the south Indian state of Kalinga caused Asoka to reevaluate his view of warfare. He forswore offensive operations, converted to Buddhism, and turned away from military conquest to "spiritual conquest": the spreading of the principles of Buddhism and a practical focus on good government.

Between them, this set of readings provides a wide range of reactions, moral and practical, to the encounter of imperial peoples with others through war and with warfare itself. Look for how different peoples answered the questions posed by warfare: Why do individuals and states go to war? Are they justified in doing so? What restrictions do societies place on the waging of warfare? What was the effect of warfare when it was waged? These issues are as relevant today as they were in 300 BCE.

1. As a group, do these sources take an approach to analyzing warfare that tends more to the moral or to the practical?
2. What are the major motivations for warfare in these sources, and how do they differ from tradition to tradition? Do some seem more motivated by reasons of state and some more motivated by personal reasons?
3. What is the balance between state and individual in these writings on war? How do these two levels of analysis intersect?
4. What conventions do you see with regard to proper behavior in waging war in these sources? In particular, what are the roles of rational calculation versus emotion in conducting war "correctly"?
5. Which source seems most applicable to your own view of warfare? Which offers the best advice to a United States facing conflict in the twenty-first century?

THE CHINESE TRADITION
Conducting Warfare

The Warring States era (464 to 221 BCE) was a crucial turning point in Chinese history. During this time, the many effectively independent states into which China had become divided were at war with each other constantly. But unlike the constant warfare of the period 770 to 453 BCE, which had been aristocratic, based on extracting tribute and admissions of suzerainty, and which had involved small armies of charioteers, Warring States warfare evolved rapidly into a deadly contest of political survival. Some rulers began raising larger, infantry-based armies with which they conducted campaigns of conquest against their neighbors. To raise and support such armies, they refashioned their administrative systems and enhanced the power of kingship against their aristocracies. The fundamental outlines of the later Chinese imperial state were created during this age of military competition.

As rulers looked for every military advantage they could get, there arose a class of military experts who wrote advice on how best to use the new, larger armies in this life-or-death environment. The most famous of these many writers, Sun Tzu, is a shadowy figure about whom we know very little. He lived during the latter half of the Warring States period. Sun Tzu was a scholar of war, and he takes his place with Confucius, Lao Tzu (founder of Taoism), and Han Fei Tzu (founder of Legalism) as one of the Chinese masters. Indeed, the influence of Confucian, Taoist, and Legalist ideas can be seen in Sun Tzu's principles of war. The scholarly nature of Sun Tzu's work and the other Warring States military manuals is important in two ways. First, it shows that the study of warfare and its place in statecraft was taken seriously by Chinese intellectuals. But, second, the intellectualization of war fit into the antiaristocratic, centralizing trends of Chinese states in this age. Sun Tzu and others constructed leadership—and indeed soldierly qualities—in warfare as a matter not of heroism and practical knowledge (as it had been for aristocratic-led armies earlier) but as the implementation of rational principles by a single trained expert; they saw good soldiers as obedient followers of this enlightened leadership. The implications of this model of military leadership for the structure of the state are clear.

The unification of China by the Ch'in in 221 BCE resulted from the successful application of Sun Tzu's principles. It thus proved itself to be a very practical set of principles, so practical that Mao Zedong in the twentieth century read and followed Sun Tzu's advice in his campaigns, and Sun Tzu is still required reading in United States military academies today. But also note that the edition we read includes commentaries by later Chinese scholars on the basic text. These commentaries illustrate the living, expanding nature of the Chinese philosophical tradition and point to the even wider metaphorical use of Sun Tzu's work beyond the military sphere—it has been used as a manual for business executives, for example. It is, in short, a rich text that will repay close study.

QUESTIONS TO CONSIDER

1. What basic principles of warfare does Sun Tzu advocate? How does economics (or logistics—the art of feeding and supplying armies) shape these principles? What role does psychology play in them?
2. What seems to be the ultimate goal of warfare in the Chinese tradition? How does this relate to the downplaying of glory and bravery in the text?
3. What appear to be the influences of Confucian thought on Sun Tzu? Of Taoist thought? Of Legalist thought? Do these schools of thought show up in the commentaries as well?
4. What are the qualities of good military leadership for Sun Tzu? How do these qualities relate to the philosophical influences on the text? Would you have wanted to serve as a spy under a Sun Tzu–trained general?
5. Why has Sun Tzu remained so popular into modern times? How is his advice applicable beyond the problems of warfare?

THE ART OF WARFARE

Sun Tzu

Chapter 1. Estimates

Sun Tzu said:

1. War is a matter of vital importance to the state; the province of life or death; the road to survival or ruin. It is mandatory that it be thoroughly studied.

   > *Li Ch'üan**: "Weapons are tools of ill omen." War is a grave matter; one is apprehensive lest men embark upon it without due reflection.

Source: From Sun Tzu, *The Art of War*, trans. Samuel B. Griffith. Copyright © 1963 by Oxford University Press, Inc. Used by permission of Oxford University Press, Inc.

*This and the other names before indented paragraphs are the names of later Chinese commentators on the text, followed by their commentary.

2. Therefore, appraise it in terms of the five fundamental factors and make comparisons of the seven elements later named. So you may assess its essentials.

3. The first of these factors is the Tao; the second, weather; the third, terrain; the fourth, command; and the fifth, law.

4. By the Tao I mean that which causes the people to be in harmony with their leaders, so that they will accompany them in life and unto death without fear of mortal peril.

> *Chang Yü:* When one treats people with humanity, justice, and righteousness, and reposes confidence in them, the army will be united in mind and all will be happy to serve their leaders.

5. By weather I mean the interaction of *yin* and *yang;* the effects of winter's cold and summer's heat and the conduct of military operations in accordance with the seasons.

6. By terrain I mean distances, whether the ground is traversed with ease or difficulty, whether it is open or constricted, and the chances of life or death.

7. By command I mean the general's qualities of wisdom, sincerity, humanity, courage, and strictness.

8. By law I mean organization, control, assignment of appropriate ranks to officers, regulation of supply routes, and the provision of principal items used by the army.

9. There is no general who has not heard of these five matters. Those who master them win; those who do not are defeated.

. . .

15. If a general who heeds my strategy is employed, he is certain to win. Retain him! When one who refuses to listen to my strategy is employed, he is certain to be defeated. Dismiss him!

. . .

17. All warfare is based on deception.

18. Therefore, when capable, feign incapacity; when active, inactivity.

19. When near, make it appear that you are far away; when far away, that you are near.

20. Offer the enemy a bait to lure him; feign disorder and strike him.

> *Tu Mu:* The Chao general Li Mu released herds of cattle with their shepherds; when the Hsiung Nu [Huns] had advanced a short distance he feigned a retirement, leaving behind several thousand men as if abandoning them. When the Khan heard this news, he was delighted, and at the head of a strong force marched to the place. Li Mu put most of his troops into formations on the right and left wings, made a horning attack, crushed the Huns and slaughtered over one hundred thousand of their horsemen.*

21. When he concentrates, prepare against him; where he is strong, avoid him.

22. Anger his general and confuse him.

---

*The Hsiung Nu [Huns] were nomads who caused the Chinese trouble for centuries. The Great Wall was constructed to protect China from their incursions.

23. Pretend inferiority and encourage his arrogance.

24. Keep him under a strain and wear him down.

25. When he is united, divide him.

> *Chang Yü:* Sometimes drive a wedge between a sovereign and his ministers; on other occasions separate his allies from him. Make them mutually suspicious so that they drift apart. Then you can plot against them.

26. Attack where he is unprepared; sally out when he does not expect you.

> *Ho Yen-hsi:* Li Ching of the T'ang* proposed ten plans to be used against Hsiao Hsieh, and the entire responsibility of commanding the armies was entrusted to him. In the eighth month he collected his forces at K'uei Chou.
>
> As it was the season of the autumn floods the waters of the Yangtze were overflowing and the roads by the three gorges were perilous, Hsiao Hsieh thought it certain that Li Ching would not advance against him. Consequently he made no preparations.
>
> In the ninth month Li Ching took command of the troops and addressed them as follows: "What is of the greatest importance in war is extraordinary speed; one cannot afford to neglect opportunity. Now we are concentrated and Hsiao Hsieh does not yet know of it. Taking advantage of the fact that the river is in flood, we will appear unexpectedly under the walls of his capital. As is said: "When the thunder-clap comes, there is no time to cover the ears.' Even if he should discover us, he cannot on the spur of the moment devise a plan to counter us, and surely we can capture him."
>
> He advanced to I Ling and Hsiao Hsieh began to be afraid and summoned reinforcements from south of the river, but these were unable to arrive in time. Li Ching laid siege to the city and Hsieh surrendered.

27. These are the strategist's keys to victory. It is not possible to discuss them beforehand.

> *Mei Yao-ch'en:* When confronted by the enemy respond to changing circumstances and devise expedients. How can these be discussed beforehand?

28. Now if the estimates made in the temple before hostilities indicate victory, it is because calculations show one's strength to be superior to that of his enemy; if they indicate defeat, it is because calculations show that one is inferior. With many calculations, one can win; with few one cannot. How much less chance of victory has one who makes none at all! By this means I examine the situation and the outcome will be clearly apparent.

Chapter 2. Waging War

Sun Tzu said:

1. Generally, operations of war require one thousand fast four-horse chariots, one thousand four-horse wagons covered in leather, and one hundred thousand mailed troops.

---

*Li Ching was a general for the T'ang Dynasty (618–907). The names of people and places in this and other accounts in the commentaries are less important than the general principles the episode illustrates.

> *Tu Mu:* . . . In ancient chariot fighting, "leather-covered chariots" were both light and heavy. The latter were used for carrying halberds, weapons, military equipment, valuables, and uniforms. The Ssu-ma Fa said: "One chariot carries three mailed officers; seventy-two foot troops accompany it. Additionally, there are ten cooks and servants, five men to take care of uniforms, five grooms in charge of fodder, and five men to collect firewood and draw water. Seventy-five men to one light chariot, twenty-five to one baggage wagon, so that taking the two together one hundred men compose a company."

2. When provisions are transported for a thousand *li,** expenditures at home and in the field, stipends for the entertainment of advisers and visitors, the cost of materials such as glue and lacquer, and of chariots and armor, will amount to one thousand pieces of gold a day. After this money is in hand, one hundred thousand troops may be raised.

> *Li Ch'uan:* Now when the army marches abroad, the treasury will be emptied at home.

3. Victory is the main object in war. If this is long delayed, weapons are blunted and morale depressed. When troops attack cities, their strength will be exhausted.

4. When the army engages in protracted campaigns, the resources of the state will not suffice.

5. When your weapons are dulled and ardor damped, your strength exhausted and treasure spent, neighboring rulers will take advantage of your distress to act. And even though you have wise counselors, none will be able to lay good plans for the future.

6. Thus, while we have heard of blundering swiftness in war, we have not yet seen a clever operation that was prolonged.

> *Tu Yu:* An attack may lack ingenuity, but it must be delivered with supernatural speed.

7. For there has never been a protracted war from which a country has benefited.

8. Thus those unable to understand the dangers inherent in employing troops are equally unable to understand the advantageous ways of doing so.

9. Those adept in waging war do not require a second levy of conscripts nor more than one provisioning.

10. They carry equipment from the homeland; they rely for provisions on the enemy. Thus the army is plentifully provided with food.

11. When a country is impoverished by military operations it is due to distant transportation; carriage of supplies for great distances renders the people destitute.

12. Where the army is, prices are high; when prices rise the wealth of the people is exhausted. When wealth is exhausted, the peasantry will be afflicted with urgent exactions.

---

*Unit of distance; Chinese equivalent of a mile.

13. With strength thus depleted and wealth consumed, the households in the central plains will be utterly impoverished and seven-tenths of their wealth dissipated.

> *Li Ch'üan:* If war drags on without cessation, men and women will resent not being able to marry, and will be distressed by the burdens of transportation.

14. As to government expenditures, those due to broken-down chariots, worn-out horses, armor and helmets, arrows and crossbows, lances, hand and body shields, draft animals and supply wagons will amount to sixty per cent of the total.

15. Hence the wise general sees to it that his troops feed on the enemy, for one bushel of the enemy's provisions is equivalent to twenty of his; one hundredweight of enemy fodder to twenty hundredweight of his.

16. The reason troops slay the enemy is because they are enraged.

17. They take booty from the enemy because they desire wealth.

. . .

19. Treat the captives well, and care for them.

> *Chang Yü:* All the soldiers taken must be cared for with magnanimity and sincerity so that they may be used by us.

20. This is called "winning a battle and becoming stronger."

21. Hence what is essential in war is victory, not prolonged operations. And therefore the general who understands war is the Minister of the people's fate and arbiter of the nation's destiny.

> *Ho Yen-hsi:* The difficulties in the appointment of a commander are the same today as they were in ancient times.

Chapter 13. Employment of Secret Agents

5. Now there are five sorts of secret agents to be employed. These are native, inside, double, expendable, and living.

. . .

7. Native agents are those of the enemy's country people whom we employ.

8. Inside agents are enemy officials whom we employ.

9. Double agents are enemy spies whom we employ.

10. Expendable agents are those of our own spies who are deliberately given fabricated information.

11. Living agents are those who return with information.

12. Of all those in the army close to the commander none is more intimate than the secret agent; of all rewards none more liberal than those given to secret agents; of all matters none is more confidential than those relating to secret operations.

> *Mei Yao-ch'en:* Secret agents receive their instructions within the tent of the general, and are intimate and close to him.

13. He who is not sage and wise, humane and just, cannot use secret agents. And he who is not delicate and subtle cannot get the truth out of them.

. . .

23. And therefore only the enlightened sovereign and the worthy general who are able to use the most intelligent people as agents are certain to achieve great things. Secret operations are essential in war; upon them the army relies to make its every move.

> *Chia Lin:* An army without secret agents is exactly like a man without eyes or ears.

Interpreting Warfare

Sima Qian (c. 145 to after 91 BCE) is to Chinese history writing what Herodotus and Thucydides combined are to Western historical writing. A scholar and official under the Han, he began collecting historical records and sources early in his career. He was eventually appointed Grand Historian of the Han Court in 107 BCE, in which office he composed the *Records of the Grand Historian*. Based on extensive research in the Imperial Library and on the sources he collected, this monumental work traces Chinese history from the legendary Five Sage Emperors down to Sima Qian's own times.

A central section of the work deals with the rise and fall of the Qin (pronounced "chin") dynasty (221 to 206 BCE) and its founder, the fearsome First Emperor, Qin Shi Huangdi (256 to 210 BCE). Military conquest played a central role in the Qin rise and the unification of China, but the Chinese attitude toward war, especially on the part of scholars such as Sima Qian, remained ambivalent. The reputation of the First Emperor is therefore not as favorable as it might have been in other cultures. Compare, for example, the Roman sources later in this chapter for Augustus. It is interesting to note that, to outsiders, the name of China refers to the Qin dynasty, but that the Chinese refer to themselves as "the people of Han."

The Han dynasty under which Sima Qian wrote replaced the Qin after widespread revolts under the second Qin emperor. Although the Han abolished many of the Qin's harshest Legalist measures, especially those aimed against Confucian scholars such as Sima Qian, in many ways it retained the structure of government set in place by the Qin, including uniform government districts, standardized weights and measures, strict law codes, and antiaristocratic measures. But it cloaked the iron hand of the Chinese state in a Confucian velvet glove, founding a Confucian Academy and promoting scholars such as Sima Qian to positions in the bureaucracy. (It also implemented, for a time, a rather Taoist—what we might call laissez-faire—economic policy that worked for a time to promote prosperity.) It was this synthesis, rather than the naked Legalism of the Qin, that would survive into subsequent dynasties, in part because of the view of history promoted by Sima Qian and his successors as official court historians.

QUESTIONS TO CONSIDER

1. In what ways did the First Emperor follow Sun Tzu's advice on conducting warfare, according to this account? How does that advice fit with the Legalist philosophy that guided the First Emperor?

2. The First Emperor was a great conqueror and unifier. In other civilizations he might have been regarded as a martial hero (perhaps, for instance, medieval Western Europe, whose Charlemagne bears some resemblance to the First Emperor). Why is he not seen this way in the Chinese tradition?

3. Sima Qian writes that "the power to attack, and the power to retain what one has thereby won, are not the same." What are the implications of such a view for the role of the military in Chinese government?

4. Given that Sima Qian is writing from the perspective of the dynasty that succeeded the Qin (and that favored scholars such as himself), how reliable and fair does his account seem to you?

5. What can a civilian-run government such as the modern United States learn from Sima Qian's account about the role of the military and the conduct of warfare?

RECORDS OF THE GRAND HISTORIAN

Sima Qian

The First Emperor

. . . [W]hen the power of the Zhou dynasty waned,* the Qin rose to prominence, building its capital in the western borderland. From the time of Duke Mu on,† it gradually ate away at the domains of the other feudal rulers until the process was finally completed by the First Emperor. . . . In the case of Qin, however, while it was in a flourishing state, its manifold laws and stern punishments caused the empire to tremble. But when its power declined, then the people eyed it with hatred and the whole area within the seas rose up in revolt.

Duke Xiao of Qin,‡ relying upon the strength of Mt. Yao and the Hangu Pass and basing himself in the area of Yongzhou,§ with his ministers held fast to his land and eyed the house of Zhou, for he cherished a desire to roll up the empire like a mat, to bind into one the whole world, to bag all the land within the four seas; he had it in his heart to swallow up everything in the eight directions. At this time he was aided by Lord Shang,** who at home set up laws for him, encouraged agriculture and weaving, and built up the instruments of war, and abroad contracted military alliances and

---

Source: Sima Qian, *Records of the Grand Historian*, trans. Burton Watson, 74–83. Copyright © 1993. Reprinted by permission of Columbia University Press.

*The Eastern Zhou (770–256 BCE) lost even nominal control of China during the Warring States era; the last Zhou king was deposed in 256 BCE.

†Mid-seventh century BCE.

‡381–338 BCE.

§The state of Qin was in the west of China and was protected from its enemies by mountain ranges.

**The chief minister of the Qin ruler.

attacked the other feudal lords.* Thus the men of Qin were able with ease to acquire territory east of the upper reaches of the Yellow River.

After the death of Duke Xiao, kings Huiwen and Wu carried on the undertakings of their predecessor and, following the plans he had laid, seized [a state] in the south and [states] in the west, and acquired rich land in the east and provinces of strategic value. The other feudal lords in alarm came together in council to devise some plan to weaken Qin, sparing nothing in gifts of precious objects and rich lands to induce men from all over the empire to come and join with them in a "vertical alliance," and pool their strength. . . . [The leading] four lords were all men of intelligence and loyalty, generous and kind to others, who honored worthy men and took good care of their followers. They rejected the Horizontal Alliance and instead formed the Vertical Alliance, which united all the forces of [nine] states. . . . With a force of 1,000,000 soldiers drawn from an area ten times that of Qin, they beat upon the Pass and pressed forward toward Qin. But the men of Qin opened the Pass to entice the enemy in, and the armies of the Nine States fled and did not dare advance. Qin, without expending a single arrow or losing a single arrowhead, threatened the feudal rulers of the entire empire.

With this the Vertical Alliance collapsed, its treaties came to naught, and the various states hastened to present Qin with parts of their territory as bribes for peace. With its superior strength Qin pressed the crumbling forces of its rivals, pursued those who had fled in defeat, and overwhelmed and slaughtered the army of 1,000,000 until their shields floated upon a river of blood. Following up the advantages of its victory, Qin gained mastery over the empire and divided up its mountains and rivers. The powerful states begged to submit to its sovereignty and the weaker ones paid homage at its court.

Then followed kings Xiaowen and Zhuangxiang, whose reigns were short and uneventful. After this came the First Emperor who, carrying on the glorious spirit of his six predecessors, cracked his long whip and drove the universe before him, swallowed up the eastern and western Zhou, and overthrew the feudal lords. He ascended the throne of honor and ruled the six directions, scourging the world with his lash, and his might shook the four seas. In the south he seized the land of the hundred tribes . . . and made of it [two] provinces, and the lords of the hundred [tribes] bowed their heads, hung halters from their necks, and pleaded for their lives with the lowest officials of Qin. Then he sent [a general] north to build the Great Wall and defend the borders, driving back the Xiongnu over 700 *li*, so that the barbarians no longer ventured to come south to pasture their horses and their men dared not take up their bows to vent their hatred.

Thereupon he discarded the ways of the former kings and burned the books of the hundred schools of philosophy in order to make the black-headed people[†] ignorant. He destroyed the walls of the great cities, put to death the powerful leaders, and collected all the arms of the empire, which he had brought to his capital at Xianyang, where the spears and arrowheads were melted down and cast to make twelve human

---

*"Feudal lords" refers to the rulers of the various states of Warring States China, nominally under the rule of the Zhou king.

†That is, the Chinese.

statues. All this he did in order to weaken the black-headed people. After this he ascended and fortified Mt. Hua, set up fords along the Yellow River, and strengthened the heights and precipices overlooking the fathomless valleys, in order to secure his position. He garrisoned the strategic points with skilled generals and strong cross-bowmen and stationed trusted ministers and well-trained soldiers to guard the land with arms and question all who passed back and forth. When he had thus pacified the empire, the First Emperor believed in his heart that, with the strength of his capital within the passes and his walls of metal extending 1,000 miles, he had established a rule that would be enjoyed by his sons and grandsons for 10,000 generations.

For a while after the death of the First Emperor the memory of his might continued to awe the common people. Yet Chen She, born in a humble hut with tiny windows and a wattle door, a day laborer in the fields and a garrison conscript, whose abilities could not match even the average, who had neither the worth of Confucius . . . nor wealth . . . , stepped from the ranks of the common soldiers, rose up from the paths of the fields, and led a band of some hundred poor, weary soldiers in revolt against Qin. They cut down trees to make their weapons and raised their flags on garden poles, and the whole world gathered like a cloud, answered like an echo to a sound, brought them provisions, and followed after them as shadows follow a form. In the end the leaders east of the mountains rose up together and destroyed the house of Qin.

. . . Qin, beginning with an insignificant amount of territory, reached the power of a great kingdom and for 100 years made the ancient eight provinces pay homage at its court. Yet, after it had become master of the six directions and established its palaces within the passes, a single commoner opposed it and its seven ancestral temples toppled, its ruler died by the hands of men, and it became the laughing stock of the world. Why? Because it failed to rule with humanity and righteousness, and did not realize that the power to attack, and the power to retain what one has thereby won, are not the same.

. . . [T]he First Emperor was greedy and short-sighted, confident in his own wisdom, never trusting his meritorious officials, never getting to know his people. He cast aside the kingly Way and relied on private procedures, outlawing books and writings, making the laws and penalties much harsher, putting deceit and force foremost and humanity and righteousness last, leading the whole world in violence and cruelty. In annexing the lands of others, one may place priority on deceit and force, but insuring peace and stability in the lands one has annexed calls for a respect for authority. Hence I say that seizing, and guarding what you have seized, do not depend upon the same techniques.

. . . So it is said, a people who feel secure may be led into righteous ways, but a people who feel threatened easily turn to evil. . . .

THE GREEK TRADITION

Greek warfare in the Archaic and Classical, or Hellenic, periods (600 to 323 BCE) was not connected with large empires as Chinese, Roman, and Indian warfare came to be after 200 BCE. But Greek attitudes toward war influenced much of southwest Asia after the conquests of Alexander the Great and also influenced the Romans. Greek warfare occurred between small city-states and was conducted by *hoplite phalanxes.* Hoplites were infantrymen armed with bronze body armor, large shields, and spears. They were also the well-off members of the city-state, arming themselves and serving mostly out of civic duty as a militia force. They stood shoulder to shoulder with their friends and neighbors in dense blocks called phalanxes. Two phalanxes would meet on a level piece of ground, charge each other, and push until one side gave way. Such battles were brief but bloody, especially among the front ranks and during the short pursuit after one side broke and ran, and they tested the community solidarity of a city's citizens. Hoplite warfare and its communal virtues were closely connected to the varyingly collective forms of government, from dual monarchies and limited aristocracies to broader oligarchies and even to the democracy of Athens, practiced by Greek city-states. However, the fairly elite character in the small Greek world of those who could afford the hoplite panoply, even if they were only independent farmers, should not be forgotten.

Here we present two poetic visions of hoplite warfare. The first is by Tyrtaeus, a Spartan from c. 650 BCE. Sparta had the most professional and effective of all the phalanx armies, mostly because Sparta based its economy on a large population of rural slaves, called *helots,* who both made possible (through their agricultural production) and necessitated (by their numbers and thus the possibility of a massive revolt) Sparta's maintenance of a full-time, professional force of soldiers. Tyrtaeus praises the virtues that made the trained Spartan phalanx such a formidable force in the Greek world. The second poem is by Archilochus, a contemporary of Tyrtaeus' from the Aegean island of Paros. He served as a mercenary rather than in a regular civic phalanx; mercenary service, or service for pay by members of one *polis* for another, would become increasingly important after 400 BCE in the wake of the Peloponnesian War.

QUESTIONS TO CONSIDER

1. What is the key military virtue for Tyrtaeus? What does this imply about styles of warfare? How does it compare with military virtues in Sun Tzu?

2. What does this style of warfare imply about Greek attitudes toward political participation more broadly? Was participation in warfare an "ennobling" act for Greeks?

3. What does Tyrtaeus' poem tell us about the social setting of warfare—the impact warfare had on the families, friends, and community of the soldiers?

4. What does Archilochus' poem tell us about the potential difference between the ideals and the realities of Greek warfare? How much is his view influenced by his mercenary status?

5. How would these accounts of participation in warfare fit into Chinese warfare as described by Sun Tzu and Sima Qian? How would a Warring States general view a body of Greek hoplites?

PRAISE OF THE VIRTUOSITY OF THE CITIZEN SOLDIER

Tyrtaeus

I would not say anything for a man nor take account of him
for any speed of his feet or wrestling skill he might have.
Not if he had the size of a Cyclops and strength to go with it,
not if he could outrun Boreas, the North Wind of Thrace.
Not if he were more handsome and gracefully formed than Tithonos,
or had more riches than Midas had, or Kinyras too,
nor if he were more of a king than Tantalid Pelops,
or had the power of speech and persuasion Adrastos had,
not if he had all the splendors except for a fighting spirit.
For no man ever proves himself a good man in war
unless he can endure to face the blood and the slaughter,
go close against the enemy and fight with his hands.
Here is courage, mankind's finest possession,
here is the finest prize that a young man can endeavor to win.

And it is a good thing his city and all the people share with him
when a man plants his feet and stands in the foremost spears relentlessly, all thought
    of foul flight completely forgotten,
and has well trained his heart to be steadfast and to endure,
and with words encourages the man who is stationed beside him.
Here is a man who proves himself to be valiant in war.
With a sudden rush he turns to flight the rugged battalions
of the enemy and sustains the beating waves of the assault.

And he who so falls among the champions and loses his sweet life,
so blessing with honor his city, his father, and all his people,
with wounds in his chest, where the spear that he was facing has transfixed that
    massive guard of his shield,
and gone through his breastplate as well.
Why, such a man is lamented alike by the young and the elders,
and all his city goes into mourning and grieves for his loss.
His tomb is pointed out with pride and so are his children,
and his children's children,
and afterward all the race that is his.
His shining glory is never forgotten, his name is remembered,
and he becomes an immortal, though he lies under the ground,
a brave man who has been killed by the furious War God
standing his ground and fighting hard for his children and land.

Source: Richmond Lattimore, *Greek Lyrics,* 2nd ed., 1960, pp. 14–15. Reprinted by permission of The University of Chicago Press.

But if he escapes the doom of death, the destroyer of bodies,
and wins his battle and bright renown for the work of his spear,
all men give place to him alike, the youth and the elders,
and much joy comes his way before he goes down to the dead.
Aging he has reputation among his citizens.
No one tries to interfere with his honors or all he deserves.
All men withdraw before his presence and yield their seats to him:
Youth and the men of his age and even those older than he.
Thus a man should endeavor to reach this high place of courage
with all his heart and so trying never be backward in war.

ELEGY

Archilochus

Some barbarian is waving my shield, since I was obliged to
    Leave that perfectly good piece of equipment behind
under a bush. But I got away, so what does it matter?
    Let the shield go; I can buy another one equally good.

THE ROMAN TRADITION
The Benefits of Warfare

After nearly a century of civil war and a series of dictatorships that shook the Roman Republic between about 100 and 27 BCE, Octavian, great-nephew and adopted son of Julius Caesar, last of the dictators, defeated his rivals for power and initiated the era of the *Pax Romana* (Roman Peace). Accorded the title *Augustus* (Revered One, implying divine authority), he is known to us as Augustus Caesar, First Citizen and effectively first emperor of Rome, though he never took that title himself and maintained the outward forms of Republican rule while concentrating all real power in his own hands.

Augustus was a successful military leader, both in civil wars against foes such as Marc Antony (of Cleopatra fame) and against foreign foes (though a general named Varus did lose three of Augustus's legions to Germanic tribes in an ambush in southern Germany in 9 CE), and equally on land and at sea (his final battle against Marc Antony was a naval battle at Actium, off the coast of Greece). The military establishment that Augustus led consisted of a large army of several hundred thousand men organized in legions posted to strategically located bases in

Source: Richmond Lattimore, *Greek Lyrics*, 2nd ed., 1960, p. 2. Reprinted by permission of The University of Chicago Press.

the empire. Movement of the legions was facilitated by the fine Roman road system. (Walls for border defense, such as Hadrian's Wall in Britain, mostly postdate Augustus' time.) The soldiers were full-time professionals who enrolled as young men and served until age sixty, at which point they received their own land, often in a new colony settled by retired soldiers and their families; soldiers also received periodic bonuses from generous emperors, following an example set by Augustus.

Near the end of his reign (27 BCE to 14 CE), Augustus had the following account of his accomplishments engraved on two bronze pillars and set in front of his mausoleum in Rome. The original of "The achievements of the Divine Augustus, by which he brought the world under the empire of the Roman people, and of the expenses which he bore for the state and people of Rome" are lost but are known from copies in Asia Minor. After his death Augustus was worshipped as a diety.

QUESTIONS TO CONSIDER

1. What is Augustus's view of warfare? Is there more to it than a utilitarian tool for establishing peace? How does it compare with Sun Tzu's view? With the Greek view?
2. What is Augustus's relationship to the Roman army? What sorts of measures does Augustus take to ensure the loyalty of the army? What does this tell you about Roman political structures?
3. How does Augustus, as a "first emperor," compare with Qin Shi Huangdi, the Chinese First Emperor? Why are their reputations so different in their own cultures?
4. What does this source tell us about the place of warfare and the Roman army in the Roman world? Were the Romans "militaristic"?
5. What lessons does this source hold for a civilian government such as the United States for civil–military relations? For the exercise of power as an imperial nation?

RES GESTAE DIVI AUGUSTI (THE ACHIEVEMENTS OF THE DIVINE AUGUSTUS)

1) At the age of nineteen [44 BC] on my own responsibility and at my own expense I raised an army, with which I successfully championed the liberty of the republic when it was oppressed by the tyranny of a faction. . . .

Source: Res Gestae Divi Augusti (The Achievements of the Divine Augustus). Edited with an introduction and commentary by P. A. Brunt and J. M. Moore (Oxford, UK: Oxford University Press, 1967).

2) I drove into exile the murderers of my father,* avenging their crime through tribunals established by law [43 BC]; and afterwards, when they made war on the republic, I twice defeated them in battle [42 BC].

3) I undertook many civil and foreign wars by land and sea throughout the world, and as victor I spared the lives of all citizens who asked for mercy. When foreign peoples could safely be pardoned I preferred to preserve rather than to exterminate them. The Roman citizens who took the soldier's oath of obedience to me numbered about 500,000. I settled rather more than 300,000 of these in colonies or sent them back to their home towns after their period of service; to all these I assigned lands or gave money as rewards for their military service. I captured six hundred ships, not counting ships smaller than triremes.

4) . . . On fifty-five occasions the senate decreed that thanksgivings should be offered to the immortal gods on account of the successes on land and sea gained by me or by my legates acting under my auspices. . . . In my triumphs nine kings or children of kings were led before my chariot. . . .

. . .

13) It was the will of our ancestors that the gateway of Janus Quirinus should be shut when victories had secured peace by land and sea throughout the whole empire of the Roman people; from the foundation of the city down to my birth, tradition records that it was shut only twice, but while I was the leading citizen the senate resolved that it should be shut on three occasions.

. . .

15) To each member of the Roman plebs I paid under my father's will 300 sesterces†
[44 BC], and in my own name I gave them 400 each from the booty of war in my fifth consulship [29 BC], and once again in my tenth consulship [24 BC]. . . . In my fifth consulship [29 BC] I gave 1,000 sesterces out of booty to every one of the colonists drawn from my soldiers; about 120,000 men in the colonies received this largesse at the time of my triumph. . . .

16) I paid cash to the towns for the lands that I assigned to soldiers in my fourth consulship. . . . The sum amounted to about 600,000,000 sesterces paid for lands in Italy, and about 260,000,000 disbursed for provincial lands. Of all those who founded military colonies in Italy or the provinces I was the first and only one to have done this in the recollection of my contemporaries. Later, . . . I paid monetary rewards to soldiers whom I settled in their home towns after completion of their service, and on this account I expended about 400,000,000 sesterces.

17) . . . when the military treasury was founded by my advice for the purpose of paying rewards to soldiers who had served for twenty years or more, I transferred to it from my own patrimony 170,000,000 sesterces.

. . .

21) I built the temple of Mars the Avenger and the Forum Augustum on private ground from the proceeds of booty. . . . From the proceeds of booty I dedicated gifts in the

---

*Julius Caesar, his adoptive father.

†A small bronze or silver coin.

Capitol and in the temples of the divine Julius, of Apollo, of Vesta and of Mars the Avenger; this cost me about 100,000,000 sesterces. . . .

22) I gave three gladiatorial games in my own name and five in that of my sons or grandsons; at these games some 10,000 men took part in combat. . . .

23) I produced a naval battle as a show for the people at the place across the Tiber now occupied by the grove of the Caesars, where a site 1,800 feet long and 1,200 broad was excavated. There thirty beaked triremes or biremes and still more smaller vessels were joined in battle. About 3,000 men, besides the rowers, fought in these fleets.

. . .

25) I made the sea peaceful and freed it of pirates. In that war I captured about 30,000 slaves who had escaped from their masters and taken up arms against the republic, and I handed them over to their masters for punishment. The whole of Italy of its own free will swore allegiance to me and demanded me as the leader in the war in which I was victorious at Actium. The Gallic and Spanish provinces, Africa, Sicily and Sardinia swore the same oath of allegiance. More than seven hundred senators served under my standards at that time, including eighty-three who previously or subsequently (down to the time of writing) were appointed consuls, and about one hundred and seventy who were appointed priests.

26) I extended the territory of all those provinces of the Roman people on whose borders lay peoples not subject to our government . . . without waging an unjust war on any people. . . . At my command and under my auspices two armies were led almost at the same time into Ethiopia and Arabia Felix; vast enemy forces of both peoples were cut down in battle and many towns captured. . . .

. . .

29) By victories over enemies I recovered in Spain and in Gaul, and from the Dalmatians several standards lost by other commanders. I compelled the Parthians* to restore to me the spoils and standards of three Roman armies and to ask as suppliants for the friendship of the Roman people. Those standards I deposited in the innermost shrine of the temple of Mars the Avenger.

Maintaining Imperial Rule

Not all the subjects of the Roman Empire were happy with its rule, despite the peace and prosperity of the *Pax Romana*. The Jews, whose exclusive monotheism prevented them from participating in the cult of Augustus, were uncomfortable subjects of the Roman Empire, though the Romans were in fact fairly tolerant of the Jewish population, recognizing their separate religious tradition and allowing them to practice it. Nonetheless, religious and ethnic tensions fanned the flames of Jewish discontent, and the population broke into open revolt in 70 CE.

---

*Originally nomadic horsemen who ruled an empire based in Persia that was Rome's major opponent in the east.

The war that followed was chronicled by a remarkable historian, Flavius Josephus (c. 37–100 CE). Born in Jerusalem as Joseph ben Matthias, Josephus was developing a career as a scholar and rabbi when he went to Rome on a diplomatic mission to the Emperor Nero. On his return he was drafted into a command position of the emerging revolt. Captured by the Roman general Vespasian, he earned the trust of the soon-to-be emperor by prophesying Vespasian's rise to rule. The emperor adopted Josephus into his family, the Flavians, and Josephus became an advisor to the Roman war effort, now led by Vespasian's son Titus. Unable to persuade his coreligionists to surrender, he witnessed the sack and destruction of Jerusalem and its temple. His account of the war is factual but also flattered his patron the emperor and served as a warning to other peoples who might consider revolt against the might of the Roman imperium.

Josephus seems from the beginning to have considered the Jewish revolt doomed, and it is not hard to see why in objective, material terms. Rome was, along with the Han Empire and the Parthians, one of the world's great powers; Parthia was contained at this time, and China was so far away as to be nearly legendary (save for the flow of Chinese silk to the Roman elites); thus Rome ruled nearly the whole world known to Josephus and had proved its military prowess repeatedly against many foes. The Jews were outnumbered and outorganized—Josephus had spent much of his time as a commander settling factional disputes within the Jewish camp, whereas the Romans obeyed a divine emperor. But the Jews, too, had their notions of divine assistance, and thus this revolt saw a clash of cultures as much as a clash of politics.

In this selection, Titus, son of Emperor Vespasian and commander of the Roman forces, exhorts his men before a battle with the Jewish rebels. Note in particular the motivations for fighting Titus ascribes to each side and which he thinks is more powerful.

QUESTIONS TO CONSIDER

1. What does Titus present as the key motivation for Roman soldiers in battle? How does this compare with the Jewish motives for going to war, and how does he rank them?

2. What is the balance between passion and rational calculation in what Titus says to inspire his troops? Which ultimately seems more important?

3. What does Titus's speech say about the role of warfare in the maintenance of order in the empire? How does this compare with Augustus's vision half a century earlier?

4. How would Sun Tzu evaluate the Roman conduct of this campaign? What advice might he have given the Jewish forces, faced with a vastly superior foe?

5. Does the cultural clash visible in this war hold any lessons for current-day conflicts? Are Roman attitudes about war useful for a modern superpower?

THE JEWISH WARS

Josephus

Book III
Chapter 10

2. But when Titus perceived that the enemy was very numerous, he sent to his father, and informed him that he should want more forces. But as he saw a great many of the horsemen eager to fight, and that before any succor could come to them, and that yet some of them were privately under a sort of consternation at the multitude of the Jews, he stood in a place whence he might be heard, and said to them,

"My brave Romans! for it is right for me to put you in mind of what nation you are, in the beginning of my speech, that so you may not be ignorant who you are, and who they are against whom we are going to fight. For as to us, Romans, no part of the habitable earth hath been able to escape our hands hitherto; but as for the Jews, that I may speak of them too, though they have been already beaten, yet do they not give up the cause; and a sad thing it would be for us to grow wealthy under good success, when they bear up under their misfortunes. As to the alacrity which you show publicly, I see it, and rejoice at it; yet am I afraid lest the multitude of the enemy should bring a concealed fright upon some of you: let such a one consider again, who we are that are to fight, and who those are against whom we are to fight. Now these Jews, though they be very bold and great despisers of death, are but a disorderly body, and unskillful in war, and may rather be called a rout than an army; while I need say nothing of our skill and our good order; for this is the reason why we Romans alone are exercised for war in time of peace, that we may not think of number for number when we come to fight with our enemies: for what advantage should we reap by our continual sort of warfare, if we must still be equal in number to such as have not been used to war. Consider further, that you are to have a conflict with men in effect unarmed, while you are well armed; with footmen, while you are horsemen; with those that have no good general, while you have one; and as these advantages make you in effect manifold more than you are, so do their disadvantages mightily diminish their number. Now it is not the multitude of men, though they be soldiers, that manages wars with success, but it is their bravery that does it, though they be but a few; for a few are easily set in battle-array, and can easily assist one another, while over-numerous armies are more hurt by themselves than by their enemies. It is boldness and rashness, the effects of madness, that conduct the Jews. Those passions indeed make a great figure when they succeed, but are quite extinguished upon the least ill success; but we are led on by courage, and obedience, and fortitude, which shows itself indeed in our good fortune, but still does not for ever desert us in our ill fortune. Nay, indeed, your fighting is to be on greater motives than those of the Jews; for although they run the hazard of war for liberty, and for their country, yet what can be a greater motive to us than glory? and that it may never be said, that after we have got dominion

Source: Flavius Josephus, *The Works of Flavius Josephus,* trans. William Whiston (Auburn and Buffalo: John E. Beardsley, 1895).

of the habitable earth, the Jews are able to confront us. We must also reflect upon this, that there is no fear of our suffering any incurable disaster in the present case; for those that are ready to assist us are many, and at hand also; yet it is in our power to seize upon this victory ourselves; and I think we ought to prevent the coming of those my father is sending to us for our assistance, that our success may be peculiar to ourselves, and of greater reputation to us. And I cannot but think this an opportunity wherein my father, and I, and you shall be all put to the trial, whether he be worthy of his former glorious performances, whether I be his son in reality, and whether you be really my soldiers; for it is usual for my father to conquer; and for myself, I should not bear the thoughts of returning to him if I were once taken by the enemy. And how will you be able to avoid being ashamed, if you do not show equal courage with your commander, when he goes before you into danger? For you know very well that I shall go into the danger first, and make the first attack upon the enemy. Do not you therefore desert me, but persuade yourselves that God will be assisting to my onset. Know this also before we begin, that we shall now have better success than we should have, if we were to fight at a distance."

3. As Titus was saying this, an extraordinary fury fell upon the men; and as Trajan was already come before the fight began, with four hundred horsemen, they were uneasy at it, because the reputation of the victory would be diminished by being common to so many. Vespasian had also sent both Antonius and Silo, with two thousand archers, and had given it them in charge to seize upon the mountain that was over against the city, and repel those that were upon the wall; which archers did as they were commanded, and prevented those that attempted to assist them that way; And now Titus made his own horse march first against the enemy, as did the others with a great noise after him, and extended themselves upon the plain as wide as the enemy which confronted them; by which means they appeared much more numerous than they really were. Now the Jews, although they were surprised at their onset, and at their good order, made resistance against their attacks for a little while; but when they were pricked with their long poles, and overborne by the violent noise of the horsemen, they came to be trampled under their feet; many also of them were slain on every side, which made them disperse themselves, and run to the city, as fast as every one of them were able. So Titus pressed upon the hindmost, and slew them; and of the rest, some he fell upon as they stood on heaps, and some he prevented, and met them in the mouth, and ran them through; many also he leaped upon as they fell one upon another, and trod them down, and cut off all the retreat they had to the wall, and turned them back into the plain, till at last they forced a passage by their multitude, and got away, and ran into the city.

THE INDIAN TRADITION
Questioning Warfare

Asoka (304–232 BCE) was third king of the Mauryan dynasty. After taking the throne, he initially pursued the expansionist policies of his father Bindusara and his grandfather Chandragupta Maurya. The Mauryan Empire maintained a large, professional army, complete with an impressive (though militarily unreliable) corps of trained war elephants, supported by a large bureaucratic machine, much like the Han and Roman empires, and indeed the range of terrains and climates in which Mauryan armies campaigned probably exceeded those in either China or the Roman Empire. It is probably this geographic diversity, including the presence within agricultural districts of large tracts of semidesert and scrub land good at best for pastoralism but incapable of supporting agriculture, that accounts for political division, rather than imperial unity, being the rule in India before and even after the Mauryas, by contrast certainly with China and even with Rome (especially the eastern half of the Empire) in later centuries.

It is thus especially noteworthy that, with the conquest of the kingdom of Kalinga on India's southeastern coast, Asoka brought almost the whole of the subcontinent under Mauryan rule. But the cost of that campaign in human lives and misery led Asoka to a spiritual crisis and conversion to Buddhism. He forswore offensive warfare (but did retain his large army and the will to use it defensively when necessary) and instead committed himself and his government to spiritual conquest, the welfare of his subjects, and the promotion of *dharma* (sacred duty, though the term has a number of meanings in Hindu and Buddhist tradition and Asoka construed it broadly and with toleration for religious variety). Adopting the reign name *Priyadarsi* ("One who looks after the welfare of others"), he had stone pillars erected throughout his realms inscribed with his precepts on *dharma*. This selection comes from those Rock and Pillar Edicts and is more about the impact of and reaction to war than about war itself.

QUESTIONS TO CONSIDER

1. What aspects of warfare on the ground most bother Asoka? What are the implications of this list for his view of the world?

2. What view of human nature seems to lie behind Asoka's reaction to warfare and his subsequent policies? Is it one that could be applied elsewhere?

3. A cynic might say that encouraging Buddhism (a pacifist religion) among his subjects would benefit Asoka by reducing resistance to government edicts. How might Asoka answer this charge?

4. What would Sun Tzu say about Asoka's policy of nonaggression? What about Augustus? How would Asoka answer them?

5. Is the moral alternative to warfare expressed here applicable to today's world? How? Is nonaggression a desirable stance for a great power? Is it a possible one?

ROCK AND PILLAR EDICTS

Asoka

Rock Edict XIII

Beloved-of-the-Gods, King Priyadarsi, conquered the Kalingas eight years after his coronation. One hundred and fifty thousand were deported, one hundred thousand were killed and many more died (from other causes). After the Kalingas had been conquered, Beloved-of-the-Gods came to feel a strong inclination towards the Dharma, a love for the Dharma and for instruction in Dharma. Now Beloved-of-the-Gods feels deep remorse for having conquered the Kalingas.

Indeed, Beloved-of-the-Gods is deeply pained by the killing, dying and deportation that take place when an unconquered country is conquered. But Beloved-of-the-Gods is pained even more by this—that Brahmans, ascetics, and householders of different religions who live in those countries, and who are respectful to superiors, to mother and father, to elders, and who behave properly and have strong loyalty towards friends, acquaintances, companions, relatives, servants and employees—that they are injured, killed or separated from their loved ones. Even those who are not affected (by all this) suffer when they see friends, acquaintances, companions and relatives affected. These misfortunes befall all (as a result of war), and this pains Beloved-of-the-Gods.

There is no country, except among the Greeks, where these two groups, Brahmans* and ascetics, are not found, and there is no country where people are not devoted to one or another religion. Therefore the killing, death or deportation of a hundredth, or even a thousandth part of those who died during the conquest of Kalinga now pains Beloved-of-the-Gods. Now Beloved-of-the-Gods thinks that even those who do wrong should be forgiven where forgiveness is possible.

Even the forest people, who live in Beloved-of-the-Gods' domain, are entreated and reasoned with to act properly. They are told that despite his remorse Beloved-of-the-Gods has the power to punish them if necessary, so that they should be ashamed of their wrong and not be killed. Truly, Beloved-of-the-Gods desires non-injury, restraint and impartiality to all beings, even where wrong has been done.

Now it is conquest by Dharma that Beloved-of-the-Gods considers to be the best conquest. And it (conquest by Dharma) has been won here, on the borders, even six hundred yojanas away, where the Greek king Antiochos rules, beyond there where the four kings named Ptolemy, Antigonos, Magas and Alexander rule,[†] likewise in the south among the Cholas, the Pandyas, and as far as Tamraparni.[‡] Here in the king's domain among the Greeks, the Kambojas, the Nabhakas, the Nabhapamkits, the Bho-

---

Source: The Edicts of King Ashoka, trans. Ven. S. Dhammika. Copyright © 1993 Buddhist Publication Society, Kandy, Sri Lanka. Reprinted by permission of Dhamma Books.

*The priestly class of Hindu society.

†Antiochus, Ptolemy, and the others were Alexander's generals (and their successors) who had divided Alexander's empire into four Successor kingdoms after Alexander's death.

‡Kingdoms in the far south of India, the one area of the subcontinent not under direct Mauryan rule.

jas, the Pitinikas, the Andhras and the Palidas,* everywhere people are following Beloved-of-the-Gods' instructions in Dharma. Even where Beloved-of-the-Gods' envoys have not been, these people too, having heard of the practice of Dharma and the ordinances and instructions in Dharma given by Beloved-of-the-Gods, are following it and will continue to do so. This conquest has been won everywhere, and it gives great joy—the joy which only conquest by Dharma can give. But even this joy is of little consequence. Beloved-of-the-Gods considers the great fruit to be experienced in the next world to be more important.

I have had this Dharma edict written so that my sons and great-grandsons may not consider making new conquests, or that if military conquests are made, that they be done with forbearance and light punishment, or better still, that they consider making conquest by Dharma only, for that bears fruit in this world and the next. May all their intense devotion be given to this which has a result in this world and the next.

---

*The various ethnic and linguistic groups encompassed by the empire.

CHAPTER 6

Women in the Ancient World

INTRODUCTION

In his comedy *Lysistrata* (411 BCE), the Athenian playwright Aristophanes depicted the women of Athens bringing the Peloponnesian War to an end by means of a sex strike. They organized to abstain from sex until the men became so desperate that they made peace. His play is considered a comic masterpiece, but implicit in its plotline is a darker side of Greek society—the systematic disempowerment of women. Because they were denied active involvement in the participatory democracy of the Greek *polis,* the only means they had at their disposal to influence the councils of men was the sex act. The Greek world of the *polis* era is rightly presented as one of the wellsprings of a wide variety of significant aspects of human culture—for example, logic, philosophy, political science, democratic governance, drama, and historical writing. Yet this dynamic, creative society, to an even greater extent than did most ancient societies, relegated women to a position of extreme subordination. The contrast between the accomplishments of the Hellenic Greeks and the treatment of women in that culture throws into stark relief the experiences and roles of women in the ancient world. In the readings that follow, the reader will be asked to assess the nature of women's roles in five different cultures—those of (1) ancient Greece, (2) Rome of the pagan era (ca. 200 BCE), (3) China of the first century CE, (4) the Christian Roman subculture around 200 CE (before Christianity became the established religion of the Roman Empire), and (5) early Hindu India. Of course, questions about the proper relationship between men and women and about the correct role of women in society are still burning issues. Yet, in addition to the contemporary relevance of the exploration of gender issues, the particular subject of gender roles and gender relations allows us to examine the complex social issue of the relatively unempowered and the underclass.

Humans are social animals, and even in situations of extreme disparity in power between social groups—in circumstances such as slavery, prisons, and concentration camps, for example—there is an interaction between those who exercise power and those on whom power is exercised. All the more so, then, in less extreme cases do those lower in the hierarchy of power and status react to, shape, and contest the dominant social values and social systems. Hence, even when excluded from the formal exercise of power by being deprived of the right to participate in government, military affairs, property ownership and management, and higher culture, humans devise ways to exert influence, even if that influence is passive or reactive.

The women represented and presented here were neither completely devoid of influence nor absolutely unable to give voice to their thoughts and feelings. Nonetheless, they were also affected and influenced by the dominant male power structures (known as patriarchies). So an additional subject to examine is the extent to which those lower on the scale of social and political power are molded by and assimilate the reigning social values. Again, an issue of human social life— the complex process by which social norms are created, transmitted, internalized, and transformed—can be addressed by looking at the way women in ancient societies were neither wholly dependent on, nor completely independent of, the male-dominated system of social values.

Two other elements to pay attention to in reading these materials are (1) the common gender split between the public (male) and private or domestic (female) spheres and (2) the different interests of elite and common women. It was not uncommon for women to be accorded some privileges and power inside the walls of the family home or in matters connected with the domestic sphere, even if those matters extended beyond the home. Although it must be recognized that this is a not insignificant realm of responsibility, it still represents less than full empowerment, if the public sphere remained an exclusively or preeminently male domain. An important question to bear in mind is to what extent, if any, women were allowed to extend their influence into the public sphere and how men reacted when they did. Connected with this consideration is the differential power of elite and common women. The sources presented here are "privileged" in the direction of elite women. Penelope, the Roman women, Ban Zhao, and Perpetua all came from the upper class, and none of the authors of these sources can be said to have presented a commoner's point of view. So, again, it is essential to be aware that the situations and values presented here would apply in the first instance to elite women, while also asking ourselves which of these texts might have also affected women who were not from the upper classes.

The first selection comes from the famous epic of ancient Greece, *The Odyssey.* One of the core texts of Classical Greece, the *Odyssey* was probably produced in the 700s BCE. Its story centers on the difficult journey homeward of one of the great heroes of *The Iliad,* Odysseus. Another focus of the work is the home and family, which he struggles to return to. His kingdom and his household were managed in his absence by his faithful wife, Penelope, who has faced her own trials and troubles. Penelope's character and cleverness are displayed in the selection included here, which involves the climactic scene of Odysseus's return and the final test Penelope sets for him to prove his identity.

The second piece excerpted here revolves around a political dispute of ancient Rome. The specific point of contention was the proposal to repeal a law (the

Oppian Law) that limited the luxury items Roman women could wear in public. Although the law had been passed at a time of great crisis for Rome and that time was long past, the effort to repeal the law became a heated dispute, because women had taken to the streets to protest the law. Thus the law became a symbol of male control over women, and the debate over its repeal reflects different views of the role of women in Roman society. All of the voices in this selection are male, even that of the historian Livy from whose work the selection is taken. Hence this passage provides the dominant masculine perspective and reveals the limits imposed on women's roles in Rome, even by those who supported the women's position on this issue.

The third selection in this chapter comes from a handbook written explicitly to serve as a guide to proper behavior for women in Han China (206 BCE–220 CE) in the second century of our era. The *Nujie,* or *Lessons for Women* (ca. 110 CE), provides us with a comprehensive understanding of the proper role and behavior of women in elite Chinese society. The author, Ban Zhao (ca. 45–ca. 110 CE), was herself an exceptional individual who was chosen to serve the empress directly and whose writing places her among the ranks of the first women scholars in the history of humanity. Although written by a woman of remarkable accomplishments, *Lessons for Women* depicts as the ideal a thoroughly subordinate role for women within the Confucian value system.

The next source in this chapter comes from the prison diary of a woman, Vibia Perpetua, who was executed for her Christian beliefs around 200 CE in the Roman city of Carthage in North Africa. This is a most unusual and distinctive source. Here we have an otherwise unknown woman, speaking to us in her own voice across the centuries. Her decision not to recant her faith when faced with execution and her defiance of her father in the process presents to us a circumstance in which a woman asserted the ultimate power. In a sense, her story demonstrates that, although women in the ancient world were not free to choose the way they lived, they still retained the power to choose the way they died. In addition, her story allows us to examine the role of women in the early Christian world.

The final source in this chapter reflects Hindu religious and social values. It comprises entries in the *Code of Manu* relating to the special responsibilities of women. The *Code of Manu* has been interpreted as an attempt to restore order after a period of turmoil. Although Hindus do not view it as a divinely revealed text, they do believe that the *Code of Manu* is consistent with the proper order of the universe and with the values revealed by the gods in other sources. In that regard, the restrictions and limitations it imposes on women and wives are thought to be divinely sanctioned and to rest on the ultimate authority of the gods.

In different voices and from different cultures and different time periods, the sources excerpted here reveal the social roles of women in the ancient world and the social value systems that defined those roles. Although none of these women were "liberated" in anything like the modern sense, they were not completely disempowered, either. Moreover, even from their inferior position in the power pyramid of the ancient world, they asserted themselves and shaped in significant, though still subordinate, ways the contours of their lives. Their experiences allow us to examine the specific issue of women's role in society and the broader theme

of the encounter between the relatively unempowered in society and the dominant social and political systems that constrain them.

CHAPTER QUESTIONS

1. Identify and compare the position of elite women in the different cultures presented here. In what ways do the women presented here exercise power? Are
   there any differences in the power women exercise in the public sphere versus
   the private sphere?
2. How do the selections composed by women (Perpetua and Ban Zhao) differ
   from those written by men? How might the voices of nonelite women differ
   from the voices of these women?
3. How do the men presented here react to the women? How do the behaviors
   and opinions of the men differ and what, if anything, do they have in
   common?
4. In which culture does the elite woman have the most power and privileges?
   In which the least? Can the difference be explained?
5. What general conclusions can you draw about power relations, based on these
   readings? What limits are there on the power exercised by the dominant parties,
   and in what ways is power exercised by those in subordinate social positions?

WOMEN IN THE HOMERIC WORLD: *THE ODYSSEY*

The Odyssey as a literary work is a mixture of fact and fiction. It was probably composed late in the eighth century BCE (i.e., the 700s BCE), but it may have originated even later. Authorship, composition date, and historical accuracy of this text
are all highly controversial subjects among classicists. Our concern here is not
with these issues, but with the view *The Odyssey* provides of gender relations in an
aristocratic society. As far as the story itself goes, *The Odyssey* tells the tale of
Odysseus's long and troubled return from the Trojan War, which was the subject
of *The Iliad*. Because he has angered Poseidon, the god of the sea, he suffers a
series of unfortunate events, such as shipwreck, capture, and escape from the Cyclops, Polyphemus, avoiding the irresistible allure of the Sirens' song, and so on.
Odysseus was famous for his judgment and his cleverness—it was he who devised
the tactic of the Trojan Horse that led to the conquest of Troy and ultimately
ended the Trojan War. His cleverness and perseverance allow him to endure
despite his troubles and eventually to succeed in returning home.

The position of noblewomen in the world of *The Odyssey* was mixed. The
world of *The Odyssey* was not unlike that of the western Middle Ages without the
castles. Noble lords, who were great warriors, lived on self-sufficient manorial estates, worked by peasants. In that world, as in most aristocratic societies, women
were valued because of their bloodlines. Aristocracies traditionally assert their

right to rule on the basis of superior ancestry, so it was important to have noble ancestors on both the father's and the mother's sides. The noblewomen in this society also had important duties, managing the estates and their household economy, especially during the prolonged absences of the noblemen. In Penelope's case, for example, she has successfully run the estate for years in Odysseus's absence. At the same time, noblewomen could not hold property and power on their own. In *The Odyssey,* when Odysseus did not return from the Trojan War along with the other warriors, evil suitors established themselves in his household and were consuming much of what the estate produced. Although Penelope waited faithfully, in the end they would have forced her to choose one of them as her new husband. Until she remarried, she would enjoy a certain degree of autonomy. Here we can detect the ambiguous status of noblewomen: They are valued for their "pedigree," and as members of the upper class they are trained in certain managerial skills, yet ultimately they must accept a subordinate status in a marriage to a nobleman.

The passage presented here represents the culmination of both *The Iliad* and *The Odyssey,* because it returns Odysseus to the embrace of his wife and household, ending his long absence both at Troy and on the journey back. When he finally reaches home, he does not know what to expect, and he is characteristically cautious, concealing his identity until he has appraised the situation. Despite Odysseus's long absence, Penelope continues to wait for him. Hers is an unenviable task. Not only does she bear the burden of worry for her absent husband, but she also has to deal with the insistent pressure from the boorish noble suitors. She reveals an enormous strength of character throughout this ordeal.

Penelope is a worthy match for Odysseus. She demonstrates her own shrewdness in a variety of ways. For example, she devises stratagems to delay the day of decision about a new husband. One way she puts off the suitors is to unravel every night the cloth that she is weaving for her wedding. Her faithfulness and steadfastness has made her name a synonym for fidelity. Another test she uses to hold off the suitors is to require them to string an enormous and extremely powerful bow. In the following scene, she reveals similar cleverness and sagacity in posing one final test for Odysseus to prove his identity.

The suitors are dealt with in the following fashion. Odysseus, still disguised as a homeless wanderer, is allowed by the mocking suitors to have a go at stringing the bow. Of course, he alone is powerful enough to string it, and, after he does so, he uses it to slay all the suitors. At this point, he reveals his true identity to Penelope. Penelope has had her suspicions that this man might actually be her long-lost husband, but she has not endured the long years on her own without developing her own internal resources and caution. She who has held out so long refuses to accept his declaration without first setting him a test. Central to that test is knowledge of the fact that the house was built by Odysseus himself around an olive tree that was topped off and used as a supporting pillar in the middle of the bedroom.

She is fearful, after all her years of faithful waiting, of some trick that would lead her to yield to a clever stranger posing as Odysseus. There are numerous mistaken-identity scenes in both *The Iliad* and *The Odyssey,* often involving deception by the gods. To be sure of his identity, she sets a test for him, ordering her servants to move Odysseus's bed out of the main bedroom. She knows, as the real Odysseus will also know, that the bed is connected to the olive-tree pillar and cannot be moved.

QUESTIONS TO CONSIDER

1. List the elements of Penelope's character that are revealed in this scene. Compare them with the character traits of Odysseus that emerge in this passage.
2. Who holds the power? How is that power utilized? Does this scene involve power in the public or in the private sphere?
3. Odysseus was characterized as "the best of the Achaeans [i.e., Greeks]" because of his wisdom, courage, caution, and cleverness. Assess whether Odysseus demonstrates those attributes in this scene. Analyze Penelope's behavior using those four attributes. Who is "the best of the Achaeans" in this scene?
4. What description does *The Odyssey* provide of Penelope's emotions once she is convinced of Odysseus's identity? How does this description equate her experiences during her husband's long absence with Odysseus's own experiences?
5. Having read the whole passage, how would you describe the relations between Odysseus and Penelope? Is one in a dominant position, or is the relationship on more of an equal footing?

THE ODYSSEY

Homer

The upper servant Eurynome washed and anointed Odysseus in his own house and gave him a shirt and cloak, while Athene* made him look taller and stronger than before; she also made the hair grow thick on the top of his head, and flow down in curls like hyacinth blossoms; she glorified him about the head and shoulders just as a skillful workman who has studied art of all kinds under Hephaestus[†] or Athene—and his work is full of beauty—enriches a piece of silver plate by gilding it. He came from the bath looking like one of the immortals, and sat down opposite his wife on the seat he had left. "My dear," said he, "heaven has endowed you with a heart more unyielding than woman ever yet had. No other woman could bear to keep away from her husband when he had come back to her after twenty years of absence, and after having

---

Source: The Odyssey of Homer, trans. Samuel Butler, 287–90. Copyright © 1944 Walter J. Black, New York.
*Goddess of Wisdom. Odysseus is one of her favorites.
[†]God of fire and volcanoes, and also of metalworking and smiths.

gone through so much. But come, nurse, get a bed ready for me; I will sleep alone, for this woman has a heart as hard as iron."

"My dear," answered Penelope, "I have no wish to set myself up, nor to depreciate you; but I am not struck by your appearance, for I very well remember what kind of a man you were when you set sail from Ithaca. Nevertheless, Euryclea,* take his bed outside the bed chamber that he himself built. Bring the bed outside this room, and put bedding upon it with fleeces, good coverlets, and blankets."

She said this to try him, but Odysseus was very angry and said, "Wife, I am much displeased at what you have just been saying. Who has been taking my bed from the place in which I left it? He must have found it a hard task, no matter how skilled a workman he was, unless some god came and helped him to shift it. There is no man living, however strong and in his prime, who could move it from its place, for it is a marvelous curiosity which I made with my very own hands. There was a young olive growing within the precincts of the house, in full vigor, and about as thick as a bearing-post. I built my room round this with strong walls of stone and a roof to cover them, and I made the doors strong and well-fitting. Then I cut off the top boughs of the olive tree and left the stump standing. This I dressed roughly from the root upwards and then worked with carpenter's tools well and skillfully, straightening my work by drawing a line on the wood, and making it into a bed-prop. I then bored a hole down the middle, and made it the center-post of my bed, at which I worked till I had finished it, inlaying it with gold and silver; after this I stretched a hide of crimson leather from one side of it to the other. So you see I know all about it, and I desire to learn whether it is still there, or whether any one has been removing it by cutting down the olive tree at its roots."

When she heard the sure proofs Odysseus now gave her, she fairly broke down. She flew weeping to his side, flung her arms about his neck, and kissed him. "Do not be angry with me Odysseus," she cried, "you, who are the wisest of mankind. We have suffered, both of us. Heaven has denied us the happiness of spending our youth, and of growing old, together; do not then be aggrieved or take it amiss that I did not embrace you thus as soon as I saw you. I have been shuddering all the time through fear that someone might come here and deceive me with a lying story; for there are many very wicked people going about. Zeus's[†] daughter Helen[‡] would never have yielded herself to a man from a foreign country, if she had known that the sons of Achaeans[§] would come after her and bring her back. Heaven put it in her heart to do wrong, and she gave no thought to that sin, which has been the source of all our sorrows. Now, however, that you have convinced me by showing that you know all about our bed (which no human being has ever seen but you and I and a single maid servant, . . . who was given me by my father on my marriage, and who keeps the doors of our room) hard of belief though I have been I can mistrust no longer."

---

*A domestic slave of Odysseus's father and the woman who wet-nursed Odysseus as a baby.

[†]God of the sky and lightning, king of the gods.

[‡]Helen of Troy ran away from her husband with Paris, son of the king of Troy, which caused the Trojan War.

[§]The Greeks from mainland Greece. They are the ones who attacked Troy.

Then Odysseus in his turn melted, and wept as he clasped his dear and faithful wife to his bosom. As the sight of land is welcome to men who are swimming towards the shore, when Poseidon* has wrecked their ship with the fury of his winds and waves—a few alone reach the land, and these, covered with brine, are thankful when they find themselves on firm ground and out of danger—even so was her husband welcome to her as she looked upon him, and she could not tear her two fair arms from about his neck. Indeed they would have gone on indulging their sorrow till rosy-fingered morn appeared, had not Athene determined otherwise, and held night back in the far west, while she would not suffer Dawn[†] to leave Oceanus, nor to yoke the two steeds Lampus and Phaethon that bear her onward to break the day upon mankind. . . .

Thus did they converse. Meanwhile Eurynome and the nurse took torches and made the bed ready with soft coverlets; as soon as they had laid them, the nurse went back into the house to go to her rest, leaving the bed chamber woman Eurynome to show Odysseus and Penelope to bed by torch light. When she had conducted them to their room she went back, and they then came joyfully to the rites of their own old bed. Telemachus,[‡] Philoetius,[§] and the swineherd now left off dancing, and made the women leave off also. They then laid themselves down to sleep in the cloisters.

When Odysseus and Penelope had had their fill of love they fell talking with one another. She told him how much she had had to bear in seeing the house filled with a crowd of wicked suitors who had killed so many sheep and oxen on her account, and had drunk so many casks of wine. Odysseus in his turn told her what he had suffered, and how much trouble he had himself given to other people. He told her everything, and she was so delighted to listen that she never went to sleep till he had ended his whole story.

A PUBLIC PROTEST DEMONSTRATION
BY ELITE ROMAN WOMEN

The second piece excerpted here comes from Titus Livy's *History of Rome.* Livy was born in the last century BCE (either 59 or 64 BCE) in northern Italy. Livy was a Roman patriot, and his history reflected his pride in Rome's accomplishments. Unfortunately, only about a quarter of his original *History* survives. Nonetheless, it is still the best single source for Roman history, and for the parts of his *History* that survive, Livy is an irreplaceable primary source.

---

*God of the Sea.

[†]To the Greeks, Dawn was a goddess who lived in the east by the waters of Oceanus, the body of water that surrounded the land mass in Greek understanding of geography. Every morning, two steeds, Lampus and Phaethon, draw her chariot across the sky.

[‡]The son of Odysseus and Penelope. He was only a baby when Odysseus left for the Trojan War and is still a young man at the time of his father's return. He and Philoetius help Odysseus fight the evil suitors.

[§]An old and loyal servant of Odysseus.

The incident related in the passage presented here involves an extremely rare instance of public political protest on the part of the women of Rome. The issue was the proposed repeal of the *Lex Oppia,* or Oppian Law. In 215 BCE during the Second Punic Wars, one of Rome's three great conflicts with Carthage over dominance in the western Mediterranean, the famous Carthaginian general Hannibal inflicted a devastating defeat on the Romans at the battle of Cannae. In the wake of that defeat, the Oppian Law was passed, prohibiting women from having more than half an ounce of gold, wearing clothes in public adorned with expensive purple dye, or riding in a carriage except on religious holidays. These restrictions were implemented to suppress public displays of wealth at a time when Romans were forced by Hannibal's successes to undergo enormous sacrifices in order to raise and equip new armies. In 195 BCE a movement arose, supported by public demonstrations by women, to repeal the restrictions. The women appealed to the consuls.[1] One of them, Marcus Porcius Cato, adamantly opposed repeal, and the other consul, Lucius Valerius, supported repeal.

Women were denied political rights in Rome. In fact, Roman law invested the father of the family with extraordinarily broad powers (*patria potestas*), including even the right to kill unwanted children at birth. During the Republic, women were ordinarily under the control (*manus*) of their husbands, and other women had guardians who made all major decisions. The protest was a real-life effort by women to make themselves heard.

For various reasons, the repeal seemed threatening to some Roman leaders. The long Roman wars had left Roman women relatively independent because of their husbands' absences or deaths. In addition, Roman conquests brought a flood of new wealth into the city. Rome was a victim of its own success, and widespread change might transform Roman society beyond recognition. This new wealth, combined with the repeal of Oppian Law restrictions on women's luxury items, called into question the traditional control men wielded over women in Rome.

The most vehement opponent of the repeal of the restrictive law was Marcus Porcius Cato (234–149 BCE), commonly referred to as Cato the Elder. In his remarkable career, Cato had led Roman armies to victory over Carthaginian forces in Spain and had risen to the position of consul. He was known as Cato the Censor for his hard-bitten opposition to what he perceived to be moral decline. Cato opposed displays of wealth and luxury, rigorously enforced laws, and resisted anything he connected with a decline in public morals, including elements of Greek culture, which he deemed to be inferior and effeminate. His objections and arguments were responded to by Lucius Valerius, also consul in 195 but a figure of much less prominence in Roman history and about whom much less is known.

It is also worth mentioning that the Romans carefully studied histories such as Livy's, considering history to be "philosophy teaching by examples." Thus works such as Livy's did not just gather dust on a shelf but were part of the education of the ruling classes in Rome, so the values represented in this selection helped shape Roman attitudes toward women. The circumstances surrounding this public protest by women in Rome constitute an ideal opportunity for us to assess Roman ideas about women and their proper place in the social and political life of humanity.[2]

1. Considering the restrictions that were being protested, what class of Roman women was probably involved? How might the social class of these women affect the way the male leadership of Rome responded to the protests?

2. What are Cato's arguments for maintaining the ban on gold, purple cloth, and carriages? Is he more concerned with the law itself or with the public protest by the women against it?

3. What distinctions are raised in these passages between the public and the private spheres? Did women have more power in the private sphere in Roman society or were they equally disempowered in both areas?

4. If men are superior to women, as Cato argues, why is it necessary to have a law to enforce rules? Can you identify any ways in which Cato ironically argues that women are actually superior to men? Conversely, although Valerius supports the repeal of the Oppian Law, does he paint a flattering picture of women?

5. The Oppian Law was repealed. In your opinion, does this show that women actually had power in Roman society? How does their power compare with that of Penelope?

HISTORY OF ROME, BOOK XXXIV I-H

Livy

Cato . . . spoke as follows in defense of the law: "If we had, each one of us, made it a rule to uphold the rights and authority of the husband in our own households we should not now have this trouble with the whole body of our women. As things are now our liberty of action, which has been checked and rendered powerless by female despotism at home, is actually crushed and trampled on here in the Forum, and because we were unable to withstand them individually we have now to dread their united strength. . . . [T]here is no class of women from whom the gravest dangers may not arise, if once you allow intrigues, plots, secret cabals to go on. . . .

"It was not without a feeling of shame that I made my way into the Forum through a regular army of women. Our ancestors would have no woman transact even private business except through her guardian, they placed them under the tutelage of parents or brothers or husbands. We suffer them now to dabble in politics and mix themselves up with the business of the Forum and public debates and election contests. . . . Give the reins to a headstrong nature, to a creature that has not been tamed, and then hope that they will themselves set bounds to their license if you do not do it

Source: From Livy in *History of Rome,* Book XXXIV 1-H, Roland Mellor, ed., *The Historians of Ancient Rome,* 1998, 332–33, 335–36, 338. Reprinted with permission of Routledge, a division of Taylor & Francis Books, LTD.

yourselves. . . . What they really want is . . . license, and if they win on this occasion what is there that they will not attempt? . . .

"If you allow them to . . . finally put themselves on an equality with their husbands, do you imagine that you will be able to tolerate them? From the moment that they become your fellows they will become your masters. . . ."

After this . . . Valerius made the following speech in defense of his proposal: "M. Porcius [Cato] . . . spent . . . more time in castigating the matrons than in arguing against the bill. . . . I shall defend the measure. . . . Because we are now enjoying the blessings of peace and the commonwealth is flourishing and happy, the matrons are making a public request to you that you will repeal a law which was passed against them under the pressure of a time of war. He denounces this action of theirs as a plot, a seditious movement, and he sometimes calls it a female secession. I know how these and other strong expressions are selected to bolster up a case, and . . . Cato is a powerful speaker and sometimes almost menacing. What innovation have the matrons been guilty of by publicly assembling in such numbers for a cause which touches them so closely? Have they never appeared in public before? I will quote your own *Origines** against you. [H]ow often they have done this and always to the benefit of the State."

[Valerius cites several instances from Roman history in which the women of Rome came to its defense.]

"You say that they were actuated by different motives then. It is not my purpose to establish the identity of motives, it is sufficient to clear them from the charge of strange unheard-of conduct. And yet, in matters which concern men and women alike, their action occasioned surprise to no one; why then should we be surprised at their taking the same action in a cause which especially interests them? But what have they done? We must, believe me, have the ears of tyrants if, whilst masters condescend to listen to the prayers of their slaves we deem it an indignity to be asked a favor by honorable women. . . .

"You husbands are at liberty to wear a purple wrap over your dress, will you refuse to allow your wives to wear a purple mantle? Are the trappings of your horses to be more gorgeous than the dress of your wives? . . . No, but most certainly there is general grief and indignation felt among them when they see the wives of our Latin allies† permitted to wear ornaments which they have been deprived of, when they see them resplendent in gold and purple and driving through the City while they have to follow on foot, just as though the seat of empire was in the Latin cities and not in their own. This would be enough to hurt the feelings of men, what then think you must be the feelings of poor little women who are affected by small things? Magistracies, priestly functions, triumphs, military decorations and rewards, spoils of war— none of these fall to their lot. Neatness, elegance, personal adornment, attractive

---

*A seven-volume encyclopedic history of Rome by Cato.

†Non-Roman Latin-speaking peoples of central Italy.

appearance and looks—these are the distinctions they covet, in these they delight and pride themselves; these things our ancestors called the ornament of women. . . . I suppose you think that if you repeal the Oppian Law, and should wish to forbid anything which the law forbids now, it will not be in your power to do so, and that some will lose all legal rights over their daughters and wives and sisters. No; women are never freed from subjection as long as their husbands and fathers are alive; they deprecate the freedom which orphanhood and widowhood bring. They would rather leave their personal adornment to your decision than to that of the law. It is your duty to act as their guardians and protectors and not treat them as slaves; you ought to wish to be called fathers and husbands, instead of lords and masters. . . . Whatever decision you come to, they in their weakness will have to submit to it. The greater your power, so much the more moderate ought you to be in exercising it."

WOMEN AND CONFUCIAN VALUES IN CHINA

The remarkable woman whose work is presented here, Ban Zhao, was born somewhere between 45 and 48 CE and died some time before 120 CE. Later in Chinese history, Ban Zhao was respected for both her scholarship and her ability.[3] Her father, who died when she was a young girl, had begun work on an important imperial history, known as the *Han Shu*. His work was left incomplete at his death, and one of his sons took up the task of completing the father's work, at which he was assisted for a while by his brother. When he also died, Ban Zhao was entrusted with the completion of the work. Although the exact nature of what she added to the final product is a matter of dispute, her contributions were significant, and she ranks as China's earliest woman historian and one of the first woman scholars in world history. She must have had a character as impressive as her scholarly abilities, because she was honored with selection as the governess of the empress and her ladies-in-waiting. The work from which the following extract was taken is the *Nujie,* or *Lessons for Women,* which she wrote somewhere around 110 CE.

As she indicates in the work, it was written as a guide for her own daughters, so that they would have a pattern for their behavior. As such, it is written very much in the Confucian tradition, emphasizing respect for ancestors, elders, and other superiors and the importance of proper behavior to the smooth and correct functioning of society. Although Ban Zhao reached positions of great influence, she highlights the necessity for women to respect and be submissive to other family members, in addition to her husband. These included not only her father- and mother-in-law, but also her brothers- and sisters-in-law. The Confucian system insisted on the recognition of sharply distinguished social hierarchies, and, although a woman might have standing as a member of a high-born family, within the family web itself, she could easily find herself at the base of the pyramid.

By the time of Ban Zhao, Confucianism was firmly rooted in Chinese culture and thought. To review, Confucius, the Western variant of the title Kung Fu Tzu, or "Master Kung," lived from 551 to 479 BCE. His teachings emphasized *li* (proper behavior) and *jen* (true manliness) as the foundation of harmony in society and life. Confucianism is a sophisticated extension of the ideas behind the Mandate of Heaven to all aspects of human life, essentially arguing that a harmonious and balanced existence is based on proper personal and ritual behavior. Five key relationships have to be conducted correctly. They are ruler–subject, parents–children, husband–wife, brother–brother, and friend–friend. In virtually every one of these relationships (except for parents/parents-in-law and children) women occupy an inferior position. That *jen* means "true manliness" is equivalent to the linguistic connection between virility and virtue (both with the common Latin root of *vir*, or "man"), and this serves to underline the subordinate position of women in the Confucian value system. At the same time, however, Confucianism emphasizes proper and respectful behavior and criticizes abusive behavior. Moreover, for the system to function properly, women must fulfill their roles and relationships in the correct fashion. Once again, although women occupy secondary and passive roles, Confucianism accords a respectful place to women and attaches significant consequences, both positive and negative, to women's behavior.

QUESTIONS TO CONSIDER

1. According to Ban Zhao, what should be the foremost concerns of a woman? In general terms, how ought she strive to relate to others?

2. What are the two Chinese concepts of *Yin* and *Yang*, and how are they connected to the issue of the proper behavior of women? In your opinion, did the concepts of *Yin* and *Yang* accord women more power in the private sphere as compared with the public sphere, or was the amount of power consistent in both the public and private arenas?

3. Although this work focuses on the obligations of women, judging by it, how ought men to behave in their role as husbands? Does the subordinate role allocated to women in this system have any compensating benefits in the way that men are supposed to behave?

4. Ban Zhao argues that women ought to receive some education and training, just as men do. How can the insistence in the Confucian system that women serve men be used to justify better education and training for women? What class of women do you think would have benefited most if restrictions on education of women had been lifted?

5. How does the position of women in ancient Chinese society compare with that of women in the other societies and cultures presented in this chapter? Would the behavior of Penelope, the Roman women, or Perpetua have been possible in Chinese society? Would she have agreed with the *Code of Manu*?

LESSONS FOR WOMEN

Ban Zhao

Introduction

I, the unworthy writer, am unsophisticated, unenlightened, and by nature unintelligent, but I am fortunate both to have received not a little favor from my scholarly father, and to have had a (cultured) mother and instructresses upon whom to rely for a literary education as well as for training in good manners. More than forty years have passed since at the age of fourteen I took up the dustpan and the broom in the Cao family.* During this time with trembling heart I feared constantly that I might disgrace my parents, and that I might multiply difficulties for both the women and the men (of my husband's family). Day and night I was distressed in heart, (but) I labored without confessing weariness. Now and hereafter, however, I know how to escape (from such fears).

Being careless, and by nature stupid, I taught and trained (my children) without system. Consequently I fear that my son Gu may bring disgrace upon the Imperial Dynasty by whose Holy Grace he has unprecedentedly received the extraordinary privilege of wearing the Gold and the Purple,† a privilege for the attainment of which (by my son, I) a humble subject never even hoped. Nevertheless, now that he is a man and able to plan his own life, I need not again have concern for him. But I do grieve that you, my daughters, just now at the age for marriage, have not at this time had gradual training and advice; that you still have not learned the proper customs for married women. I fear that by failure in good manners in other families you will humiliate both your ancestors and your clan. I am now seriously ill, life is uncertain. As I have thought of you all in so untrained a state, I have been uneasy many a time for you. At hours of leisure I have composed in seven chapters these instructions under the title, "Lessons for Women." . . .

From this time on everyone of you strive to practice these (lessons).

Chapter I Humility

On the third day after the birth of a girl the ancients observed three customs: (first) to place the baby below the bed; (second) to give her a potsherd with which to play; and (third) to announce her birth to her ancestors by an offering. Now to lay the baby below the bed plainly indicated that she is lowly and weak, and should regard it as her primary duty to humble herself before others. To give her potsherds with which to play indubitably signified that she should practice labor and consider it her primary duty to be industrious.

Source: Lessons for Women (Nujie) in Nancy Lee Swann, *Pan Chao: Foremost Woman Scholar of China* (New York: The Century Co., 1932), 82–90.

*Her husband's family.

†Colors of imperial service.

To announce her birth before her ancestors clearly meant that she ought to esteem as her primary duty the continuation of the observance of worship in the home.

These three ancient customs epitomize a woman's ordinary way of life and the teachings of the traditional ceremonial rites and regulations. Let a woman modestly yield to others; let her respect others; let her put others first, herself last. Should she do something good, let her not mention it; should she do something bad, let her not deny it.

Let her bear disgrace; let her even endure when others speak or do evil to her. Always let her seem to tremble and to fear. [T]hen she may be said to humble herself before others.

Let a woman retire late to bed, but rise early to duties; let her not dread tasks by day or by night. Let her not refuse to perform domestic duties whether easy or difficult. That which must be done, let her finish completely, tidily, and systematically. Then she may be said to be industrious.

Let a woman be correct in manner and upright in character in order to serve her husband. Let her live in purity and quietness (of spirit), and attend to her own affairs. Let her love not gossip and silly laughter. Let her cleanse and purify and arrange in order the wine and the food for the offerings to the ancestors. Then she may be said to continue ancestral worship.

No woman who observes these three (practices) has ever had a bad reputation or has fallen into disgrace. If a woman fail to observe them, how can her name be honored; how can she but bring disgrace upon herself?

Chapter II Husband and Wife

The Way of husband and wife is intimately connected with *Yin* and *Yang,* and relates the individual to gods and ancestors.* Truly it is the great principle of Heaven and Earth, and the great basis of human relationships. . . . For these reasons the relationship cannot but be an important one.

If a husband be unworthy then he possesses nothing by which to control his wife. If a wife be unworthy, then she possesses nothing with which to serve her husband. If a husband does not control his wife, then the rules of conduct manifesting his authority are abandoned and broken. If a wife does not serve her husband, then the proper relationship (between men and women) and the natural order of things are neglected and destroyed. As a matter of fact the purpose of these two (the controlling of women by men, and the serving of men by women) is the same.

Now examine the gentlemen of the present age. They only know that wives must be controlled, and that the husband's rules of conduct manifesting his authority must be established. They therefore teach their boys to read books and (study) histories. But they do not in the least understand that husbands and masters must (also) be served, and that the proper relationship and the rites should be maintained.

---

*Yin and yang were two cardinal principles in Chinese philosophy of the Han period. Yin and yang were opposing, but mutually necessary and complementary, principles. Yang is the male principle; it is dominant and is also associated with the sun, heat, light, and Heaven. Yin, the female principle, is characterized by yielding and submission. It is connected with the moon, cold, and darkness (winter and fall, for example). Each of them helps create and complement the other, and excess of one principle actually leads into the other. Acting together, they provide harmony and completeness.

Yet only to teach men and not to teach women,—is that not ignoring the essential relation between them? According to the "Rites,"* it is the rule to begin to teach children to read at the age of eight years, and by the age of fifteen years they ought then to be ready for cultural training. Only why should it not be (that girls' education as well as boys' be) according to this principle?

Chapter III Respect and Caution

As *Yin* and *Yang* are not of the same nature, so man and woman have different characteristics. The distinctive quality of the *Yang* is rigidity; the function of the *Yin* is yielding. Man is honored for strength; a woman is beautiful on account of her gentleness. Hence there arose the common saying: "A man though born like a wolf may, it is feared, become a weak monstrosity; a woman though born like a mouse may, it is feared, become a tiger."

Now for self-culture nothing equals respect for others. To counteract firmness nothing equals compliance. Consequently it can be said that the Way of respect and acquiescence is woman's most important principle of conduct. . . . Those who are steadfast in devotion know that they should stay in their proper places; those who are liberal and generous esteem others, and honor and serve (them). . . .

The correct relationship between husband and wife is based upon harmony and intimacy, and (conjugal) love is grounded in proper union. Should actual blows be dealt, how could matrimonial relationship be preserved? Should sharp words be spoken, how could (conjugal) love exist? If love and proper relationship both be destroyed, then husband and wife are divided.

Chapter IV Womanly Qualifications

A woman (ought to) have four qualifications: (1) womanly virtue; (2) womanly words; (3) womanly bearing; and (4) womanly work. Now what is called womanly virtue need not be brilliant ability, exceptionally different from others. Womanly words need be neither clever in debate nor keen in conversation. Womanly appearance requires neither a pretty nor a perfect face and form. Womanly work need not be work done more skillfully than that of others. . . .

These four qualifications characterize the greatest virtue of a woman. No woman can afford to be without them. In fact they are very easy to possess if a woman only treasure them in her heart. The ancients had a saying: "Is Love afar off? If I desire love, then love is at hand!" So can it be said of these qualifications.

Chapter V Whole-hearted Devotion

Now in the "Rites" is written the principle that a husband may marry again, but there is no Canon that authorizes a woman to be married the second time. Therefore it is said of husbands as of Heaven, that as certainly as people cannot run away from Heaven, so surely a wife cannot leave (a husband's home).

If people in action or character disobey the spirits of Heaven and of Earth, then Heaven punishes them. Likewise if a woman errs in the rites and in the proper mode

---

*There were a number of classical texts that all scholar-officials knew intimately. One of the so-called "Five Classics" was the *Classic of Rites* that discussed court ceremonies and social norms.

of conduct, then her husband esteems her lightly. The ancient book, "A Pattern for Women," says: "To obtain the love of one man is the crown of a woman's life; to lose the love of one man is to miss the aim in woman's life." For these reasons a woman cannot but seek to win her husband's heart. Nevertheless, the beseeching wife need not use flattery, coaxing words, and cheap methods to gain intimacy. . . .

Chapter VI Implicit Obedience

Now "to win the love of one man is the crown of a woman's life; to lose the love of one man is her eternal disgrace." This saying advises a fixed will and a whole-hearted devotion for a woman. Ought she then to lose the hearts of her father- and mother-in-law?

There are times when love may lead to differences of opinion (between individuals); there are times when duty may lead to disagreement. . . . Nothing is better than an obedience which sacrifices personal opinion. Whenever the mother-in-law says, "Do not do that," and if what she says is right, unquestionably the daughter-in-law obeys. Whenever the mother-in-law says, "Do that," even if what she says is wrong, still the daughter-in-law submits unfailingly to the command.

Let a woman not act contrary to the wishes and the opinions of parents-in-law about right and wrong; let her not dispute with them what is straight and what is crooked. Such (docility) may be called obedience which sacrifices personal opinion. Therefore the ancient book, "A Pattern for Women," says: "If a daughter-in-law (who follows the wishes of her parents-in-law) is like an echo and a shadow, how could she not be praised?"

Chapter VII Harmony with Younger Brothers- and Sisters-in-law

In order for a wife to gain the love of her husband, she must win for herself the love of her parents-in-law. To win for herself the love of her parents-in-law, she must secure for herself the good will of younger brothers- and sisters-in-law. . . . The "Book of Changes"* says:

> "Should two hearts harmonize,
> The united strength can cut gold.
> Words from hearts which agree,
> Give forth fragrance like the orchid."

This saying may be applied to (harmony in the home). . . .

Modesty is virtue's handle; acquiescence is the wife's (most refined) characteristic. All who possess these two have sufficient for harmony with others. In the "Book of Poetry"† it is written that "here is no evil; there is no dart." So it may be said of (these two, modesty and acquiescence).

---

* *Yi jing* (*I Ching*). One of the "Five Classics."
† *Shi jing*, another of the "Five Classics."

A MARTYRED CHRISTIAN WOMAN
IN ROMAN NORTH AFRICA

A most fascinating instance of a woman's empowerment is that of Vibia Perpetua, who was executed for her beliefs in 202 or 203 CE in Carthage in Roman North Africa. Very little is known about Perpetua, except that she was still a catechumen—that is, she had not yet been baptized—at the time of her arrest. Her father, who figures prominently in her diary, was a pagan, but her mother and two brothers were Christians. She was executed along with five others who publicly asserted their Christian faith, despite, or perhaps because of, the assurance of execution. As the diary and accompanying materials make clear, Perpetua was a leader and was looked up to as having special spiritual gifts. The supposed day of her death, March 7, is still celebrated as her feast day in the Roman Catholic Church.

The complexity of the issue of women's role in society is very vividly represented in Christianity. On the one hand, Eve is blamed for the fall from grace and the expulsion from the Garden into the troubles of this world. On the other hand, Mary was honored by her selection as the woman who would bear the god-child, Jesus, and the sorrows she endured watching her son be tortured and crucified have earned her unique respect and affection among Christians. Given the subordinate role that women have experienced in almost all cultures, Jesus' special recognition and blessing of the meek in the Sermon on the Mount gave Christianity an additional appeal among women. Yet despite the fact that Christian congregations have often numbered more women than men, most Christian religions have not accorded women equal status. This can be seen very clearly in religion's policies concerning women clergy. Christianity has historically been dominated by men, who are still the only ones deemed worthy of being priests or preachers in the majority of Christian denominations.

This separate and inferior status for women began as early as the Apostle Paul. Paul was arguably the most important founder of the Christian church. He was a converted Jew. Indeed, he was one of the main opponents of the new Christian offshoot of Judaism before his conversion on the Damascus road. He was also a Roman citizen and a man well educated in both rabbinical Judaism and classical Greek learning. As a result, he was exceptionally well placed for and, after his conversion, extraordinarily energetic in organizing and directing the new Christian communities that sprang up across the Mediterranean region and the Middle East. It was primarily Paul who ensured that the new belief would not remain a Jewish sect but would be accessible to non-Jews who did not follow traditional Jewish practices, such as eating kosher foods and practicing circumcision (as even adult male converts to Judaism had to do). As regards women, he established their secondary status in his First Letter to the Corinthians, in which he wrote:

> Be imitators of me, as I am of Christ. . . . But I want you to understand that the head of every man is Christ, the head of a woman is her husband, and the head of Christ is God. . . . For a man . . . is the image and glory of God; but woman is the glory of man. (For man was not made from woman, but woman from man.

> Neither was man created for woman, but woman for man.) . . . Nevertheless, in
> the Lord woman is not independent of man nor man of woman; for as woman
> was made from man, so man is now born of woman. And all things are from
> God.[4]

Although it is simplistic to cite one source as the complete depiction of something
as complex as women's proper role in human secular and religious affairs, Paul's
characterization of male–female relations in 1 Corinthians is a fair representation
of Christian beliefs about gender roles throughout much of the history of that religious system.

Despite the common beliefs to the contrary, there were only two great persecutions of Christians in the Roman Empire, the first of which came in 250 CE. In
fact, it was nearly a century after Jesus' death before the Christians reached numbers great enough to get sufficient attention from the Roman authorities as being
distinguished from Jews, who had a special religious status under the Romans. It
is important to remember that the Romans were religiously, as in most other ways,
an extraordinarily pragmatic people, who worshiped an incredible number and variety of gods and spirits. They assumed that their success was due to the patronage
of these gods and spirits, who had been properly placated by the Romans in the
punctilious public ceremonies honoring the gods. After some time, the Romans
had permitted the Jews not to attend these ceremonies, accepting in their stead
Jewish prayers to their god on behalf of the emperor. They accepted this in part
because Judaism was a small, ancestral religion.

Even though the Roman authorities were opposed to extending these privileges to the Christians, any persecutions of Christians were largely local affairs,
erupting under a specific governor in a particular region and then running its
course with relatively few victims. In 111 CE Pliny the Younger, who was governor of Bithynia at the time, wrote to the Emperor Trajan for advice on how to
handle this new sect. Trajan's response is a model of pragmatism and moderation:

> Do not go looking for Christians. If they are brought before you and the charge
> is proven, they must be punished; with the proviso that if someone denies they
> are Christian and gives proof of it, by offering reverence to our gods, they shall
> be acquitted on the grounds of repentance. . . . Anonymous written accusations
> shall be disregarded as evidence.[5]

Many Christians avoided conflict by bribing an official for a document that indicated the bearer had performed prayers for the Roman gods (which Christians
could not do and be true to their belief in one God), by getting servants to perform the rituals, or merely by doing it and keeping their reservations to themselves. In the case that we have this extraordinary record of—Perpetua's prison
diary—she refused to recant or to compromise in any way. As a result, she finally
got the martyrdom that, as her diary reveals, she so avidly embraced. This record
is remarkable for both its rarity and its intimacy. In the rare prison diaries of a female martyr, Perpetua, of early Christianity, we can examine the contradictory
empowerment and independence that someone possesses who is willing to give
up her life for her beliefs. Her trial, imprisonment, and death throw into stark relief the normal power relations of the late Roman world.

1. What evidence can you find that indicates that a general persecution of Christians was not underway? What other Christians besides Perpetua and her fellow prisoners do we encounter and what are they doing?

2. How do Perpetua's family members react to her imprisonment, and how can you explain any differences in their behaviors? How would you feel if a member of your family gave herself over to a religion in the way that Perpetua does?

3. How does Perpetua's decision to maintain her faith publicly give her power? How does it change the normal power relations in Roman society? Does it also affect her power in the private sphere?

4. How does Perpetua's power differ from that of Penelope and of the women who protested the Oppian Law in Rome roughly four hundred years earlier? Who had more power, Perpetua, Penelope, or the Roman women?

5. How do you read the scene in Perpetua's vision in which she fights a gladiatorial contest with an Egyptian fighter? Can it be seen as a metaphor for the transformation in power relationships that occurred when Perpetua decided her own fate as a Christian martyr?

THE MARTYRDOM OF PERPETUA, A CHRISTIAN WOMAN IN ROMAN NORTH AFRICA (circa 200 CE)

A number of young catechumens were arrested . . . and with them Vibia Perpetua, a newly married woman of good family and upbringing. Her mother and father were still alive and one of her two brothers was a catechumen like herself. She was about twenty-two years old and had an infant son at the breast. (Now from this point on the entire account of her ordeal is her own, according to her own ideas and in the way that she herself wrote it down.)

While we were still under arrest (she said) my father out of love for me was trying to persuade me and shake my resolution. "Father," said I, "do you see this vase here, for example, or waterpot or whatever?"

"Yes, I do," said he.

And I told him: "Could it be called by any other name than what it is?"

And he said: "No."

"Well, so too I cannot be called anything other than what I am, a Christian."

Source: The Acts of the Christian Martyrs, trans. Herbert Musurillo, 109, 111, 113, 115, 117, 119. Copyright © 1972 by Oxford University Press, Inc. Used by permission of Oxford University Press, Inc.

At this my father was so angered by the word "Christian" that he moved towards me as though he would pluck my eyes out. But he left it at that and departed, vanquished along with his diabolical arguments.

For a few days afterwards I gave thanks to the Lord that I was separated from my father, and I was comforted by his absence. During these few days I was baptized, and I was inspired by the Spirit not to ask for any other favor after the water but simply the perseverance of the flesh. A few days later we were lodged in the prison; and I was terrified, as I had never before been in such a dark hole. What a difficult time it was! With the crowd the heat was stifling; then there was the extortion of the soldiers; and to crown all, I was tortured with worry for my baby there.

Then Tertius and Pomponius, those blessed deacons who tried to take care of us, bribed the soldiers to allow us to go to a better part of the prison to refresh ourselves for a few hours. Everyone then left that dungeon and shifted for himself. I nursed my baby, who was faint from hunger. In my anxiety I spoke to my mother about the child, I tried to comfort my brother, and I gave the child in their charge. I was in pain because I saw them suffering out of pity for me. These were the trials I had to endure for many days. Then I got permission for my baby to stay with me in prison. At once I recovered my health, relieved as I was of my worry and anxiety over the child. My prison had suddenly become a palace, so that I wanted to be there rather than anywhere else.

Then my brother said to me: "Dear sister, you are greatly privileged; surely you might ask for a vision to discover whether you are to be condemned or freed."

Faithfully I promised that I would, for I knew that I could speak with the Lord, whose great blessings I had come to experience. And so I said: "I shall tell you tomorrow." Then I made my request and this was the vision I had:

I saw a ladder of tremendous height made of bronze, reaching all the way to the heavens, but it was so narrow that only one person could climb up at a time. To the sides of the ladder were attached all sorts of metal weapons: there were swords, spears, hooks, daggers, and spikes; so that if anyone tried to climb up carelessly or without paying attention, he would be mangled and his flesh would adhere to the weapons.

At the foot of the ladder lay a dragon of enormous size, and it would attack those who tried to climb up and try to terrify them from doing so. And Saturus* was the first to go up, he who was later to give himself up of his own accord. He had been the builder of our strength, although he was not present when we were arrested. And he arrived at the top of the staircase and he looked back and said to me: "Perpetua, I am waiting for you. But take care; do not let the dragon bite you."

"He will not harm me," I said, "in the name of Christ Jesus."

Slowly, as though he were afraid of me, the dragon stuck his head out from underneath the ladder. Then, using it as my first step, I trod on his head and went up.

Then I saw an immense garden, and in it a gray-haired man sat in shepherd's garb; tall he was, and milking sheep. And standing around him were many thousands

---

*Another Christian.

of people clad in white garments. He raised his head, looked at me, and said: "I am glad you have come, my child."

He called me over to him and gave me, as it were, a mouthful of the milk he was drawing; and I took it into my cupped hands and consumed it. And all those who stood around said: "Amen!" At the sound of this word I came to, with the taste of something sweet still in my mouth. I at once told this to my brother, and we realized that we would have to suffer, and that from now on we would no longer have any hope in this life.

A few days later there was a rumor that we were going to be given a hearing. My father also arrived from the city, worn with worry, and he came to see me with the idea of persuading me.

"Daughter," he said, "have pity on my grey head—have pity on me your father, if I deserve to be called your father, if I have favored you above all your brothers, if I have raised you to reach this prime of your life. Do not abandon me to be the reproach of men. Think of your brothers, think of your mother and your aunt, think of your child, who will not be able to live once you are gone. Give up your pride! You will destroy all of us! None of us will ever be able to speak freely again if anything happens to you."

This was the way my father spoke out of love for me, kissing my hands and throwing himself down before me. With tears in his eyes he no longer addressed me as his daughter but as a woman. I was sorry for my father's sake, because he alone of all my kin would be unhappy to see me suffer.

I tried to comfort him saying: "It will all happen in the prisoner's dock as God wills; for you may be sure that we are not left to ourselves but are all in his power."

And he left me in great sorrow.

One day while we were eating breakfast we were suddenly hurried off for a hearing. We arrived at the forum, and straight away the story went about the neighborhood near the forum and a huge crowd gathered. We walked up to the prisoner's dock. All the others when questioned admitted their guilt. Then, when it came my turn, my father appeared with my son, dragged me from the step, and said: "Perform the sacrifice—have pity on your baby!"

Hilarianus the governor . . . said to me: "Have pity on your father's grey head; have pity on your infant son. Offer the sacrifice for the welfare of the emperors."

"I will not," I retorted.

"Are you a Christian?" said Hilarianus.

And I said: "Yes, I am."

When my father persisted in trying to dissuade me, Hilarianus ordered him to be thrown to the ground and beaten with a rod. I felt sorry for father, just as if I myself had been beaten. I felt sorry for his pathetic old age.

Then Hilarianus passed sentence on all of us: we were condemned to the beasts, and we returned to prison in high spirits. . . .

The day before we were to fight with the beasts I saw the following vision. Pomponius the deacon came to the prison gates and began to knock violently. I went out and opened the gate for him. He was dressed in an unbelted white tunic, wearing elaborate sandals. And he said to me: "Perpetua, come; we are waiting for you."

Then he took my hand and we began to walk through rough and broken country. At last we came to the amphitheatre out of breath, and he led me into the centre of the arena.

Then he told me: "Do not be afraid. I am here, struggling with you." Then he left.

I looked at the enormous crowd who watched in astonishment. I was surprised that no beasts were let loose on me; for I knew that I was condemned to die by the beasts. Then out came an Egyptian against me, of vicious appearance, together with his seconds, to fight with me. There also came up to me some handsome young men to be my seconds and assistants.

My clothes were stripped off, and suddenly I was a man. My seconds began to rub me down with oil (as they are wont to do before a contest). Then I saw the Egyptian on the other side rolling in the dust. Next there came forth a man of marvelous stature, such that he rose above the top of the amphitheater. He was clad in a beltless purple tunic with two stripes (one on either side) running down the middle of his chest. He wore sandals that were wondrously made of gold and silver, and he carried a wand like an athletic trainer and a green branch on which there were golden apples.

And he asked for silence and said: "If this Egyptian defeats her he will slay her with the sword. But if she defeats him, she will receive this branch." Then he withdrew.

We drew close to one another and began to let our fists fly. My opponent tried to get hold of my feet, but I kept striking him in the face with the heels of my feet. Then I was raised up into the air and I began to pummel him without as it were touching the ground. Then when I noticed there was a lull, I put my two hands together linking the fingers of one hand with those of the other and thus I got hold of his head. He fell flat on his face and I stepped on his head.

The crowd began to shout and my assistants started to sing psalms. Then I walked up to the trainer and took the branch. He kissed me and said to me: "Peace be with you, my daughter!" I began to walk in triumph towards the Gate of Life. Then I awoke. I realized that it was not with wild animals that I would fight but with the Devil, but I knew that I would win the victory. So much for what I did up until the eve of the contest. About what happened at the contest itself, let him write of it who will.

———————————

WOMEN IN CLASSICAL HINDU CULTURE

The last source details the obligations and status of women in the Hindu culture that developed in the Indus Valley. The material included here comes from the *Code of Manu*, which dates from the second to third century CE. The *Code of Manu* deals with many different features of Hindu life, such as the proper behavior of different castes and methods for ritual purification. The "Manu" referred to in the title is the legendary "first man" of Hindu culture (*Manu* and the English word *man* are related linguistically) and also as the first lawgiver. Thus, the *Code of Manu* is thought of within Hinduism as a text based on human traditions (*Smriti*), but it is also believed to be consistent with the values included in texts that are divinely revealed (*Shruti*), such as the "Purusha Hymn." As a result, it restates and reaffirms traditional values and structures, but it does so on the basis of religious authority.

The responsibilities described for women in the *Code of Manu* need to be understood within the context of Hinduism. As was discussed in chapter 2, a central component of Hinduism is the concept of *dharma*. The root meaning of the word *dharma* is "to sustain." Hindus believe that by living up to the religious and social responsibilities attached to one's social position (caste and gender), one sustains the proper order of the universe, gains good karma, and moves up the scale of reincarnation toward unity with the Brahman, or World Soul. Composed following a period of unrest, the *Code of Manu* represents a rigorous attempt to reestablish order within the Hindu world.

QUESTIONS TO CONSIDER

1. What are the duties of a good woman/wife, according to the *Code of Manu?* In general, how would a good woman behave, according to these codes? How would proper behavior differ for an elite woman as opposed to a woman who was not from the upper class?
2. How should men relate to women, according to the *Code?* It has been said that the *Code* was intended to restore order. In what ways are men asked, in their relationships with women, to keep order? Is there any distinction here between the public and private spheres?
3. How would women, by following the codes presented here, adhere to the Hindu concept of *dharma* and help to "sustain" the world?
4. How are women rewarded for behaving the way the *Code* instructs them to? How are the rewards connected with the Hindu belief in reincarnation and *karma?*
5. How does the ideal behavior of a woman and a wife, according to the *Code of Manu,* compare with the standards established for women in the other texts in this chapter? Would it be more desirable to be a woman in Hindu society or in one of the other social systems presented in this chapter?

CODE OF MANU

Hear now the duties of women.

By a girl, by a young woman, or even by an aged one, nothing must be done independently, even in her own house.

Source: The Law of Manu, in *The Sacred Books of the East,* vol. XXV, trans. G. Bühler (Oxford, UK: Clarendon Press, 1886), 194–97, 328–30, 332, 335, 344–45.

In childhood a female must be subject to her father, in youth to her husband, when her lord is dead to her sons; a woman must never be independent.

She must not seek to separate herself from her father, husband, or sons; by leaving them she would make both (her own and her husband's) families contemptible.

She must always be cheerful, clever in (the management of her) household affairs, careful in cleaning her utensils, and economical in expenditure.

Him to whom her father may give her, or her brother with the father's permission, she shall obey as long as he lives, and when he is dead, she must not insult (his memory). . . .

[B]etrothal (by the father or guardian) is the cause of (the husband's) dominion (over his wife).

The husband who wedded her with sacred texts, always gives happiness to his wife, both in season and out of season, in this world and in the next.

Though destitute of virtue, or seeking pleasure (elsewhere), or devoid of good qualities, (yet) a husband must be constantly worshipped as a god by a faithful wife.

No sacrifice, no vow, no fast must be performed by women apart (from their husbands); if a wife obeys her husband, she will for that (reason alone) be exalted in heaven.

A faithful wife, who desires to dwell (after death) with her husband, must never do anything that might displease him who took her hand, whether he be alive or dead. . . .

[L]et her emaciate her body by (living on) pure flowers, roots, and fruit; but she must never even mention the name of another man after her husband has died.

Until death let her be patient (of hardships), self-controlled, and chaste, and strive (to fulfill) that most excellent duty which (is prescribed) for wives who have one husband only.

A virtuous wife who after the death of her husband constantly remains chaste, reaches heaven, though she have no son, just like those chaste men.

But a woman who from a desire to have offspring violates her duty towards her (deceased) husband, brings on herself disgrace in this world, and loses her place with her husband (in heaven). . . .

By violating her duty towards her husband, a wife is disgraced in this world, (after death) she enters the womb of a jackal, and is tormented by diseases (the punishment of) her sin. . . .

[A] female who controls her thoughts, speech, and actions, gains in this (life) highest renown, and in the next (world) a place near her husband.

Women must particularly be guarded against evil inclinations, however trifling (they may appear); for, if they are not guarded, they will bring sorrow on two families. . . .

No man can completely guard women by force; but they can be guarded by the . . . (following) expedients: Let the (husband) employ his (wife) in the collection and expenditure of his wealth, in keeping (everything) clean, in (the fulfilment of) religious duties, in the preparation of his food, and in looking after the household utensils.

Women, confined in the house under trustworthy and obedient servants, are not (well) guarded; but those who of their own accord keep guard over themselves, are well guarded. . . .

Through their passion for men, through their mutable temper, through their natural heartlessness, they become disloyal towards their husbands, however carefully they may be guarded in this (world).

(When creating them) Manu allotted to women (a love of their) bed, (of their) seat and (of) ornament, impure desires, wrath, dishonesty, malice, and bad conduct. . . .

The production of children, the nurture of those born, and the daily life of men, (of these matters) woman is visibly the cause.

Offspring, (the due performance of) religious rites, faithful service, highest conjugal happiness and heavenly bliss for the ancestors and oneself, depend on one's wife alone.

He only is a perfect man who consists (of three persons united), his wife, himself, and his offspring; thus (says the Veda), and (learned) Brahmanas propound this (maxim) likewise, "The husband is declared to be one with the wife." . . .

The husband receives his wife from the gods, (he does not wed her) according to his own will; doing what is agreeable to the gods, he must always support her (while she is) faithful.

"Let mutual fidelity continue until death," this may be considered as the summary of the highest law for husband and wife.

Let man and woman, united in marriage, constantly exert themselves, that (they may not be) disunited (and) may not violate their mutual fidelity.

NOTES

1. When Rome changed from a monarchy to a republic, the main responsibilities of the king, including military command, were divided between two consuls who shared those powers and duties and who were elected to one-year terms.

2. It was not uncommon for historians in that era to put words into the mouths of historical figures. That is the case in this excerpt, because no record of this speech was available at the time Livy wrote his *History*. Nonetheless, the opinions expressed in this passage still represent Roman views regarding the status and behavior of women.

3. See Arthur Cotterell, *China: A Cultural History* (New York: New American Library, 1988), 117–18.

4. *The Bible*, Revised Standard Version, Paul, 1 Corinthians 11.

5. Cited in Anthony Kamm, *The Romans: An Introduction* (London, UK: Routledge, 1995).

PART THREE

THE
TRADITIONAL
WORLD:
300 CE TO 1100 CE

Encounters with the "Other"

Nomads and Sedentary Societies

INTRODUCTION

On Halloween night, 1938, Orson Welles and his Mercury Theater broadcast a radio adaptation of H. G. Wells's classic 1898 novel, *War of the Worlds*. Welles transferred the story to Grovers Mill, New Jersey, and dramatized it as a live news broadcast of the invasion of Earth by aliens from Mars—playing it convincingly enough to cause mass panic in some parts of the country. "Alien invasion" stories have since been a staple of science fiction and have entered the mainstream of popular culture through movies such as *Alien, Close Encounters of the Third Kind*, and *Independence Day* and TV shows such as *The X Files*. Outside of a fringe of "Roswell true believers," however, most people recognize such stories as fictional. They may express our fears and hopes about encounters with the ultimate "Other," some imagined extraterrestrial form of life, but we haven't had to face the reality.

In some ways, though, the inhabitants of many traditional civilizations did face invasions from another world, invasions as strange and terrifying as the rampage of Welles's Martians and much more real. For, periodically, most of the major Eurasian areas of settled agriculture and the states and cultures built on farming encountered the fierce, alien nomads of the central Asian steppes, herders of animals who appeared so strange and savage that they might as well have been from another planet. Similar encounters arose, though less intensely, in parts of sub-Saharan Africa and in Mesoamerica. The ongoing interaction, often though not always hostile, between sedentary peoples (settled agriculturalists) and nomadic pastoralists constituted for traditional worlds the principal encounter with truly significant Others. It was the divide that generated for most societies the distinction between "civilized" and "barbarian." And like the fears and hopes invested in our own celluloid E.T.s, the fears, hopes, and values of traditional settled societies are made visible to us in their images of the nomadic Other.

The topic of this chapter, then, is not just the historical patterns of actual activity between nomads and sedentary societies, patterns that ranged from raiding to trading and from hostility to cultural exchange and accommodation. It is even more about perceptions, mental images, and the thought world of traditional societies. Our theme is a question: How did settled peoples view nomads, and what does this tell us about the cultures of those settled peoples and of the nomads? There is an evident one-sidedness to this question, for we have not asked what the nomads thought of their settled neighbors. There is an obvious reason for this: Most nomadic societies did not write and have thus left us no records of their thoughts about their settled neighbors. We can sometimes get secondhand reports, or more accurately clues, from literate visitors to the steppes who recorded what they learned of their hosts. But this remains a decidedly "unfair" chapter, biased of necessity toward the views of settled, literate societies.

The division between the worlds of pastoral nomads and of farmers is an ancient one, dating to the beginnings of agriculture and the domestication of animals 10,000 years ago, and whose major distinction is based in geography. The central Asian steppes, a vast area of grassland stretching from northwest of China past southern Russia, is too dry for agriculture but ideal for grazing herds. With the domestication of horses around 4000 BCE, the herders who lived there gained mobility and military potential expressed first in the use of chariots. The development of the compound bow, a powerful missile weapon short enough to be used from horseback, turned nomadic tribes into formidable military forces.

Yet the numbers of nomads were always relatively small—herding supports far fewer people than agriculture—and much of their military effort was turned against each other in tribal battles for grazing land. It was only when nomadic tribes combined that they posed a real threat to their settled neighbors, and combinations were often unstable and short lived. The constant churning of nomadic populations means that telling the various named groups of nomads from each other—Scyths, Huns, Turks, and so on—is problematic and at times artificial. Ironically, nomadic coalitions tended to be strongest in proximity to strong settled states, as successful nomadic leaders used the wealth obtained from trading with and raiding rich states to build their own power bases. Most of the time, the combination of a strong Chinese state and the restriction of access to lands farther west created by the Gobi Desert created the most favorable environment for the formation of nomadic chiefdoms and proto-states at the eastern end of the steppes. Thus most historical movement on the steppes was east to west, as losers in the eastern power struggles migrated westward, where frontiers were more open.

Nomadic incursions into the settled world therefore came only periodically. The most significant waves of activity peaked around 1000 BCE, 400 CE, 1050 CE, and 1250 CE. Each saw the creation through conquest of nomadic empires, but such empires tended not to last long in unified form, as the ecological divide between farmland and grazing land was too great for traditional states and their limited resources to bridge successfully for long. Some conquerors founded dynasties and gave up pastoralism; others simply returned to the steppes, preferring the nomadic life. The last wave, around 1250, saw the creation of the Mongol Empire, the greatest of the nomadic conquest empires and in some ways the last. A further wave of nomadic influence around 1550 saw the creation of hybrid nomad-settled empires by the Ottomans, Manchus, and Mughals before nomadic independence

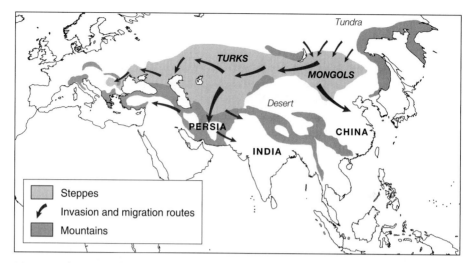

Map 7.1 The Central Asian Steppes

finally succumbed after about 1700 to the growing demographic and technological advantages, including gunpowder weapons, deployed by the settled states. But for two millennia the threat, if not always the activity, of invasion by steppe nomads created a living Other for settled societies. Again, not all the interaction between these two worlds was hostile. Nomads traded with sedentary states, sometimes adopted aspects of sedentary cultures (the steppes became a great meeting ground of world religions over time), and acted as intermediaries between settled worlds—the Silk Road, after all, ran through the steppes. Diplomatic intermarriage along the frontier was not uncommon. But these more peaceful sorts of interactions tended to be overshadowed in the imaginations and diplomatic calculations of settled peoples by the otherworldly military threat posed by the nomads.

We look at five views of nomadic invaders, spread widely over time and space. First, a first-century BCE description of the Xiongnu, the archetypal nomadic peoples of the Chinese world. Second, a late-fourth-century Roman view of the Huns, one of the barbarian groups that invaded the Roman empire (under Attila they campaigned in Gaul and Italy in 449–451, eventually being defeated at the Battle of Chalons in 451). Next, a description of the steppe nomads by the tenth-century Byzantine Emperor Constantine Porphyrogenitus that reflects both Byzantine experience and the classical legacy of Greek and Roman views and terms. Ibn Al-Athir gives us an early-thirteenth-century Muslim view of the Mongol attacks on the Islamic world, and Marco Polo, a European who lived for years at the Mongol court, gives us something of an "outside insider's" view of Mongol life.

As you read these selections, bear in mind the problem posed by all these sources: how does one describe people from "another world," and what do the choices made in describing such folk say about the observers? In other words, descriptions of nomads tell us as much about the hopes, fears, and assumptions of different sedentary peoples as they do about the nomads themselves. And there is a valuable lesson in this even today about how to read descriptions of any people (or even imaginary aliens). H. G. Wells's Martians could only cause panic because Americans saw themselves in them.

CHAPTER QUESTIONS

1. What characteristics of nomadic life stand out to all these authors—that is, what do they agree on about the nomads? What differences appear in the different accounts?
2. Do the differences result from the different perspectives of the different authors, from differences among nomadic peoples, or both? Is there evidence for change over time among the nomads (are the Mongols significantly different from the Xiongnu, for example)?
3. What do the different authors' sources of knowledge about the nomads tell us about the various ways in which the nomadic and sedentary worlds came into contact with and related to each other?
4. How was each world influenced and perhaps transformed by their relationships with the other? Was influence more significant in one direction or the other? Why?
5. What do these readings tell you about the hopes, fears, and assumptions about the world common in sedentary societies? How do their accounts of nomadic life seem distorted or unreal because of their prior assumptions?

DESCRIBING THE OTHER

The Chinese had to deal with nomadic neighbors on their northwestern frontier from an early date, and many of the patterns of that relationship were established, or at least explored, under the Han dynasty (202 BCE–220 CE). The Xiongnu was the Chinese name of the peoples, more or less politically united at different times, who were the dominant nomadic power on the frontier during Han rule. In addition to Chinese agricultural goods and metallurgy, the Xiongnu had developed a taste for Chinese silk, which became the principal luxury item used by nomadic leaders to build their political coalitions on the steppes: the more silk a leader could give away, the larger a following he could create.

As with all government business under the Han and subsequent Chinese dynasties, voluminous records were kept of court deliberations over policy with regard to the frontier and of diplomatic correspondence with the Xiongnu, whose leader had the title *Shen-yu*. Official court historians used these records extensively when writing their histories. The following selections are from one of these official histories and give much detail about Chinese attitudes toward the "barbarians" who caused them so much trouble, as well as opening a few windows into the attitudes of the nomads themselves. Although colored by Chinese assumptions, the descriptions are generally accurate, receiving confirmation from other written sources and from archaeology.

The selections describe an early period in Han relations with the Xiongnu, before 140 BCE, that can be described as conciliatory, being characterized by the payment of tribute by the Chinese to the Xiongnu (though the Chinese sources tend to call the goods "gifts"), use of diplomatic marriages, and other techniques designed to acculturate the "barbarians" to Chinese ways. Later, under the martial emperor Han Wudi (140 to 87 BCE), the Han adopted a more aggressive policy of expansion and control. This worked for a time but proved unsustainably expensive. Thereafter, Chinese policy under subsequent dynasties tended to oscillate between the poles of conciliation and passive defense (marked, among other things, by construction or extension of frontier walls that eventually joined to become the Great Wall) and active management of the frontier via aggression and, at times, conquest.

QUESTIONS TO CONSIDER

1. What characteristics of the Xiongnu way of life stand out to Chinese observers? Why are these characteristics significant?
2. How did the Xiongnu view the Chinese way of life? What were the attractions of Chinese goods? What were the disadvantages and dangers of closer contact with China?
3. How might Chinese diplomacy with the Xiongnu have contributed to the origins of the Silk Road, the great trans-Asian trade route of the classical world?
4. What did the Chinese see as the advantages and disadvantages of the main diplomatic paths—aggression and conciliation—that were available to them in dealing with the Xiongnu? What were the advantages and disadvantages of these strategies from the Xiongnu perspective?
5. What sources of information did the Chinese have about the Xiongnu? How accurate do you think the reports in these histories are? Was there an incentive to accuracy on the Chinese side? In other words, what was the purpose of these histories, and what do they tell us about the Chinese worldview of the time?

HAN SHU: HAN CHINESE DESCRIPTIONS OF THE XIONGNU

The Customs of the Xiongnu

Previous to the time of Yao and Shun* we hear of a race called the mountain Jung. These were the Xiongnu, who inhabited the northern regions, and removed from place to place, according to the pasturage for their flocks and herds. The bulk of their

Source: Excerpted from "Han Shu," trans. A. Wylie, *Journal of the Anthropological Institute of Great Britain and Ireland,* 3 (1874), 401–50.

*Yao and Shun were semilegendary rulers from China's early history.

stock consisted of horses, oxen and sheep; but in smaller numbers they bred likewise camels, asses, mules, horse-ass hybrids, wild horses and hybrids of the same. Removing their herds to find water and pasturage, they had no fixed cities, but dwelt on their rural patrimonies, each family having its allotted portion of land. They had no written characters, but performed oral contracts. The children rode on sheep, and shot birds and squirrels with the bow and arrow. When a little bigger, they shot foxes and hares, the flesh of which they ate. On reaching manhood, when able to bend a bow, they were fully equipped and mounted on horseback. In time of peace they hunted for their living; but when harassed by war, they cultivated martial exercises, to fit them for invasion or attack, which was agreeable to their disposition. The taller troops were armed with bows and arrows; the shorter with swords and spears. When successful in the contest, they pressed forward; but on meeting with a reverse, they retreated, and thought it no shame to run away. On gaining a victory they showed no regard to propriety or equity. From the king downwards all ate the flesh of domestic animals, and clothed themselves with the skins, wearing a fur covering over all. The able-bodied ate the fat and choice portions, while the aged ate and drank what was left. The strong and robust were held in esteem, while the old and feeble were treated with contempt. When a father died, they married their widowed mother; and when a brother died, it was customary to marry his widow. Their names were not transmitted to their descendants.

According to their laws, he who drew a sword a foot in length against another was put to death; anyone guilty of highway robbery was deprived of his family possessions. Small crimes were punished with the rack; and greater crimes with death. The longest imprisonment did not amount to ten days; and all the prisoners in the country only numbered a few individuals.

Early in the morning the Shen-yu [the chief of the Xiongnu] went outside the camp to worship the rising sun, and in the evening he worshipped the moon. . . . In funerals they used coffins and cases containing gold, silver and clothing; but they had no grave-mound, trees or mourning apparel. Several tens or even hundreds of near dependants and concubines were accustomed to follow their master's funeral.

In undertaking any military enterprise, they were always guided by the moon. When the moon was about full, they would engage in battle; but when on the wane, they withdrew from the contest. When one beheaded a captive in battle, he received a goblet of wine, and was allowed to retain the booty. Captives were given as slaves to their captors; so that in war, every man was struggling for personal profit. They were clever at leading the enemy into an ambuscade, and then surrounding them. The eagerness of the scramble was like birds flocking to the prey; but when calamity overtook them, they were dispersed like scattered tiles or passing clouds. Any one bringing home the body of a man slain in battle, got the property of the deceased.

Diplomacy Across the Frontier

[Xiongnu raids were] a cause of much anxiety to the Chinese, and eventually led the Emperor to adopt the notable expedient of sending a princess of the imperial house to Maou-tun,* for his consort.

---

*Shun-yu Maou-tun (209 to 174 BCE), the first great leader of the Xiongnu.

The lady Ung-choo was selected, and conveyed to the home of her new lord by Liw King.* It was hoped that the issue of this union might be more imbued with Chinese susceptibilities and tendencies, and thus be the more easily brought under control. In pursuance of the same policy, the Chinese sent yearly presents of raw and woven silk, wine, and food, thus aiming to cultivate Chinese tastes among them; and on each occasion the fraternal bond of peace and amity was renewed, so that for a time there was a cessation of Maou-tun's incursions. . . .

[In the year 176 BCE] Shen-yu resolved on a dispatch to the Emperor, to the following effect: "The Great Shen-yu, by the will of God ruler of the Xiongnu nation, respectfully salutes the Emperor of China. Formerly your Majesty was pleased to express your gratification on the conclusion of a treaty of peace and amity. In the same spirit the Right Sage prince† bore without complaint the menacing insults of the Chinese officials on the border; till the matter assumed such dimensions, that it became a question of deliberation . . . how to avoid a breach of the treaty and maintain the fraternal relations. Once and again letters of remonstrance were received from Your Majesty; but when I dispatched an envoy with a reply, he did not return, nor was there any messenger from Your Majesty, while the case was treated by you as a cause for war. Now in consequence of a slight breach of the treaty by some petty officials, you pursued the Right Sage prince, till he was driven westward into the territories of [a rival nomad people]. There, however, heaven favored our cause: our officers and troops were loyal and true; our horses were strong and spirited; and by slaughter, decapitation, subjugation and pacification, our army effected the complete reduction of [these rivals]; while . . . adjacent kingdoms, to the number of twenty-six in all, without exception, submitted to the Xiongnu; and thus all the bowmen nations are united as one family. Having also tranquillized the northern lands, we are now desirous that there should be a cessation of hostilities, and that the troops should send their horses to pasture. Let the past be forgotten and the treaty renewed; that the people on the borders may enjoy peace as it was in the days of old; and so the young may attain to maturity; the aged may live unmolested, and uninterrupted happiness prevail from age to age."

About the same time, the Chinese Emperor would seem to have been troubled with some suspicions regarding the Xiongnu, and dispatched a commissioner with a letter, in which he requested Shen-yu to send him a camel, two riding horses and two studs of carriage horses. Uneasy about the approach of the Xiongnu to the stockades, he ordered all the officials and people dwelling on the borders to remove their habitations to a considerable distance. Shen-yu on his part complied with the Emperor's request, and sent forward the offerings with the above epistle. On the arrival of the missive at the Chinese court, during the summer of 175, a consultation was held to discuss the expediency of attacking the Xiongnu or renewing the treaty of peace with them. Peaceful counsels prevailed; it was the general opinion that Shen-yu having just acquired the prestige of victory over [his rivals], it would be impolitic to make an attack on them then. Besides it was argued by some that the conquest of the Xiongnu territory would be of little advantage to China; the waters were salt and the country

---

*A high official in the Imperial Court.

†That is, Maou-tun himself.

uninhabitable; so that the far wiser method would be to renew the treaty. The Emperor acceded to the suggestion.

Consequent on these deliberations, the following year an envoy was dispatched to the Xiongnu. The envoy took a letter to the effect: "The Emperor of China respectfully salutes the Shen-yu of the Xiongnu. My envoy has brought me a letter, in which you say that you are desirous that there should be a cessation of hostilities, that the past should be forgotten and the treaty renewed, that the people on the borders may enjoy peace, and uninterrupted happiness prevail from age to age. All this has my perfect approbation, being in accordance with the policy of the sage Monarchs of ancient times. When China entered into a fraternal treaty with the Xiongnu, the Shen-yu was treated with the greatest liberality. The breach of the treaty and the interruption of amicable relations has always been on the side of Xiongnu. But the trespass of the Right Sage prince having already been pardoned, I will not now accumulate reproaches. If you really entertain the feelings expressed in this letter, let strict injunctions be given to all your officers, to beware of breaking the treaty in future, and that they manifest fidelity and respect in accordance with the tenor of your epistle. We hear from the envoy, the great merit you have acquired by your military enterprises, in subjugating the nations; and in recognition of your arduous achievements, I now beg to present you with a light figured lining imperial embroidered robe, a light long embroidered tunic, and a light variegated gown; also a golden hair comb, a gold ornamented waist-belt, and a buffalo-horn belt fastening; also ten pieces of twilled silk, thirty pieces of variegated silk, and forty pieces each of carnation satin and green silk." These articles were then handed over to the proper functionary, who caused them to be conveyed to the Shen-yu.

Chinese and Xiongnu Customs

In the 10th month of this year, Maou-tun died, and was succeeded by his son Ke-yuh, who assumed the title of "Venerable high" Shen-yu. On his accession, the Emperor Wandi, following up the example and policy of his ancestor, sent a princess of the imperial house for a consort to the newly-elevated chieftain, and appointed the eunuch Chung-hing Yue to escort her to her new home. Yue would fain have excused himself, but the monarch overruled all his objections. "If I am compelled to go," he said, "it will be an unfortunate day for the house of Han." On reaching the Xiongnu camp, Yue, having resolved to make good his words, tendered his submission to the Shen-yu, who became much attached to him. The confidence thus established ensured to Yue a certain liberty of speech; and when he saw the Shen-yu giving way to a fondness for the dress and the food of China, he did not fail to raise a warning voice, and thus addressed his chief: "The entire Xiongnu population is not equal to that of one Chinese province; but one cause of their strength is the simplicity of their dress and food, in which they are independent of China. Now should your Highness change the national customs, and introduce a taste for Chinese luxuries, while the supply of these are only sufficient to meet about one fifth of the requirements, the Xiongnu will all go over to the Chinese. Suppose your people were clothed in Chinese silk, in riding about among the thorns and brush-wood their robes and tunics would be unavoidably torn and destroyed; and it is evident that for strength and durability they are not to be compared to good skin garments. It will be wise also to give up Chinese table delicacies, which are neither so convenient nor so wholesome as good milk and cream." Yue also instructed the officers of the Shen-yu in the art of keeping records, in order that they might preserve a register of the people and the cattle.

When the Emperor of China sent a letter eleven inches in length, inscribed "The Emperor respectfully salutes the Shen-yu of the Xiongnu," with presents and complimentary expressions, Chung-hing Yue induced the Shen-yu to send a return letter twelve inches long, with a larger and longer seal, and audaciously worded "The great Shen-yu of the Xiongnu, the offspring of heaven and earth, ordained by the sun and moon, respectfully salutes the Emperor of the Han," with the usual presents and complimentary expressions. When the Chinese envoy disparagingly remarked that the Xiongnu were wanting in their duty towards the aged,* Chung-hing Yue replied, "You Chinese employ agricultural troops to defend the borders; but when they are sent on a military expedition, so miserably are they found in necessaries, is it not a fact that their aged parents deprive themselves of their warm clothing and comforts to supply their sons with requisite food during the campaign?" The envoy assented, and Yue continued, "The Xiongnu make war the business of life. The aged and infirm being unable to fight, the choice food is given to the healthy and robust, that they may be able to stand the fatigues of the camp. Thus father and sons are helpful to each other. How then can you say that the Xiongnu are wanting in their duty towards the aged?" Continuing the discussion, the envoy remarked, "Among the Xiongnu, father and son sleep in the same cabin. When the father dies, the son takes the mother to wife. When a brother dies, his widow is taken by a surviving brother. They neither wear cap nor sash, and know nothing of the rites of the entrance-hall or the guest-chamber."† "As to that," replied Yue, "the Xiongnu live on their flocks and herds, and clothe themselves with the skins. The flocks being dependent on the herbage and water, it is necessary, from time to time, to remove to fresh localities. Hence, in time of danger, the men practice equestrian archery; and in the seasons of security, they live at ease and free from care. They have few restraints, and are unembarrassed by conventional forms. The intercourse of prince and subject is simple and durable; and the government of the nation is consolidated as that of a single body. When a father or elder brother dies, the son or younger brother takes the widow to wife, as they abhor the mixture of families. Hence although there are disorders among the Xiongnu, yet they preserve the family stem untainted. Now in China, though they do not openly take the widows of their fathers and brothers to wife, yet while matrimonial etiquette requires more distant alliances, this is a fruitful source of murders; and even the change of the surname frequently arises from this custom. Then as to defects in the rites, the ill-feeling that is generated by stringency in the intercourse between superiors and inferiors is such that it may be said, by the time the edifice reaches the summit, the strength of the builders is utterly exhausted. The husbandman spends his force in the labors of tillage and mulberry culture, to procure a supply of food and clothing; and you build cities and outposts for self-defense. But in time of danger the people are not trained to warlike exercises; and in time of peace every one is taken up with his own business. Pshaw! People living in mud huts, with but half a costume and scarcely the

---

*A reference to filial piety, a cardinal Chinese virtue.

†A reference to Chinese ceremonial dress and ritual.

power of intelligible speech, what have they to do with caps!" After that when the envoy wished to discuss the merits of Chinese civilization, Yue abruptly cut him short, saying, "Let not the Han envoy spend his words. The presentation of silks and grain from the Han to the Xiongnu is merely a clever device to estimate their numbers. Nor are these gifts in themselves without their drawbacks. On the contrary, when the grain is ripe, it is trodden down by mounted troops, and there is an end of their harvest, much misery and distress being the natural result."

A ROMAN VIEWS THE HUNS

The Roman Empire in the fourth century was in difficulty. Barbarian invasions by both steppe nomads and seminomadic farmers and herders from the forests of northern Europe exacerbated problems of population decline, civil war for the throne, and economic disruption. Into this situation burst the Huns, a coalition of nomadic peoples who threatened the Roman world for more than half a century. Their initial effect was to drive other peoples, such as the Goths, before them, forcing them across Roman borders. Many of these in fact took up service as allies and auxiliaries in the Roman army, but others pillaged, and Rome was forced to deal with them in various ways, from bribing them to go away to fighting them to settling them in Roman territory. The Huns therefore contributed both indirectly and directly to Roman troubles in the fourth and fifth centuries, until their last great coalition under the infamous Attila met defeat at the Battle of Chalons in 451 and the Huns disappeared from history.

Ammianus Marcellinus, the author of this account of the Huns, was an officer in the Roman army in the second half of the fourth century. He was Greek, born to noble parents between 325 and 330 in Antioch. In retirement he wrote copiously on the history and politics of the empire he knew. His *Res Gestae* starts in the year 96, picking up where Tacitus left off, though the first part of his history is now lost. What we have covers the years 353 to 378 and focuses on the last pagan emperor, Julian, who is something of a hero to Ammianus, himself a follower of the old cults though not a harsh critic of Christianity. Still, sections of his work decry the cultural decline he saw in Rome itself and the burdens of taxation, corruption, and military inefficiency that threatened the empire's continued existence. He also describes the various enemies Rome faced beyond (and increasingly within) its borders, surveying parts of the world in a style that owes much more to Herodotus than to Tacitus. He witnessed the great Roman defeat at Adrianople in 378 at the hands of the Goths, where the Emperor Valens died and where Ammianus's history ends, though his account was written more than ten years later (he died sometime after 391).

It was in narrating the events leading up to Adrianople that Ammianus came to his description of the Huns, because their flight from the Huns brought the Goths to the borders of Rome on the Danube. The arrival of the Goths in the empire, therefore, represents a case of the sort of "domino effect" common on the steppes in which tribes displaced each other westward under pressure from farther east. His description, although exhibiting the prejudice of Romans (and sedentary people in general) against "uncivilized" nomads, is by Roman standards reasonably fair and, to the extent that it can be checked against archaeological records, seems to be fairly accurate.

QUESTIONS TO CONSIDER

1. What characteristics of the Huns stand out most to Ammianus? What is significant about these characteristics? How does his description compare with the Chinese description of the Xiongnu?

2. What sort of tone does he use to describe these characteristics? Is there anything he admires about the Huns?

3. Ammianus often describes the Huns in terms of negatives: "they do not have X; they do not do Y." What does this sort of description tell you about Ammianus himself and the way an educated Roman saw the world?

4. Given this style of negative description, what do you think Ammianus might have missed in describing the Huns? That is, what might be the inaccuracies of omission rather than commission in this account?

5. Given what Ammianus says about them, what do you think a Hunnish counterpart to Ammianus would have said about the Romans?

RES GESTAE

Ammianus Marcellinus

1. . . . the seed and origin of all the ruin and various disasters that the wrath of Mars* aroused, putting in turmoil all places with unwonted fires, we have found to be this. The people of the Huns, but little known from ancient records, dwelling beyond the Maeotic Sea† near the ice-bound ocean, exceed every degree of savagery.

2. Since the cheeks of the children are so deeply furrowed with the steel from their very birth, in order that the growth of hair, when it appears at the proper time, may be checked by the wrinkled scars, they grow old without beards and without any beauty, like eunuchs. They all have compact, strong limbs and thick necks, and are so monstrously ugly and misshapen, that one might take them for two-legged beasts or for the stumps, rough-hewn into images, that are used in putting sides to bridges.

3. But although they have the form of men, however ugly, they are so hardy in their mode of life that they have no need of fire nor of savory food, but eat the roots of wild plants and the half-raw flesh of any kind of animal whatever, which they put between their thighs and the backs of their horses, and thus warm it a little.

Source: Ammianus Marcellinus, *Res Gestae* 31.2 (available at http://www.thelatinlibrary.com/ammianus/31.shtml); trans. Michael Pavkovic and Stephen Morillo.

*The god of war.

†The Black Sea; in other words, the Huns come from the steppes north and east of that sea.

4. Never sheltering themselves with roofed houses, they avoid them as people avoid sepulchers as not fit for common use. Not even a cabin thatched with reeds is to be found among them; but they wander, traveling through mountains and woods, and accustom themselves to put up with frost and hunger and thirst from the cradle. These wanderers do not live under roofs unless under the greatest necessity, for they do not count their safety to be under roofs. . . .

. . .

6. They cover their heads with round caps and protect their hairy legs with goatskins; their shoes are formed upon no lasts, and so prevent their walking with free step. For this reason they are not at all adapted to battles on foot, but they are almost glued to their horses, which are hardy, it is true, but ugly, and sometimes they sit them women-fashion and thus perform their ordinary tasks. From their horses by night or day every one of that nation buys and sells, eats and drinks, and bowed over the narrow neck of the animal relaxes into a sleep so deep as to be accompanied by many dreams.

7. And when deliberation is called for about weighty matters, they all consult as a common body in that fashion. They are subject to no royal restraint, but they are content with the disorderly government of their important men, and led by them they force their way through every obstacle.

8. They also sometimes fight when provoked, and then they enter the battle drawn up in wedge-shaped masses, while their medley of voices makes a savage noise. And as they are lightly equipped for swift motion, and unexpected in action, they purposely divide suddenly into scattered bands and attack, rushing about in disorder here and there, dealing terrific slaughter; and because of their extraordinary rapidity of movement they are never seen to attack a rampart or pillage an enemy's camp.

9. And on this account you would not hesitate to call them the most terrible of all warriors, because they fight from a distance with missiles having sharp bone, instead of their usual points, joined to the shafts with wonderful skill; then they gallop over the intervening spaces and fight hand to hand with swords, regardless of their own lives; and while the enemy are guarding against wounds from the sabre-thrusts, they throw strips of cloth plaited into nooses over their opponents and so entangle them that they fetter their limbs and take from them the power of riding or walking.

10. None of them plow nor even touch a plow handle, for they live without settled abode, but constantly wander without home, law or stable source of food, with the wagons in which they live, like people always fleeing. . . .

BYZANTIUM AND BARBARIANS

The Roman Empire in the west dissolved under the twin pressures of external invasion and internal decay, but the richer, more urban eastern half of the empire survived. Transformed by Christianity, truncated by the early Islamic conquests, and predominantly Greek rather than Latin in culture, what became known as the Byzantine Empire was nonetheless the direct heir of Rome and preserved Roman wisdom about dealing with peoples like the Huns—peoples Byzantine writers often referred to as *Scyths,* using the Classical Greek name for the steppe nomads of Herodotus's time. In short, Byzantine dealings with steppe powers was informed by a combination of practical politics and learning based on literary tradition. And the need for successful relations with the steppe powers north of the Black Sea was pressing between 600 and 900, a period when Byzantium was largely on the defensive against the vastly superior power of the Islamic caliphate while also facing threats in the Balkans and in Italy. Alliance with the nomadic power of the moment in order to provide a counterthreat to Arab power was a necessity of survival.

One of the best examples of Byzantine official culture, containing a clear statement of these diplomatic imperatives, is the treatise called *De Administrando Imperio* ("On the Administration of the Empire") by the Emperor Constantine VII Porphyrogenitus (905–959). *Porphyrogenitus* means "born in the purple"—that is, the legitimate heir of a reigning emperor—and Constantine took his heritage seriously. He came to the throne early in life, but achieved full power, free from the domination of regents representing the military aristocracy, only in middle age. In the meantime, he had become a student of classical literature and a prolific writer and compiler, mostly of treatises such as this one, composed between 948 and 952, that were aimed at educating his own son Romanus in the duties and intricacies of running the empire. The selections here focus on the Pechenegs, the dominant steppe power north of the Black Sea in Constantine's time, and form part of a survey of the lands and peoples surrounding the empire that stands, like Ammianus's work, in the ethnographic tradition of Herodotus. Yet the origin, purpose, and tone of the treatise are more like the Chinese *Han Shu* than Ammianus's independent history.

QUESTIONS TO CONSIDER

1. What characteristics of the Pechenegs seem most important to Constantine? Is he interested in them as a culture?

2. What are the main diplomatic tools and options the Byzantines have in dealing with the Pechenegs?

3. What are the similarities and differences between Byzantine and Chinese diplomacy with regard to their respective nomadic neighbors? Which power had more options, and why?

4. What seem to be the sources of Constantine's knowledge about the Pechenegs? How accurate do you think the information in this treatise is? Was there an incentive to accuracy on the Byzantine side? How useful would such a treatise have been to a new emperor?

5. How do you think the Pechenegs would have viewed the Byzantines? What motives, incentives, and options did the Pechenegs have in dealing with the Byzantines?

DE ADMINISTRANDO IMPERIO

Constantine Porphyrogenitus

1. Of the Pechenegs, and how many advantages accrue from their being at peace with the emperor of the Romans.

Hear now, my son, those things of which I think you *should* not be ignorant, and be wise that you may attain to government. For I maintain that while learning is a good thing for all the rest as well, who are subjects, yet it is especially so for you, who are bound to take thought for the safety of all, and to steer and guide the laden ship of the world. And if in setting out my subject I have followed the plain and beaten track of speech and, so to say, idly running and simple prose, do not wonder at that, my son. For I have not been studious to make a display of fine writing or of an Atticizing style,* swollen with the sublime and lofty, but rather have been eager by means of every-day and conversational narrative to teach you those things of which I think you should not be ignorant and which may without difficulty provide that intelligence and prudence which are the fruit of long experience.

I conceive, then, that it is always greatly to the advantage of the emperor of the Romans to be minded to keep the peace with the nation of the Pechenegs and to conclude conventions and treaties of friendship with them and send every year to them from our side a diplomatic agent with presents befitting and suitable to that nation, and to take from their side sureties, that is, hostages and a diplomatic agent, who shall be collected together under charge of the competent minister in this city protected of God, and shall enjoy all imperial benefits and gifts suitable for the emperor to bestow.

This nation of the Pechenegs is neighbor to the district of Cherson,† and if they are not friendly disposed towards us, they may make excursions and plundering raids against Cherson, and may ravage Cherson itself and the so called Regions.

2. Of the Pechenegs and the Russians.

The Pechenegs are neighbors to and march with the Russians also, and often, when the two are not at peace with one another, raid Russia, and do her considerable harm and outrage.

The Russians also are much concerned to keep the peace with the Pechenegs. For they buy of them horned cattle and horses and sheep, whereby they live more easily and comfortably, since none of the aforesaid animals is found in Russia. Moreover, the Russians are quite unable to set out for wars beyond their borders unless they are at peace with the Pechenegs, because while they are away from their homes, these may come upon them and destroy and outrage their property. And so the Russians, both to avoid being harmed by them and because of the strength of that nation, are the more

---

Source: Selections from Constantine Porphyrogenitus, *De Administrando Imperio,* ed. Gy. Moravcsik, trans. R. J. H. Jenkins, rev. ed., 49–55, 167–71. Copyright © 1967 Dumbarton Oaks. Reprinted with permission.

*That is, a style imitating that of classical Greek authors; there is some unintentional irony in this claim.

†Byzantine city and province on the north shore of the Black Sea, in the region of the Crimean Peninsula. Cherson was a significant center of Byzantine trade with the steppes and Russia.

concerned always to be in alliance with them and to have them for support, so as both to be rid of their enmity and to enjoy the advantage of their assistance.

Nor can the Russians come at this imperial city of the Romans, either for war or for trade, unless they are at peace with the Pechenegs, because when the Russians come with their ships to the barrages of the river and cannot pass through unless they lift their ships off the river and carry them past by portaging them on their shoulders, then the men of this nation of the Pechenegs set upon them, and, as they cannot do two things at once, they are easily routed and cut to pieces.

3. Of the Pechenegs and Turks.

The tribe of the Turks,* too, trembles greatly at and fears the said Pechenegs, because they have often been defeated by them and brought to the verge of complete annihilation. Therefore the Turks always look on the Pechenegs with dread, and are held in check by them.

4. Of the Pechenegs and Russians and Turks.

So long as the emperor of the Romans is at peace with the Pechenegs, neither Russians nor Turks can come upon the Roman dominions by force of arms, nor can they exact from the Romans large and inflated sums in money and goods as the price of peace, for they fear the strength of this nation which the emperor can turn against them while they are campaigning against the Romans. For the Pechenegs, if they are leagued in friendship with the emperor and won over by him through letters and gifts, can easily come upon the country both of the Russians and of the Turks, and enslave their women and children and ravage their country.

5. Of the Pechenegs and the Bulgarians.

To the Bulgarians† also the emperor of the Romans will appear more formidable, and can impose on them the need for tranquility, if he is at peace with the Pechenegs, because the said Pechenegs are neighbors to these Bulgarians also, and when they wish, either for private gain or to do a favour to the emperor of the Romans, they can easily march against Bulgaria, and with their preponderating multitude and their strength overwhelm and defeat them. And so the Bulgarians also continually struggle and strive to maintain peace and harmony with the Pechenegs. For from having frequently been crushingly defeated and plundered by them, they have learned by experience the value and advantage of being always at peace with them.

6. Of the Pechenegs and Chersonites.

Yet another folk of these Pechenegs lies over against the district of Cherson; they trade with the Chersonites, and perform services for them and for the emperor in Russia and Chazaria‡ . . . and all the parts beyond: that is to say, they receive from the Chersonites a prearranged remuneration in respect of this service proportionate to their labor and trouble, in the form of pieces of purple cloth, ribbons, loosely woven cloths, gold brocade, pepper, scarlet or "Parthian" leather,§ and other commodities which

---

*Nomadic peoples to the east of the Pechenegs.

†The Bulgars were of nomadic origin but had settled in the Balkan Peninsula north and west of Byzantine frontiers, establishing the major Bulgar-Slavic State of the region.

‡The lands of the Chazars (or Khazars), another nomadic group east of the Pecheneg lands.

§The Parthians were a nomadic people who had ruled an empire based in Persia in the first and second centuries; they were major rivals of Rome in the Near East.

they require, according to a contract which each Chersonite may make or agree to with an individual Pecheneg. For these Pechenegs are free men and, so to say, independent, and never perform any service without remuneration.

7. Of the dispatch of imperial agents from Cherson to Patzinacia.

When an imperial agent goes over to Cherson on this service, he must at once send to Patzinacia* and demand of them hostages and an escort, and on their arrival he must leave the hostages under guard in the city of Cherson, and himself go off with the escort to Patzinacia and carry out his instructions. Now these Pechenegs, who are ravenous and keenly covetous of articles rare among them, are shameless in their demands for generous gifts, the hostages demanding this for themselves and that for their wives, and the escort something for their own trouble and some more for the wear and tear of their cattle. Then, when the imperial agent enters their country, they first ask for the emperor's gifts, and then again, when these have glutted the menfolk, they ask for the presents for their wives and parents. Also, all who come with him to escort him on his way back to Cherson demand payment from him for their trouble and the wear and tear of their cattle.

. . .

37. The Nation of the Pechenegs

Originally, the Pechenegs had their dwelling on the river Atil, and likewise on the river Geïch, having common frontiers with the Chazars and the so-called Uzes.[†] But fifty years ago the so-called Uzes made common cause with the Chazars and joined battle with the Pechenegs and prevailed over them and expelled them from their country, which the so-called Uzes have occupied till this day. The Pechenegs fled and wandered round, casting about for a place for their settlement; and when they reached the land which they now possess and found the Turks living in it, they defeated them in battle and expelled and cast them out, and settled in it, and have been masters of this country, as has been said, for fifty-five years to this day.

The whole of Patzinacia is divided into eight provinces with the same number of great princes. . . . After their [the princes'] deaths their cousins succeeded to their rule. For law and ancient principle have prevailed among them, depriving them of authority to transmit their ranks to their sons or their brothers, it being sufficient for those in power to rule for their own lifetime only, and when they die, either their cousin or sons of their cousins must be appointed, so that the rank may not run exclusively in one branch of the family, but the collaterals also inherit and succeed to the honor; but no one from a stranger family intrudes and becomes a prince. The eight provinces are divided into forty districts, and these have minor princelings over them.

Four clans of the Pechenegs . . . lie beyond the Dnieper river towards the eastern and northern parts. . . . The other four clans lie on this side of the Dnieper river, towards the western and northern parts, that is to say . . . Bulgaria, . . . Turkey, . . . Russia, and . . . the tributary territories of the country of Russia . . . and the rest of the Slavs. . . .

---

*The land of the Pechenegs.

†These are rivers and peoples of the steppes farther east.

At the time when the Pechenegs were expelled from their country, some of them of their own will and personal decision stayed behind there and united with the so-called Uzes, and even to this day they live among them, and wear such distinguishing marks as separate them off and betray their origin and how it came about that they were split off from their own folk: for their tunics are short, reaching to the knee, and their sleeves are cut off at the shoulder, whereby, you see, they indicate that they have been cut off from their own folk and those of their race.

On this side of the Dniester river, towards the part that faces Bulgaria, at the crossings of this same river, are deserted cities. . . . Among these buildings of the ancient cities are found some distinctive traces of churches, and crosses hewn out of porous stone, whence some preserve a tradition that once on a time Romans had settlements there.

The Pechenegs are also called "Kangar," though not all of them, but only the folk of [three named provinces], for they are more valiant and noble than the rest: and that is what the title "Kangar" signifies.

ISLAM AND THE MONGOL SCOURGE

The greatest of the nomadic conquerors were the Mongols. They were united in 1206 by the remarkable leader Temujin, who took the title Genghis Khan, or "Great Leader." Son of a tribal leader, Genghis had spent the first forty years of his life securing his own position of leadership against rivals and betrayals and then forging a unified Mongol state on the steppes. Uniquely among steppe leaders to that time, he issued a written code of law, the Jasagh, that governed Mongol society and organized the Mongol military. The two were intertwined: He organized his people and army into decimally based units drawn from artificial "tribes" that he created to erase old divisions among the Mongols and among the many Turkish nomads he came to dominate and incorporate into his system. His success is attested in the amazing scope of Mongol conquests and their staying power—the Mongol Empire, the largest land empire in world history, lasted (though in divided form) nearly 150 years after its founder's death in 1227.

Indeed, Genghis Khan initiated the Mongol conquests, taking the seminomadic kingdoms of north China in the decade after 1206. He then turned his attention westward. Unfortunately for the Islamic world, the first Islamic ruler he sent envoys to, the Khwarazmshah (ruler of the area around modern Pakistan, Afghanistan, and Iran), executed the envoys and insulted the Khan. Not only did the Khwarazmshah pay with his life and kingdom, but he earned Islam the intense hostility of the normally fairly religiously tolerant Mongols (themselves shamanistic polytheists). The Mongols under Genghis and his successors therefore attacked further Islamic lands with special fury, eventually destroying Baghdad and ending the caliphate there. It was this onslaught that Ibn al-Athir witnessed.

Ibn al-Athir was a Muslim scholar whose most important work was *al-Kamil fi at-tarikh* ("The Complete History"), a history of the world. Born in Jazirat in 1160, he lived most of his life in Mosul but traveled widely in the Muslim lands of southwest Asia, including several trips to Baghdad, and later lived in Aleppo and Damascus. As a young man he spent time with Saladin's army in Syria as Saladin fought the Crusader states. He died in 1233 in Mosul.

His history was influential at the time and is an important source for Islamic history in the period of the Crusades and Mongol invasions. In these selections, he writes about the Mongol attacks in 1220–1221 on the heart of the Muslim world. His view is personal and apocalyptic, closer in tone to Ammianus's account of the Huns than to the official court documents generated by the Han and Byzantine governments, but his focus is somewhat less ethnographic than Ammianus's and much more moralistic. In many ways, this view of a steppe nomadic invasion is closest emotionally to the Orson Welles radio broadcast of *War of the Worlds* in its shock at the otherworldliness of the invaders. And Ibn al-Athir did not even live to see the culmination of the Mongol assault on the Islamic world— the destruction of Baghdad and its resident caliphate in 1258.

QUESTIONS TO CONSIDER

1. What characteristics of the Mongols stand out for Ibn al-Athir? What tone does he take in describing their attacks?
2. What factors, for the author, account for Mongol success in overrunning the Islamic world?
3. What is the moral of the story? Or put another way, what is the purpose of this history? How does it compare in this respect with the Chinese and Byzantine documents?
4. What are the author's sources? How reliable do you think his account is? Does he have the same stake in reliability that the other sources do?
5. How might the Mongols describe the Muslim world and its people?

DESCRIPTION OF THE MONGOL CONQUESTS

Ibn al-Athir

The Horror

For some years I continued averse from mentioning this event, deeming it so horrible that I shrank from recording it, and ever withdrawing one foot as I advanced the other. To whom, indeed, can it be easy to write the announcement of the death-blow of Islam and the Muslims, or who is he on whom the remembrance thereof can weigh lightly? O would that my mother had not born me, or that I had died and become a forgotten thing ere this befell! Yet withal a number of my friends urged me to set it

Source: Edward G. Browne, *A Literary History of Persia* (Cambridge, UK: Cambridge University Press, 1902), ii, 427–31.

down in writing, and I hesitated long; but at last came to the conclusion that to omit this matter could serve no useful purpose. I say, therefore, that this thing involves the description of the greatest catastrophe and the most dire calamity (of the like of which days and nights are innocent) which befell all men generally, and the Muslims in particular; so that, should one say that the world, since God Almighty created Adam until now, hath not been afflicted with the like thereof, he would but speak the truth.

For indeed history doth not contain aught which approaches or comes nigh unto it. For of the most grievous calamities recorded was what Nebuchadnezzar inflicted on the children of Israel by his slaughter of them and his destruction of Jerusalem; and what was Jerusalem in comparison to the countries which these accursed miscreants destroyed, each city of which was double the size of Jerusalem? Or what were the children of Israel compared to those whom these slew? For verily those whom they massacred in a single city exceeded all the children of Israel. Nay, it is unlikely that mankind will see the like of this calamity, until the world comes to an end and perishes, except the final outbreak of Gog and Magog.

For even Antichrist will spare such as follow him, though he destroy those who oppose him; but these spared none, slaying women and men and children, ripping open pregnant women and killing unborn babes. Verily to God do we belong, and unto Him do we return, and there is no strength and no power save in God, the High, the Almighty, in face of this catastrophe, whereof the sparks flew far and wide, and the hurt was universal; and which passed over the lands like clouds driven by the wind.

The Mongol Conquests

For these were a people who emerged from the confines of China, and attacked the cities of Turkistan, like Kashghar and Balasaghun,* and thence advanced on the cities of Transoxiana, such as Samarqand, Bukhara and the like,† taking possession of them, and treating their inhabitants in such ways as we shall mention; and of them one division then passed on into Khurasan,‡ until they had made an end of taking possession, and destroying, and slaying, and plundering, and thence passing on to Ray, Hamadan and the Highlands,§ and the cities contained therein, even to the limits of Iraq, whence they marched on the towns of Adharbayjan and Arraniyya,** destroying them and slaying most of their inhabitants, of whom none escaped save a small remnant; and all this in less than a year; this is a thing whereof the like hath not been heard.

And when they had finished with Adharbayjan and Arraniyya, they passed on to Darband-i-Shirwan, and occupied its cities, none of which escaped save the fortress wherein was their King; wherefore they passed by it to the countries of the Lan and the Lakiz and the various nationalities which dwell in that region, and plundered, slew, and destroyed them to the full. And thence they made their way to the lands of

---

*Centers of the Turkish heartland of the western steppes.

†Transoxiana, the region "beyond the Oxus River," was the steppe region just beyond the range of sedentary culture, north and northeast of Persia.

‡An important "transitional" province, partly pastoral and partly agricultural, in the north of Persia bordering Transoxiana.

§Of Persia.

**In eastern Mesopotamia.

Qipchaq, who are the most numerous of the Turks, and slew all such as withstood them, while the survivors fled to the fords and mountain-tops, and abandoned their country, which these Tartars overran. All this they did in the briefest space of time, remaining only for so long as their march required and no more.*

Another division, distinct from that mentioned above, marched on Ghazna and its dependencies, and those parts of India, Sistan and Kirman which border thereon, and wrought therein deeds like unto the other, nay, yet more grievous.†

Now this is a thing the like of which ear hath not heard; for Alexander, concerning whom historians agree that he conquered the world, did not do so with such swiftness, but only in the space of about ten years; neither did he slay, but was satisfied that men should be subject to him. But these Tartars conquered most of the habitable globe, and the best, the most flourishing and most populous part thereof, and that whereof the inhabitants were the most advanced in character and conduct, in about a year; nor did any country escape their devastations which did not fearfully expect them and dread their arrival. Moreover they need no commissariat, nor the conveyance of supplies, for they have with them sheep, cows, horses, and the like quadrupeds, the flesh of which they eat, [and] naught else. As for their beasts which they ride, these dig into the earth with their hoofs and eat the roots of plants, knowing naught of barley. And so, when they alight anywhere, they have need of nothing from without.

As for their religion, they worship the sun when it arises, and regard nothing as unlawful, for they eat all beasts, even dogs, pigs, and the like; nor do they recognize the marriage-tie, for several men are in marital relations with one woman, and if a child is born, it knows not who is its father.

Therefore Islam and the Muslims have been afflicted during this period with calamities wherewith no people hath been visited. These Tartars (may God confound them!) came from the East, and wrought deeds which horrify all who hear of them, and which thou shalt, please God, see set forth in full detail in their proper connection.

Muslim Weakness

As for these Tartars, their achievements were only rendered possible by the absence of any effective obstacle; and the cause of this absence was that Muhammad Khwarazmshah‡ had overrun the [other Muslim] lands, slaying and destroying their Kings, so that he remained alone ruling over all these countries; wherefore, when he was defeated by the Tartars, none was left in the lands to check those or protect these, that so God might accomplish a thing which was to be done.

It is now time for us to describe how they first burst forth into the lands. "Stories have been related to me," he says, "which the hearer can scarcely credit, as to the terror of them which God Almighty cast into men's hearts; so that it is said that a single one of them would enter a village or a quarter wherein were many people, and would continue to slay them one after another, none daring to stretch forth his hand against

---

*These areas stretched from northern Mesopotamia into Asia Minor.

†The areas to the east of their north Persian entry point into settled territory.

‡Ruler of the areas of Afghanistan and southern Iran.

this horseman. And I have heard that one of them took a man captive, but had not with him any weapon wherewith to kill him; and he said to his prisoner, "Lay your head on the ground and do not move"; and he did so, and the Tartar went and fetched his sword and slew him therewith.

Another man related to me as follows: "I was going," said he, "with seventeen others along a road, and there met us a Tartar horseman, and bade us bind one another's arms. My companions began to do as he bade them, but I said to them, 'He is but one man; wherefore, then, should we not kill him and flee?' They replied, 'We are afraid.' I said, 'This man intends to kill you immediately; let us therefore rather kill him, that perhaps God may deliver us.' But I swear by God that not one of them dared to do this, so I took a knife and slew him, and we fled and escaped." And such occurrences were many.

A VENETIAN VISITS THE MONGOLS

By 1260 the Mongol Empire in the west stopped expanding; in the east the conquest of southern Song China in 1278 by Genghis Khan's grandson Kubilai effectively ended Mongol expansion. Even before this time, however, the Mongols had shifted from brutal plundering conquerors to clever administrators. They employed subjects from all over their lands to assist them in the task, always difficult for nomads, of ruling settled territories, drawing Persian administrators to China and vice versa. The second half of the thirteenth century has sometimes been called the "Pax Mongolica," the Mongol peace, as their rule secured the safety of the trade routes across the steppes and encouraged the exchange of goods and ideas throughout their vast empire and beyond.

It was in this setting that undoubtedly the most famous visitor to the world of the steppe nomads, the Venetian Marco Polo (c. 1253–1324), made his career. Marco's father and uncle were merchants who had visited the court of Kubilai Khan, grandson of Ghengis Khan and emperor of China, between about 1260 and 1269, returning with a request from the Great Khan for Christian missionaries. They set out again in 1271 with two Dominican friars (who gave up almost immediately) and young Marco. They arrived back at Kubilai's capital in northern China in 1274 or 1275, and Marco entered into service in the Mongol government, traveling widely through the empire for nearly twenty years. Although doubts have been raised about whether Marco actually did travel to China (or even existed), none of the doubts are well founded, and we can accept the picture he paints of his travels as largely accurate. He and the elder Polos left in the early 1290s, reaching Venice again in 1295.

Marco Polo's account of the Mongol life is therefore informed and sympathetic—Marco may well have identified more with his hosts than with his home in Venice, where he had grown up with his father absent and which he had left while still a teenager. He and his family were certainly among the mercantile "nomadic fringe" of the settled civilizations, in a tradition stretching back to the early days of the Silk Road. But his account is also complicated by the fact that the Mongols he knew were rulers of a great empire, with a capital city on the steppes (Karakorum) and other capitals in the conquered territories. Some of them were, in other words, at least partly sedentarized nomads and so perhaps less strange than they might have been. And by the time Marco came to Kubilai's court, the Mongol government was cosmopolitan, employing officials from across the world.

Marco told his account in a Genoese prison to a romance writer named Rustichello of Pisa, who tried to shape Marco's largely utilitarian accounts of cities, goods, and travel routes into a tale of adventure and strange lands. The stylistic result is far from successful, but the book was nonetheless a huge success in a Europe at the height of its medieval prosperity and eager for more information about the largely mysterious world around it. It remained popular, influencing explorers (including Christopher Columbus) for several centuries, its images becoming part of Western culture, most famously perhaps in Samuel Taylor Coleridge's poem "Kubla Khan":

> *In Xanadu did Kubla Khan*
> *A stately pleasure-dome decree:*
> *Where Alph, the sacred river, ran*
> *Through caverns measureless to man*
> *Down to a sunless sea.*

In this selection, however, Marco Polo describes not the magnificent court of the ruler of the Yüan dynasty of China but the customs of the nomadic population of the Mongols as he knew them.

QUESTIONS TO CONSIDER

1. What characteristics of the Mongols stand out most to Marco Polo? What is his tone in describing these characteristics?
2. How does his description compare with the others you have read? Are the differences in the observer, or are the Mongols different from their nomadic predecessors?
3. Marco is an eyewitness—he is his own best source, in other words. But even eyewitnesses can miss things or be misled, and his account is filtered through a romance writer's pen. Does his picture strike you as accurate? What might be missing or mistaken in this description?
4. This source stands in sharpest contrast to Ibn al-Athir's description of the Mongols. What factors explain the differences between these two sources?
5. How do you think the Mongols viewed their long-term guest and employee? How do you think they viewed the various subject peoples of their empire?

TRAVELS

Marco Polo

Chapter 51. Of Those Who Reigned after Genghis Khan, and of the Customs of the Tartars

Now the next that reigned after Genghis Khan, their first Lord, was Güyük Khan, and the third Prince was Batu Khan, and the fourth was Hülegü Khan, the fifth Möngke Khan, the sixth Kubilai Khan,* who is the sovereign now reigning, and is more potent than any of the five who went before him; in fact, if you were to take all those five together, they would not be so powerful as he is. Nay, I will say yet more; for if you were to put together all the Christians in the world, with their Emperors and their Kings, the whole of these Christians—aye, and throw in the Saracens to boot—would not have such power, or be able to do so much as this Kubilai, who is the Lord of all the Tartars in the world, those of the Levant and of the Orient included; for these are all his vassals and subjects. I mean to show you all about this great power of his in this book of ours.

You should be told also that all the Grand Khans, and all the descendants of Genghis their first Lord, are carried to a mountain that is called Altai to be interred. Wherever the Sovereign may die, he is carried to his burial in that mountain with his predecessors; no matter, if the place of his death were 100 days' journey distant, thither must he be carried to his burial.

Let me tell you a strange thing too. When they are carrying the body of any Emperor to be buried with the others, the convoy that goes with the body puts to the sword all whom they fall in with on the road, saying: "Go and wait upon your Lord in the other world!" For they do in truth believe that all such as they slay in this manner do go to serve their Lord in the other world. They do the same too with horses; for when the Emperor dies, they kill all his best horses, in order that he may have the use of them in the other world, as they believe. And I tell you as a certain truth, that when Möngke Khan died, more than 200,000 persons, who chanced to meet the body on its way, were slain in the manner I have told.

Chapter 52. Concerning the Customs of the Tartars

Now that we have begun to speak of the Tartars, I have plenty to tell you on that subject. The Tartar custom is to spend the winter in warm plains where they find good pasture for their cattle, whilst in summer they betake themselves to a cool climate among the mountains and valleys, where water is to be found as well as woods and pastures.

Source: Selections from *The Book of Ser Marco Polo*, trans. Henry Yule (London, 1874), i, 241–60, modernized by S. Morillo.

*Marco Polo is in error about several of these. The title "Great Khan" descended from Genghis (1206–27) to Ögödei (1227–41) to Güyük (1246–50) to Möngke (1251–59) to Kubilai (1260–94). Batu was khan of the Golden Horde, the subdivision of the empire encompassing Russia and the western steppes, and Hülegü was khan of the Persian subdivision of the empire.

Their houses are circular, and are made of wands covered with felts. These are carried along with them wherever they go; for the wands are so strongly bound together, and likewise so well combined, that the frame can be made very light. Whenever they erect these huts the door is always to the south. They also have wagons covered with black felt so efficaciously that no rain can get in. These are drawn by oxen and camels, and the women and children travel in them. The women do the buying and selling, and whatever is necessary to provide for the husband and household; for the men all lead the life of gentlemen, troubling themselves about nothing but hunting and hawking, and looking after their goshawks and falcons, unless it be the practice of warlike exercises.

They live on the milk and meat which their horses supply, and on the produce of the chase; and they eat all kinds of flesh, including that of horses and dogs, and Pharaoh's rats, of which last there are great numbers in burrows on those plains. Their drink is mare's milk.

They are very careful not to meddle with each other's wives, and will not do so on any account, holding that to be an evil and abominable thing. The women too are very good and loyal to their husbands, and notable housewives as well. Ten or twenty of them will dwell together in charming peace and unity, nor shall you ever hear an ill word among them.

The marriage customs of Tartars are as follows. Any man may take a hundred wives if he so please, and if he be able to keep them. But the first wife is ever held most in honor, and as the most legitimate, and the same applies to the sons whom she may bear. The husband gives a marriage payment to his wife's mother, and the wife brings nothing to her husband. They have more children than other people, because they have so many wives. They may marry their cousins, and if a father dies, his son may take any of the wives, his own mother always excepted; that is to say the eldest son may do this, but no other. A man may also take the wife of his own brother after the latter's death. Their weddings are celebrated with great ado.

Chapter 53. Concerning the God of the Tartars

This is the fashion of their religion. They say there is a Most High God of Heaven, whom they worship daily with censers and incense, but they pray to Him only for health of mind and body. But they have also a certain other god of theirs called Natigai, and they say he is the god of the Earth, who watches over their children, cattle, and crops. They show him great worship and honor, and every man has a figure of him in his house, made of felt and cloth; and they also make in the same manner images of his wife and children. The wife they put on the left hand, and the children in front. And when they eat, they take the fat of the meat and grease with it the god's mouth, as well as the mouths of his wife and children. Then they take of the broth and sprinkle it before the door of the house; and that done, they deem that their god and his family have had their share of the dinner.

Their drink is mare's milk, prepared in such a way that you would take it for white wine; and a right good drink it is, called by them *Kemiz*.

The clothes of the wealthy Tartars are for the most part of gold and silk stuffs, lined with costly furs, such as sable and ermine, squirrel and fox-skin, in the richest fashion.

Chapter 54. Concerning the Tartar Customs of War

All their harness of war is excellent and costly. Their arms are bows and arrows, sword and mace; but above all the bow, for they are capital archers, indeed the best that are known. On their backs they wear armor of hardened leather, prepared from buffalo and other hides, which is very strong. They are excellent soldiers, and passing valiant in battle. They are also more capable of hardships than other nations; for many a time, if need be, they will go for a month without any supply of food, living only on the milk of their mares and on such game as their bows may win them. Their horses also will subsist entirely on the grass of the plains, so that there is no need to carry store of barley or straw or oats; and they are very docile to their riders. These, in case of need, will abide on horseback the livelong night, armed at all points, while the horse will be continually grazing.

Of all troops in the world these are they which endure the greatest hardship and fatigue, and which cost the least; and they are the best of all for making wide conquests of country. And this you will perceive from what you have heard and shall hear in this book; and (as a fact) there can be no manner of doubt that now they are the masters of the biggest half of the world. Their troops are admirably ordered in the manner that I shall now relate.

You see, when a Tartar prince goes forth to war, he takes with him, say 100,000 horse. Well, he appoints an officer to every ten men, one to every hundred, one to every thousand, and one to every ten thousand, so that his own orders have to be given to ten persons only, and each of these ten persons has to pass the orders only to another ten, and so on; no one having to give orders to more than ten. And every one in turn is responsible only to the officer immediately over him; and the discipline and order that comes of this method is marvelous, for they are a people very obedient to their chiefs. Further, they call the corps of 100,000 men a *Tuk;* that of 10,000 they call a *Toman;* the thousand they call . . . ; the hundred *Guz;* the ten. . . .* And when the army is on the march they have always 200 horsemen, very well mounted, who are sent a distance of two marches in advance to reconnoiter, and these always keep ahead. They have a similar party detached in the rear, and on either flank, so that there is a good lookout kept on all sides against a surprise. When they are going on a distant expedition they take no gear with them except two leather bottles for milk; a little earthenware pot to cook their meat in, and a little tent to shelter them from rain. And in case of great urgency they will ride ten days on end without lighting a fire or taking a meal. On such an occasion they will sustain themselves on the blood of their horses, opening a vein and letting the blood jet into their mouths, drinking till they have had enough, and then staunching it.

They also have milk dried into a kind of paste to carry with them; and when they need food they put this in water, and beat it up till it dissolves, and then drink it. It is prepared in this way: they boil the milk, and when the rich part floats on the top they skim it into another vessel, and of that they make butter; for the milk will not become solid till this is removed. Then they put the milk in the sun to dry. And when they go on an expedition every man takes some ten pounds of this dried milk with him. And

---

*The terms for thousand and ten are missing in the original manuscripts.

of a morning he will take a half pound of it and put it in his leather bottle, with as much water as he pleases. So, as he rides along, the milk-paste and the water in the bottle get well churned together into a kind of pap, and that makes his dinner.

When they come to an engagement with the enemy, they will gain the victory in this fashion. They never let themselves get into a regular melee, but keep perpetually riding round and shooting into the enemy. And as they do not count it any shame to run away in battle, they will sometimes pretend to do so, and in running away they turn in the saddle and shoot hard and strong at the foe, and in this way make great havoc. Their horses are trained so perfectly that they will double hither and thither, just like a dog, in a way that is quite astonishing. Thus they fight to as good purpose in running away as if they stood and faced the enemy, because of the vast volleys of arrows that they shoot in this way, turning round upon their pursuers, who are fancying that they have won the battle. But when the Tartars see that they have killed and wounded a good many horses and men, they wheel round bodily, and return to the charge in perfect order and with loud cries; and in a very short time the enemy are routed. In truth they are stout and valiant soldiers, and inured to war. And you perceive that it is just when the enemy sees them run, and imagines that he has gained the battle, that he has in reality lost it; for the Tartars wheel round in a moment when they judge the right time has come. And after this fashion they have won many a fight.

All this that I have been telling you is true of the manners and customs of the genuine Tartars. But I must add also that in these days they are greatly degenerated; for those who are settled in Cathay have taken up the practices of the Idolaters of the country, and have abandoned their own institutions; whilst those who have settled in the Levant have adopted the customs of the Saracens.*

Chapter 55. Concerning the Administration of Justice Among the Tartars

The way they administer justice is this. When any one has committed a petty theft, they give him, under the orders of authority, seven blows of a stick, or seventeen, or twenty-seven, or thirty-seven, or forty-seven, and so forth, always increasing by tens in proportion to the injury done, and running up to one hundred and seven. Of these beatings sometimes they die. But if the offence be horse-stealing, or some other great matter, they cut the thief in two with a sword. However, if he be able to ransom himself by paying nine times the value of the thing stolen, he is let off. Every Lord or other person who possesses beasts has them marked with his peculiar brand, be they horses, mares, camels, oxen, cows, or other great cattle, and then they are sent abroad to graze over the plains without any keeper. They get all mixed together, but eventually every beast is recovered by means of its owner's brand, which is known. For their sheep and goats they have shepherds. All their cattle are remarkably fine, big, and in good condition.

They have another notable custom, which is this. If any man have a daughter who dies before marriage, and another man have had a son also die before marriage, the parents of the two arrange a grand wedding between the dead lad and lass. And marry them they do, making a regular contract! And when the contract papers are

---

*That is, the Mongols in China and neighboring lands generally converted to Buddhism; whereas with a certain irony that would have astounded Ibn al-Athir, the rest became Muslim.

made out they put them in the fire, in order (as they will have it) that the parties in the other world may know the fact, and so look on each other as man and wife. And the parents thenceforward consider themselves sib to each other just as if their children had lived and married. Whatever may be agreed on between the parties as dowry, those who have to pay it cause to be painted on pieces of paper and then put these in the fire, saying that in that way the dead person will get all the real articles in the other world.

Now I have told you all about the manners and customs of the Tartars; but you have heard nothing yet of the great state of the Grand Khan, who is the Lord of all the Tartars and of the Supreme Imperial Court. All that I will tell you in this book in proper time and place, but meanwhile I must return to my story which I left off in that great plain when we began to speak of the Tartars.

CHAPTER 8

Encountering Transcendent Reality

The Rise of the Salvation Religions

INTRODUCTION

In the 2003 baseball playoffs, both the Boston Red Sox and the Chicago Cubs found themselves up by three runs and only five outs from the promised land of the World Series. Boston had not won a world championship since 1918, Chicago since 1908. Throughout those long wanderings in the wilderness, during which each team was supposedly marked by a "curse," their devoted fans had kept the faith, religiously wearing the regalia—caps, jerseys, t-shirts—of their favorites. They made daily pilgrimages to their Meccas—Fenway Park and Wrigley Field—for every home game. There they worshipped their heroes, sang hymns to them ("Take me out to the ballgame . . ."), and chanted incantations against evil ("Yankees s—". . . well, you get the idea). Surely this year one of the "curses" had to be lifted, and at least one set of baseball faithful would reach nirvana and be rewarded for their suffering.

Alas, it was not to be. Both lost. Lamentations were raised to the sky in the Hub and the Windy City. Boston sacrificed a manager. And yet, in some important way it didn't matter. Their faithful still worship, and they cite the scripture of eternal hope known to baseball fans everywhere: Wait till next year.

This is a chapter about eternal hope. That the story of the 2003 baseball playoffs can be plausibly (if a bit obviously) written in the language of religious devotion shows us the importance of organized sports in the modern world. But it also tells us about the impact that the world's great salvation religions have had on cultural imagination and imagery everywhere. What are the "salvation religions"? They are that set of the world's many religions that promise salvation—eternal life, heavenly rewards, hope for a better existence than this mortal earth offers—to their followers. The four major ones are Mahayana Buddhism, Christianity, Islam, and Devotional Hinduism. All arose sometime in the period 100 BCE to 630 CE, with the major period of development coming after 200 CE. Each offered a version of eternal hope to its followers, a message that proved to have wide resonance in the troubled period of world history between 200 and 700 CE when the age of great empires came to an end, at least partly under pressures from nomadic invaders (see chapters 5 and 7). But invasions and political troubles simply aggravated the uncertainties and problems that have always beset common people in traditional societies, living from harvest to harvest and subject to varying degrees of taxation or rent from those holding power over them. Life for women, too, not just among peasants but at every social level, was full of restrictions (see chapter 6). The major philosophies and religions we examined in chapter 4 addressed some of these problems, but in ways that were not always intellectually accessible to the illiterate masses—they were the philosophies and religions of elites, and in many ways they continued to be so. Creeds that offered hope to the common people, therefore, found a ready audience in this world, though they also found ready converts among the ruling class.

That these faiths found a wide audience was intentional, for a central characteristic of the salvation religions is that their message was meant to be universal and available to all. This was partly a matter of their breaking a "tribal" or inherited notion of membership in a religious community that defined the southwest Asian religions of Persian Zoroastrianism and Hebrew Judaism (see chapter 4).[1] Both Zoroastrianism and Judaism stand as ancestors of or influences on the salvation religions, but each remained the exclusive religion of its people. The salvation religions reached out to different peoples and cultures. Another reason they found a large audience was that they made their message intentionally accessible and their practice "user friendly," to use the computer term. Each of the salvation religions offered a simple message of hope and a straightforward path to salvation. The message was presented not just textually in religious literature but also artistically, through art and architecture, and socially, through community practice and preaching. As a result, they spread widely in the troubled world following the age of empires, and they remain to this day, in one form or another, the most widely practiced religions in the world. In this chapter we present materials related to the spread of these faiths, and, in the next chapter, to the conversion encounters they provoked. In this chapter we look at their doctrines and messages themselves, in terms of both substance and method of presentation.

We include for each of the four religions presented here both a fundamental text and a small selection of visual sources. Neither Buddhism nor Hinduism has a single canonical scripture in the way that Christianity and Islam do, but each had popular texts that shaped the most widely followed Salvationist sects of each faith. For Buddhism, we have excerpted part of *The Lotus Sutra*. *The Lotus Sutra* expounded the fundamental beliefs that came to characterize Mahayana Buddhism, especially the way that Buddhist saints, called *bodhisattvas,* aided humans in the transition up the ten levels of existence to nirvana. The text we use comes from a fifth-century Chinese translation of the work. *The Lotus Sutra* is accompanied by pictures of statues of the sort used in popular Buddhist worship. They show *bodhisattvas,* whose role is explained in *The Lotus Sutra.*

For Hinduism, we present a section of the *Vishnu Purana,* which is the oldest and most important of the holy texts of Devotional Hinduism. The *Vishnu Purana* guides the reader into the way of devotion to Vishnu, the most popular of the Hindu gods in this form of worship. *Puranas* are collections of myth, folk tales, and teachings, transmitting the belief of Devotional Hinduism that salvation could be achieved through worship of a god. The selection we include is the concluding dialogue of the *Vishnu Purana.* It is not only one of the oldest of the *Puranas,* dating from the 100s CE, but it is also one of the most important. It too is accompanied by pictures of two statues, one of Vishnu and one of Ganesh, another popular Hindu god.

The New Testament of the Bible is the canonical text of Christianity. From it, we present selections from two of its most significant sections: the Book of Romans and the Gospel of Matthew. The passages presented contain the core beliefs of Christianity as laid out in the Sermon on the Mount. In addition, the understanding that Paul had of Christianity and its meaning was crucial to the development of the religion and to Christian beliefs about the nature of and path toward salvation. Both of the selections date from after the death of Jesus. Paul's epistles (letters) to the Romans date from the mid-50s CE, and the date for Matthew's Gospel is usually given as around the 70s CE. In addition, images of early Christian art are included: a mosaic of Christ healing the blind and an icon of Jesus' mother, enthroned and holding the infant Jesus.

Finally, we present passages from the Qur'an, the sacred text of Islam. Muslims believe the Qur'an to be the will and words of God as revealed to Muhammad, the last of his prophets. Scholars think, however, that the Qur'an is the product of the teachings of Muhammad, as shaped by early followers. As was true of the Gospels, a significant passage of time intervened between the death of the religion's founder and the emergence of a canonical text. However that may be, the Qur'an lays out the fundamental beliefs and duties of followers of Islam, and we have excerpted passages central to the salvation message of the faith. These passages are followed by an example of Arab calligraphy, an art form that did not violate Islam's prohibition against representational art.

Hope in the salvation religions was presented as an encounter with a transcendent reality, a higher realm of existence. Suffering in this world would be rewarded in another, better life, a life not bounded by the harsh realities of this material world. Because of the centrality of belief in humans' ability to transcend the physical world, the religions differed among and within themselves on the actual importance of this world and action in this life. They all accommodated some range of both practical, community-based spiritual expression (charity, kindness, and so forth) and more mystical expressions of connection to the divine and even withdrawal from this world. As you read these selections and look at the art associated with them, think about the different ways this encounter with transcendence was conceived of in each tradition, as well as the similarities across all the salvation religions. Above all look for the form in which hope was presented. For all of them offered hope, something to look forward to when the forces of evil and despair seemed triumphant. Wait till next year.

1. What elements of belief are common to all these faiths? That is, what do they agree on about life, the universe, and the divine? What elements differ?
2. What elements of practice, of the paths to salvation people could take, are common to all these faiths? That is, what do they agree on about what people should do to achieve a lasting encounter with transcendence? What elements differ? How are the religious practices connected with the belief system?
3. How do the images associated with these texts reinforce or represent the doctrines presented in the written texts? Are there common elements to "salvationist" art?
4. What sort of hope does each salvation religion offer? That is, can you characterize in a word or two the central message of each religion, through which hope appears?
5. Do the similarities or the differences between these faiths seem more important to you? Why have the differences seemed to matter more to the practitioners of these faiths historically?

MAHAYANA BUDDHISM

Buddhism had begun to spread widely within India after the conversion of Asoka (see chapter 5) and his promotion of the religion as part of a syncretic (a combination of elements from different beliefs) emphasis on *dharma* (sacred duty) as the bond between his government and his subjects. It may have been these efforts at popularizing the religion that gave impetus to tendencies within the religion that eventually carried it in a new direction. By the first century CE, these tendencies had begun to come together into a self-conscious new school of Buddhism, described by its practitioners as *Mahayana,* or the Greater Vehicle—meaning that this sect promised to carry far more people to salvation than the older version could. Followers of Mahayana Buddhism referred to the older version as *Hinayana,* or Lesser Vehicle. The followers of the older version, though, preferred to refer to their religion as *Theravada,* or the Teaching of the Elders. This religion continued to exist and itself spread to parts of southeast Asia. It was the Mahayana version of Buddhism that first became widely popular in India and then, during the early centuries CE, spread all over central and East Asia.

In its early form, and largely in the Theravada school, Buddhism was non-theistic—the Buddha was simply a mortal, though a special one—and the search for Enlightenment was a matter of individual practice and achievement, as laid out in the Four Noble Truths and the Noble Eightfold Path (see chapter 4). The tendency to revere the Buddha as a god probably arose even during his own life. The large number of gods and the way that divinity was woven into everyday existence in the Hindu tradition (unlike the separation of divinity and creation in the southwest Asian religious traditions) made "godliness" a not uncommon phenomenon. In Mahayana belief, the Buddha has become an all-knowing being, somewhere between a divine person—a mortal man who achieves immortality— and a god, to whom even Hindu gods offer respect. His wisdom surpasses that of the other gods, because he recognizes the uncreated and infinite nature of the universe, whereas some of them imagine themselves as creators.

Accompanying the rise of belief in the Buddha's divinity was a belief in a class of beings known as *bodhisattvas,* or Wise Beings. Essentially these are people who had reached the edge of nirvana, release from the cycle of death and rebirth, only to compassionately turn back to help others cross over into bliss. Nirvana itself evolved from the somewhat abstract notion of "extinguishment"—of the soul becoming one with the cosmos and escaping the illusion of individuality—to a notion of a heavenly paradise.[2] The image often used to explain the role of the bodhisattva is of a ferryman who repeatedly carries masses of devout worshippers over to salvation on his giant barge, while Theravada Buddhists cross the river one at a time and each one only once.

One of the most popular of the bodhisattvas was *Avalokitesvara,* or "Perceiver of the World's Sounds," who first shows up in a book called *The Lotus Sutra,* one of the earliest and most influential of the sacred texts of Mahayana Buddhism. *The Lotus Sutra* describes the ten cosmic levels of existence, from hell up to nirvana, with bodhisattvas on the ninth level working to remove the suffering of the world and to carry people to the highest level. Avalokitesvara is prominent among the bodhisattvas of *The Lotus Sutra,* and his cult spread with the dissemination of the text. The work was first translated into Chinese in 255 CE, and a Chinese translation made in 406 is the basis for this English translation. One interesting note about the transmission of Buddhism to China is that in later centuries Avalokitesvara, called *Guanyin* in China, was transformed into a female. In either form, Perceiver of the World's Sounds illustrates the central characteristics of Mahayana Buddhism's encounter with the transcendent.

QUESTIONS TO CONSIDER

1. What does someone who needs the help of Perceiver of the World's Sounds have to do to get it? How difficult is it to get this help? Are the things a worshipper must do personal or communal?

2. Generate a list of the sorts of help Perceiver of the World's Sounds can offer. What does this list tell you about the concerns and activities of people at the time?

3. How is this Buddhism different from the Buddhism presented in chapter 4? Is its philosophy and practice easier or harder to grasp or perform? What is the significance of the difference?

4. What characteristics of the statues of Amita Buddha and of Avalokitesvara stand out to you? What message do they convey, and how does this message reflect or complement the message of the text?

5. Taking the text and the art together, what strikes you as the central message of Mahayana Buddhism? That is, what is the main avenue to hope in Mahayana Buddhism? What is the appeal of that message?

THE LOTUS SUTRA

At that time the Bodhisattva Inexhaustible Intent immediately rose from his seat, bared his right shoulder, pressed his palms together and, facing the Buddha, spoke these words: "World Honored One, this Bodhisattva Perceiver of the World's Sounds—why is he called Perceiver of the World's Sounds?"

The Buddha said to Bodhisattva Inexhaustible Intent: "Good man, suppose there are immeasurable hundreds, thousands, ten thousands, millions of living beings who are undergoing various trials and suffering. If they hear of this Bodhisattva Perceiver of the World's Sounds and single-mindedly call his name, then at once he will perceive the sound of their voices and they will all gain deliverance from their trials.

"If someone, holding fast to the name of Bodhisattva Perceiver of the World's Sounds, should enter a great fire, the fire could not burn him. This would come about because of this bodhisattva's authority and supernatural power. If one were washed away by a great flood and call upon his name, one would immediately find himself in a shallow place.

"Suppose there were a hundred, a thousand, ten thousand, a million living beings who, seeking for gold, silver, lapis lazuli, seashell, agate, coral, amber, pearls, and other treasures, set out on the great sea, and suppose a fierce wind should blow their ship off course and it drifted to the land of rakshasas* demons. If among those people there is even just one who calls the name of Bodhisattva Perceiver of the World's Sounds, then all those people will be delivered from their troubles with the rakshasas. This is why he is called Perceiver of the World's Sounds.

"If a person who faces imminent threat of attack should call the name of Bodhisattva Perceiver of the World's Sounds, then the swords and staves wielded by his attackers would instantly shatter into so many pieces and he would be delivered.

"Though enough . . . rakshasas to fill all the thousand-million-fold world should try to come and torment a person, if they hear him calling the name of Bodhisattva Perceiver of the World's Sounds, then these evil demons will not even be able to look at him with their evil eyes, much less do him harm.

"Suppose, in a place filled with all the evil-hearted bandits of the thousand-million-fold world, there is a merchant leader who is guiding a band of merchants carrying valuable treasures over a steep and dangerous road, and that one man shouts out

---

Source: The Lotus Sutra, trans. Burton Watson, 298–303. Copyright © 1993 Columbia University Press. Reprinted with permission.

*Divine beings. In the cosmic scheme of things, they are evil, but they also use their powers to protect Buddhism.

these words: 'Good men, do not be afraid! You must single-mindedly call on the name of Bodhisattva Perceiver of the World's Sounds. This bodhisattva can grant fearlessness to living beings. If you call his name, you will be delivered from these evil-hearted bandits!' When the band of merchants hear this, they all together raise their voices, saying, 'Hail to the Bodhisattva Perceiver of the World's Sounds!' And because they call his name, they are at once able to gain deliverance. Inexhaustible Intent, the authority and supernatural power of the Bodhisattva and Mahasattva* Perceiver of the World's Sounds are as mighty as this!

"If there should be living beings beset by numerous lusts and cravings, let them think with constant reverence of Bodhisattva Perceiver of the World's Sounds and then they can shed their desires. If they have great wrath and ire, let them think with constant reverence of Bodhisattva Perceiver of the World's Sounds and then they can shed their ire. If they have great ignorance and stupidity, let them think with constant reverence of Bodhisattva Perceiver of the World's Sounds and they can rid themselves of stupidity.

"Inexhaustible Intent, the Bodhisattva Perceiver of the World's Sounds possesses great authority and supernatural powers, as I have described, and can confer many benefits. For this reason, living beings should constantly keep the thought of him in mind.

"If a woman wishes to give birth to a male child, she should offer obeisance† and alms to Bodhisattva Perceiver of the World's Sounds and then she will bear a son blessed with merit, virtue, and wisdom. And if she wishes to bear a daughter, she will bear one with all the marks of comeliness,‡ one who in the past planted the roots of virtue and is loved and respected by many persons.

"Inexhaustible Intent, suppose there is a person who accepts and upholds the names of as many bodhisattvas as there are sands in sixty-two million Ganges, and for as long as his present body lasts, he offers them alms in the form of food and drink, clothing, bedding and medicines. What is your opinion? Would this good man or good woman gain many benefits or would he not?"

Inexhaustible Intent replied, "They would be very many, World-Honored One."

The Buddha said: "Suppose also that there is a person who accepts and upholds the name of Bodhisattva Perceiver of the World's Sounds and even just once offers him obeisance and alms. The good fortune gained by these two persons would be exactly equal and without difference. . . . Inexhaustible Intent, if one accepts and upholds the name of Bodhisattva Perceiver of the World's Sounds, he will gain the benefit of merit and virtue that is as immeasurable and boundless as this!"

Bodhisattva Inexhaustible Intent said to the Buddha, "World-Honored One, Bodhisattva Perceiver of the World's Sounds—how does he come and go in this saha§ world? How does he preach the Law for the sake of living beings? How does the power of expedient means apply in this case?"

---

*"Great being."

†Respect.

‡Beauty.

§The saha world is this world, which one must endure in suffering.

The Buddha said to Bodhisattva Inexhaustible Intent: "Good man, if there are living beings in the land who need someone in the body of a Buddha in order to be saved, Bodhisattva Perceiver of the World's Sounds immediately manifests himself in a Buddha body and preaches the Law for them. If they need someone in a pratyekabuddha's* body in order to be saved, immediately he manifests a pratyekabuddha's body and preaches the Law to them. If they need a voice-hearer to be saved, immediately he becomes a voice-hearer and preaches the Law for them. If they need King Brahma† to be saved, immediately he becomes King Brahma and preaches the Law for them. If they need the lord Shakra‡ to be saved, immediately he becomes the lord Shakra and preaches the Law for them. If they need the heavenly being Freedom to be saved, immediately he becomes the heavenly being Freedom and preaches the Law for them. If they need a great general of heaven to be saved, immediately he becomes a great general of heaven and preaches the Law for them. . . . If they need a petty king to be saved, immediately he becomes a petty king and preaches the law for them.

If they need a rich man to be saved, immediately he becomes a rich man and preaches the Law for them. If they need a householder to be saved, immediately he becomes a householder and preaches the Law for them. If they need a chief minister to be saved, immediately he becomes a chief minister and preaches the Law for them. If they need a Brahman to be saved, immediately he becomes a Brahman and preaches the Law for them. If they need a monk, a nun, a layman believer, or a laywoman believer he becomes these and preaches the Law for them. If they need the wife of a rich man, of a householder, a chief minister, or a Brahman to be saved, immediately he becomes those wives and preaches the Law for them. If they need a young boy or a young girl he becomes these and preaches the Law for them. If they need a heavenly being, a dragon, . . . he becomes all of these and preaches the Law for them. . . .

"Inexhaustible Intent, this Bodhisattva Perceiver of the World's Sounds has succeeded in acquiring benefits such as these and, taking on a variety of different forms, goes about among the lands saving living beings. For this reason you and the others should single-mindedly offer alms to Bodhisattva Perceiver of the World's Sounds who can bestow fearlessness on those who are in fearful, pressing or difficult circumstances. That is why in this saha world everyone calls him Bestower of Fearlessness."

Bodhisattva Inexhaustible Intent said to the Buddha, "World-Honored One, now I must offer alms to Bodhisattva Perceiver of the World's Sounds."

Then he took from his neck a necklace adorned with numerous precious gems, worth a hundred or a thousand taels§ of gold, and presented it to [the bodhisattva], saying, "Sir, please accept this necklace of precious gems as a gift in the Dharma."

At that time Bodhisattva Perceiver of the World's Sounds was unwilling to accept the gift.

Inexhaustible Intent spoke once more to Bodhisattva Perceiver of the World's Sounds, saying, "Sir, out of compassion for us, please accept this necklace."

---

*A Buddhist sage who reaches Enlightenment and achieves nirvana without stopping to help others as a bodhisattva does.

†The Hindu god of creation, a protective deity for Mahayana Buddhists.

‡Indra, Hindu god of thunder; another protector deity of Mahayana Buddhists.

§A tael is about one and a half ounces.

Then the Buddha said to Bodhisattva Perceiver of the World's Sounds, "Out of compassion for this Bodhisattva Inexhaustible Intent and for the four kinds of believers, the heavenly kings, . . . human and nonhuman beings, you should accept this necklace."

Thereupon Bodhisattva Perceiver of the World's Sounds, having compassion for the four kinds of believers and the heavenly beings, dragons, human and nonhuman beings and the others, accepted the necklace and, dividing it into two parts, presented one part to Shakyamuni Buddha* and presented the other to the tower[†] of the Buddha Many Treasures.

At that time Bodhisattva Inexhaustible Intent posed this question in verse form:

World-Honored One replete with wonderful features,
I now ask you once again
for what reason that Buddha's son
is named Bodhisattva Perceiver of the World's Sounds?
The honored One endowed with wonderful features
replied to Inexhaustible Intent in verse:
Listen to the actions of the Perceiver of Sounds,
how aptly he responds in various quarters.
He has attended many thousands and millions of Buddhas,
setting forth his great pure vow.
I will describe him in outline for you—
listen to his name, observe his body,
bear him in mind, not passing the time vainly,
for he can wipe out the pains of existence.
Suppose you are surrounded by evil-hearted bandits,
each brandishing a knife to wound you.
Think on the power of that Perceiver of Sounds
and at once all will be swayed by compassion!
If living beings encounter weariness or peril,
immeasurable suffering pressing them down,
the power of the Perceiver of Sounds' wonderful wisdom
can save them from the sufferings of the world.
He sends down the sweet dew, the Dharma rain,
to quench the flames of earthly desires.
Endowed with all benefits,
he views living beings with compassionate eyes.

At that time the Bodhisattva Earth Holder immediately rose from his seat, advanced, and said to the Buddha, "World-Honored One, if there are living beings who hear this chapter on Bodhisattva Perceiver of the World's Sounds, on the freedom of his actions, his manifestation of a universal gateway, and his transcendental powers, it should be known that the benefits these persons gain are not few!"

---

*A title for the Buddha, founder of Buddhism.

†A temple.

Figure 8.1 Amita Buddha at Kamakura.

Figure 8.2 Bronze Statue of Avalokitesvara.

Amita Buddha, or Buddha of profound enlightenment (Figure 8.1), is portrayed sitting in the classic meditation position in this 42-foot-tall bronze statue in Kamakura, Japan, cast beginning in 1252. Amita was the bodhisattva Dharmakara, who attained Buddhahood partly by promising to assist others to achieve enlightenment. Amita Buddha is the Buddha of the Pure Land.

Avalokitesvara, Bodhisattva Perceiver of the World's Sounds (Figure 8.2), is shown in this fifteenth-century bronze from Nepal. Done in a style dating back to the sixth century, it shows the bodhisattva with his emblem, a lotus blossom, growing up on either side of him. The lotus was a favorite symbol of enlightenment because its flower rose from muddy waters, as enlightenment rises from the suffering of existence; the wavy form of the stems represents the winding path to enlightenment. Avalokitesvara himself supports a Buddha on his head, making him the literal intermediary between lower and higher planes of existence and the path along which aspirants to enlightenment may rise. His jewelry and other trappings show his ties to this world, meaning that he will not rise to the Pure Land without his followers.

DEVOTIONAL HINDUISM

The development of Mahayana Buddhism represented a serious challenge to Hinduism's position as the predominant form of religion in India. Hinduism met that challenge with the development of a form of worship called *bhakti,* or devotion, meaning unconditional devotion to a god. Devotional Hinduism built on the *yoga,* or discipline, of devotion that was already one of its central practices. For example, the discipline of devotion was revealed to the warrior Arjuna by his charioteer Krishna in the *Bhagavad-Gita.* Krishna was in reality an *avatar,* or incarnation, of the god Vishnu (see chapter 4). Unlike the Yoga of Action, which required strict and selfless attention to duty at all times, and the Yoga of Knowledge, which required the leisure and temperament for extended study and meditation, the Yoga of Devotion offered salvation to anyone who would worship a god unconditionally. In Devotional Hinduism, the form of that salvation was *moksha,* or release from the cycle of death and rebirth and reunion with Brahman, the universal soul. Because of the salvation that it promised and because it was accessible to everyone, it appealed to many of the same groups who found Mahayana Buddhism attractive, including members of lower castes, women, and others to whom the more traditional, priestly paths toward salvation were largely closed. Bhakti spread rapidly in the period after 300, and in fact by 1500 the combination of resurgent Hinduism and the inroads made by Islam had reduced Buddhism in India to a few scattered outposts.

Sometimes the three main gods of Hinduism are called the Hindu Trinity: namely, Brahma, the Creator; Vishnu, the Preserver; and Shiva, the Destroyer. They are thought to embody the three main aspects of Brahman, the Universal Soul or One. Vishnu and Shiva emerged during this period as the dominant, though not exclusive, subjects of devotional worship throughout India and tended to absorb many of the lesser gods of the Hindu pantheon over time. Though Brahma was thought to be somewhat distant and aloof, having completed his job of creation, Vishnu took an active interest in the world, appearing in different incarnations when he was needed, and Shiva was seen as a loving and interventionist god whose powers of destruction were seen as creative, purifying, and regenerative.

Accompanying the development of the new practice of devotionalism was the rise, between 300 and 100 BCE, of a new body of sacred literature that explained and promoted that practice. These works, known as *puranas,* are compilations of myth, folklore, simplified teachings, and other stories aimed at popular audiences. They were probably meant to be read or recited aloud. Their central message was that unconditional devotion to the worship of a single god would bring salvation. They are long, sometimes disjointed, but full of colorful images and easy-to-grasp ideas. There are eighteen major puranas; the *Vishnu Purana,* which recounts the ten incarnations of the great Vishnu, is one of the oldest and most important of the set. It probably dates to as early as the second century CE. This selection comes from the last chapter of the *Purana* and is in the form of a dialogue between a teacher, Parasara, and his disciple Maitreya. Because of its ideas and its antiquity, it is one of the most important texts for understanding the specific ways that Devotional Hinduism addressed the encounter with transcendence.

QUESTIONS TO CONSIDER

1. What must a worshipper do to receive the blessings of Vishnu? How difficult is it to get these blessings? Are the things a worshipper must do personal or communal?

2. What are the blessings bestowed by devotion to Vishnu? How do they compare with the list of concerns shown in *The Lotus Sutra*?

3. How are the practices required of a good follower of Devotional Hinduism related to its belief system? How did the beliefs and practices combine to offer a more accessible path to salvation than the Hinduism of the *Bhagavad-Gita*? How do the beliefs and practices presented in the *Vishnu Purana* compare with those embodied in Mahayana Buddhism and *The Lotus Sutra*?

4. What characteristics of the statues of Vishnu and the god Ganesh stand out to you? What message do they convey and how does this message reflect or complement the message of the text? How are they similar to or different from the Buddhist statues?

5. Taking the text and art together, what strikes you as the central message of Devotional Hinduism? That is, what is the main avenue to hope in Devotional Hinduism? What is the appeal of that message?

THE *VISHNU PURANA*

Parasara.   I have now explained to you, Maitreya, the third kind of worldly dissolution, or that which is absolute and final, which is liberation and resolution into eternal spirit. . . . I have repeated to you, in short, who were desirous of hearing it, the imperishable Vaishnava Purana,* which is destructive of all sins, the most excellent of all holy writings, and the means of attaining the great end of man.

If there is anything else you wish to hear, propose your question, and I will answer it.

Maitreya.   Holy teacher, you have, indeed, related to me all that I wished to know; and I have listened to it with pious attention. I have nothing further to inquire. The doubts inseparable from the mind of man have all been resolved by you; and, through your instructions, I am acquainted with the origin, duration, and end of all things. . . . Of all this have I acquired a knowledge, through your favor; and nothing else is worthy to be known, when it is once understood that Vishnu and this world are not (mutually) distinct. Great Muni,† I have obtained, through your kindness, all I desired—the dissipation of my doubts. . . . There is nothing else, venerable Brahman, that I have to inquire of you. And forgive me, if your answers to my questions have

---

Source: The *Vishnu Purana*, trans. H. H. Wilson, vol. 5 (New York and London: Garland Publishing, 1981), 244–55 [facsimile reprint of 1870 ed., London, Trübner & Co.].

*The Purana of Vishnu.

†Teacher, holy man.

imposed upon you any fatigue. Pardon me the trouble that I have given you, through that amiable quality of the virtuous which makes no distinction between a disciple and a child.

Parasara.   I have related to you this Purana, which is equal to the Vedas* (in sanctity), and by hearing which, all faults and sins whatever are expiated.[†] In this have been described to you the primary and secondary creation, [the hierarchy of heavenly beings and earthly kings]; the (distinctions of the) four castes, and the actions of the most eminent amongst men; holy places on the earth, holy rivers and oceans, sacred mountains, and legends of the (truly) wise; the duties of the different tribes, and the observances enjoined by the Vedas. By hearing this, all sins are at once obliterated. In this, also, the glorious Hari[‡] has been revealed—the cause of the creation, preservation, and destruction of the world; the soul of all things, and himself all things; by the repetition of whose name man is, undoubtedly, liberated from all sins, which fly like wolves that are frightened by a lion. The repetition of his name with devout faith is the best remover of all sins; destroying them, as fire purifies the metal from the dross. The stain of the Kali age,[§] which ensures to men sharp punishments in hell, is, at once, effaced by a single invocation of Hari. He who is all that is—the whole egg of Brahma,** with [all the divine beings], the stars, asteroids, planets, . . . men, Brahmans, and the rest, animals tame and wild, insects, birds, ghosts and goblins, trees, woods, mountains, rivers, oceans, the subterranean regions, the divisions of the earth, and all perceptible objects, he who is all things, who knows all things, who is the form of all things, being without form himself, and of whom whatever is, from Mount Meru[††] to an atom, all consists—he, the glorious Vishnu, the destroyer of all sin—is described in this Purana. By hearing this Purana an equal recompense is obtained to that which is derived from the performance of an Aswamedha sacrifice,[‡‡] or from fasting at the holy places. . . . Hearing this Purana but once is as efficacious as the offering of oblations in a perpetual fire for a year. The man who, with well-governed passions, bathes at [a holy place and time], and beholds the image of Hari, obtains a great recompense; so does he who, with mind fixed upon [Vishnu], attentively recites this Purana. . . . The same degree of merit that a man reaps from [a series of traditional devotions] and effecting the liberation of his progenitors by offering to them on such an occasion obsequial cakes,[§§] he derives, also, from hearing, with equal devotion, a section of this Purana. This Purana is the best of all preservatives for those who

---

*The Vedas, or "Wisdoms," are the earliest religious texts of Hinduism, dating from somewhere around 1000 BCE (see chapter 2).

[†]Atoned for.

[‡]Vishnu.

[§]The last of four repeating ages of the universe, a period of 360,000 years of corruption and decline named for Kali, the goddess consort of Shiva. Shiva's destruction ends the Kali Age, and the universe is then reborn to an age of virtue. The Puranas all assert that we are living in the Kali Age.

**The universe.

[††]Home of the Gods.

[‡‡]An ancient Aryan horse sacrifice.

[§§]Offerings at funeral rites for ancestors.

are afraid of worldly existence, a certain alleviation of the sufferings of men and remover of all imperfections.

This Purana . . . was communicated by Brahma to [a series of gods, monarchs and holy men, through whom] it came to my knowledge; and I have, now, Maitreya, faithfully imparted it to you. . . . Whoever hears this great mystery, which removes the contamination of the Kali, shall be freed from all his sins. He who hears this every day, acquits himself of his daily obligations to ancestors, gods, and men. The great and rarely attainable merit that a man acquires by the gift of a brown cow he derives from hearing ten chapters of this Purana. He who hears the entire Purana, contemplating in his mind Achyuta*—who is all things, and of whom all things are made; who is the stay of the whole world, the receptacle of spirit; who is knowledge, and that which is to be known; who is without beginning or end, and the benefactor of the gods—obtains, assuredly, the reward that attends the uninterrupted celebration of the Aswamedha rite. He who reads and retains with faith this Purana, in the beginning, middle, and end of which is described the glorious Achyuta, the lord of the universe in every stage, the master of all that is stationary or moveable, composed of spiritual knowledge, acquires such purity as exists not in any world—the eternal state of perfection which is Hari. The man who fixes his mind on Vishnu goes not to hell. He who meditates upon him regards heavenly enjoyment only as an impediment; and he whose mind and soul are penetrated by him thinks little of the world of Brahma;† for, when present in the minds of those whose intellects are free from soil, he confers upon them eternal freedom. What marvel it is, therefore, that the sins of one who repeats the name of Achyuta should be wiped away? Should not that Hari be heard of whom those devoted to acts‡ worship with sacrifices continually as the god of sacrifice; whom those devoted to meditation§ contemplate as primary and secondary, composed of spirit; by obtaining whom, man is not born, nor nourished, nor subjected to death; who is all that is, and that is not, who is both cause and effect; who, as the progenitors, receives the libations made to them; who, as the gods, accepts the offerings addressed to them; the glorious being who is without beginning or end; . . . who is the abode of all spiritual power; in whom the limits of finite things cannot be measured; and who, when he enters the ear, destroys all sin?

[Closing prayer to Vishnu:]

I adore him, that first of gods, Purushottama,** who is without end and without beginning, without growth, without decay, without death; who is substance that knows not change. I adore that ever inexhaustible spirit who assumed sensible qualities;††

---

*Another name for Vishnu, meaning "The Unfallen One."

†In other words, the material world created by Brahma.

‡Those who follow the Discipline (*yoga*) of Action (see *Bhagavad-Gita*, chapter 4) to obtain *moksha*, or release from the cycle of death and rebirth.

§Those who follow the Discipline of Knowledge.

**"The Substance of Purusha" (see "Purusha Hymn," chapter 2); that is, the original material from which the universe was created; another name for Vishnu.

††Who appears as various avatars such as Krishna, the charioteer of the *Bhagavad-Gita*.

who, though one, became many; who, though pure, became as if impure, by appearing in many and various shapes; who is endowed with divine wisdom and is the author of the preservation of all creatures. I adore him, who is the one conjoined essence and object of both meditative wisdom and active virtue; who is watchful in providing for human enjoyments; who is one with the three qualities;* who, without undergoing change, is the cause of the evolution of the world; who exists of his own essence, ever exempt from decay. I constantly adore him, who is entitled heaven, air, fire, water, earth, and ether; who is the bestower of all the objects which give gratification to the senses; who benefits mankind with the instruments of fruition; who is perceptible, who is subtle, who is imperceptible. May that unborn, eternal Hari, whose form is manifold, and whose essence is composed of both nature and spirit, bestow upon all mankind that blessed state which knows neither birth nor decay!

Figure 8.3 Vishnu   **Figure 8.4** Ganesh

---

*Creation, preservation, destruction, the qualities of Brahma, Vishnu, and Shiva, the Hindu "trinity."

The Vishnu statue in Figure 8.3 is from the early Chola period, around 850; it is a bronze figure just over 14 inches tall. It shows the god standing in repose and reaching out one of his four arms in blessing and assistance. The Chola kingdom was in the southeast part of India and thrived between about 850 and 1100. Vishnu, Shiva, and Ganesh were all popular figures in Chola art.

The Ganesh in Figure 8.4 is high Chola, from around 1071, and stands almost 20 inches tall. Ganesh is one of the most popular of the non-Trinity gods. According to the legend in the *Shiva Purana,* one version of many, he was the son of Shiva and his consort Parvati, who created him to guard her rooms after Shiva had interrupted her bath. Shiva beheaded the boy when he blocked his way the next time, but when Parvati proved inconsolable, he replaced the missing boy's head with that of an elephant and brought him back to life. He is revered as a protector of families and as the Remover of Obstacles; he is thus worshipped at the commencement of important activities (including the worship of other gods) and projects (such as term papers). He holds an axe from Shiva in his upper right arm, his own tusk in the lower right arm, a noose that snares delusion in the upper left arm, and a sweet that he tastes with his trunk (thus the large belly) in the lower right arm.

CHRISTIANITY

The eastern Mediterranean around the beginning of the first century CE was a world of religious ferment. In addition to the civic and emerging imperial cults of the ruling Roman Empire, mystery religions—often secret groups who looked to some particular god for eternal life, Truth, and so forth, usually by means of sacrificial ceremonies and other rituals—were gaining popularity. Prominent also were many of the ideas associated with Persian Zoroastrianism (see chapter 4) and a variety of dualistic, proto-salvationist faiths influenced by it. Finally, a number of Jewish sects took varying approaches to the problem posed by Roman control of Palestine, the land they believed had been promised to them by their god. A militant strain in Judaism would rise in revolt against Rome in 69 CE, leading to the war chronicled by Josephus (see chapter 5). But before then, a different sort of Jewish rabbi, or teacher, and his followers had already made their mark on the religious world.

Joshua, or Jesus in Greek, of Nazareth (c. 4 BCE–c. 30 CE) was a prophet in the tradition of Second Isaiah (chapter 4), who preached the coming, not of a military Messiah (Anointed One, a sacred leader) who would lead the Jews to repossession of the promised land, but of the coming of a spiritual Messiah who would lead not just Jews but all of mankind to the promised land of salvation and heavenly reward. At some point, his followers became convinced that he was that Messiah. Despite his emphasis on a heavenly Kingdom, his popularity among the Jewish population made both the Romans and the leaders of the Jewish community (who had no desire to irritate the Romans) nervous, and they had him executed by crucifixion. His followers, however, believed that he rose from the dead and ascended to his Father in heaven, promising to return to sit in judgment on mankind.

The teachings of Jesus himself clearly formed the basis of what became a new religion, Christianity, so called because Jesus' title of Messiah in Greek is *Christos,* and his followers were therefore Christians. But because Jesus left no writings of his own, the working out and refining of Jesus' message in theological terms, as well as defining who the message was aimed at and what constituted the community of believers, was largely the work of a Jew named Saul (3 BCE–64 or 67 CE) from Tarsus in Asia Minor. Trained as a rabbi and scholarly religious leader in the Jewish tradition, he underwent a sudden conversion experience, changed his name to Paul, and became early Christianity's most influential missionary and teacher. He wrote many epistles, or letters, to different communities of converts, explaining and developing the new faith and, most crucially, opening it up decisively to Gentiles, or non-Jews. His letter to a group of Christians in Rome is his fullest, most complete statement of the tenets of the new religion, and it came to be part of the authoritative texts of the faith. These texts, including Paul's Epistle to the Romans, came to be known collectively as the New Testament of the Bible, to distinguish it from the Old Testament, the Jewish portion of the Bible. A section of this epistle is the first reading here.

Also included as the foundation of the New Testament were accounts of Jesus' life and teachings, known as *Gospels,* or Good News. Four came to be considered canonical, with pride of place taken by that of Matthew. Early Christians attributed this book to the Matthew who was one of Jesus' original twelve Apostles, but modern scholarship places the author as a second-generation Christian, probably from Antioch, and writing around 80 CE. Included here is the section of the Gospel of Matthew known as the Sermon on the Mount, which almost certainly represents not a verbatim transcription of a single speech but Matthew's summary of Jesus' key teachings set in an appropriate setting, similar to Thucydides' account of Pericles' funeral oration (see chapter 4). Together, the writings of Paul and Matthew give a good sense of the foundations of this new salvation religion.

QUESTIONS TO CONSIDER

1. What must a worshipper do to receive the blessings of Christ? How difficult is it to receive these blessings? Are the things a worshipper must do personal or communal? What classes of people would find the message of the Sermon on the Mount attractive? Why?

2. What are the blessings bestowed by adherence to the teachings of Jesus? How do they compare with those bestowed in *The Lotus Sutra* and the *Vishnu Purana*—what are the similarities and differences?

3. What are the differences between Christianity and the Judaism of Second Isaiah? What are the differences and similarities between the doctrine developed by Paul and the doctrine presented as Jesus' by Matthew?

4. What characteristics of the mosaics of Jesus and Mary stand out to you? What message do they convey, and how does this message reflect or complement the

message of the text? How are they similar to or different from the Buddhist and Hindu statues?

5. Taking the text and art together, what strikes you as the central message of Christianity? That is, what is the main avenue to hope in Christianity? What is the appeal of that message?

THE NEW TESTAMENT

Romans 1

[1]Paul, a servant of Christ Jesus, called to be an apostle and set apart for the gospel of God. . . .

[7]To all in Rome who are loved by God and called to be saints:
Grace and peace to you from God our Father and from the Lord Jesus Christ.

[11]I long to see you so that I may impart to you some spiritual gift to make you strong— [12]that is, that you and I may be mutually encouraged by each other's faith. . . .

[14]I am obligated both to Greeks and non-Greeks, both to the wise and the foolish. [15]That is why I am so eager to preach the gospel also to you who are at Rome.

[16]I am not ashamed of the gospel, because it is the power of God for the salvation of everyone who believes: first for the Jew, then for the Gentile. [17]For in the gospel a righteousness from God is revealed, a righteousness that is by faith from first to last, just as it is written: "The righteous will live by faith."

Romans 5

[1]Therefore, since we have been justified through faith, we have peace with God through our Lord Jesus Christ, [2]through whom we have gained access by faith into this grace in which we now stand. And we rejoice in the hope of the glory of God. [3]Not only so, but we also rejoice in our sufferings, because we know that suffering produces perseverance; [4]perseverance, character; and character, hope. [5]And hope does not disappoint us, because God has poured out his love into our hearts by the Holy Spirit, whom he has given us.

[6]You see, at just the right time, when we were still powerless, Christ died for the ungodly. [7]Very rarely will anyone die for a righteous man, though for a good man someone might possibly dare to die. [8]But God demonstrates his own love for us in this: While we were still sinners, Christ died for us.

[9]Since we have now been justified by his blood, how much more shall we be saved from God's wrath through him! [10]For if, when we were God's enemies, we were reconciled to him through the death of his Son, how much more, having been reconciled, shall we be saved through his life! [11]Not only is this so, but we also rejoice in God through our Lord Jesus Christ, through whom we have now received reconciliation.

Source: The Holy Bible, Revised Standard Edition (New York: American Bible Society, 1952), Romans 1, 5, 10; Matthew 5, 6.

Romans 10

"The word is near you; it is in your mouth and in your heart," that is, the word of faith we are proclaiming: [9]That if you confess with your mouth, "Jesus is Lord," and believe in your heart that God raised him from the dead, you will be saved. [10]For it is with your heart that you believe and are justified, and it is with your mouth that you confess and are saved. [11]As the Scripture says, "Anyone who trusts in him will never be put to shame."

[12]For there is no difference between Jew and Gentile—the same Lord is Lord of all and richly blesses all who call on him, [13]for, "Everyone who calls on the name of the Lord will be saved."

[14]How, then, can they call on the one they have not believed in? And how can they believe in the one of whom they have not heard? And how can they hear without someone preaching to them? [15]And how can they preach unless they are sent? As it is written, "How beautiful are the feet of those who bring good news!"

Matthew 5

[1]Now when he saw the crowds, he went up on a mountainside and sat down. His disciples came to him, [2]and he began to teach them saying:

[3]"Blessed are the poor in spirit,
for theirs is the kingdom of heaven.
[4]Blessed are those who mourn,
for they will be comforted.
[5]Blessed are the meek,
for they will inherit the earth.
[6]Blessed are those who hunger and thirst for righteousness,
for they will be filled.
[7]Blessed are the merciful,
for they will be shown mercy.
[8]Blessed are the pure in heart,
for they will see God.
[9]Blessed are the peacemakers,
for they will be called sons of God.
[10]Blessed are those who are persecuted because of righteousness,
for theirs is the kingdom of heaven.

[11]"Blessed are you when people insult you, persecute you and falsely say all kinds of evil against you because of me. [12]Rejoice and be glad, because great is your reward in heaven, for in the same way they persecuted the prophets who were before you.

[13]"You are the salt of the earth. But if the salt loses its saltiness, how can it be made salty again? It is no longer good for anything, except to be thrown out and trampled by men.

[14]"You are the light of the world. A city on a hill cannot be hidden. [15]Neither do people light a lamp and put it under a bowl. Instead they put it on its stand, and it gives light to everyone in the house. [16]In the same way, let your light shine before men, that they may see your good deeds and praise your Father in heaven.

[17]"Do not think that I have come to abolish the Law or the Prophets; I have not come to abolish them but to fulfill them. [18]I tell you the truth, until heaven and earth disap-

pear, not the smallest letter, not the least stroke of a pen, will by any means disappear from the Law until everything is accomplished. [19]Anyone who breaks one of the least of these commandments and teaches others to do the same will be called least in the kingdom of heaven, but whoever practices and teaches these commands will be called great in the kingdom of heaven. [20]For I tell you that unless your righteousness surpasses that of the Pharisees and the teachers of the law, you will certainly not enter the kingdom of heaven.

[21]"You have heard that it was said to the people long ago, 'Do not murder, and anyone who murders will be subject to judgment.' [22]But I tell you that anyone who is angry with his brother will be subject to judgment. . . . .

[33]"Again, you have heard that it was said to the people long ago, 'Do not break your oath, but keep the oaths you have made to the Lord.' [34]But I tell you, Do not swear at all: either by heaven, for it is God's throne; [35]or by the earth, for it is his footstool; or by Jerusalem, for it is the city of the Great King. [36]And do not swear by your head, for you cannot make even one hair white or black. [37]Simply let your 'Yes' be 'Yes,' and your 'No,' 'No'; anything beyond this comes from the evil one.

[38]"You have heard that it was said, 'Eye for eye, and tooth for tooth.' [39]But I tell you, Do not resist an evil person. If someone strikes you on the right cheek, turn to him the other also. [40]And if someone wants to sue you and take your tunic, let him have your cloak as well. [41]If someone forces you to go one mile, go with him two miles. [42]Give to the one who asks you, and do not turn away from the one who wants to borrow from you.

[43]"You have heard that it was said, 'Love your neighbor and hate your enemy.' [44]But I tell you: Love your enemies and pray for those who persecute you, [45]that you may be sons of your Father in heaven. He causes his sun to rise on the evil and the good, and sends rain on the righteous and the unrighteous. [46]If you love those who love you, what reward will you get? Are not even the tax collectors doing that? [47]And if you greet only your brothers, what are you doing more than others? Do not even pagans do that? [48]Be perfect, therefore, as your heavenly Father is perfect.

Matthew 6

[1]"Be careful not to do your 'acts of righteousness' before men, to be seen by them. If you do, you will have no reward from your Father in heaven.

[2]"So when you give to the needy, do not announce it with trumpets, as the hypocrites do in the synagogues and on the streets, to be honored by men. I tell you the truth, they have received their reward in full. [3]But when you give to the needy, do not let your left hand know what your right hand is doing, [4]so that your giving may be in secret. Then your Father, who sees what is done in secret, will reward you.

[5]"And when you pray, do not be like the hypocrites, for they love to pray standing in the synagogues and on the street corners to be seen by men. I tell you the truth, they have received their reward in full. [6]But when you pray, go into your room, close the door and pray to your Father, who is unseen. Then your Father, who sees what is done in secret, will reward you. [7]And when you pray, do not keep on babbling like pagans, for they think they will be heard because of their many words. [8]Do not be like them, for your Father knows what you need before you ask him.

[9]"This, then, is how you should pray:

"'Our Father in heaven,

hallowed be your name,
^{10}your kingdom come,
your will be done
on earth as it is in heaven.
^{11}Give us today our daily bread.
^{12}Forgive us our debts,
as we also have forgiven our debtors.
^{13}And lead us not into temptation,
but deliver us from the evil one.'

^{14}For if you forgive men when they sin against you, your heavenly Father will also forgive you. ^{15}But if you do not forgive men their sins, your Father will not forgive your sins.

^{19}"Do not store up for yourselves treasures on earth, where moth and rust destroy, and where thieves break in and steal. ^{20}But store up for yourselves treasures in heaven, where moth and rust do not destroy, and where thieves do not break in and steal. ^{21}For where your treasure is, there your heart will be also.

^{22}"The eye is the lamp of the body. If your eyes are good, your whole body will be full of light. ^{23}But if your eyes are bad, your whole body will be full of darkness. If then the light within you is darkness, how great is that darkness!

^{24}"No one can serve two masters. Either he will hate the one and love the other, or he will be devoted to the one and despise the other. You cannot serve both God and Money.

^{25}"Therefore I tell you, do not worry about your life, what you will eat or drink; or about your body, what you will wear. Is not life more important than food, and the body more important than clothes? ^{26}Look at the birds of the air; they do not sow or reap or store away in barns, and yet your heavenly Father feeds them. Are you not much more valuable than they? ^{27}Who of you by worrying can add a single hour to his life? ^{28}"And why do you worry about clothes? See how the lilies of the field grow. They do not labor or spin. ^{29}Yet I tell you that not even Solomon in all his splendor was dressed like one of these. ^{30}If that is how God clothes the grass of the field, which is here today and tomorrow is thrown into the fire, will he not much more clothe you, O you of little faith? ^{31}So do not worry, saying, 'What shall we eat?' or 'What shall we drink?' or 'What shall we wear?' ^{32}For the pagans run after all these things, and your heavenly Father knows that you need them. ^{33}But seek first his kingdom and his righteousness, and all these things will be given to you as well. ^{34}Therefore do not worry about tomorrow, for tomorrow will worry about itself. Each day has enough trouble of its own."

The picture in Figure 8.5 illustrates an episode from the Gospels in which Jesus cures the blind with his touch. It is a mosaic from a wall of a church in Ravenna, Italy, and dates from around 500 CE. The picture in Figure 8.6 is an *icon,* or a painting of a religious figure intended to be carried around as an object of devotion; its beauty and subject matter were supposed to lift the attention of the

Figure 8.5 Christ Healing the Blind

Figure 8.6 Enthroned Mother of God

viewer to heaven—a sort of artistic intermediary between this world and the spiritual realm. This one comes from Mt. Sinai in Palestine and dates to about 550 CE. In it, Jesus as a baby sits on the lap of his mother Mary, who became a major object of devotion in both the eastern, Greek branch of Christianity and somewhat later in the western, Latin branch. Mary sits enthroned with a Patriarch, or high Church official, on one side of her and the Eastern Roman Emperor on the other, with archangels behind her looking up toward heaven.

ISLAM

Islam was the last of the major salvation religions to arise, and in some ways it is surprising that it did appear. Arabia is basically a vast desert that for most of its history has supported little more than nomadic Arab herders known as bedouins, with a fringe of merchant towns along the coast and some settled farmers on Arabia's northwestern edge where it joins to Palestine. The nomads of Arabia, unlike the nomads of the central Asian steppes, were too poor to generate their own political organization internally and both too poor and too few in numbers to play a major military role in most eras. Some Arab groups occasionally made alliances with the great powers of the area, but Arab leaders were more the clients than the equal allies of sedentary kings and emperors. On the other hand, Arabia lacked the constant political turnover and migration of populations that characterized the steppes and that made any ethnic, linguistic, or cultural grouping there temporary and shallowly rooted. As a result, the Arab tribes by 600 CE had a long, stable cultural history and deeply rooted group identities and divisions. Finally, a mix of religious traditions characterized pre-Islamic Arabia. Many Arabs still followed old pagan ways; Jewish communities coexisted with Arab ones; and Christianity by 600 was making major inroads. This is one reason the emergence of a new faith is surprising, for a salvation religion was already established in the area.

But a combination of circumstances derailed expectations and launched a new religion. First, Arabia between 600 and 630 became an arena of competition between the Christian Byzantine Empire and the Zoroastrian Persian Empire of the Sassanid dynasty. Engaged in a protracted struggle for dominance in southwest Asia and Egypt, the two empires both looked for Arab allies, putting new resources into Arab society and raising the political pressure in the area. At the same time, an Arab merchant from Mecca began preaching messages from Allah, *the* god—the same god of the Jews and Christians, but with a new and final message specially for the Arabs. Muhammad became the prophet of a new Arab creed. According to Muslim belief, he was the last of the line of prophets running from Abraham and Moses through Isaiah and Jesus with the final revelation from God. But his success was far from immediate. He preached for twelve years in Mecca, gaining only a small following and much opposition. In 622 he took his followers to an oasis village that became known as Medina, the City of the Prophet, and established the first *umma,* or community of the faithful. (The *hejira,* the break with Mecca and move to Medina, became the act marking the beginning of the Islamic calendar.) Now a political and military leader, as well as a prophet, Muhammad was able to attract new followers to Medina and eight years later to reenter Mecca in triumph. Almost all of Arabia fell under his leadership. Even before Muhammad's death in 632, he had begun leading his Arab coalition against the now exhausted empires on the borders of Arabia. His first two successors in leadership of the *umma,* Abu Bakr and Umar, rapidly created a vast Arab empire, swallowing religiously dissident provinces of Byzantium and the whole of the Persian Empire.

Islam means "submission," and a Muslim is one who submits to the will of Allah. The holy book of the Muslims is the Qur'an. Like Jesus, Muhammad did not write down his own teachings, though Islamic tradition holds that the Qur'an was recited by Muhammad, to whom it was revealed by Allah. But unlike Christianity, which had a single Paul to define much of its doctrine, the developed doctrines of Islam emerged from a much broader, more communal and contested recording, reordering, and refining of the words of the Prophet. What we actually know of very early Islamic doctrine is therefore minimal. But what emerged after eighty years or so has remained ever since the core of Islam, the last of the great encounters with transcendence via a salvation religion.

QUESTIONS TO CONSIDER

1. What are the key duties that a Muslim must perform to receive the blessing of Allah? How difficult are they? Are they communal or personal?

2. What are the blessings of Allah? What do they tell us of the concerns of the Arab world at the time? What punishments are reserved for those who do not seek the blessings of Allah?

3. What similarities and differences does Islam show as a salvation religion compared with the other three faiths presented in this chapter? What characteristics of Islam seem to reflect its late entry into the field, and what characteristics seem to reflect the particular historical circumstances that surrounded the emergence of Islam?

4. The greatest sin in Islam is worship of idols. How could this have influenced Muslim art in the direction of "nonrepresentational" art, such as that of the Arab calligraphy? What differences in the use of art in religion are implied by a nonrepresentational artistic tradition?

5. Considering both the text and the calligraphy, what strikes you as the central message of Islam? That is, what is the main avenue to hope in Islam? What is the appeal of that message?

THE QUR'AN

The Cow*

In the name of Allah, the Beneficent, the Merciful.

[**2.2**] This Book, there is no doubt in it, is a guide to those who guard (against evil).

[**2.3**] Those who believe in the unseen and keep up prayer and spend out of what We have given them.

[**2.4**] And who believe in that which has been revealed to you and that which was revealed before you and they are sure of the hereafter.

[**2.5**] These are on a right course from their Lord and these it is that shall be successful.

[**2.6**] Surely those who disbelieve, it being alike to them whether you warn them, or do not warn them, will not believe.

. . .

[**2.21**] O men! serve your Lord Who created you and those before you so that you may guard (against evil).

[**2.22**] Who made the earth a resting place for you and the heaven a canopy and (Who) sends down rain from the cloud then brings forth with it subsistence for you of the fruits; therefore do not set up rivals to Allah while you know.

[**2.23**] And if you are in doubt as to that which We have revealed to Our servant, then produce a chapter like it and call on your witnesses besides Allah if you are truthful.

. . .

[**2.25**] And convey good news to those who believe and do good deeds, that they shall have gardens in which rivers flow; whenever they shall be given a portion of the fruit thereof, they shall say: This is what was given to us before; and they shall

---

Source: *The Holy Qur'an*, trans. M. H. Shakir, 1983. Reprinted by permission of Tahrike Tarsile Qur'an, Inc.

*The names of sections in the Qur'an reflect items discussed in those sections. Sometimes, as in this section known as "The Cow," these strike non-Muslims, who do not know the entire text, as odd.

be given the like of it, and they shall have pure mates in them, and in them, they shall abide.

. . .

[2.28] How do you deny Allah and you were dead and He gave you life? Again He will cause you to die and again bring you to life, then you shall be brought back to Him.

. . .

[2.30] And when your Lord said to the angels, I am going to place in the earth a khalif,* they said: What! wilt Thou place in it such as shall make mischief in it and shed blood, and we celebrate Thy praise and extol Thy holiness? He said: Surely I know what you do not know.

. . .

[2.40] O children of Israel! call to mind My favor which I bestowed on you and be faithful to (your) covenant with Me, I will fulfill (My) covenant with you; and of Me, Me alone, should you be afraid.

. . .

[2.43] And keep up prayer and pay the poor-rate[†] and bow down with those who bow down.
[2.44] What! do you enjoin men to be good and neglect your own souls while you read the Book; have you then no sense?
[2.45] And seek assistance through patience and prayer, and most surely it is a hard thing except for the humble ones,
[2.46] Who know that they shall meet their Lord and that they shall return to Him.

. . .

[2.62] Surely those who believe, and those who are Jews, and the Christians, and the Sabians,[‡] whoever believes in Allah and the Last day and does good, they shall have their reward from their Lord, and there is no fear for them, nor shall they grieve.

. . .

[2.79] Woe, then, to those who write the book with their hands and then say: This is from Allah, so that they may take for it a small price; therefore woe to them for what their hands have written and woe to them for what they earn.

. . .

[2.82] And (as for) those who believe and do good deeds, these are the dwellers of the garden; in it they shall abide.

. . .

---

*Khalif, or Caliph, means "Successor of the Prophet [Muhammad]." The caliphs were the head of the Islamic community as a whole, and they therefore held a position that combined aspects of a Catholic pope and an emperor.

†The tax or tithe that embodied the Islamic duty of being charitable.

‡Gnostic, or rationalist, Christians in Persia; therefore, a "people of the book"—Jews, Christians, and Muslims—and worthy of toleration in Islamic thought, since they were not idol worshippers.

[2.87] And most certainly We gave Musa the Book and We sent apostles after him one after another; and We gave Isa, the son of Marium,* clear arguments and strengthened him with the holy spirit, What! whenever then an apostle came to you with that which your souls did not desire, you were insolent so you called some liars and some you slew.

. . .

[2.105] Those who disbelieve from among the followers of the Book do not like, nor do the polytheists, that the good should be sent down to you from your Lord, and Allah chooses especially whom He pleases for His mercy, and Allah is the Lord of mighty grace.

[2.106] Whatever communications We abrogate or cause to be forgotten, We bring one better than it or like it. Do you not know that Allah has power over all things?

[2.107] Do you not know that Allah's is the kingdom of the heavens and the earth, and that besides Allah you have no guardian or helper?

. . .

[2.110] And keep up prayer and pay the poor-rate and whatever good you send before for yourselves, you shall find it with Allah; surely Allah sees what you do.

. . .

[2.112] Yes! whoever submits himself entirely to Allah and he is the doer of good (to others) he has his reward from his Lord, and there is no fear for him nor shall he grieve.

. . .

[2.115] And Allah's is the East and the West, therefore, whither you turn, thither is Allah's purpose; surely Allah is Amplegiving, Knowing.

. . .

[2.119] Surely We have sent you with the truth as a bearer of good news and as a warner, ...

. . .

[2.125] And when We made the House a pilgrimage for men and a (place of) security, and: Appoint for yourselves a place of prayer on the standing-place of Ibrahim. And We enjoined Ibrahim and Ismail† saying: Purify My House for those who visit (it) and those who abide (in it) for devotion and those who bow down (and) those who prostrate themselves.

. . .

[2.129] Our Lord! and raise up in them an Apostle from among them who shall recite to them Thy communications and teach them the Book and the wisdom, and purify them; surely Thou art the Mighty, the Wise.

---

*Musa is Moses; Isa is Jesus, and Marium is Mary.

†Ibrahim is Abraham, and Ismail is Ishmail. The Arabs considered themselves the descendants of Abraham through his son Ishmail, whom he had with the slave girl Hagar, while the Jews were Abraham's descendants through Isaac, his son by his wife Sarah.

[2.130] And who forsakes the religion of Ibrahim but he who makes himself a fool, and most certainly We chose him in this world, and in the hereafter he is most surely among the righteous.

[2.131] When his Lord said to him, Be a Muslim, he said: I submit myself to the Lord of the worlds.

. . .

[2.147] The truth is from your Lord, therefore you should not be of the doubters.

[2.148] And every one has a direction to which he should turn, therefore hasten to (do) good works; wherever you are, Allah will bring you all together; surely Allah has power over all things.

[2.149] And from whatsoever place you come forth, turn your face towards the Sacred Mosque; and surely it is the very truth from your Lord, and Allah is not at all heedless of what you do.

[2.150] And from whatsoever place you come forth, turn your face towards the Sacred Mosque; and wherever you are turn your faces towards it, so that people shall have no accusation against you, except such of them as are unjust; so do not fear them, and fear Me, that I may complete My favor on you and that you may walk on the right course.

[2.151] Even as We have sent among you an Apostle* from among you who recites to you Our communications and purifies you and teaches you the Book and the wisdom and teaches you that which you did not know.

[2.152] Therefore remember Me, I will remember you, and be thankful to Me, and do not be ungrateful to Me.

[2.153] O you who believe! seek assistance through patience and prayer; surely Allah is with the patient.

[2.154] And do not speak of those who are slain in Allah's way as dead; nay, (they are) alive, but you do not perceive.

[2.155] And We will most certainly try you with somewhat of fear and hunger and loss of property and lives and fruits; and give good news to the patient,

[2.156] Who, when a misfortune befalls them, say: Surely we are Allah's and to Him we shall surely return.

[2.157] Those are they on whom are blessings and mercy from their Lord, and those are the followers of the right course.

[2.158] Surely the . . . whoever makes a pilgrimage to the House or pays a visit (to it), there is no blame on him if he goes round them both; and whoever does good spontaneously, then surely Allah is Grateful, Knowing.

. . .

[2.190] And fight in the way of Allah with those who fight with you, and do not exceed the limits, surely Allah does not love those who exceed the limits.

[2.191] And kill them wherever you find them, and drive them out from whence they drove you out, and persecution is severer than slaughter, and do not fight with them

---

*Muhammad.

at the Sacred Mosque until they fight with you in it, but if they do fight you, then slay them; such is the recompense of the unbelievers.

[2.192] But if they desist, then surely Allah is Forgiving, Merciful.

[2.193] And fight with them until there is no persecution, and religion should be only for Allah, but if they desist, then there should be no hostility except against the oppressors.

. . .

[2.196] And accomplish the pilgrimage and the visit for Allah, but if, you are prevented, (send) whatever offering is easy to obtain, and do not shave your heads until the offering reaches its destination; but whoever among you is sick or has an ailment of the head, he (should effect) a compensation by fasting or alms or sacrificing, then when you are secure, whoever profits by combining the visit with the pilgrimage (should take) what offering is easy to obtain; but he who cannot find (any offering) should fast for three days during the pilgrimage and for seven days when you return; these (make) ten (days) complete; this is for him whose family is not present in the Sacred Mosque, and be careful (of your duty) to Allah, and know that Allah is severe in requiting (evil).

. . .

[2.263] Kind speech and forgiveness is better than charity followed by injury; and Allah is Self-sufficient, Forbearing.

. . .

[2.270] And whatever alms you give or (whatever) vow you vow, surely Allah knows it; and the unjust shall have no helpers.

[2.271] If you give alms openly, it is well, and if you hide it and give it to the poor, it is better for you; and this will do away with some of your evil deeds; and Allah is aware of what you do.

. . .

[2.277] Surely they who believe and do good deeds and keep up prayer and pay the poor-rate they shall have their reward from their Lord, and they shall have no fear, nor shall they grieve.

. . .

[2.284] Whatever is in the heavens and whatever is in the earth is Allah's; and whether you manifest what is in your minds or hide it, Allah will call you to account according to it; then He will forgive whom He pleases and chastise whom He pleases, and Allah has power over all things.

Alms

In the name of Allah, the Beneficent, the Merciful.

[107.1] Have you considered him who calls the judgment a lie?

[107.2] That is the one who treats the orphan with harshness,

[107.3] And does not urge (others) to feed the poor.

[107.4] So woe to the praying ones,

[107.5] Who are unmindful of their prayers,

[107.6] Who do (good) to be seen,

[107.7] And withhold the necessaries of life.

(a)

Figure 8.7 Arabic Calligraphy: the Name of Allah

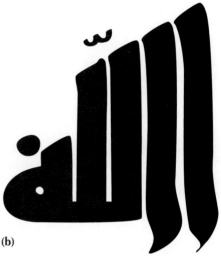

(b)

   Islam, like Judaism, taught that the making of representational images of Allah, people, or animals was a form of idolatry that was therefore prohibited. But this does not mean that Islamic religion was without artistic expression. In addition to a long tradition of beautiful abstract geometric decorations on buildings and in the margins of manuscripts, calligraphy, or the art of beautiful handwriting, became a means of artistic expression in itself, not just a means of conveying the written word. (A similar calligraphic tradition had already evolved in China, whose ideographic system of writing lent itself to expressive textual production, though in China calligraphy often accompanied and complemented a thriving tradition of representational art.) The two pictures in Figure 8.7 both show the name of Allah written in Kufic script. Figure 8.7a is a detail of a mosaic inscription from a mosque in Samarqand in Central Asia, Figure 8.7b is calligraphy from the Maghrib in North Africa, written on gazelle skin.

NOTES

1. To some extent, Hinduism remained largely a religion one was born into as well, but the size and variety of the population that embraced this manifold tradition distinguished it from these other two faiths, and Hinduism did spread, if only in somewhat limited ways, beyond India into southeast Asia.

2. For example, it is called the "Pure Land" in the Mahayana Buddhist sect of that name.

CHAPTER 9

Conversion Encounters

The Spread of the Salvation Religions

INTRODUCTION

In the late nineteenth century, baseball came to Japan, brought by "baseball missionaries" from the United States, where the game was invented. The Japanese took readily to *beisu boru,* which became one of the cultural cornerstones of the push for Westernization that characterized the period in Japan. Organized teams appeared, national leagues arose, and the league champions met in an annual Japanese championship series. By the 1920s, American major league all-star teams, featuring the demigods of the baseball pantheon of the time, including Babe Ruth, Ty Cobb, and others, regularly toured Japan during the off season, playing Japanese all-star teams in exhibition series. It appeared that "America's pastime," which, as was discussed at the beginning of chapter 8, many Americans follow with religious devotion, had converted the Japanese.

But the game had not been unaffected by its adoption in the Land of the Rising Sun. The teams in Japanese leagues, rather than bearing the names of the cities where they played, often instead bore the names of the large corporations that sponsored them. This remains true today: the Nippon Ham Fighters are not the "Ham Fighters"—whatever those would be!—from Nippon, but the "Fighters" from the Nippon Ham company. In addition, some of the rules of the game had changed in the trip across the Pacific. The oddest change, from an American perspective, is that Japanese baseball allowed for tie games. Indeed, ties were almost an ideal outcome, because a tie meant that neither team was defeated and "lost face."[1] In other words, in moving to Japan baseball had accommodated itself, through what might be called a set of conversion encounters, to its new environment. In the Japanese economic and political power structures, corporate identity plays a larger role than urban communal identity, so teams are named after companies. Japanese culture stresses consensus and hierarchy more than the individualism and competitiveness of U.S. culture, so ties are allowed. In other words, Japan had converted to baseball, but in the process baseball had been translated into Japanese.

This chapter is about the similar conversion encounters that resulted from the spread of the salvation religions (whose basic doctrines were introduced in chapter 8). It examines the conflicts and accommodations these religions made with local power structures and with local cultures and religious beliefs in the course of their expansion. It also looks at the changes in the religions that resulted from these conversion encounters. While allowing us to explore the historically significant transmission of the salvation religions' belief systems and values, the chapter also enables us to consider the broader issue of cultural transmission and reception and the complex phenomenon of human cross-cultural interaction. In multicultural and globalized contemporary societies, these issues clearly continue to have relevance.

The spread of the great salvation religions in the period between about 200 and 1000 CE was impressive. During this time Mahayana Buddhism traveled along the Silk Road from its home in north India, reaching China in the second century CE and spreading widely within China during the next several centuries. It also spread to Tibet, and from China it had reached Korea, Japan, and parts of southeast Asia by 1000. In other parts of southeast Asia, Theravada Buddhism had arrived directly from south India; the same areas also saw a more limited spread of Devotional Hinduism. Meanwhile, Christianity was spreading slowly within the Roman Empire, although its expansion quickened considerably after the conversion of the Emperor Constantine in 312 CE. The centuries up to 1000 saw the gradual evangelization of much of western Europe. After 800, large parts of Slavic eastern Europe also converted to Christianity. But the period after 630 also saw the loss of significant Christian lands in north Africa and Iberia to the spread of the newest of the salvationist faiths, Islam. The explosive growth of the Islamic empire also encompassed much of southwest Asia, including Persia, and extended to the borderlands of India and into the steppes of central Asia. In another direction, Islam spread along Saharan and coastal trade routes into sub-Saharan Africa.

The salvation religions spread in different ways. The obvious way for a religion to spread is through missionary activity, and missionaries did play a role in converting new populations to these faiths. Sometimes missionaries worked directly with common people, but even more effective was the practice of converting a local leader, whose people would then follow his lead. Such conversions could result from missionary work. But they also sometimes stemmed from diplomatic contacts, and, hence, they represented the moral aspect of a political alliance. War also frequently played a part in the spread of the salvation religions. Victory in battle could demonstrate the power of a new god, adding to political conversions of the type just discussed: Constantine himself converted after winning a battle under the sign of the Christian God. War could also lead to conquest and the gradual conversion of a subject population who recognized the advantages of aligning their religion with that of their new rulers.[2] Finally, religious beliefs often spread with trade: merchants carried their beliefs with them, and merchant communities established in distant lands could end up influencing the peoples with whom they traded. Conversely, merchants from lands that the salvation religions had not yet reached often found it advantageous to convert in order to facilitate contacts with merchants from lands to which the faith had already spread. All these methods were at work in this period, and by 1000 vast portions of the Afro-Eurasian world were divided among the four major salvation religions, at the expense of numerous local religious traditions.

But just as local beliefs affected the form that baseball took in Japan, local beliefs did not simply disappear in the face of the new faiths but shaped their reception and form in a variety of ways. One important result was syncretism, or the blending of beliefs. Whether it was the cross-fertilization of Chinese Taoism with Buddhism when the latter reached the Middle Kingdom, the incorporation of pagan midwinter festivals (and tree-decorating rituals) into the timing and form of the celebration of Christ's birthday in the Christian calendar of religious festivals, or the emergence of Persian as the second literary language of the Islamic world, the salvation religions adopted attributes of prior belief systems and cultures, molding those beliefs to their central doctrinal messages and adapting their message and practice to local ways.

The result of this process of syncretism was twofold and, in some ways, apparently contradictory. First, syncretism certainly made the expansion of the salvation religions easier and so contributed to the creation of large cultural worlds connected by their common faiths. Buddhist monks traveled from Japan and China to India and southeast Asia, Christian bishops corresponded with and visited with their colleagues from Norway to Constantinople, and Muslim merchants traveled from Spain to Afghanistan, while pilgrims came from Ghana to Mecca. A common religion made such contacts both desirable and more readily possible.

Yet precisely because syncretism operated at the level of sometimes very local or regional cultures, it also produced a host of local variations on the central themes of the salvation religions. Korean Buddhism was not exactly the same as Chinese Buddhism; the armed Buddhist monks of some Japanese religious houses looked odd to both. Irish monasticism differed in organization from Italian monasticism; on a larger scale, western, Latin-based Christianity came to differ in a number of notable ways from eastern, Greek-based Christianity. Similarly, the division between Sunni and Shia variants of Islam, though dating ideologically to early in the religion's history, showed up most clearly in the widespread adoption of Shiism in Persia, the one area of the new Muslim empire not dominated by Arabs. As these cases show, religious difference in the worlds of the salvation religions could express political and cultural differences that the uniformity of faith had masked. The doctrinal structure of the religions affected the form of this sort of religious identity formation. For example, Buddhism, with no central text or single authoritative religious leader, divided into numerous sects. Meanwhile, Christianity, with its almost legalistically defined creed, struggled instead with heresies encompassed within a broad Christian denomination. But the underlying principle remained the same—that religions adapted to cultures and cultures to religions—and was one result of the wide spread of the salvation religions to very different cultural areas.

We examine these issues through a variety of texts. The spread of Buddhism to China is presented through two texts. The first is known as *The Disposition of Error.* Exact information about the author and date of this document is lacking, but from internal evidence it has been dated to the fifth century CE. It comes from southern China, and it presents Buddhist answers in response to Confucian and traditionalist objections raised against the new religion. The main orientation of this text is to argue that Buddhism is consistent with traditional Chinese values and beliefs. The second source is called *The Platform Scripture of the Sixth Patriarch*. This document describes the process by which an important figure in Chinese Buddhism, the so-called Sixth Patriarch (or master) Hui-neng, was selected. *The Platform Scripture* derives from the meditational form of Buddhism, known as Ch'an in China and Zen in Japan. Meditational Buddhism emphasized an individual, mystical connection with the divine, and so this text shows a different side of the transmission of Buddhism to China. We stand on firmer ground in dating this text, which derives from around the time of Hui-neng's death in 713 CE.

The spread of Buddhism to Japan was very different from its diffusion into China. This was due in part to the fact that Japan was far less developed than China at that point and also to the related fact that the Japanese political system was less unified and sophisticated. As a result, Buddhism in Japan became entwined with the emergence of the imperial system and with Japanese cultural borrowing from China and Korea. These imported systems had to be reconciled with existing Japanese religious practices, known as Shinto. The best source on this process of transmission and transformation is the *Nihongi,* the semiofficial historical chronicle of Yamato Japan, which was finished in 720, and which we excerpt below.

The spread of Christianity is presented from two perspectives. The first is the story of the conversion to Roman Catholicism of the Franks, one of the main Germanic peoples of northwestern Europe in the centuries after the collapse of the Roman Empire in the west. The most significant event in this process was the conversion of their king, Clovis, in 496 CE. Clovis hesitated and resisted before converting. That saga is unfolded for us in Gregory of Tours' *History of the Franks*. Gregory (539–594) was one of the foremost churchmen of the region and a confidant of the Frankish kings of his time. His history undoubtedly bears some bias, but it is a generally reliable account of the conversion process in the rough world of western Europe.

Meanwhile, the story of the spread of Christianity—this time Greek Orthodox Christianity—in eastern Europe is detailed here through excerpts from a work known as the *Russian Primary Chronicle*. The *Primary Chronicle* is one of the most important historical sources for a region known as Kievan Rus'. This region was a loosely unified political and trading zone, stretching from the Baltic to the Black Sea, dating from the ninth to the thirteenth centuries. The leading political figure was the Grand Prince of Kiev (contemporary Kyiv). In the 980s, Vladimir was Grand Prince, and we excerpt here the discussion of the conversion process of Vladimir to Eastern Orthodoxy. The *Primary Chronicle* dates from the twelfth century, but it is based on chronicles compiled centuries earlier.

Finally, two sources demonstrate some of the issues of conversion and assimilation raised by the spread of Islam. *The Pact of Umar* shows early Islam's policy toward conquered people. Unlike the other texts in this chapter, *The Pact of Umar* describes how the dominant Muslim population dealt with a population that in many ways it did not want to see converted. Hence, it operates a bit like a photographic negative. By highlighting the ways that Muslims tried to stay separate from and dominant over the native Christian populations, it reveals the many different aspects of the conversion experience. The text itself is supposed to be a copy of a contract, or *dhimma*, from ca. 737 between the Caliph Umar (r. 634–644) and a Christian community in Syria. In reality, this text dates from somewhere in the early 800s, the false "backdating" serving to add authority and legitimacy to it.

An example of the cultural and religious differences that endure after a culture adopts a new, alien religion is available to us in Ibn Battuta's *Donation to Those Interested in Curiosities* (1355). Ibn Battuta (1304–1369) was one of the great travelers in world history before the modern era. His journeys carried him throughout the core Islamic territories of southwest Asia and north Africa and as far east as China. One of his last journeys was to Mali in west Africa, and he has left us a vivid description of the quite different Islamic culture that held sway in Mali, a description told from the perspective of traditional Islamic culture.

Thus this chapter has a number of themes, foremost of which is conversion encounters of different types and the resulting syncretism. That particular encounter theme allows us to deal with the historical experience out of which broad cultural worlds united by faith were created at the same time that religious differences appeared within these broad cultural worlds. The impact of this set of encounters on world history is immeasurable, affecting as it did the areas that adopted the spreading faiths, as well as the faiths themselves and their homelands. Imagining baseball played today under the conditions of Babe Ruth's day—no African American, Latin American, or Asian players, no international competitions such as the Olympics and the Little League World Series—only hints at the transformative impact of conversion encounters such as these.

CHAPTER QUESTIONS

1. In all these accounts, what characteristics of the salvation religions seem most important in their spread? What is their appeal to people encountering them for the first time? What explains the adaptability or appeal of a particular religion to a given culture (for example, why was Buddhism more attractive in China than in the Middle East)?

2. What sorts of resistance do the salvation religions meet among new populations? How do those opposed to the adoption of the new faiths argue against them? Can you identify any broad cultural factors behind this resistance?

3. In both their appeal and the reasons for resistance to them, what is the balance of spiritual and material factors (for example, the appeal of eternal salvation versus immediate political advantage)? Does one seem more important than the other? In what ways do spiritual and material factors complement each other?

4. All of these accounts are written from within the salvationist faiths. Do they seem biased in such a way as to be unreliable sources for the history of conversion encounters? How might we read such texts so as to account for such

bias—can we read between the lines and get closer to the truth of what happened, if necessary?

5. What is your reaction to these stories of conversion? Do the reasons for which people converted (or resisted conversion) strike you as compelling? How are these stories similar to or different from "conversion experiences" (religious or otherwise) that you are familiar with today?

THE SPREAD OF BUDDHISM
Buddhism in China

Mahayana Buddhism spread from its homeland in northern India along the trade routes of central Asia known as the Silk Road. When it spread to such areas and to Tibet, parts of southeast Asia, Korea, and Japan, it helped introduce writing and other characteristics of the sedentary societies in which it had arisen. In other words, it came wrapped in the prestige of "civilization" and often helped build political hierarchies in those places more complex than had existed before, all of which added to its spiritual appeal. When Buddhism reached China, however, it encountered an already established civilization with deeply rooted literary and intellectual traditions. In addition, the scholarly elite of China was somewhat hostile to "foreign" influence. On the other hand, in the troubled times that followed the fall of the Han dynasty in 220 CE, Buddhism's promise of a better hereafter proved powerful among common people, while some rulers of the regional dynasties that replaced the Han saw in Buddhism a way to buttress their authority. Finally, Chinese intellectuals looked to it as a new source for magical elixirs of longevity or immortality (a path down which Taoism had already traveled by this time) and of metaphysical speculation. Major translation projects were undertaken in the period 200–500, and knowledge of Buddhism spread through these texts and owing to the building of temples and the founding of Buddhist communities of monks.[3] By the 400s Buddhism had become established widely enough to cause concern among traditionalist Chinese, especially among the Confucian scholarly elite, and to provoke counterattacks in the form of government persecution in the north and of tracts attacking the faith in the south.

The first of the following texts, whose author and exact date of composition are unknown, takes the form of a Buddhist answer to some of the common lines of attack contained in such tracts.[4] From that internal evidence, and knowing something about the reaction against Buddhism in China, we can safely assert that it comes from southern China during the fifth century CE. In order to win the Chinese over to Buddhism, the followers of the new faith had to address, among other things, significant aspects of existing Chinese culture—for example, the importance of ancestor worship and of the five relationships of Confucianism. The author of the first text pursues one of the logical lines to take when recommending something new to a culture: He argues that the practice of Buddhism is compatible with traditional Chinese values and that the ideas in Buddhist texts are similar to those in the Chinese classics. Buddhism, he asserts, complements and extends Chinese cultural practices rather than contradicting them.

The second source, on the other hand, represents another path that Chinese Buddhists took in trying to establish the compatibility of their faith with the existing body of Chinese literature and culture. That alternative path was based in the Buddhist emphasis on individual enlightenment by means of meditation. Meditation and contemplation had been important practices in Buddhism since the Buddha himself attained enlightenment by meditating under a bo tree. In addition, a School of Meditation arose as one stream of Mahayana Buddhism, emphasizing meditation as the central path to enlightenment. Known as Ch'an in China and later as Zen in Japan, this school tended to discount the importance of texts in favor of practice and the direct transmission of the Buddhist Law from one master (or patriarch) to another. The foundational text for this school is *The Platform Scripture of the Sixth Patriarch*.[5] The Sixth Patriarch, Hui-neng (638–713), was the key figure in Ch'an Buddhism's rise to prominence as one of the most influential Buddhist schools in China. The text appears to be a lecture by Hui-neng recorded by one of his pupils and dates to the early eighth century, around or shortly after Hui-neng's death. Our selection covers Hui-neng's early career as a monk and his recognition by the Fifth Patriarch as the next in the line of transmission of the Law.

These two sources, then, embody two different understandings of Buddhism and also represent two alternative ways of transmitting and adapting complex ideas and value systems to new cultures, which is the theme of this chapter. Between these two texts, we get a glimpse into the variety and complexity of the conversion encounters between Buddhism and Chinese culture.

QUESTIONS TO CONSIDER

1. What objections are raised against Buddhism in *The Disposition of Error*? How do these objections reflect the values and worldview of classical Chinese culture?

2. What characteristics of Buddhism does Mou Tzu emphasize in order to make it appear acceptable to Chinese scholars? How does he use Lao Tzu's Taoism and other parts of Chinese culture to refute Confucian objections to Buddhism?

3. What is the central message of *The Platform Scripture*? How does it compare with the message of *The Disposition of Error*? Which text strikes you as more "intellectual," and why? How do you account for the difference?

4. What barriers to the spread of Buddhism are presented in these two texts? Why does the initiation of Hui-neng as Sixth Patriarch have to take place in secret? Are the objections to Buddhism based more on spiritual factors or on practical considerations?

5. If these barriers existed, why was Buddhism so successful in spreading to the Chinese cultural zone? What aspects of Buddhism seem similar to elements of the Chinese culture that existed at that time, Confucianism and Taoism in particular?

THE DISPOSITION OF ERROR

Mou Tzu

[The form of this text is a passage stating an objection to Buddhism followed by Mou Tzu's Buddhist response.]

The questioner said: If the way of the Buddha is the greatest and most venerable of ways, why did Yao, Shun, the Duke of Chou,* and Confucius not practice it? . . . You, sir, are fond of the *Book of Odes* and the *Book of History,*† and you take pleasure in rites and music. Why, then, do you love the way of Buddha and rejoice in outlandish arts? Can they exceed the Classics and commentaries and beautify the accomplishments of the sages?

Mou Tzu said: All written works need not necessarily be the words of Confucius, and all medicine does not necessarily consist of the formulae of [the famous physician] P'ien-ch'üeh. What accords with principle is to be followed, what heals the sick is good. The gentleman-scholar draws widely on all forms of good, and thereby benefits his character. . . . [Other sages are not mentioned in the Five Classics, yet are accepted.] How much less, then, may one reject the Buddha, whose distinguishing marks are extraordinary and whose superhuman powers know no bounds! How may one reject him and refuse to learn from him? . . .

The questioner said: Now of felicities there is none greater than the continuation of one's line, of unfilial conduct there is none worse than childlessness. The monks forsake wife and children, reject property and wealth. Some do not marry all their lives. How opposed this conduct is to felicity and filial piety! . . .

Mou Tzu said: Wives, children, and property are the luxuries of the world, but simple living and inaction are the wonders of the Way. Lao Tzu has said, "Of reputation and life, which is dearer? Of life and property, which is worth more?" . . . The monk practices the way and substitutes that for the pleasures of disporting himself in the world. He accumulates goodness and wisdom in exchange for the joys of wife and children.

The questioner said: The Buddhists say that after a man dies he will be reborn. I do not believe in the truth of these words. . . .

Mou Tzu said: . . . The spirit never perishes. Only the body decays. The body is like the roots and leaves of the five grains, the spirit is like the seeds and kernels of the five grains. When the roots and leaves come forth they inevitably die. But do the seeds and kernels perish? Only the body of one who has achieved the Way perishes. . . .

Someone said: If one follows the Way one dies. If one does not follow the Way one dies. What difference is there?

Source: From Mou Tzu in *The Disposition of Error* by DeBary, et al., *Sources of the Chinese Tradition,* 274–80. Copyright © 1960 Columbia University Press. Reprinted with permission.

*These were semilegendary early rulers of China, who were idealized by Confucian scholars as the founders and models of Chinese culture and good government.

†Two of the Five Classics, the core texts that Chinese Confucian culture was based on.

Mou Tzu said: You are the sort of person who, having not a single day of goodness, yet seeks a lifetime of fame. If one has the Way, even if one dies one's soul goes to an abode of happiness. If one does not have the Way, when one is dead one's soul suffers misfortune.

The questioner said: . . . You, sir, at the age of twenty learned the way of Yao, Shun, Confucius, and the Duke of Chou. But now you have rejected them, and instead have taken up the arts of the barbarians. Is this not a great error?

Mou Tzu said: . . . According to the Buddhist scriptures, above, below, and all around, all beings containing blood belong to the Buddha-clan. Therefore I revere and study these scriptures. Why should I reject the Way of Yao, Shun, Confucius, and the Duke of Chou? Gold and jade do not harm each other, crystal and amber do not cheapen each other. . . .*

The questioner said: Of those who live in the world, there is none who does not love wealth and position and hate poverty and baseness, none who does not enjoy pleasure and idleness and shrink from labor and fatigue. . . . But now the monks wear red cloth, they eat one meal a day, they bottle up the six emotions, and thus they live out their lives. What value is there in such an existence?

Mou Tzu said: "Wealth and rank are what a man desires, but if he cannot obtain them in a moral way, he should not enjoy them. Poverty and meanness are what a man hates, but if he can only avoid them by departing from the Way, he should not avoid them."† Lao Tzu has said, "The five colors make men's eyes blind, the five sounds make men's ears deaf, the five flavors dull the palate, chasing about and hunting make men's minds mad, possessions difficult to acquire bring men's conduct to an impasse. The sage acts for his belly, not for his eyes." Can these words possibly be in vain? . . .

The questioner said: You, sir, say that the scriptures are like the rivers and the sea, their phrases like the brocade and embroidery. Why, then, do you not draw on the Buddhist scriptures to answer my questions? Why instead do you refer to the books of *Odes* and *History,* joining together things that are different to make them appear the same?

Mou Tzu said: . . . I have quoted those things, sir, which I knew you would understand. Had I preached the words of the Buddhist scriptures or discussed the essence of nonaction, it would have been like speaking to a blind man of the five colors or playing the five sounds to a deaf man.

The questioner said: The Taoists say that Yao, Shun, the Duke of Chou, and Confucius and his seventy two disciples did not die, but became immortals. The Buddhists say that men must all die, and that none can escape. What does this mean?

Mou Tzu said: Talk of immortality is superstitious and unfounded; it is not the word of the sages. Lao Tzu says, "Even Heaven and earth cannot be eternal. How much the less can man!" Confucius says, "The wise man leaves the world, but humanity and filial piety last forever." . . . I make the Classics and the commentaries my authorities and find my proof in the world of men. To speak of immortality, is this not a great error?

---

*One valuable thing does not reduce the worth of another valuable thing.

†*Analects* IV, 5.

THE PLATFORM SCRIPTURE
OF THE SIXTH PATRIARCH

[The Fifth Patriarch] asked Hui-neng: "Whence have you come to pay homage to me? What do you want from me?"

Hui-neng answered: "Your disciple is from Lingnan ["South of the Mountain Ranges," in the region of present Canton]. A citizen of Hang-chou, I have come a great distance to pay homage, without seeking anything except the Law of the Buddha."

The Great Master reproved him, saying: "You are from Lingnan and, furthermore, you are a barbarian. How can you become a Buddha?"

Hui-neng answered: "Although people are distinguished as northerners and southerners, there is neither north nor south in Buddha-nature. In physical body, the barbarian and the monk are different. But what is the difference in their Buddha-nature?"

The Great Master intended to argue with him further, but, seeing people around, said nothing. Hui-neng was ordered to attend to duties among the rest. It happened that one monk went away to travel. Thereupon Hui-neng was ordered to pound rice, which he did for eight months.

One day the Fifth Patriarch [Hung-jen] suddenly called all his pupils to come to him. As they assembled, he said: "Let me say this to you. Birth and death are serious matters. You people are engaged all day in making offering [to the Buddha], going after blessings and rewards only, and you make no effort to achieve freedom from the bitter sea of life and death. Your self-nature seems to be obscured. How can blessings save you? Go to your rooms and examine yourselves. He who is enlightened use his perfect vision of self-nature and write me a verse. When I look at his verse, if it reveals deep understanding, I shall give him the robe and the Law and make him the Sixth Patriarch. Hurry, hurry!"

At midnight Shen-hsui, holding a candle, wrote a verse on the wall of the south corridor, without anyone knowing about it, which said:

Our body is the tree of Perfect Wisdom,
And our mind is a bright mirror.
At all times diligently wipe them,
So that they will be free from dust.

The Fifth Patriarch said: "The verse you wrote shows some but not all understanding. You have arrived at the front door but you have not entered it. Ordinary people, by practicing in accordance with your verse, will not degenerate. But it will be futile to seek the Supreme Perfect Wisdom while holding to such a view. One must enter the door and see his self-nature. Go away and come back after one or two days of thought. If you have entered the door and seen your self-nature, I shall give you the robe and the Law."

Source: From *The Platform Scripture of the Sixth Patriarch* by DeBary, et al., *Sources of the Chinese Tradition,* 350–52. Copyright © 1960 Columbia University Press. Reprinted with permission.

Shen-hsui went away and for several days could not produce another verse. Hui-neng also wrote a verse . . . which says:

The tree of Perfect Wisdom is originally no tree.
Nor has the bright mirror any frame.
Buddha-nature is forever clear and pure.
Where is there any dust?

Another verse:

The mind is the tree of Perfect Wisdom.
The body is the clear mirror.
The clear mirror is originally clear and pure.
Where has it been affected by any dust?

Monks in the hall were all surprised at these verses. Hui-neng, however, went back to the rice-pounding room. The Fifth Patriarch suddenly realized that Hui-neng was the one of good knowledge but was afraid to let the rest learn it. He therefore told them: "This will not do." The Fifth Patriarch waited till midnight, called Hui-neng to come to the hall, and expounded the *Diamond Sutra*.* As soon as Hui-neng heard this, he understood. That night the Law was imparted to him without anyone knowing it, and thus the Law and the robe [emblematic] of Sudden Enlightenment were transmitted to him. "You are now the Sixth Patriarch," said the Fifth Patriarch to Hui-neng.

The Fifth Patriarch told Hui-neng: "From the very beginning, the transmission of the Law has been as delicate as a hanging thread of silk. If you remain here, someone might harm you. You had better leave quickly."

[Hui-neng, having returned South, said]: "I came and stayed in this place [Canton] and have not been free from persecution by government officials, Taoists, and common folk. The doctrine has been transmitted down from past sages; it is not my own idea. Those who wish to hear the teachings of the past sages should purify their hearts. Having heard them, they should first free themselves from their delusions and then attain enlightenment."

Buddhism in Japan

Japan before 500 CE consisted of a mass of farmers living at a Neolithic (late Stone Age) level—little better than mud huts—and ruled over by the powerful men of a set of aristocratic clans. Japanese belief centered on Shinto, the native Japanese religious tradition. Shinto is animist, seeing gods or spirits throughout the natural world, as in trees and streams. As the traditional and very ancient Japanese belief system, it lacked either a central text or a founder. Its religious practices emphasized rituals, prayers, and shrines.

---

*The "Diamond Sutra," so called because it could cut like a diamond through any obstacle on the path to enlightenment, was one of the most popular of Mahayana texts, especially in the Ch'an school, because of its discussion of the nature of reality, illusion, and perception.

Around 500, though, a wave of immigrants and cultural influence from the Korean kingdom of Paekche entered Japan from the southwest, bringing with it new technology for metal weapons. The influx stimulated the rise of a new Japanese state, the Kingdom of Yamato, centered on modern-day Osaka, and further militarized the aristocratic clans. The key elements of this wave of cultural borrowing were Chinese writing, Confucianism (the first Confucian scholar came to Yamato in 513), and Buddhism. Buddhism arrived in force in 552 when Paekche sent an image of the Buddha, some scriptures, and a Buddhist priest to the Yamato court with which it was allied. All these elements entered at the instigation of the Yamato kings, who sought to use them as tools to strengthen and centralize their rule against the resistance of the clan-based aristocracy.

This process heightened in the reign of the Empress Suiko (r. 592–628) and her regent Prince Shotoku (573–621). Prince Shotoku was a devout Buddhist who consciously imported T'ang Chinese models of government in reaction to the breakdown of the Paekche alliance and growing armed aristocratic resistance. He wrote a constitution for the Japanese government that was largely Confucian in its principles but the second article of which required devotion to Buddhism on the part of Japan's rulers. Finally, a coup against Shotoku and his Soga clan brought to power Kotoku Tenno, or "The Divine Emperor" Kotoku, in 645. His reforms, sponsored by Confucians and Buddhists at the Imperial Court, represent the true birth of the Japanese imperial government and the incorporation of the clans and their aristocrats into centralized rule.

This history is recounted in the *Nihongi*, a semiofficial history of Yamato Japan completed in 720. It emphasized both the divine origins of the imperial family and the part of Buddhism in the construction of the imperial system. The establishment of Buddhism in Japan, then, was inseparable from the emergence of centralized, imperial authority, and the following source deals with the twinned processes by which imperial authority and Buddhism were promoted. Moreover, it demonstrates that Buddhism and Shintoism could coexist, each contributing to the authority and legitimacy of the emperor, as Shinto elements appear in the text in the references to gods, plagues, and demons. Thus the encounter between Buddhism and the Japanese system was very different from the Chinese encounter with Buddhism.

QUESTIONS TO CONSIDER

1. How is Buddhism displayed at the Japanese Imperial Court? Given the opposition of the aristocratic clans to imperial power, what functions might such displays have played in the system of government?

2. How do the edicts on the organization of Buddhism in Japan relate to the edicts on other aspects of government? Why would the emperor mix reforms of the organization of Buddhism in with control of the country in terms of censuses, tax collection, land use, and the other issues presented here?

3. Despite the text's assertion that Kotoku "despised the Way of the Gods" (that is, Shinto), how does he in fact appeal to both Shinto and Buddhist religious traditions in explaining his reforms? How do the two traditions complement each other?

4. How does the coming of Buddhism to Japan compare with its arrival in China? Does the process of transmission to Japan seem easier and less contested than what occurred in China? What differences seem most important to you, and how do you explain them?

5. What role do spiritual factors play in the conversion encounter between Buddhism and Japanese culture, according to the material in this text? What part do practical considerations of government and political power play? How are tangible aspects of art and culture used to root Buddhism in Japanese society?

NIHONGI, BOOK XXV

The Emperor [Kotoku] honored the religion of Buddha and despised the Way of the Gods* (as is instanced by his cutting down the trees of [a sacred] shrine). He was of a gentle disposition, and loved men of learning. He made no distinction of noble and mean, and continually dispensed beneficent edicts.

. . .

The Emperor . . . summoned together the Ministers under the great tsuki tree, and made an oath appealing to the gods of Heaven and Earth, and saying:

"Heaven covers us: Earth upbears us: the Imperial way is but one. But in this last degenerate age, the order of Lord and Vassal was destroyed, until Supreme Heaven by Our hands put to death the traitors. Now, from this time forward, both parties shedding their hearts' blood, the Lord will eschew double methods of government, and the Vassal will avoid duplicity in his service of the sovereign! On him who breaks this oath, Heaven will send a curse and earth a plague, demons will slay them, and men will smite them. This is as manifest as the sun and moon."

. . .

(645 CE) . . . 1st year, Autumn, 8th month, 5th day. Governors of the Eastern provinces were appointed. Then the Governors were addressed as follows: "In accordance with the charge entrusted to Us by the gods of Heaven, We propose at this present for the first time to regulate the myriad provinces.

"When you proceed to your posts, prepare registers of all the free subjects of the State and of the people under the control of others, whether great or small. Take account also of the acreage of cultivated land. As to the profits arising from the gardens and ponds, the water and land, deal with them in common with the people.

Source: W. G. Ashton, "Nihongi: Chronicle of Japan from the Earliest Times to AD 697," *Transactions and Proceedings of the Japan Society, London,* supplement i (1896). References to AD have been changed to CE for clarity and consistency.

*Shinto.

Moreover, it is not competent for the provincial Governors, while in their provinces, to decide criminal cases, nor are they permitted by accepting bribes to bring the people to poverty and misery. . . .

"Moreover, on waste pieces of ground let arsenals be erected, and let the swords and armor, with the bows and arrows of the provinces and districts, be deposited together in them. . . .

"You Governors of provinces, take careful note of this and withdraw. Accordingly presents were made them of silk and cloth, which varied in the case of each person." . . .

8th day. A messenger was sent to the Great Temple to summon together the Buddhist priests and nuns, and to address them on the part of the Emperor, saying: "In [552], [the] King of Pekche* reverently transmitted the Law of Buddha to our great Yamato. At this time the Ministers in a body were opposed to its transmission. Only Soga no Iname no Sukune believed in this Law, and the Emperor accordingly instructed him to receive it with reverence. In the reign of the [next] Emperor . . . , Soga no Mumako no Sukune, influenced by the reverence for his deceased father, continued to prize highly the doctrines of Buddha. But the other Ministers had no faith in it, and its institutes had almost perished when the Emperor instructed Mumako no Sukune reverently to receive this Law. In the reign of the Empress Suiko[†]. . . , Mumako no Sukune, on behalf of the Empress, made an embroidered figure of Buddha sixteen feet high and a copper image of Buddha sixteen feet high. He exalted the doctrine of Buddha and showed honor to its priests and nuns. It is Our desire anew to exalt the pure doctrine and brilliantly to promulgate great principles. We therefore appoint as professors the following ten persons, [names listed], chief priests of temples. We separately appoint [a priest], chief priest of the Temple of Kudara.[‡]

"Let these ten professors well instruct the priests in general in the practice of the teachings of [Buddha]. It is needful that they be made to comply with the Law. If there is a difficulty about repairing temples built by any from the Emperor down to [local magistrates], We will in all cases assist in doing so. We shall also cause Temple Commissioners and Chief Priests to be appointed, who shall make a circuit to all the temples, and having ascertained the actual facts respecting the priests and nuns, their male and female slaves, and the acreage of their cultivated lands, report all the particulars clearly to us."

19th day. Commissioners were sent to all the provinces to take a record of the total numbers of the people. The Emperor on this occasion made an edict, as follows: . . . "At the present time, the people are still few. And yet the powerful cut off portions of land and water and converting them into private ground, sell it to the people, demanding the price yearly. From this time forward the sale of land is not allowed. Let no man without due authority make himself a landlord, engrossing to himself that which belongs to the helpless."

The people were greatly rejoiced. . . .

---

*The easternmost of the three Korean kingdoms, allied during this time with the Japanese kingdom of Yamato.

†592 to 628.

‡The Imperial temple.

(CE 650.) Winter, 10th month. . . . In this month the construction was begun of an embroidery figure of Buddha sixteen feet in height. . . .

In this year, [an artist at the Imperial Court], in obedience to an Imperial order, carved one thousand images of Buddha.

(CE 651.) Winter, 12th month, last day. More than 2100 priests and nuns were invited to the Palace . . . , and made to read [Sutras].

That night over 2700 lights were lit in the courtyard of the Palace, and there were caused to be read [various] Sutras. . . .

THE SPREAD OF CHRISTIANITY
The Latin Church in Western Europe

Christianity spread slowly through the Roman Empire during the first and second centuries CE. By the end of the third century Christians constituted perhaps 10 percent of the population of the empire, concentrated mostly in cities, which made them more prominent in the more urbanized eastern empire than in the more rural west. But in 312, a general named Constantine, involved in a struggle for the throne, saw the Christian sign of the cross in the sky, accompanied by the message *in hoc signo vincet*—"under this sign you will conquer"—before a battle with his rivals. He won, and as emperor issued an Edict of Toleration ending the sporadic persecutions the new faith had suffered previously. He also promoted the religion, even presiding over the first council of all Christian bishops at Nicea in 324, where the fundamental Christian statement of belief, the Nicene Creed, was formulated. Eventually, he converted to Christianity. A century later, Christianity was the official religion of the empire, and a slim majority of the empire's population was now Christian.

Constantine had also founded a new capital city, which he immodestly named Constantinople, on the Bosporus straits separating Europe from Asia Minor; he also divided the administration of the empire into eastern and western halves based in Constantinople and Rome. In the course of the fourth and fifth centuries, the differences between the richer, more urbanized and Greek-speaking east and the poorer, more rural, Latin-speaking west grew more pronounced. Effective imperial government continued to be exercised from Constantinople, but it gradually fell apart in Rome. Incursions by various barbarian tribes, mostly of Germanic origin, contributed to the decline. The City, as Rome was called, was itself sacked in 410. The collapse of imperial government in the west and its continuance in the east would have profound consequences for the course of Christianity's conversion encounters in the two areas. We consider the Latin West first.

In the absence of effective systems of Roman imperial defense, Christianity in the west was forced to deal with the Germanic successor kingdoms that divided up Roman territory. Much energy and attention was focused on trying to convert these new groups to the faith. In their efforts at converting the Germanic successor states to their faith, the Christian leaders in the west had several advantages, all of which were rooted in the desire of most Germanic kings to imitate Roman ways as far as they could. Christianity could thus present itself as the faith of the Romans, connected to and conveying imperial prestige. In practical terms, it offered an urban-based system of organization that mirrored and reinforced the remains of Roman secular administration. The Catholic Church also controlled the clergy, which was the most significant literate group left in the west. On the other hand, Christianity faced competition from Roman and German pagans, who promoted their belief systems. Even more intense competition came from within Christianity itself, as various heresies spread in the politically weak and fragmented west.[6] It was in this context that one of the key conversion encounters of the period—that of the Franks—took place.

The Franks had become in the course of the fifth century one of the most powerful of the Germanic successor kingdoms. While some other Germanic rulers converted to Arianism, a Christian heresy, perhaps to distinguish themselves from their subject Roman populations, the Frankish kings remained pagan until 496, when their king Clovis converted to Catholic Christianity. This event was therefore a crucial turning point in the political and religious history of the medieval west, building an alliance between the Church and the Frankish state that benefited both sides. There are several accounts of Clovis's conversion, including this one by Gregory of Tours in his *History of the Franks*. Gregory (539–594) was a prominent churchman—as bishop of Tours he was the leading prelate in what had been Roman Gaul—and a representative of the old Roman aristocracy of the area. He was personally acquainted with several of the Frankish kings of his own day, and he wrote his history partly to flatter them. Despite this bias, he is generally a reliable, if somewhat naïve, chronicler.

Here, then, is another encounter between a salvation religion and a different cultural and religious system. The pagan and warrior ways of Clovis, as the leader of the Germanic Franks, are shown responding and ultimately going over to the new Catholic faith of the west. But note, as well, that Clovis embraces this religion on his own terms. As has been stated, one of the things that makes conversion encounters so interesting is the way that the receiving culture and the religious system adapt to each other.

QUESTIONS TO CONSIDER

1. What influences brought Christianity to Clovis's attention? What are the important features of the faith as they are presented to Clovis?
2. What is Clovis's initial reaction to what he learns of Christianity? Why do you think he reacts the way he does? What changes his mind?
3. How does Clovis's personal conversion connect with and influence the larger conversion of the Frankish ruling class? What are Clovis's doubts about this connection, and how are they dispelled? Do you think Gregory has given us the full story here?
4. Both early medieval Europe and Yamato Japan had an underdeveloped economy, a weak political structure, and the presence of a foreign imperial

tradition. How does Clovis's conversion compare with the coming of Buddhism to Japan in the *Nihongi*? Are the similarities or the differences more striking to you?

5. How important are practical considerations of military power and cultural sophistication to this conversion encounter? What role do purely spiritual considerations play? What is the relationship between spiritual and material forces in the conversion encounter between Christianity and Germanic Europe?

HISTORY OF THE FRANKS

Gregory Bishop of Tours

As Clovis often sent embassies to Burgundy, the maiden Clotilda was found by his envoys. And when they saw that she was of good bearing and wise, and learned that she was of the family of the king, they reported this to King Clovis, and he sent an embassy to [the Burgundian king] without delay asking her hand in marriage. And [the Burgundian king] was afraid to refuse, and surrendered her to the men, and they took the girl and brought her swiftly to the king. The king was very glad when he saw her, and married her. . . .

He had a first-born son by Queen Clotilda, and as his wife wished to consecrate him in baptism, she tried unceasingly to persuade her husband, saying: "The gods you worship are nothing, and they will be unable to help themselves or any one else. For the names you have given them are names of men and not of gods, as Saturn, who is declared to have fled in fear of being banished from his kingdom by his son; as Jove himself, the foul perpetrator of all shameful crimes, committing incest with men, mocking at his kinswomen, not able to refrain from intercourse with his own sister. . . . What could Mars or Mercury do? They are endowed rather with the magic arts than with the power of the divine name. But he ought to be worshipped who created by his word heaven and earth, the sea and all that is in them out of a state of nothingness, who made the sun shine, and adorned the heavens with stars, who filled the waters with creeping things, the earth with living things and the air with creatures that fly, at whose nod the earth is decked with growing crops, the trees with fruit, the vines with grapes, by whose hand mankind was created, by whose generosity all that creation serves and helps man whom he created as his own." But though the queen said this the spirit of the king was by no means moved to belief, and he said: "It was at the command of our gods that all things were created and came forth, and it is plain that your God has no power and, what is more, he is proven not to belong to the family of the gods." Meantime the faithful queen made her son ready for baptism; she gave command to adorn the church with hangings and curtains, in order that he who could not be moved by persuasion might be urged to belief by this mystery. The

Source: From Gregory Bishop of Tours, *History of the Franks,* trans. Ernest Brehaut, 38–41. Copyright © 1965 Columbia University Press. Reprinted with permission.

boy, whom they named Ingomer, died after being baptized, still wearing the white garments in which he became regenerate.* At this the king was violently angry, and reproached the queen harshly, saying: "If the boy had been dedicated in the name of my gods he would certainly have lived; but as it is, since he was baptized in the name of your God, he could not live at all." To this the queen said: "I give thanks to the omnipotent God, creator of all, who has judged me not wholly unworthy, that he should deign to take to his kingdom one born from my womb. My soul is not stricken with grief for his sake, because I know that, summoned from this world as he was in his baptismal garments, he will be fed by the vision of God."

After this she bore another son, whom she named Chlodomer at baptism; and when he fell sick, the king said: "It is impossible that anything else should happen to him than happened to his brother, namely, that being baptized in the name of your Christ, he should die at once." But through the prayers of his mother, and the Lord's command, he became well.

The queen did not cease to urge him to recognize the true God and cease worshipping idols. But he could not be influenced in any way to this belief, until at last a war arose with the Alamanni,† in which he was driven by necessity to confess what before he had of his free will denied. It came about that as the two armies were fighting fiercely, there was much slaughter, and Clovis's army began to be in danger of destruction. He saw it and raised his eyes to heaven, and with remorse in his heart he burst into tears and cried: "Jesus Christ, whom Clotilda asserts to be the son of the living God, who art said to give aid to those in distress, and to bestow victory on those who hope in thee, I beseech the glory of thy aid, with the vow that if thou wilt grant me victory over these enemies, and I shall know that power which she says that people dedicated in thy name have had from thee, I will believe in thee and be baptized in thy name. For I have invoked my own gods, but, as I find, they have withdrawn from aiding me; and therefore I believe that they possess no power, since they do not help those who obey them. I now call upon thee, I desire to believe thee, only let me be rescued from my adversaries." And when he said this, the Alamanni turned their backs, and began to disperse in flight. And when they saw that their king was killed, they submitted to the dominion of Clovis, saying: "Let not the people perish further, we pray; we are yours now." And he stopped the fighting, and after encouraging his men, retired in peace and told the queen how he had merit to win the victory by calling on the name of Christ. This happened in the fifteenth year of his reign.

Then the queen asked Remi, bishop of Rheims, to summon Clovis secretly, urging him to introduce the king to the word of salvation. And the bishop sent for him secretly and began to urge him to believe in the true God, maker of heaven and earth, and to cease worshipping idols, which could help neither themselves nor anyone else. But the king said: "I gladly hear you, most holy father; but there remains one thing: the people who follow me cannot endure to abandon their gods; but I shall go and speak to them according to your words." He met with his followers, but before he could speak the power of God anticipated him, and all the people cried out to-

---

*Received baptism.

†A Germanic tribe.

gether: "O pious king, we reject our mortal gods, and we are ready to follow the immortal God whom Remi preaches." This was reported to the bishop, who was greatly rejoiced, and bade them get ready the baptismal font. The squares were shaded with tapestried canopies, the churches adorned with white curtains, the baptistery set in order, the aroma of incense spread, candles of fragrant odor burned brightly, and the whole shrine of the baptistery was filled with a divine fragrance: and the Lord gave such grace to those who stood by that they thought they were placed amid the odors of paradise. And the king was the first to ask to be baptized by the bishop. Another Constantine advanced to the baptismal font. . . . And of his army more than 3000 were baptized.

The Greek Church in Eastern Europe

Unlike the western Church, which was forced to reach out to barbarian populations in order to survive, the eastern Church (known as Eastern Orthodoxy or the Orthodox Church) was sheltered behind the protection of late Roman imperial administration and sometimes saw barbarian invaders more as threats to its Christian population than as opportunities for converts. Heresy also became a problem in the east. For example, the populations of Syria and Egypt expressed their dissatisfaction with the dominance of Constantinople by adhering to Monophysitism, a heresy that denied Christ's humanity.[7] Eastern Orthodoxy's defensive mentality became stronger with the rise of Islam, which stripped away Syria and Egypt from the empire and put Byzantium (as the eastern empire after the rise of Islam is generally known) on the defensive militarily for centuries (see chapter 12). As a result of these influences, the Orthodox Church tended to view its Byzantine adherents as a new Chosen People. Therefore, it was slower than its western Catholic counterpart to develop strong missionary activity beyond the borders of the empire. Reinforcing this reluctance was the problem of what conversion to Orthodoxy meant politically to potential convert populations. In the fragmented west, conversion to Christianity often served as a marker of a group's achievement of political autonomy under the spiritual umbrella of the Church headed by the pope. In Byzantium, on the other hand, the subordination of the Church to the government and of the patriarch of Constantinople to the emperor implied that outside converts would also accept Byzantine political domination, a condition they were often reluctant to agree to. Only slowly did conversion to Orthodoxy become separated from subordination to Constantinople. Interestingly, these restrictions relaxed and Orthodox missionary activity increased after about 800, when the empire was no longer so desperately on the defensive.

Because Byzantium faced Islamic populations on its eastern borders, the main opportunities for conversion of pagan populations initially came in the west, among the Slavic peoples of the Balkan peninsula. The brothers Cyril and Methodius led this effort, inventing an alphabet for the writing of Slavic (the Cyrillic alphabet) so that the Gospels could be translated. The spread of Christianity to the Slavs achieved its greatest success in the 980s when the leading Russian prince, Vladimir, converted.[8] The region is usually referred to as Kievan Rus', and it was under the control of different members of a single princely family. Vladimir occupied the most prestigious and powerful position as Grand Prince of Kiev. Agriculture was the basis of the economy. The political unity of the area, however, was based on an extensive trading system that linked the Baltic and Black Seas via rivers and short overland portages between them. The trade system was known as the road "between the Variangians [Vikings] and the Greeks [Constantinople]." Thus Byzantium was the most important political, military, and economic power in the region.

The story of Vladimir's conversion comes from *The Russian Primary Chronicle*, a compilation of earlier chronicles from the principalities of Kiev and Novgorod that covers the years 850 to 1110 and probably first appeared shortly after 1110, though the earliest manuscript copy dates to several hundred years later. The *Primary Chronicle* undoubtedly overstates the military power of Vladimir, although he did enjoy some military success against the Byzantines. In essence, though, this source presents an accurate picture of the political, military, diplomatic, and cultural factors at work in the conversion encounter between Kievan Rus' and Eastern Orthodoxy. It also helps us appreciate the attraction and power of salvation religions in general, as Vladimir was going to convert to one of them. The only question was which one.

QUESTIONS TO CONSIDER

1. How did Vladimir first hear of Christianity? What was his motivation for looking further into the question of converting to one of the religions brought to his attention?

2. How does Vladimir go about deciding which religion to adopt? What features of Greek Orthodoxy appeal to him most when he finally decides? What is the role of culture in this process?

3. What is the relationship of Vladimir's conversion to the conversion of his people as a whole? How is this connection similar to and different from that between the conversion of Clovis and of the Franks as a whole? What do you think the conversion experience of the common people was, in these circumstances?

4. How does this conversion encounter in Russia compare with the one in Japan and the one in western Europe? In China? How does the active role of Byzantium in this encounter make a difference to the way it develops?

5. What is the role of military and diplomatic power in this conversion experience? How did marital politics play a part in the story? On the basis of this text, what do you think Vladimir's strongest motivation was for converting to Eastern Orthodoxy?

POVEST' VREMENNYKH LET: THE RUSSIAN PRIMARY CHRONICLE

987: Vladimir summoned together his vassals and the [Kiev] city elders, and said to them: "Behold, the Bulgars* came before me urging me to accept their religion [Islam]. Then came the Germans and praised their own faith [western Catholicism]; and after them came the Jews. Finally the Greeks appeared, criticizing all other faiths but commending their own, and they spoke at length, telling the history of the whole world from its beginning. Their words were artful, and it was wondrous to listen and pleasant to hear them. They preach the existence of another world. 'Whoever adopts our religion and then dies shall arise and live forever. But whosoever embraces another faith, shall be consumed with fire in the next world.' What is your opinion on this subject, and what do you answer?" The vassals and the elders replied: "You know, O Prince, that no man condemns his own possessions, but praises them instead. If you desire to make certain, you have servants at your disposal. Send them to inquire about the ritual of each and how he worships God." Their counsel pleased the prince and all the people, so that they chose good and wise men to the number of ten, and directed them to go first among the Bulgars and inspect their faith. The emissaries went their way, and when they arrived at their destination they beheld the disgraceful actions of the Bulgars and their worship in the mosque; then they returned to their own country. Vladimir then instructed them to go likewise among the Germans, and examine their faith, and finally to visit the Greeks. They thus went into Germany, and after viewing the German ceremonial, they proceeded to Constantinople where they appeared before the emperor. He inquired on what mission they had come, and they reported to him all that had occurred. When the emperor heard their words, he rejoiced, and did them great honor on that very day.

On the morrow, the emperor sent a message to the patriarch† to inform him that a Russian delegation had arrived to examine the Greek faith, and directed him to prepare the church and the clergy, and to array himself in his sacerdotal robes, so that the Russians might behold the glory of the God of the Greeks. When the patriarch received these commands, he bade the clergy assemble, and they performed the customary rites. They burned incense, and the choirs sang hymns. The emperor accompanied the Russians to the church,‡ and placed them in a wide space, calling their attention to the beauty of the edifice, the chanting, and the offices of the archpriest and the ministry of the deacons, while he explained to them the worship of his God. The

---

Source: Samuel H. Cross, "The Russian Primary Chronicle," *Harvard Studies and Notes in Philology and Literature*, 12 (1930), 170–177.

*An Islamic people, who occupied the lower reaches of the Volga River east of Kiev.

†The Patriarch of Constantinople, the head of the Orthodox Church.

‡Hagia Sophia, or the church of Divine Wisdom in Constantinople. It was the Byzantines' greatest cathedral, known for its size and its beautiful mosaics. After the conquest of Byzantium in 1453 by the Ottoman Turks, it was turned into an Islamic mosque.

Russians were astonished, and in their wonder praised the Greek ceremonial. Then the Emperors Basil and Constantine* invited the envoys to their presence, and said, "Go hence to your native country," and thus dismissed them with valuable presents and great honor. Thus they returned to their own country, and the prince called together his vassals and the elders. Vladimir then announced the return of the envoys who had been sent out, and suggested that their report be heard. He thus commanded them to speak out before his vassals. The envoys reported: "When we journeyed among the Bulgars, we beheld how they worship in their temple, called a mosque, while they stand ungirt. The Bulgarian bows, sits down, looks hither and thither like one possessed, and there is no happiness among them, but instead only sorrow and a dreadful stench. Their religion is not good. Then we went among the Germans, and saw them performing many ceremonies in their temples; but we beheld no glory there. Then we went on to Greece, and the Greeks led us to the edifices where they worship their God, and we knew not whether we were in heaven or on earth. For on earth there is no such splendor or such beauty, and we are at a loss how to describe it. We know only that God dwells there among men, and their service is fairer than the ceremonies of other nations. For we cannot forget that beauty. Every man, after tasting something sweet, is afterward unwilling to accept that which is bitter, and therefore we cannot dwell longer here." Then the vassals spoke and said, "If the Greek faith were evil, it would not have been adopted by your grandmother Olga, who was wiser than all other men." Vladimir then inquired where they should all accept baptism, and they replied that the decision rested with him.

After a year had passed, in 988, Vladimir marched with an armed force against Kherson,† a Greek city, and the people of Kherson barricaded themselves therein. Vladimir halted at the farther side of the city beside the bay, a bowshot from the town, and the inhabitants resisted energetically while Vladimir besieged the town. Eventually, however, they became exhausted, and Vladimir warned them that if they did not surrender, he would remain on the spot for three years. When they failed to heed this threat, Vladimir marshalled his troops and ordered the construction of an earthwork in the direction of the city. While this work was under construction, the inhabitants dug a tunnel under the city wall, stole the heaped-up earth, and carried it into the city, where they piled it up in the centre of the town. But the soldiers kept on building, and Vladimir persisted. Then a man of Kherson, Anastasius by name, shot into the Russian camp an arrow on which he had written: "There are springs behind you to the east, from which water flows in pipes. Dig down and cut them off." When Vladimir received this information, he raised his eyes to heaven and vowed that if this hope was realized, he would be baptized. He gave orders straightway to dig down above the pipes, and the water supply was thus cut off. The inhabitants were accordingly overcome by thirst, and surrendered.

Vladimir and his retinue entered the city, and he sent messages to the Emperors Basil and Constantine, saying: "Behold, I have captured your glorious city. I have also

---

*Basil II, "The Bulgar Slayer," who would conquer the Balkan Bulgars around 1114, and his brother Constantine VIII. Basil held the real power.

†Kherson was a Greek city on the Black Sea, the main trade connection between the Byzantine Empire and the Russian principalities.

heard that you have an unwed sister. Unless you give her to me to wife, I shall deal with your own city as I have with Kherson." When the emperors heard this message, they were troubled, and replied: "It is not meet for Christians to be given in marriage to pagans. If you are baptized, you shall have her to wife, inherit the kingdom of God, and be our companion in the faith. Unless you do so, however, we cannot give you our sister in marriage." When Vladimir learned their response, he directed the envoys of the emperors to report to the latter that he was willing to accept baptism, having already given some study to their religion, and that the Greek faith and ritual, as described by the emissaries sent to examine it, had pleased him well. When the emperors heard this report, they rejoiced, and persuaded their sister Anna to consent to the match. They then requested Vladimir to submit to baptism before they should send their sister to him, but Vladimir desired that the princess should herself bring priests to baptize him. The emperors complied with his request, and sent forth their sister, accompanied by some dignitaries and priests. Anna, however, departed with reluctance. "It is as if I were setting out into captivity," she lamented; "better were it for me to die here." But her brothers protested: "Through your agency God turns the Russian land to repentance, and you will relieve Greece from the danger of grievous war. Do you not see how much evil the Russians have already brought upon the Greeks? If you do not set out, they may bring on us the same misfortunes." It was thus that they overcame her hesitation only with great difficulty. The princess embarked upon a ship, and after tearfully embracing her kinfolk, she set forth across the sea and arrived at Kherson. The natives came forth to greet her, and conducted her into the city, where they settled her in the palace.

By divine agency, Vladimir was suffering at that moment from a disease of the eyes, and could see nothing, being in great distress. The princess declared to him that if he desired to be relieved of this disease, he should be baptized with all speed, otherwise it could not be cured. When Vladimir heard her message, he said, "If this proves true, then of a surety is the God of the Christians great," and gave order that he should be baptized. The Bishop of Kherson, together with the princess's priests, after announcing the tidings, baptized Vladimir, and as the bishop laid his hand upon him, he straightway received his sight. Upon experiencing this miraculous cure, Vladimir glorified God, saying, "I have now perceived the one true God." When his followers beheld this miracle, many of them were also baptized.

Vladimir was baptized in the Church of St. Basil, which stands at Kherson upon a square in the centre of the city, where the Khersonians trade. The palace of Vladimir stands beside this church to this day, and the palace of the princess is behind the altar. After his baptism, Vladimir took the princess in marriage. . . . As a wedding present for the princess, he gave Kherson over to the Greeks again, and then departed for Kiev.

When the prince arrived at his capital, he directed that the idols should be overthrown and that some should be cut to pieces and others burned with fire. . . .

Thereafter Vladimir sent heralds throughout the whole city to proclaim that if any inhabitant, rich or poor, did not betake himself to the river, he would risk the prince's displeasure. When the people heard these words, they wept for joy, and exclaimed in their enthusiasm, "If this were not good, the prince and his boyars would not have accepted it." On the morrow the prince went forth to the Dnepr with the priests of the princess and those from Kherson, and a countless multitude assembled. They all went into the water: some stood up to their necks, others to their breasts, the younger near the bank, some of them holding children in their arms, while the adults waded farther out. The priests stood by and offered prayers. There was joy in heaven and upon earth to behold so many souls saved. But the devil groaned, lamenting: "Woe is me! how am I driven out hence! For I thought to have my dwelling place here, since the apostolic teachings do not abide in this land. Nor did this people know God, but I rejoiced in the service they rendered unto me. But now I am vanquished by the ignorant, not by apostles and martyrs, and my reign in these regions is at an end."

When the people were baptized, they returned each to his own abode. Vladimir, rejoicing that he and his subjects now knew God himself, looked up to heaven and said: "O God, who hast created heaven and earth, look down, I beseech thee, on this thy new people, and grant them, O Lord, to know thee as the true God, even as the other Christian nations have known thee. Confirm in them the true and unalterable faith, and aid me, O Lord, against the hostile adversary, so that, hoping in thee and in thy might, I may overcome his malice." Having spoken thus, he ordained that churches should be built and established where pagan idols had previously stood. . . . He began to found churches and to assign priests throughout the cities, and to invite the people to accept baptism in all the cities and towns. He took the children of the best families, and sent them to schools for instruction in book learning.

THE SPREAD OF ISLAM
Conquest and Conversion in the Early Caliphate

Buddhism was born as a universal truth; the development of Mahayana Buddhism simply reinforced its message of salvation open to anyone. Its spread via conversion encounters was therefore an expression of its philosophy. Christianity started as a sect of Judaism, but Paul opened it to Gentiles, and it followed a universalist course thereafter (though the experience of Byzantium during its defensive centuries shows that a more exclusive notion of a "Chosen People" could still lurk in expressions of the faith). But Islam began, on the model of Judaism (from which it in part derived), as a faith for a particular people, the Arabs, despite its conception of Allah as the sole god of the universe. It developed a universalist mission of conversion more slowly, under the conditions of rapid and widespread conquest that installed Muslims as the rulers of large non-Muslim populations. What were Muslims to do about such populations?

Though there is scattered evidence for forced conversions, especially of non-Muslim Arabs, in the early stages of the conquest, forced conversion ended up being prohibited in the Qur'an. The prohibition reflected both a central tenet of the faith (that submission to Allah must be a voluntary, individual choice) and practical concerns about admitting non-Arabs to the faith and about maintaining the cultural distinction between conquerors and conquered. Arabs who wished to convert voluntarily presented little problem. But what of non-Arab populations who submitted to the political rule of Muslims but did not wish (or were not immediately invited) to convert?

A contract, or *dhimma,* that Muhammad himself had created in Arabia with a Jewish Arab tribe in 628 formed one model: The non-Muslims accepted the protection of the Muslims in return for freedom to practice their own faith, submission to Islamic rule, and payment of tribute. The form that tribute commonly came to assume was a poll tax. This was a tax on people, called a *jizya,* paid by the *dhimmis,* those under the protection of and bound by a *dhimma.* These contracts specified somewhat different restrictions and penalties in different places and times, but they shared broad common features. Perhaps the most famous is the source presented here, the *Pact of Umar,* which claims to be a *dhimma* of around 637 between the Caliph Umar (r. 634–644) and the Christians of Syria. In fact, it is a later, more developed form of the *dhimma* dating from the early 800s but backdated to legitimize it.

Though it is about populations that did not convert, *The Pact of Umar,* and other agreements like it, formed an important context for Islamic conversion encounters. For, although it recognized and tolerated the right of subject populations, especially of Christians and Jews,[9] to practice their religions—a level of toleration well beyond anything seen in Christian lands, it might be noted—it nevertheless placed restrictions and financial penalties on *infidels,* or unbelievers who had not submitted to Allah. These restrictions and penalties tended, over time, to encourage conversion, though it was not their intent. Conversion, after all, removed a source of income from the government, because those who converted no longer had to pay the poll tax. Another feature of such pacts should also be noted: They are made with communities of common people. Islamic powers made virtually no effort to convert the aristocracies of conquered populations, because they identified Persian and Roman aristocrats with the hostile, infidel imperial civilizations they had conquered. As a result, stories such as those of Clovis and Vladimir are almost nonexistent in early Islamic history, and conversion became a bottom-up phenomenon. Contracts such as *The Pact of Umar* are also the context for this feature of Islamic conversion encounters.

Hence what is presented here is the inverse of what we have seen so far. It is, in effect, a nonconversion encounter. In the way that Islamic authorities set subject, non-Islamic populations off from the dominant Islamic ruling peoples, they reveal the ways that they sought to prevent the subject peoples and cultures from influencing their culture and faith. They are implicitly recognizing what we have argued in this chapter, that conversion encounters involve mutual adaptation and evolution between the belief system and people converting to it.

QUESTIONS TO CONSIDER

1. What restrictions does the *Pact* put on nonbelievers? How onerous do they seem? Why do you think physical aspects of the separation of the non-Muslim community play such a prominent role in the *Pact?*
2. What provisions of the *Pact* seem to encourage conversion to Islam? What provisions seem to discourage it? What is the balance between the two, in your opinion?

3. What do you think the effect of the *Pact's* being aimed at essentially leaderless communities, rather than at groups under clearly recognized leaders, was in encouraging or discouraging conversion?

4. How do the conditions for conversions created and reflected in the *Pact* compare with those prevailing in Japan, western Europe, and Russia? Are they more like the conditions facing Buddhism in China? Why?

5. Taking the *Pact* as a whole, what role do practical political considerations play in setting the boundaries of conversion encounters between Islam and its subject populations? What role do spiritual factors play?

THE PACT OF UMAR

In the name of God, the Merciful and Compassionate. This is a writing* to 'Umar b. al-Khattab from the Christians of such-and-such a city. When you marched against us, we asked of you protection for ourselves, our posterity, our possessions, and our co-religionists; and we made this stipulation† with you

That we will not erect in our city or the suburbs any new monastery, church, [monk's] cell or hermitage.

That we will not repair any of such buildings that may fall into ruins, or renew those that may be situated in the Muslim quarters of the town.

That we will not refuse the Muslims entry into our churches either by night or by day.

That we will open the gates wide to passengers and travelers.

That we will receive any Muslim traveler into our houses and give him food and lodging for three nights.

That we will not harbor any spy in our churches or houses, or conceal any enemy of the Muslims.

That we will not teach our children the Qur'an.

That we will not make a show of the Christian religion nor invite anyone to embrace it.‡

That we will not prevent any of our kinsmen from embracing Islam, if they so desire.

That we will honor the Muslims and rise up in our assemblies when they wish to take their seats.

That we will not imitate them in our dress, either in the cap, turban, sandals, or parting of the hair.

That we will not make use of their expressions of speech,§ nor adopt their surnames.

Source: T. W. Arnold, trans., *The Preaching of Islam*, 2nd ed. (London, 1913), 57–59. Some of the punctuation and formatting has been changed for clear presentation here.

*Letter.

†Commitment.

‡Try to convert anyone.

§That is, use Qur'anic verses to greet one another.

That we will not ride on saddles, or gird on swords, or take to ourselves arms or wear them.

Or engrave Arabic inscriptions on our rings.*

That we will not sell wines.†

That we will shave the front of our heads.

That we will keep to our own style of dress, wherever we may be. That we will wear girdles round our waists.‡

That we will not display the cross upon our churches or display our crosses or our sacred books in the streets of the Muslims or in their marketplaces.

That we will strike the bells in our churches lightly.

That we will not recite our services in a loud voice when a Muslim is present.

That we will not carry palm branches or our images in procession in the streets.

That at the burial of our dead we will not chant loudly or carry lighted candles in the streets of the Muslims or their market places.

That we will not take slaves that have already been in the possession of Muslims, nor spy into their houses.

And that we will not strike any Muslim.

All this we promise to observe, on behalf of ourselves and our co-religionists, and receive protection from you in exchange. And if we violate any of the conditions of this agreement, then we forfeit your protection and you are at liberty to treat us as enemies and rebels.

Travel, Trade, and Conversion in the Islamic World

After the initial explosion of Muslim conquests had subsided, expansion of the community of Islam occurred mainly along trade routes. Islamic rulers were generally friendly to merchant activity, and the central position of Islam among the great Afro-Eurasian civilizations made it a crossroads of lucrative trade routes. Non-Muslim merchants, therefore, often saw conversion to Islam as a way to increase their connections to this valuable world of trade. Although merchant communities did not consistently lead the rest of their society into converting, their own conversion allowed them to stand in two worlds, that of their original culture and that of the wider world of Islam.

That wider world encouraged travel in other ways as well, fostering both conversion encounters and cultural encounters of the converted. The duty of pilgrimage to Mecca laid upon Muslims in the Qur'an fostered travel; common faith and the common Arab tongue in which that faith was learned and expressed facilitated communication across diverse cultures. Yet the cultural differences that survived and colored the various conversion encounters that expanded the Islamic world persisted under the commonalities, to be discovered and navigated by travelers within Islam.

---

*For use as seals, for correspondence and legal documents.

†Consumption of alcohol is prohibited in Islam.

‡A belt of leather; Muslims wore silk sashes.

One of the most famous of such travelers is Ibn Battuta (1304–1369). Born into the scholarly elite of Morocco in northern Africa, he studied Islamic law and in his twenties began a series of travels, prompted first by pilgrimages to Mecca, that took him throughout southwest Asia, India (where he served as an Islamic judge for eight years), southeast Asia, and even China (see chapter 15). Finally, late in his traveling career, he crossed the Sahara to the kingdom of Mali in west Africa. On his return he dictated an account of his many travels. His *Donation to Those Interested in Curiosities* became one of the most popular examples of the Islamic genre of travel literature. If the previous sources in this chapter have explored the process of conversion, this account gives a glimpse of the cultural aftermath of conversion, both the links created between diverse cultures by a common faith and the differences that remain despite these common links. Read it, if you will, as an account by an American baseball fan of attending a game in Japan.

QUESTIONS TO CONSIDER

1. What seems familiar to Ibn Battuta in Mali? That is, what connections has Islam forged for him that transcend particular cultures?
2. What seems strange or unfamiliar to him? That is, what practices, customs, or beliefs color the local varieties of Islam in ways that surprise him, and what aspects of local culture remain apparently untouched by Islam?
3. Are there aspects of Mali's culture that Battuta finds apparently familiar but that from our perspective look like his misunderstandings? What does he approve of and disapprove of (as opposed to finding familiar or not)?
4. How do Battuta's experiences in Mali resemble the experiences of Buddhists in China?
5. How deeply do you think conversion to Islam affected the culture and people of Mali?

A DONATION TO THOSE INTERESTED IN CURIOSITIES

Ibn Battuta

Thus I reached the city of Malli [Mali], the capital of the king of the blacks. I stopped at the cemetery and went to the quarter occupied by the whites,* where I asked for Muhammad ibn al-Faqih. I found that he had hired a house for me and went there. His son-in-law brought me candles and food, and next day Ibn al-Faqih himself came

Source: Ibn Battuta, *Travels in Asia and Africa 1325–1354,* tr. and ed. H. A. R. Gibb (London: Broadway House, 1929), 323–35.
*North African Arabs and Berber merchants.

to visit me, with other prominent residents. I met the qadi* of Malli, 'Abd ar-Rahman, who came to see me; he is a negro, a pilgrim, and a man of fine character. I met also the interpreter Dugha, who is one of the principal men among the blacks. All these persons sent me hospitality—gifts of food and treated me with the utmost generosity—may God reward them for their kindnesses!

. . .

The sultan of Malli is Mansa Sulayman,† "mansa" meaning sultan, and Sulayman being his proper name. He is a miserly king, not a man from whom one might hope for a rich present. It happened that I spent these two months without seeing him, on account of my illness. Later on he held a banquet in commemoration of our master Abu'l-Hasan,‡ to which the commanders, doctors, qadi and preacher were invited, and I went along with them. Reading-desks were brought in, and the Koran was read through, then they prayed for our master Abu'l-Hasan and also for Mansa Sulayman.

. . .

On certain days the sultan holds audiences in the palace yard, where there is a platform under a tree, with three steps; this they call the "pempi." It is carpeted with silk and has cushions placed on it. [Over it] is raised the umbrella, which is a sort of pavilion made of silk, surmounted by a bird in gold, about the size of a falcon. The sultan comes out of a door in a corner of the palace, carrying a bow in his hand and a quiver on his back. On his head he has a golden skull-cap, bound with a gold band which has narrow ends shaped like knives, more than a span in length. His usual dress is a velvety red tunic, made of the European fabrics called "mutanfas." The sultan is preceded by his musicians, who carry gold and silver guimbris,§ and behind him come three hundred armed slaves. He walks in a leisurely fashion, affecting a very slow movement, and even stops from time to time. On reaching the pempi he stops and looks round the assembly, then ascends it in the sedate manner of a preacher ascending a mosque-pulpit. As he takes his seat the drums, trumpets, and bugles are sounded. Three slaves go out at a run to summon the sovereign's deputy and the military commanders, who enter and sit down. Two saddled and bridled horses are brought, along with two goats, which they hold to serve as a protection against the evil eye. Dugha stands at the gate and the rest of the people remain in the street, under the trees.

The negroes are of all people the most submissive to their king and the most abject in their behaviour before him. They swear by his name, saying "Mansa Sulayman ki".** If he summons any of them while he is holding an audience in his pavilion, the person summoned takes off his clothes and puts on worn garments, removes his turban and dons a dirty skullcap, and enters with his garments and trousers raised knee-high. He goes forward in an attitude of humility and dejection and knocks the ground hard with his elbows, then stands with bowed head and bent back listening to what he says. If anyone addresses the king and receives a reply from him, he uncovers his

---

*Religious judge, the position Battuta had held in India.
†Ruled Mali 1341–1360.
‡The late sultan of Morocco, ruled 1331–1351.
§Two-stringed guitars.
**"The emperor Sulayman has commanded."

back and throws dust over his head and back, for all the world like a bather splashing himself with water. I used to wonder how it was they did not blind themselves. If the sultan delivers any remarks during his audience, those present take off their turbans and put them down, and listen in silence to what he says.

Sometimes one of them stands up before him and recalls his deeds in the sultan's service, saying, "I did so-and-so on such a day," or, "I killed so-and-so on such a day." Those who have knowledge of this confirm his words, which they do by plucking the cord of the bow and releasing it [with a twang], just as an archer does when shooting an arrow. If the sultan says, "Truly spoken," or thanks him, he removes his clothes and "dusts." That is their idea of good manners.

. . .

I was at Malli during [Ramadan].* On these days the sultan takes his seat on the pempi after the mid-afternoon prayer. The armor-bearers bring in magnificent arms— quivers of gold and silver, swords ornamented with gold and with golden scabbards, gold and silver lances, and crystal maces. At his head stand four amirs driving off the flies, having in their hands silver ornaments resembling saddle-stirrups. The commanders, qadi and preacher sit in their usual places.

The interpreter Dugha comes with his four wives and his slave-girls, who are about a hundred in number. They are wearing beautiful robes, and on their heads they have gold and silver fillets, with gold and silver balls attached. A chair is placed for Dugha to sit on. He plays on an instrument made of reeds, with some small calabashes at its lower end, and chants a poem in praise of the sultan, recalling his battles and deeds of valor. The women and girls sing along with him and play with bows. Accompanying them are about thirty youths, wearing red woolen tunics and white skullcaps; each of them has his drum slung from his shoulder and beats it. Afterwards come his boy pupils who play and turn wheels in the air. . . . They show a marvellous nimbleness and agility in these exercises and play most cleverly with swords. Dugha also makes a fine play with the sword. Thereupon the sultan orders a gift to be presented to Dugha and he is given a purse containing two hundred mithqals[†] of gold dust and is informed of the contents of the purse before all the people. The commanders rise and twang their bows in thanks to the sultan. The next day each one of them gives Dugha a gift, every man according to his rank. Every Friday after the [afternoon] prayer, Dugha carries out a similar ceremony to this that we have described.

On feast-days after Dugha has finished his display, the poets come in. Each of them is inside a figure resembling a thrush, made of feathers, and provided with a wooden head with a red beak, to look like a thrush's head. They stand in front of the sultan in this ridiculous make-up and recite their poems. I was told that their poetry is a kind of sermonizing in which they say to the sultan: "This pempi which you occupy was that whereon sat this king and that king, and such and such were this one's noble actions and such and such the other's. So do you too do good deeds whose memory will outlive you." After that the chief of the poets mounts the steps of the pempi and lays his head on the sultan's lap, then climbs to the top of the pempi and lays his head first on the sultan's right shoulder and then on his left, speaking all the while in their

---

*The Muslim month of fasting from sunrise to sunset.

†One *mithqal* equals 4.72 grams of gold.

tongue, and finally he comes down again. I was told that this practice is a very old custom amongst them, prior to the introduction of Islam, and that they have kept it Up.

. . .

The negroes possess some admirable qualities. They are seldom unjust, and have a greater abhorrence of injustice than any other people. Their sultan shows no mercy to anyone who is guilty of the least act of it. There is complete security in their country. Neither traveler nor inhabitant in it has anything to fear from robbers or men of violence. They do not confiscate the property of any white man who dies in their country, even if it be uncounted wealth. On the contrary, they give it into the charge of some trustworthy person among the whites, until the rightful heir takes possession of it. They are careful to observe the hours of prayer, and assiduous in attending them in congregations, and in bringing up their children to them.

. . .

On Fridays, if a man does not go early to the mosque, he cannot find a corner to pray in, on account of the crowd. It is a custom of theirs to send each man his boy [to the mosque] with his prayer-mat; the boy spreads it out for his master in a place befitting him [and remains on it] until he comes to the mosque. Their prayer-mats are made of the leaves of a tree resembling a date-palm, but without fruit.

Another of their good qualities is their habit of wearing clean white garments on Fridays. Even if a man has nothing but an old worn shirt, he washes it and cleans it, and wears it to the Friday service. Yet another is their zeal for learning the Koran by heart. They put their children in chains if they show any backwardness in memorizing it, and they are not set free until they have it by heart. I visited the qadi in his house on the day of the festival. His children were chained up, so I said to him, "Will you not let them loose?" He replied, "I shall not do so until they learn the Koran by heart."

. . .

Among their bad qualities are the following. The women servants, slave-girls, and young girls go about in front of everyone naked, without a stitch of clothing on them. Women go into the sultan's presence naked and without coverings, and his daughters also go about naked. Then there is their custom of putting dust and ashes on their heads, as a mark of respect, and the grotesque ceremonies we have described when the poets recite their verses. Another reprehensible practice among many of them is the eating of carrion, dogs, and asses.

NOTES

1. "Losing face" is the term for the shame and humiliation that Japanese associate with failure in competition.
2. It should be noted that religion could also, however, provide a motive for continued resistance to a conqueror.
3. An example of the difficulty and complexity of transmitting religious ideas and beliefs to different cultures is the translation of Buddhist texts into Chinese. Translation is always difficult, but it was made especially so in China, owing to the ideographic Chinese

writing system. Hence, Indian concepts and terms could not easily be transliterated (represented merely by its sounds, with meaning to be filled in by context) but had to be represented in terms of analogous Chinese concepts.

4. The attribution of the text to "Mou Tzu" is traditional, but nothing is known about such an individual.

5. It is a nice Zen paradox that a school that deemphasizes texts has its own foundational text.

6. Heresies were versions of Christian belief different from the Catholic, or "universal," faith approved by the official Church hierarchy.

7. *Monophysite* means "one nature." That is, they held that Christ was God, but not man.

8. The terms "Russian" and "Russia" have to be used advisedly, because the people were organized in clans and tribes and had no consciousness of being "Russian." In fact, the territory of this region is now divided between Russia, Ukraine, and Belarus, and Vladimir's capital, Kiev, is now called Kyiv and is the capital of Ukraine.

9. For Muslims, "People of the Book" are all those who share the books of revealed truth from God—Muslims, Christians, and Jews. Of course, Muslims believe that God's final revelation was given to Muhammad.

CHAPTER 10

The Artist Encounters Life

Literature and Social Values

INTRODUCTION

In a famous formulation, Supreme Court Justice Potter Stewart asserted, "I shall not today attempt further to define . . . [pornography] . . . but I know it when I see it." Justice Stewart was trying to distinguish between art and pornography, and his statement echoes the common American assertion that "I don't know art, but I know what I like." In the same way that the Supreme Court found Justice Stewart's formulation inadequate to the task of defining pornography—the issues of free speech proved too thorny—the common attempt to reduce arguments about art to issues of aesthetics (the study of the beautiful) has not really succeeded in defining art. Art and its role in human society is simply too complex an issue to sum up adequately in the saying "Beauty is in the eye of the beholder." One reason for this is that beauty is not the only dimension to art. Another way of looking at art is to consider what function art plays in human societies. The question then becomes, "What is (the role of) art?" An individual work would then be "art" only if it performed whatever role one thinks art should perform.

Many different answers have been given to that problem. One response is captured in the expression *Ars gratia ars,* which appears under the roaring lion at the beginning of movies produced by MGM. It is a Latin expression, meaning "Art for art's sake." According to this understanding, art performs no other function than to embody the human need to express itself in artistic creation. Another consideration concerning the role of art is that art must perform a positive social function. This is both a traditional religious view of art and a contemporary modern understanding. Art, from this perspective, must instill correct values and hold up proper models, whatever those are judged to be. Clearly, this point of view rejects the idea of "art for art's sake," and it maintains that art has a "higher" function. Some anthropologists take an entirely different tack, in assessing the role of art in human life as a form of playful self-expression. In all of these understandings, art is a fundamental part of the human encounter with the world.

These three ways of viewing art can be summarized as (1) art as an independent and natural process of human self-expression, (2) art as shaper of social values, and (3) art as a complex form of human play. In this chapter, we address the relationship of art to human life, keeping in mind these three understandings of what constitutes art. We do so by considering selections from four "classics" of world literature: Murasaki Shikibu's *The Tale of Genji,* the famous *Arabian Nights, The Song of Roland,* and Geoffrey Chaucer's *The Canterbury Tales.* The works and the passages from them have been chosen to represent a variety of cultures and of social groups within those cultures. An additional consideration taken into account is the genesis of the works themselves, the way these artistic works were created. These selections allow you to sample eminent elements of the global cultural heritage, as well as to grapple with the relationship between art and human social values. Whether it is true, as it is often said, that "art imitates life," it is undoubtedly true that art encounters life, and this chapter is devoted to that encounter.

Our first text comes from Murasaki Shikibu's *The Tale of Genji.* This text from Heian Japan (794–1185 CE) is very interesting for a number of reasons. First of all, it was written by a lady-in-waiting for the empress. As a result, it provides a unique "interior" perspective of elite Japanese values of that time period from the point of view of a woman. Furthermore, because sexual politics were a prominent part of Heian elite culture, gender issues are even more dramatically highlighted. Because of the absence in that time period of significant military threats, elite Japanese reflected highly sophisticated artistic standards. The selection presented here comes from a chapter titled "The Picture Competition," so considerations of art's role in human life come into play on several levels of this text.

Our second selection comes from the *Arabian Nights,* one of the most famous pieces of world literature. The story we present here is "The Story of Ali Cogia, a Merchant of Bagdad." As the title indicates, this tale involves the ethics and practices of the merchant and trading culture of the Middle East. In addition, it allows us to glimpse the values that structured the behavior of political authorities. Finally, the story incorporates children playing a game as a key part of the resolution of the conflict, so that another aspect of art is foregrounded in the narrative itself. In general, this story incorporates the values of Middle Eastern culture in a rich, vibrant, and sophisticated Islamic era.

Following *Arabian Nights,* we present excerpts from a classic epic of medieval western Europe, *The Song of Roland.* The tale is about an incident that occurred in the late eighth century, but the text we have is an Anglo-Norman version, composed around 1100 CE. The world and the values represented here are those of the armed nobility of the Middle Ages. The tension and narrative in *Roland* revolve around the issue of what constitutes a good vassal. Insofar as it, too, deals with the problem of "true" nobility, *Roland* has similarities with both *Genji* and the selection from *The Canterbury Tales.* In addition, although the warrior spirit of *Roland* gives it a very different feel from *The Tale of Genji,* it also involves a competition—in this case a very deadly game of trial by combat.

The final text is "The Wife of Bath's Tale" from Geoffrey Chaucer's *The Canterbury Tales.* Chaucer composed these tales between 1387 and his death in 1400. The overall work was left incomplete at his death, but the tale we include in this chapter is in finished form. Like two of the other works included here, it involves a nobleman and a discussion—playful, to be sure—of what true nobility entails. In addition, like *Genji,* it raises gender issues. Perhaps more than any of the other texts, Chaucer's piece poses for us the question of whether this work of art embodies the human need to express itself in artistic form (art for art's sake), an enduring human effort to use art to shape social values, or an artistic instance of the recurring human attribute of playfulness. Art encounters life in a variety of forms and expressions, and to that encounter we now turn.

CHAPTER QUESTIONS

1. Which works or which parts of each work seem to you to represent "art for art's sake"? Identify those aspects of the works here that seem to involve art as a form of human self-expression. What benefit or purpose do you think the artist who composed these works might have sought or achieved through the process of creating these works?

2. In what ways do the following works seek to identify and hold up for imitation certain values? Do the works represent different, perhaps conflicting, values? If so, how are they reconciled, or how is the tension between them handled?

3. What role does the seemingly irrepressible human instinct for play occupy in these works of elite literature? How do the authors utilize play to move the action of their narratives? How is play used to represent and promote certain values?

4. What is distinctive about the cultures and societies that produced these works of art? What common elements do they have? How does the culture and society affect the nature of the art that is produced? What is the role of gender in these works and societies, and how does its role differ from contemporary social practices?

5. How does the treatment of human cultures and social values in these works differ from the way those subjects are dealt with in other works (for example, the Bible or the Qur'an)? Can you identify with the subjects and issues dealt with in these works? Do they speak to you across the ages and the cultural divides? In what ways?

ELITE VALUES IN HEIAN JAPAN

Murasaki Shikibu's *The Tale of Genji* is a product of Japan's Heian period (794–1185). In that era, Japan was greatly influenced by Chinese governmental and cultural forms, which were nativized and adapted to fit the Japanese environment. For example, the extreme centralization and imperial power of the Chinese system were never replicated in Japan. Because Japan consists of islands and faced no great foreign threat at that time, the emperor and the central government ruled in concert with a powerful aristocracy organized on clan lines. In fact, over time a branch of one of the leading aristocratic clans, the northern Fujiwara, succeeded in dominating the emperors and effectively ruling Japan in their place (866–1068). Ultimately, the Fujiwara were outmaneuvered and some imperial autonomy was restored, but nothing approaching the Chinese system ever existed. Similarly, Chinese culture in the forms of written language, the Buddhist religion, and art and architecture exercised a powerful attraction for the Japanese. In the seventh century, the Chinese system of writing was adopted as the first written language in Japan, used for government, laws, records, and histories. Around 900 CE a written, phonetic Japanese script (*hiragana*) was devised, and a lively literary culture evolved.

As in most other societies before modern times, Japan was dominated politically and culturally by the aristocratic elite, especially the court notables. One remarkable feature of Japanese elite culture in this era is the prominent position occupied by a couple of extraordinary women. Although knowledge and use of written Chinese had been largely restricted to men and to male-dominated fields, such as government and law, *hiragana* was more accessible to aristocratic women, and it was more suitable to the intimate and personal issues—especially marital politics—that played a central role in their lives. The two literary products of the Heian era that are best known in the West—Sei Shonagon's *Pillow Book* and Murasaki's *The Tale of Genji*—were written by aristocratic women. As was true in the political system, the absence of external military threat allowed the Japanese elite the luxury of concentrating on aristocratic cultural aesthetics and court politics. In this environment, and equipped with the flexible and familiar *hiragana,* women writers could assume a prominence unheard of in other systems.

The Tale of Genji is a remarkable work written by a remarkable woman, Murasaki Shikibu, who is so completely identified with this work that she actually earned the name "Murasaki" as a nickname based on the name of the leading female character in *Genji*. She was born around 973 into a minor branch of the Fujiwara clan, the powerful aristocratic family that dominated politics in Heian Japan from 866 to 1068 CE, and she died sometime after 1031. Her father served in minor posts, such as provincial governor, but, as far back as her great-grandfather, the family had enjoyed a certain literary eminence. After the death of her husband, she became a sort of lady-in-waiting tutor of a young empress, so she was ideally placed to observe the highly stylized but fiercely pursued sexual politics of the Japanese court. The Fujiwara had achieved dominance by succeeding in marrying a succession of daughters to the emperors, who were in turn pressured by the Fujiwara to abdicate early. As a result, there was usually more than one fairly young former emperor in the background of the political picture, and the ruling emperor was often a minor, for whom the senior Fujiwara served as guardian and effective ruler of the country. The combination of this political constellation with the relatively lax sexual mores of the Heian upper class meant that there were at any given moment a number of currents of sexual and marital intrigue swirling about the court. Such are the court politics and aristocratic characters that make up the crux of Murasaki's story.[1]

The Tale of Genji has been called with some justification the world's first novel. It is the story of an especially gifted son of an emperor, Genji. In the course of the story, Genji evolves from a sort of courtly playboy who is most concerned with court conquests and politics to a man who finds his greatest pleasure with his wife and who understands the impermanence of this world. For most of the novel, though, he exists in the rarified atmosphere of the higher realms of Heian aristocratic and court life. It was a world of exquisite cultural nuance and extraordinary sensibility to aesthetic (that is, relating to beauty) distinctions and etiquette, not unlike that of Louis XIV's Versailles. The complex interrelations in the story are worthy of a modern-day soap opera, and they can be somewhat dizzying. Here is the basic outline. Genji's father was an emperor who fell in love with a woman of inappropriate rank, Genji's mother. Ultimately, Genji's father's first wife, Lady Kokiden, a powerful Fujiwara, forces him to declare Genji ineligible to become an emperor (that is what *Genji* means). Lady Kokiden's son becomes emperor Suzaku, though by the time of the passage excerpted here he has already abdicated, and so he is the ex-emperor. Genji's mother is persecuted and dies. Eventually, another woman becomes the emperor's wife and replaces Genji's mother in his affections. She is Fujitsubo, who has her own complex relations with Genji. Genji adopts a young woman, Murasaki, who it turns out is Fujitsubo's niece. In the passage included here, Murasaki's presentation at court has been arranged by Genji, who seeks to promote her interests by introducing her to the underage current emperor. (Ultimately, Genji will decide that he is in love with Murasaki; he will take her as his wife and find sincere happiness with her.) His main rival at the court is To no Chujo, Genji's brother-in-law (Genji is married to his sister, but he neglects her in favor of relationships with other women) and at this time still his close friend. The main point of contention becomes showing the young emperor that his ward, Murasaki, has greater sensitivity and cultural sophistication connected with painting than does To no Chujo's daughter.

The characters in this selection are

Genji

the young emperor

Murasaki[2]—Genji's ward and eventually his main wife

Fujitsubo—Genji's father's wife and surrogate mother to him; also Murasaki's aunt

To no Chujo—Genji's brother-in-law, friend, and rival

Princess Chujo—To no Chujo's young daughter, the young current emperor's favorite court lady

Emperor Suzaku—a young ex-emperor, Genji's stepbrother

QUESTIONS TO CONSIDER

1. Identify all the traits or behaviors in the characters presented in this selection that seem to be represented as desirable or admirable. Define the attributes of an ideal individual in that society based on the traits you have identified.

2. As the chapter title indicates, the action revolves around a "picture competition." Assess the kinds of subjects and treatments that they valued most in paintings.

3. In your opinion, what values, if any, was Murasaki Shikibu holding up for imitation? Perhaps she was presenting values and behaviors in order to criticize them. Do you see any of that at work in this selection? How do the values presented here compare with those of modern American society?

4. The anthropological understanding of the role of art in human society also includes "play." In this selection, play is presented as a competition between Genji and To no Chujo. Assess the way each one conducts himself in this competition. How might this depiction have "shaped" or affected the behavior of subsequent generations of Japanese? How does it compare with American competitive behavior?

5. Finally, art has also been understood as "an independent and natural process of human self-expression." Murasaki Shikibu was widowed young and assigned to the service of a limited and prudish imperial wife. What might *The Tale of Genji* have allowed her to express? What kind of outlet might the process of literary creation have provided for her? If you have produced any art, what purposes did the creative process serve for you?

THE TALE OF GENJI, "THE PICTURE COMPETITION"

Murasaki Shikibu

To no Chujo had presented his daughter at Court with the express intention that she should one day share the Throne. The presence of this formidable rival at the Palace could not fail to cause him considerable anxiety. . . .

[The Emperor's] favor seemed to be pretty equally divided between the two existing claimants. He was particularly interested in pictures and had as a result of this taste himself acquired considerable skill. It happened that Murasaki painted very charmingly, and so soon as he discovered this the Emperor began constantly sending for her to paint pictures with him. Among the serving-women in the Palace he had always taken an interest in any who were said to be fond of pictures; and it was natural that when he discovered painting to be the favorite occupation of the pretty princess he should become very much attached to her. Hers were not solemn pictures, but such clever, quick sketches; so that just to watch her do them was an exciting game. And when, sitting so charmingly beside him on the divan, she paused and held her brush in the air for a moment wondering where to put the next stroke, she looked so daring that the little Emperor's heart was completely captivated. Soon he was going to her rooms at all hours, and To no Chujo became seriously alarmed lest his own daugh-

Source: Murasaki Shikibu, *The Tale of Genji*, trans. Arthur Waley (New York: The Modern Library, 1960), 331, 332–34, 336–37, 338–39, 341–42.

ter should lose her primacy. But he was determined not to be outdone, and being of an extremely ingenious and resourceful nature he soon had a plan for putting an end to this menacing situation. He sent for all the most skillful painters in the land and under strict bond of secrecy set them to work upon a collection of pictures which was to be like nothing that had ever been seen before. They were to be illustrations to romances, which would be preferable to purely ingenious subjects, the significance being more easily grasped by a young mind and all the most interesting and exciting stories were chosen. In addition to these illustrations there was to be a set of "Months," a very attractive subject, with texts specially written for the occasion. In due time Princess Chujo showed them to the Emperor, who was naturally very much interested and soon afterwards asked for them again, saying that he thought Murasaki would like to see them. At this Princess Chujo began to make difficulties, and though His Majesty promised to show them to no one else and carry them with the greatest care straight to the other princess's apartments, she refused to part with them. Genji heard of this and was amused to see that To no Chujo could still throw himself into these absurd conspiracies with the same childish excitement as in their young days. "I am very sorry," he said to the Emperor, "to hear that Princess Chujo hides her pictures from you and will not let you take them away and study them at your ease. It seems, too, that she was quite cross and quarrelsome about it, which was most reprehensible. But I have some very nice pictures, painted a long while ago. I will send them to you: . . . there were whole cupboards full of pictures both old and new. Taking Murasaki with him he now inspected their contents and together they went through the whole collection, putting on one side those which were most likely to appeal to modern taste. . . . [I]t occurred to Genji that his own sketches made during his sojourn at Suma and Akashi might be of interest, and sending for the box in which they were kept he took advantage of this occasion to go through them with Murasaki. Even someone seeing them without any knowledge of the circumstances under which they were painted would, if possessed of the slightest understanding of such matters, have at once been profoundly moved by these drawings. . . .

On hearing of the preparations that were taking place . . . , To no Chujo went through his pictures again and had them all fitted out with the most elegant ivory-rollers, backings and ribbons. It was about the tenth day of the third month. The weather was delightful, things were looking at their best and everyone was in a good temper; moreover it was a time at which no particular fetes or ceremonies occupied the Court, so that uninterrupted attention could be now given to those lighter pastimes in which the Emperor so much delighted, and whole days were spent unrolling painting after painting. The one ambition of everyone at Court was to rout out and bring to the Palace some picture which should particularly catch the young Emperor's fancy. Both Murasaki's partisans and those of Lady Chujo had brought forward vast numbers of scrolls. On the whole, illustrated romances proved to be the most popular. Murasaki's side was strongest in ancient works of well-established reputation; while Lady Chujo patronized all the cleverest modern painters, so that her collection, representing as it did all that most appealed to the fashionable tastes of the moment, made at first sight a more dazzling impression. . . .

It happened that Fujitsubo was paying one of her periodical visits to the Court, and having given a casual inspection to the exhibits of both parties she decided to suspend her usual religious observances and devote herself to a thorough study of all these works, for painting was a matter in which she had always taken a deep interest. Hearing the animated discussions which were taking place between the supporters of modern and ancient art, she suggested that those present should be formed into two teams [Murasaki's and Lady Chujo's]. . . . These were considered the cleverest women of the day, and Fujitsubo promised herself very good entertainment from such an interchange of wit and knowledge as their rivalry was likely to afford. . . .

Presently Genji arrived at the Palace and was greatly diverted by the spectacle of this disorderly and embittered combat. "If you will get up another competition," he said, "I will arrange for the Emperor to be present and will myself make the awards." In preparation for this event, which he had indeed been contemplating for some time, he made a further selection from the pictures which he had recently put aside, and having done so he could not resist inserting among them the two scrolls of his sketches made at Suma and Akashi. To no Chujo meanwhile, determined not to be outdone, was straining every nerve in preparation for the new contest. It was indeed a moment in the history of our country when the whole energy of the nation seemed to be concentrated upon the search for the prettiest method of mounting paper-scrolls. In arranging the conditions of the contest Genji had said: "My idea is that it should be confined to paintings already in existence; we do not want a lot of new work hurriedly executed for this special purpose. . . ." But To no Chujo could not resist the temptation to set some of his favorite masters to work, and improvising a little studio with a secret door he strove to steal a march on his rivals. The secrecy was not however as well maintained as he could have desired; even Suzaku, in his secluded apartments, heard the story and determined to put his own collection at the service of Murasaki. He had a series of "Festivals All the Year Round," painted by various famous old masters; texts explaining these pictures had been added by no less a hand than that of the [former] Emperor Daigo. . . .

When the great day came, though there had not been much time for preparation everything was arranged in the most striking and effective manner. The ladies-in-waiting belonging to the two sides stood drawn up in line on either side of the Imperial Throne; the courtiers, very much on the alert, were ranged up in the verandah of the small back room. Lady Chujo's party (the left) exhibited their pictures in boxes of purple sandalwood mounted on sapanwood stands, over which was thrown a cover of Chinese brocade worked on a mauve ground. The carpet on which the boxes stood was of Chinese fine-silk, dyed to the color of grape-juice. Six little girls were in attendance to assist in handling the boxes and scrolls; they were dressed in mantles with white scarves lined with pink; their tunics were of scarlet, worn with facings blue outside and light green within.

Murasaki's boxes were of aloeswood arranged on a low table of similar wood, but lighter in color. The carpet was of Korean brocade on a blue-green ground. The festoons hanging round the table and the design of the table-legs were carefully thought out and in the best taste. The little girls in attendance wore blue mantles, with willow-colored scarves; their tunics, brown outside and yellow within. When all the boxes were duly arranged on their stands, the Emperor's own ladies took up their places, some with Lady Chujo's supporters, some with the opposing side. At the summons of the herald Genji and To no Chujo now appeared. . . . An amazing collection of paintings had been assembled and assuredly the task of the judges was no light one. A great impression was made when Murasaki's side produced the famous series of "Four Seasons" by noted masters of antiquity. Both the charming fancy displayed in the choice of episodes for illustration and the easy, flowing character of the brushstrokes rendered these works highly attractive; and the modern paintings on paper, being necessarily limited in size, sometimes, especially in landscape, made a certain impression of incompleteness. Yet the far greater richness both of brushwork and invention gave even to the more trivial of these modern works a liveliness which made them compare not unfavorably with the masterpieces of the past. Thus it was very difficult indeed to reach any decision, save that today, as on the previous occasion, both sides had produced many works of absorbing interest. . . .

At last the moment arrived when there was only one more picture to show on each side. Amid intense excitement Murasaki's side produced the roll containing Genji's sketches at Suma. To no Chujo was aghast. His daughter's side too had reserved for their last stroke one of the most important works at their disposition; but against the prospect of so masterly a hand working at complete leisure and far from the distracting influences which beset an artist in town, Lady Chujo's supporters at once knew that they could not hope to prevail. An additional advantage was given to Genji's paintings by the pathos of the subject. That during those years of exile he had endured a cheerless and monotonous existence those present could well conjecture. But when they saw, so vividly presented, both the stern manner of his life and in some sort even the feelings which this rustic life had aroused in one used to every luxury and indulgence, they could not but be deeply moved, and there were many . . . who could scarcely refrain from tears. Here were presented in the most vivid manner famous bays and shores of the Suma coast, so renowned in story yet to these city folk so utterly unknown and unimagined. The text was written in cursive Chinese characters, helped out here and there with a little native script, and unlike the business day-to-day journals that men generally keep it was varied by the insertion of an occasional poem or song. The spectators now clamored only for more specimens of Genji's handiwork, and it would have been impossible at that moment to interest them in anything else. It seemed to them as though all the interest and beauty of the many pictures which they had been examining had in some strange manner accumulated and attached themselves to this one scroll. By universal and ungrudging consent Murasaki's side was awarded the victory. . . .

Genji gave instructions that the Suma scroll should be left with Fujitsubo. Hearing that it was only one of a series, she begged to be shown the rest. "You shall see them all in good time," Genji said; "there are far too many of them to go through at one sitting." The little Emperor, too, seemed to have thoroughly enjoyed the proceedings, which was a great comfort to those who had engineered them.

When To no Chujo saw with what zest Genji supported his ward Murasaki even in such trifling matters as this contest he again became a little uneasy about Lady Chujo's position. But observing the situation closely, he noted that the young Emperor, who certainly began by being very deeply attached to his little playmate, after his first excitement of recognizing this new companion with her interesting grownup accomplishments had passed away, settled down again quite happily to his old love. For the present at any rate there was no need for anxiety.

THE *ARABIAN NIGHTS* AND ISLAMIC CULTURE

With the possible exception of the Qur'an itself, no other work of Arab–Muslim culture is as widely known in the west as is the *Arabian Nights*. The story that we present here, "The Story of Ali Cogia, a Merchant of Bagdad," is included to represent the culture of the Arab Muslim world before 1000 CE. This era is one of the golden ages of the Arab Islamic zone, a time when a sophisticated, vibrant, and cohesive culture permeated much of the Muslim world, the *dar al-Islam*. Within a hundred years of the death of Muhammad in 632 CE, the region from Persia across North Africa to Spain was under the control of Muslim rulers. Most of the former Persian and Byzantine empires were Islamic in faith and governance, and Islamic thinkers absorbed the Persian and Greek intellectual and cultural legacies. Its dynamic economy included some of the richest and most productive portions of the Persian and Mediterranean worlds, and the Islamic world enjoyed high levels of both urbanization and literacy. The region was far in advance of western Europe. Caliph Harun al-Rashid, who figures prominently in many of the stories in the *Arabian Nights* and who is famous for a magnificent and enlightened reign in the late 700s and early 800s, is emblematic of the brilliant, culturally synthetic intellectual life of medieval Islam.

The history of the text of the *Arabian Nights* is a long, complex story in itself. By 1000 CE a version of the *Arabian Nights* existed, though we do not know what its exact contents were. The current version consists of stories that were versions of older, pre-Islamic tales and some that were added after the year 1000 and even from other collections. As a result, it has been called a "book without authors," and we cannot assert with any certainty either the individual author or in many cases even the origin of many stories in the *Arabian Nights*. Hence, as opposed to *The Tale of Genji*, there is no biography of an author on the basis of which we can conjecture about authorial intent or the process of self-expression. What we can say about the *Arabian Nights* is that a variety of genres is represented, such as heroic epics, fables, and humorous tales. Many of the stories, such as those involving Aladdin, Ali Baba, and Sinbad, are already well known in the west. The pretext for the telling of these diverse tales is the story of the narrator herself, Sheherazade. The story is that a cruel king, Shariyar, had women killed after he had slept with them one time. When it was her turn, Sheherazade told him an unfinished story, and he put off having her killed in order to hear the end of it. This story telling cycle continued for the thousand and one nights, after which Shariyar had decided not to have her beheaded. As regards the overall explanation for a series of unrelated tales and in terms of the use of narratives within narratives, the *Arabian Nights* resembles Chaucer's *The Canterbury Tales*.

The *Nights* is a very useful source for the social history of the Islamic Middle East in that era. Thus we can examine material from the *Nights* as both shaping and reflecting Muslim social values. The story presented here involves a Baghdad merchant and his search for justice from the caliph for a wrong done to him while he is on an extended journey that includes his pilgrimage to Mecca. Learning of other trading opportunities, he travels widely in the Islamic world and is away for several years, during which time his supposed friend steals some gold from him. The story involves the social status and values of the merchantry in Islamic society, an Islamic religious element, and a representation of governmental authority. It is important to note that the merchantry enjoyed a higher status in Islamic society than was true of the Christian West until relatively recent times. Both the Prophet Muhammad himself and many of his leading early followers came from trading families. At the time of this story, 'Abbasid Baghdad was the economic, political, and cultural center of Islam, and the apex of 'Abbasid power and eminence occurred under Caliph Harun al-Rashid (786–809), who is also known as a great patron of the arts. Finally, the practice of taking items to sell in order to finance the pilgrimage, or *hajj,* to Mecca was considered quite acceptable. Ali Cogia was following good Muslim practice.

QUESTIONS TO CONSIDER

1. Because of its moral, we can assume that this story "encodes" certain social messages about proper behaviors and values in Muslim society of that era. By examining the actions of both Ali Cogia and the man with whom he left the jar of "olives," describe how a merchant should behave in Muslim society. How does it compare with contemporary American values concerning merchants?

2. One element that the anthropological interpretation of art insists on is "play." How is play incorporated into this story? How does play in this story compare with that in "The Picture Competition" from *The Tale of Genji?*

3. Consider the way that political authority is represented in this story. How many different instances can you identify in which authority is represented as responsive and legitimate? How do the political concerns presented here compare with the ideal behavior expected of a merchant?

4. How do the caliph and his subordinates compare with the political elite presented in *The Tale of Genji?* Which system and sets of behaviors seems closer to our own? Why? What do Ali Cogia's travels tell us about the nature of Islamic society in that era?

5. How does this story compare with "The Picture Competition" from *The Tale of Genji?* Does it have a different "artistic" feel? How would you describe any difference you detect? What do you think explains any difference?

THE STORY OF ALI COGIA, A MERCHANT OF BAGDAD

In reign of the caliph Haroun Alraschid, there lived at Bagdad a merchant, whose name was Ali Cogia, that was neither one of the richest nor meanest sort. He was a bachelor, and lived master of his own actions, in the house which was his father's, very well content with the profit he made of his trading; but happening to dream for three nights together that a venerable old man came to him, and, with a severe look reprimanded him for not having made a pilgrimage to Mecca, he was very much troubled.

As a good Muslim, he knew he was obliged to undertake a pilgrimage; but as he had a house, shop, and goods, he always believed that they might stand for a sufficient reason to excuse him, endeavoring by his charity, and good deeds, to atone for that neglect. But after this dream, his conscience was so much pricked, that the fear lest any misfortune should befall made him resolve not to defer it any longer; and, to be able to go that year, he sold off his household goods, his shop, and with it the greatest part of his merchandises; reserving only some which he thought might turn to a better account at Mecca; and meeting with a tenant for his house, let* that also.

Things being thus disposed, he was ready to go when the Bagdad caravan set out for Mecca; the only thing he had to do, was to secure a sum of a thousand pieces of gold, which would be troublesome to carry along with him, besides the money he had set apart to defray his expenses. To this end he made choice of a jar, of a proportionable size, put the thousand pieces of gold into it, and covered them over with olives. When he had closed the mouth of the jar, he carried it to a merchant, a particular friend of his, and said to him, You know, brother, that in two or three days time I set out with the caravan on my pilgrimage to Mecca; and I beg the favor of you, that you would take upon you the charge of keeping a jar of olives for me till I return. The merchant promised him he would, and in an obliging manner said, Here, take the key of my warehouse, and set your jar where you please; I promise you shall find it there when you come again.

On the day the caravan was to set out, Ali Cogia added himself to it, with a camel, (loaded with what merchandises he thought fit to carry along with him,) which served him to ride on, and arrived safe at Mecca, where he visited, along with other pilgrims, the temple so much celebrated and frequented by all Muslims every year, who come from all parts of the world and observe religiously the ceremonies prescribed them; and when he had acquitted himself of the duties of his pilgrimage, he exposed the merchandises he had brought with him, to sell or exchange them.

Two merchants passing by, and seeing Ali Cogia's goods, thought them so fine and choice, that they stopped some time to look at them, though they had no occasion for them; and when they had satisfied their curiosity, one of them said to the

Source: *Arabian Nights' Entertainment*, ed. Robert L. Mack, 787–96. Copyright © 1995 Oxford University Press, Inc. Used by permission of Oxford University Press, Inc. Spelling has been modified to accord with standard American usage, and *mussulman* has been changed to *Muslim* for clarity.

*He rented his house.

other, as they were going away, If this merchant knew to what profit these goods would turn at Cairo, he would carry them thither, and not sell them here, though this is a good market.

Ali Cogia heard these words; and as he had often heard talk of the beauties of Egypt, he was resolved to take the opportunity of seeing them, and take a journey thither; therefore, after having packed up his goods again, instead of returning to Bagdad, he set out for Egypt with a caravan to Cairo; and when he came thither, he found his account in his journey, and in a few days sold all his goods to a greater advantage than he hoped for. . . .

[Using his profits to buy goods for sale back in Baghdad, he journeys homeward, but is lured into visiting other places by curiosity and business opportunity. Hence, he is gone from Baghdad for a long time.]

All this time, his friend, with whom he had left his jar of olives, neither thought of him nor them; but . . . one evening, when this merchant was supping at home with his family, and the discourse happening to fall upon olives, his wife was desirous to eat some, saying, that she had not tasted any for a long while. Now you talk of olives, said the merchant, you put me in mind of a jar which Ali Cogia left with me seven years ago, when he went to Mecca, and put it himself in my warehouse, for me to keep it for him against he returned; and what is become of him I know not; though, when the caravan came back, they told me he was gone for Egypt. Certainly he must be dead, since he has not returned in all this time; and we may eat the olives, if they prove good. Lend me a plate and a candle, and I will go and fetch some of them, and we will see.

For God's sake, good husband, said the wife, do not commit so base an action; you know that nothing is more sacred than what is committed to one's care and trust: you say Ali Cogia has been gone to Mecca, and is not returned; and they say, that he is gone to Egypt; and how do you know but that he may be gone farther? As you have no news of his death, he may return to-morrow, for any thing you can tell; and what a disgrace would it be to you and your family, if he should come, and you not restore him his jar in the same condition he left it? I declare I have no desire for the olives, and will not taste of them; for when I mentioned them, it was only by way of discourse; besides, do you think that they can be good, after they have been kept so long? They must be all moldy, and spoiled; and if Ali Cogia should return, as I have a great fancy he will, and should find they have been opened, what will he think of your honor? I beg of you to let them alone.

The wife had not argued so long with her husband, but that she read his obstinacy in his face. In short, he never regarded what she said, but got up, took a candle and a platter, and went into the warehouse. Well, husband, said the wife again, remember I have no hand in this business, and that you cannot lay any thing to my charge if you should have cause to repent of this action.

The merchant's ears were deaf to these remonstrances of his wife, and he still persisted in his design. When he came into the warehouse, he opened the jar, and found the olives all moldy; but, to see if they were all so at the bottom, he turned the jar topsy-turvy upon the plate; and by shaking the jar, some of the gold tumbled out.

At the sight of the gold, the merchant, who was naturally covetous, looked into the jar, and perceived that he had shaken out almost all the olives, and what remained was gold coin fast wedged in: he immediately put the olives into the jar again, and returned to his wife. Indeed, my dear, said he, you was [sic] in the right to say that the olives were all moldy; for I have found it so, and have made up the jar just as Ali Cogia left it; so that he will not perceive that they have been touched, if he should return. You had better have taken my advice, said the wife, and not meddled with them: God grant that no mischief may come of it.

The merchant was not in the least affected with his wife's last words, but spent almost the whole night in thinking how he might appropriate Ali Cogia's gold to his own use, in case Ali Cogia should return, and ask him for the jar. The next morning he went and bought some olives of that year, took out the old, with the gold, and filled the jar with the new, covered it up, and put it in the same place.

About a month after the merchant had committed so base an action, (for which he ought to pay dear,) Ali Cogia arrived at Bagdad. . . .

The next morning, Ali Cogia went to pay a visit to the merchant his friend, who received him in the most obliging manner imaginable, and expressed a great deal of joy at his return, after so many years absence; telling him that he had begun to lose all hopes of ever seeing him again.

After the usual compliments on such a meeting, Ali Cogia desired the merchant to return him the jar of olives which he had left with him, and to excuse the liberty he had taken in giving him so much trouble.

My dear friend, Ali Cogia, replied the merchant, you are to blame to make all these apologies on such an occasion; I should have made as free with you; there, take the key of the warehouse, go and take it; you will find it in the same place where you left it.

Ali Cogia went into the merchant's warehouse, took his jar, and after having returned him the key, and thanks for the favor he had done, returned with it to the inn where he lodged; and opening the jar, and putting his hand down to the bottom, to see for his gold, was very much surprised to find none. At first he thought he might perhaps be mistaken; and, to discover the truth, poured out all the olives, without so much as finding one single piece of money. His astonishment was so great, that he then stood for some time motionless: lifting up his hands and eyes to heaven, he cried out, Is it possible that a man whom I took for my very good friend, should be guilty of so base an action?

Ali Cogia, cruelly frightened at so considerable a loss, returned immediately to the merchant. My good friend, said he, do not be surprised to see me come back so soon: I own the jar of olives to be the same put into your magazine; but with the olives I put a thousand pieces of gold into it, which I do not find: Perhaps you might have had an occasion for them, and used them in your traffic: if so, they are at your service; only put me out of my pain, and give me an acknowledgment, and pay me them again at your own convenience.

The merchant, who expected that Ali Cogia would come with such a complaint, had meditated upon a ready answer. Friend Ali Cogia, said he, when you brought your jar of olives to me, I never touched it, but gave you the key of my warehouse, whither you carried it yourself; and did not you find it in the same place, and covered in the same manner as when you left it? And if you put gold in it, you have found it again: You told me that they were olives, and I believed so. This is all I know of the matter; and you may believe me, if you please, for I never touched them.

Ali Cogia made use of all the mild ways he could think of, to oblige the merchant to do him right. I love peace and quietness, said he to him, and shall be very sorry to come to those extremities which will bring the greatest disgrace upon you: Consider, that merchants, as we are, ought to forsake all interest to preserve a good reputation. Once again, I tell you, I should be very much concerned, if your obstinacy should oblige me to force you to do me justice; for I would rather, almost, lose what is my right, than have recourse to law.

Ali Cogia, replied the merchant, you agree that you left the jar of olives with me; and now you have taken it away, you come and ask me for a thousand pieces of gold. Did you ever tell me that such a sum was in the jar? I knew nothing but that they were olives. I wonder you do not as well ask me for diamonds and pearls: Be gone about your business, and do not raise a mob about my shop.

These last words were pronounced in so great an heat and passion, as not only made those who stood about the shop already, stay longer, and created a great mob, but made the neighboring merchants come out of their shops to see what was the difference between Ali Cogia and the merchant, and endeavor to reconcile them; and when Ali Cogia had informed them of his grievance, they asked the merchant what he had to say.

The merchant owned that he had kept the jar for Ali Cogia in his warehouse, but denied that ever he meddled with it, and swore, that he knew nothing but that it was full of olives, as Ali Cogia told him, and bid them all bear witness of the insult and affront offered him. You bring it upon yourself, said Ali Cogia, taking him by the arm; but since you use me so basely, I cite you according to the law of God: Let us see whether you will have the assurance to say the same thing before the cady.*

The merchant could not refuse this summons, which every good Muslim is bound to observe, or be declared a rebel against his religion; but said, With all my heart, we shall soon see who is in the wrong.

Ali Cogia carried the merchant before the cady, before whom he accused him of cheating him of a thousand pieces of gold, which he had left with him. The cady asked him if he had any witnesses; to which he replied that he had not taken that necessary precaution, because he believed the person he trusted his money with, to be his friend, and always took him for an honest man.

The merchant made the same defense he had done before the merchants his neighbors, offering to make oath that he never had the money he was accused of, and that he did not so much as know there was such a sum; upon which the cady took his oath, and afterwards dismissed him.

Ali Cogia, extremely mortified to find that he must sit down with so considerable a loss, protested against the sentence the cady gave, declaring that he would appeal to the caliph Haroun Alraschid, who would do him justice; which protestation the

---

*An Islamic judge.

cady only looked upon as the effect of the common resentment of all those who lose their cause; and thought he had done his duty, in acquitting a person accused without witnesses.

While the merchant returned home, triumphing over Ali Cogia, and overjoyed at his good fortune, Ali Cogia went to get a petition drawn up; and the next day, observing the time when the caliph came from prayers in the afternoon, he placed himself in the street he was to pass through; and holding out his hand with the petition, an officer appointed for that purpose, who always goes before the caliph, came and took it from him.

As Ali Cogia knew that it was the caliph's custom to read the petitions as he went into the palace, he went into the court, and waited till the officer came out of the caliph's apartment, who told him the hour the caliph had appointed to hear him; and then asking him where the merchant lived, he sent to him to signify the caliph's pleasure.

The same evening, the caliph, the grand visier Giafar, and Mesrour, the chief of the eunuchs,* went all disguised through the town, as . . . it was usual so to do; and passing through a street, the caliph heard a noise, and mending his pace, he came to a gate which led into a little court, where, through a hole, he perceived ten or twelve children playing by moon-light.

The caliph, who was curious to know at what play these children played, sat down upon a bench which he found just by; and still looking through the hole, he heard one of the briskest and liveliest of the children say, Come, let us play at the cady. I will be cady; bring Ali Cogia and the merchant who cheated him of the thousand pieces of gold before me.

These words of the child put the caliph in mind of the petition Ali Cogia had given him that day, and made him redouble his attention. As Ali Cogia's affairs and the merchant's made a great noise, and were in every body's mouth in Bagdad, it had not escaped the children, who all accepted the proposition with joy, and agreed on the parts each was to act; not one of them refused him that made the proposal to be cady; and when he had taken his seat, which he did with all the seeming gravity of a cady, another, as an officer of the court, presented two before him; one as Ali Cogia, and the other as the merchant against whom he complained.

Then the pretended cady, directing his discourse to the feigned Ali Cogia, asked him what he had to lay to that merchant's charge?

Ali Cogia, after a low bow, informed the young cady of the fact, and related every particular, and afterwards begged that he would use his authority, that he might not lose so considerable a sum of money.

Then the cady, turning about to the merchant, asked him why he did not return the money which Ali Cogia demanded of him.

The young merchant alleged the same reasons as the real merchant had done before the cady himself, and proffered to confirm it by an oath, that what he had said was truth.

---

*The grand vizier was a sort of prime minister. Eunuchs were frequently used in palaces, because they had no family interests to promote.

Not so fast, replied the pretended cady; before you come to your oath, I should be glad to see the jar of olives. Ali Cogia, said he, addressing himself to the lad who acted that part, have you brought the jar? No, replied he: Then go and fetch it immediately.

The pretended Ali Cogia went immediately, and returning as soon, feigned to bring a jar before the cady, telling him, that it was the same he left with the accused person, and took away again. But to omit no part of the formality, the supposed cady asked the merchant if it was the same; and as, by his silence, he seemed not to deny it, he ordered it to be opened. He that represented Ali Cogia, seemed to take off the cover, and the pretended cady made as if he looked into it. They are fine olives, said he; let me taste them; and then pretending to eat of them, added, they are excellent: But, continued he, I cannot think that olives will keep seven years, and be so good: Send for two olive merchants, and let me hear what is their opinion. Then the two boys, as olive merchants, presented themselves. Are you olive merchants, said the sham cady? Tell me how long olives will keep to be fit to eat.

Sir, replied the two merchants, let us take what care we can, they will hardly be worth any thing at the third year; for they have neither taste nor colour. If it be so, answered the cady, look into that jar, and tell me how old those olives are.

The two merchants pretended to examine and to taste the olives, and told the cady they were new and good. You are deceived, said the young cady; there is Ali Cogia, who says they were put into the jar seven years ago.

Sir, replied the merchants, we can assure you they are of this year's growth; and we will maintain, there is not a merchant in Bagdad but will say the same.

The sham merchant that was accused would fain have objected against the evidence of olive merchants; but the cady would not suffer him. Hold your tongue, said he; you are a rogue, and ought to be hanged. Then the children put an end to their play, by clapping their hands with a great deal of joy, and seizing the criminal, to carry him to execution.

I cannot express how much the caliph Haroun Alraschid admired the wisdom and sense of the boy who had passed so just a sentence, in an affair which was to be pleaded before him the next day; and rising up off the bench he sat on, he asked the grand visier, who heard all that passed, what he thought of it. Indeed, Commander of the True Believers, answered the grand visier Giafar, I am surprised to find so much sense in one so young.

But, answered the caliph, dost thou know one thing? I am to pronounce sentence in this very cause tomorrow, and that the true Ali Cogia presented his petition to me today: And do you think, continued he, that I can judge better? I think not, answered the visier, if the case is as the children represented it. Take notice then of this house, said the caliph, and bring the boy to me tomorrow, that he may judge of this affair in my presence; and also order the cady who acquitted the roguish merchant to attend, to take example by a child: Besides, take care to bid Ali Cogia bring his jar of olives with him, and let two olive merchants be present. After this charge, he pursued his rounds, without meeting with any thing worth his attention.

The next day, the visier went to the house where the caliph had been a witness of the children's play, and asked for the master of it; but he being abroad, his wife came to him. He asked her if she had any children. To which she answered, she had three; and called them. My brave boys, said the visier, which of you was the cady, when you played together last night? The eldest made answer, he was: But not knowing why he asked the question, colored.* Come along with me, child, said the grand visier, the Commander of the Faithful wants to see you.

The mother was in a great fright when she saw the grand visier would take her son with him, and asked him upon what account the caliph wanted him. The grand visier promised her that he should return again in an hour's time, when he would tell her; assuring her he should come to no harm. But pray, sir, said the mother, give me leave to dress him first, that he may be fit to appear before the Commander of the Faithful; which the visier readily complied with.

As soon as the child was dressed, the visier carried him, and presented him to the caliph, at the time he had appointed Ali Cogia and the merchant. The caliph, who saw that the boy was dashed,† to encourage him, said, Come to me, child, and tell me if it was you that determined the affair between Ali Cogia and the merchant that cheated him of his money. I saw and heard you, and am very well pleased with you. The boy answered modestly, that it was he. Well, my dear, replied the caliph, come and sit down by me, and you shall see the true Ali Cogia and the true merchant.

Then the caliph set him on the throne by him, and asked for the two parties. When they were called, they came and prostrated themselves before the throne, bowing their heads quite down to the tapestry. Afterwards, the caliph said to them, Plead both of you your causes before this child, who shall do you both justice; and if he be at any loss, I will rectify it.

Ali Cogia and the merchant pleaded one after the other, as before; but when the merchant proposed his oath, the child said, It is too soon; it is proper that we should see the jar of olives.

At these words, Ali Cogia presented the jar, placed it at the caliph's feet, and opened it. The caliph looked upon the olives, and took one, and tasted of it. Afterwards the merchants were called, who examined the olives, and reported that they were good, and of that year. The boy told them, that Ali Cogia assured him that it was seven years since he put them up; and they returned the same answer as the children who represented them the night before.

Though the merchant who was accused saw plainly that these merchants' opinion would condemn him, yet he would say something in his own justification: When the child, instead of ordering him to be hanged, looked upon the caliph, and said, Commander of the Faithful, this is no jesting matter; it is your majesty that must condemn him to death, and not me, though I did it yesterday in my play.

The caliph, fully satisfied of the merchant's villany,‡ gave him into the hands of the ministers of justice, to be hanged; which sentence was executed upon him, after he had confessed where he had hid the thousand pieces of gold, which were re-

---

*Blushed.

†Awed by being in the presence of the caliph and the court.

‡Crime.

stored to Ali Cogia. Then the monarch, who was all just and equitable, turning to the cady, bid him learn of the child how to acquit himself of his duty; and embracing the boy, sent him home with a purse of a hundred pieces of gold, as a token of his liberality.*

FEUDAL VALUES IN MEDIEVAL WESTERN EUROPE: *THE SONG OF ROLAND*

The contrast between the two cultures of Heian Japan and medieval Islam and that of the medieval west could hardly be greater. Even under Roman rule, western Europe had never been as urban and developed as the eastern Mediterranean lands. But the period dealt with in *The Song of Roland* is not known as the Dark Ages for no reason. Economic life, public administration and safety, cities, and even the population itself were cratering. The population of England, for example, fell from about 4.5 million in the Roman period to a low of about 1.5 million. Such higher culture as existed was restricted to monasteries, as the collapse of the Roman system, a cycle of bad weather, and devastating invasions reduced life to very basic levels. The great lord of *Roland* is Charlemagne, who was indeed the most powerful and dynamic ruler in the west for hundreds of years. Yet despite the mini-Renaissance that occurred during his reign, Charlemagne himself was illiterate and, at 20,000 inhabitants, his capital of Aachen was a provincial burg compared with the caliph's Baghdad, with nearly half a million residents. By 1100, when *Roland* was composed somewhere in the Anglo-Norman realms of England or northern France, Europe had rebounded a great deal from the worst experiences of the Early Middle Ages. Still, it would be some time yet before western Europe passed the Islamic world of the Middle East in wealth, knowledge, population, and power. Although some aspects of so-called courtly love and medieval romances could be compared with aspects of the *Genji* tale and the romantic intrigues of the Heian court, there is nothing in the west to compare with the aesthetic sophistication and style of the medieval Japanese aristocracy.

As Charlemagne was the greatest ruler of the Early Middle Ages, it is only fitting that the greatest epic of that era should involve an expedition launched by him into northern Spain in 778. One of the Moorish rulers of Iberia had invited Charlemagne into Spain to help him against a rival. The main French action was the siege of the northern Iberian city of Saragossa, which siege Charlemagne was forced to lift prematurely because of a revolt in his northern territories. As his forces were leaving Spain through the Pyrenees pass at Roncesvalles, a Basque force attacked and destroyed the rear guard in retaliation for destruction caused

---

*Generosity.

by Charlemagne and his forces. This attack occurred on August 15, 778, and it became the basis for the medieval *chanson de geste,* or epic poem, known as *The Song of Roland.* As indicated, it was probably written down close to 1100 CE, either in Normandy or in Anglo-Norman England.

The events as depicted in *The Song of Roland* diverge from the actual historical record. Essentially, the story of the *chanson* goes as follows: The campaign of Charlemagne in northern Spain has lasted seven years, and only Saragossa, under the Moorish king Marsile, remains to be conquered. To preserve himself and his kingdom, Marsile gives Charlemagne expensive gifts and prominent hostages and promises (falsely) to come north later to be baptized into Christianity and to become Charlemagne's vassal. The great warrior Roland, who is Charlemagne's nephew and his favorite vassal, counsels him to refuse, suspecting treachery, because earlier two negotiators had been killed by Marsile. Roland's stepfather and rival Ganelon urges Charlemagne to accept. Ganelon then becomes very angry when Roland suggests that he be Charlemagne's emissary to Marsile, an indication that he does not truly believe Marsile. Ganelon hatches a plot to ensure that Roland will lead a relatively small rear guard, allowing Marsile's forces to destroy them. The plan works; Roland and his force are destroyed. But Ganelon is arrested by Charlemagne, who knows he is responsible. After Charlemagne has avenged Roland's death by capturing Saragossa, he subjects Ganelon to trial by combat.

Two great clashes occur in *The Song of Roland,* one religious and the other political. The first is the relatively straightforward struggle between Christianity and infidels. Although the attacking force in the real events of 778 were Christian Basques, by the time of the composition of *The Song of Roland* the enemy has become the Muslims of Spain. They are variously referred to as "Saracens" and "pagans," and there are confusing references to "their gods, Tervagant and Muhammad/And Apollo."[3] This aspect of the poem may provide a justification for the recently launched First Crusade to "regain" the Holy Land. Moreover, Charlemagne prays for and receives divine help in making the day last longer, so that he can catch and destroy Marsile's forces. He is also visited and aided by "saint Gabriel." After Saragossa has been taken:

> He has the city searched by a thousand Franks,
> The synagogues and the mosques as well.
> With iron hammers and hatchets which they held
> They shatter the statues and all the idols.
> Neither sorcery nor falseness will be left there.
> The king believes in God; he wants to hold a service
> And his bishops bless the water.
> They take the pagans up to the baptistery;
> If there is anyone who withstands Charles,
> He has him hanged or burned or put to death.
> More than a hundred thousand are baptized
> True Christians, with the exception of the queen.
> She will be taken as a captive to fair France;
> The king wishes her to become a convert through love.[4]

Clearly, *The Song of Roland* is intended in part to show that, as Roland put it, "The pagans are wrong and the Christians are right."[5]

The second and more central contest in *Roland* involves the more complicated issue of what constitutes a true or faithful vassal. Roland's father had already died, and his mother—Charlemagne's sister—married Ganelon. Despite this connection, there is no love lost between Roland and Ganelon. Roland is Ganelon's rival for primacy among Charlemagne's vassals. Moreover, Ganelon has a son by Roland's mother, and it is to this boy, Baldwin, that he bequeaths his lands when he sets out on the mission to Marsile. Ganelon has evil in his heart from the outset. He first recommends that Roland be sent on the mission, but Charlemagne will not hear of it. Then, when Roland suggests Ganelon as the emissary, his stepfather's hatred bursts into the open. He states to Charlemagne:

> . . . "this is all Roland's doing;
> As long as I live, I shall have no love for him,
> Nor Oliver, since he is his companion,
> Nor the twelve peers, because they love him so.
> I challenge them here, lord, in your presence."[6]

To Ganelon, all of Roland's actions are those of a rival feudal lord. When Roland offers to go in his place, he responds, "You will not go in my place; You are not my vassal and I am not your lord."[7] Hence, for Ganelon, his act of vengeance against Roland is a private feud between two independent feudal lords and has no bearing on Ganelon's relationship to Charlemagne as vassal.

The story of *The Song of Roland,* then, is about what constitutes true or faithful behavior and who is a better nobleman—Roland or Ganelon. It is also a story about the contest for power among members of the elite. In that regard it resembles the *Genji* tale, but in a far different culture with vastly different values. As the action begins, Roland, his faithful friend Oliver, and Archbishop Turpin (who is also a warrior knight) realize that they face an enormous army and that they have been set up. Oliver has thrice asked Roland to blow his great horn to summon Charlemagne and the main forces to return and face the Saracens with them, and three times Roland has refused. They will eventually be overwhelmed by the sheer size of the Moorish force, but not before killing incredible numbers of the enemy.

QUESTIONS TO CONSIDER

1. According to the title, Roland is the hero of this piece. Describe his most important attributes and assess what they tell us about ideal behavior of knights and vassals, according to this work.

2. Ganelon is Roland's archenemy. Identify how he is treated by Charlemagne and by others in these passages, and interpret what values the author is trying to impart by having him dealt with in these ways.

3. What do the other knights think of Ganelon's justification of his own actions? What do you make of the fact that only one knight will come forward to serve as Charlemagne's champion in the trial by combat?

4. This tale was part of an oral tradition and then was given shape by a single, unknown author around 1100. Hence it has aspects of the long oral tradition behind the *Arabian Nights* and the singular, authorial voice of *The Tale of Genji*. How does it compare artistically with those two works? Does it seem more similar to one than to the other to you? Or is it distinctive, and, if so, what in your opinion distinguishes it?

5. Here again, we have a different sort of elite, representing a different cultural tradition. Compare the warrior values depicted in this tale with the courtly ways of Heian Japan and the Islamic values of medieval Baghdad. Are there any common elements among the different elites? In the ways that authority is represented? How justice is determined?

THE SONG OF ROLAND

Roland is brave and Oliver is wise;
Both are marvelous vassals.
Now that they are armed and mounted
    on their horses,
Neither will avoid the fray for fear of
    death.
The counts are brave and their words
    lofty;
The treacherous pagans ride on in great
    fury.
Oliver said: "Roland, just see all this;
The enemy is near us, Charles is so far
    away.
You did not deign to blow your horn;
If the king were here, we should suffer
    no harm.
Look up towards the Spanish pass;
The rearguard, as you see, is in a sorry
    plight.
Those who are part of this one will never
    form another."
Roland replies: "Do not speak of such
    outrage;
A curse on the heart which cowers in
    the breast!
We shall stand firm and hold our
    ground,

It is we who shall deal the blows and
    hack men down."

88

When Roland sees that battle will begin,
He becomes fiercer than a lion or a
    leopard.
He hails the Franks and calls to Oliver:
"Lord companion, friend, such words
    should not be spoken;
The emperor who left the Franks with us
Allotted us twenty thousand men,
And to his knowledge there was not a
    coward amongst them.
For his lord a vassal must suffer great
    hardship
And endure both great heat and great
    cold;
He must also part with flesh and blood.
Strike with your lance and I with
    Durendal,
My good sword, which was a gift from
    the king.
If I die here, the man who owns it next
    can say
That it belonged to a noble vassal."

Source: The Song of Roland, trans. Glyn Burgess, 64–65, 87, 148–55. Copyright © 1990 Penguin Books. Used by permission of Penguin Putnam Group (USA) Inc.

89

Archbishop Turpin, some way across the
field,
Spurs on his horse and gallops up a hill.
With these solemn words he calls upon
the Franks:
"Lord barons, Charles has left us here;
For our king we must be prepared to die.
Help us now to sustain the Christian
faith:
You will have to engage in battle, as you
well know;
For you see the Saracens with your own
eyes.
Confess your sins, pray for the grace
of God;
To save your souls I shall absolve you all.
If you die, you will be blessed martyrs
And take your place in paradise on
high."
The Franks dismount and kneel upon
the ground;
In God's name the archbishop blessed
them.
As penance he orders them to strike.

90

The Franks rise and get to their feet;
They are fully absolved and freed of
their sins
And the archbishop in God's name has
blessed them.
Then they mounted their swift war-
horses,
Armed in knightly fashion
And all well equipped for battle.
Count Roland summons Oliver:
"Lord companion, you realized full well
That Ganelon has betrayed us all.
He has accepted gold, riches and
money;
It is the emperor's duty to avenge us.
King Marsile has struck a bargain for
our lives;

But he will have to pay for it with the
sword."

*[Finally, when it has become evident
that the Moorish army will defeat them
unless help arrives, Roland blows his
mighty horn. It is too late, but even
then Ganelon counsels Charlemagne
not to turn back, because it is just
Roland calling attention to himself.
Charlemagne realizes what has happened, and, before turning his forces
around to ride to Roland's defense,
he orders Ganelon arrested.]*

137

The evening sky becomes brighter
And their weapons gleam in the sun;
Hauberks and helmets give off dashes
of light,
And so do their shields, which are richly
painted with flowers,
And their spears and their gilded
pennons.
Full of wrath the emperor rides
And the Franks as well, grieving and
sorrowful.
There is no one who does not weep
profusely
And they are greatly afraid for Roland.
The king has Count Ganelon seized
And he handed him over to his
household cooks.
He summons the master cook, Besgun:
"Guard him for me well, as befits a
criminal;
He has betrayed my household."
The cook takes him and assigns to
the task
A hundred scullions, both best and
worst.
They pluck out his beard and his
moustache
And each gives him four blows with
his fist.

They beat him soundly with sticks and
staves;
They put an iron collar round his neck
And place him in fetters like a bear.
To his shame they set him upon a pack-
horse,
Guarding him until they deliver him to
Charles.

[Having defeated the Moorish armies,
captured Saragossa and avenged Roland,
Charlemagne returns north, and he turns
to the task of dealing with Ganelon. It
turns out, though, that Charlemagne's
greatest vassals now think that punishment of Ganelon would be pointless. They recommend leniency and
restoration of Ganelon to his noble
position. One of Ganelon's vassals,
Pinabel, has offered to step forward for
Ganelon in a trial by combat that will
determine Ganelon's fate. Only one
knight, Thierry, comes forward to back
Charlemagne, and he offers to represent
the king in the trial by combat. This
action, the combat itself and the judgement that befell Ganelon are presented
in the section that follows.]

276

The emperor has returned to Aix;
Ganelon the traitor, in iron chains,
Is in the citadel before the palace.
The servants have tied him to a post;
They bind his hands with thongs of
deer-hide
And beat him thoroughly with sticks and
staves.
He has not deserved a different fate;
In great anguish he awaits his trial there.

277

It is written in the ancient chronicle
That Charles summons vassals from
many lands.

They are assembled in the chapel in Aix.
The day is solemn, the festival is great;
Many say it was Saint Sylvester's day.
Then the trial and the case begin
Of Ganelon who committed treason.
The emperor had him dragged before
him.

278

"Lord barons," said King Charlemagne,
"Give me a true judgement with regard
to Ganelon.
He came with me in my army as far as
Spain
And robbed me of twenty thousand of
my Franks
And my nephew, whom you will never
see again,
Oliver too, the brave and the courtly.
He betrayed the twelve peers for money."
Ganelon said: "A curse on me, if I
conceal this!
Roland wronged me in respect of gold
and wealth;
For which reason I sought his death and
his woe.
But I admit to no treason in this act."
The Franks reply: "Now we shall hold a
council."

279

Ganelon stood there before the king;
His body is robust, his face of noble hue;
If he were loyal, he would seem the
perfect baron.
He sees the men of France and all the
judges
And thirty of his kinsmen who are with
him.
Then he shouted out loudly in clear
tones:
"For the love of God, listen to me,
barons.
Lords, I was in the army with the
emperor;

I served him in faith and in love.
Roland his nephew conceived a hatred
      for me
And nominated me for death and woe.
I was a messenger to King Marsile;
Through my wisdom I managed to
      escape.
I challenged Roland the warrior
And Oliver and all his companions;
Charles heard it and his noble barons.
I avenged myself, but there is no treason
      in it."
The Franks reply: "We shall begin our
      council."

280

When Ganelon sees that his great trial
      is under way,
He had thirty of his kinsmen with him;
There is one to whom the others pay
      attention
He is Pinabel from Castel de Sorence.
He is a skilled talker and a good
      spokesman
And also a good vassal for defending
      his arms.

281

Ganelon said: "In you . . . friend . . .
Now save me from death and from this
      accusation."
Pinabel said: "You will soon be free.
There is no Frank who dares sentence
      you to hang,
To whom, if the emperor brings us
      together,
I shall not give the lie with my steel
      sword."
In thanks Count Ganelon kneels at
      his feet.

282

Bavarians and Saxons have gone to
      the council

And Poitevins and Normans and Franks.
There are many Germans and Teutons
      there.
Those from the Auvergne are the most
      skilled in law;
Because of Pinabel they are inclined to
      peace.
They said to each other: "It is best to let
      matters drop.
Let us abandon the trial and beseech the
      king
To absolve Ganelon this time;
Let him then serve him in love and
      faith.
Roland is dead, never will you see him
      again.
He will not be recovered for gold or any
      sum of money;
Anyone who fought over this would be a
      fool."
There is no one who does not grant this
      and agree,
Except for Thierry, the brother of Lord
      Geoffrey.

283

Charlemagne's barons return to him;
They say to the king: "Lord, we beseech
      you
To absolve Count Ganelon,
Then let him serve you in faith and love.
Let him live, for he is a very noble man.
Never, even if he dies, will this baron
      [i.e., Roland] be seen again
And no amount of money will ever get
      him back for us."
The king said: "You are traitors to me."

284

When Charles sees that everyone has
      failed him,
He bows his head and keeps his face
      down low;
The sorrow he feels makes him bewail
      his fate.

But see, before him stands a knight, Thierry,
The brother of Geoffrey, a duke of Anjou.
His body was spare and slim and slender,
His hair black and his face somewhat tanned.
He is not big, but nor is he too small.
In courtly fashion he spoke to the emperor:
"Fair lord king, do not distress yourself so.
You know that I have served you very well;
By virtue of my ancestors I must make this case:
Whatever Roland may have done to Ganelon,
The act of serving you should have protected him.
Ganelon is a traitor in that he betrayed him;
He committed perjury against you and wronged you.
For this I judge that he be hanged and put to death
And his body should be placed . . .
As befits a man who has committed treason.
If he now has a kinsman who would give me the lie,
With this sword I have girded on
I am willing to uphold my verdict at once."
The Franks reply: "You have spoken well."

285

Pinabel then came before the king.
He is tall and strong, brave and swift;
The man he strikes has come to the end of his days.
He said to the king: "Lord, this trial is yours;
Order that this confusion should cease.
I see Thierry here who has given judgement;

I declare it false and shall do battle with him."
He places in the king's hand his right deerskin gauntlet;
The emperor said: "I required good surety."
So thirty kinsmen make a pledge of loyalty;
The king said: "And I shall set him at liberty."
He has them guarded until the trial takes place.

286

When Thierry sees that there will now be a battle,
He presented his right gauntlet to Charles.
The emperor secures him with hostages;
Then he has four benches brought on to the spot.
Those who are to fight take their seats there;
They are summoned to battle by the agreement of the rest.
Ogier of Denmark explained the procedures;
And then they ask for their horses and their arms.

287

Now that the battle is arranged,
They make confession and are absolved and blessed.
They hear mass and receive communion
And place generous offerings in the churches.
Then they both came back before Charles.
They have their spurs fitted to their feet
And don shining hauberks, strong and light;
Their bright helmets are fastened upon their heads.

They gird on their swords with pommels
of pure gold;
Around their necks they hang their
quartered shields
And in their right hands they carry their
sharp spears.
Then they mounted their swift war-
horses,
Whereupon a hundred thousand knights
began to weep.
Because of Roland they feel pity for
Thierry.
God well knows how it will all end.

288

Beneath Aix the meadow is very broad;
The combat between the two barons has
begun.
They are valiant men of great courage
And their horses are swift and lively.
They spur them on well, letting go the
reins;
With all their might they go to strike
each other.
Their entire shields are shattered and
smashed;
They tear their hauberks and burst their
saddle girths.
Their bows are turned round and their
saddles fall;
A hundred thousand men weep as they
watch them.

289

Both the knights are together on the
ground,
Swiftly they jump back on to their feet.
Pinabel is strong and swift and agile;
They attack each other without their
horses.
With swords whose pommels are of
pure gold
They strike repeatedly on their steel
helmets.

Mighty are the blows which tear apart
the helmets;
Great is the lament of the Frankish
knights.
"O God," said Charles, "make justice
shine forth!"

290

Pinabel said: "Thierry, surrender;
I shall become your vassal in love and
faith
And shall give you as much as you
desire of my wealth.
But let Ganelon be reconciled with the
king."
Thierry replies: "I shall not hear of it.
A curse on me, if I ever agree to this.
Let God show this day which of us is
right."

291

Thierry said: "Pinabel, you are very
brave;
You are tall and strong and your body is
well formed.
Your peers recognize your courage.
Let this combat cease right now;
I shall reconcile you with Charlemagne.
Justice will be done to Ganelon;
No day will dawn without it being
spoken of."
Pinabel said: "May the Lord God forbid!
I want to support all my kinsmen
And shall not surrender for any man
alive.
I should sooner die than be reproached
for this."
With their swords they renew their blows
On their helmets, studded with pure
gold and gems;
Bright sparks fly up towards heaven.
It is not possible to separate them now;
Only when one of them is dead will the
battle end.

292

Pinabel of Sorence is very brave
And he strikes Thierry on his helmet
    from Provence;
The sparks fly on to the grass, setting
    it alight.
The point of his sword of steel bears
    down
On his forehead . . .
He brings it right down on to his face;
His right cheek is covered in blood.
His hauberk is burst open right down
    to his waist;
God protects him from being cast
    down dead.

293

Thierry sees that he is wounded in the
    face;
The clear blood falls on to the grassy
    meadow.
He strikes Pinabel on his helmet of
    burnished steel;
He broke and split it right down to the
    nasal.
His brains spilled forth from his head;
Thierry raised his sword and flung him
    dead.
With this blow the combat is won.
The Franks shout out: "God has
    performed a miracle.
It is right for Ganelon to be hanged
And his kinsmen who upheld his suit."

294

When Thierry has won his combat,
The Emperor Charles came up to him,
Together with forty of his barons,
Duke Naimes, Ogier of Denmark,
Geoffrey of Anjou and William of Blaye.
The king took Thierry in his arms;
He wipes his face with his great marten
    skins;

He lays these aside, then they put others
    on him.
They disarm the knight very gently
And sit him astride a mule from Arabia.
He returns in joy and jubilation.
They arrive at Aix and dismount in the
    square.
At that time the execution of the others
    commences.

295

Charles addresses his counts and his
    dukes:
"What is your advice concerning those
    whom I detained?
They came to support Ganelon in his
    trial;
For Pinabel they agreed to become
    hostages."
The Franks reply: "Not a single one shall
    live."
The king commands his provost,
    Basbrun:
"Go and hang them all from the gallows-
    tree.
By this beard whose hair is hoary white,
If one escapes, you are dead and ruined."
He replies: "What else could I do?"
With a hundred serving-men he leads
    them away by force;
There are thirty of them who were
    hanged.
A traitor kills himself and his fellows.

296

Then the Bavarians and the Germans
    came back,
Together with the Poitevins, Bretons and
    Normans.
Above all others the Franks agreed
That Ganelon should die in terrible
    agony.
They have four war-horses brought
    forward;

Then they bind him by his hands and feet.
The horses are mettlesome and swift;
Four servants goad them on
Towards a stream which flows through a
  field.
Ganelon was given over to total
  perdition.

All his ligaments are stretched taut
And he is torn limb from limb;
His clear blood spills out on to the green
  grass.
Ganelon died a traitor's death.
A man who betrays another has no right
  to boast of it.

ELITE VALUES IN GEOFFREY CHAUCER'S *CANTERBURY TALES*

By Chaucer's day (ca. 1340–1400), both England and western Europe had changed a great deal. They were still probably less advanced than the Muslim world, and warfare continued to bedevil the region. Nonetheless, they were wealthier, both more urban and more urbane, and had come a long way from the worst period of the great collapse in the Early Middle Ages. The great events of Chaucer's era were the Hundred Years' War and the onset of the bubonic plague. The former would not end till 1453, its conclusion greatly accelerated, as was the Ottoman conquest of Constantinople, by the impact of gunpowder weapons. It marked an important transition in politics, ending the Anglo-Norman arrangements that had the English king with holdings both in Britain and on the mainland in France. The latter was an unprecedented demographic disaster, cutting the population nearly in half in 1348–1349. The socioeconomic development, geopolitical transformations, and demographic convulsions of this time period sent shock waves through the theoretically static and unchanging social hierarchy of medieval England. Workers immediately benefited from the drastic drop in the labor force, as wages rose precipitously. Peasant life was affected as well, and by 1381 the social unrest contributed to the Peasants' Revolt (see chapter 12) led by Wat Tyler. By the time of Chaucer's death in 1400, the Renaissance would be under way across Europe. The simplistic estate structure of an earlier day that had divided the population into "those who pray, those who fight, and those who work" no longer coincided in even the remotest fashion to the social diversity and dynamism of Western Europe.

    This most interesting of times found a fitting chronicler in the author of *The Canterbury Tales*. Geoffrey Chaucer was born in 1340 or later, the first child of John Chaucer, a reasonably successful rising man, who pursued both court and business interests. Chaucer himself served in a variety of court and government posts in his lifetime, even holding briefly a position as a member of Parliament. He knew a variety of languages. His government work involved him in missions to the continent, including to Italy, and he was strongly influenced by Italian writers, especially Boccaccio. From 1387 onward (perhaps up to the very end of his life), Chaucer worked on *The Canterbury Tales*. Although he authored other works, it is for this great collection of stories that he is best known. After his death in 1400, he was buried in Westminster Abbey, the first resident of a section that came to be known as "Poet's Corner."

The Canterbury Tales begins with a prologue that introduces the reader to the twenty-nine pilgrims who are joined together on this common journey, and Chaucer reveals much of the character of each in his brief capsule summaries. The work shares certain features with both the *Arabian Nights* in general and the story of Ali Cogia in particular. It has in common with the *Arabian Nights* the presence of multiple stories within the story. Chaucer's device for introducing the tales is a sort of wager or competition proposed to lighten their journey by having each member of the company tell tales on their journey to Canterbury and on the way back. The traveler whose story is judged the best by the general company will be hosted to a sumptuous dinner on the completion of their journey. And like the tale of Ali Cogia, it involves a pilgrimage, in this case to the sacred shrine of Thomas à Becket at Canterbury Cathedral. Also similar to *Arabian Nights* is the presence of characters from diverse social groups. We provide here his characterization of one of his more memorable personalities, the Wife of Bath, followed by her tale.

QUESTIONS TO CONSIDER

1. List the main character traits and life experiences of the Wife of Bath. How does she compare with the female characters in the other stories? Do you think she represents an "ideal woman" of the time?

2. What is the role of play in Chaucer's work in general and in this story in particular? Do you think that the message of this story is intended to be taken seriously, or does the "playful" element undercut the message?

3. How is the knight depicted in this story? What kind of "quest" is the knight on, and how does it compare with the heroic ideal of knighthood presented in *Roland*? What does the fairy-hag have to say about the nobility and commoners? And how does this compare with the image of the noble elite in the other stories?

4. As has been discussed, Chaucer lived in an era of change in politics to more of a national orientation and also a time of great social stress. In that context, is the Wife of Bath's story subversive of traditional medieval values? Does it "encode" a new set of values in terms of gender and class roles? How do the gender and class roles presented in this story compare with the traditional understanding of those roles?

5. Most commentators agree that the narrator of the story represents Chaucer's point of view. What do you think of the artistic self-expression as relates to the character and story of the Wife of Bath? Is Chaucer merely creating a saucy and vital character who tells a humorous story, or does he take seriously both the woman herself and the messages implicit in her story?

"THE WIFE OF BATH'S TALE" FROM *THE CANTERBURY TALES*

Geoffrey Chaucer

A worthy woman there was from near
    the city
Of Bath, but somewhat deaf, and more's
    the pity
For weaving she possessed so great a
    bent
She outdid the people of Ypres and of
    Ghent.
No other woman dreamed of such a
    thing
As to precede her at the offering,
Or if any did, she fell in such a wrath
She dried up all the charity in Bath.
She wore fine kerchiefs of old-fashioned
    air,
And on a Sunday morning, I could
    swear,
She had ten pounds of linen on her
    head.
Her stockings were of finest scarlet-red,
Laced tightly, and her shoes were soft
    and new.
Bold was her face, and fair, and red in
    hue.
She had been an excellent woman all
    her life.
Five men in turn had taken her to wife,
Omitting other youthful company—
But let that pass for now! Over the sea
She had traveled freely; many a distant
    stream
She crossed, and visited Jerusalem
Three times. She had been at Rome and
    at Boulogne,
At the shrine of Compostella, and at
    Cologne.

She had wandered by the way through
    many a scene.
Her teeth were set with little gaps
    between.
Easily on her ambling horse she sat.
She was well wimpled, and she wore a
    hat
As wide in circuit as a shield or targe.
A skirt swathed up her hips, and they
    were large.
Upon her feet she wore sharp-roweled
    spurs.
She was a good fellow; a ready tongue
    was hers.
All remedies of love she knew by name,
For she had all the tricks of that old
    game.

The Wife of Bath's Tale

In the old days when King Arthur ruled
    the nation,
Whom Welshmen speak of with such
    veneration,
This realm we live in was a fairy land.
The fairy queen danced with her jolly
    band
On the green meadows where they held
    dominion.
This was, as I have read, the old opinion;
I speak of many hundred years ago.
But no one sees an elf now, as you
    know,
For in our time the charity and prayers
And all the begging of these holy friars
Who swarm through every nook and
    every stream

Source: Geoffrey Chaucer, *The Portable Chaucer,* ed. Theodore Morrison, 73–74, 243–53. Copyright © 1967 Penguin Books. Used by permission of Viking Books, a division of Penguin Putnam Group (USA) Inc.

Thicker than motes of dust in a sunbeam,
Blessing our chambers, kitchens, halls,
   and bowers
Our cities, towns, and castles, our high
   towers,
Our villages, our stables, barns, and
   dairies,
They keep us all from seeing any fairies,
For where you might have come upon
   an elf
There now you find the holy friar himself
Working his district on industrious legs
And saying his devotions while he begs.
Women are safe now under every tree.
No incubus is there unless it's he,
And all they have to fear from him is
   shame.
     It chanced that Arthur had a knight
     who came
Lustily riding home one day from
   hawking,
And in his path he saw a maiden
   walking
Before him, stark alone, right in his
   course.
This young knight took her maidenhead
   by force,
A crime at which the outcry was so keen
It would have cost his neck, but that the
   queen,
With other ladies, begged the king so
   long
That Arthur spared his life, for right or
   wrong,
And gave him to the queen, at her own
   will,
According to her choice, to save
   or kill.
     She thanked the king, and later
     told this knight.
Choosing her time, "You are still in such
   a plight
Your very life has no security.
I grant your life, if you can answer me
This question: what is the thing that most
   of all

Women desire? Think, or your neck will
   fall
Under the ax! If you cannot let me know
Immediately, I give you leave to go
A twelvemonth and a day, no more, in
   quest
Of such an answer as will meet the test.
But you must pledge your honor to
   return
And yield your body, whatever you may
   learn."
     The knight sighed; he was rueful
     beyond measure.
But what! He could not follow his own
   pleasure,
He chose at last upon his way to ride
And with such answer as God might
   provide
To come back when the year was at the
   close.
And so he takes his leave, and off he
   goes.
     He seeks out every house and
     every place
Where he has any hope, by luck or
   grace,
Of learning what thing women covet
   most.
But it seemed he could not light on any
   coast
Where on this point two people would
   agree,
For some said wealth and some said
   jollity,
Some said position, some said sport in
   bed
And often to be widowed, often wed.
Some said that to a woman's heart what
   mattered
Above all else was to be pleased and
   flattered.
That shaft, to tell the truth, was a close
   hit.
Men win us best by flattery, I admit,
And by attention. Some say our greatest
   ease

Is to be free and do just as we please,
And not to have our faults thrown in our
   eyes,
But always to be praised for being wise.
And true enough, there's not one of us all
Who will not kick if you rub us on a gall.
Whatever vices we may have within,
We won't be taxed with any fault or sin.
   Some say that women are
      delighted well
If it is thought that they will never tell
A secret they are trusted with, or
   scandal.
But that tale isn't worth an old rake
   handle;
We women, for a fact, can never hold
A secret. Will you hear a story told?
Then witness Midas! For it can be read
In Ovid that he had upon his head
Two ass's ears that he kept out of sight
Beneath his long hair with such skill and
   sleight
That no one else besides his wife could
   guess.
He loved her well, and trusted her no
   less.
He begged her not to make his blemish
   known,
But keep her knowledge to herself alone.
She swore that never, though to save her
   skin,
Would she be guilty of so mean a sin,
And yet it seemed to her she nearly died
Keeping a secret locked so long inside.
It swelled about her heart so hard and
   deep
She was afraid some word was bound to
   leap
Out of her mouth, and since there was
   no man
She dared to tell, down to a swamp she
   ran—
Her heart, until she got there, all agog—
And like a bittern booming in the bog
She put her mouth close to the watery
   ground:

"Water, do not betray me with your
   sound!
I speak to you, and you alone," she said.
"Two ass's ears grow on my husband's
   head!
And now my heart is whole, now it is
   out.
I'd burst if I held it longer, past all
   doubt."
Safely, you see, awhile you may confide
In us, but it will out; we cannot hide
A secret. Look in Ovid if you care
To learn what followed; the whole tale
   is there.
   This knight, when he perceived he
      could not find
What women covet most, was low in
   mind;
But the day had come when homeward
   he must ride,
And as he crossed a wooded countryside
Some four and twenty ladies there by
   chance
He saw, all circling in a woodland
   dance,
And toward this dance he eagerly drew
   near
In hope of any counsel he might hear.
But the truth was, he had not reached
   the place
When dance and all, they vanished into
   space.
No living soul remained there to be seen
Save an old woman sitting on the green,
As ugly a witch as fancy could devise.
As he approached her she began to rise
And said, "Sir knight, here runs no
   thoroughfare.
What are you seeking with such anxious
   air?
Tell me! The better may your fortune be.
We old folk know a lot of things," said
   she.
   "Good mother," said the knight,
      "my life's to pay,
That's all too certain, if I cannot say

What women covet most. If you could tell
That secret to me, I'd requite you well."
    "Give me your hand," she answered. "Swear me true
That whatsoever I next ask of you,
You'll do it if it lies within your might
And I'll enlighten you before the night."
    "Granted, upon my honor," he replied.
"Then I dare boast, and with no empty pride,
Your life is safe;" she told him. "Let me die
If the queen herself won't say the same as I.
Let's learn if the haughtiest of all who wear
A net or coverchief upon their hair
Will be so forward as to answer 'no'
To what I'll teach you. No more; let us go."
With that she whispered something in his ear,
And told him to be glad and have no fear.
    When they had reached the court, the knight declared
That he had kept his day, and was prepared
To give his answer, standing for his life.
Many the wise widow, many the wife,
Many the maid who rallied to the scene,
And at the head as justice sat the queen.
Then silence was enjoined; the knight was told
In open court to say what women hold
Precious above all else. He did not stand
Dumb like a beast, but spoke up at command
And plainly offered them his answering word
In manly voice, so that the whole court heard.
    "My liege and lady, most of all," said he,
"Women desire to have the sovereignty

And sit in rule and government above
Their husbands, and to have their way in love.
This is what most you want. Spare me or kill
As you may like; I stand here by your will."
    No widow, wife, or maid gave any token
Of contradicting what the knight had spoken.
He should not die; he should be spared instead;
He was worthy of his life, the whole court said.
    The old woman whom the knight met on the green
Sprang up at this. "My sovereign lady queen,
Before your court has risen, do me right!
It was I who taught this answer to the knight,
For which he pledged his honor in my hand,
Solemnly, that the first thing I demand,
He would do it, if it lay within his might.
Before the court I ask you, then, sir knight,
To take me," said the woman, "as your wife,
For well you know that I have saved your life.
Deny me, on your honor, if you can."
    "Alas," replied this miserable man,
"That was my promise, it must be confessed.
For the love of God, though, choose a new request!
Take all my wealth, and let my body be."
    "If that's your tune, then curse both you and me,"
She said. "Though I am ugly, old, and poor,
I'll have, for all the metal and the ore
That under earth is hidden or lies above,

Nothing, except to be your wife and
   love."
     "My love? No, my damnation, if
     you can!
Alas," he said, "that any of my clan
Should be so miserably misallied!"
     All to no good; force overruled his
     pride,
And in the end he is constrained to wed,
And marries his old wife and goes to
   bed.
     Now some will charge me with an
     oversight
In failing to describe the day's delight,
The merriment, the food, the dress at
   least.
But I reply, there was no joy nor feast;
There was only sorrow and sharp misery.
He married her in private, secretly,
And all day after, such was his distress,
Hid like an owl from his wife's ugliness.
     Great was the woe this knight had
     in his head
When in due time they both were
   brought to bed.
He shuddered, tossed, and turned, and
   all the while
His old wife lay and waited with a smile.
"Is every knight so backward with a
   spouse?
Is it," she said, "a law in Arthur's house?
I am your love, your own, your wedded
   wife.
I am the woman who has saved your life.
I have never done you anything but
   right.
Why do you treat me this way the first
   night?
You must be mad, the way that you
   behave!
Tell me my fault, and as God's love can
   save,
I will amend it, truly, if I can."
     "Amend it?" answered this
     unhappy man.
"It can never be amended, truth to tell.

You are so loathsome and so old as well,
And your low birth besides is such a
   cross
It is no wonder that I turn and toss.
God take my woeful spirit from my
   breast!"
     "Is this," she said, "the cause of
     your unrest?"
     "No wonder!" said the knight. "It
     truly is:"
"Now sir," she said, "I could amend all
   this
Within three days, if it should please me
   to,
And if you deal with me as you should
   do.
     "But since you speak of that
     nobility
That comes from ancient wealth and
   pedigree,
As if that constituted gentlemen,
I hold such arrogance not worth a hen!
The man whose virtue is pre-eminent,
In public and alone, always intent
On doing every generous act he can,
Take him—he is the greatest gentleman!
Christ wills that we should claim nobility
From him, not from old wealth or family.
Our elders left us all that they were
   worth
And through their wealth and blood we
   claim high birth,
But never, since it was beyond their
   giving,
Could they bequeath to us their virtuous
   living;
Although it first conferred on them the
   name
Of gentlemen, they could not leave that
   claim!
     "Dante the Florentine on this was
     wise:
'Frail is the branch on which man's
     virtues rise'—
Thus runs his rhyme—"God's goodness
   wills that we

Should claim from him alone nobility
Thus from our elders we can only claim
Such temporal things as men may hurt
   and maim.
      "It is clear enough that true
      nobility
Is not bequeathed along with property,
For many a lord's son does a deed of
   shame
And yet, God knows, enjoys his noble
   name.
But though descended from a noble
   house
And elders who were wise and virtuous,
If he will not follow his elders, who are
   dead,
But leads, himself, a shameful life
   instead,
He is not noble, be he duke or earl.
It is the churlish deed that makes the
   churl.
And therefore, my dear husband, I
   conclude
That though my ancestors were rough
   and rude,
Yet may Almighty God confer on me
The grace to live, as I hope, virtuously.
Call me of noble blood when I begin
To live in virtue and to cast out sin.
      "As for my poverty, at which you
      grieve;
Almighty God in whom we all believe
In willful poverty chose to lead his life,
And surely every man and maid and
   wife
Can understand that Jesus, heaven's king,
Would never choose a low or vicious
   thing.
A poor and cheerful life is nobly led;
So Seneca and others have well said,
The man so poor he doesn't have a
   stitch,
If he thinks himself repaid, I count him
   rich.
He that is covetous, he is the poor man,
Pining to have the things he never can.

It is of cheerful mind, true poverty.
Juvenal says about it happily:
'The poor man as he goes along his way
And passes thieves is free to sing and
   play.'
Poverty is a good we loathe, a great
Reliever of our busy worldly state,
A great amender also of our minds
As he that patiently will bear it finds.
And poverty, for all it seems distressed,
Is a possession no one will contest.
Poverty, too, by bringing a man low,
Helps him the better both God and self
   to know,
Poverty is a glass where we can see
Which are our true friends, as it seems to
   me.
So, sir, I do not wrong you on this score;
Reproach me with my poverty no more.
      "Now, sir, you tax me with my age;
      but, sir,
You gentlemen of breeding all aver
That men should not despise old age, but
   rather
Grant an old man respect, and call him
   'father':
      "If I am old and ugly, as you have
      said,
You have less fear of being cuckolded,
For ugliness and age, as all agree,
Are notable guardians of chastity.
But since I know in what you take
   delight,
I'll gratify your worldly appetite.
      "Choose now, which of two
      courses you will try:
To have me old and ugly till I die
But evermore your true and humble
   wife,
Never displeasing you in all my life,
Or will you have me rather young and
   fair
And take your chances on who may
   repair
Either to your house on account of me
Or to some other place, it well may be.

Now make your choice, whichever you
　　prefer."
　　　　The knight took thought, and
　　　　sighed, and said to her
At last, "My love and lady, my dear wife,
In your wise government I put my life.
Choose for yourself which course will
　　best agree
With pleasure and honor, both for you
　　and me.
I do not care, choose either of the two;
I am content, whatever pleases you."
　　　　"Then have I won from you the
　　　　sovereignty,
Since I may choose and rule at will?"
　　said she.
　　　　He answered, "That is best, I think,
　　　　dear wife."
　　　　"Kiss me," she said. "Now we are
　　　　done with strife,
For on my word, I will be both to you,
That is to say, fair, yes, and faithful too.
May I die mad unless I am as true
As ever wife was since the world was
　　new.
Unless I am as lovely to be seen
By morning as an empress or a queen
Or any lady between east and west,
Do with my life or death as you think best.

Lift up the curtain, see what you may
　　see."
　　　　And when the knight saw what
　　　　had come to be
And knew her as she was, so young, so
　　fair,
His joy was such that it was past
　　compare.
He took her in his arms and gave her
　　kisses
A thousand times on end; he bathed in
　　blisses.
And she obeyed him also in full measure
In everything that tended to his pleasure.
　　　　And so they lived in full joy to the
　　　　end.
And now to all us women may Christ
　　send
Submissive husbands, full of youth in
　　bed,
And grace to outlive all the men we
　　wed.
And I pray Jesus to cut short the lives
Of those who won't be governed by their
　　wives;
And old, ill-tempered niggards who hate
　　expense,
God promptly bring them down with
　　pestilence!

NOTES

1. Richard Bowring, *Muraski Shikibu: The Tale of Genji* (Cambridge and New York: Cambridge University Press, 1988), 4–5.

2. In the original, she is also referred to as Princess Akikonomu. To make the already complicated story a little less confusing, we refer to her as Murasaki throughout.

3. *The Song of Roland*, trans. Glyn Burgess (London: Penguin Books, 1990), 114.

4. Ibid., 145–46.

5. Ibid., p. 61.

6. Ibid., p. 39.

7. Ibid., p. 38.

PART FOUR

TOWARD A GLOBAL WORLD: 1100 CE TO 1500 CE

CHAPTER 11

The Encounter between War and Religion

INTRODUCTION

In the wake of September 11, 2001, President George W. Bush called for a "crusade" against terrorism. The crusading label was almost instantly withdrawn and repudiated because of the very problematic historical resonances it raised for the Islamic world, whose cooperation would be necessary in any attempt to deal with global terrorism. But in the Bush Administration's "war on terrorism" and in the subsequent real wars in Afghanistan and Iraq, the idea of a "clash of civilizations" (to use Samuel P. Huntington's simplistic phrase), of a set of wars at least partially informed by differences in religion, lurked just below the surface of official rhetoric and received explicit expression by religious extremists on both sides.

Yet talk of "holy war" in the modern world makes many people uncomfortable. The idea of aggressive warfare, in particular, being sanctioned by major religions whose central message focuses on peace, love, and brotherhood in a world whose United Nations Charter calls for religious freedom, tolerance, and respect for human rights strikes many as anachronistic and wrongheaded. In other words, war and religion in our modern world do not mix well. The very history that made President Bush's use of the term *crusade* problematic, however, shows that religion and warfare have long been linked historically—that religion and warfare encountered each other from early on. Why? And what was the nature of this encounter? This chapter explores some of the answers to those questions and examines the ways in which religious precepts, religiously inspired worldviews, and religiously based theories of "Just War" encountered and interacted with the practice of war itself.

Even before the rise of the salvation faiths, religion had been central to the worldview of most traditional civilizations, as we saw in chapter 4. This centrality became even more pronounced after the rise of the salvation religions, which we examined in chapters 8 and 9, as these religions assumed important roles even in areas such as China, where a dominant strand of that civilization's worldview was based in a secular philosophy, Confucianism. As a central part of a civilization's worldview, religion not only explained the cosmos and guided ethical thinking but also tended to be a, if not the, pillar of legitimacy for the governments of traditional states. This is where it came into contact with war making, for as we saw in chapter 5, and in a different form in chapter 7, states (and their nomadic neighbors) invariably and consistently conducted warfare for a whole range of reasons. What was a religion, especially one adopted as the official creed of an empire, to say about making war? The rise of the salvation religions, with their universalist claims, had the potential to raise the stakes in terms of government and warfare, for the outcome of wars could be seen from this perspective as signaling God's divine favor for one political faction or faith over another—religion and war could now produce, in short, "holy war." One key, then, to understanding the relationship of war and religion is to understand the relationship of religion to states, or the encounter of faith and power.

Attitudes compatible with holy war have their roots, especially in southwest Asia, in presalvationist religions that were closely tied to a particular people and so to a particular state. The Hebrew Scriptures are full of tales of God smiting the foes of the Israelites or ordering His people to fight for a homeland or their freedom. This sanctioning of warfare worked most easily when a Hebrew kingdom still existed, of course; once it ceased to, prophets such as Isaiah reinterpreted warfare in terms of God's universal plan for history. Yet the Persians, beneficiaries of this reinterpretation, already had their own universal-seeming but essentially exclusive religion in Zoroastrianism that also sanctioned the warfare of the Persian state unproblematically. In a similar but more restricted way in south Asia, Hinduism also sanctioned warfare on the part of the warrior caste, as represented in the *Bhagavad-Gita* and its tale of Arjuna's ethical dilemma. While subordinating warrior authority to priestly authority, at least in theory, Hindu thought still carved out a place for warfare among the tools of statecraft. (See chapter 4 for the *Gita,* Zoroastrianism, and Isaiah.)

The attitudes of Christianity, Islam, and Buddhism toward warfare were more complicated, and they are explored in the sources for this chapter. They stem from the "foundational events" of each religion, discussed in the introduction to chapter 9: the conversion of the Mauryan emperor Asoka in 261 BCE, the conversion of the Roman emperor Constantine in 312, and the career of Muhammad in the 620s. After his conversion, Asoka forswore offensive warfare, and as a rule afterward Buddhism had little to do with direct sanctioning of warfare, though in Japan after c. 1000 Buddhism, especially though not exclusively in its Zen form, came to be associated with the ethos of the *bushi,* the Japanese warrior class. But the tradition of *in hoc signo vinces*—"under this sign you will conquer"—established by Constantine linked Christianity with warfare from its earliest days as a state-favored religion, and Muhammad fought from early in his career to establish his community of believers, again linking warfare to the religion from its inception. It is not accidental that both religions between 300 and 1000 developed conceptions of holy war unknown in Buddhism. Some historians identify the first Christian "crusade" in the campaigns of the East Roman emperor Heraclius in the early 600s against the Persians, who themselves campaigned under the banner of a militant Zoroastrianism. The first wave of Islamic *jihad* then burst on both sides, swallowing the Persians and reducing the Byzantine Empire to a Holy Land under siege.

Still, there is a subtle but important difference in the way each religion was connected to warfare. Christianity always accepted the existence (indeed the necessity) of the state, having grown up under the Roman Empire at its height. Even as a minority and sometimes persecuted religion, the notion of "rendering unto Caesar" recognized the state and its functions, including warfare. (Christian pacifism was always the view only of a small minority.) Once Christianity became the state religion, the efforts of Christian thinkers were directed not toward arguing against war but toward arguing about when it was justified. Christian Just War theory was largely a product of the writings of Augustine of Hippo (354–430) and equated warfare with the other exercise of coercive force on the part of the state, law and justice. In short, Christianity accepted the state and therefore had to accept (and justify) at least some warfare.

Islam, on the other hand, developed from Arab tribal traditions that set themselves against the imperial state structures of Rome and Persia that dominated Southwest Asia in 600. Thus, as the scholars and jurists of the Islamic *ulema* came to define Islam in the two centuries after the initial Islamic conquests, a curious result emerged. Warfare in the form of *jihad* (literally "struggle") against unbelievers was unproblematic as an activity of the Islamic community, having been established by the Prophet himself. But the state, because it usually resembled by necessity the imperial structures of the Romans and Persians against whom the *ulema* defined Islam, came easily to be seen as essentially illegitimate, though not by definition. This left Islamic warfare as being acceptable in itself (though not against other Muslims), while the only structure capable of organizing such warfare was often not acceptable. As a result, there was a significant strain of Muslim thought that defined *jihad* in terms of the internal, individual struggle of individuals against evil, not in terms of a state-organized activity. At the same time, Islamic military systems came to rely on slave soldiers and frontier tribes—groups outside the mainstream of Islamic society—for manpower. In short, by rejecting the state (at least practical states), Islam made problematic the practice of warfare by Islamic communities.

Ironically, it was the Crusades, the culmination of the development of Christian notions of holy war, that by bringing holy war to Islam did much to revive the alternate tradition of *jihad* as real warfare rather than individual struggle. The First Crusade (1097–1101) is thus a crucial episode in the history of holy war for both Christianity and Islam, and it set the tone for relationships between the two civilizations for the next 400 years and beyond.

Despite all these differences, however, Christianity, Islam, and Buddhism all attempted in various ways to place restrictions on warfare—in practice, for example, Muslim Just War theory came to resemble Christian Just War theory fairly closely. On the other hand, religious differences often seemed not to restrict but to inflame the passions of war when peoples of different faiths fought each other. Our exploration of the encounter between religion and warfare in the period from 1100 to 1500 will examine both the similarities and the important divergences in the connection between war and different religions.

CHAPTER QUESTIONS

1. What is the relationship in each religion between cosmic order and earthly order? That is, what role does the religion take in ensuring peace in this life, as well as salvation in the next?
2. What impact does this connection have for individual followers of each religion in terms of waging warfare? Is it a duty? A necessary evil? A desired activity?
3. How did the nature of a belief system affect its interpretation of war? Did the ethical values of each religion require adjustment in the encounter with war? What are the overall similarities and differences in each religion's relationship to warfare compared with the others?
4. What do you think accounts for these similarities and differences?
5. Which view of the connection of religion and warfare seems most applicable to warfare in the twenty-first century? Why?

CHRISTIANITY AND WAR

Thomas Aquinas (1224–1274) was the greatest medieval Christian theologian, a teacher at universities in Paris and Rome and a prolific writer. His masterpiece, the *Summa Theologiae,* or *Summation of Theology,* explored Catholic Christian scholarship in a huge range of fields and represents the highpoint of the medieval synthesis of faith and reason. He wrote during the second century of crusading, when the major Crusades were being led by Louis IX of France. (Louis earned sainthood for his piety, not necessarily for the results of his crusades, which were consistently disasters.) He was therefore very familiar with the theological and ethical questions surrounding the exercise of force by Christian states.

Drawing on a number of sources, but most crucially on various writings of St. Augustine, Aquinas summarized Christian theories of Just War in one small part of the *Summa.* The structure of this section, like all the sections of the *Summa,* presents first the views with which Aquinas disagrees, stated as answers to a specific question (in this case "Is it always a sin to wage war?"). Aquinas then cites, under the heading "On the Other Hand," a quote from Scripture or some earlier theologian that calls the opposing position into question. Finally, under the heading "Reply," he presents his own case, which answers the points presented initially.

QUESTIONS TO CONSIDER

1. What conditions does Aquinas say are necessary for a war to be waged justly? What kinds of Christian behaviors must a warrior practice in order to make war just, according to Aquinas?
2. Do Aquinas's justifications of war answer adequately the arguments for war as a sin presented in the first part of the reading? How does this encounter between Christianity and war result in a "Christianized" ideal of warfare?

3. What sorts of authorities or sources back up his argument? In other words, how does the history of Christianity inform his answers? How important does religion seem to this theory?

4. How easy to fulfill are the conditions Aquinas lays out? Are they sufficient? Too restrictive? Not restrictive enough? In your opinion, is it possible while engaged in actual combat to maintain the Christian principles Aquinas lays out?

5. Are Aquinas's conditions universal? That is, do they work to describe the just-ness of modern wars, even if they are not waged by Christian states, or is this a culturally restricted view of the justness of war?

SUMMA THEOLOGIAE

Thomas Aquinas

Second Part of the Second Part, Question 40: Concerning War
Article 1. Is it always a sin to wage war?

THE FIRST POINT: 1. It would seem that it is always a sin to wage war. Punishments are meted out only for sin. But our Lord named the punishment for people who wage war when he said, "All who draw the sword will die by the sword" (Matthew 26.52). Every kind of war, then, is unlawful.

2. Moreover, whatever goes against a divine command is a sin. But war does that. Scripture says, "But I say this to you, offer the wicked man no resistance." (Matthew 5.39). Also, "Not revenging yourselves, my dearly beloved, but give place to [the] wrath [of God]" (Romans 12.19). War is always a sin then.

3. Besides, the only thing that stands as a contrary to the act of virtue is a sin. Now war is the contrary of peace. Therefore, it is always a sin.

4. Besides, if an action is lawful, practicing for it would be lawful, as is obvious in the practice involved in the sciences [e.g. medicine]. But warlike exercises which go on in tournaments are forbidden by the church, since those killed in such trials are de-nied ecclesiastical burial. Consequently, war appears to be plainly wrong.

ON THE OTHER HAND, Augustine says [commenting on John the Baptist's advice to the Roman soldiers in Luke 3.14], "If Christian teaching forbade war altogether, those looking for the salutary advice of the Gospel would have been told to get rid of their arms and give up soldiering. But instead they were told, 'Do violence to no man, be content with your pay.' If this ordered them to be satisfied with their pay, then it did not forbid a military career."

REPLY: Three things are required for any war to be just. The first is the authority of the sovereign on whose command war is waged. Now, a private person has no business

---

Source: Thomas Aquinas, *Summa Theologiae* in *Latin Text and English Translation, Introductions, Notes, Appendices, and Glossaries* (New York: McGraw-Hill, 1964–), Pt. 2, Qu. 40, Art. 1.

declaring war. He can seek redress by appealing to the judgment of his superiors. Nor can he summon together whole people, which has to be done to fight a war. Since the care of the commonweal is committed to those in authority, they are the ones to watch over the public affairs of the city, kingdom, or province in their jurisdiction. And just as they use the sword in lawful defense against domestic disturbance when they punish criminals, as Paul says—"He does not bear the sword in vain, for he is God's minister, an avenger to execute wrath upon him that does evil" (Romans 13.4)—so they lawfully use the sword of war to protect the commonweal from foreign attacks. Thus it is said to those in authority, "Rescue the weak and the needy, save them from the clutches of the wicked" (Psalms 82.3). Hence Augustine writes, "The natural order conducive to human peace demands that the power to counsel and declare war belongs to those who hold the supreme authority."

Secondly, a just cause is required, namely that those who are attacked are attacked because they deserve it on account of some wrong they have done. So Augustine says, "We usually describe a just war as one that avenges wrongs, that is, when a nation or state has to be punished either for refusing to make amends for outrages done by its subjects, or to restore what it has seized injuriously."

Thirdly, the right intention of those waging war is required, that is, they must intend to promote the good and to avoid evil. Hence Augustine writes, "Among true worshippers of God, those wars are looked on as peace-making which are waged neither from aggrandizement nor cruelty, but with the object of securing peace, of repressing the evil and supporting the good." Now it can happen that, even given a legitimate authority and a just cause for declaring war, it may yet be wrong because of a perverse intention. So again Augustine says, "The craving to hurt people, the cruel thirst for revenge, the unappeased and unrelenting spirit, the savageness of fighting on, the lust to dominate, and suchlike—all these are rightly condemned in wars."

Hence: 1. On the first point, as Augustine says, "'To draw the sword' is to arm oneself and to spill blood without command or permission of superior or lawful authority." But if a private person uses the sword by the authority of the sovereign or judge, or a public person uses it through zeal for justice, and by the authority, so to speak, of God, then he himself does not 'draw the sword,' but is commissioned by another to use it. He thus does not deserve punishment. Still, even those who do use it sinfully are not always slain with the sword. Yet they will always 'die by the sword,' since they will be punished eternally for their sinful use of it unless they repent.

2. On the second point, these words, as Augustine says, must always be borne in readiness of mind, so that a man must always be prepared to refrain from resistance or self-defense if the situation calls for it. Sometimes, however, he must act otherwise for the common good or even for the good of his opponents. Thus Augustine writes, "One must do many things with a kind of benign severity with those who must be punished against their will. Now whoever is stripped of the lawlessness of sin is overcome for his own good, since nothing is unhappier than the happiness of sinners. It encourages guilty impunity, and strengthens bad will, the enemy inside us."

3. On the third point, even those who wage a just war intend peace. They are not then hostile to peace, except that evil peace which our Lord "did not come to send on the earth" (Matthew 10.34). So Augustine again says, "We do not seek peace in order to

wage war, but we go to war to gain peace. Therefore be peaceful even while you are at war, that you may overcome your enemy and bring him to the prosperity of peace."

4. On the fourth point, warlike exercises are not completely forbidden—only those which are excessive and dangerous, and end in killing and looting. In olden time, they presented no such danger. So, as Jerome writes, they were called "practices of arms" or "wars without blood."*

CHRISTIAN ACCOUNTS OF THE FIRST CRUSADE

In response to requests from the Byzantine Empire for mercenaries to help them fight the Sejuk Turks, who had overrun the heart of Asia Minor and taken much of the Holy Land in the decades after defeating the Byzantines at Manzikert in 1071, Pope Urban II (1088–1099) called for an armed pilgrimage to Jerusalem to free the Holy Land from the hands of the Saracens. Preaching first at Claremont, in France, in 1095, his call met an immediate and overwhelmingly enthusiastic response. A crusade (so called from the crosses those who took the pledge sewed onto their surcoats) resulted, the first of many, as it turned out. Our first selection is one version (of five that we have) of the speech Pope Urban II gave at Claremont in 1095 that launched the First Crusade.

It took two years for the expedition to get under way, and it was led not by any of the kings of Europe but by a motley assortment of second-rank rulers, mostly French, including the Count of Aquitaine and the Duke of Normandy. It achieved success beyond any reasonable expectation, defeating several Turkish armies along the way and surviving a ten-month siege at Antioch, the major city of northern Syria, in 1097–1098. After a siege during which the Crusaders nearly starved to death, they captured the city, only to be besieged in turn by a Turkish Muslim army under the Turkish amir of Mosul, Kerbogha. With morale at a critical low, the events described in the third selection took place. In June 1099 they reached Jerusalem, which was captured in a bloody massacre on July 15, 1099. Fulk of Chartres, the author of our fourth selection, participated in the storming of the city. This victory capped the creation of a set of Christian-ruled states along the eastern Mediterranean seaboard.

QUESTIONS TO CONSIDER

1. What are Pope Urban's reasons for urging the Franks (a term for the French and for western Europeans generally in much Crusading literature) to take up arms and go to the Holy Land? Could someone motivated to join the

---

*This is actually from a treatise on Roman military practices called *A Summary of Military Matters,* written around 400 CE by an imperial Roman administrator named Flavius Vegetius Renatus, and widely studied in the Middle Ages.

Crusade by Urban's speech approach the war in the way that Aquinas required for just war?

2. What is the tone of his speech in presenting these reasons? Is this a rational appeal, or an emotional one? Or both? How important is religion in the appeal? What motivations other than religious ones does Urban give? Does his presentation of the reasons for this war conform to the requirements for a Just War laid out by Aquinas?

3. How does the religion of Aquinas and Pope Urban compare with the popular conception of the connection of religion and war seen in the events at Antioch?

4. Does what happened at Jerusalem strike you as a logical outcome of Urban's appeal? Is it in conformity with Aquinas's conditions for a Just War?

5. What is the relationship of Christianity and warfare as it appears in this set of sources?

POPE URBAN PREACHES THE FIRST CRUSADE (1095)

The Version of Robert the Monk

Oh, race of Franks, race from across the mountains, race chosen and beloved by God as shines forth in very many of your works, set apart from all nations by the situation of your country, as well as by your catholic faith and the honor of the holy church! To you our discourse is addressed and for you our exhortation is intended. We wish you to know what a grievous cause has led us to your country, what peril threatening you and all the faithful has brought us.

From the confines of Jerusalem and the city of Constantinople a horrible tale has gone forth and very frequently has been brought to our ears, namely, that a race from the kingdom of the Persians,* an accursed race, a race utterly alienated from God, a generation forsooth which has not directed its heart and has not entrusted its spirit to God, has invaded the lands of those Christians and has depopulated them by the sword, pillage and fire; it has led away a part of the captives into its own country, and a part it has destroyed by cruel tortures; it has either entirely destroyed the churches of God or appropriated them for the rites of its own religion. They destroy the altars, after having defiled them with their uncleanness. They circumcise the Christians, and the blood of the circumcision they either spread upon the altars or pour into the vases of the baptismal font. When they wish to torture people by a base death, they perforate their navels, and dragging forth the extremity of the intestines, bind it to a stake; then with flogging they lead the victim around until the viscera having gushed forth the victim falls prostrate upon the ground. Others they bind to a post and pierce with arrows. Others they compel to extend their necks and then, attacking them with naked swords, at-

Source: Selected from Dana C. Munro, "Urban and the Crusaders," *Translations and Reprints from the Original Sources of European History*, Vol 1:2 (Philadelphia: University of Pennsylvania, 1895), 5–8.
*An archaic way of referring to the Turks.

tempt to cut through the neck with a single blow. What shall I say of the abominable rape of the women? To speak of it is worse than to be silent.* The kingdom of the Greeks is now dismembered by them and deprived of territory so vast in extent that it can not be traversed in a march of two months. On whom therefore is the labor of avenging these wrongs and of recovering this territory incumbent, if not upon you? You, upon whom above other nations God has conferred remarkable glory in arms, great courage, bodily activity, and strength to humble the hairy scalp of those who resist you.

Let the deeds of your ancestors move you and incite your minds to manly achievements; the glory and greatness of king Charles the Great,† and of his son Louis, and of your other kings, who have destroyed the kingdoms of the pagans, and have extended in these lands the territory of the holy church. Let the holy sepulcher of the Lord our Savior, which is possessed by unclean nations, especially incite you, and the holy places which are now treated with ignominy and irreverently polluted with their filthiness. Oh, most valiant soldiers and descendants of invincible ancestors, be not degenerate, but recall the valor of your progenitors.

But if you are hindered by love of children, parents and wives, remember what the Lord says in the Gospel, "He that loveth father or mother more than me, is not worthy of me." "Every one that hath forsaken houses, or brethren, or sisters, or father, or mother, or wife, or children, or lands for my name's sake shall receive an hundred-fold and shall inherit everlasting life." Let none of your possessions detain you, no solicitude for your family affairs, since this land which you inhabit, shut in on all sides by the seas and surrounded by the mountain peaks, is too narrow for your large population; nor does it abound in wealth; and it furnishes scarcely food enough for its cultivators. Hence it is that you murder one another, that you wage war, and that frequently you perish by mutual wounds. Let therefore hatred depart from among you, let your quarrels end, let wars cease, and let all dissensions and controversies slumber. Enter upon the road to the Holy Sepulcher; wrest that land from the wicked race, and subject it to yourselves. That land which as the Scripture says "floweth with milk and honey," was given by God into the possession of the children of Israel. Jerusalem is the navel of the world; the land is fruitful above others, like another paradise of delights. This the Redeemer of the human race has made illustrious by His advent, has beautified by residence, has consecrated by suffering, has redeemed by death, has glorified by burial. This royal city, therefore, situated at the center of the world, is now held captive by His enemies, and is in subjection to those who do not know God, to the worship of the heathens. She seeks therefore and desires to be liberated, and does not cease to implore you to come to her aid. From you especially she asks succor, because, as we have already said, God has conferred upon you above all nations great glory in arms. Accordingly undertake this journey for the remission of your sins, with the assurance of the imperishable glory of the kingdom of heaven.

When Pope Urban had said these and very many similar things in his urbane discourse, he so influenced to one purpose the desires of all who were present, that they cried out, "It is the will of God! It is the will of God!" When the venerable Roman pontiff heard that, with eyes uplifted to heaven he gave thanks to God and, with his hand commanding silence, said:

---

*This list of charges is vastly exaggerated.

†Charlemagne.

Most beloved brethren, today is manifest in you what the Lord says in the Gospel, "Where two or three are gathered together in my name there am I in the midst of them." Unless the Lord God had been present in your spirits, all of you would not have uttered the same cry. For, although the cry issued from numerous mouths, yet the origin of the cry was one. Therefore I say to you that God, who implanted this in your breasts, has drawn it forth from you. Let this then be your war-cry in combats, because this word is given to you by God. When an armed attack is made upon the enemy, let this one cry be raised by all the soldiers of God: It is the will of God! It is the will of God!

And we do not command or advise that the old or feeble, or those unfit for bearing arms, undertake this journey; nor ought women to set out at all, without their husbands or brothers or legal guardians. For such are more of a hindrance than aid, more of a burden than advantage. Let the rich aid the needy; and according to their wealth, let them take with them experienced soldiers. The priests and clerks of any order are not to go without the consent of their bishop; for this journey would profit them nothing if they went without permission of these. Also, it is not fitting that laymen should enter upon the pilgrimage without the blessing of their priests.

Whoever, therefore, shall determine upon this holy pilgrimage and shall make his vow to God to that effect and shall offer himself to Him as a living sacrifice, holy, acceptable unto God, shall wear the sign of the cross of the Lord on his forehead or on his breast. When, truly, having fulfilled his vow be wishes to return, let him place the cross on his back between his shoulders. Such, indeed, by the twofold action will fulfill the precept of the Lord, as He commands in the Gospel, "He that taketh not his cross and followeth after me, is not worthy of me."

THE FINDING OF THE HOLY LANCE
AT ANTIOCH (1098)

The Account of the Gesta Francorum

There was a certain pilgrim of our army, whose name was Peter, to whom before we entered the city St. Andrew, the apostle, appeared and said: "What art thou doing, good man?"

Peter answered, "Who art thou?"

The apostle said to him: "I am St. Andrew, the apostle. Know, my son, that when thou shalt enter the town, go to the church of St. Peter. There thou wilt find the Lance of our Saviour, Jesus Christ, with which He was wounded as He hung on the arm of the cross." Having said all this, the apostle straightway withdrew.

But Peter, afraid to reveal the advice of the apostle, was unwilling to make it known to the pilgrims.

Source: August C. Krey, *The First Crusade: The Accounts of Eyewitnesses and Participants* (Princeton, NJ: Princeton University Press, 1921), 174–76.

However, he thought that he had seen a vision, and said: "Lord, who would believe this?" But at that hour St. Andrew took him and carried him to the place where the Lance was hidden in the ground. When we were a second time situated in such (straits) as we have stated above, St. Andrew came again, saying to him: "Wherefore hast thou not yet taken the Lance from the earth as I commanded thee? Know verily, that whoever shall bear this Lance in battle shall never be overcome by an enemy." Peter, indeed, straightway made known to our men the mystery of the apostle.

The people, however, did not believe (it), but refused, saying: "How can we believe this?" For they were utterly terrified and thought that they were to die forthwith. Thereupon, this man came forth and swore that it was all most true, since St. Andrew had twice appeared to him in a vision and had said to him: "Rise, go and tell the people of God not to fear, but to trust firmly with whole heart in the one true God and they will be everywhere victorious. Within five days the Lord will send them such a token that they will remain happy and joyful, and if they wish to fight, let them go out immediately to battle, all together, and all their enemies will be conquered, and no one will stand against them." Thereupon, when they heard that their enemies were to be overcome by them, they began straightway to revive and to encourage one another, saying: "Bestir yourselves, and be everywhere brave and alert, since the Lord will come to our aid in the next battle and will be the greatest refuge to His people whom He beholds lingering in sorrow."

Accordingly, upon hearing the statements of that man who reported to us the revelation of Christ through the words of the apostle, we went in haste immediately to the place in the church of St. Peter which he had pointed out. Thirteen men dug there from morning until vespers. And so that man found the Lance, just as he had indicated. They received it with great gladness and fear, and a joy beyond measure arose in the whole city.

BATTLE WITH KERBOGHA OUTSIDE ANTIOCH (1098)

The Account of the Gesta Francorum

[Inspired by the "discovery" of the Holy Lance, the Crusaders sallied out to do battle with their besiegers.]

At length, when the three days fast had been fulfilled, and a procession had been held from one church to another, they confessed their sins, were absolved, and faithfully took the communion of the body and blood of Christ; and when alms had been given they celebrated mass. Then six battle lines were formed from the forces within the city [taking the Holy Lance with them]. . . . Our bishops, priests, clerics, and monks, dressed in holy vestments, came out with us with crosses, praying and

Source: August C. Krey, *The First Crusade: The Accounts of Eyewitnesses and Participants* (Princeton, NJ: Princeton University Press, 1921), 182–85.

beseeching the Lord to make us safe, guard us, and deliver us from all evil. Some stood on the wall of the gate, holding the sacred crosses in their hands, making the sign (of the cross) and blessing us. Thus were we arrayed, and, protected with the sign of the cross, we went forth through the gate which is before the mosque.

After Kerbogha saw the lines of the Franks, so beautifully formed, coming out one after the other, he said: "Let them come out, that we may the better have them in our power!" But after they were outside the city and Kerbogha saw the huge host of the Franks, he was greatly frightened. He straightway sent word to his Emir, who had everything in charge, that if he saw a light burn at the head of the army he should have the trumpets sounded for it to retreat, knowing that the Turks had lost the battle. . . . Duke Godfrey, the Count of Flanders, and Hugh the Great rode near the water, where the enemy's strength lay. These men, fortified by the sign of the cross, together attacked the enemy first. When the other lines saw this, they likewise attacked. The Turks and the Persians in their turn cried out. Thereupon, we invoked the Living and True God and charged against them, and in the name of Jesus Christ and of the Holy Sepulchre we began the battle, and, God helping, we overcame them. But the terrified Turks took to flight, and our men followed them to the tents. Thereupon, the knights of Christ chose rather to pursue them than to seek any spoils. . . . The enemy, indeed, left their pavilions there, gold, silver, and many ornaments, also sheep, cattle, horses, mules, camels, asses, grain, wine, butter, and many other things which we needed. When the Armenians and Syrians who dwelt in those regions heard that we had overcome the Turks, they ran to the mountain to meet them and killed as many of them as they could catch. We, however, returned to the city with great joy and praised and blessed God, who gave the victory to His people. . . .

This battle was fought on the fourth day before the Kalends of July, on the vigil of the apostles Peter and Paul, in the reign of our Lord Jesus Christ, who has honor and glory forever and ever. Amen. And after our enemies had now been completely conquered, we gave fitting thanks to God, Three and One, and the Highest. Some of the enemy, exhausted, others, wounded in their flight hither and thither, succumbed to death in valley, forest, fields, and roads. But the people of Christ, that is, the victorious pilgrims, returned to the city, rejoicing in the happy triumph over their defeated foes.

THE SIEGE AND CAPTURE OF JERUSALEM
(1099)

On the seventh of June the Franks besieged Jerusalem. . . . The Saracens defended themselves vigorously, and, with slings, very skillfully hurled back burning firebrands,

Source: Fulk (or Fulcher) of Chartres, *Gesta Francorum Jerusalem Expugnantium [The Deeds of the Franks Who Attacked Jerusalem]*, in Frederick Duncan and August C. Krey, eds., *Parallel Source Problems in Medieval History* (New York: Harper & Brothers, 1912), pp. 109–15.

which had been dipped in oil and fresh fat. Many on both sides, fighting in this manner, often found themselves in the presence of death.

. . . On the following day the work again began at the sound of the trumpet, and to such purpose that the rams, by continual pounding, made a hole through one part of the wall. The Saracens suspended two beams before the opening, supporting them by ropes, so that by piling stones behind them they would make an obstacle to the rams. However, what they did for their own protection became, through the providence of God, the cause of their own destruction. For, when the tower was moved nearer to the wall, the ropes that supported the beams were cut; from these same beams the Franks constructed a bridge, which they cleverly extended from the tower to the wall. About this time one of the towers in the stonewall began to burn, for the men who worked our machines had been hurling firebrands upon it until the wooden beams within it caught fire. The flames and smoke soon became so bad that none of the defenders of this part of the wall were able to remain near this place. At the noon hour on Friday, with trumpets sounding, amid great commotion and shouting "God help us," the Franks entered the city. When the pagans saw one standard planted on the wall, they were completely demoralized, and all their former boldness vanished, and they turned to flee through the narrow streets of the city. Those who were already in rapid flight began to flee more rapidly.

Count Raymond and his men, who were attacking the wall on the other side, did not yet know of all this, until they saw the Saracens leap from the wall in front of them. Forthwith, they joyfully rushed into the city to pursue and kill the nefarious enemies, as their comrades were already doing. Some Saracens, Arabs, and Ethiopians took refuge in the tower of David, others fled to the temples of the Lord and of Solomon. A great fight took place in the court and porch of the temples, where they were unable to escape from our gladiators. Many fled to the roof of the temple of Solomon, and were shot with arrows, so that they fell to the ground dead. In this temple almost ten thousand were killed. Indeed, if you had been there you would have seen our feet colored to our ankles with the blood of the slain. But what more shall I relate? None of them were left alive; neither women nor children were spared.

This may seem strange to you. Our squires and poorer footmen discovered a trick of the Saracens, for they learned that they could find byzants [note: a gold coin] in the stomachs and intestines of the dead Saracens, who had swallowed them. Thus, after several days they burned a great heap of dead bodies, that they might more easily get the precious metal from the ashes. Moreover, Tancred broke into the temple of the Lord and most wrongfully stole much gold and silver, also precious stones, but later, repenting of his action, after everything had been accounted for, be restored all to its former place of sanctity.

The carnage over, the crusaders entered the houses and took whatever they found in them. However, this was all done in such a sensible manner that whoever entered a house first received no injury from any one else, whether he was rich or poor. Even though the house was a palace, whatever he found there was his property. Thus many poor men became rich.

Afterward, all, clergy and laymen, went to the Sepulcher of the Lord and His glorious temple, singing the ninth chant. With fitting humility, they repeated prayers and made their offering at the holy places that they had long desired to visit.

ISLAM AND WAR

The fountainhead of any Islamic theory is the Qur'an. In the Qur'an, the Prophet Muhammad sanctioned warfare as one form of *jihad,* or the struggle to establish and spread the peace and justice of an Islamic community. By the time of the Crusades, Islamic jurists had developed the tenets of an Islamic theory of Just War. In this view, the world was divided into *Dar al-Islam,* the realm of peace and justice, and *Dar al-Harb,* the realm of chaos and war that brings misery to its inhabitants and whose continued existence poses an ongoing threat to the security of *Dar al-Islam.* It was the duty of true Islamic states to expand the realm of *Dar al-Islam* by preaching, writing, and if necessary conquest, so as to bring Muslim law and its benefits of peace and justice to the whole world. But certain conditions had to be met before a *jihad* was justified. There had to be a just cause for starting the war— note the essentially defensive injunction in Sura 2 in the reading. The targets of the *jihad* had first to be invited to convert or to pay tribute to the Islamic authority. A properly constituted Islamic authority had to declare the *jihad* (though what constituted a "proper Islamic authority" was open to dispute). Finally, the war had to be conducted according to broader Islamic values.

The selections from the Qur'an presented here are the key ones relating directly to warfare. As you read them, bear in mind the passages from the Qur'an presented in chapter 8 that define those broader Islamic values.

QUESTIONS TO CONSIDER

1. What are the key elements of *jihad* as presented in these passages? Is this about warfare alone?
2. Do they seem to support the Islamic theory of Just War outlined in the introduction to the selection? Do alternate interpretations seem possible?
3. How do these passages compare with Aquinas's writings in terms of the place of warfare in a faith-based world? Is religion more or less important than in Aquinas's theory?
4. Are the Qur'anic conditions for Just War universal? That is, do they work to describe the justness of modern wars, even if they are not waged by Muslim states, or is this a culturally restricted view of the justness of war? How do they compare with Aquinas in this sense?

THE QUR'AN

2. The Cow

In the name of God,
Most Gracious, Most Merciful

190. Fight in the cause of God
Those who fight you,
But aggress not.
For God does not love aggressors.

191. And slay them
Wherever you catch them,
And turn them out
From where they have
Turned you out.
For tumult and oppression
Are worse than slaughter.
But do not fight them
At the Sacred Mosque,
Unless they first
Fight you there.
But if they fight you,
Slay them.
Such is the reward
Of those who suppress
faith.

192. But if they cease,
God is Oft-forgiving,
Most Merciful.

193. And fight them on
Until there is no more
Tumult or oppression,
And there prevail
Justice and faith in God.
But if they cease,
Let there be no hostility,
Except to those
Who practice oppression.

9. The Repentance

5. But when the forbidden months
Are past, then fight and slay
The pagans wherever you find
them,
And seize them, beleaguer
them,
And lie in wait for them
In every stratagem of war.
But if they repent
And establish regular prayers
And practice regular charity,
Then open the way for them.
For God is Oft-Forgiving,
Most Merciful.

6. If one amongst the pagans
Ask you for asylum,
Grant it to him,
So that he may hear the Word
Of God. And then escort him
To where he can be secure.
That is because they are
Men without knowledge.

22. Pilgrimage

In the name of God,
Most Gracious, Most Merciful

78. And strive [*jihad*] in His cause
As you ought to strive,
With sincerity and under
discipline.
He has chosen you, and has
Imposed no difficulties on you
In religion. It is the cult
Of your father Abraham.
It is He Who has named
You Muslims, both before

Source: The Holy Qur'an, trans. M. H. Shakir, 1983. Reprinted by permission of Tahrike Tarsile Qur'an, Inc.

And in this Revelation,
That the Messenger may be
A witness for you, and you
Be witnesses for mankind!
So establish regular prayer,
Give regular charity,
And hold fast to God.
He is your Protector—
The best to protect
And the best to help.

25. The Criterion

In the name of God,
Most Gracious, Most Merciful

47.   And He it is Who makes
The night as a robe
For you, and sleep as repose
And makes the day
As if it were a resurrection.

48.   And He it is Who sends
The winds as heralds
Of glad tidings, going before
His Mercy, and We send down
Pure water from the sky—

49.   That with it, We may give
Life to a dead land,
And slake the thirst
Of things We have created—
Cattle and men in great numbers.

50.   And We have distributed
The water amongst them,
in order
That they may celebrate
Our praises, but most men
Are averse to anything but
Rank ingratitude

51.   Had it been Our Will,
We could have sent
A warner to every center
Of population,

52.   Therefore listen not
To the Unbelievers,
But strive [*jihad*]
Against them with the utmost
Strenuousness, with the
Qur'an.

Muslim Accounts of the First Crusade

Ibn al-Athir, whom we met in chapter 7 describing the Mongol attacks on Islamic lands, was a Muslim scholar whose most important work was *al-Kamil fi at-tarikh* ("The Complete History"), a history of the world. Born in Jazirat in 1160, he lived most of his life in Mosul but traveled widely in the Muslim lands of southwest Asia, including several trips to Baghdad, and later lived in Aleppo and Damascus. As a young man he spent time with Saladin's army in Syria as Saladin fought the Crusader states. He died in 1233 in Mosul. Here he tells the story of the origin of the Crusades as he had it and then describes the Frankish conquest of Jerusalem in 1099.

QUESTIONS TO CONSIDER

1. What were the causes of the Frankish attack on Muslim lands, according to al-Athir? What specific events characterize the events at Antioch and the conquest of Jerusalem for al-Athir?

2. How do his descriptions of these causes and events compare with the Christian accounts of the launching of the First Crusade, the siege of Antioch, and the conquest of Jerusalem? What are the differences and similarities? Al-Athir describes the same incidents as do the Western sources cited previously. What does his account tell us about Muslim attitudes concerning Just War?

3. Are the values and ideas expressed in the poem al-Athir quotes consistent with the Muslim ideal of Just War presented in the passages from the Qur'an? Can the values in this passage be reconciled with al-Athir's condemnation of the Christian Crusaders?

4. Does al-Athir think Muslim actions in these wars accord with Islamic values and the duty to *jihad?* Why or why not? Is this a Just War from the Muslim perspective? How do al-Athir's ideas on war compare with those expressed in the Qur'an? How do they compare with those expressed in Aquinas?

5. What is the relationship of Islam and warfare as it appears in this set of sources?

THE COMPLETE HISTORY

Ibn al-Athir

Origin of the Franks' Attack on Islam

The power of the Franks first became apparent when in the year 478/1085–86* they invaded the territories of Islam and took Toledo and other parts of Andalusia, as was mentioned earlier. Then in 484/1091 they attacked and conquered the island of Sicily[†] and turned their attention to the African coast. Certain of their conquests there were won back again but they had other successes, as you will see.

In 490/1097 the Franks attacked Syria. This is how it all began: Baldwin, their King,[‡] a kinsman of Roger the Frank who had conquered Sicily, assembled a great army and sent word to Roger saying: "I have assembled a great army and now I am on my way to you, to use your bases for my conquest of the African coast. Thus you and I shall become neighbours."

Roger called together his companions and consulted them about these proposals. "This will be a fine thing both for them and for us!" they declared, "for by this means these lands will be converted to the Faith!" At this Roger raised one leg and farted loudly and swore that it was of more use than their advice.[§] "Why?" "Because if

Source: From Francesco Gabrieli, *Arab Historians of the Crusades*, 3–4, 7–9, 10–12. Copyright © 1957 The Regents of the University of California. Reprinted with permission.

*Islamic date followed by CE date.

[†]This date clearly refers to the end of the Norman conquest [of Sicily].

[‡]This Baldwin (Bardawīl) is a composite character, compounded of the various Baldwins of Flanders and Jerusalem; or else the first Baldwin is mistakenly thought to have been already a king in the West.

[§]It is disagreeable to find the great count acting like a barbarian on the very first page, but the passage is characteristic of the contemptuous crudity with which the Muslims usually spoke of their enemies, as well as giving a fairly accurate picture of Roger's political acumen.

this army comes here it will need quantities of provisions and fleets of ships to transport it to Africa, as well as reinforcements from my own troops. Then, if the Franks succeed in conquering this territory they will take it over and will need provisioning from Sicily. This will cost me my annual profit from the harvest. If they fail they will return here and be an embarrassment to me here in my own domain. As well as all this Tamīm* will say that I have broken faith with him and violated our treaty, and friendly relations and communications between us will be disrupted. As far as we are concerned, Africa is always there. When we are strong enough we will take it."

He summoned Baldwin's messenger and said to him: "If you have decided to make war on the Muslims your best course will be to free Jerusalem from their rule and thereby win great honour. I am bound by certain promises and treaties of allegiance with the rulers of Africa." So the Franks made ready and set out to attack Syria.

Another story is that the Fatimids of Egypt were afraid when they saw the Seljuqids extending their empire through Syria as far as Gaza, until they reached the Egyptian border and Atsiz† invaded Egypt itself. They therefore sent to invite the Franks to invade Syria and so protect Egypt from the Muslims.‡ But God knows best.

The Finding of the Holy Lance and the Battle at Antioch

When Kerbogha heard that the Franks had taken Antioch he mustered his army and advanced into Syria. . . . All the Turkish and Arab forces in Syria rallied to him except for the army from Aleppo. . . . When the Franks heard of this they were alarmed and afraid, for their troops were weak and short of food. The Muslims advanced and came face to face with the Franks in front of Antioch. Kerbogha, thinking that the present crisis would force the Muslims to remain loyal to him, alienated them by his pride and ill-treatment of them. They plotted in secret anger to betray him and desert him in the heat of battle.

After taking Antioch the Franks camped there for twelve days without food. The wealthy ate their horses and the poor ate carrion and leaves from the trees. Their leaders, faced with this situation, wrote to Kerbogha to ask for safe-conduct through his territory but he refused, saying "You will have to fight your way out." . . . There was also a holy man [among the Franks] who had great influence over them, a man of low cunning, who proclaimed that the Messiah had a lance buried in the Qusyin, a great building in Antioch. "And if you find it you will be victorious and if you fail you will surely die." Before saying this he had buried a lance in a certain spot and concealed all trace of it. He exhorted them to fast and repent for three days, and on the fourth day he led them all to the spot with their soldiers and workmen, who dug everywhere and found the lance as he had told them. Whereupon he cried "Rejoice! For victory is secure." So on the fifth day they left the city in groups of five or six. The Muslims said to Kerbogha: "You should go up to the city and kill them one by one as they come out; it is easy to pick them off now that they have split up." He replied: "No, wait until

---

*The Zirid amir of Tunisia, Tarmīm ibn Mu'izz.

†A general of the Seljuqid [Turkish] Sultan Malikshāh, who in 1076 attacked Egypt from Palestine.

‡Of course the Fatimids [rulers of Egypt] were also Muslims, but they were *shi'a* "heretics" and so opposed to the rest of *sunni* Islam.

they have all come out and then we will kill them." He would not allow them to attack the enemy and when some Muslims killed a group of Franks, he went himself to forbid such behaviour and prevent its recurrence. When all the Franks had come out and not one was left in Antioch, they began to attack strongly, and the Muslims turned and fled. This was Kerbogha's fault, first because he had treated the Muslims with such contempt and scorn, and second because he had prevented their killing the Franks. The Muslims were completely routed without striking a single blow or firing a single arrow. . . . The only Muslims to stand firm were a detachment of warriors from the Holy Land, who fought to acquire merit in God's eyes and to seek martyrdom. The Franks killed them by the thousand and stripped their camp of food and possessions, equipment, horses and arms, with which they re-equipped themselves.

The Franks Conquer Jerusalem

Taj ad-Daula Tutūsh* was the Lord of Jerusalem but had given it as a fief to the amir Suqmān ibn Artūq the Turcoman. When the Franks defeated the Turks at Antioch the massacre demoralized them, and the Egyptians, who saw that the Turkish armies were being weakened by desertion, besieged Jerusalem under the command of al-Afdal ibn Badr al-Jamali.[†] Inside the city were Artūq's sons, Suqmān and Ilghazi, their cousin Sunij and their nephew Yaquti. The Egyptians brought more than forty siege engines to attack Jerusalem and broke down the walls at several points. The inhabitants put up a defense, and the siege and fighting went on for more than six weeks. In the end the Egyptians forced the city to capitulate, in sha'bān 489/August 1096.[‡] Suqmān, Ilghazi and their friends were well treated by al-Afdal, who gave them large gifts of money and let them go free. They made for Damascus and then crossed the Euphrates. Suqmān settled in Edessa and Ilghazi went on into Iraq. The Egyptian governor of Jerusalem was a certain Iftikhār ad-Daula, who was still there at the time of which we are speaking.

After their vain attempt to take Acre by siege, the Franks moved on to Jerusalem and besieged it for more than six weeks. They built two towers, one of which, near Sion, the Muslims burnt down, killing everyone inside it. It had scarcely ceased to burn before a messenger arrived to ask for help and to bring the news that the other side of the city had fallen. In fact Jerusalem was taken from the north on the morning of Friday 22, sha'bān 492/15 July 1099. The population was put to the sword by the Franks, who pillaged the area for a week. A band of Muslims barricaded themselves into the Oratory of David[§] and fought on for several days. They were granted their lives in return for surrendering. The Franks honoured their word, and the group left by night for Ascalon. In the Masjid al-Aqsa the Franks slaughtered more than 70,000

---

*A Syrian Seljuqid, Malikshlāh's brother.

†The Fatimid vizier.

‡If this date were correct, the connection with the fall of Antioch would no longer exist. In fact, the date given here is wrong: the Egyptians took Jerusalem in August 1098.

§The *Mihrāb Dawūd*, called the Tower of David in the European sources, is the citadel at Jerusalem. Not to be confused with a small sanctuary of the same name in the Temple precinct.

people, among them a large number of Imams and Muslim scholars, devout and ascetic men who had left their homelands to live lives of pious seclusion in the Holy Place. The Franks stripped the Dome of the Rock* of more than forty silver candelabra, each of them weighing 3,600 drams, and a great silver lamp weighing forty four Syrian pounds, as well as a hundred and fifty smaller silver candelabra and more than twenty gold ones, and a great deal more booty. Refugees from Syria reached Baghdad in Ramadan, among them the qadi Abu Sa'd al Hārawi. They told the Caliph's ministers a story that wrung their hearts and brought tears to their eyes. On Friday they went to the Cathedral Mosque and begged for help, weeping so that their hearers wept with them as they described the sufferings of the Muslims in that Holy City: the men killed, the women and children taken prisoner, the homes pillaged. Because of the terrible hardships they had suffered, they were allowed to break the fast.

It was the discord between the Muslim princes, as we shall describe, that enabled the Franks to overrun the country. Abu l-Muzaffar al-Abiwardi[†] composed several poems on this subject, in one of which he says:

We have mingled blood with flowing tears, and there is no room left in us
    for pity(?)
To shed tears is a man's worst weapon when the swords stir up the embers of war.
Sons of Islam, behind you are battles in which heads rolled at your feet.
Dare you slumber in the blessed shade of safety, where life is as soft as an orchard
    flower?
How can the eye sleep between the lids at a time of disasters that would waken any
    sleeper?
While your Syrian brothers can only sleep on the backs of their chargers, or in
    vultures' bellies!
Must the foreigners feed on our ignominy, while you trail behind you the train of a
    pleasant life, like men whose world is at peace?
When blood has been spilt, when sweet girls must for shame hide their lovely faces
    in their hands!
When the white swords' points are red with blood, and the iron of the brown lances
    is stained with gore!
At the sound of sword hammering on lance young children's hair turns white.
This is war, and the man who shuns the whirlpool to save his life shall grind his teeth
    in penitence.
This is war, and the infidel's sword is naked in his hand, ready to be sheathed again
    in men's necks and skulls.

---

*The rock from which, the Muslims believe, Muhammad ascended into heaven. Over it was built the so-called Mosque of 'Umar, the chief Islamic monument in Jerusalem. It was from this mosque that the conquerors took their booty. Nearby, but separate from it, is the 'Farthest Mosque' (al-Masjid al-Aqsa), where according to Ibn al-Athir the armies of the Cross showed even greater barbarity. The two sanctuaries are often confused in both Arabic and European sources.

†An Iraqi poet of the eleventh and twelfth centuries.

This is war, and he who lies in the tomb at Medina seems to raise his voice and cry: "O sons of Hashim!*

I see my people slow to raise the lance against the enemy: I see the Faith resting on feeble pillars.

For fear of death the Muslims are evading the fire of battle, refusing to believe that death will surely strike them."

Must the Arab champions then suffer with resignation, while the gallant Persians shut their eyes to their dishonour?

BUDDHISM AND WARFARE

The closest association between Buddhism and warfare developed in Japan. Because it was imported as the religion of the ruling courtly class, Buddhism was attractive for political reasons to the rural warrior class, the *bushi,* that began to emerge into prominence as the military arm of the court in the eleventh and twelfth centuries. Mahayana sects such as Pure Land Buddhism also carried the promise of life after death to a class whose profession forced it to face death frequently, though later, in the thirteenth and fourteenth centuries, Zen, which emphasized the ephemeral nature of life and laid stress on personal discipline and living each moment fully, became the most popular form of Buddhism for the *bushi.* Yet the promise of salvation carried a price, for Buddhism, like the other salvation religions, considered killing a sin, and made fewer concessions to the worldly, essentially political necessity that states exercise coercive force to maintain order. The potential conflicts this created for warriors whose role in government involved killing are illustrated in this selection.

The Tale of the Heike is the most famous of a whole set of medieval Japanese war tales. It tells the story of the Gempei War (1180–1185), the culmination of a civil war that split Japan between 1156 and 1185. It takes its name from the Chinese name of the losing side, a coalition of families led by the Heike (or Taira, in Japanese)—the Japanese war tales often focus on heroic losers rather than winners. Though initially successful, the Taira eventually met defeat at the hand of a set of clans led by the Genji (*Minamoto* in Japanese), whose leader, Minamoto Yoritomo, became Japan's first shogun in 1185. Even on the winning side, however, the emphasis is on tragic heroes, for the central figure of the tale is the Genji general Yoshitsune, Yoritomo's cousin, a brilliant general but naïve politician. After leading the Genji forces to victory, he is eliminated by Yoritomo as a potential rival. As you read this selection, think about the image of winners and losers from the perspective of Buddhist religious precepts.

---

*The Prophet, who from the tomb raises his voice to rebuke his descendants (the sons of Hashim), that is, the unworthy Caliphs whose opposition to the Crusades is only halfhearted.

1. As it is shown here, what is the attitude of Japanese warriors toward killing and death?
2. What are the key precepts of Buddhism as the warriors understood them? How do these relate to their attitudes toward waging warfare?
3. How is the relationship of Japanese warriors to their religion and their duty similar to or different from that of Christian and Muslim warriors? Can you imagine a Christian Crusader anguishing over killing a foe in the way that Naozone does? Why or why not?
4. Given what we see here, do you think there could be a Buddhist theory of Just War?
5. What is the relationship of Buddhism and warfare as it appears in this set of sources?

THE TALE OF THE HEIKE

9.16. The Death of Atsumori

[Naozone, a warrior on the Genji side of the battle, captures Atsumori, a young court aristocrat from the Heike side. The following exchange then takes place.]

"I would like to spare you," he said, restraining his tears, "but there are Genji warriors everywhere. You cannot possibly escape. It will be better if I kill you than if someone else does it, because I will offer prayers on your behalf."

"Just take my head and be quick about it."

Overwhelmed by compassion, Naozone could not find a place to strike. His senses reeled, his wits forsook him, and he was scarcely conscious of his surroundings. But matters could not go on like that forever: in tears, he took his head.

"Alas, no lot is as hard as a warrior's. I would never have suffered such a dreadful experience if I had not been born into a military house. How cruel I was to kill him!"

He pressed his sleeve to his face and shed floods of tears. . . .

After that, Naozone thought increasingly of becoming a monk.

10.5. A Statement of Precepts

[Shigehira, a leader of the defeated Heike side, is captured. When he learns he is to be sent to the Genji headquarters to be executed, he requests of his captors that he be allowed to enter religious life.]

He summoned Toi no Jirō Sanehira. "I would like to become a monk. Do you think it could be arranged?"

Source: From *The Tale of the Heike*, trans. Helen Craig McCullough, 317, 333–35. Copyright © 1988 Stanford University Press. Reprinted with permission.

Sanehira transmitted the request to Yoshitsune, who reported it to Retired Emperor Go-Shirakawa. "We can probably do something about that after Yoritomo interviews him. It cannot be allowed at present," the Retired Emperor said.

"In that case," Shigehira said when he was told, "might I see a holy man who has been my teacher for many years? I would like to talk to him about the next life."

"What is his name?"

"He is the man known as Hōnenbō of Kurodani."

Sanehira assented. "I see no objection."

Overjoyed, the Middle Captain sent for the monk. "I must have been taken prisoner because I was destined to meet you again," he said in tears. "What ought I to do about the life to come? In the days when I was a man of some importance, I let myself be distracted by official duties and fettered by public affairs, too proud and arrogant to worry about my fate in the next world. And it was even worse after our luck ended and the disorders broke out: battling here and contending there, I was hampered by the evil desire to destroy others and save myself, perpetually unable to achieve purity of heart. In particular, there is the matter of the burning of the southern capital. Under orders from the court and the military, and because I could not refuse to serve the Emperor or to comply with the demands of the times, I went to Nara to end the monks' violence. The destruction of the temples was quite unanticipated—quite beyond anyone's power to prevent—but I was Commander-in-Chief at the time; and that, I suppose, is why all the blame fell on me. (I hear there is a saying, 'The man at the top is the man responsible,' or something of the sort.) I have come to realize that these present dreadful humiliations must all be regarded as punishments.

"Now I would like to shave my head, receive the precepts, and devote myself heart and soul to religious pursuits, but a man in my situation is not free to do as he pleases. Alas! Because today or tomorrow may bring my end, I fear I can perform no pious acts that would suffice to erase a single one of my sins. When I review my life, I understand that my evil deeds tower higher than Mount Sumeru, that my good ones amount to less than a speck of dust. Beyond any question, I am doomed to the Three Evil Paths if I die in this state. Please, Your Holiness, be compassionate and merciful. If there is a way to save such a sinner, tell me of it."

The holy man remained silent for a time, choked with tears. By and by, he began to speak. "It is a sorrow beyond sorrow that you should face the prospect of returning to the Three Evil Paths after having enjoyed the rare good fortune of being born a man. But the Buddhas of the Three Worlds must surely feel happiness because you have now abandoned wicked thoughts and embraced good ones, desirous of rejecting the impure world and achieving rebirth in the Pure Land. There are various ways of escaping from the world of illusion, but in these unclean, tumultuous latter days of the Law, the best one is to recite the name of Amida Buddha. The goal, the Pure Land, has been divided into nine grades, and the necessary pious acts have been compressed into six syllables, which even the most slow witted person can chant.* You must not depreciate yourself because you think you have committed grave sins: even those who are guilty of the Ten Evils and the Five Deadly Sins can attain rebirth if they

---

* *Namu amida butsu* ("Hail, Amida Buddha!").

repent. Nor must you lose hope because you think you have performed few meritorious acts: Amida will come to meet anyone who has it in his heart to intone the sacred name one time or ten times. It is explained, 'He who intones the sacred name with all his heart will enter the Western Paradise.' It is taught, 'To intone Amida's name is to repent sins constantly.' Demons cannot approach the person who trusts in the words, 'Amida's name is a sharp sword.' It is written that a man's sins will all vanish if he recites, 'A single Buddha invocation washes away all sins.'

"I have tried to summarize the essential elements of the Pure Land faith: these quotations may be considered its basic teachings. But belief is the key to rebirth. You must believe with all your heart: never, never entertain a doubt. If you believe these teachings without reservation, and if you meditate on Amida Buddha in your heart and keep his name on your lips, always and everywhere, whether you are walking, standing, sitting, or lying down, there can be no doubt that at the hour of death you will leave this cruel world for the Pure Land from which there is no return."

The instructive discourse delighted the Middle Captain. "I would like to receive the commandments now. May I do so without becoming a monk?"

"It is quite common for a layman to receive them." The holy man touched a razor to Shigehira's forehead, made shaving motions, and administered the Ten Commandments. Shigehira received the precepts with tears of joy streaming down his face, and Hōnen also wept as he spoke, moved by deep compassion and sympathy.

Shigehira told Tomotoki to fetch a certain inkstone, one he had deposited with a samurai whose house he had frequented for poetry and music sessions. Then he presented it to the holy man as a pious offering. "Please do not give this away," he said, weeping. "Keep it where you can see it always, and whenever you remember, 'That object belonged to Shigehira once,' think of it as though it were myself and recite the sacred name. I would be truly grateful if you could chant an occasional scroll of holy writ on my behalf when you have the time." Unable to reply, Hōnen put the inkstone in his bosom and went home in tears, wringing the sleeves of his black robe.

CHAPTER 12

Land, Law, and Lordship

INTRODUCTION

Every year by April 15, millions of United States taxpayers figure out their income taxes and file their Form 1040s. At the head of that form is a space where taxpayers fill in their names (as well as the names of their spouses on joint returns) and their addresses. At the foot of the form, where they sign, they also fill in their professions. Built into the tax code are significant deductions for paying interest on home loans, for various home improvements, and, in the tax codes of some states, deductions for rent paid. Tax day is therefore an annual reminder of citizens' role in paying for the state and of the role of the state in structuring and regulating its citizens' lives, including their housing and employment. Put another way, tax day is a visible encounter of the populace with the authority of the state, with the laws by which the state regulates society, and with the fiscal demands of the state, organized in large part around ownership and use of property. The attention politicians pay to the tax code, constantly tinkering with deductions, incentives, penalties, and favors for special interests, demonstrates how central the fiscal function of the state is and the extent to which social power, or what might be called class interests, shapes the fiscal functioning of the state. Indeed, revenue collection and disbursement takes its place with keeping domestic order (ideally through an orderly system of policing, courts, and justice) and maintaining military forces as one of the most fundamental tasks of a functioning government.

In preindustrial societies, where the great majority of the wealth produced by society derived more or less directly from farming, the relationship of the state and its fiscal mechanisms to land ownership and use, expressed in law and in the social and economic relationships of rural class structures and production, formed one of the most important sets of encounters such a society had to deal with. The various ways different societies constructed those encounters can therefore tell us much about the lives of everyday people in such societies, a topic for which direct evidence in the form of written testimony by farmers is usually close to nonexistent.

Laws, tax codes, and land surveys are a rare window into the social structure of peasant villages and into the ways those villages were connected to the larger political and economic patterns and developments of their societies. Given that the rural peasant population usually formed at least 80 percent of the total population, and sometimes upward of 95 percent of it, this is important evidence. We examine in this chapter some examples of this sort of difficult and indirect evidence and what it can say about the encounter of preindustrial societies and their states in fiscal and legal terms.

One complication in looking at this sort of evidence for preindustrial societies, however—aside from the inherent difficulty of the sorts of evidence we possess—is that the lines between what we would call the public and the private exercise of authority are often less clear than they are in our world. Another way of putting this is that the distinction between a landlord who charges rent from a peasant family for their use of a piece of land, on the one hand, and a government official who collects tax from a peasant family for use of a piece of land, on the other hand, was in some societies neither clearly defined nor even conceptualized as a possible distinction. The informal social power of the landlord merged imperceptibly into the formal administrative power of the official. The implications of this for government power and for our understanding of the social and class structures of traditional societies cannot be underestimated. The power of landholding elites was a constant and central factor in the lives of the peasants over whom the elites lorded it (in a very literal way).

Nor was this always a matter of the interests of the elite simply capturing state power to their own advantage, though this was not an uncommon outcome—the state in effect becoming the formalized and legitimized enforcer of the interests of landlords against the interests of peasant farmers. One common problem of such an outcome for the state as an independent entity was that it could lead to severe fiscal problems for the state. Rich, legally privileged landlords were much more able to avoid paying taxes than were peasants, whether by using their wealth and influence to obtain legal exemptions or simply by being able to monopolize the exercise of force in the locality, effectively shutting other officials or representatives of state interest out of the area. This could lead the state to raise taxes on the peasant farmers it could still reach, making their lives difficult or impossible to sustain and perhaps driving them and their lands into the arms of locally powerful lords in exchange for protection. (We recognize, of course, how rich, powerful entities such as multinational corporations in our time obtain favorable legal and tax treatment, at the expense of average taxpayers, from modern, democratic governments.) Recognizing this danger, some states took measures to protect their interests in the peasant population against the interests of powerful landed elites. The state's interests (largely for its own fiscal health), of course, were not exactly congruent with the interests of the peasants, who might have preferred getting rid of both state and landlords. But the state's interest in stable tax income could dovetail with a more benevolent interest in the organization of rural life for the benefit of peasant cultivators. Thus the interplay of interests visible in the evidence of laws, tax policies, and structures of land use and rural production tends to reflect a shifting and unstable balance of the interests of all three groups: state, elites, and peasants. Again, how those balances played out can tell us crucial things about the organization and practical beliefs of different societies.

Another complication is that our notions of private property often do not translate well into the terms of rural land use in traditional societies. "Ownership" might not be clearly defined by our standards. Peasant cultivators might have rights guaranteeing them occupancy of a piece of land, but without the right to alienate the land, or such rights might be limited in terms of who the cultivator could sell to or exchange with, where exchanged land had to be, and so forth. Even more restrictively, many peasants had no right to leave the land. The "peasant cultivator" was often taken, as well, to be not an individual but an extended family unit, all of whom had to agree to the transaction. If there were a landlord, he too might have rights over the land that were collectively held or restricted in various ways. At the top of the system of landholding, the state or king might claim ultimate ownership of all land or assert the right to approve all land transactions, especially large transfers among the elite. One must bear in mind when reading sources such as those in this chapter that "ownership" is more accurately read as a shifting and multivalent collection of rights to the use of, income from, jurisdiction over, and/or disposal of pieces of land and the cultivators who lived on them.

We look at examples of law codes, policy statements, and economic documents from four civilizations, covering times ranging from about 700 to 1500. First, we present a collection of Byzantine laws dating from the eighth century, collectively known as the Farmer's Law, that give a picture of life among communities of small independent farmers in the middle period of the empire. During this time, the empire was on the defensive against the powerful Arab caliphate, whose armies regularly raided the Anatolian plateau (the middle of modern Turkey) that formed the agricultural heartland of Byzantine territory. Defense of the empire depended on units of the Byzantine army stationed throughout the *themes*, or provinces, of Anatolia and supported from the local produce and tax revenues generated by the farming population; the whole system gained its coherence and continuity from the central role of the government in Constantinople in recruiting the armies, collecting the taxes, and regulating the landholding on which both were based. Powerful aristocratic landholding families, though present in the empire at this point, make only a token appearance in this law, and in general they were at a low point in their influence over Byzantine government and society because of the vulnerability of their landholdings in common with those of the independent peasantry, which tended to align their interests with those of the central government. The Byzantine arrangements of land, law, and lordship visible in this source therefore reflect a world characterized by a relatively strong central government ruling over a relatively poor and economically limited society.

Second, we present a pair of reform proposals from Song China in the eleventh century. The reforms are concerned with land distribution among the peasantry and with the excessive power of great landowners and moneylenders over the peasants that threatened government income. The Song dynasty (960–1279) put the empire together after the civil wars that brought down the militaristic Tang dynasty. Though deliberately antimilitarist and often on the defensive against steppe nomads in the north (the dynasty eventually fell to the Mongols), the Song presided over a dynamic period of Chinese history. China was the world leader in technology during this time: gunpowder, block printing on paper, and navigational advances, including use of magnetic compasses, were all invented under the Song, and steel production in eleventh-century north China dwarfed the output of the rest of the world combined. The insecurity of the northern frontier encouraged merchant activity centered in the southeast, which connected China with southeast Asia and the Indian Ocean trade routes. Printing, in turn, formed part of the context for a renaissance period for Chinese culture. In particular, printing made copies of the Confucian classics far more widely available and led to a Neo-Confucian revival that made serious inroads into the popularity of Buddhism, as well as expanding the pool of educated men capable of competing in the civil service exams that staffed the government bureaucracy. The old military aristocracy was no longer a threat to government stability, having destroyed itself at the end of the Tang. Yet despite this prosperity and progressive cultural atmosphere, problems remained in the countryside. New, fast-ripening breeds of rice introduced early in the dynasty essentially doubled agricultural productivity, fueling the economic boom, but rapid population growth quickly ate up the gains on a per capita basis. Peasant unrest, a factor in the fall of the Tang, continued to show up regularly, provoked by high taxation to support the huge (though closely controlled and therefore inefficient) Song army and the demands of large landowners and moneylenders. Song arrangements of land, law, and lordship, therefore, reflect a world characterized by a strong central government ruling over a rich and varied society.

Next we present a legal primer from early-fourteenth-century Japan. It was designed to guide landholding warrior families through the intricacies of suits over land possession. Like the Chinese memorials, it therefore presents a somewhat indirect picture of rural life but a more direct look at the concerns of those who depended on landed income for their position and status. Japan in 1300 was ruled by a somewhat odd combination of two governments: a civil government, headed by the emperor, with its capital at Kyoto in south central Japan and a military government (or *bakufu,* literally "tent government") headquartered at Kamakura, in the east near what is now Tokyo, and headed by a shogun. Although the shogunate derived its legitimacy from the civil government, its monopoly of military power meant that since the founding of the shogunate in 1190 its local power had gradually increased at the expense of the civil aristocracy. Both the civil and military elites lived off the income rights from landed estates, and so the adjudication of land disputes was central to power and status. By 1300 the legal and governmental system was under increasing strain, an indirect effect of the Mongol invasions of 1274 and 1281. The Kamakura shogunate had led a successful (and lucky) defense of the islands, but it could not meet the subsequent demands of all its warriors for land rewards. After earlier internal wars the winners got the losers' lands; but this war had been defensive, and no new land was available for redistribution. Thus our source may present a somewhat idealized picture of a legal system approaching crisis. Finally, Japanese farming, based largely on wet-field rice agriculture, was productive in certain areas but was geographically limited by the islands' many mountains, and the economy as a whole was not as developed or sophisticated as many economies in mainland Asia at this time. Japanese arrangements of land, law, and lordship therefore reflect a world characterized by a somewhat weak and divided government ruling over a relatively poor and limited economy.

Finally, we present two sources relating to the peasant unrest in England in the mid-fourteenth century. The first is a law reacting to the effects of the labor shortage immediately after the Black Death. The second is a chronicle account of the Peasants' Revolt of 1381. The mid-fourteenth century was a troubled time for western European civilization, and the troubles focused on its two biggest kingdoms, England and France. The two were at war with each other from 1337 to 1453, with only periodic truces, a conflict known as the Hundred Years' War. The war took place mostly on French soil and saw English armies conduct economic warfare by riding repeatedly through the French countryside pillaging, burning, and looting. But the high costs of the war affected both governments, which found themselves constantly searching for money and devoting so much of their resources to the war that they neglected the maintenance of internal order and justice. The war took place against the backdrop of the Black Death (see chapter 14), which killed nearly a third of the European population in the three years after 1348. The plague hit a population already weakened by famines brought about in part by climatic change that brought cooler, wetter weather to much of the continent after 1300. The class antagonisms visible in the sources were aggravated by the fact that the roots of European governments grew in part from the informal social and political ties between members of the warrior aristocracy, meaning that elite and government interests were fairly congruent, though the limitations on government power that stemmed from those same roots mitigated the oppressive power of states somewhat. Despite this gloomy picture, however, the European economy exhibited underlying strengths resulting from three centuries of growth before 1300. European arrangements of land, law, and lordship, therefore, reflect a world characterized by relatively weak governments ruling over a rich and varied society.

As you read these four case studies in the structures of rural life and the encounter between land, law, and lordship, look carefully at several issues. First, figuring out the purpose of these documents—why they seem to have been written, what agenda they were trying to promote, and whose interests they served—is crucial to understanding what these sources have to say. Second, figuring out the purpose of these documents will give greater insight into the evidence they present for social classes, social relations, and the structures of rural life. Finally, because rural production and the social relationships that surrounded it were so central to the organization of every preindustrial civilization, these documents tell us something important about the cultural traditions and worldviews of these four societies.

CHAPTER QUESTIONS

1. Are there common elements in the arrangements of landholding, law, and lordship in the accounts from these four very different societies? What are they?

2. The arrangements of landholding, law, and lordship in these accounts reflect various balances between three interests: those of the state, those of the landholding elite, and those of peasants. Whose interests seem dominant in these accounts? Why? How are these interests expressed in culturally specific ways?

3. Do the variations in state strength and economic prosperity across these four societies correlate with variations in whose interests seem to dominate in these encounters? Does weak versus strong government or poor versus rich society seem to matter more in affecting the balance of interests?

4. What do the commonalities and balances of interests in these accounts tell you about preindustrial societies generally? How are they different from our society today in terms of land ownership, social class interests, and government fiscal and social policies?

5. What lessons do these accounts hold for the making of modern policy with regard to state power, revenue collection, and class interests?

BYZANTIUM
Regulating New Settlements

The Farmer's Law cannot be dated with certainty, nor is its exact authorship known. But internal evidence points to a date in the seventh or eighth century, probably right around 700. This was a period in which the Byzantine state had to scrape together the financial and manpower resources it needed to defend itself—especially Anatolia, its agricultural heartland in the center of Asia Minor—against the armies of the far larger and richer Arab caliphate to its southeast (see Map 12.1). Its strategy of defense, based on its inferiority, allowed Arab armies to enter Byzantine territory, hoping simply to harass them, prevent them taking any major cities (especially the capital at Constantinople), and wait for them to go home at the end of the campaigning season. This was, obviously, hard on the rural population of the area, and many regions contained abandoned fields and settlements that the government then attempted to repopulate with migrants from other areas. The organization of such new settlements was a large part of what the Farmer's Law regulated.

The law is certainly the work not of a private compiler or commentator but of a government official composing or recording what we would call legislation. The law consists of eighty-five sometimes repetitive short chapters or provisions, of which we present a selection. The first twenty-two deal with cultivation practices and the relations of farmers in a community with each other. These chapters have the character of civil law and are almost certainly the new part of the legislation, as they do not parallel provisions in earlier Roman law. The rest of the chapters deal variously with problems associated with cattle, dogs, and miscellaneous buildings and farm implements. These have the character of criminal law and are derivative of earlier Roman legal codes.

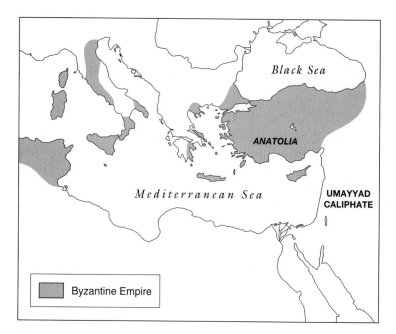

Map 12.1 Byzantine Empire, c. 700.

The law is not a complete regulation for all rural classes and types of communities. Most important, large landowners, lay or ecclesiastical, who would have rented out portions of their land to tenant farmers or employed serf or slave labor do not appear in the law except tangentially in chapter 9[1] and chapter 10 as "the grantor" (that is, the person making a land grant in exchange for a fixed rent and set of labor services). Large landowners would have suffered from the insecurity of landholding during this period, reducing their status and significance in the social and political life of the empire, and were furthermore dealt with in other law codes. Instead, this law is aimed at regulating a new (or newly important) sort of community of small, independent farmers; the law suggests, in provisions mentioning division of the land, that these were sometimes new settlements—agricultural colonies, as it were, on land newly reclaimed after being abandoned earlier during the various invasions that threatened the empire's existence in the seventh century.

The small farmers covered by the law were not Jeffersonian homesteaders, owning their land and free to do with it as they pleased. In the larger scope of Roman law they held a status barely above slavery: They were not free to leave the land and were subject to the jurisdiction of the magistrate of the district. But their lack of freedom reflects, ironically to us perhaps, their importance to the state as its primary source of tax income for supporting its armies. Note that several provisions refer, at least indirectly, to the fact that the tax burden fell on the community as a whole: If a farmer fled his homestead, the rest of the community had to make up his share of the common tax burden.

1. Based on the provisions of this law, describe rural life in Byzantium in these centuries. What features stand out to you?

2. What are the main sorts of disputes and problems arising in a community of small farmers such as this? What concerns on the part of the farmers do these problems reflect?

3. In addition to landholding farmers, agricultural wage earners and slaves also appear as types of people in these communities. What jobs did they do? How does their status compare with that of the farmers'?

4. What principles does the law seem to apply in resolving disputes or punishing crimes? Does the law strike you as fair and just? As harsh? Both?

5. Where does the balance of interests between state, elite, and peasants lie in this law? What does the overall purpose of the law seem to be? How does it reflect its historical context?

THE FARMER'S LAW

I. The farmer who is working his own field must be just and must not encroach on his neighbor's furrows. If a farmer persists in encroaching and docks a neighboring lot—if he did this in plowing-time, he loses his plowing; if it was in sowing-time that he made this encroachment, he loses his seed and his husbandry and his crop—the farmer who encroached.

2. If a farmer without the landowner's cognizance enters and plows or sows, let him not receive either wages for his plowing or the crop for his sowing—no, not even the seed that has been cast.

3. If two farmers agree one with the other before two or three witnesses to exchange lands and they agreed for all time, let their determination and their exchange remain firm and secure and unassailable.

4. If two farmers, A and B, agree to exchange their lands for the season of sowing and A draws back, then, if the seed was cast, they may not draw back; but if the seed was not cast they may draw back; but if A did not plow while B did, A also shall plow.

5. If two farmers exchange lands either for a season or for all time, and one plot is found deficient as compared with the other, and this was not their agreement, let him who has more give an equivalent in land to him who has less; but if this was their agreement, let them give nothing in addition.

6. If a farmer who has a claim on a field enters against the sower's will and reaps, then, if he had a just claim, let him take nothing from it; but if his claim was baseless, let him provide twice over the crops that were reaped.

Source: Walter Ashburner, "The Farmer's Law (continued)," *Journal of Hellenistic Studies,* 32 (1912): 68–95.

7. If two territories contend about a boundary or a field, let the judges consider it and they shall decide in favor of the territory which had the longer possession; but if there is an ancient landmark, let the ancient determination remain unassailed.

8. If a division wronged people in their lots or lands, let them have license to undo the division.*

9. If a farmer on shares reaps without the grantor's consent and robs him of his sheaves, as a thief shall he be deprived of all his crop.†

10. A shareholder's portion is nine bundles, the grantor's one: he who divides outside these limits is accursed.

11. If a man takes land from an indigent farmer and agrees to plow only and to divide, let their agreement prevail; if they also agreed on sowing, let it prevail according to their agreement.

12. If a farmer takes from some indigent farmer his vineyard to work on a half-share and does not prune it as is fitting and dig it and fence it and dig it over, let him receive nothing from the produce.

13. If a farmer takes land to sow on a half-share, and when the season requires it does not plow but throws the seed on the surface, let him receive nothing from the produce because he played false and mocked the land-owner.

14. If he who takes on a half-share the field of an indigent farmer who is abroad changes his mind and does not work the field, let him restore the produce twice over.

15. If he who takes on a half-share changes his mind before the season of working and gives notice to the landowner that he has not the strength and the landowner pays no attention, let the man who took on a half-share go harmless.

16. If a farmer takes over the farming of a vineyard or piece of land and agrees with the owner and takes earnest-money and starts and then draws back and gives it up, let him give the just value of the field and let the owner have the field.

17. If a farmer enters and works another farmer's woodland,‡ for three years he shall take its profits for himself and then give the land back again to its owner.

18. If a farmer who is too poor to work his own vineyard takes flight and goes abroad, let those from whom claims are made by the public treasury gather in the grapes, and the farmer if he returns shall not be entitled to mulct them [demand forfeiture from them] in the wine.

19. If a farmer who runs away from his own field pays every year the extraordinary taxes of the public treasury, let those who gather in the grapes and occupy the field be mulcted [fined] twofold.

20. If a man cuts another's wood without its owner's cognizance and works and sows it, let him have nothing from the produce.

21. If a farmer builds a house or plants a vineyard in another's field or plot and after a time there come the owners of the plot, they are not entitled to pull down the house or root up the vines, but they may take an equivalent in land. If the man who

---

*The division referred to here would have been an initial division of the land in a new settlement.

†This and the next provision are the only ones that refer to tenant farming involving a rich absentee landlord (the "grantor" of the land) and a long-term rental agreement (shares). Such agreements also undoubtedly required labor services of the tenant in addition to the shares of the crops produced.

‡Unlike in c. 2, this refers to a farmer entering another farmer's woodland with the owner's permission.

built or planted on the field that was not his own stoutly refuses to give an equivalent, the owner of the plot is entitled to pull up the vines and pull down the house.

22. If a farmer at digging-time steals a spade or a hoe, and is afterwards recognized, let him pay its daily hire twelve folles; the same rule applies to him who steals a pruning-knife at pruning-time, or a scythe at reaping-time, or an axe at wood-cutting time.

Concerning Herdsmen.

23. If a neatherd [cow herder] in the morning receives an ox from a farmer and mixes it with the herd, and it happens that the ox is destroyed by a wolf, let him explain the accident to its master and he himself shall go harmless.

. . .

25. If a herdsman receives an ox from a farmer in the morning and goes off and the ox gets separated from the mass of oxen and goes off and goes into cultivated plots or vineyards and does harm, let him not lose his wages, but let him make good the harm done.

26. If a herdsman in the morning receives an ox from a farmer and the ox disappears, let him swear in the Lord's name that he has not himself played foul and that he had no part in the loss of the ox and let him go harmless.

. . .

28. If a herdsman on occasion of the loss of an ox or its wounding or blinding makes oath and is afterwards by good evidence proved a perjurer, let his tongue be cut out and let him make good the damage to the owner of the ox.

. . .

30. If a man cuts a bell from an ox or a sheep and is recognized as the thief, let him be whipped; and if the animal disappears, let him make it good who stole the bell.

31. If a tree stands on a lot, if the neighboring lot is a garden and is overshadowed by the tree, the owner of the garden may trim its branches; but if there is no garden, the branches are not to be trimmed.

. . .

33. If a guardian of fruit* is found stealing in the place which he guards, let him lose his wages and be well beaten.

34. If a hired shepherd is found milking his flock without the owner's knowledge and selling them, let him be beaten and lose his wages.

. . .

36. If a man takes an ox or an ass or any beast without its owner's knowledge and goes off on business, let him give its hire twice over; and if it dies on the road, he shall give two for one, whatever it may be.

. . .

38. If a man finds an ox doing harm in a vineyard or in a field or in another place, and does not give it back to its owner, on the terms of recovering from him all the destruction of his crops, but kills or wounds it, let him give ox for ox, ass for ass, or sheep for sheep.

. . .

---

*Guardians were appointed either by the farmer to guard against thieves or by the landlord to ensure an equal division of the fruit between landlord and tenant in a share arrangement, as in c. 9 and 10.

42. If while a man is trying to steal one ox from a herd, the herd is put to flight and eaten by wild beasts, let him be blinded.

. . .

45. If a slave kills one ox or ass or ram in a wood, his master shall make it good.

46. If a slave, while trying to steal by night, drives the sheep away from the flock in chasing them out of the fold, and they are lost or eaten by wild beasts, let him be hanged as a murderer.

47. If a man's slave often steals beasts at night, or often drives away flocks, his master shall make good what is lost on the ground that he knew his slave's guilt, but let the slave himself be hanged.

. . .

49. If a man finds a pig doing harm or a sheep or a dog, he shall deliver it in the first place to its master; when he has delivered it a second time, he shall give notice to its master; the third time he may cut its tail or its ear or shoot it without incurring liability.

. . .

55. If a man kills a sheepdog and does not make confession but there is an inroad of wild beasts into the sheepfold, and afterwards he who killed the dog is recognized, let him give the whole flock of sheep together with the value of the dog.

. . .

64. Let those who set fire to a threshing-floor or stacks of corn by way of vengeance on their enemies be burnt.

. . .

81. If a man who is dwelling in a district ascertains that a piece of common ground is suitable for the erection of a mill and appropriates and then, after the completion of the building, if the commonalty of the district complain of the owner of the building as having appropriated common ground, let them give him all the expenditure that is due to him for the completion of the building and let them share it in common with its builder.

82. If after the land of the district has been divided, a man finds in his own lot a place which is suitable for the erection of a mill and sets about it, the farmers of the other lots are not entitled to say anything about the mill.

83. If the water which comes to the mill leaves dry cultivated plots or vineyards, let him make the damage good; if not, let the mill be idle.

84. If the owners of the cultivated plots are not willing that the water go through their plots, let them be entitled to prevent it.

SONG CHINA
Proposals for Land Reform

The two documents presented here give us a piece of a debate with a long history in China. As in Byzantium, the fiscal health of the government depended on the existence of a large class of independent farmers. But periodically, especially in times of economic prosperity from which some benefited more than others, the power of great landowners threatened both the livelihoods of independent farmers and state tax revenues. At these times, proposals for land reform—for some scheme by which to redistribute land to the poor away from the rich—surfaced.

The late eleventh century was such a period for the Song dynasty. Economic prosperity based on much increased rice production and booming trade and manufacturing sectors greatly enlarged the class of people in the empire with enough money to entertain ambitions of government service and social respectability. Government service was available through education in the Confucian classics, but social respectability entailed not just an official position but the proper sort of private income. Though many merchants became wealthy, merchant activity was frowned on in Confucian doctrine, and so some successful merchants attempted to invest their earnings in land. This put pressure on small peasant landholders, as well as threatening the ability of the government to collect the full share of taxes from the land. At the same time, the empire was facing aggressive enemies on its northern frontier. Distrusting the sort of powerful generals and strong armies that had brought the Tang dynasty down in civil war, the Song relied instead on a vast and carefully controlled military establishment. Unfortunately, both its size and the greater number of civilian officials that it demanded to control it meant such an army was very expensive. In such circumstances, proposals for land reform came to the fore.

When they did, the point of reference for such reforms was the past, specifically the (semimythical) age of the Sage Emperors Yao and Shun and the later age of the Chou dynasty and the system of landholding supposedly in force at that time, the well-field system. Under this scheme, all the land of the empire was divided into square plots, which were in turn subdivided into nine square subplots (like a tic-tac-toe board). Eight families would occupy the outer plots; the inner square would be reserved for the communal well and other buildings. This scheme was supposed to have ensured a livelihood for all families, regularized the collection of taxes, and made for a happy utopia in the countryside. Though they recognized that times had changed, all reformers tended to take what they saw as the principles and effects of the well-field system as their model for reform.

The first source offers a viewpoint on the feasibility of well-field-style land reform under the Song dynasty. Su Hsün (1009–1066) was a government official famous for his writings that defend the Song system against charges of overtaxation and attempts to prove the well-field system infeasible. In doing so he gives a summary of the views of other reformers who advocated the reestablishment of the well-field system.

Second, Wang An-shih (1021–1086) was in effect the prime minister of China under the Emperor Shen-tsung (r. 1068–1085). He instituted, with the emperor's support, a wide-ranging set of reforms more ambitious than any before the rule of the Communists, reforms that touched on the organization of landholding and tax assessment, the civil service exams, and many other areas of governance. In this edict he proposes expanding an experimental reform measure already tried in one province. Although he took his inspiration from the Confucian classics, his interpretation of Confucianism, which stressed the authority of the central government to impose changes for the good of society, aroused significant opposition among other Confucian scholars, as well as those whose vested interests came under attack. Eventually, almost all his reform measures were repealed.

1. From the somewhat indirect evidence of these sources, what was life like in the Chinese countryside under the Song? How does it compare with life in eighth-century Byzantium?

2. What are the key issues for these reformers? Do they seem motivated more by concern for the welfare of the people or by fears for the fiscal health of the state?

3. What principles guide the thinking of these writers, even when they disagree about details or practicality?

4. Why was this a recurring issue in China? Can you think of other ways to achieve reform that might have worked in this society?

5. Where does the balance of interests between state, elite, and peasants lie in Chinese society? Where would the reformers like it to lie?

THE LAND SYSTEM—A DISSENTING VIEW

Su Hsün

At the height of the Chou dynasty the heaviest taxes ran to as much as one part in four [that is, a tax of 25 percent of the harvest], the next heaviest to one part in five, and then on down to rates as low as one part in ten or below. Taxes today, though never as low as one part in ten, likewise do not exceed one part in four or one in five, provided that the local magistrate is not rapacious and grasping. Thus there is not a great difference in the rate of taxation between Chou times and our own. . . .

However, during the Chou dynasty the people of the empire sang, danced, and rejoiced in the benevolence of their rulers, whereas our people are unhappy, as if they were extracting their very muscles and peeling off their very skins to meet the needs of the state. The Chou tax was so much, and our tax is likewise so much. Why, then is there such a great difference between the people's sadness today and their happiness then? There must be a reason for this.

During Chou times, the well-field system was employed. Since the well-field system was abolished, the land no longer belongs to the cultivators, and those who own the land do not cultivate. Those who do cultivate depend for their land upon the rich people. The rich families possess much land and extensive properties; the paths linking their fields run on and on. They call in the migratory workers and assign each a piece of their land to till, whipping and driving them to work, and treating them as slaves. Sitting there comfortably, they look around, give commands, and demand services. In the summer the people hoe for them, in the fall they harvest for them. No one disobeys their commands. The landowner amuses himself and yet draws half the

Source: DeBary, et al., eds., *Sources of Chinese Tradition*, vol. 1, 406–08. Copyright © 1960 Columbia University Press. Reprinted with permission.

income of the land, while the other half goes to the cultivator. For every landowner there are ten cultivators. Thus the landowner accumulates his half share day by day and so becomes rich and powerful; the cultivators eat their half share day by day and so become poor and hungry, without means of appeal. . . .

Alas, the poor cultivate and yet are not free from hunger. The rich sit with full stomachs and amuse themselves and yet are not free from resentment over taxes. All these evils arise from the abolition of the well-fields. If the well-fields were restored, the poor would have land to till, and not having to share their grain and rice with the rich, they would be free from hunger. The rich, not being allowed to hold so much land, could not hold down the poor. Under these circumstances those who did not till would not be able to get food. Besides, having the whole product of the land out of which to pay their taxes to the local magistrate, they would not be resentful. For this reason all the scholars of the empire outdo themselves calling for the restoration of the well-fields. And some people say: "If the land of the rich were taken away and given to those who own no land, the rich would not acquiesce in it, and this would lead to rebellion. After such a great cataclysm, when the people were decimated and vast lands lay unused, it would be propitious for instituting the well-field system at once. When Emperor Kao of Han overthrew the Ch'in dynasty or when Emperor Kuang-wu succeeded the Former Han, it could have been done and yet was not. This is indeed to be regretted!"

I do not agree with any of this. Now even if all the rich people offered to turn their lands over to the public, asking that they be turned into well-fields, it still could not be done. Why?

[Su Hsün proceeds to describe in detail the system of land organization, irrigation, and local administration associated with the well-field system as it is set forth in the Rites of Chou. He concludes that such an intricate system could never be reproduced under existing conditions.]

When the well-fields are established, [a corresponding system of] ditches and canals would have to be provided. . . . This could not be done without filling up all the ravines and valleys, leveling the hills and mountains, destroying the graves, tearing down the houses, removing the cities, and changing the boundaries of the land. Even if it were possible to get possession of all the plains and vast wildernesses and then lay them out according to plan, still we would have to drive all the people of the empire, exhaust all the grain of the empire, and devote all our energy to this alone for several hundred years, without attending to anything else, if we were ever to see all the land of the empire turned into well-fields and provided with ditches and canals. Then it would be necessary to build houses within the well-fields for the people to settle down and live in peace. Alas, this is out of the question. By the time the well-fields were established, the people would have died and their bones would have rotted away. . . .

Although the well-field [system] cannot be put into effect, nevertheless, it actually would offer certain advantages in the present situation. Now if there were something approximating the well-field [system], which could be adopted, we might still be able to relieve the distress of the people.

[At this point Su reviews the proposals made in the Han dynasty for a direct limitation of land ownership, and the reasons for their failure.]

I want to limit somewhat the amount of land which one is allowed to hold, and yet not restrict immediately those whose land is already in excess of my limit, but only make it so that future generations would not try to occupy land beyond that limit. In short, either the descendants of the rich would be unable to preserve their holdings after several generations and would become poor, while the land held in excess of my limit would be dispersed and come into the possession of others; or else as the descendants of the rich came along they would divide up the land into several portions. In this way, the land occupied by the rich would decrease and the surplus land would increase. With surplus land in abundance, the poor would find it easy to acquire land as a basis for their family livelihood. They would not have to render service to others, but each would reap the full fruit of the land himself. Not having to share his produce with others, he would be pleased to contribute taxes to the government. Now just by sitting at court and promulgating the order throughout the empire, without frightening the people, without mobilizing the public, without adopting the well-field system, still all the advantages of the well-fields would be obtained. Even with the well-fields of the Chou, how could we hope to do better than this?

MEMORIAL ON THE CROP LOANS MEASURE

Wang An-shih

In the second year of Hsi-ning [1069], the Commission to Coordinate Fiscal Administration presented a memorial as follows:

The cash and grain stored in the Ever-Normal and the Liberal-Charity granaries of the various circuits,* counting roughly in strings of cash and bushels of grain, amount to more than 15,000,000. Their collection and distribution are not handled properly, however, and therefore we do not derive full benefit from them. Now we propose that the present amount of grain in storage should be sold at a price lower than the market price when the latter is high; and that when the market price is low, the grain in the market should be purchased at a rate higher than the market price. We also propose that our reserves be made interchangeable with the proceeds of the land tax and the cash and grain held by the Fiscal Intendants, so that conversion of cash and grain may be permitted whenever convenient.

With the cash at hand, we propose to follow the example set by the crop loan system in Shensi province. Farmers desirous of borrowing money before the harvest should be granted loans, to be repaid at the same time as they pay their tax, half with the summer payment and half with the autumn payment.† They are free to repay either in kind or in cash, should they prefer to do so if the price of grain is high at the time of repayment. In the event disaster strikes, they should be allowed to defer payment

---

Source: DeBary, et al., eds., *Sources of Chinese Tradition,* vol. 1, 420–21. Copyright © 1960 Columbia University Press. Reprinted with permission.

*Government granaries intended to provide grain to the poor during times of shortage.

†Interest of 2 percent per month (24 percent per annum) was to be charged for the loans. Private moneylenders generally charged more, but this was still an interest rate high enough to create a serious burden on peasant borrowers.

until the date when the next harvest payment would be due. In this way not only would we be prepared to meet the distress of famine, but, since the people would receive loans from the government, it would be impossible for the monopolistic houses* to exploit the gap between harvests by charging interest at twice the normal rate.

Under the system of Ever-Normal and Liberal-Charity granaries, it has been the practice to keep grain in storage and sell it only when the harvest is poor and the price of grain is high. Those who benefit from this are only the idle people in the cities.

Now we propose to survey the situation in regard to surpluses and shortages in each circuit as a whole, to sell when grain is dear and buy when it is cheap, in order to increase the accumulation in government storage and to stabilize the prices of commodities. This will make it possible for the farmers to go ahead with their work at the proper season, while the monopolists will no longer be able to take advantage of their temporary stringency. All this is proposed in the interests of the people, and the government derives no advantage therefrom. Moreover, it accords with the idea of the ancient kings who bestowed blessings upon all impartially and promoted whatever was of benefit by way of encouraging the cultivation and accumulation of grain.

This proposal was adopted by the emperor, and put into effect first in [certain provinces], as suggested by the Commission to Coordinate Fiscal Administration. The results obtained were later considered to justify extension of the system to other areas.

KAMAKURA JAPAN
A Fourteenth-Century Law Primer

The *Sata Mirensho* is an introduction to the procedures of the courts that administered land law under the Kamakura *bakufu*, the military government of Japan that had been founded, alongside the imperial civil government in Kyoto, in 1190 by Minamoto Yoritomo. The *bakufu* was headed by a shogun, a military ruler (Yoritomo was the first shogun), and was responsible for two areas of government above all others. First was the defense of the kingdom. It had to defend against foreign enemies only twice, in 1274 and 1281, both times against massive Mongol invasions. Both times it succeeded, in large part (especially the first time) because lucky storms destroyed the Mongol fleets. The *bakufu* also included maintaining internal peace as part of defense, and it fought a civil war in 1221 against the ambitions of a retired emperor to restore direct imperial rule.

Second, the *bakufu* was the branch of the state that governed the warrior class of Japan that constituted Japan's military forces. The *bakufu* was, in fact, born out of a war between factions of the warrior class who had emerged as the rurally based military arm of the older civil aristocracy but who by the end of that war in 1190 asserted effective (if not formal) equality with the Kyoto-based civil families. Governing the warriors entailed regulating the social and political ties that held the class together, ties expressed in terms of bonds of vassalage (to use a fairly analo-

---

*Moneylenders and others who in the government's view tried to monopolize wealth.

gous European term) between families. Such ties created what this source calls "samurai status," that is, the status of families who served other families (the root of *samurai* is the verb *saburu*, "to serve") in a military capacity. The hierarchy of vassalage and service led to the family of the shogun, whose highest, most trusted retainers received appointments as *jito*, or military governors of large districts. Usually, all such ties were cemented by grants of land (or more technically, of income from specified pieces of land), and it was regulating the landholdings of the warrior class that was the second responsibility of those governing the warriors, as reflected in this source. The aftermath of the Mongol invasions had complicated this task significantly, for warriors who had served in those campaigns expected to be rewarded with new landed income by the *bakufu*, but unlike after the civil war of 1221, when the lands of the defeated faction were confiscated, there was no new land to distribute. Our source, therefore, comes from a period in which the *bakufu* struggled to maintain its own income and to moderate increasingly sharp legal disputes over land among its warrior retainers.

The advice of the *Sata Mirensho* is thus procedural, but it also gives us some of the substance of common disputes. Written by a legal expert working for the government, probably between 1319 and 1322, it was aimed at members of the warrior class who needed to deal with the land courts, whether as litigants in disputes over their own land, as administrators of justice appointed by the *bakufu* to run local courts (and thus preside over local disputes between peasants and over disputes between landowners), or as managers of the estates of civil aristocrats or religious institutions. It focuses mostly on legal procedures and terminology, but its explanations of these also give some insight into the substance of common sorts of cases and into the sorts of people and social status the courts dealt with.

Such a primer was necessitated in part by the sophistication and complexity of the Kamakura legal system. Two very different approaches to law informed the courts of Kyoto, where the civil government and the emperor resided, and those of Kamakura, where the military government was headquartered. The former based law in Chinese legal theory and principles, whereas the latter had developed precedent-based, customary laws as pragmatic responses to the problems of warrior landholding that had arisen with the establishment of the shogunate. In much the same way that Roman law informed the codification of Germanic customary law in Europe after the eleventh century, the cross-fertilization of different legal systems in Japan added to the legal precision of both, as well as honing the analytic abilities of Kamakura lawyers.

QUESTIONS TO CONSIDER

1. What information do we have about rural life and agricultural production in Japan from this source? What crops were grown, and what taxes and duties did peasants owe to the government?
2. What are the main sorts of problems and disputes that seem to come before the court system? How do these differ from the issues that appear in the Byzantine Farmer's Law?

3. What is the attitude of the source (and the system) toward peasants? Does this attitude express a close attachment to the doings of the rural population or a more distanced relationship focused mainly on secure income? What do you think the effect of this attitude was on peasant life compared with the attention paid to peasants in Byzantium and China?

4. What principles, including principles of evidence, seem to guide the courts in settling legal disputes? What do these principles say about Japanese society and culture during this period?

5. Where does the balance of interests lie between state, elite, and peasant in Kamakura Japan? Why do you think the author advises his readers not to show this document to "outsiders"?

SATA MIRENSHO

14. *Shomusata* are suits concerning titles of ownership of paddy, dry fields, and other property. . . .

15. *Zatsumusata* are suits concerning money loans with interest, grain loans with interest, bills of exchange payable in money or grain, mortgage in the guise of a sale for a limited period, things borrowed with or without interest, deposited objects, deeds of sale, sale of paddy fields (except matters concerning title, for these are *shomusata*), slaves, semi-free workers, and abduction of servants. Suits of these and similar kinds are all called *zatsumusata*. The *monchūjo* court tries them in the Kanto* where the bakufu is in direct control; . . . Within Kamakura, however, *zatsumusata* cases come under the *mandokoro* secretariat of the shogun, as also all cases concerning the administration of corvée and taxes due to the shogun.

. . .

17. *Kendansata* are suits concerning rebellion, night attacks, robbery with violence, secret theft, brigandry in the mountains, piracy, homicide, wounding with a sharp weapon, arson, battery and assault by beating or kicking, robbery with threat of violence, daylight robbery (violence committed while hunting down a robber comes under *shomusata* procedure); further, footpadding (robbing people on the road), or creating a panic and stealing valuables which people may drop when running away; or seizing and raping women, or harvesting another's paddy or dry field. Trials for such and similar activities are called *kendansata*. In the Kanto, the *samuraidokoro* (the bakufu office for war and vassals) has the competence to try such cases; in the Kyoto [area], such cases come under the special criminal judges of the bakufu.

18. On the deadlines for compliance with summons: . . . allowance for the distance of the provinces must be made.†

Source: Carl Steenstrup, "Sata Mirensho: A Fourteenth-Century Law Primer," in *Monumenta Nipponica,* 35 (1980): 405–35. Reprinted with permission.

*The plain in eastern Japan, now dominated by Tokyo, where warrior power was strongest.

†Between ten and thirty days was standard, depending on the distance from the court.

. . .

37. On confirmation of land possession. The decision lies with Kamakura, and three judges have been appointed for this task. If a man believes [he has a right to be confirmed in his holdings], he makes application to them. First, they investigate all the documents—original bakufu grants, series of successive deeds, genealogical tables proving a hereditary title to land, etc. All these documents should be submitted to the aforementioned office. If the claim is considered reasonable, official letters are sent . . . to the constable [military governor] of the province [where the land is] or to the claimant's relatives, asking whether he is in actual possession of the land or not. . . . If nobody objects, or the answers received . . . tally [with what the claimant says], then he receives his confirmation. (Nowadays, this is done in the following way: the [bakufu officials] place their seals in the margin of the deed and it is called "margin confirmation"). But if somebody raises objections, then the matter must be transferred to [another court] whose turn it is to try the case, and [it] will decide the rights and wrongs of the matter. Further, the *monchūjo* (see Article 15) is the competent authority for confirming land acquired by purchase.

. . .

43. *Jito* are those who have succeeded each other in the service of the shoguns since the time of Yoritomo and have received benefices [land] from the shoguns.

44. *Shinpo jito* are those who received grants of confiscated land, etc., at the time of the Jokyu war [1221].* (Their shares of landed income are spelled out in detail in bakufu documents.)

45. On combining the benefits of an original *jito* and a *shinpo jito.* "Cumulated perquisites" means that a man is already an original *jito* and has full rights over and benefits from some land, and then in addition he takes the shares allowed a *shinpo jito.* This is pluralism and will be punished.

46. A *gokenin* is a man whose ancestors held since time immemorial ownership of land because they cleared it and received a bakufu edict confirming them as land-holding warriors. ("Ownership because of land clearance" simply means "original private holding").

47. A *higokenin* is a man who has samurai status but holds no lands in return for vassal duties to the bakufu.

48. *Honchitsu* is the name which the ancestors of a *jito* or a *gokenin* bore during their lifetimes. Anyone, even a man who in recent years has been given a confirmation of possession [Article 37] or has regularly paid dues in grain or labor to the Kamakura offices, who on investigation is found to possess no edict from the shoguns, is classed as a *higokenin.* (However, if the most favored heir of the family keeps the family edict, and the other heirs have no edicts of their own, then they are considered to have the same *honchitsu* as the favored heir.)

. . .

51. *Go-anchi* is land granted by the shoguns in return for services rendered to the shogunate for many generations.

---

*A civil war triggered by the ambitions of a retired emperor. The winning faction received the lands of the losing faction.

52. *Honryo* is paddy or dry or other land which a man owns because his ancestors cleared it and obtained a bakufu edict confirming them as landholding warriors (it is also called "private holding").

. . .

54. On headmen, bailiffs, managers, collectors, surveyors, and sheriffs (the last-named have the police and magistrate rights and duties of jurisdiction in the area and are also called Police Commissioners). These and other estate officials are managed by the *jito* who employed them ("managed" implies hiring and dismissal). However, anyone holding an individual bakufu benefice by edict is not bound by private orders issued by *jito* except in matters concerning the dues and rents that he owes them.

55. *Kō-otsunin* [nondescript people] are peasants and other civilians.

56. Only *jito* and *gokenin* can bring cases before bakufu courts as they please. Estate officials [Article 54] and those below them can sue only when they obtain letters of recommendation from the local *jito*. However, a general manager [far away] in western Japan can litigate for himself; but in order to prevent abuse of this freedom, the law has it that if a proxy commits some fault, then his master is also held responsible, even though he was unaware of what his proxy did.

. . .

77. A *kokyakujō* is a letter by which a paddy, dry, or other land is bought and sold.

78. A *kabegaki* is a letter by which a judge forbids a party to press his litigation when the other party is in taboo [e.g., in mourning].

. . .

122. *Ichoku* means disobedience toward a judgment made by courtiers. (However, *ichoku* cannot be committed by warriors or their employees.)*

. . .

145. In cases of litigation over a money loan with interest, or things borrowed against interest, when there is documentary proof thereof: if the parties say that the conditions were different from [those set out in] the document, their arguments should not be heard, no matter whether the parties are courtiers or warriors. Oath-taking should not be admitted; adjudication can be made only on the basis of the [loan] document itself.

146. On agreements with strangers. If a man gives property, such as fields or weapons, to brothers or relatives who are not his descendants, his gift is irrevocable. This is called "an agreement with strangers". (Regarding gifts to descendants, the more recent of two conflicting documents stands; but as regards gifts to relatives or other "strangers", the earlier of the two documents should be relied on.)

147. On private agreements. Whatever the terms of a private agreement the parties may have drawn up out of court concerning their dispute, the court will not regard these terms as binding. But once the parties have a letter of agreement [duly approved by a law court] between them, then this agreement will be strictly upheld by the courts.

. . .

---

*Because they took their orders from the bakufu.

150. I have written down privately the above points concerning bakufu jurisdiction from my own experience; those with some training may learn everything from these lines, inexperienced people with none may well take them to heart. The main point as to rules of law is this: . . . for customary law, study old judgments and the extant copies of parties' pleadings. The competent administrator carefully weighs the basic issues of right and wrong in each case, concentrating on solving the *whole* case, considering both what is useful in the short run and what is the considered [legal] opinion of the era. He should not make a decision until he has worked his way through the case in this way. He should not consider acquaintance with the parties or their status. As for "basic issues of right and wrong", he should hold lawful precedents in high esteem. And although he may feel quite sure where justice lies, he should withhold his decision and reconcile the parties if the defendant is in a mood to bend; and even more so if the case is doubtful. He should ponder this point deeply. He should respect powerful families, help the poor, take care of his kin, show respect to strangers, and never grow fond of litigation but earnestly strive for the reconciliation of litigants, and concentrate on equitable decisions. Such a person will be protected by the gods and conform with the will of the Buddha. He should eschew sharp practices. An administrator who follows the good old customs goes for reconciliation, the less reliable one goes for judgment. The administrator's skill consists of knowing many points of law, for the law prevails over judgments, but a judgment should not prevail over the rules of the law. An old book says, "No law should be broken because of a single individual." How true this is. In decision-making, the legal rules are what matters most; but decisions also aim at practicality, so make an end to useless litigation. Weighty matters should not be settled by one man's understanding, but right and wrong should be determined after group discussion. Success or defeat in court depends on the parties' good or bad luck, and so, when you are about to decide a case, whether big or small, make a point of praying and appealing to the gods and buddhas,* and never show any lack of care.

And so I have recorded here my naive views. Do not show them to outsiders.

WESTERN EUROPE
Labor Law, Taxes, and the English Peasants' Revolt of 1381

Peasant unrest is an explicit factor in but not the focus of the Chinese land reform documents, and it lurks somewhere behind the legal sources for Byzantium and Japan. Here we turn to direct legal and chronicle evidence of peasant activity in England in the mid-fourteenth century. The first source is a law, the Ordinance of Laborers, passed by Parliament in 1349. It responds to the concerns of the landed classes who were represented in Parliament. Because of the labor shortages caused by the plague, working folk, including peasant serfs, were demanding (and receiving)

---

*That is, the Shinto, as well as the Buddhist, deities.

much higher wages than they had been accustomed to receiving before the plague. A revised version of the law, the Statute of Laborers, specifying acceptable wages, was passed in 1351, a clear indication that the measures were failures, ignored by workers and employers alike. Wages, in both real and nominal terms, shot up in the decades after the plague. Perhaps because the Ordinance was a dead letter, it seems to have provoked little organized resistance.

The second source is an account of the great Peasants' Revolt that hit England thirty years after the passage of the Statute of Laborers. It comes from the *Chronicles* of Jean Froissart (1337–1410). Froissart claims that "it was because of the abundance and prosperity in which the common people then lived that this rebellion broke out," and there is some truth to this claim. Rising wages after the plague raised standards of living, and with overpopulation definitively eliminated, the diets of everyday people got more varied and nutritious. It is interesting to consider why it was the prosperous peasants of 1381, and not the less well-off peasants of 1300, who revolted. One answer (though not the only one) was that having failed to regulate wages successfully in 1351, in 1381 the royal government tried exploiting the new wealth of the peasantry by instituting a Poll Tax—essentially a head tax, or amount levied on each person in the kingdom. The tax was new and widely hated and triggered the revolt (note that Froissart fails to mention it).

Born in the independent county of Hainault, Froissart spoke and wrote in French but had connections with the English royal court. His work therefore reflects the pan-European culture of the warrior aristocracy for whom he wrote—notably great deeds of arms and displays of chivalry. He began writing his chronicles in 1369, using both earlier chronicles and material he had gathered over the years in official capacities, as well as his own memories and notes of events he had witnessed. He was revising the fourth book of the *Chronicles* when he died in 1410. Though he was not an eyewitness to the revolt of 1381, and although some details of his account differ from other sources, his chronicles give us a clear picture of the attitudes of the landed classes toward the peasants they ruled. Although the account ends with the defeat of the rebels and the king's promise of revenge, it should be noted that only the ringleaders were executed, unlike the mass slaughter that accompanied the suppression of the Jacquerie, a great peasant revolt in France in 1358, itself much more violent and triggered by the misery of the peasants caused by the Hundred Years' War. And in the long run the rebels' cause carried the day: serfdom virtually disappeared in England in the century after the great revolt.

QUESTIONS TO CONSIDER

1. What details of rural life do these two accounts give? How are they similar to, and how do they differ from, the pictures provided by the Byzantine, Chinese, and Japanese sources?
2. What is the relationship between the concerns of the landed elite and the government expressed in the Ordinance and the concerns of the peasants as they appear in Froissart's chronicle? Are the concerns of the latter causally related to the circumstances that prompted the Ordinance?

3. In almost any preindustrial society on which we could find evidence (including, for example, the evidence about Byzantium in the Farmer's Law), labor shortages would be correlated with losses in peasant freedom rather than rising wages: that is, states and elites would meet potential labor shortages by locking in the available labor. What does it tell you about fourteenth-century England that this response was not successful?

4. How is the economics of labor tied in England to people's views of social hierarchy and state legitimacy? How did such views affect the outcome of the Peasants' Revolt?

5. Where does the balance of interests lie between state, elite, and peasant in fourteenth-century England? Does the balance strike you as being less settled than in the other sources? How might this be significant?

THE ORDINANCE OF LABORERS (1349)

The king to the sheriff of Kent, greeting. Because a great part of the people, and especially of workmen and servants, lately died of the pestilence, many [of the survivors] seeing the necessity of masters, and great scarcity of servants, will not serve unless they may receive excessive wages, and some rather willing to beg in idleness, than by labor to get their living; we, considering the grievous incommodities, which of the lack especially of ploughmen and such laborers may hereafter come, have upon deliberation and treaty with the prelates and the nobles, and learned men assisting us, of their mutual counsel ordained:

That every man and woman of our realm of England, of what condition he be, free or bond [serf], able in body, and within the age of threescore years, not living in merchandise [by trade], nor exercising any craft, nor having [anything] of his own whereof he may live, nor proper land, about whose tillage he may himself occupy, and not serving any other, if he in convenient service, his estate considered, be required to serve, he shall be bound to serve him who shall him require; and take only the wages, livery, recompense, or salary, which were accustomed to be given in the places where he aims to serve, in the twentieth year of our reign of England [that is, in 1347, before the plague], or five or six other common years just before. Provided always, that their lords be preferred before others by their bondmen or their land tenants, so to be retained in their service; so that nevertheless the said lords shall retain no more than be necessary for them; and if any such man or woman, being so required to serve, will not do the same, and that being proved by two true men before the sheriff or the constables of the town where the same shall happen, he shall anon be taken by them or any of them, and committed to the next jail, there to remain under strait keeping, till he find surety to serve in the form aforesaid.

Source: Albert Beebe White and Wallace Notestein, eds., *Source Problems in English History* (New York: Harper and Brothers, 1915), some wording modified by S. Morillo.

Item, if any reaper, mower, or other workman or servant, of whatever estate or condition that he be, retained in any man's service, departs from the said service without reasonable cause or license, before the term agreed, he shall have pain of imprisonment. And that none under the same pain presume to receive or to retain any such in his service.

Item, that no man pay, or promise to pay, any servant any more wages, liveries, recompense, or salary than was wont, as afore is said; nor that any man in another manner shall demand or receive the same, upon pain of paying double that amount that so shall be paid, promised, required, or received, to him which thereof shall feel himself grieved [that is, to another employer offering customary wages or seeking to retain an employee]. . . .

Item, if the lords of the towns or manors presume in any point to come against this present ordinance either by them, or by their servants, then pursuit shall be made against them in the counties, wapentakes, tithings [different sorts of courts of law], or such other courts, for the treble pain paid or promised by them or their servants in the form aforesaid; and if anyone before this present ordinance has contracted with anyone so to serve for more wages, he shall not be bound by reason of the same contract to pay more than at any other time was wont to be paid to such person; nor upon the said pain shall presume to pay any more.

Item, that saddlers, skinners, white-tawers [tanners who made white leather using alum and salt], cordwainers, tailors, smiths, carpenters, masons, tilers, [shipwrights], carters, and all other artificers and workmen, shall not take for their labor and workmanship above the same that was wont to be paid to such persons the said twentieth year, and other common years next before, as afore is said, in the place where they shall happen to work; and if any man take more, he shall be committed to the next jail, in manner as afore is said.

Item, that butchers, fishmongers, hostelers, brewers, bakers, and all other sellers of all manner of victual, shall be bound to sell the same victual for a reasonable price, having respect to the price that such victual be sold at in the places adjoining, so that the same sellers have moderate gains, and not excessive, reasonably to be required according to the distance of the place from whence the said victuals be carried; and if any sell such victuals in any other manner, and thereof be convicted in the manner and form aforesaid, he shall pay the double the price that he so received, to the injured party, or, in default of him, to any other that will pursue in this behalf: and the mayors and bailiffs of cities, boroughs, merchant-towns, and others, and of the ports and places of the sea, shall have power to inquire of all and singular which shall in any thing offend the same, and to levy the said pain to the use of them at whose suit such offenders shall be convicted; and in case that the same mayors or bailiffs be negligent in doing execution of the premises, and thereof be convicted before our justices, by us to be assigned, then the same mayors and bailiffs shall be compelled by the same justices to pay the treble of the thing so sold to the injured party, or to any other in default of him that will pursue; and nevertheless toward us they shall be grievously punished.

Item, because many healthy beggars, as long as they may live by begging, refuse to labor, giving themselves to idleness and vice, and sometime to theft and other abominations; none upon the said pain of imprisonment shall, under the color of pity or alms, give any thing to one who may labor, or presume to favor them toward their desires, so that thereby they may be compelled to labor for their necessary living.

We command you, firmly enjoining, that in all the premises in the cities, boroughs, market towns, seaports, and other places in your bailiwick, where you shall think expedient, within liberties [holdings outside normal jurisdiction] as well as without, you do cause to be publicly proclaimed, and to be observed and duly put in execution aforesaid; and this by no means omit, as you regard us and the common weal of our realm, and would save yourself harmless. Witness the king at Westminster, the 18th day of June. By the king himself and the whole council.

Like writs are directed to the sheriffs throughout England.

The king to the reverend father in Christ W. by the same grace bishop of Winchester, greeting. "Because a great part of the people," as before, until "for their necessary living," and then thus: And therefore we entreat you that the premises in every of the churches, and other places of your diocese, which you shall think expedient, you do cause to be published; directing the parsons, vicars, ministers of such churches, and others under you, to exhort and invite their parishioners by salutary admonitions, to labor, and to observe the ordinances aforesaid, as the present necessity requires: and that you do likewise moderate the stipendiary chaplains of your said diocese, who, as it is said, do now in like manner refuse to serve without an excessive salary; and compel them to serve for the accustomed salary, as it behooves them, under the pain of suspension and interdict. And this by no means omit, as you regard us and the common weal of our said realm. Witness, etc. as above. By the king himself and the whole council.

Like letters of request are directed to the several bishops of England, and to the keeper of the spiritualities of the archbishopric of Canterbury, during the vacancy of the see, under the same date.

THE PEASANTS' REVOLT OF 1381

While these negotiations and discussions were going on,* there occurred in England great disasters and uprisings of the common people, on account of which the country was almost ruined beyond recovery. Never was any land or realm in such great danger as England at that time. It was because of the abundance and prosperity in which the common people then lived that this rebellion broke out, just as in earlier days the

---

Source: Jean Froissart, *Chronicles,* ed. and trans. Geoffrey Brereton, 211–13, 226–28. Copyright © 1968 Penguin Books. Used by permission of Penguin Putnam Group (USA) Inc.

*Between John of Gaunt, Duke of Lancaster, and the Scots, with a view to renewing the truce between England and Scotland.

Jack Goodmans rose in France and committed many excesses, by which the noble land of France suffered grave injury.*

These terrible troubles originated in England from a strange circumstance and a trivial cause. That it may serve as a lesson to all good men and true, I will describe that circumstance and its effects as I was informed of them at the time.

It is the custom in England, as in several other countries, for the nobles to have strong powers over their men and to hold them in serfdom: that is, that by right and custom they have to till the lands of the gentry, reap the corn and bring it to the big house, put it in the barn, thresh and winnow it; mow the hay and carry it to the house, cut logs and bring them up, and all such forced tasks; all this the men must do by way of serfage to the masters. In England there is a much greater number than elsewhere of such men who are obliged to serve the prelates and the nobles. And in the counties of Kent, Essex, Sussex and Bedford in particular, there are more than in the whole of the rest of England.

These bad people in the counties just mentioned began to rebel because, they said, they were held too much in subjection, and when the world began there had been no serfs and could not be, unless they had rebelled against their lord, as Lucifer did against God; but they were not of that stature, being neither angels nor spirits, but men formed in the image of their masters, and they were treated as animals. This was a thing they could no longer endure, wishing rather to be all one and the same;† and, if they worked for their masters, they wanted to have wages for it. In these machinations they had been greatly encouraged originally by a crack-brained priest of Kent called John Ball, who had been imprisoned several times for his reckless words by the Archbishop of Canterbury. This John Ball had the habit on Sundays after mass, when everyone was coming out of church, of going to the cloisters or the graveyard, assembling the people round him and preaching thus:

"Good people, things cannot go right in England and never will, until goods are held in common and there are no more villeins‡ and gentlefolk, but we are all one and the same.§ In what way are those whom we call lords greater masters than ourselves? How have they deserved it? Why do they hold us in bondage? If we all spring from a single father and mother, Adam and Eve, how can they claim or prove that they are lords more than us, except by making us produce and grow the wealth which they spend? They are clad in velvet and camlet lined with squirrel and ermine, while we go dressed in coarse cloth. They have the wines, the spices and the good bread: we have the rye, the husks and the straw, and we drink water. They have shelter and ease in their fine manors, and we have hardship and toil, the wind and the rain in the fields. And from us must come, from our labor, the things which keep them in luxury. We are called serfs and beaten if we are slow in our service to them, yet we have no

---

*This refers to the Jacquerie, the French Peasants' Revolt of 1358, so called because the nobility called its participants "Jack Goodmans," or in French "Jacques Bonhommes," a derogatory term something like "Joe Sixpack" today, but with more negative overtones.

†Since Froissart uses no word exactly corresponding to *equal*, it has been avoided in translation. His phrase is: *mais vouloient être tout un.* See also footnote §.

‡Serfs or commoners.

§Or "unified." Froissart: *tout-unis.*

sovereign lord we can complain to, none to hear us and do us justice. Let us go to the King—he is young—and show him how we are oppressed, and tell him that we want things to be changed, or else we will change them ourselves. If we go in good earnest and all together, very many people who are called serfs and are held in subjection will follow us to get their freedom. And when the King sees and hears us, he will remedy the evil, either willingly or otherwise."

These were the kind of things which John Ball usually preached in the villages on Sundays when the congregations came out from mass, and many of the common people agreed with him. Some, who were up to no good, said: "He's right!" and out in the fields, or walking together from one village to another, or in their homes, they whispered and repeated among themselves: "That's what John Ball says, and he's right."

The Archbishop of Canterbury, being informed of all this, had John Ball arrested and put in prison, where he kept him for two or three months as a punishment. It would have been better if he had condemned him to life imprisonment on the first occasion, or had him put to death, than to do what he did; but he had great scruples about putting him to death and set him free; and when John Ball was out of prison, he went on with his intrigues as before. The things he was doing and saying came to the ears of the common people of London, who were envious of the nobles and the rich. These began saying that the country was badly governed and was being robbed of its wealth by those who called themselves noblemen. So these wicked men in London started to become disaffected and to rebel and they sent word to the people in the counties mentioned to come boldly to London with all their followers, when they would find the city open and the common people on their side. They could then so work on the King that there would be no more serfs in England.

These promises incited the people of Kent, Essex, Sussex, Bedford and the neighboring districts and they set off and went towards London. They were a full sixty thousand and their chief captain was one Wat Tyler. With him as his companions were Jack Straw and John Ball. These three were the leaders and Wat Tyler was the greatest of them. He was a tiler of roofs, and a wicked and nasty fellow he was.

[The crowd marches through Canterbury, sacking the palace of the Archbishop on the way, and makes its way to London, where they have several meetings with King Richard II, at the time only fourteen years old, and some of his leading nobles. At one of these, in a field outside of London at Smithfield, the king with perhaps sixty supporters, virtually surrounded by the rebel mob, entered into negotiations with Wat Tyler, who (according to this account) was acting belligerently and seemed to be trying to provoke a fight with the king's supporters.]

Just then the Lord Mayor of London arrived on horseback with a dozen others, all fully armed beneath their robes, and broke through the crowd. He saw how Tyler was behaving and said to him in the sort of language he understood: "Fellow, how dare you say such things in the King's presence? You're getting above yourself." The King lost his temper and said to the Mayor: "Lay hands on him, Mayor." Meanwhile Tyler was answering: "I can say and do what I like. What's it to do with you?" "So, you stinking boor," said the Mayor, who had once been a King's Advocate, "you talk like that in the presence of the King, my natural lord? I'll be hanged if you don't pay for it."

With that he drew a great sword he was wearing and struck. He gave Tyler such a blow on the head that he laid him flat under his horse's feet. No sooner was he down than he was entirely surrounded, so as to hide him from the crowds who were there, who called themselves his men. One of the King's squires called John Standish dismounted and thrust his sword into Tyler's belly so that he died.

Those crowds of evil men soon realized that their leader was dead. They began to mutter: "They've killed our captain. Come on, we'll slay the lot!" They drew themselves up in the square in a kind of battle-order, each holding before him the bow which he carried. Then the King did an extraordinarily rash thing, but it ended well. As soon as Tyler was dispatched, he left his men, saying: "Stay here, no one is to follow me," and went alone towards those half-crazed people, to whom he said : "Sirs, what more do you want? You have no other captain but me. I am your king, behave peaceably." On hearing this, the majority of them were ashamed and began to break up. They were the peace-loving ones. But the bad ones did not disband; instead they formed up for battle and showed that they meant business. The King rode back to his men and asked what should be done next. He was advised to go on towards the country, since it was no use trying to run away. The Mayor said: "That is the best thing for us to do, for I imagine that we shall soon receive reinforcements from London, from the loyal men on our side who are waiting armed in their houses with their friends."

While all this was going on, a rumor spread through London that the King was being killed. Because of it, loyal men of all conditions left their houses armed and equipped and made for Smithfield and the fields nearby, where the King now was. Soon they were some seven or eight thousand strong. Among the first to arrive were Sir Robert Knollys and Sir Perducat d'Albret, accompanied by a strong force of men, and nine of the London aldermen with over six hundred men-at-arms, and also an influential London citizen called Nicholas Brembre, who received an allowance from the King, and now came with a powerful company of men-at-arms. As they arrived they all dismounted and drew up in battle formation near the King, on one side. Opposite were all those evil men, drawn up also, showing every sign of wanting a fight, and they had the King's banners with them. There and then the King created three new knights. One was William Walworth, Mayor of London, the second John Standish and the third Nicholas Brembre. The leaders conferred together, saying: "What shall we do? These are our enemies who would gladly have killed us if they thought they had the advantage." Sir Robert Knollys argued frankly that they should go and fight them and kill them all, but the King refused to agree, saying that he would not have that done. "But," said the King, "I want to have my banners back. We will see how they behave when we ask for them. In any case, by peaceful means or not, I want them back." "You're right," said the Earl of Salisbury. So the three new knights were sent over to get them. They made signs to the villeins not to shoot, since they had something to discuss. When they were near enough for their voices to be heard, they said: "Now listen, the King commands you to give back his banners, and we hope that he will have mercy on you." The banners were handed over at once and taken back to the King. Any of the villeins who had obtained royal letters* were also ordered in the King's name to give them up, on pain of death. Some did so, but not all. The King had them taken and torn up in front of them. It may be said that as soon

---

*Letters granting an end to serfdom, obtained from the king in earlier negotiations.

as the royal banners had been removed, those bad men became just a mob. Most of them threw down their bows and they broke formation and started back for London. Sir Robert Knollys was more than angry that they had not been attacked and all killed. But the King would not hear of it, saying that he would take full vengeance later, as he did.

NOTES

1. Legal chapter, or numbered section of a legal code.

CHAPTER 13

Intellectual Traditions

INTRODUCTION

The invention of quantum mechanics in the first half of the twentieth century introduced ideas that challenged many scientists' (and nonscientists') traditional assumptions about the physical world. Propositions such as "something cannot be in two places at once," "something cannot be one thing and a different thing at the same time," and "the behavior of objects is predictable at least in theory" seemed (and still seem) so basically commonsensical as to be the equivalent of articles of faith, yet each is untrue in quantum physics. Subatomic particles can, in some way, be in two places at once, can be both waves and particles, and do behave in ways that are statistically describable but not predictable. The encounter between scientific rationality and faith in common sense challenged even some of the greatest minds: Albert Einstein himself could not accept the implications of statistical randomness built into quantum mechanics, saying "God does not play dice with the universe." And yet practical applications of quantum theory, especially in electronics and computing, prove the theory not only true but also useful in the commonsense world.

This chapter explores some earlier encounters between reason and tradition and the efforts of some great thinkers to reconcile them in useful ways. As we have already seen in previous chapters, human communities readily form traditions, both secular and religious, intellectual and popular, that encompass and shape the views of the world that members of those communities hold. The formation of such traditions, which met needs as diverse as explaining nature, regulating social relationships, and providing hope if not for this life then in one to follow, reflects humankind's ability to think rationally and communicate the results of such thought through symbolic language. This ability is one of the things that sets people apart from other animals—indeed, the ability and how it operates, that is, what the "mind" is and how it comes to know the world around it, is one of the themes we explore in the writings of these thinkers. Yet that same ability could lead to the questioning of traditional answers that were seen to no longer work or to need re-explaining in the face of new challenges. Sometimes those challenges arose from an encounter with an alternate tradition that provided different answers or even answered different questions and that thus needed to be incorporated into or reconciled with the old tradition.

Specifically, we look at the writings of three men whose careers were shaped in various ways by the encounter of reason and tradition. First, we present the writings of the Chinese philosopher, scholar, and sometime government official Chu Hsi (1130–1200). Chu lived during the Southern Song dynasty, a time of ongoing threats of barbarian invasion from the north. Nevertheless, despite these threats and sometimes military losses, Song China also witnessed significant economic development. Faster ripening strains of rice introduced from southeast Asia doubled agricultural production and supported a booming and increasingly urbanized population. Merchant activity flourished. The broadening of the well-to-do class that this development allowed was met by the invention of movable-type printing, which put many more copies of classic literature into circulation. The combined effect of these developments was to widen access both to education and to the government positions available to the educated through the system of civil service exams.

The philosophical content of the exams had been shaped by the canon of Confucian classic texts (see chapter 4) since Han times, but Confucianism had been eclipsed in importance by Buddhism, one of the great salvation religions (see chapter 9), after the fall of the Han in 220 CE through the early years of the Tang dynasty. Confucianism had begun to reassert itself later in the Tang, and by Song times was again the dominant ideology of China's ruling scholarly elite. But the challenge to the homegrown Chinese philosophical tradition presented by Buddhism and by the developments in China's mystical religion, Taoism (see chapter 4), stimulated by contact with Buddhism, could not simply be dismissed. Confucianism was a fundamentally secular philosophy of personal improvement, social relationships, and good government. What it lacked, by contrast with Buddhism and Taoism, was a comprehensive cosmology and metaphysics: accounts of the structure of the universe and how the fundamental principles of the universe connected to and shaped the individual and his ethical concerns. Many scholars of the Song period turned their attention to working out an alternate cosmology and metaphysics compatible with and informed by Confucian ideals. Their efforts eventually coalesced into what became known as Neo-Confucianism. This movement was well developed by the time Chu Hsi entered the field. His achievement was to synthesize and systematize Neo-Confucian philosophy into a system of thought that remained dominant in China until the challenge of Western imperialism and ideas in the nineteenth century. What we see in the work of Chu Hsi, therefore, are the results of an encounter between an essentially secular tradition and a religious challenge, worked out through Chu Hsi's powers of reason.

The second thinker we examine is the medieval European philosopher and teacher Thomas Aquinas (1224–1274). Aquinas lived during a thirteenth century that was in many ways the high point of medieval European civilization. Unlike China, Europe faced no serious external threat during this time and in fact posed more of a threat to its own, especially Muslim, neighbors through Crusades in the Near East and in Iberia. But, like China, it was experiencing a long economic expansion accompanied by urbanization, a rise in trade, and a significant broadening and deepening of education among the population, marked above all by the founding and growth of universities.

The Catholic Church had long dominated education and literacy in medieval Europe, and the Christian religion as interpreted by the Church remained the cornerstone of learning even in the universities, which were not, strictly speaking, part of official Church organization (many having been founded instead as teaching guilds, and even as student-run learning guilds). But the air of academic freedom the universities fostered had already stimulated new modes of inquiry that were not always comfortable for the guardians of the creed, especially the application of the science of logic, derived from some small pieces of Aristotle's writings rediscovered in the twelfth century, to questions of Christian dogma. The level of challenge to tradition and the curriculum embodied in it went up immeasurably, however, with the introduction from Muslim Spain (a frontier of cultural exchange as much as of warfare) of vast chunks of the Aristotelian corpus long lost to European scholars. This material, along with extensive Arabic commentaries on it, entered European universities in the decades just before Aquinas's academic career began. Aristotle was already thought of as The Philosopher, the man who knew everything, before this influx. Thus the challenge presented by his inquiries into everything—from logic, metaphysics, and cosmology to biology, poetics, and politics—to Christian tradition could not be ignored. But nor could they be adopted uncritically: after all, Aristotle was a pre-Christian pagan. It was to synthesizing Christian and Aristotelian thought, to combining Faith and Reason, that the Scholastics, the university-based thinkers of medieval civilization, turned themselves in the thirteenth century. It was Aquinas who most comprehensively and successfully achieved this synthesis, formulating what became official Catholic doctrine until well into the twentieth century. What we see in Aquinas's work, therefore, are the results of an encounter between an essentially religious tradition and a secular challenge, worked out through Aquinas's powers of reason.

The third and final thinker we examine is the great Muslim historian, philosopher, sociologist, and sometime government official Ibn Khaldun (1332–1406). Khaldun lived mostly in North Africa during somewhat troubled times for the various Islamic states of the world. Like China, North Africa faced external pressure on at least one frontier as the Christian Reconquista in Spain advanced. Khaldun's family, though originally of south Arabian origin, had for centuries lived in southern Spain, but Khaldun's great-great-grandfather had moved to North Africa after a series of Christian victories in the area. His father died in the great Black Death epidemic of 1348–1349 that swept the Muslim and Christian worlds alike. And political instability plagued the emirates of Algeria and Tunisia, where Khaldun spent much of his life before moving to Egypt. He lived to see the victories of Tamerlane over the emerging Ottoman sultanate and even met the Great Conqueror in person.

Ibn Khaldun's context is therefore both more personal and more troubled than Chu Hsi's and Thomas Aquinas's. The response of much of the Muslim world to the upheavals of this age leaned toward mysticism (especially Sufism) and withdrawal from politics, as well as a turning back toward the basic religious tenets of the Islamic faith. Ibn Khaldun, on the other hand, seems to have identified himself with the Spanish elements in Islam that were disappearing, as well as the scientific strain in Islamic culture that was in retreat in the face of mysticism and fundamentalism, and to have constructed himself as a semidetached insider in his own culture. He certainly managed to achieve a sort of objectivity about his world that is remarkable. Interestingly (and probably significantly for this "scientific" outlook), his rationalism had its roots in the same works of Aristotle, adopted enthusiastically by the Islamic world centuries before, that played so important a role in Aquinas's career. And although Khaldun was widely admired (and sometimes disliked) in the broad community of Islamic scholars and officials within which he moved, and although his most famous book, *The Muqaddimah*, remained influential for centuries, his uniqueness prevented his having the same impact on orthodoxy that Chu Hsi had in China or Aquinas had in Catholic Europe. What we see in Ibn Khaldun's work, therefore, are the results of an encounter between a tradition with both religious and secular elements and a troubled world context, refracted through the reasoning of one man.

All three of these men wrote on a vast array of topics in books many volumes long. In order to facilitate comparison of their methods and of the encounter of traditions with reason, we have focused our selections from each man's work on two topics. First, fittingly for an examination of the encounter of reason and tradition, each man wrote on what the human "mind" is and how it comes to apprehend and understand the world around it. These discussions of theories of mind and epistemology (the science of how we know what we know) are in each case intimately tied up with each man's cosmology, and so they offer a small window into the deeper philosophical structures and traditions within which each man worked. Second, as an example of how such theories can be applied to problems in the everyday world, we present some of what each man wrote about problems of social organization and governance.

It might seem that the writings of thinkers as powerful and sophisticated as Chu Hsi, Aquinas, and Ibn Khaldun could not possibly be representative of the broader intellectual traditions and worldviews of a whole civilization. What relevance do such writings have for our understanding of the culture of common people in Song China, medieval Europe, and Muslim North Africa? In one sense, this is a good objection: These men are not representative even of the academics of their days—they stand above them, and their thoughts must be taken as their own, sometimes idiosyncratic, reactions to the encounter of tradition and reason. But their very prominence meant that they were influential within their traditions, in the cases of Chu Hsi and Aquinas coming to define those traditions for centuries afterward. And if that influence was confined to the educated elite within their traditions, the political and social power of that elite meant that these writers' influence was transmitted to and affected the everyday lives of common people within those traditions at least indirectly. This is not so different from today. After all, very few people today really understand quantum physics, but that does not stop them using the electronic gadgets spawned from the discoveries of those who do understand it.

CHAPTER QUESTIONS

1. How does each man explain the human mind? How does each theory of mind reveal a deeper theory of the universe?

2. What does each man have to say about government and social organization? How is each presentation of this topic related to the more theoretical grounding of how minds work?

3. Do these accounts of mind and governance tend to affirm or critique the intellectual tradition and practices of government in each man's society? How is each author's attitude to his own tradition related to his context and position in society?

4. These are all, in their traditions, rational, scholarly examinations of these subjects. What is similar in the approach of these three thinkers? What is different? Do the similarities outweigh the differences? What does this say about the universality of human reason?

5. Whose accounts of these subjects seem most "rational" to you? (What do you mean by "rational"?) Which account is most convincing? Is it the same one you find most rational? Why or why not?

SONG CHINA
Chu Hsi and the Neo-Confucian Synthesis

Chu Hsi (1130–1200) was the son of a local official in Song China, during a time of barbarian threats on the northern frontier but also of economic growth and intellectual ferment. Chu showed early promise as a scholar, attaining the rough equivalent of a doctorate at eighteen, when most at that level were at least thirty-five. He served off and on as an official himself, gaining a reputation for scrupulous honesty that at times earned him enemies. As a result, he refused public appointments and the factional politics that went with them for large portions of his career, devoting himself instead to writing. He built on the work of a group of scholars known as the Neo-Confucian school, whose main project was to respond to the challenge of Buddhism and Taoism. His synthesis of Neo-Confucianism became the standard version of this dominant philosophy thereafter.

Chu's aim was to put traditional Confucian ethics on a firm metaphysical foundation, linking morality to the structure of the universe. Several key elements in Chu's philosophy allowed him to work out this problem. At the physical–metaphysical level, the universe reflects the interaction of *li*, translated as "principle," and *ch'i*, translated as "universal energy" (or just "energy"). *Li* is the transcendent pattern or principle that lies behind all objects in the universe and determines their form. But to become real objects, *li* must be actualized by *ch'i*, the universal energy that gives objects their substance. Thus each person or object is both a specific and unique product of the interaction of *li* and *ch'i*, and a piece of two universal and morally positive elements of the cosmos. In terms of the human mind, *li* shows up as "nature," the part of human nature that reflects that universal goodness, unsullied by the energy of creation, while *ch'i*, that energy, shows up as feelings and emotions.

Through strenuously cultivating one's "nature" and through self-purification, one can use the "nature" in mind to perfect and realize *ren*, translated as "humanity," one of the four cardinal virtues (along with rectitude, propriety, and wisdom), and the one from which all others spring. In ethical practice, that is, in dealing with other people, *ren* shows up as the sense of compassion, but it also serves as a transcendent moral standard connected to *Tao*, the universal pattern of action and standard of morality that completes (with *li* and *ch'i*) the fundamental characteristics of nature. Thus for Chu it is the operations of the mind that consciously bring human action (including good governance) into harmony with a "Heaven," or cosmos, whose principles are visible to the mind. The mind is thus what guides people to moral goodness; sages are those people who best achieve this.

QUESTIONS TO CONSIDER

1. How does Chu explain the nature and functioning of the human mind? What images or metaphors does he use?
2. How does his discussion of the human mind shape his discussion of good government? What are the philosophical and practical (or personal) points of connection?
3. Is Chu critical of his own tradition? Why or why not?
4. What do you think of the style of argument or presentation Chu uses to convey his ideas? Does the discussion of mind clarify the discussion of good government? What general logical or intellectual principles underlie Chu's analysis of mind, morality, and governance?
5. Do you find this account convincing? Why or why not?

FURTHER REFLECTIONS ON THINGS AT HAND

Chu Hsi

The Essence of Tao

12. Master Chu said: The beginning [of anything] is the beginning of [its] energy. The birth [of anything] is the beginning of [its] form.

13. Master Chu said: If the nature of heaven's endowment is lacking in material substance, then there is no place where it can be. It is like a spoonful of water: if there

Source: Selections from Chu Hsi, *Further Reflections on Things at Hand*, trans. by Allen Wittenborn, 60–66, 129–34, 138. Copyright © 1991 University Press of America. Reprinted by permission of Rowman and Littlefield Publishers.

is nothing to hold it, then there is nowhere for the water to be. Ch'eng said, "It is incomplete to discuss the nature of something without discussing energy, and it is vague to discuss energy without discussing nature. To consider these as two [distinct] principles simply will not do. Therefore, it is a great accomplishment to clarify the idea left incomplete by the sages of antiquity." Generally speaking, this principle has never been clearly perceived. In fact, ever since the Ch'in and Han periods all the various written records have been little more than interpretations of dreams. . . .

· · ·

15. Master Chu said: Nature is what is not yet moved. Feelings are what is already moved. The mind contains both what is already moved and what is not yet moved. What is not yet moved in the mind is nature, and what is already moved is feelings, and what we call the mind governs nature and feelings. Desire is the feelings released. The mind is like water: nature is like the stillness of water, feelings are the flow of water. Desire is turbulent waves, but waves which can be both good and bad. A good desire is like the kind when I desire humanity. A bad one just rushes out like seething breakers. Generally, a bad desire will destroy the universal principle, just as when pent-up water [is suddenly released] there is nothing it does not destroy. Mencius* said that the feelings can be good. This is to speak of the uprightness of feelings, and the feelings that flow out from one's nature are originally all good. So in asking about the desire of "what is desirable is called good" I say that this is not the desire of feelings, but the idea of what can be loved.

16. Master Chu said: Nature is like a ray of sunshine: that which people and things receive is different, just as the ray of sunlight shining through an opening can be either large or small. Humans and things are fixed by their form and matter, and once they are, it is difficult to change them. It is like the cricket and the ant being so small that they only know the difference between superior and inferior and that's all.

17. Master Chu said: When people and things are born, the form of their natural endowment is leaning or upright; from the very beginning they are completely different. However, even within their leaning or upright dispositions, there are differences of being clear, turbid, vague, and distinct.

18. Master Chu said: Every blade of grass and every single tree is imbued with the energy of universal harmony.

19. Master Chu said: It is essential to understand that the un-stimulated [phase of the mind] is nature, and that the stimulated [phase of the mind] is feelings. The mind links movement and stillness and there is nothing it does not exist in. In *Understanding Words* it says, "Nature sets up what there is in the world, while feelings affect the movement of everything in the universe. The mind contains the virtues of nature and feelings." These words are concise and thorough.

· · ·

22. Master Chu said: Nature is not some conspicuous thing that can be seen. It is simply to [inquire] exhaustively into principle and to investigate things. Nature naturally lies in these and need not be sought later. This is why the sage rarely speaks about nature.

---

*Meng Tzu (372–289 BCE) is known in the Chinese intellectual tradition as the "second sage," because he promoted and developed Confucius's thought. The Latinized form of his name is Mencius.

23. Master Chu said: Human nature is analogous to water: originally it is pure. If we fill a clear vessel then the water will be clear, but if we fill a dirty vessel then the water will be sullied. Its original purity is always there, but once it becomes dirty or turbid it is very difficult to regain its purity. Therefore, although stupidity can eventually become intelligent, and although weakness can eventually be made strong, it takes a great deal of effort.

24. Master Chu said: Nature is the principle of the mind, and feelings are the movement of the mind. Talent is the feelings' ability to do something. Feelings and talent are definitely very close to each other. But feelings issue forth when something is encountered, and pass through the twists and turns of the road to the end. Talent is what enables [feelings] to do this. In short, all things in their complications and ramifications come from the mind.

. . .

27. Master Chu said: Intelligence controls the distinctions in our knowledge. Intention controls the planning of our actions. Intelligence is close to nature and substance. Intention is close to feelings and function.

28. Master Chu said: Only mind is absolute.

29. Master Chu said: Heaven has only spring, summer, autumn, and winter. Humans have only humanity, rectitude, propriety, and wisdom. These four are those four. Mind is what functions. There are only these four principles. There is nothing else.

. . .

32. Master Chu said: What heaven imparts to people and things is called endowment. What people and things receive [from heaven] is called nature. What governs a body is called mind. What is received from heaven and is bright and upright is called illuminating virtue.

. . .

36. Master Chu said: Mencius spoke about "humanity being a person's mind." This is a most fitting remark. Mind is naturally a humane thing. So long as we preserve this mind, then there is no need to worry that such a person will be inhuman.

. . .

44. Someone asked, when a person is free from all cares, inside he is empty, clear, and unobstructed. Is this the natural movement of his energy, or is this his nature?

Master Chu answered: Empty, clear, and unobstructed is the mind. When principle is complete and sufficient within [the mind] and without the slightest deficiency, this is one's nature. When it is stimulated by things to movement, then it is feelings. . . . Combining nature and consciousness gives the term 'mind.' This is to speak in particular about humans and things.

. . .

49. Master Chu said: Nature is the principle of heaven. All things innately receive it. There is not one thing that does not contain principle. Mind is the body's ruler. Intention is what the mind releases. The feelings are the movement of the mind. Will is where the mind goes; it is much stronger than either the feelings or intention. Energy is the life force that fills our body. Compared to the others, energy has form and function and is relatively coarse.

He also said, without the mind, there is no way to perceive nature. Discard nature and there is no way to perceive the mind.

Governing the State

2. Master Chu said: It is only the sage who completes human relations, and it is only the ideal monarch who completes the rules of government. Certainly the common people do not reach up to this. However, in establishing the root of the mind, those who have completed them should be taken as a model, but those who do not complete them should not be taken as a standard.

3. Master Chu said: World affairs involve both ordinary and urgent matters, and court government concerns both ordinary and urgent events. If you handle ordinary matters as urgent everything becomes unduly critical and relentlessly faultfinding with no means of preserving the overall organization, while at court the atmosphere becomes very strained. But if you treat urgent affairs as ordinary you will become lax and negligent with no way of attending to critical matters, while world affairs daily grow worse. By balancing them, both problems will be gone.

4. Master Chu said: The senior officers determine the moral qualities and intellectual capabilities of those recommended to the ruler to carry out the affairs of state. They should not become sympathetic or friendly, but rather be completely objective about them. Their only concern is the nation, and in no way must they inject their own ideas lest they be unable to assist in this undertaking.

5. Master Chu said: Even though all things in the world are always inconstant and changing, they are imbued with innumerable implications, still there is nothing that is not the ruler's concern.

The ruler's august person lies deep within the palace. Though the inner workings of his mind are not to be known, the results become manifest. They are like "what all eyes see and what all fingers point to," and can never be concealed.

This is why in ancient times the former sages and kings were cautious and wary and kept a firm grip on themselves. Whether they were in turbulent and unstable times, or in isolated and far-away places, they would focus and concentrate their mind, conquer and recover it. Like facing the spirits or approaching a steep precipice, there was not the slightest negligence.

6. Master Chu said: World order was not established by itself. The calculations of the ruler must be fair and just, impartial and unbiased, and only then will this order become interconnected and secure. Nor can the monarch correct it himself. He must be close to good and wise statesmen but keep distant from mean and selfish characters. By clearly explaining the attributes of rectitude and principle, and by blocking the road to selfishness and perversity, all of this can be realized and made right.

. . .

9. Master Chu said: Anyone who is to be prime minister must prepare his one heart and two eyes. When the eyes are clear then one can know the honest and the dishonest. When the heart is impartial then one can advance the honest and retire the dishonest.

10. Someone asked about the comment that in the art of ruling one should know the essentials.

Master Chu said: Just so. If one is to manage a district or a county he should punish those who expose secrets, root out thieves and brigands, promote agriculture and sericulture [the raising of silkworms], and restrict the lower professions. If one attends court he must be open to the people, be familiar with the feelings of the people, and eliminate special interest groups and cliques. If one is going to be a senior official he must recruit wise and talented men, get rid of corrupt bureaucrats, remove extortion, and equally distribute power and labor. All of these measures follow an established form and should be handled in this way. If one is to be a close advisor to the emperor he should be outspoken and direct, as well as composed and taciturn. If one is going to administer a town or a village, he should be confidential and exercise self-control, and be personally incorrupt and reserved. But if you still move forward and do things [arrogance and pride] will injure the essentials.

. . .

12. Master Chu said: The art of governing does not lie in exerting one's own strengths, but rather values the empire's excellence.

13. Master Chu said: The ruler should concentrate on the truth of intelligence and not seek merely the name of intelligence. Trusting senior officials, daily planning affairs, constantly analyzing arguments, all in order to determine the most appropriate line of action: this is the truth of intelligence. Being inattentive to one's advisors and unquestioningly accepting their words: this is the name of intelligence.

. . .

16. Master Chu said: When it comes to the affairs of state there is not one man with the intelligence and ability who can execute them single handedly. This is why the ancient exemplars, even though their moral undertakings and resourceful methods were enough to do the job, still drew widely from the abilities of others in order to benefit. But before they used this acquired ability they gathered together their disciples to encourage and commend their accomplishments to build a large pool of them. So when the time came to use them they recommended their achievements, and displayed their abilities, and there was nothing that was not done.

17. Master Chu said: The most urgent aim of all the ancient exemplary individuals was nothing other than to gather throughout the world wise and virtuous men. The reason why they so urgently sought such wise and virtuous ones was not simply a desire to have their works compiled and edited by them, or to have their services to mankind praised just for appearance's sake. But it was in order to broaden their knowledge and thinking to heights never before reached, and to extend their thinking further than ever before. There were some who had not perfected goodness who used [the worthies] to correct it. Therefore, search for them as widely as possible, respect them as magnanimously as possible, and treat them as sincerely as possible. They had to have the worthies of the empire, known and unknown, all gladly come before them to correct their mistakes. After that, in their moral achievements, they never felt remorse about some hidden indignity. Rather, they were completely immersed in greatness.

. . .

28. Master Chu said: In ancient times the learning of sage emperors and enlightened kings always began with pursuing the principles of things to the furthest extent and perfecting knowledge to the highest degree. If you make moral principles completely clear without even a hair of darkness, then naturally your intentions will be sincere and your mind upright, and they will respond to the affairs of the empire.

Laws and Regulations

1. Master Chu said: Systems the world over are neither completely beneficial nor completely harmful, and so we must determine to what extent they are so.

2. Master Chu said: If we fail to observe whether someone is good or evil, or loyal or corrupt, but simply concerned with sectarian affairs, then the petty conniver will come up with schemes which are meant only to cover up his deeds. On the other hand, the gentleman relies only on impartiality and straight dealing, and is never devious. Frequently, however, there may be some discrimination and factionalism. Such cases that have occurred in the Han and Tang, and even in our own era, are not all that distant.

3. Master Chu said: Systems are easily talked about, but where is there anyone to make them work?

4. Master Chu said: The gentleman should at all costs refrain from being excessively angry or spiteful with the mean man, but neither is there any reason to engage in close relations.

. . .

20. Some students were discussing the demerits of the local government and feudal systems. Master Chu said: Generally speaking, any law must have its drawbacks. No law is perfect. The important thing lies in having the right men. If there are the right men, even though the laws are no good, there are still many benefits. But if there are the wrong men, there may be excellent laws, but of what benefit would they be? . . .

MEDIEVAL WESTERN EUROPE
Thomas Aquinas and the Scholastic Synthesis

Thomas Aquinas (1224–1274) was the youngest son of a southern Italian noble family during a time of economic growth, cultural flowering, and intellectual ferment. Like Chu an intellectual prodigy, he joined the Dominicans, an order of itinerant friars who were the leading academicians of the day, against his family's wishes (the order was too new and radical for them). He studied at various schools in Italy, Germany, and eventually Paris, where he completed his equivalent of a doctorate early and was appointed a professor of theology at the University of Paris. He therefore joined the Scholastics, or school men, thinkers whose self-appointed project was to reconcile Christian doctrine with logic and the use of reason, above all as contained in the newly discovered works of Aristotle. Aquinas's own writings were produced either as responses to specific requests from his superiors (as for a handbook for missionaries) or as "textbooks" for his own teaching purposes. The *Summa Theologiae*, his most famous and comprehensive work, began as his introductory text for teaching theology. But it turned into an encyclopedia of Catholic doctrine that remained fundamental for centuries.

Aquinas shows a great gift for systematic organization and exposition of problems. The *Summa*, as a teaching text, is divided into questions, which are followed variously by arguments, replies to the arguments, and sometimes responses to the replies. An early convert to the philosophy of Aristotle, he used Aristotelian principles to explicate Christian doctrine while pointing out those places where reason could not go and only faith could guide. Among the most important aspects of Aristotelianism that shaped Aquinas's thinking were Aristotle's four-part categorization of causation (material, formal, efficient, and final) and, above all, the interpretation of Aristotle by the Muslim scholar Avicenna (Ibn Sina) that stressed the distinction between the "nature" of living things (their fundamental essence, analogous to *li* in Chu's thought) and their *esse*, or "act of being," which was only an imperfect instantiation of their nature (somewhat like the product of uniting *li* and *ch'i* in Chu's system). In God, on the other hand, nature and *esse* were identical: He was the perfect instantiation of his own perfect nature. And for Aquinas, this metaphysical conception of the universe shaped his view of the human mind: the rational soul formed for him the first stage in the actualization of the human body, the first product of the movement of nature to *esse*. The soul's simultaneous material existence and connection to divinely inspired nature was one key to the ability of the human mind to perceive the universe and comprehend it as evidence of God's role as rational designer and final cause.

Aristotle's analysis of types of political organization also informed Aquinas's own exposition of this subject, which (given the role of God's design in the world) is basically a defense of monarchy as the best form of government.

QUESTIONS TO CONSIDER

1. How does Aquinas explain the nature and functioning of the human mind? How does his exposition compare with Chu's?
2. How does Aquinas's discussion of the mind connect with his discussion of government? Are they consistent with each other? Does he apply his theory of knowledge to his analysis of kingship?
3. Is Aquinas critical of (or objective about) his own tradition? Why or why not?
4. What do you think of Aquinas's style of argument? What general logical or intellectual principles underlie Aquinas's analysis of mind, morality, and governance? How are they similar to, and different from, the Chinese principles of Chu Hsi?
5. Do you find this account convincing? Why or why not?

SUMMA THEOLOGIAE AND ON KINGSHIP

Thomas Aquinas

On Human Nature

Is the active intellect part of the human soul?
Arguments:

2. The philosopher [Aristotle] . . . states that the active intellect "does not understand at certain times and not understand at other times." But our soul is not constantly

Source: Selections from *The Essential Aquinas: Writings of Philosophy, Religion and Society,* translated with introduction by John Y. B. Hood, 72–78, 193–97. Copyright © 2002 Praeger Publishers. Reprinted by permission of Greenwood Publishing Group, Westport, CT.

engaged in understanding, but rather does so at certain times and does not at others. Therefore the active intellect is not part of our soul.*

I answer that the active intellect the philosopher speaks of is in fact part of the soul. As evidence for this, consider the fact that it is necessary that we posit a superior intellect over and above the human, one from which the human intellect obtains the capacity for understanding. Now for everything that participates in something else and that is imperfect and subject to change, there preexists something else that essentially possesses the participated-in quality and is perfect and unchanging. And the human soul is commonly said to possess the power of understanding via participation. Signs of this are that it is not the soul in its entirety that understands, but only a part of it; it comes to the understanding of truth not immediately but via argument and the discursive movement of the mind; and it has only imperfect understanding, both in that it does not understand everything and in that its understanding moves from potential to actuality. Therefore there must be some higher intellect that helps bring the soul to understanding. For this reason certain persons identify this separate intellect with the active intellect, claiming that, so to speak, it "illuminates" sense images, rendering them intelligible.

But even if there were such a separate active intellect, it would still be necessary to posit some power within the human soul that actualized these intelligible objects. This is also the case with other natural objects, which, in addition to universal causal agents, also have specific powers implanted within themselves that are derived from the universal agent. Thus it is not the sun alone that causes reproduction in humans; rather, there is also a procreative power that belongs to individual humans. The case is similar with other animals that are complete in their own nature. For among sublunar [i.e., earthly] entities, nothing is more perfect than the human soul. Hence we must say that the soul contains within itself a power—derived from the higher intellect—which enables it to illuminate sense images. . . .

Now the "separate mind," according to our Faith, is none other than God himself, who creates the soul and, as I will make clear later . . . , in whom the soul finds perfect happiness. Hence the human soul participates in the intellectual light of God, in accord with Psalm 4.7: , "The light of your countenance is sealed upon us as a sign, O Lord."

Can the mind understand by means of intelligible structures within itself without reference to sense images?
Response:

In our present state of life, in which we are joined to a body, it is impossible for our mind to understand anything without reference to sense images. . . . For we see that when imagination is impeded by some injury to a bodily organ (e.g., with epilepsy), or when memory is impeded (e.g., with lethargy), the mind is also impeded in its ability to understand what it previously learned. . . .

Are the intelligible structures abstracted from sense images the objects of our understanding?
Response:

Thus we should say rather that intelligible structures are the *means* by which we understand. The following will make this clear. For, as [Aristotle] states, there are two

---

*This first paragraph states the opposition case, which Aquinas then proceeds to prove wrong.

types of action: *intransitive,* such as seeing and understanding; and *transitive,* like heating or cutting. And each type occurs according to its own nature or structure. And just as the structure involved in transitive action includes a certain similarity between actor and object (i.e., the heat in the agent that causes heat *is* the same as that received by the object), so too in intransitive action there is a similarity between actor and object. Hence we see via a likeness of the visible object, and our minds understand via an intelligible structure.

Now since our minds are capable of self-reflection, we can, via such reflection, both understand and understand the means by which we understand. Thus *in* a secondary sense these intelligible structures become the objects of understanding. But the primary object of understanding remains the [external] objects to which the intelligible structures are similar.

On Kingship

Prologue:

As I was pondering what offering I might make your Royal Highness that would be in accord with my vocation and position, it occurred to me that the most appropriate gift would be to compose, to the best of my ability, a book for the king in which I would carefully describe the origins of kingship and the duties of a king as they are presented in Sacred Scripture, in the teaching of the philosophers, and in the praiseworthy deeds of rulers, trusting for help in the beginning, progress, and conclusion of this work in him who is King of Kings and Lord of Lords: God, the Great Lord and King over all gods, through whom all kings rule.

Chapter 1: It is necessary for humans living in community to be governed by a diligent ruler.

We must begin by explaining what the term "king" means. In all things directed toward a goal, if there are various possible ways of proceeding, there must be someone in charge if the goal is to be achieved. For instance, a ship that may be blown here and there by contrary winds will never reach port unless it is guided by a competent helmsman. The fact that man has a goal or purpose, to which his life and all his actions are directed by his mind, is clear from the fact that he acts purposefully. But men pursue their goals or purposes in diverse ways, as the variety of their purposes and actions indicates. Therefore each person needs something to direct him. Now each naturally possesses the light of reason to guide him toward his goals. And if man were suited to a solitary life, as many animals are, he would not require anyone to direct him toward his goal; rather, each would be ruler of himself, subordinate only to the highest King, God, who infused in him the divine light of reason that directs his actions.

But man, more than any other animal, is social and political, and it is natural for him to live in community. Natural necessity declares this. For nature provides other animals with food, fur, and either means of defense—tooth, horn, or claw—or else speed for flight. She gives man none of these, but in their place grants him reason, which enables him to fashion substitutes for these defenses. But an individual cannot do all this himself; one man alone cannot procure the necessities of life. Therefore he naturally lives in society.

Moreover, other animals know by instinct what is helpful or harmful. For example, sheep naturally know that the wolf is an enemy, while other animals know which plants are medicinal as well as other things essential to their well-being. But for man such things are naturally known only in community. For the process of reasoning, from first principles to specifics, on such matters cannot be accomplished by a single individual. Thus man must live in community so that each can help the other via specialization, for example, one is a physician while others perform other jobs.

This is also obvious from the fact that it is a specific property of man to use speech to communicate the totality of his conceptions. True, other animals express their feelings in various ways, for example, dogs express anger by barking, but man communicates even more than the most gregarious animals, such as cranes, ants, and bees. Thus Ecclesiastes 4.9: "It is better that there be two than one, for each shall have benefit of the other's society."

If therefore it is natural that man live in society, it is also necessary that there be someone to regulate the community. For when many people live together in close proximity, they will often work at cross-purposes unless there is someone to care for the common good, just as the physical processes of the body would tend to disintegrate without some regulatory power that controls all the actions and processes of the body. Thus Solomon said, "Without a ruler the people are scattered" (Proverbs 11.14).

And it is rational that this occur, since the good of the individual is not identical with the good of the many. In their individual good they are divided, while the common good unites them. Now things that differ have distinct causes. Therefore in addition to something that moves one toward his individual good, there must be someone who moves individuals toward the common good. For this reason, whenever many things are directed toward one goal or purpose we find that there is someone who rules them. For in the physical universe all bodies, by divine providence, are ruled by the primary body—namely, the heavens—and all physical bodies are ruled by rational creatures. And in an individual the soul rules the body, and among the faculties of the soul the spirited and desiring parts are ruled by the rational. Similarly, within the body itself there is one organ that is primary vis-a-vis the others and moves them, namely, the heart or the brain. Therefore in every multitude there must be a ruler.

Chapter 2: Various types of rulership or kingship.

Things directed toward a goal or purpose may proceed correctly or incorrectly. This is why we find instances of correct and incorrect rulership. Good rulership occurs when subjects are directed toward their true goal; poor rulership occurs when they are not. Now the goal appropriate to free men differs from that appropriate to slaves. For a free man is his own cause, whereas whatever a slave is or has belongs to another. If therefore a ruler guides a community of free men to the goal or purpose of such a community, his regime is right and just, but if he guides it toward his own private advantage, his regime is unjust and perverse. Thus at Ezekiel 34.2 the Lord threatens such rulers: "Woe to those shepherds who fed themselves"—that is, sought their own advantage. "Ought not the herd be fed by the shepherd?" For shepherds should pursue the well-being of their flock, and rulers that of the peoples subject to them.

If an unjust regime headed by a single ruler uses the regime to pursue his own advantage rather than the good of the populace, he is called a "tyrant." The term is derived from that for courage, though in this case he uses his power to oppress rather than to rule in accordance with justice. (Among the ancients, all who ruled of their own accord were called "tyrants.") If the unjust regime is headed not by a single ruler, however, but by a few, it is called an "oligarchy." In such regimes a few wealthy men oppress the many. This differs from tyranny only in the number of rulers. If the regime is controlled by the many, it is called a "democracy," that is, the rule of the populace. This occurs when the plebeians rule in order to plunder the rich. Only the plurality of rulers distinguishes such a regime from a tyranny.

We may make similar terminological distinctions among just regimes. If power in such a regime is held by many, it is usually termed a "polity." An example would be when the warrior class held power in a city or province. If a just regime is headed by a small number of virtuous rulers, it is called an "aristocracy," which means rule of the good or best, who for this reason are called "the nobility."

But if a just regime is headed by a single ruler, he is properly termed a "king." Hence in Ezekiel the Lord says, "My servant David shall be king over all, and they shall all have one shepherd." From this it is clear that it is the nature of the king to rule as one and to be a shepherd caring for the common good rather than for his own advantage.

Since man in solitude cannot obtain the necessities of life and it is thus proper for him to live in a community, it necessarily follows that the more self-sufficient a community is, the more perfect it is. Now a family residing in a home is sufficient for some of life's necessities, such as nutrition and the bearing of children, and so on. For the mere physical artifacts needed, a neighborhood or village is sufficient. And for a complete community providing all the necessities of life, a city is required. But better still is a nation to provide for self-defense. Hence one who governs a perfect community (either a city or a nation) is termed a king, while he who governs a household is a *paterfamilias* [father of the family]. There is, however, a similarity between the two, as can be seen from the fact that a king is sometimes called "father of his country."

From these considerations we may define a king as "one who rules the populace of a city or nation for the sake of the common good." Hence Solomon (at Eccl. 5.8): "The king reigns over all the lands subject to him."

Chapter 3: It is better for a community to be ruled by a single king than by a plurality of rulers.

It follows from what has been stated that we ought to consider whether it is better for a nation or city to be ruled by one or by many. We may examine this by considering the goal or purpose of rulership. Now just as the intention of a captain is to preserve his ship from the perils of the sea by bringing it into a safe harbor, so too the intention of every ruler should be to achieve the salvation of his subjects.

The good and salvation of a society is that its unity, or peace, be preserved. If this is lost, the well-being of the city is imperiled, since strife among the populace makes life difficult. Thus, above all, a ruler must seek the unity of peace. Whether or not to seek to keep or restore peace is a question that should not even arise, any more than it should be a question for a doctor whether or not to heal a patient committed to his care. For deliberation ought not be about the goal, but about the means. Thus the Apostle commends unity of faith among the people: "Take care to preserve the unity of the Spirit in the bonds of peace" (Ephesians 4.3). Therefore the better a polity keeps peace, the more effective it is. For we term a thing "effective" to the extent that it achieves its goal.

Obviously something that is intrinsically unified can preserve unity better than a plurality. Similarly, a thing that is intrinsically hot is more efficient at heating. Therefore the rule of one is more effective than the rule of many.

Furthermore, nature does everything in the best possible way. But in nature, rulership is always entrusted to one. Thus among the limbs and organs of the body the heart moves them all, and among the powers of the soul reason moves all. So too with bees there is one king, and God, maker of the entire universe, is its king. This is only reasonable, since all multiplicity ultimately derives from unity. So, if things made by human design imitate nature, and if that artist is best who best imitates nature, it necessarily follows that it is best when human communities have a single ruler.

This is also clear from experience. For cities and nations that do not have a single ruler labor under dissension and violence. This fulfills the lament the Lord uttered through the prophet (Jeremiah 12.10): "Many shepherds have destroyed my vineyard." By contrast, cities and nations wherein there is one ruler enjoy peace and prosperity, and justice flourishes. Hence through the prophet the Lord promises, as a great benefit, that he will grant them one head, and will put one prince in their midst.

Chapter 4: It may be proved by many considerations and arguments that, while when the ruler is just, the rule of one is best, so too when the ruler is unjust this regime is the worst.

Just as the rule of a king is the best regime, the rule of a tyrant is the worst. As stated, a republic and a democracy are rule of the many, aristocracy and oligarchy are rule of the few, and kingship and tyranny are the rule of one. And it has been shown already that kingship is the best polity. Therefore if the worst is the opposite of the best, tyranny is necessarily the worst polity.

What's more, a united force is more effective than a dispersed or divided one. For many gathered as one can pull a load that each individually cannot. Therefore just as a united force is more effective in bringing about good, so too the harm brought about is greater if the force for evil is united rather than dispersed or divided.

An unjust regime works to the detriment of the many by pursuing not the common good, but rather what is advantageous to the ruler alone. Therefore, while in a just regime, the greater the unity the more effective the polity, so that monarchy is better than aristocracy and aristocracy is better than a republic, in an unjust regime the opposite is the case: the more unified the regime, the greater the harm done to the populace. Thus a tyranny does more harm than an oligarchy, and an oligarchy does more harm than a democracy.

ISLAMIC NORTH AFRICA
Ibn Khaldun and Muslim Rationalism

Ibn Khaldun (1332–1406) was the son of an Islamic scholar, descendant of a long line of scholar-officials of the dynasties of southern Spain and northwest Africa. These were troubled times for the Iberian Muslim kingdoms, as the Christian Reconquista steadily reduced the extent of Muslim possessions in Spain. Political disunity and instability plagued much of the Muslim world, not to mention the devastation wrought by the real plague, the Black Death, that swept the Muslim world in the 1340s.

Khaldun was seventeen when his father died in the plague. He studied traditional subjects such as the Qur'an and Qur'anic studies under a series of prominent teachers, and he continued to study with and under experts in various fields for years while becoming an acknowledged member of the scholarly community in his own right. He served in a number of official capacities, but like Chu Hsi spent periods out of government due to factional quarrels. His writing reflects and is an influential example of an Islamic scholarly tradition that emphasized the communal development of knowledge and a leading social and pseudo-governmental role for the community of scholars in the wider Muslim world, a role similar to that played by rabbis in Jewish communities. It also reflects the efforts of Muslim scholars to deal with troubled times in terms of their intellectual traditions.

The Muqaddimah is the product of one of Ibn Khaldun's later periods of retirement, and it was the first substantial piece of original scholarship he published. Originally, it constituted the introduction and first book of a planned world history. Although he did complete the rest of the history in several large volumes, the Muqaddimah, or introduction, gained a life of its own due to its unique character. Rather than setting in with narrative, Khaldun first wrote on historiography, or the history of writing history itself. He then developed a theoretical framework for the analysis of history based on the influences of geography, climate, social organization, and so forth on the rise and fall of different kingdoms and civilizations. Finally, he finished this "introduction" with a systematic discussion of the trades and crafts by which humans make a living and the sciences by which they understand their world, including the nature and functioning of the human mind itself. The Muqaddimah is thus much more than a work of history, though it is informed by a tradition of Arab historiography that emphasized the transmission of knowledge in a scholarly community and thus paid attention to the reliability and bias of individual historians. It is even more a work of social science and philosophy of history.

Khaldun's discussion of government is therefore of a different character from the theoretical and moral observations of Chu and Aquinas on this topic. And although he shares with Aquinas a grounding in the work of Aristotle, visible especially in his discussion of mind, in the area of government he breaks free of the Aristotelian mold far more clearly than Aquinas does. Ibn Khaldun's work is thus a product of his scholarly method and is a fine example of another intellectual tradition of the medieval world.

QUESTIONS TO CONSIDER

1. How does Khaldun explain the nature and functioning of the human mind? How does his exposition compare with Chu's and Aquinas's?
2. How does Khaldun's discussion of the mind connect with his discussion of government? Does his analysis of government reflect the principles he lays out for human knowledge?

3. Is Khaldun critical of (or objective about) his own tradition? Why or why not?
4. What do you think of Khaldun's style of argument? What general logical or intellectual principles underlie Khaldun's analysis of mind, morality, and governance? How is his method similar to and different from the Chinese and Western Christian traditions?
5. Do you find this account convincing? Why or why not?

THE MUQADDIMAH

Ibn Khaldun

The Various Kinds of Sciences

Man's ability to think.

It should be known that God distinguished man from all the other animals by an ability to think which He made the beginning of human perfection and the end of man's noble superiority over existing things.

This comes about as follows: Perception—that is, consciousness, on the part of the person who perceives, in his essence of things that are outside his essence—is something peculiar to living beings to the exclusion of all other beings and existent things. Living beings may obtain consciousness of things that are outside their essence through the external senses God has given them, that is, the senses of hearing, vision, smell, taste, and touch. Man has this advantage over the other beings that he may perceive things outside his essence through his ability to think, which is something beyond his senses. It is the result of (special) powers placed in the cavities of his brain. With the help of these powers, man takes the pictures of the *sensibilia* [things perceived by the senses], applies his mind to them, and thus abstracts from them other pictures. The ability to think is the occupation with pictures that are beyond sense perception, and the application of the mind to them for analysis and synthesis. This is what is meant by the word *af'idah* "hearts" in the Qur'an: "He gave you hearing and vision and hearts." *Af'idah* "hearts" . . . means here the ability to think.

The ability to think has several degrees. The first degree is man's intellectual understanding of the things that exist in the outside world in a natural or arbitrary order, so that he may try to arrange them with the help of his own power. This kind of thinking mostly consists of perceptions. It is the discerning intellect, with the help of which man obtains the things that are useful for him and his livelihood, and repels the things that are harmful to him.

The second degree is the ability to think which provides man with the ideas and the behavior needed in dealing with his fellow men and in leading them. It mostly

Source: Selections from Ibn Khaldun in *The Muqaddimah: An Introduction to History,* translated by Franz Rosenthal, Bollingen Series XLIII, 1: 89–93, 313–24, 472–73; 2: 411–22. Copyright © 1958 Princeton University Press. Reprinted by permission of Princeton University Press.

conveys apperceptions, which are obtained one by one through experience, until they have become really useful. This is called the experimental intellect.

The third degree is the ability to think which provides the knowledge, or hypothetical knowledge, of an object beyond sense perception without any practical activity (going with it). This is the speculative intellect. It consists of both perceptions and apperceptions. They are arranged according to a special order, following special conditions, and thus provide some other knowledge of the same kind, that is, either perceptive or apperceptive. Then, they are again combined with something else, and again provide some other knowledge. The end of the process is to be provided with the perception of existence as it is, with its various genera, differences, reasons, and causes. By thinking about these things, (man) achieves perfection in his reality and becomes pure intellect and perceptive soul. This is the meaning of human reality.

The world of the things that come into being as the result of action, materializes through thinking.

It should be known that the world of existent things comprises pure essences, such as the elements, the things resulting from their influence, and the three things that come into being from the elements, namely, minerals, plants, and animals. All these things are connected with the divine power.

It also comprises actions proceeding from living beings, that happen through their intentions, and are connected with the power that God has given them. Some of their actions are well arranged and orderly. Such are human actions. Others are not well arranged and orderly. They are the actions of living beings other than man. . . .

For instance, if a man thinks of bringing into existence a roof to shelter him, he will progress in his mind (from the roof) to the wall supporting the roof, and then to the foundation upon which the wall stands. Here, his thinking will end, and he will then start to work on the foundation, then (go on to) the wall, and then (to) the roof, with which his action will end. This is what is meant by the saying: "The beginning of action is the end of thinking, and the beginning of thinking is the end of action."

Thus, human action in the outside world materializes only through thinking about the order of things, since things are based upon each other. After (he has finished thinking), he starts doing things. His thinking starts with the thing that comes last in the causal chain and is done last. His action starts with the first thing in the causal chain, which thinking reaches last. Once this order is taken into consideration, human actions proceed in a well-arranged manner.

On the other hand, the actions of living beings other than man are not well arranged. They lack the thinking that acquaints the agent with the order of things governing his actions. Animals perceive only with the senses. Their perceptions are disconnected and lack a connecting link, since only thinking can constitute such (a connecting link).

The sciences (knowledge) of human beings and the sciences (knowledge) of angels.

We observe in ourselves through sound intuition the existence of three worlds.

The first of them is the world of sensual perception. We become aware of it by means of the perception of the senses, which the animals share with us.

Then, we become aware of the ability to think which is a special quality of human beings. We learn from it that the human soul exists. This knowledge is necessitated by the fact that we have in us scientific perceptions which are above the perceptions of the senses. They must thus be considered as another world, above the world of the senses.

Then, we deduce (the existence of) a third world, above us, from the influences that we find it leaves in our hearts, such as volition and an inclination toward active motions. Thus, we know that there exists an agent there who directs us toward those things from a world above our world. That world is the world of spirits and angels. It contains essences that can be perceived because of the existence of influences they exercise upon us, despite the gap between us and them.

Often, we may deduce (the existence of) that high spiritual world and the essences it contains, from visions and things we had not been aware of while awake but which we find in our sleep and which are brought to our attention in it and which, if they are true (dreams), conform with actuality. We thus know that they are true and come from the world of truth. "Confused dreams," on the other hand, are pictures of the imagination that are stored inside by perception and to which the ability to think is applied, after (man) has retired from sense perception.

We do not find any clearer proof than this for (the existence of) the spiritual world. Thus, we have a general knowledge of it, but no particulars. The metaphysicians make conjectures about details concerning the essences of the spiritual world and their order. . . . However, none of it is certain, because the conditions of logical argumentation as established in logic do not apply to it. One of these conditions is that the propositions of the argument must be primary and essential, but the spiritual essences are of an unknown essentiality. Thus, logical argumentation cannot be applied to them. Our only means of perceiving something of the details of these worlds are what we may glean from matters of religious law, as explained and established by religious faith. . . .

"God taught man what he did not know."

Human Civilization in General

First prefatory discussion

Human social organization is something necessary. The philosophers [specifically, Aristotle] expressed this fact by saying: "Man is 'political' by nature." That is, he cannot do without the social organization for which the philosophers use the technical term "town" (*polis*).

This is what civilization means. (The necessary character of human social organization or civilization) is explained by the fact that God created and fashioned man in a form that can live and subsist only with the help of food. He guided man to a natural desire for food and instilled in him the power that enables him to obtain it.

However, the power of the individual human being is not sufficient for him to obtain (the food) he needs, and does not provide him with as much food as he requires to live. Even if we assume an absolute minimum of food—that is, food enough for one day, (a little) wheat, for instance—that amount of food could be obtained only after much preparation such as grinding, kneading, and baking. Each of these three operations requires utensils and tools that can be provided only with the help of several crafts, such as the crafts of the blacksmith, the carpenter, and the potter. Assuming that a man could eat unprepared grain, an even greater number of operations would be necessary in order to obtain the grain: sowing and reaping, and threshing to separate it from the husks of the ear. Each of these operations requires a number of tools and many more crafts than those just mentioned. It is beyond the power of one man alone to do all that, or (even) part of it, by himself. Thus, he cannot do without a combination of many powers from among his fellow beings, if he is to obtain food for himself and for them. Through cooperation, the needs of a number of persons, many times greater than their own (number), can be satisfied.

Likewise, each individual needs the help of his fellow beings for his defense, as well. When God fashioned the natures of all living beings and divided the various powers among them, many dumb animals were given more perfect powers than God gave to man. The power of a horse, for instance, is much greater than the power of man, and so is the power of a donkey or an ox. The power of a lion or an elephant is many times greater than the power of (man).

Aggressiveness is natural in living beings. Therefore, God gave each of them a special limb for defense against aggression. To man, instead, He gave the ability to think, and the hand. With the help of the ability to think, the hand is able to prepare the ground for the crafts. The crafts, in turn, procure for man the instruments that serve him instead of limbs, which other animals possess for their defense.

Lances, for instance, take the place of horns for goring, swords the place of claws to inflict wounds, shields the place of thick skins, and so on. There are other such things. They were all mentioned by Galen [classical Greek physician] in *De usu partium.* The power of one individual human being cannot withstand the power of any one dumb animal, especially not the power of the predatory animals. Man is generally unable to defend himself against them by himself. Nor is his (unaided) power sufficient to make use of the existing instruments of defense, because there are so many of them and they require so many crafts and (additional) things. It is absolutely necessary for man to have the co-operation of his fellow men. As long as there is no such co-operation, he cannot obtain any food or nourishment, and life cannot materialize for him, because God fashioned him so that he must have food if he is to live. Nor, lacking weapons, can he defend himself.

Thus, he falls prey to animals and dies much before his time. Under such circumstances, the human species would vanish. When, however, mutual co-operation exists, man obtains food for his nourishment and weapons for his defense. God's wise plan that man(kind) should subsist and the human species be preserved will be fulfilled.

When mankind has achieved social organization, as we have stated, and when civilization in the world has thus become a fact, people need someone to exercise a restraining influence and keep them apart, for aggressiveness and injustice are in the animal nature of man. The weapons made for the defense of human beings against the aggressiveness of dumb animals do not suffice against the aggressiveness of man to man, because all of them possess those weapons. Thus, something else is needed for defense against the aggressiveness of human beings toward each other. It could not come from outside, because all the other animals fall short of human perceptions and inspiration. The person who exercises a restraining influence, therefore, must be one of themselves. He must dominate them and have power and authority over them, so that no one of them will be able to attack another. This is the meaning of royal authority.

It has thus become clear that royal authority is a natural quality of man which is absolutely necessary to mankind. The philosophers mention that it also exists among certain dumb animals, such as the bees and the locusts. One discerns among them the existence of authority and obedience to a leader. They follow the one of them who is distinguished as their leader by his natural characteristics and body. However, outside of human beings, these things exist as the result of natural disposition and divine guidance, and not as the result of an ability to think or to administrate. "He gave everything its natural characteristics, and then guided it."

The philosophers go further. They attempt to give logical proof of the existence of prophecy and to show that prophecy is a natural quality of man. In this connection, they carry the argument to its ultimate consequences and say that human beings absolutely require some authority to exercise a restraining influence. They go on to say that such restraining influence exists through the religious law (that has been) ordained by God and revealed to mankind by a human being. (This human being) is distinguished from the rest of mankind by special qualities of divine guidance that God gave him, in order that he might find the others submissive to him and ready to accept what he says. Eventually, the existence of a (restraining) authority among them and over them becomes a fact that is accepted without the slightest disapproval or dissent.

This proposition of the philosophers is not logical, as one can see. Existence and human life can materialize without (the existence of prophecy) through injunctions a person in authority may devise on his own or with the help of a group feeling that enables him to force the others to follow him wherever he wants to go. People who have a (divinely revealed) book and who follow the prophets are few in number in comparison with (all) the Magians* who have no (divinely revealed) book. The latter constitute the majority of the world's inhabitants. Still, they (too) have possessed dynasties and monuments, not to mention life itself. They still possess these things at this time in the intemperate zones to the north and the south. This is in contrast with human life in the state of anarchy, with no one to exercise a restraining influence. That would be impossible.

This shows that (the philosophers) are wrong when they assume that prophecy exists by necessity. The existence of prophecy is not required by logic. Its (necessary character) is indicated by the religious law, as was the belief of the early Muslims.

God gives success and guidance.

Royal authority and large dynastic (power) are attained only through a group and group feeling.

This is because, as we established in the first chapter, aggressive and defensive strength is obtained only through group feeling which means (mutual) affection and willingness to fight and die for each other.

Now, royal authority is a noble and enjoyable position. It comprises all the good things of the world, the pleasures of the body, and the joys of the soul. Therefore, there is, as a rule, great competition for it. It rarely is handed over (voluntarily), but it may be taken away. Thus, discord ensues. It leads to war and fighting, and to attempts

---

*"Magians" originally meant the Zoroastrians. In later Islam they were considered as people who followed a kind of prophet but did not have Scriptures as did the Christians and the Jews. Thus they occupied a position somewhere between the latter and polytheists. The term was eventually used to denote the general idea of pagans.

to gain superiority. Nothing of all this comes about except through group feeling, as we have also mentioned.

This situation is not at all understood by the great mass. They forget it, because they have forgotten the time when the dynasty first became established. They have grown up in settled areas for a long time. They have lived there for successive generations. Thus, they know nothing about what took place with God's help at the beginning of the dynasty. They merely notice that the coloring of the men of the dynasty is determined, that people have submitted to them, and that group feeling is no longer needed to establish their power. They do not know how it was at the beginning and what difficulties had to be overcome by the founder of (the dynasty). . . .

God has power to do what He wishes.

When a dynasty is firmly established, it can dispense with group feeling.

The reason for this is that people find it difficult to submit to large dynastic (power) at the beginning, unless they are forced into submission by strong superiority. (The new government) is something strange. People are not familiar with, or used to, its rule. But once leadership is firmly vested in the members of the family qualified to exercise royal authority in the dynasty, and once (royal authority) has been passed on by inheritance over many generations and through successive dynasties, the beginnings are forgotten, and the members of that family are clearly marked as leaders. It has become a firmly established article of faith that one must be subservient and submissive to them. People will fight with them in their behalf, as they would fight for the articles of faith. By this time, (the rulers) will not need much group (feeling to maintain) their power. It is as if obedience to the government were a divinely revealed book that cannot be changed or opposed. . . .

(The rulers) maintain their hold over the government and their own dynasty with the help, then, either of clients and followers who grew up in the shadow and power of group feeling, or (with that) of tribal groups of a different descent who have become their clients.

Dynasties of wide power and large royal authority have their origin in religion based either on prophecy or on truthful propaganda.

This is because royal authority results from superiority. Superiority results from group feeling. Only by God's help in establishing His religion do individual desires come together in agreement to press their claims, and hearts become united. God said: "If you had expended all the treasures on earth, you would have achieved no unity among them." The secret of (this) is that when the hearts succumb to false desires and are inclined toward the world, mutual jealousy and widespread differences arise. (But) when they are turned toward the truth and reject the world and whatever is false, and advance toward God, they become one in their outlook. Jealousy disappears. There are few differences. Mutual cooperation and support flourish. As a result, the extent of the state widens, and the dynasty grows, as we shall explain now.

Religious propaganda gives a dynasty at its beginning another power in addition to that of the group feeling it possessed as the result of the number of its (supporters).

As we have mentioned before, the reason for this is that religious coloring does away with mutual jealousy and envy among people who share in a group feeling, and causes concentration upon the truth. When people (who have a religious coloring) come to have the (right) insight into their affairs, nothing can withstand them, because their outlook is one and their object one of common accord. They are willing to die for (their objectives). (On the other hand,) the members of the dynasty they attack may be many times as numerous as they. But their purposes differ, in as much as they are false purposes, and (the people of the worldly dynasty) come to abandon each other, since they are afraid of death. Therefore, they do not offer resistance to (the people with a religious coloring), even if they themselves are more numerous. They are over-powered by them and quickly wiped out, as a result of the luxury and humbleness existing among them, as we have mentioned before.

Remarks on the words "Pope" and "Patriarch" in the Christian religion and on the word "Kohen" used by the Jews.

It should be known that after the removal of its prophet, a religious group must have someone to take care of it. (Such a person) must cause the people to act according to the religious laws. In a way, he stands to them in the place (*khalifah,* caliph) of their prophet, in as much as (he urges) the obligations which (the prophet) had imposed upon them. Furthermore, in accordance with the afore-mentioned need for political leadership in social organization, the human species must have a person who will cause them to act in accordance with what is good for them and who will prevent them by force from doing things harmful to them. Such a person is the one who is called ruler.

In the Muslim community, the holy war is a religious duty, because of the univer-salism of the (Muslim) mission and (the obligation to) convert everybody to Islam ei-ther by persuasion or by force. Therefore, caliphate and royal authority are united in (Islam), so that the person in charge can devote the available strength to both of them at the same time.

The other religious groups did not have a universal mission, and the holy war was not a religious duty to them, save only for purposes of defense. It has thus come about that the person in charge of religious affairs in (other religious groups) is not concerned with power politics at all. (Among them,) royal authority comes to those who have it, by accident and in some way that has nothing to do with religion. It comes to them as the necessary result of group feeling, which by its very nature seeks to obtain royal authority, as we have mentioned before, and not because they are under obligation to gain power over other nations, as is the case with Islam. They are merely required to establish their religion among their own (people).

CHAPTER 14

Illness and Therapy in the Plague Years

INTRODUCTION

"Ring around the rosies, a pocketful of posies,
Ashes, ashes, we all fall down."

What seems like an innocent children's rhyme is actually a grim description of the infection and mortality caused by the dreadful plague known as the "Black Death."[1] Spreading from Asia to much of medieval Europe, the Middle East, and North Africa in the mid-fourteenth century, the plague may have killed half of the population in the most seriously afflicted regions. In the view of many historians, the plague was one of the greatest biomedical crises ever experienced by mankind, whose impact dramatically altered world history. From the perspective of those unfortunate fourteenth-century individuals who experienced the plague firsthand, it was an age of confusion, fear, and social upheaval. The disaster was so extreme and shocking that it seemed to herald the end of the world. As described in the somber words of Ibn Khaldun, an Islamic historian who survived the plague, "Civilization both in the East and West was visited by a destructive plague which devastated nations and caused populations to vanish. It swallowed up many of the good things of civilization and wiped them out in the entire world."[2]

The history of the plague (or any other epidemic) can provide a variety of unique and revealing perspectives on human society. The way a disease spreads in a particular society or region, for example, may tell us something about people's lifestyles, their social conditions, patterns of mobility, and relationships with nature. From another perspective, illness and its therapies are social phenomena. The ways we define, treat, and assess conditions of sickness are directly shaped by our scientific etiologies,[3] social structures, and cultural values. And lastly, our reactions to disease, particularly to maladies as deadly and mysterious as the Black Death, are shaped by some of our most basic instincts, most notably the fear of death and the drive for self-preservation. Our goal in this chapter, therefore, is to study the fourteenth-century pestilence for the many insights it can provide us about history, culture, and the human condition. Using documents from both medieval Europe and the Islamic Middle East, we may also compare disease experiences and perceptions from two different cultures and assess how this unprecedented human encounter with disease challenged belief systems, social institutions, and interpersonal relationships.

What was the plague? According to modern biomedical science,[4] it was a severe infection of the lymphatic system caused by *Pasteurella pestis,* a bacillus[5] carried principally by fleas that thrive on animals, particularly rodents such as rats. The most common variant in the fourteenth century was bubonic plague, caused by the bite of an infected flea. In one or two days, victims quickly developed the telltale symptoms: fevers, dark red splotches on the skin ("rosies") caused by epidermal hemorrhaging, and grossly swollen, orange-sized lymph nodes ("buboes") at the neck, armpits, and groin. The bubonic variety of plague killed approximately 60 percent of those infected, usually within a week marked by excruciating pain. A more lethal variant was the pneumonic plague that attacked the respiratory system, causing the victim to cough and spit blood, which invariably helped to spread it to others. Pneumonic plague killed nearly all of its victims, usually in one to two days. Outbreaks of bubonic plague continue to the present, and the World Heath Organization reports between 1,000 and 3,000 cases every year, including some in the United States.[6] But with the advent of modern antibiotics, together with more extensive public health services than existed in the past, patients with the disease can generally be cured, and outbreaks can be contained.

The plague of the fourteenth century was not the world's first major pandemic.[7] Records from ancient China, as well as the Bible and Qur'an, recount recurring and devastating epidemics. In the latter years of the Roman Empire, a major outbreak of plague struck the Mediterranean, killing nearly a quarter of the population between 541 and 544. But the fourteenth-century plague was a far larger and more deadly pandemic. Researchers believe the plague originated in central Asia, where the bacillus was endemic[8] to the local rodent population. From there, it spread east to China, south to the Indian subcontinent, and west to Europe, the Middle East, and North Africa. By 1350, the plague had even spread as far as Ireland and Scandinavia, more than 5,000 miles from where it is thought to have begun.

Historians attribute the rapid and extensive spread of the plague to three important factors. First, the plague spread quickly along commercial land and sea routes that linked peoples (and their diseases) more closely than ever before. In Asia, the creation of the Mongol Empire provided the political stability that helped to promote long-distance trade, and trading caravans carried goods (and infected fleas) to China, India, and the Black Sea. Once at the Mediterranean, an extensive network of maritime trade carried the disease (via rats in cargo holds) to ports in Europe and North Africa, where it spread once again by trading routes to major cities and towns.

The spread of disease was also facilitated by additional environmental and social conditions. In Europe and the Middle East, the plague found new animal hosts (the common black rat) and a vulnerable human population. Lacking previous exposure to the bacillus, people in the Middle East and Europe had few natural defenses against the disease, and the deaths of millions resulted. In some regions, such as medieval France, the health of the population was further weakened by recurrent famines and destructive wars in the thirteenth century, which increased people's susceptibility to disease.

Lastly, the plague pandemic was unwittingly assisted by popular conceptions of and therapies for the disease. Although many observers in Europe and the Middle East recognized that the illness was somehow contagious, they did not recognize the flea-rat-human connection, perhaps because there was no knowledge of disease-causing bacillus, or perhaps because rats and fleas were such a ubiquitous feature of everyday life. Instead, the search for explanations and remedies centered on elaborate theories concerning poisonous miasmas[9] and divine retribution. These ideas helped to determine responses and therapies. In Europe and the Middle East, individual patients were commonly bled to eliminate the toxic poisons in their bodies, while entire communities organized mass processions and prayers that unwittingly helped to spread the disease to others.

But neither medicinal treatments nor prayers seemed to help. Although statistics are incomplete, the mortality estimates of the plague are staggering. In China, an estimated 13 million people were killed in the fourteenth century, which reduced the overall population by an estimated 30 percent. In Egypt, eyewitness accounts claimed that more than a third of the population perished in the first two years (1347–1349) of the epidemic, whereas in Europe, approximately 25 million people died between 1348 and 1375. Nor did the plague go away. Subsequent periodic outbreaks continued to cause widespread havoc and destruction for generations afterward.[10]

The economic and social impact of such population losses was often dramatic. In both Europe and the Middle East, the depopulation of large areas initially caused severe labor shortages, growing impoverishment, and general economic decline. But here the similarities between the two regions seems to end. Some historians assert that in Europe, the shortage of labor in the rural areas helped to end feudalism and encourage the development of a proto-capitalist system based on wage labor. In this interpretation, the European economy soon rebounded, as did the population, setting the stage for the European Renaissance and the growth of capitalist economies.[11] In the Middle East, the depopulation of the countryside did not lead to widespread social reforms; instead, old regimes such as the Mamluk dynasty in Egypt lost crucial labor and revenues and eventually lost power to the Ottomans, a dynamic new power emanating from modern-day Turkey. Similarly, many historians believe that the high mortality suffered by the Mongols significantly undermined the strength and stability of their empire in Asia.

This chapter examines the impact of the plague, but on a much more intimate scale. Our primary concern is to examine how the disease was perceived by local populations, doctors, and religious leaders and to assess how those ideas affected social institutions, spiritual beliefs, and personal behavior. Our two case studies focus on fourteenth-century medieval Europe and the Middle East, and our evidence dates primarily from the first decades of the epidemic, when the disease was the most mysterious and lethal. In both case studies, we begin with contemporary perspectives on the causes of the epidemic, which include both natural and supernatural explanations. We then use additional eyewitness accounts to examine social reactions and consequences. The readings and themes of this chapter are challenging, for we are investigating illness as a cultural phenomenon, one that is largely defined and treated within the context of social values and cultural beliefs. In order to obtain this understanding, one must read the texts carefully and look for clues concerning modes of interpretation and public reactions. As we investigate the importance of disease in human history, we may also gain a better understanding of the human condition when faced with disease, misfortune, and death—insights that may be both useful and relevant for comprehending the current AIDS pandemic.

CHAPTER QUESTIONS

1. In both medieval Europe and the Middle East, explanations for the plague included environmental theories. How do these theories compare between the two regions? How do they compare with our modern biomedical definitions?

2. Both cultures also attributed the plague in part to "God's will." Why might both cultures seek answers in the supernatural? How close are the two interpretations? Are the differences significant?

3. What range of responses do you find in the two case studies? What might be the attitudes or beliefs that explain the differing responses? How do you explain the persecution of scapegoats?

4. How did the plague seem to affect regions and communities? How did it affect individuals? In your assessment, which impact was greater: depopulation or fear? What evidence supports your view?

5. Some people have called AIDS the great modern plague of the twentieth and twenty-first centuries. In your opinion, how have modern American definitions of and responses to AIDS compared with those found in medieval Europe or the Middle East? Has modern biomedical science replaced religious explanations of disease?

THE PLAGUE IN MEDIEVAL EUROPE
A Medical Explanation

Europeans were not prepared for the death and devastation caused by the plague. In some regions of France, for example, villages lost more than two-thirds of their residents, and in Paris, more than 800 people died each day during the height of the pestilence in 1348. In response to this unprecedented and unknown crisis, King Philip VI of France sought information and answers from the esteemed medical faculty at the University at Paris, one of the most respected and influential universities in all of Europe. Their report, issued in 1348, reflects the guiding precepts and principles of medieval European medical theory and practice.

To provide some additional background, medieval medicine in fourteenth-century Europe was shaped by two primary considerations. The first was a strong reliance on classical medical theory, particularly the ideas of Galen (130–200), a Greek physician. Galen believed that ill health was the result of an imbalance between an individual's physical constitution, the environment (especially temperature and air quality), and excessive eating and drinking. One's physical constitution, in turn, was conditioned by a balance between the body's four humors: blood, phlegm, yellow bile from the liver, and black bile from the spleen. If poor environmental conditions or improper eating or drinking habits upset the balance of bodily humors, illness was the result. From these ideas, Galen formed a comprehensive model of sickness and health that explained all maladies and eliminated the need for alternative explanations.

The other major influence on medicine was the theology and authority of the Christian Church. In most of medieval Europe, it was the Church that regulated medical education and training in the universities. Under their tutelage, students memorized the unassailable classical texts and Christian philosophy more than they practiced experimental science. The deference of science to religion was also seen in medical practice. Generally, a doctor commenced his treatment of a patient only after the priest had finished with his bedside prayers and devotionals. Physicians were widely respected in society for their knowledge and treatments, but they were also considered somewhat inconsequential for the most urgent matters of life and death.

The irrelevancy of doctors may have increased during the plague in proportion to their inability to cure plague victims. Using Galen's theory of illness, they recommended three main strategies. First, healthy individuals were cautioned to avoid bad air and sick people, which may have unwittingly encouraged panic and flight. Second, physicians recommended cleansing the air of its poisons with strong odors. Individuals carried around bundles of dried herbs and flowers ("pocketful of posies") and inhaled through them, and communities were instructed to light aromatic, smoky bonfires ("ashes, ashes") to cleanse the atmosphere. And lastly, plague victims were treated with bleeding, lancing of buboes, and special diet. But none of these actions was sufficient to stem the rising tide of plague victims, a fact that, in the opinion of some historians, helped to inspire major reforms in medical science and practice in later centuries.[12]

The selection from *The Report of the Paris Medical Faculty* (1348) that follows illustrates the dominant roles played by both classical thought and Christian doctrine in medieval medical theory. The reading comes from the first section of the *Report,* which discusses the principal causes of the plague, and it provides a revealing insight into the medieval understanding of the natural and supernatural worlds. Given the esteemed reputation of the University of Paris, these views were widely accepted and repeated in subsequent plague reports throughout Europe for several generations.

1. According to the Paris medical faculty, what environmental conditions caused the plague? How did the faculty come to these conclusions?
2. In the medieval view, how did environmental changes and conditions affect people's health? Who were deemed to be the most vulnerable? How accurate are these theories?
3. Based on their theories, what actions or therapies might these physicians recommend? Might any prove useful?
4. The *Report* ends with a reference to God. What do you find significant in this conclusion? How might it reflect the medical community's views of the natural and supernatural worlds?
5. Overall, how do you assess this report? Would you call it "scientific"? Why, or why not?

THE REPORT OF THE PARIS MEDICAL FACULTY (1348)

Seeing things which cannot be explained, even by the most gifted intellects, initially stirs the human mind to amazement; but after marveling, the prudent soul next yields to its desire for understanding and, anxious for its own perfection, strives with all its might to discover the causes of the amazing events. For there is within the human mind an innate desire to seize on goodness and truth. As the Philosopher makes plain, all things seek for the good and want to understand. To attain this end we have listened to the opinions of many modern experts on astrology and medicine about the causes of the epidemic which has prevailed since 1345. However, because their conclusions still leave room for considerable uncertainty, we, the masters of the faculty of medicine at Paris, inspired by the command of the most illustrious prince, our most serene lord, Philip, King of France, and by our desire to achieve something of public benefit, have decided to compile, with God's help, a brief compendium of the distant and immediate causes of the present universal epidemic (as far as these can be understood by the human intellect) and of wholesome remedies; drawing on the opinions of the most brilliant ancient philosophers and modern experts, astronomers as well as doctors of medicine. And if we cannot explain everything as we would wish, for a sure explanation and perfect understanding of these matters is not always to be had . . . , it is open to any diligent reader to make good the deficiency. . . .

We say that the distant and first cause of this pestilence was and is the configuration of the heavens. In 1345, at one hour after noon on 20 March, there was a major

Source: From "The Report of the Paris Medical Faculty, October 1348." Found in *The Black Death,* translated and edited by Rosemary Horrox, 158–63. Copyright © 1994 Manchester University Press. Reprinted with permission. Most of the notes in this text come from Horrox's text.

conjunction of three planets in Aquarius.* This conjunction, along with other earlier conjunctions and eclipses, by causing a deadly corruption of the air around us, signifies mortality and famine—and also other things about which we will not speak here because they are not relevant. Aristotle testifies that this is the case in his book *Concerning the causes of the properties of the elements,*† in which he says that mortality of races and the depopulation of kingdoms occur at the conjunction of Saturn and Jupiter. . . .

Although major pestilential illnesses can be caused by the corruption of water or food, as happens at times of famine and infertility, yet we still regard illnesses proceeding from the corruption of the air as much more dangerous. This is because bad air is more noxious than food or drink in that it can penetrate quickly to the heart and lungs to do its damage. We believe that the present epidemic or plague has arisen from air corrupt in its substance, and not changed by attributes.‡ By which we wish it be understood that air, being pure and clear by nature, can only become putrid or corrupt by being mixed with something else, that is to say, with evil vapors. What happened was that the many vapors which had been corrupted at the time of the [planetary] conjunction were drawn up from the earth and water, and were then mixed with the air and spread abroad by frequent gusts of wind in the wild southerly gales, and because of these alien vapors which they carried the winds corrupted the air in its substance, and are still doing so. And this corrupted air, when breathed in, necessarily penetrates to the heart and corrupts the substance of the spirit there and rots the surrounding moisture, and the heat thus caused destroys the life force, and this is the immediate cause of the present epidemic.§

And moreover these winds, which have become so common here, have carried among us (and may perhaps continue to do so in the future) bad, rotten and poisonous vapors from elsewhere: from swamps, lakes, and chasms, for instance, and also (which is even more dangerous) from unburied or unburnt corpses—which might well have been a cause of the epidemic. Another possible cause of corruption, which needs to be borne in mind, is the escape of the rottenness trapped in the center of the earth as a result of earthquakes—something which has indeed recently occurred. But the conjunctions could have been the universal and distant cause of all these harmful things, by which air and water have been corrupted.

Unseasonable weather is a particular cause of illness. For the ancients, notably Hippocrates, are agreed that if the four seasons run awry, and do not keep their proper course, the plagues and mortal passions are engendered that year. . . . It is because

---

*The houses of the zodiac are each associated with one of the elements. Aquarius is one of the air signs, and therefore hot and wet.

†This work, although credited to Aristotle in the Middle Ages, was not by him. It was the subject of a commentary by Albertus Magnus (Albert the Great, d. 1280).

‡They do not mean by this that the nature of the air changed, but that it was corrupted by being mixed with bad vapors.

§"Spirit" in these medical tracts has a very precise meaning. It was a substance created by the heart from inhaled air, and was envisioned as extremely thin, light vapor, which was carried through the body by the arteries. It was, in a literal and immediate sense, the life force, and without it the body would die.

the whole year here—or most of it—was warm and wet that the air is pestilential.*
For it is a sign of pestilence for the air to be warm and wet at unseasonable times. . . .

On the other hand, the susceptibility of the body of the patient is the most immediate cause in the breeding of illnesses, and therefore no cause is likely to have an effect unless the patient is susceptible to its effects. . . .

The bodies most likely to take the stamp of this pestilence are those which are
hot and moist, for they are the most susceptible to putrefaction. The following are
also more at risk: bodies bunged up with evil humors, because the unconsumed waste
matter is not being expelled as it should; those following a bad life style, with too
much exercise, sex, and bathing; the thin and weak, and persistent worriers; babies,
women, and young people; and corpulent people with a ruddy complexion. However those with dry bodies, purged of waste matter, who adopt a sensible and suitable
regimen, will succumb to the pestilence more slowly.

We must not overlook the fact that any pestilence proceeds from the divine will,
and our advice can therefore only be to return humbly to God. But this does not mean
forsaking doctors. For the Most High created earthly medicine, and although God
cures the sick, he does so through the medicine which in his generosity he provided.
Blessed be the glorious and high God, who does not refuse his help, but has clearly
set out a way of being cured for those who fear him. . . .

A Religious Explanation

It is perhaps not surprising that a disaster as vast and as devastating as the Black
Death would lead to the widespread belief that it was a punishment from God, a
sign of his displeasure with humankind. After all, Europeans had several precedents to refer to in their Judeo-Christian heritage. The Bible recorded that God
sent a plague upon the ancient Egyptians for refusing to free their Israelite slaves
and later used disease to punish King David and his people for disobedience.[13]
And during the great Roman epidemic in 590, Pope Gregory the Great attributed
the affliction to man's wickedness, and he led holy processionals around the city
to ask for forgiveness. Consequently, it is not unusual that clerics of the fourteenth
century would find meaning and possible remedies for the plague in these historical and biblical precedents. The majority of people were convinced that the plague
was certainly the work of God, and in September 1348, Pope Clement VI
(1291–1352) agreed. In a papal edict, he specifically referred to "this pestilence
with which God is affecting the Christian people."

To appease God's anger, the papacy supported a variety of actions. Bishops
and clergy were ordered to make solemn processions, ringing bells, carrying relics,
and chanting litanies. Special plague prayers and masses were composed, and pilgrimages were organized to visit holy shrines (as witnessed in Chaucer's *Canterbury Tales*). Above all, individuals were exhorted to repent in advance of death

---

*Historical research does suggest that the climate of the early fourteenth century was cooler and wet-
ter than normal, which may have shortened the growing season and lessened harvests.

and their final judgment. The failure of the Church to stem the tide of plague may have lessened its authority, but it did not necessarily weaken religious fervor. In some regions of Europe, people turned to more extreme and radical solutions in defiance of the Church. One of the best known was the flagellants, people who practiced self-scourging in order to appease God. Marching from town to town, the flagellants also frequently took the lead in organizing massacres against local Jews, whom they accused of poisoning the wells of Christians.

The perspective of the Christian Church on the plague is well represented in the following reading. William Edendon, Bishop of Winchester, sent copies of this letter to abbots, priors, chaplains, and vicars in his diocese in 1348, when the plague was just beginning to spread into England. Although the bishop claims that no one can truly know the will of God, he nonetheless offers his own interpretation, as well as his instructions for appropriate therapy.

QUESTIONS TO CONSIDER

1. The bishop entitled his letter *Vox in Rama*, or *A Voice in Rama*. What does this mean? Why might he open his letter in this manner? How is it significant to our understanding of his views?

2. According to the bishop, the plague is a form of punishment. How does he explain this punishment? Why, in his view, are all people deserving of punishment? How might this explanation reflect the character of plague infection?

3. What remedies does the bishop recommend? What are they meant to do?

4. In return for their devotionals, the bishop promises a grant of indulgences to those who participate. What is an indulgence? Why might these be offered at this time?

5. What conception of God is evident in this letter? Wrathful? Merciful? Vengeful? Just? How do you explain these views?

VOX IN RAMA [A VOICE IN RAMA] (1348)

William Edendon

A voice has been heard in Rama and much lamentation and mourning has echoed through various parts of the world.* Nations, bereft of their children, alas, in the abyss of unprecedented pestilence, refused to be comforted. For, what is terrible to hear,

---

Source: William Edendon, *Vox in Rama [A Voice in Rama]*, 24 October 1348. Found in *The Black Death*, translated and edited by Rosemary Horrox, 115–17. Copyright © 1994 Manchester University Press. Reprinted with permission.

*This is a reference to a passage in Matthew 2:18, which describes the massacre of male Jewish infants ordered by King Herod after he learned that a new "King of the Jews" [Jesus] had been born. "A voice was heard in Rama, wailing and loud lamentation, Rachel weeping for her children; she refused to be consoled, because they were no more." The actual passage echoes a prophecy found in Jeremiah 31:15.

cities, towns, castles and villages, which until now rejoiced in their illustrious residents (their wisdom in counsel, their splendid riches, their great strength, the beauty of their womenfolk), which rang with the abundance of joy, to which crowds of people poured from far and wide for succour, pleasure and comfort, have now been suddenly and woefully stripped of their inhabitants by this most savage pestilence, more cruel than a two-edged sword. As a result no one dares to enter these places, but instead flees far from them, as if from the caves of wild animals, so that all joy within them ceases, all sweetness is dammed up and the sound of mirth silenced, and they become instead places of horror and desolate wastelands. Broad, fruitful acres lie entirely abandoned now that their farmers have been carried off, and might as well be barren.

We report with anguish the serious news which has come to our ears, that this cruel plague has now begun a similarly savage attack on the coastal areas of England. We are struck by terror lest (may God avert it!) this brutal disease should rage in any part of our city or diocese.

Although God often strikes us, to test our patience and justly punish our sins, it is not within the power of man to understand the divine plan. But it is to be feared that the most likely explanation is that human sensuality—that fire which blazed up as a result of Adam's sin and which from adolescence onwards is an incitement to wrong doing—has now plumbed greater depths of evil, producing a multitude of sins which have provoked the divine anger, by a just judgement, to this revenge. But because God is benign and merciful, long-suffering, and above malice, it may be that this affliction, which we richly deserve, can be averted if we turn to him humbly and with our whole hearts, and we therefore earnestly urge you to devotion. We beg you in God's name, and firmly command you by the obedience which you owe us, that you present yourselves before God through contrition and the proper confession of your sins, followed by the making of due satisfaction through the performance of penance, and that every Wednesday and Sunday, assembled in the choir of your monastery, you humbly and devoutly recite the 7 penitential psalms and the 15 psalms of degrees on your knees.*

We also order that every Friday you should go solemnly in procession through the marketplace at Winchester, singing these psalms and the great litany instituted by the fathers of the church for use against the pestilence and performing other exercises of devotion, together with the clergy and people of the city, whom we wish to be summoned to attend. They are to accompany the procession with bowed heads and bare feet, fasting, with a pious heart and lamenting their sins (all idle chatter entirely set aside), and as they go they are to say devoutly, as many times as possible, the Lord's Prayer and the Hail Mary. They are to remain in earnest prayer until the end of the mass which we wish you to celebrate in your church at the end of each procession, trusting that if they persevere in their devotions with faith, rectitude and firm trust in the omnipotence and mercy of the Savior they will soon receive a remedy and timely help from heaven.

---

*The Penitential Psalms are numbers 6, 31, 37, 50, 101, 129, and 142. The Psalms of Degrees are numbers 119–133.

[The letter ends with the grant of an indulgence* of forty days to those taking part in the procession and mass and praying there for a successful expedition for the king, the safety of his family and subjects and of all Christians, the peace of the Church, England and Christendom, and for the end of the plague; and thirty days indulgence to those making similar prayers elsewhere.]

Reactions to the Plague

The historian is fortunate to have numerous fourteenth-century eyewitness commentaries on the plague in Europe. Ranging from private diaries to local histories, these records provide essential information about the spread of the epidemic and its severity and mortality in different regions. But more important for our purposes, these accounts also offer crucial insights into how people coped with the devastating pestilence. Using the two examples in this section, we may begin to analyze reactions to the plague and to assess what these responses might tell us about illness beliefs, cultural values, and/or human psychology.

One of the most famous and celebrated eyewitness accounts comes from Giovanni Boccaccio's *The Decameron,* a semifictional story of the plague in Florence, Italy. Boccaccio (1313–1375) was an aspiring Florentine writer when the plague struck his native city in the spring of 1348. Within a year, nearly half of the population was gone, carried off by either disease or fearful flight. Fascinated by people's varied reactions to the pestilence, Boccaccio began *The Decameron,* a collection of human drama stories that take place against the backdrop of the plague. In the tale, ten affluent young people from Florence seek refuge from the disease at a country estate, where they entertain themselves by each telling a story on a different day (hence, the meaning of the title *Decameron,* or "Ten Days Work"). The stories of unhappy love, promiscuous relationships, and the uncertainties of life and fortune made it popular in its day, no doubt because these themes paralleled the life experiences of so many Florentines in the 1340s and 1350s. Although scholars have typically praised *The Decameron* as a literary masterpiece, our concern is from the perspective of a cultural historian: to determine what it reveals about values, attitudes, and beliefs.

An additional perspective comes from Jean de Venette, a Carmelite monk who chronicled the spread and impact of plague in France. When the plague struck France in 1348, the country was already in the midst of a series of monumental crises, which included famine and the devastation wrought by the Hundred Years' War with England (1337–1453). Consequently, when the plague began to spread more death and fear among a beleaguered population, many wondered whether this was God's final act of destruction. In the excerpt that follows, Jean de Venette describes two of the more radical responses to the plague: the flagellant movement and the massacre of Jews.

---

*An indulgence is the remission of time spent in purgatory for one's sins, granted by the Church in the exercise of its divinely inherited powers, for some just and pious action.

QUESTIONS TO CONSIDER

1. According to Boccaccio and Venette, what are the causes of the plague? How did it spread? How do their accounts compare with *The Report of the Paris Medical Faculty*?

2. In Boccaccio's account, how did people respond to the plague? What attitudes or conditions affected people's differing reactions, choices, and behaviors? Why is he so concerned about burial customs?

3. Using both accounts, what impact did the plague have on social institutions and city life? How did it affect the economy? How did it affect the Church?

4. Who are the flagellants? What beliefs might explain their actions? Why would the Church oppose their religious fervor?

5. As Jean de Venette's chronicle relates, some communities accused Jews of spreading the plague. What ideas and emotions seem to create the need for a scapegoat? In your opinion, why were Jews frequently targeted as scapegoats?

THE DECAMERON (1348–1353)

Giovanni Boccaccio

In the year 1348 after the fruitful incarnation of the Son of God, that most beautiful of Italian cities, noble Florence, was attacked by deadly plague. It started in the East either through the influence of the heavenly bodies or because God's just anger with our wicked deeds sent it as a punishment to mortal men; and in a few years killed an innumerable quantity of people. Ceaselessly passing from place to place, it extended its miserable length over the West. Against this plague all human wisdom and foresight were vain. Orders had been given to cleanse the city of filth, the entry of any sick person was forbidden, much advice was given for keeping healthy; at the same time humble supplications were made to God by pious persons in processions and otherwise. And yet, in the beginning of the spring of the year mentioned, its horrible results began to appear, and in a miraculous manner.

The symptoms were not the same as in the East, where a gush of blood from the nose was the plain sign of inevitable death; but it began both in men and women with certain swellings in the groin or under the armpit. They grew to the size of a small apple or an egg, more or less, and were vulgarly called tumors. In a short space of time these tumors spread from the two parts named to all over the body. Soon after this the symptoms changed and black or purple spots appeared on the arms or thighs or any other part of the body, sometimes a few large ones, sometimes many little ones.

Source: Giovanni Boccaccio, *The Decameron*, trans. Richard Aldington (Garden City, NY: Garden City Publishing Company, 1930), 1–6.

These spots were a certain sign of death, just as the original tumor had been and still remained.

No doctor's advice, no medicine could overcome or alleviate this disease. An enormous number of ignorant men and women set up as doctors in addition to those who were trained. Either the disease was such that no treatment was possible or the doctors were so ignorant that they did not know what caused it, and consequently could not administer the proper remedy. In any case very few recovered; most people died within about three days of the appearance of the tumors described above, most of them without any fever or other symptoms.

The violence of this disease was such that the sick communicated it to the healthy who came near them, just as a fire catches anything dry or oily near it. And it even went further. To speak to or go near the sick brought infection and a common death to the living; and moreover, to touch the clothes or anything else the sick had touched or worn gave the disease to the person touching.

What I am about to tell now is a marvelous thing to hear; and if I and others had not seen it with our own eyes I would not dare to write it, however much I was willing to believe and whatever the good faith of the person from whom I heard it. So violent was the malignancy of this plague that it was communicated, not only from one man to another, but from the garments of a sick or dead man to animals of another species, which caught the disease in that way and very quickly died of it. One day among other occasions I saw with my own eyes (as I said just now) the rags left lying in the street of a poor man who had died of the plague; two pigs came along and, as their habit is, turned the clothes over with their snouts and then munched at them, with the result that they both fell dead almost at once on the rags, as if they had been poisoned.

From these and similar or greater occurrences, such fear and fanciful notions took possession of the living that almost all of them adopted the same cruel policy, which was entirely to avoid the sick and everything belonging to them. By so doing, each one thought he would secure his own safety.

Some thought that moderate living and the avoidance of all superfluity would preserve them from the epidemic. They formed small communities, living entirely separate from everybody else. They shut themselves up in houses where there were no sick, eating the finest food and drinking the best wine very moderately, avoiding all excess, allowing no news or discussion of death and sickness, and passing the time in music and suchlike pleasures. Others thought just the opposite. They thought the sure cure for the plague was to drink and be merry, to go about singing and amusing themselves, satisfying every appetite they could, laughing and jesting at what happened. They put their words into practice, spent day and night going from tavern to tavern, drinking immoderately, or went into other people's houses, doing only those things which pleased them. This they could easily do because everyone felt doomed and had abandoned his property, so that most houses became common property and any stranger who went in made use of them as if he had owned them. And with all this bestial behavior, they avoided the sick as much as possible.

In this suffering and misery of our city, the authority of human and divine laws almost disappeared, for, like other men, the ministers and the executors of the laws were all dead or sick or shut up with their families, so that no duties were carried out. Every man was therefore able to do as he pleased.

Many others adopted a course of life midway between the two just described. They did not restrict their victuals so much as the former, nor allow themselves to be drunken and dissolute like the latter, but satisfied their appetites moderately. They did not shut themselves up, but went about, carrying flowers or scented herbs or perfumes in their hands, in the belief that it was an excellent thing to comfort the brain with such odors; for the whole air was infected with the smell of dead bodies, of sick persons and medicines.

Others again held a still more cruel opinion, which they thought would keep them safe. They said that the only medicine against the plague-stricken was to go right away from them. Men and women, convinced of this and caring about nothing but themselves, abandoned their own city, their own houses, their dwellings, their relatives, their property, and went abroad or at least to the country around Florence, as if God's wraith in punishing men's wickedness with this plague would not follow them but strike only those who remained within the walls of the city, or as if they thought nobody in the city would remain alive and that its last hour had come. Not everyone who adopted any of these various actions died, nor did all escape. Some when they were still healthy had set the example of avoiding the sick, and, falling ill themselves, died untended.

One citizen avoided another, hardly any neighbor troubled about others, relatives never or hardly ever visited each other. Moreover, such terror was struck into the hearts of men and women by this calamity, that brother abandoned brother, and the uncle his nephew, and the sister her brother, and very often the wife her husband. What is even worse and nearly incredible is that fathers and mothers refused to see and tend their children, as if they had not been theirs. . . .

In this way many people died who might have been saved if they had been looked after. Owing to the lack of attendants for the sick and the violence of the plague, such a multitude of people in the city died day and night that it was stupefying to hear of, let alone to see. From sheer necessity, then, several ancient customs were quite altered among the survivors.

The custom had been (as we still see it today), that women relatives and neighbors should gather at the house of the deceased, and there lament with the family. At the same time the men would gather at the door with the male neighbors and other citizens. Then came the clergy, few or many according to the dead person's rank; the coffin was placed on the shoulders of his friends, and carried with funeral pomp of lighted candles and dirges to the church which the deceased had chosen before dying. But as the fury of the plague increased, this custom wholly or nearly disappeared, and new customs arose. Thus, people died, not only without having a number of women near them but without a single witness. Very few indeed were honored with the piteous laments and bitter tears of their relatives, who, on the contrary, spent their time in mirth, feasting and jesting. Even the women abandoned womanly pity and adopted this custom for their own safety. Few were they whose bodies were accompanied to church by more than ten or a dozen neighbors. Nor were these grave and honorable citizens but grave-diggers from the lowest of the people who got themselves called sextons, and performed the task for money. They took up the bier and hurried it off, not to the church chosen by the deceased but to the church nearest, preceded by four or six of the clergy with few candles and often none at all. With the aid of the grave-diggers, the clergy huddled the bodies away in any grave they could find, without giving themselves the trouble of a long or solemn burial service.

The plight of the lower and most of the middle classes was even more pitiful to behold. Most of them remained in their houses, either through poverty or in hopes of safety, and fell sick by thousands. Since they received no care and attention, almost all of them died. Many ended their lives in the streets both at night and during the day; and many others who died in their houses were only known to be dead because the neighbors smelled their decaying bodies. Dead bodies filled every corner. Most of them were treated in the same manner by the survivors, who were more concerned to get rid of their rotting bodies than moved by charity towards the dead. With the aid of porters, if they could get them, they carried the bodies out of the houses and laid them at the doors, where every morning quantities of the dead might be seen. They then were laid on biers, or, as these were often lacking, on tables. . . . Nor were these dead honored by tears and lighted candles and mourners, for things had reached such a pass that people cared no more for dead men than we care for dead goats. Thus it plainly appeared that what the wise had not learned to endure with patience through the few calamities of ordinary life, became a matter of indifference even to most ignorant people through the greatness of this misfortune.

Such was the multitude of corpses brought to the churches every day and at every hour that there was not enough consecrated ground to give them burial, especially since they wanted to bury each person in the family grave, according to the old custom. Although the cemeteries were full they were forced to dig huge trenches, where they buried the bodies by hundreds. Here they stowed them away like bales in the hold of a ship and covered them with a little earth, until the whole trench was full.

Not to pry any further into all the details of the miseries which afflicted our city, I shall add that the surrounding country was spared nothing of what befell Florence. The villages on a smaller scale were like the city; in the fields and isolated farms the poor wretched peasants and their families were without doctors and any assistance, and perished in the highways, in their fields and houses, night and day, more like beasts than men. Just as the townsmen became dissolute and indifferent to their work and property, so the peasants, when they saw that death was upon them, entirely neglected the future fruits of their past labors both from the earth and from cattle, and thought only of enjoying what they had. Thus it happened that cows, asses, sheep, goats, pigs, fowls and even dogs, those faithful companions of man, left the farms and wandered at their will through the fields, where the wheat crops stood abandoned, unreaped and ungarnered. . . .

Returning from the country to the city, it may be said that such was the cruelty of Heaven, and perhaps in part of men, that between March and July more than one hundred thousand persons died within the walls of Florence, what between the violence of the plague and the abandonment in which the sick were left by the cowardice of the healthy. And before the plague it was not thought that the whole city held so many people.

Oh, what great palaces, how many fair houses and noble dwellings, once filled with attendants and nobles and ladies, were emptied to the meanest servant! How many famous names and vast possessions and renowned estates were left without an heir! How many gallant men and fair ladies and handsome youths, whom Galen, Hippocrates and Aesculapius themselves would have said were in perfect health, at noon dined with their relatives and friends, and at night supped with their ancestors in the next world!

CHRONICLE OF JEAN DE VENETTE (1356–1358)

Jean de Venette

In A.D. 1348, the people of France and of almost the whole world were struck by a blow other than war. For in addition to the famine which I described in the beginning [of this *Chronicle*] and to the wars* which I described in the course of this narrative, pestilence and its other attendant tribulations appeared again in various parts of the world. In the month of August, 1348, after Vespers when the sun was beginning to set, a big and very bright star appeared above Paris, toward the west. It did not seem, as stars usually do, to be very high above our hemisphere but rather very near. As the sun set and night came on, this star did not seem to me or to many other friars who were watching it to move from one place. At length, when night had come, this big star, to the amazement of all of us who were watching, broke into many different rays and, as it shed these rays over Paris toward the east, totally disappeared and was completely annihilated. Whether it was a comet or not, whether it was composed of airy exhalations and was finally resolved into vapor, I leave to the decision of astronomers. It is, however, possible that it was a presage of the amazing pestilence to come, which, in fact, followed very shortly in Paris and throughout France and elsewhere, as I shall tell. All this year and the next, the mortality of men and women, of the young even more than the old, in Paris and the kingdom of France, and also, it is said, in other parts of the world, was so great that it was almost impossible to bury the dead. People lay ill little more than two or three days and died suddenly. . . . He who was well one day was dead the next and being carried to his grave. Swellings appeared suddenly in the armpit or in the groin—in many cases both—and they were infallible signs of death. This sickness or pestilence was called an epidemic by doctors. Nothing like the great numbers who died in the years 1348 and 1349 has been heard of or seen or read of in times past. This plague and disease came from . . . association and contagion, for if a well man visited the sick he only rarely evaded death. Wherefore in many towns timid priests withdrew, leaving the exercise of their ministry to such of the religious who were more daring. . . . A very great number of the saintly sisters of the Hotel-Dieu who, not fearing to die, nursed the sick in all sweetness and humility,

---

Source: From Jean de Venette, *The Chronicle of Jean de Venette*, in *Records of Civilization: Sources and Studies*, trans. Jean Birdsall, ed. Richard A. Newhall, 48–51. Copyright © 1953 Columbia University Press. Reprinted with permission.

*He is referring to his account of the Hundred Years' War in the French countryside.

with no thought of honor, a number too often renewed by death, rest in peace with Christ, as we may piously believe.

This plague, it is said, began among the unbelievers, came to Italy, and then crossing the Alps reached Avignon, where it attacked several cardinals and took from them their whole household. Then it spread, unforseen, to France, through Gascony and Spain, little by little, from town to town, from village to village, from house to house, and finally from person to person. It even crossed over to Germany, though it was not so bad there as with us. During the epidemic, God of His accustomed goodness deigned to grant this grace, that however suddenly men died, almost all awaited death joyfully. Nor was there anyone who died without confessing his sins and receiving the holy *viaticum*. To the even greater benefit of the dying, Pope Clement VI through their confessors mercifully gave and granted absolution from penalty to the dying in many cities and fortified towns. Men died the more willingly for this and left many inheritances and temporal goods to churches and monastic orders, for in many cases they had seen close heirs and children die before them.

In the year 1349, while the plague was still active and spreading from town to town, men in Germany, Flanders, Hainaut, and Lorraine uprose and began a new sect on their own authority. Stripped to the waist, they gathered in large groups and bands and marched in procession through the crossroads and squares of cities and good towns. There they formed circles and beat upon their backs with weighted scourges, rejoicing as they did so in loud voices and singing hymns suitable to their rite and newly composed for it. Thus for thirty-three days they marched through many towns doing their penance and affording a great spectacle to the wondering people. They flogged their shoulders and arms with scourges tipped with iron points so zealously as to draw blood. But they did not come to Paris nor to any part of France, for they were forbidden to do so by the king of France, who did not want them. He acted on the advice of the masters of theology of the University of Paris, who said that this new sect had been formed contrary to the will of God, to the rites of Holy Mother Church, and to the salvation of all their souls. That indeed this was and is true appeared shortly. For Pope Clement VI was fully informed concerning this fatuous new rite by the masters of Paris through emissaries reverently sent to him and, on the grounds that it had been damnably formed, contrary to law, he forbade the Flagellants under threat of anathema to practice in the future the public penance which they had so presumptuously undertaken. . . .

Some said that this pestilence was caused by infection of the air and waters, since there was at this time no famine nor lack of food supplies, but on the contrary great abundance. As a result of this theory of infected water and air as the source of the plague the Jews were suddenly and violently charged with infecting wells and water and corrupting the air. The whole world rose up against them cruelly on this account. In Germany and other parts of the world where Jews lived, they were massacred and slaughtered by Christians, and many thousands were burned everywhere, indiscriminately. The unshaken, if fatuous, constancy of the men and their wives was remarkable. For mothers hurled their children first into the fire that they might not be baptized and then leaped in after them to burn with their husbands and children. It is said that many bad Christians were found who in a like manner put poison into wells. But in truth, such poisonings, granted that they actually were perpetrated, could not have caused so great a plague nor have infected so many people. There were other causes; for example, the will of God and the corrupt humors and evil inherent in air and earth. Perhaps the poisonings, if they actually took place in some localities, re-enforced these causes. The plague lasted in France for the greater part of the years 1348 and 1349 and then ceased. Many country villages and many houses in good towns remained empty and deserted. Many houses, including some splendid dwellings, very soon fell into ruins. Even in Paris several houses were thus ruined, though fewer here than elsewhere. . . .

Art from the Plague Years

In this section, we consider some examples of art shaped by the plague epidemic in Europe. For the historian, art can be a wonderfully revealing source that sup-plements information gained from traditional written documentation. Paintings, prints, and drawings, for example, can tell a pictorial narrative that illuminates specific events, people, or conditions at the time. Artistic works can also reflect local culture and tell us much about contemporary beliefs, attitudes, and values. And perhaps most significantly for our purposes, art is emotive. The visual impact of pictures can frequently express moods and feelings more dramatically than words alone. The examples of plague art found in this section may help us to bet-ter understand and appreciate the psychological impact of the Black Death.

European art from the mid-fourteenth to the sixteenth centuries embodies a wide range of styles, themes, and moods, and it includes some of the greatest mas-terpieces of the Renaissance. Yet there is also an unmistakable legacy of the plague found in the many works that appear to be preoccupied with human suffering, retribution, and death. Plague-related art took the form of Church altarpieces and paintings, procession banners (*gonfaloni*), and smaller paintings and woodblock prints (*pestblatter*) for private worship and devotionals.[14] Most works are somber and tragic, reflecting the overwhelming fear and pessimism that must have capti-vated the mind of the painter, as well as the public. As you examine the following images, keep in mind three levels of analysis: (1) What is the image about? What characters are portrayed? Is there anything remarkable about the style? (2) What is the meaning of the picture? What story, ideas, and/or values does it express? (3) What is the emotional impact of the painting? What mood or sentiments does it convey? How does art reflect the psychological impact of the plague?

The Virgin of Mercy Devotional images of the Virgin Mary long predate the ar-rival of the fourteenth-century plague, but they gained a new significance and a new interpretation with the epidemic. Previous to the epidemic, the Virgin was commonly portrayed as sitting on an elevated throne, an artistic composition that projected a separation of the Virgin from the viewer/worshipper. Later represen-tations created during the plague years, however, witness a modification in her role and relationship with humankind. This is clearly seen in the *Plague Madonna della Misericordia* (Figure 14.1) painted by the Italian Benedetto Bonfigli in 1464.

Figure 14.1 Benedetto Bonfigli, *Plague Madonna della Misericordia,* 1464. Perugia, San Francesco al Prado.

In this altarpiece, Mary uses her mantle to envelop and protect devout Christians from the plague arrows and swords of God's angels, while Death stalks the streets below her presence.

QUESTIONS TO CONSIDER

1. Who are the various characters portrayed in Figure 14.1? What are they doing? What is significant about the way the artist arranged the picture?
2. What are the stories and morals expressed in this painting? Who was this painting for?
3. In this image, God is portrayed as the executer of Justice, while Mary is the source of Mercy. What does this tell us about medieval religious ideas? What might this also say about people's efforts to explain and cope with the plague?

The Cult of Saint Sebastian   In addition to the Virgin, the other major defender against the plague was St. Sebastian, the fourth-century Roman martyr. According to legend, Sebastian had once commanded a unit in the emperor's Praetorian Guards before he was arrested and sentenced to die for his Christian beliefs. To set an example for others, the Roman Emperor Diocletian (284–305) ordered him to be bound to a stake, shot full of arrows, and left to die. But miraculously, the arrow wounds did not kill him, and that night, he was rescued by Christians and nursed back to health. When Sebastian recovered and returned to the impe-

rial palace to plead for the lives of other Christians, he was once again arrested and sentenced to be beaten to death by clubs, and his corpse thrown into the river. This time, Sebastian was killed, but his body was again rescued and given a Christian burial in the catacombs. Later, the Church of St. Sebastian of Rome was built over the spot.

In the fourteenth century, the veneration of Saint Sebastian became widespread. His image adorned processional banners, altarpieces, and personal devotionals, and he remained a popular figure for later Renaissance painters as well. Most historians believe that Sebastian's popularity in the plague years was due in part to his persecution with arrows, which in the Western tradition have long had an association with disease.[15] The image of Sebastian in Figure 14.2, from an altarpiece painted by Giovanni del Biondo in the immediate aftermath of the plague's arrival in Italy, depicts the saint at the stake, his body fully pierced with arrows, yet remaining fully conscious and alive.

Figure 14.2 Giovanni del Biondo, *Altarpiece of Saint Sebastian*, 1370s. Florence, Museo dell'Opera del Duomo.

1. Examine the composition of Figure 14.2. What is important about the arrangement of the figures?
2. What might be the relationship between the arrows and Sebastian's Christ-like pose at the stake? What role does the divinity have in this story?
3. How might people take comfort from the story implied in this painting? Why did his image adorn so many plague procession banners?

The Triumph and Dance of Death   It should not be too surprising that in an age when plague devastated the population of medieval Europe many paintings and prints reflected a preoccupation with death. But the horrific representations and the continuation of such themes in later centuries clearly show the deep and lasting impact of the Black Death on popular attitudes and outlooks toward life.

One of the greatest paintings representing the triumph of death was an enormous fresco painted at the Camposanto, the cemetery next to the Pisa Cathedral in Italy. Unfortunately, this magnificent work, commonly attributed to Francesco Traini, was badly damaged in a fire in 1944. Instead, we have substituted a similarly themed painting (Figure 14.3) by Pieter Bruegel the Elder, the great Flemish painter, who completed his *Triumph of Death* around 1562.

Figure 14.3 Pieter Bruegel the Elder, *The Triumph of Death,* 1562. Museo del Prado, Madrid.

QUESTIONS TO CONSIDER

1. What are the stories being told in this painting (Figure 14.3)?
2. How does Bruegel use color, composition, and imagery to create a certain mood?
3. How does this painting reflect attitudes about life and about religion?

One of the more macabre artistic themes of the plague era was "the Dance of Death," in which all members of society found themselves caught up in a dance led by Death himself. Although there were many variations on this theme, perhaps the most famous is a series of forty-one wood engravings created by Hans Holbein the Younger. In his series, Death pays a visit to all members of society, from the pope and monarch to the simple peasant and tradesman. In our first example, titled *The Priest* (Figure 14.4), Holbein depicts a priest on his way to visit a sick person, accompanied by Death. In *The Physician* (Figure 14.5), Death takes a urine sample from the sick man and passes it to the doctor.

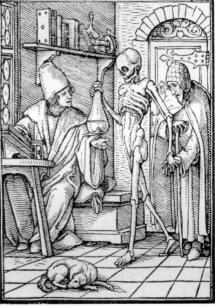

Figure 14.4. Hans Holbein the Younger, *The Priest*, 1526

Figure 14.5 Hans Holbein the Younger, *The Physician*, 1526

QUESTIONS TO CONSIDER

1. How is Death represented by Holbein in Figures 14.4 and 14.5? How does he interact with the living?
2. What is the meaning of these prints? How might it reflect attitudes about religion and medicine in the age of the plague?
3. In what ways have such images been perpetuated in modern culture? Do such images mean the same thing?

Therapies and Reactions   The final three images convey additional information about society's attempt to cope with the plague. Figure 14.6, *Physician in Plague Costume,* illustrates the clothing and apparatus used to help protect doctors from the disease. Most notable is the hood with the prominent "beak," which was filled with sweet or strong-smelling herbs or flowers. Figure 14.7, *The Plague Patient,* is a woodblock cut that shows a physician taking the pulse of a plague victim. A woman approaches the patient from the other side of the bed, holding a bowl for the bleeding of the patient. Next to the doctor stands a young man holding a censer, used for burning aromatic herbs or spices.

Figure 14.6 *Physician in Plague Costume*   **Figure 14.7** *The Plague Patient*

QUESTIONS TO CONSIDER

1. What do Figures 14.6 and 14.7 tell us about medical theories and therapies?
2. Examine *The Plague Patient* carefully. How might the patient have caught the disease?

Figure 14.8 comes from a fifteenth-century German woodblock cut that shows the burning of Jews accused of spreading the plague. The persecution of Jews by Christians occurred in Italy, France, Spain, and Germany, and in many instances, large-scale pogroms ended with large massacres and public burnings.

Figure 14.8 *The Burning of Jews Accused of Spreading the Plague*

QUESTIONS TO CONSIDER

1. Why might Jews have been chosen as scapegoats for the plague?
2. In situations of social crises, what function do scapegoats fulfill?
3. As one philosopher has noted, "In order to explain their misery some men turn to murder." Do you agree? If so, what does this suggest about human psychology?

THE PLAGUE IN THE ARAB ISLAMIC WORLD
Medical Explanations

In 1347, the plague struck Egypt. Scholars believe it came via merchant ships delivering goods and grains from the Black Sea region, perhaps even on the same vessels that delivered the disease to Sicily and southern Italy. From Egypt, it spread overland to Damascus, Jerusalem, and Mecca by 1348 and by coastal ships to ports and cities on the north African coast. Within a few months, thousands of Muslims were stricken with the disease, and in their search for answers and cures, they turned to their esteemed physicians and healers.

In medieval times, the Arab Islamic world had developed a medical tradition that ranked among the most advanced in the world, both in terms of its intellectual sophistication and in actual practice. As in Europe, medical precepts were heavily influenced by the classical theories of Hippocrates and Galen. Indeed, most historians credit Muslims for translating and preserving the medical texts of antiquity that might otherwise have been lost after the fall of the Roman Empire. Equally important, Islamic doctors systematically reorganized the ancient texts with such precision and thoroughness that they provided other physicians with an intellectually consistent and practical textbook for their practice.[16] In practice, Muslims excelled over all other medieval peoples in the organization of hospitals and medical care. There were over two hundred clinics located in principal cities of Persia, Syria, Egypt, and Spain, and hospitals were forbidden to turn away patients who could not pay.[17]

In explaining the plague, Muslim physicians tended to emphasize natural causes and natural therapies. This did not mean they discounted the role of the supernatural in illness, but perhaps more than medieval European doctors, Muslim physicians believed in the efficacy of human medical therapy. They were also more aware of the relationship between the social environment and illness, recognizing that overcrowding and stressful conditions might be injurious to health. One of the most contentious issues, however, was the theory of disease contagion. Although many Islamic doctors observed that the plague could spread from person to person, religious beliefs prohibited a thorough investigation of this fact.

The two readings in this section are representative of medieval medical theory and practice in Islamic society. Both emphasize naturalistic causes but offer different explanations and recommendations. The first comes from Ibn Ridwan (998–1061), a remarkable, self-educated physician from Cairo. Although Ibn Ridwan's treatise was written well before the major outbreak of plague in the fourteenth century, his opinions and remedies profoundly shaped Islamic medical conceptions of the Black Death. The second reading comes from Ibn Khaldun (1332–1395), a Muslim historian whose monumental history of world civilization (*The Muqaddimah*) was an effort to preserve a record of human achievements in an age when the plague threatened to destroy civil society (see Chapter 13). Ibn Khaldun's work is exceedingly detailed in its organization, and it contains interesting sections on medicine and the plague.

1. According to Ibn Ridwan, what is the cause of illness? What factors can create an epidemic? What role do supernatural forces play?
2. What kinds of therapies does Ibn Ridwan recommend? In his opinion, what is the goal of therapy?
3. Both Ibn Ridwan and Ibn Khaldun attribute sickness in part to social conditions and to stress. How does this compare with medieval European accounts? How would modern biomedicine respond to their theories?
4. How does Ibn Khaldun define medicine? How does he distinguish between humoral medicine and the traditional medicine of the Bedouins? In his opinion, which is superior?
5. In your assessment, do the views of Ibn Ridwan and Ibn Khaldun constitute scientific theories? Why, or why not?

ON THE PREVENTION OF BODILY ILLS IN EGYPT (eleventh century)

Ibn Ridwan

On the Causes of Pestilence

The meaning of an epidemic illness is that it encompasses many people in one land at one time. One type is called *al-mautan,* in which the mortality rate is high. Epidemic diseases have many causes that may be grouped into four kinds: a change in the quality of the air, a change in the quality of the water, a change in the quality of the food, and a change in the quality of psychic events.

The quality of the air is changed in two ways: first is its normal variation, and this does not produce an epidemic illness. I do not call this a sickness-inducing change. Second, when the change does not follow the normal course, it creates epidemic illness. It is the same with the other causes. If they change according to habit, they do not create illness. If the change is irregular, however, epidemic illness occurs. A deviation that changes the air from its customary nature takes place when the air becomes hotter, colder, damper, drier, or when a corruption mixes with it. The state of corruption may occur from a nearby or faraway place. Hippocrates and Galen said that it is not impossible that an epidemic disease may occur in the land of the Greeks because of a corruption that accumulated in Ethiopia, ascended to the atmosphere, then descended on the Greeks, and caused epidemic illness among them. The temperament

Source: Ibn Ridwan, *Kitab Daf 'madarr al-abdan bi-ard Misr* [On the Prevention of Bodily Ills in Egypt], in *Medieval Islamic Medicine: Ibn Ridwan's Treatise "On the Prevention of Bodily Ills in Egypt,"* trans. Michael Dols, ed. Adil S. Gamal, 112–14; 138–41. Copyright © 1984 by the Regents of University of California. Reprinted with permission.

of the air may also be changed from the normal when a large group of people arrives, whose long journey has ruined their bodies and whose humors have thus become bad. Much of their humors mixes with the air, and it is transmitted to the people, so that epidemic disease becomes evident.

The water may create epidemic illness if the water is excessive in its increase or decrease, or if a corrupt substance mixes with it. The people are forced to drink it, and the air surrounding their bodies is corrupted by the water as well. This corrupt substance may mix with the water, either in a nearby or distant place, when the water's course passes by a battlefield where many dead bodies are found. Or the river passes by polluted swamps, and it carries and mixes with this stagnant water.

Foods produce epidemic illness. If blight attacks the plants, prices rise and most people are forced to change their foods.* If most of the people increase their consumption of these foods at one time, as at the festivals, dyspepsia increases and the people become ill. And if the pastureland and the water of the animals that we eat are corrupted, it will cause epidemic illness.

Psychic events create epidemic disease when a common fear of a ruler grips the people. They suffer prolonged sleeplessness and worry about deliverance or the possibility of trouble. As a result, their digestion becomes bad and their natural heat is changed. Sometimes, people are forced to violent action in such a condition. When they expect a famine in some years, they increase their hoarding. Their distress intensifies because of what they anticipate may happen.

All of these things produce epidemic illness in human bodies when many people in one country and at one time are subjected to them. It is evident that if an illness increases at one time in one city, a good deal of vapor arises from the ill bodies and changes the temperament of the air. When this vapor meets a body that is susceptible to illness, it makes that body sick, even if it were not directly subjected to what the other people had been exposed to. For example, if an epidemic illness occurs among the people because there is a rise in prices and a lack of food and there is among them someone who does not change his habit in what he eats and drinks, and if the rotten vapor of the sick reaches his body, which is susceptible to disease, he falls ill as well. . . .

Every one of these reasons produces an epidemic illness. The intensity of the illness is related to its originating cause. If more than one cause occur together, the illness is stronger, more intense, and swifter in its killing, as appeared in Egypt several years ago [1055–1062]. Many wars took place then, killing a large number of the enemy as well as our own people. A great fear of the enemy and high prices befell the Egyptians. Furthermore, the inundation of the Nile was extraordinary in both its increase and decrease. Considerable decay from the dead mixed with the water, and the air surrounding them was contaminated by the decay of these things. Famine increased, and a high mortality occurred among the people. About a third of the people died. . . .

---

*Ibn Ridwan asserts that it is not the scarcity and high prices of food that produces epidemic illnesses but the forced change in the individual's customary diet.

On the Means of Preventing Injury from Epidemic Diseases in Egypt

It is desirable at this point that you learn what Hippocrates* and Galen recommended. As for Hippocrates, he said: "It is necessary to preserve the regimen in its usual manner, unless it is itself the cause of illness." If the normal regimen causes illness, he instructed that the accustomed amount of food and drink be diminished gradually and gently. After this, it is advisable that one be disposed toward the opposite of the cause of the illness. Beware of its having the effect of weakening the body. He also instructed that efforts be made to alter the cause that produces the illness as far as possible, so that what reaches the body is completely opposite to the cause that initially altered the body. Galen stated: "it is desirable to refrain from exertion and to be cautious of thirst, overeating, and over-drinking."

If you remember what we said at the beginning, you may easily understand the reasons for epidemic illness in Egypt and know what prevents its damage. Concerning the air, when it becomes hot, it is desirable for you to sit in the rooms that are far away from the glare of the sun, and vice versa. In general, if the weather deviates from the customary in its heat, coldness, moisture, dryness, or corruption, the way to prevent its harm is to have the rooms in the houses and living rooms furnished with what is contrary to that condition.

Likewise, concerning water, if it differs from the ordinary, you should not risk drinking much of it. Water is improved by boiling; it should be boiled if it is spoiled or if much corruption is mixed with it. Then, it is purified by what opposes this corruption, and it should be protected from the putrid air. Its containers should be fumigated with mastic and . . . garlic should be dropped into the water because garlic is beneficial for the drinking of bad water. If the occurrence of epidemic illness is due to bad foods, beware of those foods. If it is because of a general fear, it is desirable that the people hearten one another and enjoin one another to relinquish their fear and despair. . . .

We have said that when the air becomes excessively hot, it can be improved by pouring out cold water, furnishing the rooms with roses, violets, myrtle, and Egyptian willow; drinking sweetened oxymel, nenuphar, Egyptian willow, prune, rose water, sour and sweet pomegranate juice, tamarind juice, and prune juice; and smelling cool oils, like the oils of roses, nenuphar, and violets. . . . In this situation, foods and other things having a hot temperament should be avoided. Sexual intercourse and fasting are to be guarded against. One should face the north wind and be seated in underground passages. If you see that the body is full, evacuate it with gentle laxatives, as tamarind, *taranjubi'n,'* and purging cassia. If one has need of bloodletting, you should bleed him immediately on the spot. . . . Do your best, so that everything that is eaten and drunk is cold and constricting. Be cautious of physical exercise and bathing in such a condition.

If the air becomes excessively cold, you should ignite fires and furnish the rooms with sweet basil, narcissus, bitter orange, sweet marjoram, gillyflower, jasmine, and wild thyme. Also, use musk, ambergris, aloeswood, saffron, mastic, frankincense, Arabian costus, and all the hot spices. Increase the hot remedies of a delicate substance, so that its heat combats the coldness of the air and the gentleness of the

---

*Hippocrates (460–377 BCE), the ancient Greek physician, is frequently called the "father of modern medicine" because he ascribed illness and disease to natural causes.

substance combats the density produced by the air. Use rose jam, electuaries, honey, drinks, physical exercise, perspiration in the bath, and everything that opens the pores of the body and diminishes the coldness of the air. . . .

Give the remedies that are cooling and constricting and that obstruct the corruption of the humors. Give what is cold and diuretic, like spices. And give a [diluting agent] for the disposition, such as drinking prune juice and herb juice, for it is beneficial in this case. Work hard in preserving the temperament and opposing the cause of the disease to the utmost of your ability, if God Almighty wills.

THE MUQADDIMAH (1377)

Ibn Khaldun

Causes of Pestilences

In the previous (discussion), it has been established that, at the beginning, dynasties are inevitably kind in the exercise of their power and just in their administration. . . . In the later [years] of dynasties, famines and pestilences become numerous. As far as famines are concerned, the reason is that most people at that time refrain from cultivating the soil. For, in the later years of dynasties, there occur attacks on property and tax revenue and, through customs duties, on trading. Or, trouble occurs as the result of the unrest of the subjects and the great number of rebels [who are provoked] by the senility of the dynasty to rebel. Therefore, as a rule, little grain is stored. . . . If for some years nothing is stored, hunger will be general.

The large number of pestilences has its reason in the large number of famines just mentioned. Or, it has its reason in the many disturbances that result from the disintegration of the dynasty. There is much unrest and bloodshed, and plagues occur. The principal reason for the latter is the corruption of the air through [too] large a civilization [population]. It results from the putrefaction and the many evil moistures with which [the air] has contact in a dense civilization. . . . If the corruption is strong, the lung is afflicted with disease. This results in epidemics, which affect the lung in particular. Even if the corruption is not strong or great, putrefaction grows and multiplies under its influence, resulting in many fevers that affect the tempers, and the bodies become sick and perish. The reason for the growth of putrefaction and evil moistures is invariably a dense and abundant civilization such as exists in the later years of a dynasty. Such civilization is the result of the good government, the kindness, the safety, and the light taxation that existed at the beginning of the dynasty. This is obvious. Therefore, it has been clarified by science in the proper place that it is necessary to have empty spaces and waste regions interspersed between civilized areas. This makes circulation of the air possible. It removes the corruption and putrefaction affecting the air after contact with living beings, and brings healthy air. This

Source: Ibn Khaldun, *The Muqaddimah, An Introduction to History,* trans. Franz Rosenthal, vol. 2, 135–37; vol. 3, 148–51. Copyright © 1958 Princeton University Press. Reprinted with permission by Princeton University Press.

also is the reason why pestilences occur much more frequently in densely settled cities than elsewhere, as, for instance, in Cairo in the East and Fez in the Maghrib. God determines whatever He wishes.

The Science of Medicine

Medicine is a craft that studies the human body in its illness and health. The physician attempts to preserve health and to cure illness with the help of medicines and diets, but first he ascertains (the illnesses) peculiar to each limb of the body, and the reasons causing them. He also ascertains the medicines existing for each illness. Physicians deduce the effectiveness of medicines from their composition and powers. They deduce the stage of an illness from signs indicating whether the illness is ripe and will accept the medicine or not. These signs show themselves in the color of the patient, the excretions, and the pulse. The physicians in this imitate the power of nature, which is the controlling element in both health and illness. They imitate nature and help it a little, as the nature of the matter underlying the illness, the season of the year, and the age of the patient may require in each particular case. The science dealing with all these things is called medicine. . . .

Civilized Bedouins have a kind of medicine which is mainly based upon individual experience. They inherit its use from the *shaykhs* and old women of the tribe. Some of it may occasionally be correct. However, that kind of medicine is not based upon any natural norm or upon any conformity of the treatment to the temper of the humors. . . .

The medicine mentioned in religious tradition is of the Bedouin type. It is in no way part of the divine revelation. Such medical matters were merely part of Arab custom and happened to be mentioned in connection with the circumstances of the Prophet [Muhammad], like other things that were customary in his generation. They were not mentioned in order to imply that that particular way of practicing medicine is stipulated by the religious law. Muhammad was sent to teach us the religious law. He was not sent to teach us medicine or any other ordinary matter. In connection with the story of the fecundation of the palms, he said: "You know more about your worldly affairs than I."

None of the statements concerning medicine that occur in sound traditions should be considered to have the force of law. There is nothing to indicate that this is the case. The only thing is that if that type of medicine is used for the sake of a divine blessing and in true faith, it may be very useful. However, that would have nothing to do with humoral medicine but would be the result of true faith. . . .

God guides to that which is correct.

Religious Explanations of the Plague

In the Islamic world, religious beliefs permeated all conceptions of illness and disease, including the most naturalistic explanations. Although the readings from Ibn Rushad and Ibn Khaldun showed some disagreements about the spread of plague, nearly all Muslims believed that the disease was an affliction willed by God. Consequently, as in medieval Christian Europe, religious explanations of the pestilence in the Middle East should not be understood as distinct from the more naturalistic point of view, no matter how irreconcilable they may appear to us today.

The major religious authority on disease and epidemics was the Prophet Muhammad himself, whose words and deeds, along with those of his close companions, are known collectively as *ahadith* (*hadith*: singular). Muslim scholars use the thousands of *ahadith* to explain the basic teachings of the Qur'an, to answer legal questions, and to clarify the duties of believers. The *ahadith* on illness and therapy carry great weight in the Muslim world, for they are perceived to be divinely inspired. Yet many scholars also believe that the Prophet's views were undoubtedly also shaped by his own personal experiences with epidemics, which periodically afflicted Arabia during his lifetime (570–632). In either case, the Islamic interpretation of plague centered on the belief that it was a martyrdom and mercy from God for Muslims but a punishment for nonbelievers. Muslims who died of plague were considered of equal esteemed rank to those who died in *jihad*, and both were guaranteed entry to Paradise. With this conception, religious leaders called for perseverence, prayer, and repentance, while also urging the healthy to give charity and comfort to the poor and sick.

Following are excerpts from *Sahih al-Bukhari*, a nine-volume collection of *ahadith* compiled and edited by the great Islamic scholar Sahih al-Bukhari in the ninth century. Al-Bukhari organized the thousands of *ahadith* into chapters according to subject matter, which included a section (Book 71) on medicine. Although some Muslim scholars have debated the historical accuracy of the *ahadith*, most acknowledge that they represent the consensus of the Muslim community on a wide range of issues. Each *hadith* begins with an attribution to the Prophet or to one of his close associates.

QUESTIONS TO CONSIDER

1. In one *hadith*, it is said that "Allah has said the truth, but your brother's abdomen has told a lie." What is the meaning of this saying? What does it tell us about Islamic conceptions of illness and therapy?

2. Another *hadith* makes mention of mangy camels. What is the implied meaning of this story? What are the medical implications?

3. According to Muslim philosophy, the plague was a punishment for nonbelievers, but a mercy and martyrdom for Muslims. How can a disease be a sign of mercy? How does this explanation reflect conceptions of the supernatural? How might it also affect public reactions?

4. Several *ahadith* urge Muslims neither to flee nor to enter plague zones. How is that explained in religious terms? How might it also reflect the realities of the disease? Is it a useful public health measure?

5. How do Islamic *ahadith* on illness and plague compare with medieval Christian views? Which are more pronounced—the similarities or the differences in interpretations?

SAHIH AL-BUKHARI

Narrated Abu Huraira:

The Prophet said, "There is no disease that Allah has created, except that He also has created its treatment." (Volume 7, Book 71, Number 582)

Narrated Aisha:

The Prophet used to treat some of his wives by passing his right hand over the place of ailment and used to say, "O Allah, the Lord of the people! Remove the trouble and heal the patient, for You are the Healer. No healing is of any avail but Yours; healing that will leave behind no ailment." (Volume 7, Book 71, Number 639)

Narrated Abu Said Al-Khudri:

A man came to the Prophet and said, "My brother has some abdominal trouble." The Prophet said to him "Let him drink honey." The man came for the second time and the Prophet said to him, 'Let him drink honey." He came for the third time and the Prophet said, "Let him drink honey." He returned again and said, "I have done that." The Prophet then said, "Allah has said the truth, but your brother's abdomen has told a lie. Let him drink honey." So he made him drink honey and he was cured. (Volume 7, Book 71, Number 588)

Narrated Aisha:

The Prophet said, "Fever is from the heat of Hell, so abate fever with water." (Volume 7, Book 71, Number 621)

Narrated Abu Huraira:

Allah's Apostle said, "There is no 'Adha (no contagion of disease from the sick to the healthy without Allah's permission), nor Safar, nor Hama." A bedouin stood up and said, "Then what about my camels? They are like deer on the sand, but when a mangy camel comes and mixes with them, they all get infected with mange." The Prophet said, "Then who conveyed the (mange) disease to the first one?" (Volume 7, Book 71, Number 615)

Narrated Aisha:

(the wife of the Prophet) I asked Allah's Apostle about the plague. He told me that it was a Punishment sent by Allah on whom he wished, and Allah made it a source of mercy for the believers, for if one in the time of an epidemic plague stays in his country patiently hoping for Allah's Reward and believing that nothing will befall him except what Allah has written for him, he will get the reward of a martyr." (Volume 4, Book 56, Number 680)

Narrated Saud:

The Prophet said, "If you hear of an outbreak of plague in a land, do not enter it; but if the plague breaks out in a place while you are in it, do not leave that place." (Volume 7, Book 71, Number 624)

Source: Sahih al-Bukhari: The Translation of the Meanings, 9 vols, ed. Muhammed Ibn Ismaiel al-Bukhari, trans. Muhammad M. Khan (Riyadh, Saudi Arabia: Darussalam, 1997). The ahadith used in this section have been cited in the traditional manner, by volume, book, and number.

Narrated Usama bin Zaid:

> Allah's Apostle said, "Plague was a means of torture sent on a group of Israelis (or on some people before you). So if you hear of its spread in a land, don't approach it, and if a plague should appear in a land where you are present, then don't leave that land in order to run away from it (i.e., plague)." (Volume 4, Book 56, Number 679)

Reactions to the Plague

Unfortunately, translated accounts of the fourteenth-century plague in the Middle East are not as plentiful as they are for medieval Europe. Most accounts, such as the ones that are included in this section, come from Islamic historians and travelers. Our selections begin with a report from Ahmad al-Maqrizi (1364–1442), a biographer and historian of the Islamic Empire. In addition to his commentaries on politics and economic conditions, Ahmad al-Maqrizi made note of the devastating impact of the plague in Cairo.

The second selection comes from the great Islamic traveler Ibn Battuta (1304–1369), who traversed the Islamic world in the fourteenth century and recorded his observations around 1355 (see Chapter 15). While visiting Damascus in July 1348, Ibn Battuta witnessed the ravages of the plague and noted how the city organized a huge procession to help alleviate the affliction. Later, he visited Jerusalem, where the plague had recently subsided. Together, the two accounts provide some insights into popular reactions to the epidemic that may at times seem inconsistent with medical theories or with the *Sahih al–Bukhari*.

QUESTIONS TO CONSIDER

1. According to Ahmad al-Maqrizi, the plague increased in the winter months. Is this consistent with the medical theories of Ibn Ridwan? What factors might explain the increase of disease in winter?

2. In Cairo, how did people react to the fear of death? Were the responses consistent with the philosophy expressed in the *ahadith*?

3. In Ahmad al-Maqrizi's account, how are funerals organized? How does his account compare with the one offered by Boccaccio? What beliefs or attitudes might explain the differences?

4. According to Ibn Battuta, the citizens of Damascus organized a large procession in response to the plague. Do these actions seem consistent with or in contrast to religious views?

5. Some historians have claimed that Muslims were apathetic in their responses to the plague. Do you agree? What evidence supports your assessment?

THE PLAGUE IN CAIRO (1364–1442)

Ahmad al-Maqrizi

News reached Cairo from Syria that the plague in Damascus had been less deadly than in Tripoli, Hama, and Aleppo. From [October 1348] death raged with intensity. 1200 people died daily and, as a result, people stopped requesting permits from the administration to bury the dead and many cadavers were abandoned in gardens and on the roads.

In New and Old Cairo, the plague struck women and children at first, then market people, and the numbers of the dead augmented. . . . The [ravages of the] plague intensified in . . . [November] in Cairo and became extremely grave during *Ramadan*** [December], which coincided with the arrival of winter. . . . The plague continued to spread so considerably that it became impossible to count how many died. . . .

In [January 1349], new symptoms developed and people began spitting up blood.[†] One sick person came down with internal fever, followed by an unrestrained need to vomit, then spat blood and died. Those around him in his house fell ill, one after the other and in one or two nights they all perished. Everyone lived with the overwhelming preoccupation that death was near. People prepared themselves for death by distributing alms to the poor, reconciled with one another, and multiplied their acts of devotion.

None had time to consult doctors or drink medicinal syrups or take other medications, so rapidly did they die. By [January 7th] bodies had piled up in the streets and markets; [town leaders] appointed burial brigades, and some pious people remained permanently at places of prayer in New and Old Cairo to recite funeral orations over the dead. The situation worsened beyond limits, and no solution appeared possible. Almost the entire royal guard disappeared and the barracks in the sultan's citadel contained no more soldiers. . . .

People began searching [for people to act as] the *Qur'an* readers at funerals, and many individuals quit their trades to recite prayers at the head of burial processions. A group of people devoted themselves to applying a coat of clay to the inner sides of the graves. Others volunteered to wash corpses, and still others to carry them. Such volunteers received substantial wages. For example, a *Qur'an* reader earned 10 *dirhams:* the moment he finished with one funeral, he ran off to another. A body carrier demanded six *dirhams* in advance, and still it was hard to find any. A gravedigger wanted 50 *dirhams* per grave. But most of them died before they had a chance to spend their earnings.

Source: From Ahmad ibn 'Ali al-Maqrizi, *kitab al-suluk li-ma 'rifat duwal al-muluk [The Guide to the Knowledge of Dynasties and Kings]*, 4 vols., ed. M. Mustafa Ziada, vol. II, part III (Cairo: Association of Authorship, Translation and Publishing Press, 1958), 779–86, in *The Middle East and Islamic Reader,* ed. Marvin E. Gettleman and Stuart Schaar, 52–53. Copyright © 2003 Grove Press. Reprinted with permission.

*The ninth month of the Islamic calendar, observed as sacred with fasting practiced daily from dawn to sunset.

†A symptom of pneumonic plague.

Family celebrations and marriages no longer took place. . . . No one had held any festivities during the entire duration of the epidemic, and no voice was heard singing. In an attempt to revive these activities, the *wazir* [prime minister] reduced by a third the taxes paid by the woman responsible for collecting dues on singers. The call to prayer was suspended at many locations, and even at the most important ones, there remained only a single *muezzin* [caller to prayer]. . . .

Most of the mosques and lodges were closed. It was also a known fact that during this epidemic no infant survived more than one or two days after his birth, and his mother usually quickly followed him to the grave.

At [the end of February], all of Upper Egypt was afflicted with the plague. . . . According to information that arrived . . . from . . . other regions, lions, wolves, rabbits, camels, wild asses and boars, and other savage beasts, dropped dead, and were found with scabs on their bodies.

The same thing happened throughout Egypt. When harvest time arrived, many farmers had already perished [and no field hands remained to gather crops]. Soldiers and their young slaves or pages headed for the fields. They tried to recruit workers by promising them half of the proceeds, but they could not find anyone to help them gather the harvest. They threshed the grain with their horses [hoofs], and winnowed the grain themselves, but, unable to carry all the grain back, they had to abandon much of it. Most craft workshops closed, since artisans devoted themselves to disposing of the dead, while others, not less numerous, auctioned off property and textiles [which the dead left behind]. Even though the prices of fabric and other such commodities sold for a fifth of their original value . . . they remained unsold. . . .

VOYAGES (1355)

Ibn Battuta

One of the celebrated sanctuaries at Damascus is the Mosque of the Footprints (*al-Aqdam*), which lies two miles south of the city, alongside the main highway which leads to the Hijaz, Jerusalem, and Egypt. It is a large mosque, very blessed, richly endowed, and very highly venerated by the Damascenes. The footprints from which it derives its name are certain footprints impressed upon a rock there, which are said to be the mark of Moses' foot. In this mosque there is a small chamber containing a stone with the following inscription "A certain pious man saw in his sleep the Chosen One [Muhammad], who said to him 'Here is the grave of my brother Moses.'"

I saw a remarkable instance of the veneration in which the Damascenes hold this mosque during the great pestilence on my return journey through Damascus, in the latter part of July 1348. The viceroy Arghun Shah ordered a crier to proclaim through

Sources: Ibn Battuta, *Travels in Asia and Africa, 1325–1354,* trans. H. A. R. Gibb (London: G. Routledge & Sons, 1929), 68–69; Ibn Battuta, *Travels,* trans. H. A. R. Gibb, vol. 1 (Cambridge: Cambridge University Press, 1958), 143–44; vol. 4 (Cambridge: Cambridge University Press, 1994), 918.

Damascus that all the people should fast for three days and that no one should cook anything eatable in the market during the daytime. For most of the people there eat no food but what has been prepared in the market. So the people fasted for three successive days, the last of which was a Thursday, then they assembled in the Great Mosque, *amirs, sharifs, qadis,* theologians, and all the other classes of the people, until the place was filled to overflowing, and there they spent the Thursday night in prayers and litanies. After the dawn prayer next morning they all went out together on foot, holding *Qurans* in their hands, and the *amirs* barefooted. The procession was joined by the entire population of the town, men and women, small and large; the Jews came with their Book of the Law and the Christians with their Gospel, all of them with their women and children. The whole concourse, weeping and supplicating and seeking the favor of God through His Books and His Prophets, made their way to the Mosque of the Footprints, and there they remained in supplication and invocation until near midday. They then returned to the city and held the Friday service, and God lightened their affliction; for the number of deaths in a single day at Damascus did not attain two thousand, while in Cairo and Old Cairo it reached the figure of twenty-four thousand a day. . . .

[In Jerusalem, Battuta met the preacher Izz ad-Din ibn Jama'ah, a relative of the chief judge of Cairo, and he was invited to a banquet.]

I asked him the reason for this and he informed me that he had vowed during the epidemic that, if it was lightened and a day passed without having to pray for any dead, he would arrange a feast. He then said to me, "Yesterday, I did not pray for any dead, so I will give the proposed feast." I found that those whom I had known among the *shaykhs* of Jerusalem had almost all ascended to God the Almighty.

NOTES

1. The rhyme specifically refers to a prominent symptom of plague (the "rosies"), two popular therapies ("pocketful of posies" and "ashes"), and the great mortality caused by the disease ("we all fall down"). According to some folklorists, the transference of the rhyme to a children's game was a coping mechanism to alleviate adult anxieties and fears.

2. Ibn Khaldun, *The Muqaddimah: An Introduction to History,* vol. 1, transl. Franz Rosenthal (Princeton, NJ: Princeton University Press, 1967), 64.

3. A branch of knowledge concerned with causes.

4. Biomedicine refers to the biologically oriented science that predominates modern Western medical thinking.

5. A disease-inducing bacterium.

6. Cases in the United States are frequently caused by disease-carrying prairie dogs in the western states.

7. An episode of disease that occurs over a wide geographical area that affects a high proportion of the population.

8. Native to a particular region or locality.

9. A heavy vaporous atmosphere believed to cause disease.

10. The last major epidemic of plague, which began in Asia in the nineteenth century and spread along international trading routes, is estimated to have killed millions of people across three continents.

11. Not all scholars have come to similar conclusions. Other historical studies have concluded that the plague had limited long-term social or political impact, despite the high death rates.

12. Some historians trace the rise of Western medical experimental science, which began during the Renaissance with a more rigorous study of human anatomy, to the failures experienced by doctors during the years of plague.

13. See Exodus 9:1–26 and 2 Samuel 24:1–18.

14. Private acts of prayer or supplication, often directed to a particular object of faith.

15. Biblical references include this promise from God to punish the wicked: "And I will heap evils upon them; and I will spend my arrows upon them; They shall be wasted with hunger, and devoured with burning heat, and poisonous pestilence" (Deuteronomy 32:23–24). In Homer's *Iliad,* the Greek army besieging Troy is struck by a plague caused by the arrows of an angry Apollo.

16. One of the most important Islamic physicians was Ibn Sina (980–1037), also known as Avicenna in medieval Europe. In his great *Al-Qanun fi'l-tibb (Canon of Medicine),* Ibn Sina listed every known disease at the time and itemized their cures. His work was translated into Latin in the twelfth century, and it served as the primary medical text of European universities until the seventeenth century.

17. In the Islamic world, charitable organizations (*waqfs*) were created to support public institutions such as hospitals and schools.

CHAPTER 15

Expanding Global Encounters in the Fourteenth through Sixteenth Centuries

INTRODUCTION

Beginning in the mid-fifteenth century, European nations began to send explorers, merchants, missionaries, and colonizers throughout the rest of the world. Historians have often called this the "Age of Discovery," in which enterprising Portuguese and Spanish explorers took the lead in developing new sailing skills to traverse the unknown seas, discovering new lands and peoples, and initiating a new phase of global encounters that was unprecedented and unmatched in human history. In other words, the so-called Age of Discovery has commonly been portrayed as exclusively European and historically unique. But such accounts of world history are misleading and incomplete. It was certainly not a unique event, for exploration and expansion are as old as the history of mankind.[1] It was also not uniquely European. Centuries before Columbus set out from Spain in 1492, Muslim and Chinese explorers and traders had pioneered routes overland and by sea that served to link together the peoples, goods, and ideas of Asia, Arabia, and Africa. Moreover, such historical accounts do not reveal much about the essence of these voyages—the motivations, attitudes, and cross-cultural perceptions that were to have long-term consequences far beyond the initial period of "discovery."

This chapter explores the theme of exploration through the voyage diaries and chronicles of four of the most widely traveled men of the fourteenth through sixteenth centuries: Ibn Battuta, whose journeys in the mid-fourteenth century took him throughout the vast extent of the Islamic world; Zheng He, a Chinese admiral who sailed as far as the coast of east Africa in the mid-fifteenth century; Vasco da Gama, the Portuguese sea captain who was the first European to reach India by sea in 1498; and Christopher Columbus, who inadvertently "discovered" the Americas as he sought a western sea route to the spice markets of Asia. The accounts of these travelers are fascinating and useful for the detailed historical information they convey about different civilizations and cultures in the fourteenth through sixteenth centuries.[2] Moreover, they allow us to examine and assess the personal motives and actions of explorers, the nature of their experiences and contacts, and, most important, the formation of cross-cultural perceptions and attitudes.

The first voyager we shall examine is Ibn Battuta (1304–1369), a Muslim from Morocco, who was so enthralled by the sights he witnessed on his way to complete the *hajj*[3] in Mecca that he afterward devoted his life to traveling throughout most of the Muslim world, covering an estimated 75,000 miles. Such distances should not be too surprising, for the Islamic world had grown to be one of the largest, wealthiest, and most dynamic civilizations in the world by the four-teenth century. In the years following Muhammad's proclamation of the new faith in Arabia during the seventh century, Islam had spread quickly westward across north Africa and into Iberia (Spain and Portugal) and eastward into Syria and Per-sia (Iran). In subsequent centuries, Islam continued to expand into northern India and Asia, along the coast of east Africa, and even across the Sahara Desert into west Africa.

Although the Islamic world was rarely unified politically, Muslims were par-tially bound by religion and commerce. Islam offered a set of common laws and values to its adherents that helped to provide a bond of unity and common identity that transcended ethnic and regional differences. Equally important, the establish-ment of long-distance trading networks linked Muslim producers and consumers from different regions, as well as with peoples of different religions. In their quest for spices, gold, and other luxury commodities, Muslim traders organized camel caravans to the frontiers of India and across the Sahara in Africa, while organizing equally profitable trade routes by sea across the Indian Ocean. By the time of the first European arrivals in the late fifteenth century, most of the lands bordering the Indian Ocean were linked together in a dynamic and prosperous trade that was under the near monopolistic control of Muslim traders and businessmen.

Such extensive trade networks had important consequences for world history. First, it promoted a parallel development in industry and export production throughout the Islamic world. By the fourteenth century, for example, Persia was renowned for its exquisite glassware, jewelry, and pottery; Morocco for its finely-worked leather goods; and Syria for its durable cotton fabrics. Trade and industry also helped to create an urban, cosmopolitan society. The hub of Islamic civiliza-tion lay in its great cities, such as Cairo, Damascus, Baghdad, Timbuktu, and Zanzibar, that straddled major trade routes. The commercial opportunities and sophisticated culture found in these cities attracted residents from far-flung re-gions, resulting in a rich intermingling of different cultures. Finally, the expansion of trade and cultural contacts helped to spread Islam and elements of Islamic cul-ture to more distant regions, such as the Delhi Sultanate (India) and the west African kingdom of Mali. In fact, some scholars suggest that one of Ibn Battuta's primary goals in his travels was to observe and record the successful expansion of Islam in much of the known world.

In terms of wealth, advanced industry, and technology, China was at least the equal of the Islamic world. But whereas Islam was expanding along with its com-merce in the mid-fourteenth century, China was just emerging from a period of foreign conquest and occupation by the Mongols.[4] Eager to assert its power and influence, the first emperors of the new Ming dynasty (1368–1644) launched an ambitious new foreign policy based on sea power. Although China has tradition-ally been viewed as a land power, it has had a long seafaring tradition, and Chi-nese vessels had sailed to India as early as the Han dynasty (202 BCE–200 CE). China also possessed important maritime technologies to make long-distance travel possible, including the compass, large multimasted ships, and shipboard rockets. Under the early Ming emperors, China organized seven major expedi-tions between 1405 and 1422, which were led by the capable and daring Chinese admiral Zheng He.

In sheer scope and scale, Zheng He far surpassed the European maritime voy-ages that occurred later. His armada was several times the size of the fleets com-manded by Columbus, and his ships were more than six times bigger. With ap-proximately 300 vessels and 27,000 sailors, Zheng He visited ports in southeast Asia, India, Persia, Arabia, and east Africa. His primary mission was political: to display Chinese might, to collect tribute from subordinate "barbarians" in other lands, and to ferry foreign diplomats to the Chinese emperor's court. In exchange for tribute, Zheng He delivered gifts of fine porcelain dishes, silks, gold and silver, and manufactured goods. But as his travel record also shows, he was prepared and able to use military force to demand deference and to assert his superiority.

After 1422, the great maritime expeditions of China ended abruptly. Histori-ans have proposed several different theories to explain this sudden halt, suggest-ing that the voyages were too costly, that funds were needed for the construction of the Great Wall, or that the expeditions were seen as counter to Confucian ideals.[5] Nonetheless, the seven voyages of Zheng He had long-term impact. They extended China's political hegemony overseas, promoted the emigration of Chi-nese into regions of southeast Asia, and reinforced an international tribute system that continued into the nineteenth century.

In comparison with Chinese and Islamic civilizations, Europe was relatively poor, undeveloped, and isolated during much of the fourteenth and fifteenth cen-turies. The economy was still small, largely agricultural, and organized to meet local needs. Although the Crusades had created a new demand for spices and lux-ury items from Asia, Europeans remained mostly dependent on Muslim merchants and middlemen. Europe was also politically fragmented, and scarce resources and manpower were spent in innumerable wars and conflicts. And finally, beginning in the mid-fourteenth century, the Black Death (bubonic plague) struck Europe, killing millions, further weakening economies, and creating a widespread climate of fear and xenophobia.[6] From a global perspective, Europe was insular, back-ward, and unsophisticated.

The initial European drive to explore and expand began in Iberia, and it was fueled by a mixture of political, religious, and commercial motives. For centuries, Portuguese and Spanish Christians had struggled to expel the Moors (Muslim Arabs) who had ruled their lands ever since the eighth century. The *Reconquista*[7] of Iberia by Christian armies created an intense religious fervor and missionary zeal among the warring Christians, and it also generated a new sense of unity and na-tional identity. With the successful expulsion of Muslims from Iberia in the four-teenth and fifteenth centuries, Spain and Portugal emerged as strong, dynamic, and consolidated monarchies, eager to continue the offensive against the hated Moors.

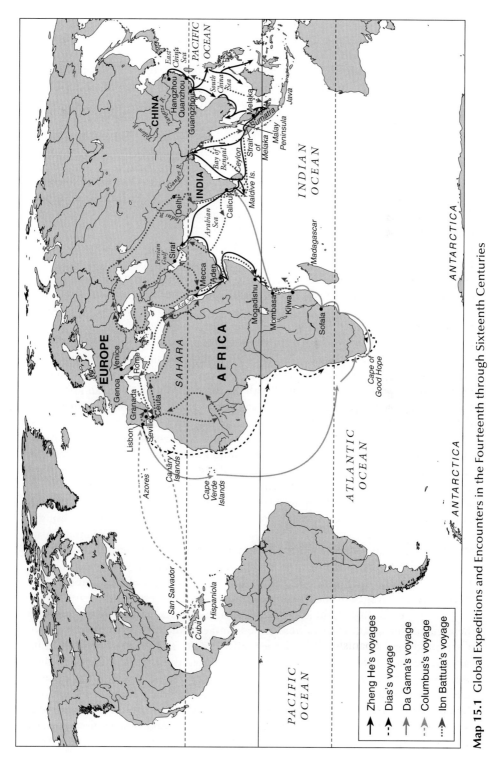

Map 15.1 Global Expeditions and Encounters in the Fourteenth through Sixteenth Centuries

One of the major proponents and patrons of expansion was Prince Henry the Navigator (1394–1460), the third son of King John I of Portugal. Under Henry's auspices, the Portuguese improved ship designs and sailing technologies that allowed voyages to venture farther from their home ports, which culminated in the 1488 voyage of Bartholomeu Dias around Africa's southern Cape of Good Hope (South Africa). Equally important, Henry provided a grand strategy to gain profit and fight the Muslim enemy at the same time by outflanking their trade routes and establishing direct European contact with the rich markets and producers of Africa and Asia. It was also Henry's goal that Europeans discover and make alliances with long-lost Christian monarchs such as Prester John, a wayward Crusader who was believed to have established a large Christian kingdom somewhere in the east. Although Prester John proved to be a myth, such intense religious ideals profoundly shaped European attitudes and actions in their initial encounters with peoples from distant lands.

Less than four decades after Prince Henry's death, Vasco da Gama departed from Portugal in 1497, determined to find a direct sea route to India and Asia. After rounding the Cape of Good Hope in four medium-sized boats with only 168 men, his first stops were at several wealthy city-states situated along the east coast of Africa in what is now Mozambique, Tanzania, and Kenya. Here he found cosmopolitan cities and a thriving trading network controlled by Muslims, but no Christians, and his stay was marked by mutual suspicion and violence. Da Gama then sailed on to India, but here his efforts to conclude commercial treaties with rulers were largely unsuccessful because European trade goods were not highly desired. Still, he returned to Portugal with his ships filled with spices and precious stones, inspiring more commercial ventures and a greater determination than ever to seize control of the Indian Ocean trade from the Muslims.

While the Portuguese were exploring eastern trade routes to India and Asia, Christopher Columbus was determined to find a western route. In 1492, after winning the patronage and financial support of the Spanish monarchy, Columbus set sail from Europe in three small ships with only 120 men. After a voyage of just over thirty days, Columbus sighted the Bahamas and then found and explored Cuba and Haiti, which he initially confused with Japan and China. Although Columbus remained disappointed that he did not find the western route to Asia (and he tried again on three more subsequent voyages), he declared himself "enchanted" with the land and peoples he "discovered," which he described in great detail in a letter to the Spanish monarchs King Fernando and Queen Ysabel.

The early voyages of the Portuguese and Spanish had immediate and long-term consequences for world history. By the sixteenth and seventeenth centuries, these initial European travelers were joined (and eventually overshadowed) by explorers and merchants from the Netherlands, Britain, and France, who joined in the conquest and colonization of the Americas and in the establishment of trading routes and depots elsewhere. With superior military might, as well as the willingness to use it, Europeans were eventually able to extend their commercial and political influence over large parts of the world. This age of expansion also initiated a process of biological exchange, whereby plants, animals, and various diseases were able to migrate beyond their original ecological environments into new areas. Historical research has shown that the so-called Columbian Exchange[8] has had a very uneven historical impact. Although the introduction of crops such as corn and the potato from the Americas to Europe may have initiated a dramatic increase in population by the eighteenth century, the global dispersion of diseases such as small-pox, syphilis, and bubonic plague decimated entire regional populations.

The readings included in this chapter provide the opportunity to explore the process of exploration and expansion in greater depth and to make comparisons between the four case studies. One of the most important themes to keep in mind is the formation and impact of cross-cultural perceptions and attitudes. Are there any commonalities in the ways people first viewed "others"? What are the most important factors that shape opinions, beliefs, and behaviors? How does one's own culture and values shape one's view of the world? What lasting impact might these initial encounters have had on subsequent meetings?

CHAPTER QUESTIONS

1. When the four travel accounts are compared, what were the most important motivations that underlay the age of expansion? How did explorers see them-selves and their mission? How did their expressed motives compare with the ones that are revealed in their descriptions of their discoveries and experiences?

2. What kinds of observations and experiences were recorded by the explorers? What do they tell us about different cultures? Existing trade routes? What kind of information seems to be missing from these accounts?

3. What role did religion play in the motives and experiences of the explorers? How were beliefs used to justify actions? What are the implications?

4. How were cross-cultural ideas formed? Were they the result of actual experiences and observations? Or were they the result of preexisting values and cultural biases? What general conclusions can be made?

5. In what ways, if any, were the European voyages of exploration unique? Examine the relationship between motives, experiences, attitudes, and long-term consequences. Do you think world history would have been radically different if China and Zheng He had "discovered" Europe in the early fifteenth century?

IBN BATTUTA'S TRAVELS IN THE ISLAMIC WORLD

Even by our modern measures, the travels of Abu Abdullah Muhammad Ibn Battuta (1304–1369) are extraordinary. Over a period of nearly thirty years, he is estimated to have traveled 75,000 miles and visited regions that now comprise over forty modern nations (see Map 15.2). Born in 1304 at Tangier, Morocco, to a family of legal scholars, Ibn Battuta initially planned to become a judge, and he pursued a legal education. But his journey to Mecca for the *hajj* when he was

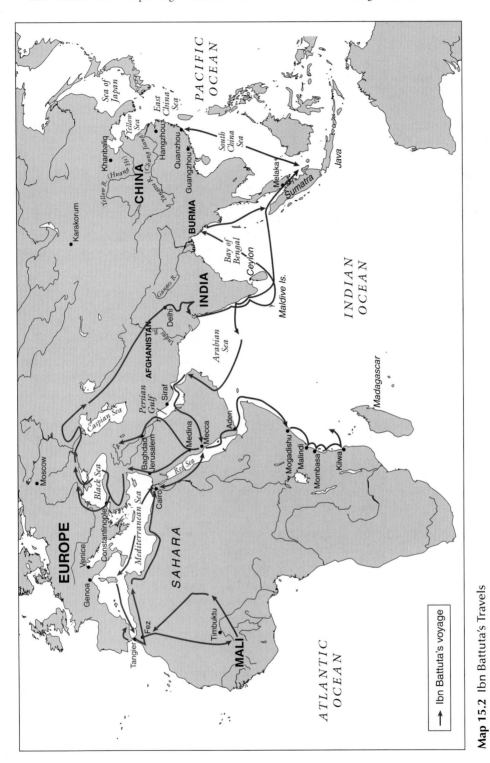

Map 15.2 Ibn Battuta's Travels

twenty-one forever changed his life. Fascinated by his long journey across north Africa, he determined to devote his entire life to traveling in different lands and observing different cultures. He reportedly had only two rules: to visit only Muslim countries, and never to travel the same road twice.

For the most part, Ibn Battuta followed his own rules. He first traveled the lands of the Middle East, crossed the Arabian desert, and visited the cities of present-day Iraq and Iran. In 1330, he changed directions and sailed down the Red Sea to the Indian Ocean, stopping along the way at trading towns situated along the coast of east Africa. Two years later, he journeyed through southern Russia and Afghanistan to India, where he was appointed a regional judge by the Sultan of Delhi. After five years' service, he recommenced his journeys and traveled to China, Burma, and Sumatra (Indonesia). After a short return home to Tangier, he departed on his last major trip in 1349, a trek across the Sahara Desert to visit the kingdom of Mali in west Africa. Upon his return, he finished writing his travel accounts while residing as an honored guest at the court of Sultan Abu Inan of Morocco. Unfortunately, little is known about the final two decades of his life before he died in 1369.

Some historians contend that Ibn Battuta's chronicles are occasionally fictional and sometimes prone to errors. Yet his record of observations and experiences provides a wealth of information about the social structures and cultural values of many different lands in the fourteenth century. In some regions of the world, such as the interior regions of Africa, his account of different African societies is one of the few remaining recorded sources for this time period. Although he focused most of his attention on the ruling classes in the areas he visited, he also recorded a wide range of human activities, from the royal ceremonies of the Malian king to farming techniques in imperial China. Indeed, some biographers of Ibn Battuta contend that it was his deep personal interest in people and their customs that led him to record and assess in such great detail the practices, beliefs, and daily life of different societies.

The reading that follows provides brief excerpts from three of Ibn Battuta's trips. The first excerpt recounts his visit to the holy sites of Medina and Mecca[9] in 1326, early in his career as a world traveler. Here his account is very favorable, focusing on the kindness and cleanliness of residents. The second excerpt includes his observations while visiting China around 1340, one of the few non-Muslim areas that he visited. Although he was impressed with the prosperity found in China, he ultimately judged that the country "did not attract me" because of its "heathendom." The final excerpt focuses on Ibn Battuta's journey to the Kingdom of Mali in west Africa, where he finds cultural attributes to praise and to condemn.

QUESTIONS TO CONSIDER

1. Compare and contrast Ibn Battuta's descriptions of Mecca, China, and Mali. What commonalities are found in each description? What does he find to praise? What does he condemn?

2. Using his descriptions as evidence, what were some of the underlying motives that inspired his travels? In what ways might these motives shape or distort his observations?

3. Identify the most important assumptions, values, or attitudes that helped shape his assessments about other cultures. Is it possible to be an "objective" world traveler?

4. Given his selective observations and value judgments, can Ibn Battuta's travel accounts be used as a reliable source of historical information?

5. Imagine that Ibn Battuta had been able to visit France or England during his travels. What kind of observations do you think he might have made? Would he have had a favorable impression of Europe during this time period? Why?

MY TRAVELS (1355)

Ibn Battuta

I left Tangier, my birthplace, on June 14, 1325, being at that time twenty-one years of age with the intention of making the Pilgrimage to the Holy House [at Mecca] and the Tomb of the Prophet [at Medina].

I set out alone, finding no companion to cheer the way with friendly intercourse, and no party of travelers with whom to associate myself. Swayed by an overmastering impulse within me, and a long-cherished desire to visit those glorious sanctuaries, I resolved to quit all my friends and tear myself away from my home. As my parents were still alive, it weighed grievously upon me to part from them, and both they and I were afflicted with sorrow. . . .

Visiting the Holy Sites of Medina & Mecca

[One] evening . . . we entered the holy sanctuary and reached the illustrious mosque, halting in salutation at the Gate of Peace; then we prayed in the illustrious garden between the tomb of the Prophet and the noble pulpit, and reverently touched the fragment that remains of the palm-trunk against which the Prophet stood when he preached. Having paid our respects to the lord of men from first to last, the intercessor for sinners, the Prophet of Mecca, Muhammad . . . we returned to our camp, rejoicing at this great favor bestowed upon us, praising God for our having reached the former abodes and the magnificent sanctuaries of His Holy Prophet, and praying [to] Him to grant that this visit should not be our last and that we might be of those whose pilgrimage is accepted.

On this journey, our stay at Medina lasted four days. We used to spend every night in the illustrious mosque, where the people, after forming circles in the courtyard and, lighting large numbers of candles, would pass the time either in reciting the Koran from volumes set on rests in front of them, or in intoning litanies, or in visiting

Source: Ibn Battuta, *Travels in Asia and Africa, 1325–1354,* trans. H. A. R. Gibb (London: Routledge, 1929), 43, 74–76, 282–84, 292, 321–25, 329.

the sanctuaries of the holy tomb. . . . We departed at night . . . with hearts full of joy at reaching the goal of our hopes, and in the morning arrived at the City of Surety, Mecca (may God ennoble her!), where we immediately entered the holy sanctuary and began the rites of pilgrimage.

The inhabitants of Mecca are distinguished by many excellent and noble activities and qualities, by their beneficence to the humble and weak, and by their kindness to strangers. When any of them makes a feast, he begins by giving food to the religious devotees who are poor and without resources, inviting them first with kindness and delicacy. The majority of these unfortunates are to be found by the public bakeries, and when anyone has his bread baked and takes it away to his house, they follow him and he gives each one of them some share of it, sending away none disappointed. Even if he has but a single loaf, he gives away a third or a half of it, cheerfully and without any ill-feeling.

Another good habit of theirs is this. The orphan children sit in the bazaar, each with two baskets, one large and one small. When one of the townspeople comes to the bazaar and buys cereals, meat and vegetables, he hands them to one of these boys, who puts the cereals in one basket and the meat and vegetables in the other and takes them to the man's house, so that his meal may be prepared. Meanwhile the man goes about his devotions and his business. There is no instance of any of the boys having ever abused their trust in this matter, and they are given a fixed fee of a few coppers.

The Meccans are very elegant and clean in their dress, and most of them wear white garments, which you always see fresh and snowy. They use a great deal of perfume and kohl and make free use of toothpicks of green arak-wood. The Meccan women are extraordinarily beautiful and very pious and modest. They too make great use of perfumes to such a degree that they will spend the night hungry in order to buy perfumes with the price of their food. They visit the mosque every Thursday night, wearing their finest apparel; and the whole sanctuary is saturated with the smell of their perfume. When one of these women goes away the odor of the perfume clings to the place after she has gone.

Voyage to China

The land of China is of vast extent, and abounding in produce, fruits, gold, and silver. In this respect there is no country in the world that can rival it. It is traversed by the river called the "Water of Life."* It is bordered by villages, fields, fruit gardens, and bazaars, just like the Egyptian Nile, only that [China] is even more richly cultivated and populous. . . . All of the fruits we have in our country are to be found here, either the same or better quality. . . . [As for Chinese pottery], it is exported to India and other countries, even reaching us as far as our own lands in the West, and it is the finest of all makes of pottery.

The Chinese themselves are infidels, who worship idols and burn their dead like the Hindus. The king of China is a Tatar [Mongol], one of the descendants of Genghis Khan. In every Chinese city there is a quarter for Muslims, in which they live by themselves, and in which they have mosques both for Friday services and for other religious

---

*Most scholars believe that Ibn Battuta is referring to China's "Grand Canal," one of the world's oldest (begun in 486 BCE) and largest (over 1,000 miles long) man-made waterways.

purposes. The Muslims are honored and respected. The Chinese infidels eat the flesh of swine and dogs, and sell it in their markets. They are wealthy folk and well-to-do, but they make no display [of wealth] in their food or their clothes. You will see a principal merchant, a man so rich that his wealth cannot be counted, wearing a coarse cotton tunic. But one thing that the Chinese do take a pride in is gold and silver plate. Everyone of them carries a stick, on which they lean in walking, and which they call the third leg. . . .

The land of China, in spite of all that is agreeable in it, did not attract me. On the contrary, I was sorely grieved that heathendom had such a strong hold over it. Whenever I went out of my house I used to see any number of revolting things, and that distressed me so much that I used to keep indoors and go out only in case of necessity. When I met Muslims in China, I always felt just as though I were meeting with my own faith and kin. . . .

Travels to the Kingdom of Mali in West Africa

When I decided to make the journey to Mali, which is reached in twenty-four days from Walata [an oasis in the Sahara] if the traveler pushes on rapidly, I hired a guide . . . for there is no necessity to travel in a company on account of the safety of that road, and set out with three of my companions. . . .

A traveler in this country carries no provisions, whether plain food or seasonings, and neither gold nor silver. He takes nothing but pieces of salt and glass ornaments, which the people call beads, and some aromatic goods. When he comes to a village the womenfolk of the blacks bring out millet, milk, chickens, pulped fruit, rice . . . and pounded beans. The traveler buys whatever of these foods he wants. . . .

Thus I reached the city of Mali, the capital of the king of the blacks. I stopped at the cemetery and went to the quarter occupied by the whites [Arab merchants], where I asked for Muhammad ibn al-Faqih. I found that he had hired a house for me and went there. His son-in-law brought me candles and food, and next day Ibn al-Faqih himself came to visit me, with other prominent residents. I met the judge of Mali, Abd ar-Rahman, who came to see me; he is a Negro, a devout Muslim, and a man of fine character. I met also the interpreter Dugha, who is one of the principal men among the blacks. All these persons sent me hospitality gifts of food and treated me with the utmost generosity. May God reward them for their kindnesses! . . .

The sultan of Mali is Mansa Sulayman, "mansa" meaning [in Mandingo*] sultan, and Sulayman being his proper name. He is a miserly king, not a man from whom one might hope for a rich present. It happened that I spent these two months without seeing him, on account of my illness. Later on he held a banquet . . . to which the commanders, doctors, judges, and preachers were invited, and I went along with them. Reading desks were brought in, and the Koran was read through, then they prayed for . . . Mansa Sulayman.

When the ceremony was over I went forward and saluted Mansa Sulayman. The judge, the preacher, and [my host] Ibn al-Faqih told him who I was, and he answered them in their tongue. They said to me, "The sultan says to you 'Give thanks to God,'"

---

*Mandingo is an African language spoken by the Malinke people who reside in the grasslands south of the Sahara Desert.

so I said, "Praise be to God and thanks under all circumstances." When I withdrew, the [sultan's] welcoming gift was sent to me. . . . Ibn al-Faqih came hurrying out of his house barefooted, and entered my room saying, "Stand up; here comes the sultan's gift to you." So I stood up, thinking that it would consist of robes of honor and money, and behold! It was three cakes of bread, and a piece of beef fried in native oil, and a calabash of sour curds. When I saw this I burst out laughing, and thought it a most amazing thing that they could be so foolish and make so much of such a paltry matter. . . .

The Negroes possess some admirable qualities. They are seldom unjust, and have a greater abhorrence of injustice than any other people. Their sultan shows no mercy to anyone who is guilty of the least act of it. There is complete security in their country. Neither traveler nor inhabitant in it has anything to fear from robbers or men of violence. They do not confiscate the property of any white man who dies in their country, even if it be uncounted wealth. On the contrary, they give it into the charge of some trustworthy person among the whites, until the rightful heir takes possession of it. They are careful to observe the hours of prayer, and assiduous in attending them in congregations, and in bringing up their children to them. On Fridays, if a man does not go early to the mosque, he cannot find a corner to pray in, on account of the crowd. It is a custom of theirs to send each man his boy [to the mosque] with his prayer-mat; the boy spreads it out for his master in a place befitting him [and remains on it] until he comes to the mosque. Their prayer-mats are made of the leaves of a tree resembling a date-palm, but without fruit.

Another of their good qualities is their habit of wearing clean white garments on Fridays. Even if a man has nothing but an old worn shirt, he washes it and cleans it, and wears it to the Friday service. Yet another is their zeal for learning the Koran by heart. They put their children in chains if they show any backwardness in memorizing it, and they are not set free until they have it by heart. I visited the *qadi* [judge] in his house on the day of the festival. His children were chained up, so I said to him, "Will you not let them loose?" He replied, "I shall not do so until they learn the Koran by heart."

Among their bad qualities are the following. The women servants, slave-girls, and young girls go about in front of everyone naked, without a stitch of clothing on them. Women go into the sultan's presence naked and without coverings, and his daughters also go about naked. Then there is their custom of putting dust and ashes on their heads, as a mark of respect, and the grotesque ceremonies we have described when the poets recite their verses. Another reprehensible practice among many of them is the eating of carrion, dogs, and asses.

THE CHINESE NAVAL EXPEDITIONS OF ZHENG HE

In 1935, a Chinese official in Fujian province found a long-forgotten stone tablet that recounted one of the greatest series of naval expeditions in world history. The tablet briefly describes the seven voyages of the Chinese admiral, explorer, and diplomat Zheng He (1371–1435), who traveled as far as Arabia and the east coast of Africa and visited more than thirty present-day countries. Born in 1371 in Yunnan (Kunyang) province, he was drafted at age ten to serve as an orderly in the army, which had just succeeded in overthrowing the Mongols and reestablishing Chinese authority under the Ming dynasty. Under the command of the Prince of Yen, Zheng He rose rapidly in rank, proving himself strong, loyal, ambitious, and a skilled junior officer. In 1403, when the Prince of Yen seized the Celestial Throne from a rival, Zheng He fought bravely on his behalf and was rewarded with an administrative position within the royal household. Two years later, he was promoted to commander in chief of one of the largest flotillas in world history.

From 1405 to 1422, Zheng He led six different expeditions that took him as far as Java, Sumatra, Vietnam, India, and Arabia and to trading centers in east Africa (see Map 15.3). For the most part, these were diplomatic missions, centered on the exchange of ambassadors, presents, and tribute. Among the gifts he brought back to China for the Yongle Emperor[10] were giraffes and lions. In exchange for tribute, Zheng He presented gifts from the emperor that included finely made porcelain dishes, rare silks, precious metals, and manufactured goods. But in places where the local "barbarians" did not adequately show deference and respect to representatives of the Celestial Empire, Zheng He and his crew used their power to impose their will on others.

When the Yongle Emperor died in 1424, Zheng He lost his most important ally and benefactor. Although he made one last great voyage in 1431, subsequent Ming emperors turned their primary attention to overland ventures and defense, most notably the construction of the Great Wall. To underscore their change in foreign policy, court officials destroyed the official travel logs of Zheng He, leaving us with only the stone tablet inscriptions and some notes kept by his crew as evidence of his achievements. The last years of his life also remain shrouded in mystery, and it is believed that he died in 1435 at the age of sixty-five.

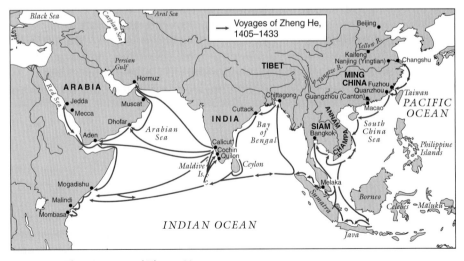

Map 15.3 The Voyages of Zheng He

1. According to the inscription, what were the goals of the voyages? In what ways might the Ming dynasty have hoped to benefit from these expeditions?

2. What role was played by the Celestial goddess? How did religious beliefs shape Zheng He's perceptions of his mission and his relations with others? How did it motivate him to leave a record of his voyages?

3. What kinds of interactions did Zheng He have with the peoples he encountered? What factors explain his different experiences and reactions?

4. In his voyage to China, Ibn Battuta was impressed with the economy and society but criticized their "heathen" practices. How might Zheng He, himself a Muslim, have responded?

5. After 1431, the Chinese abruptly stopped their overseas voyages. Based on Zheng He's account, what might have happened if they had continued into the next century? Would they have altered world history in a significant manner? What might have been different if China had "discovered" Europe, instead of Europe "discovering" China?

INSCRIPTION OF WORLD VOYAGES

Zheng He

A record of the miraculous answer [to prayer] to the goddess the Celestial Spouse.*

The Imperial Ming Dynasty unifying seas and continents, surpassing the three dynasties even goes beyond the Han and Tang dynasties. The countries beyond the horizon and from the ends of the earth have all become subjects and to the most western of the western or the most northern of the northern countries, however far they may be, the distance and the routes may be calculated. Thus the barbarians from beyond the seas, though their countries are truly distant . . . have come to audience bearing precious objects and presents.

The Emperor, approving of their loyalty and sincerity, has ordered us, Zheng He and others at the head of several tens of thousands of officers and flag-troops to ascend more than one hundred large ships to go and confer presents on them in order to make manifest the transforming power of the (imperial) virtue and to treat distant people with kindness. From the third year of Yongle† [1405] till now we have seven times received the commission of ambassadors to countries of the western ocean. The barbarian countries which we have visited are Zhancheng [Vietnam], Zhaowa [Java,

---

Source: Teobaldo Filesi, *China and Africa in the Middle Ages,* trans. David Morison, 1972, 61–65. Reprinted by Frank Cass Publishers.

*The Celestial Spouse was a goddess in Taoism, one of the major religions of China. She was considered to be the protector of travelers on the sea.

†In these inscriptions, years are measured by the emperor's reign.

Indonesia], Sanfoqi [Sumatra, Indonesia], and Xianlo [Siam] crossing straight over to Xilanshan [Sri Lanka] in South India, Calicut [India], and Kezhi [India], we have gone to the western regions of Hulumosi [Ormuz], Aden [Yemen], Mogadishu [Somalia], altogether more than thirty countries large and small. We have traversed more than one hundred thousand *li** of immense water spaces and have beheld in the ocean huge waves like mountains rising sky-high, and we have set eyes on barbarian regions far away hidden in a blue transparency of light vapors, while our sails loftily unfurled like clouds day and night continued their course rapidly like that of a star, traversing those savage waves as if we were treading a public thoroughfare. Truly this was due to the majesty and the good fortune of the Imperial Court and moreover we owe it to the protecting virtue of the divine Celestial Spouse.

The power of the goddess having indeed been manifested in previous times has been abundantly revealed in the present generation. In the midst of the rushing waters it happened that, when there was a hurricane, suddenly there was a divine lantern shining in the mast, and as soon as this miraculous light appeared[†] the danger was appeased, so that even in the danger of capsizing one felt reassured that there was no cause for fear. When we arrived in the distant countries we captured alive those of the native kings who were not respectful and exterminated those barbarian robbers who were engaged in piracy, so that consequently the sea route was cleansed and pacified and the natives put their trust in it. All this is due to the favors of the goddess.

It is not easy to enumerate completely all the cases where the goddess has answered [my prayers]. Previously in a memorial to the Court we have requested that her virtue be recognized . . . and a temple be built at Nanking on the bank of the river where regular sacrifices should be made forever. We have respectfully received an Imperial commemoration exalting her miraculous favors, which is the highest recompense and praise indeed. However, the miraculous power of the goddess resides wherever one goes. . . .

We have received the high favor of a gracious commission from our sacred Lord [the Yongle Emperor], we carry to the distant barbarians the benefits of respect and good faith [on their part]. Commanding the multitudes on the fleet and being responsible for a quantity of money and valuables in the face of the violence of the winds and the nights, our one fear is not to be able to succeed. How, then, dare we not to serve our dynasty with . . . all our loyalty and the gods with the utmost sincerity? How would it be possible not to realize what is the source of the tranquillity of the fleet and the troops and the salvation on the voyage both going and returning? Therefore, we have inscribed the virtue of the [Celestial Spouse] on stone and have also recorded the years and months of the voyages to the barbarian countries . . . in order to leave the memory forever.

---

*Scholars estimated that Zheng He traveled over 35,000 miles during his seven voyages.

†Scholars believe that this miraculous light may have been St. Elmo's fire, static electricity that is not an uncommon sight to seafarers. Because the sailors had prayed to the Taoist goddess, they believed that the light was a sign of her beneficent protection. This helps explain why Zheng He later placed a pillar of thanksgiving at the Temple of the Celestial Spouse in Fujian province.

I. In the third year of Yongle [1405] commanding the fleet we went to Calicut [India] and other countries. At that time the pirate Chen Zuyi had gathered his followers in the country of Sanfoqi [island of Sumatra], where he plundered the native merchants. When he also advanced to resist our fleet, supernatural soldiers secretly came to the rescue so that after one beating of the drum he was annihilated. In the fifth year [1407] we returned.

II. In the fifth year of Yongle [1407] commanding the fleet we went to Zhaowa [Java], Calicut, Kezhi [India], and Xianle [Siam]. The kings of these countries all sent as tribute precious objects, precious birds and rare animals. In the seventh year [1409] we returned.

III. In the seventh year of Yongle [1409] commanding the fleet we went to the countries (visited) before and took our route by the country of Xilanshan [Sri Lanka]. Its king Alagakkonara was guilty of a gross lack of respect and plotted against the fleet. Owing to the manifest answer to prayer of the goddess, [the plot] was discovered and thereupon that king was captured alive. In the ninth year [1411] on our return the captured king was presented [to the throne as a prisoner]; subsequently he received the Imperial [forgiveness and] favor of returning to his own country.

IV. In the eleventh year of Yongle [1413] commanding the fleet we went to Hulumosi [Ormuz] and other countries. In the country of Samudra [northern tip of Sumatra] there was a false king [named Sekandar] who was marauding and invading his country. The [true] king [Zaynu-'l-Abidin] had sent an envoy to the Palace Gates in order to lodge a complaint. We went there with the official troops under our command and exterminated some and arrested [other rebels], and owing to the silent aid of the goddess, we captured the false king alive. In the thirteenth year [1415] on our return he was presented [to the Emperor as a prisoner]. In that year the king of the country of Manlajia [Malacca, Malaysia] came in person with his wife and son to present tribute.

V. In the fifteenth year of Yongle [1417] commanding the fleet we visited the western regions. The country of Ormuz presented lions, leopards with gold spots and large western horses. The country of Aden [Yemen] presented [giraffes], as well as the long-horned [oryx]. The country of Mogadishu [Somalia] presented [zebras] as well as lions. The country of Brava [Somalia or Kenya] presented camels which run one thousand *li,* as well as camel-birds [ostriches]. The countries of Zhaowa [Java] and Calicut [India] presented animal *miligao* [hides]. They all vied in presenting the marvelous objects preserved in the mountains or hidden in the seas and the beautiful treasures buried in the sand or deposited on the shores. Some sent a maternal uncle of the king, others a paternal uncle or a younger brother of the king in order to present a letter of homage written on gold leaf as well as tribute.

VI. In the nineteenth year of Yongle [1421] commanding the fleet we escorted the ambassadors from Ormuz and the other countries who had been in attendance at the capital for a long time back to their countries. The kings of all these countries prepared even more tribute than previously.

VII. In the sixth year of Exeunt* [1431] once more commanding the fleet we have left for the barbarian countries in order to read to them [an Imperial edict] and to confer presents.

We have anchored in this port awaiting a north wind to take the sea, and recalling how previously we have on several occasions received the benefits of the protection of the divine intelligence we have thus recorded an inscription in stone.

VASCO DA GAMA'S VOYAGE TO AFRICA AND INDIA

Vasco da Gama's (1460–1524) two voyages to India (1497–1498; 1502–1503) are significant because they initiated direct and profitable trading routes between Europe and Asia that marked the beginning of a new phase of global commerce. Equally important, they foreshadow the use of European military power to assert its economic and political interests in new areas of the world. In both regards, Vasco da Gama played a central and pivotal role.

Born into the Portuguese nobility in 1460, da Gama received an education in mathematics and navigation and then followed his father (and most aristocrats) into the military, where he proved himself an effective officer. In the mid-1490s, when King John of Portugal ordered a naval expedition to India to open up trade, outflank the Muslims, and find new Christian allies, Vasco da Gama was placed in command of the fleet. In stark contrast to the large armada led by Zheng He more than a century earlier, da Gama had only four ships and less than two hundred men under his command when he left Lisbon in July 1497 (Map 15.4).

Five months later, as the ships rounded the tip of southern Africa, two of his vessels were leaking and many of the crew were sick with scurvy.[11] He therefore stopped along the coast of east Africa for fresh food and repairs and took the opportunity to visit some of the wealthy Swahili city-states (Mozambique, Mombasa [Kenya], Mylanta [Kenya]) that had been engaged in maritime trade with Arabia, Persia, and India for centuries.[12] But as the journal describes in great detail, the Portuguese visit to these city-states was not entirely successful nor amicable, and da Gama was frustrated in his failure to locate the lost Christian kingdom of Prester John. After a 23-day voyage across the Indian Ocean, da Gama became the first European to reach Calicut, one of the most important commercial ports of India. But his efforts to arrange a business pact with the local Hindu ruler proved unsuccessful because of mutual suspicions, the hostility of local Muslim government advisors and merchants, and, most interestingly, the general lack of interest in European trade goods. Misfortune followed da Gama after his departure from India: bad winds caused a very slow return, and many of his crew died of scurvy. Despite these setbacks, his return to Portugal in 1499 was accompanied

---

*The Emperor Zhu Zhang ordered one final voyage planned for 1431, the sixth year of his reign.

by a hero's welcome, and his prized and profitable cargoes of spices and jewels encouraged additional commercial ventures and investments.

In 1502, Vasco da Gama returned to east Africa and India with a larger, better armed fleet at his disposal. His primary mission was to avenge the murder of several Portuguese seamen who had visited Calicut in the intervening years, but his subsequent actions suggest that he was equally intent upon establishing Portuguese supremacy in the Indian Ocean. Arriving back at the east African city-state of Mombasa, da Gama threatened to burn the town and destroy its Muslim inhabitants if they did not submit to Portuguese authority (which they promptly did). The fleet then sailed to Calicut, where the Portuguese admiral demanded that all Muslims be banished from the port. To demonstrate his determination and strength, he then bombarded the city with cannon fire and routed the Muslim ships that tried to put up a fight. Following his return to Portugal in 1503, he seems to have lived in relative obscurity until called to duty again in 1524 to become a diplomat at one of the permanent outposts that the Portuguese had established in India in the meantime. But shortly after his arrival in India, he died suddenly and unexpectedly.

The original written sea logs of Vasco da Gama disappeared and are lost. Consequently, the only detailed account we possess was written by a crew member of the expedition. Although his exact identity remains somewhat a mystery, his account has been mostly verified by comparison with some of da Gama's letters and Portuguese government documents from that era. The excerpts that follow describe da Gama's experiences in the city-states of east Africa, as well as his misadventures in India. In both instances, it is valuable to examine Portuguese motives and perceptions of others, and how these shaped their particular experiences.

QUESTIONS TO CONSIDER

1. What kinds of observations and impressions are recorded in the journal? Are these shaped more by Vasco da Gama's motives and preexisting cultural values or by actual experiences? How important is physical appearance in making cultural judgments?

2. What role did religion play in shaping Portuguese motives and their views of others? How were religious beliefs used to justify their actions?

3. Why did the Swahili and Indians show such little interest in Portuguese trade goods and gifts? What dilemma did this cause? What might have been a solution to this problem?

4. In Africa and Asia, the Portuguese encountered both hospitality and hostility. What might have explained the varying reaction? To what degree, if any, did the Portuguese bring this hostility upon themselves?

5. How would you describe the cross-cultural attitudes formed during da Gama's first voyage? What kind of future relations did they portend?

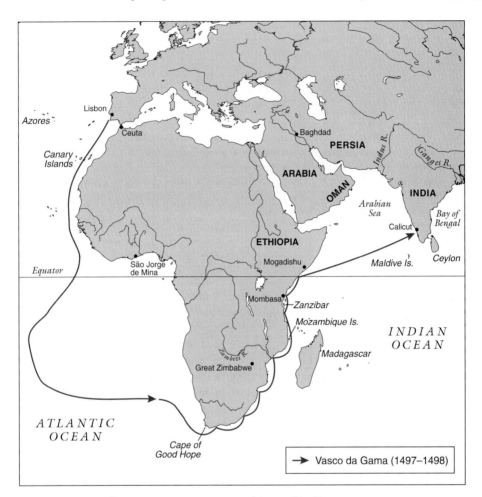

Map 15.4 Vasco da Gama's First Voyage to Africa and India

A JOURNAL OF THE FIRST VOYAGE OF VASCO DA GAMA (1497–1499)

In the name of God. Amen. In the year 1497, King Dom Manuel . . . despatched four vessels to make discoveries and go in search of spices. Vasco da Gama was the captain of these vessels. . . .

1497. Mozambique. The people of this country are of ruddy complexion and well made. They are Muhammadans [Muslims], and their language is the same as

Source: A Journal of the First Voyage of Vasco da Gama, 1497–1499, trans. E. Ravenstein, Hakluyt Society Series 1, vol. 99 (London: The Hakluyt Society, 1898), 22–25, 28–30, 34–36, 37–38, 48–68.

that of the Moors.* Their dresses are of fine linen or cotton stuffs, with variously colored stripes, and of rich and elaborate workmanship. They all wear robes with borders of silk embroidered in gold. They are merchants, and have transactions with white Moors,† four of whose vessels were at the time in port, laden with gold, silver, cloves, pepper, ginger, and silver rings, as also with quantities of pearls, jewels, and rubies, all of which are used by the people of this country. We understood them to say that all these things, with the exception of the gold, were brought thither by these Moors; and that further on to where we were going, they abounded, and that precious stones, pearls and spices were so plentiful that there was no need to purchase them as they could be collected in baskets. All this we learned through a sailor the Captain [Vasco da Gama] had with him, and who, having formerly been a prisoner among the Moors, understood their language.

These Moors, moreover, told us that along the route which we were about to follow we should meet . . . many cities along the coast, and also an island, where one half the population consisted of Moors and the other half of Christians, who were at war with each other. This island was said to be very wealthy. We were told, moreover, that Prester John resided not far from this place; that he held many cities along the coast, and that the inhabitants of those cities were great merchants and owned big ships. The residence of Prester John was said to be far in the interior, and could be reached only on the back of camels. . . . This information, and many other things which we heard, rendered us so happy that we cried with joy, and prayed God to grant us health, so that we might behold what we so much desired.

In this place and island of Mozambique, there resided a chief who had the title of Sultan. He often came aboard our ships attended by some of his people. The Captain gave him many good things to eat, and made him a present of hats, shirts, corals and many other articles. He was, however, so proud that he treated all we gave him with contempt, and asked for scarlet cloth, of which we had none. We gave him, however, of all the things we had. . . . During our stay here the Sultan of Mozambique sent word that he wanted to make peace with us and to be our friend. His ambassador was a white Moor and a nobleman, and at the same time a great drunkard. . . .

One evening, as we left the ship for the mainland to obtain drinking water, we saw about twenty men on the beach. They were armed with spears, and forbade our landing. After the Captain heard this, he ordered three bombards [small cannon] to be fired upon them, so that we might land. Having effected our landing, these men fled into the bush, and we took as much water as we wanted. [The next day], a Moor rowed out to our ships, and told us that if we wanted more drinking water, that we should go for it, suggesting that we would encounter more trouble and be forced to turn back. The Captain no sooner heard this [threat] than he resolved to go, in order to show that we were able to do them harm if we desired it. We then armed our boats, placing bombards in their poops, and started for the shore. The Moors had constructed [a defensive wall] by lashing planks together . . . [but as we approached] they were at the time walking along the beach, armed with spears, knives, bows, and slingshots,

---

*The Portuguese are describing the Swahili people of east Africa.

†"White Moors" was a term used to identify Muslim Arabs.

with which they hurled stones at us. But our bombards soon made it so hot for them that they fled behind their walls, but this turned out to their injury rather than their profit. During the three hours that we were occupied in this manner [bombarding the beach] we saw at least two men killed, one on the beach and the other behind the wall. When we were weary of this work we retired to our ships to dine. . . .

[Vasco da Gama and his fleet left Mozambique shortly thereafter and arrived two weeks later at the Swahili city-state of Mombasa.]

On Saturday, we cast anchor off Mombasa, but did not enter the port. . . . In front of the city there lay numerous vessels, all dressed in flags.* And we, anxious not to be outdone, also dressed our ships, and we actually surpassed their show. . . . We anchored here with much pleasure, for we confidently hoped that on the following day we might go on land and hear [Catholic] mass jointly with the Christians reported to live there in a neighborhood separate from that of the Moors. . . .

But those who had told us [about the Christians] had said it [to trap us], for it was not true. At midnight there approached us a *dhow* with about a hundred men, all armed with cutlasses and shields. When they came to the vessel of the Captain they attempted to board her, armed as they were, but this was not permitted, only four or five of the most distinguished men among them being allowed on board. They remained about a couple of hours, and it seemed to us that they paid us this visit merely to find out whether they might not capture one or the other of our vessels. . . .

[The next day] the King of Mombasa sent the Captain a sheep and large quantities of oranges, lemons and sugar-cane, together with a ring, as a pledge of safety, letting him know that in case of his entering the port he would be supplied with all he stood in need of. . . . The Captain sent the king a string of coral-beads as a return present, and let him know that he planned to enter the port on the following day. . . . Two men were sent by the Captain to the king, still further to confirm these peaceful assurances. . . . The king received them hospitably, and ordered that they should be shown the city. . . . When they had seen all, the king sent them back with samples of cloves, pepper and sorghum, articles he would allow us to purchase and load on our ships. . . .

That evening, the Captain questioned two Moors whom we had captured, by dropping boiling oil upon their skin, so that they might confess to any treachery intended against us. They said that orders had been given to capture us as soon as we entered the port, and thus to avenge what we had done at Mozambique. And when this torture was being applied a second time, one of the Moors, although his hands were tied, threw himself into the sea, whilst the other did so during the morning watch.

About midnight two *dhows*, with many men in them, approached. The *dhows* stood off whilst the men entered the water, swimming in the direction of our ships. . . . Our men on watch thought at first that they were fish, but when they perceived their mistake they shouted to the other vessels. They [Moors] had already boarded one ship and got hold of the rigging of the mizzen-mast, but seeing themselves discovered,

---

*The Swahili traditionally "dress" their vessels with flags and pennants to mark the feast that ends the month-long fast of Ramadan. Ramadan is an important Islamic holiday that commemorates Allah's gift of the Qur'an to mankind, a time when Muslims fast and spend more time concentrating on their faith.

they silently slipped down and fled. These and other wicked tricks were practiced upon us by these dogs, but our Lord did not allow them to succeed, because they were unbelievers.

[After a 23-day voyage across the Indian Ocean, aided by a Muslim navigator lent by the Sultan of Mozambique, the Portuguese arrived at Calicut, one of the most prosperous and important trading centers in southern India. Although the local ruler and much of the population were Hindu, there were also many merchants, traders, and government officials who were Muslims.]

After we were at anchor, four boats approached us from the land, and they asked of what nation we were. We told them, and they then pointed out Calicut to us. . . . The city of Calicut is inhabited by Christians.* They are of tawny complexion. Some of them have big beards and long hair, whilst others clip their hair short or shave the head, merely allowing a tuft to remain on the crown as a sign that they are Christians. They also wear moustaches. They pierce the ears and wear much gold in them. They go naked down to the waist, covering their lower extremities with very fine cotton stuffs. But it is only the most respectable who do this, for the others manage as best they are able.† The women of this country, as a rule, are ugly and of small stature. They wear many jewels of gold round the neck, numerous bracelets on their arms, and rings set with precious stones on their toes. All these people are well-disposed and apparently of mild temper. At first sight they seem covetous and ignorant. . . .

When we arrived at Calicut the king was away. The Captain sent two men to him with a message, informing him that an ambassador had arrived from the King of Portugal with letters. . . . [The king] sent word to the Captain bidding him welcome [and sent] a pilot . . . with orders to take us to [an anchorage] in front of the city of Calicut. We were told that the anchorage at the place to which we were to go was good . . . and that it was customary for the ships which came to this country to anchor there for the sake of safety. We ourselves did not feel comfortable . . . and we did not anchor as near the shore as the king's pilot desired. . . .

On the following morning . . . the Captain set out to speak to the king, and took with him thirteen men. We put on our best attire, put bombards [small cannon] in our boats, and took with us trumpets and many flags. On landing, the Captain was received by government officials, along with a crowd of many men, armed and unarmed. The reception was friendly, as if the people were pleased to see us, though at first appearances looked threatening, for they carried naked swords in their hands. A palanquin‡ was provided for the captain, such as is used by men of distinction in that country. . . . When we arrived [at the king's palace], men of much distinction and great lords came out to meet the Captain, and joined those who were already in attendance upon him. . . .

---

*With no prior knowledge of Indian culture or religion, Vasco da Gama and his crew mistook Hindus for Christians.

†The differences in dress witnessed by the Portuguese were most likely related to the caste system prevalent in Indian society.

‡A palanquin is a mode of transportation consisting of a chair mounted on poles and carried on the shoulders of four to six men.

The king was in a small court, reclining upon a couch covered with a cloth of green velvet, above which was a good mattress, and upon this again a sheet of cotton stuff, very white and fine, more so than any linen. . . . The Captain, on entering, saluted in the manner of the country: by putting the hands together, then raising them towards Heaven, as is done by Christians when addressing God, and immediately afterwards opening them and shutting fists quickly. . . .

And the Captain told him he was the ambassador of the King of Portugal, who was Lord of many countries and the possessor of great wealth of every description, exceeding that of any king of these parts; that for a period of sixty years his people had annually sent out vessels to make discoveries in the direction of India, as they knew that there were Christian kings there like themselves. This, he said, was the reason which induced them to order this country to be discovered, not because they sought for gold or silver, for of this they had such abundance that they needed not what was to be found in this country. . . . There reigned a king now whose name was Dom Manuel, who had ordered [da Gama] to build three vessels, of which he had been appointed Captain, and who had ordered him not to return to Portugal until he should have discovered this King of the Christians, on pain of having his head cut off. That two letters had been intrusted to him to be presented in case he succeeded in discovering him . . . and, finally, he had been instructed to say by word of mouth that he [the King of Portugal] desired to be his friend and brother.

In reply to this the king said that he was welcome; that, on his part, he held him as a friend and brother, and would send ambassadors with him to Portugal. . . . These and many other things passed between the two in this chamber, and as it was already late in the night, the king asked the Captain with whom he desired to lodge, with Christians or with Moors? And the Captain replied, neither with Christians nor with Moors, and begged as a favor that he be given a lodging by himself. The king said he would order it thus, upon which the Captain took leave of the king and came to where his men were. . . .

By that time four hours of the night had already gone . . . and the time occupied in passing through the city was so long that the captain at last grew tired, and complained to the king's advisor, a Moor of distinction, who attended him to the lodgings. The Moor then took him to his own house, and we were admitted to a court within it. . . . Many carpets had been spread, and there were two large candlesticks like those at the Royal palace. . . .

[The next morning], the captain got ready the following gifts to be sent to the king: twelve pieces of *lambel*,* four scarlet hoods, six hats, four strings of coral, a case containing six wash-hand basins, a case of sugar, two casks of oil, and two of honey. And as it is the custom not to send anything to the king without the knowledge of the Moor [his financial advisor], and other officials, the Captain informed them of his intention. They came, and when they saw the present they laughed at it, saying that it was not a thing to offer to a king, that the poorest merchant from Mecca, or any other part of India, gave more, and that if he wanted to make a present it should be in gold, as the king would not accept such things. When the Captain heard this he grew sad, and said that he had brought no gold, that, moreover, he was no merchant, but an ambassador; that he gave of that which he had, which was his own private gift and

---

*Striped cotton cloth.

not the king's; that if the King of Portugal ordered him to return he would intrust him with far richer presents; and that if the king would not accept these things he would send them back to the ships. Upon this they [the government officials] declared that they would not forward his presents, nor consent to his forwarding them himself. When they had gone there came certain Moorish merchants, and they all mocked the presents which the Captain desired to be sent to the king.

When the Captain saw that they were determined not to forward his presents, he [asked] to speak to the king, and would then return to the ships. [The officials] approved of this, and told [the Captain] that if he would wait a short time they would return and accompany him to the palace. And the Captain waited all day, but they never came back. The Captain was very angry at being among so phlegmatic and unreliable a people, and intended, at first, to go to the palace without them. On further consideration, however, he thought it best to wait until the following day. . . .

On Wednesday morning the Moors returned, and took the captain to the palace. The palace was crowded with armed men. Our Captain was kept waiting . . . for fully four long hours, outside a door, which was only opened when the king sent word to admit him. . . . The king said that he [the Captain] had claimed that he came from a very rich kingdom, and yet had brought him nothing; that he had also told him that he was the bearer of a letter, which had not yet been delivered. To this the Captain rejoined that he had brought nothing, because the object of his voyage was merely to make discoveries, but that when other ships came he would then see what they brought him; as to the letter, it was true that he had brought one, and would deliver it immediately.

The king then asked what it was he had come to discover: stones or men? If he came to discover men, as [the Captain] had claimed, why had he brought nothing? Moreover, he had been told that [the ships] carried . . . the golden image of a Santa Maria. The Captain said that the Santa Maria was not of gold, and that even if she were he would not part with her, as she had guided him across the ocean, and would guide him back to his own country. . . .

The king then asked what kind of merchandise was to be found in [Portugal]. The Captain said there was much corn, cloth, iron, bronze, and many other things. The king asked whether he had any merchandise with him. The captain replied that he had a little of each sort, as samples, and that if permitted to return to the ships he would order it to be landed, and that meantime four or five men would remain at the lodgings assigned them. The king refused [and was not interested]. The Captain might take all his people with him, securely moor his ships, land his merchandise, and attempt to sell it himself to the best advantage. Having taken leave of the king, the Captain returned to his lodgings, and we with him. As it was already late no attempt was made to depart that night.

[After two days of waiting], the Captain again asked for boats to take him to his ships. [The king's advisors] began to whisper among themselves, and said that we should have them if we would order our vessels to come nearer the shore. The Captain replied that if he ordered his vessels to approach his brother* would think that he was being held a prisoner, and would hoist the sails and return to Portugal. They said that if we refused to order the ships to come nearer we should not be permitted to

---

*Vasco da Gama's younger brother was second in command of the fleet.

leave . . . [and] they immediately closed all the doors, and many armed men entered to guard us, none of us being allowed to go outside without being accompanied by several of these guards. . . .

The Captain and we others felt very down-hearted, though outwardly we pretended not to notice what they did. . . . The Captain did not wish the ships to come within the port, for it seemed to him—as it did to us—that once inside they could easily be captured, after which they would first kill him, and us others, as we were already in their power. We passed all that day most anxiously. At night more people surrounded us than ever before, and we were no longer allowed to walk in the compound, within which we were, but confined within a small tiled court, with a multitude of people around us. We quite expected that on the following day we should be separated, or that some harm would befall us, for we noticed that our jailers were much annoyed with us. This, however, did not prevent our making a good supper off the things found in the village. Throughout that night we were guarded by over a hundred men, all armed with swords, two-edged battle-axes, shields, and bows and arrows. Whilst some of these slept, others kept guard, each taking his turn of duty throughout the night.

On the following day, these gentlemen [the Moors and government officials] came back, and this time they wore better faces. They told the Captain that . . . as it was the custom of the country that every ship on its arrival should at once land the merchandise it brought, as also the crews, and that the sellers should not return on board until the whole of it had been sold. The Captain consented, and said he would . . . see to its being done. They said this was well, and that immediately after the arrival of the merchandise he would be permitted to return to his ship. . . . At this there was great rejoicing, thanks being rendered to God for having extricated us from the hands of people who had no more sense than beasts. . . .

The merchants whom the king had sent . . . instead of buying our merchandise merely ridiculed it. The Moors no longer visited the house where the merchandise was, but they bore us no good-will, and they spat on the ground, saying "Portugal, Portugal." Indeed, from the very first they had sought to take and kill us. . . .

COLUMBUS'S FIRST VOYAGE TO THE "NEW WORLD"

Christopher Columbus (1451–1506) is probably the most famous—and infamous—explorer in world history. He has long been viewed as a heroic figure, a master navigator whose four voyages (1492–1504) across the Atlantic Ocean paved the way for the triumphant European exploration and colonization of the Americas, and his exploits have been celebrated with a national holiday, monuments and parades, and innumerable place names. But more recently, Columbus has been seen in a different, more critical perspective. He was a man driven by flawed and selfish motives, whose personal actions and ambitions opened the way for the European exploitation of the resources and peoples of the New World.

Unlike his contemporary Vasco da Gama, Columbus began life with humble origins. He was born in Genoa (Italy) in 1451, the eldest son of a Genoese wool-worker and small-time trader. He began his career on the seas in the Portuguese merchant marine, which took him as far as Iceland to the north and the coast of west Africa to the south. These experiences gave him invaluable navigation and sailing experience, and they fueled his curiosity and desire to find a western route to Asia. In 1484, he began seeking financial support for an Atlantic crossing, and he was rebuffed at least three times by the Portuguese and Spanish monarchs before he finally received support from King Fernando and Queen Ysabel in early 1492. In the initial contract, Columbus bargained to win promotion to admiral, admittance to the Spanish nobility, and a 10 percent claim to the riches of new lands discovered upon successful completion of the first voyage.

On August 3, 1492, Columbus set sail in three small ships with 120 crewmen. After a relatively uneventful voyage of thirty-three days, the fleet sighted the Bahama islands and then landed and explored parts of Cuba and Hispaniola (the island currently divided between Haiti and the Dominican Republic). With assistance of a local leader, he established a fort on Hispaniola called *Villa de Navidad* and left about forty crewmen there to guard it until his return. The Spanish monarchs were so impressed with Columbus's gifts of gold, spices, exotic birds, and human captives that he secured the financial backing for a second voyage. In 1493, Columbus left with a much larger flotilla of seventeen ships, filled with colonists, investors, and a small troop of cavalry. But his return to the fort at *Villa de Navidad* was too late, for he discovered the fort ruined and all of the crew gone.

Altogether, Columbus made four voyages across the Atlantic under the sponsorship of Fernando and Ysabel. By the end of the second voyage (1493–1496), he had sighted most of the Caribbean islands, and he rebuilt his base in Hispaniola. During the third and fourth trips (1498–1500; 1502–1504), Columbus explored the coasts of Central and South America, from present-day Honduras to Venezuela. But his last trip was marred by his difficulties with Spanish colonists, increased hostility from indigenous peoples, and his frustrating inability to discover the westward route to Asia. Back in Spain, his attempts to join the nobility and to recover his governorship of the "Indies" from King Fernando were unsuccessful. By many accounts, Columbus died a disappointed man.

The outcome of Columbus's voyages are open to interpretation and debate. His discoveries undoubtedly brought Europe and the Americas into sustained contact with each other and ultimately led to European immigration and the transplantation of their culture and values. But others might add that it also led to the exploitation and genocide of native Americans. On the island of Hispaniola, for example, Spanish actions against the indigenous population dramatically reduced their population from an estimated 250,000 in 1492 to under 500 by 1538. Moreover, the genocide of native Americans throughout the Caribbean, by conquest or disease, was one of the principal factors behind the importation of African slave labor in subsequent centuries.

We possess two accounts of Columbus's first voyage to the Americas, and excerpts from each are included in this chapter. The first source is the logbook kept by Columbus during the trip and presented in 1493 to the Spanish monarchs. The prologue to the log highlights his stated motives and objectives prior to his departure. The second source is a letter written by Columbus prior to his return, in which he summarized his discoveries and assessments, with the goal of securing additional financial support for a second voyage. The letter describes his enchantment with the natural beauty of the islands and his impressions of the "innocent" inhabitants. But it is also evident that Columbus was somewhat disappointed and remained uncertain whether he had discovered anything of great importance. He found neither great cities nor civilized peoples, and although the islands might hold potential wealth, they were not his intended object of discovery.

QUESTIONS TO CONSIDER

1. What were Columbus's primary motives, as declared in the prologue to his logbook? How do these compare with the ones revealed in his descriptions of Hispaniola and Cuba? How might one account for the differences?
2. Columbus portrays most of the island inhabitants as "innocent" and "timid." What led him to these conclusions? What impact did this perception have on his behavior? In your estimation, did Columbus take advantage of the innocence and generosity of the inhabitants?

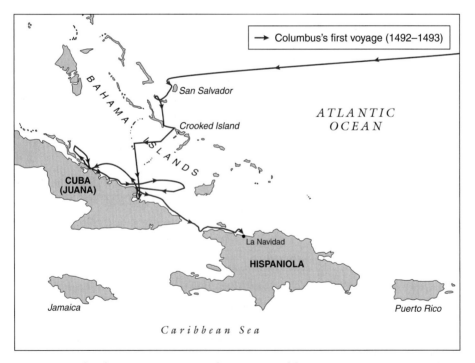

Map 15.5 Columbus's First Voyage to the "New World"

3. Columbus says of Hispaniola, "It is a land to be desired, and when seen, never to be left." What did he consider to be the attractions on Hispaniola? Did these portend future relationships between Europeans and the indigenous islanders?

4. At the end of his letter, Columbus made a direct appeal for more financial assistance from the Spanish monarchy. Might this request have affected the way in which he described his discoveries?

5. Columbus specifically noted two distinct future policies in the New World: the conversion of the indigenous peoples to Christianity and the pursuit of wealth from the accumulation of gold and other resources. Based on his own explanations, were these two goals compatible? Why or why not?

PROLOGUE TO THE LOGBOOK OF THE FIRST VOYAGE (1492)

Christopher Columbus

Most Christian and most exalted and most excellent and most mighty princes, King and Queen of the Spains* and of the islands of the sea, our sovereigns. . . . [In] this present year of 1492, your Highnesses concluded a [successful] end of the war with the Moors who reigned in Europe . . . and as Catholic Christians and as princes devoted to the holy Christian faith and its propagators, and enemies of the sect of Mahomet [Muhammad] and of all idolatries and heresies, took thought to send me, Christopher Columbus, to India, to see the princes and peoples and lands and . . . the manner which should be used to bring about their conversion to our Holy Faith. . . . I shall not go [to India] to the eastward, by which way it was the custom to go, but by way of the west, by which down to this day we do not know certainly that any one has passed. . . . [This voyage] has accorded me great rewards and ennobled me so that from that time henceforward I might style myself *Don*† and be high admiral of the Ocean Sea and [become] perpetual governor of the islands and [lands] which I should discover. . . . To this end, I thought to write all this journey very carefully . . . in which I will set all the seas and lands of the Ocean Sea in their true places. . . . And all these things will be a great enterprise.

Source: Christopher Columbus, *The Voyages of Christopher Columbus, Being the Journals of his First and Third, and the Letters Concerning his First and Last Voyages,* trans. and ed. Cecil Jane (London: Argonaut Press, 1930), 135–36.

*The marriage of King Fernando and Queen Ysabel united the formerly separate Spanish kingdoms of Aragon, Castile, and Leon.

†A title of nobility.

LETTER DESCRIBING HIS FIRST VOYAGE (1493)

Christopher Columbus

Since I know that you will be pleased at the great victory with which Our Lord has crowned my voyage, I write this to you, from which you will learn how in thirty-three days I passed from the Canary Islands to the Indies, with the fleet which the most illustrious king and queen, our sovereigns, gave to me. There I found very many islands, filled with people innumerable, and of them all I have taken possession for their Highnesses, by proclamation made and with the royal standard unfurled, and no opposition was offered to me.

To the first island which I found I gave the name "San Salvador," in remembrance of the blessed Savior, who had marvelously bestowed all this; the Indians call it "Guanahani." To the second island, I gave the name "Santa Maria de Concepcion" [Rum Cay]; to the third, "Fernandina"; to the fourth, "Isabella" . . . and so each island received a new name from me.*

When I came to Juana [Cuba], I followed its coast to the westward, and I found it to be so extensive that I thought that it must be the mainland, the province of Cathay [China]. And since there were neither towns nor villages on the seashore, but only small villages whose residents all fled immediately, I continued along the coast, thinking that I could not fail to find great cities and towns. At the end of many miles, seeing that there was no change . . . I retraced my path back to a remarkable harbor known to me. From that point, I sent two men inland to learn if there were a king or great cities. They traveled three days' journey, finding many small villages and numerous people, but nothing of importance, and so they returned.

I understood sufficiently from other Indians, whom I had previously seized there, that this land was nothing but an island, and I therefore followed its coast eastward for over three hundred miles to the point where it ended. From that point, I saw another island to the east, distant about fifty miles, and I gave it the name "Hispana" [Hispaniola].† I sailed there and followed its northern coast eastward for over five hundred miles.

This island and all the others are very fertile. . . . [Along the coast of Hispaniola] are many harbors, beyond comparison with others that I know in Christendom, and many rivers, good and large. Its lands are high, and there are many sierras and very lofty mountains. . . . [All the islands] are most beautiful, of a thousand shapes; all are accessible and are filled with trees of a thousand kinds, and so tall that they seem to touch the sky. I am told that they never lose their foliage, and this I can believe, for I saw them as green and lovely as they are in Spain in May, and some of them were

Source: Christopher Columbus, *The Voyages of Christopher Columbus, Being the Journals of his First and Third, and the Letters Concerning his First and Last Voyages,* trans. and ed. Cecil Jane (London: Argonaut Press, 1930), 259–64.

*All of these islands are part of the present-day Bahamas.

†The large island of Hispaniola is now divided between the nations of Haiti and the Dominican Republic. It is believed that Columbus's first voyage took him to the north coast of Haiti.

flowering, some bearing fruit. . . . There are six or eight kinds of palm, which are a wonder to behold on account of their beautiful variety, but so are the other trees and fruits and plants. There are also marvelous pine groves, very wide and smiling plains, birds of many kinds, and fruits and honey in great diversity. In the interior, there are mines of metals, and the population is without number.

Hispana [Hispaniola] is a marvel. The sierras and the mountains, the plains, the arable and pasture lands, are so lovely and so rich for planting and sowing, for breeding cattle of every kind, and for building towns and villages. The harbors of the sea here are such as cannot be believed to exist unless they have been seen, and so with the rivers, many and great, and of good water, the majority of which contain gold. In the trees, fruits and plants, there is a great difference from those of Juana [Cuba]. In this island, there are many spices and great mines of gold and of other metals.

The people of this island, and of all the other islands which I have found and of which I have information, all go naked, men and women, as their mothers bore them, although some of the women cover a single place with the leaf of a plant or with a net of cotton which they make for the purpose. They have no iron or steel or weapons, nor are they inclined to use them. This is not because they are not well built and of handsome stature, but because they are very timid. They have no other arms than spears made of reeds, to which they fix a small sharpened stick. They do not dare to make use of these weapons against us, for many times it has happened that I have sent ashore two or three men to some town to have speech with them, and countless people have come out to them, and as soon as they have seen my men approaching, they have fled, a father not even waiting for his son. This is not because we have done them any harm; on the contrary, at every place where I have been and have been able to have speech with them, I have given gifts to them, such as cloth and many other things, receiving nothing in exchange. But they remain by nature incurably timid.

It is true that, once they have been reassured and have lost their fear of us, they are so innocent and so generous with all that they possess, that no one would believe it who has not seen it. They refuse nothing that they possess if it be asked of them. On the contrary, they invite any one to share it and display as much love as if they would give their hearts. They are content with whatever trifle or gift that is given to them, whether it be of value or valueless. I forbade that they should be given things so worthless as fragments of broken crockery, scraps of broken glass and ends of straps, although when they were able to get them, they fancied that they possessed the best jewel in the world. A sailor once received gold equal to the weight of two and a half coins for a little piece of strap, and others received much more for other things which were worth less. . . . They took even the pieces of the broken hoops of the wine barrels and, like savages, gave what they had, but this seemed to me to be wrong and I forbade it. I gave them a thousand handsome good things, which I had brought, in order that they might conceive affection for us and, more than that, might become Christians and be inclined to the love and service of your Highnesses and of the whole Spanish nation, and strive to aid us and to give us of the things which they have in abundance and which are necessary to us.

They do not hold any creed nor are they idolaters; they only believe that power and good are in the heavens. . . . This belief is not the result of ignorance, for they are actually of a very acute intelligence, they know how to navigate the seas, and it is amazing how good an account they give of everything. [Instead], this belief is because they have never seen people clothed or ships such as ours.

As soon as I arrived in the Indies, I took by force some natives at the first island that I found in order that they might give me information about these places. And so it was that they soon understood us, and we them, either by speech or signs, and they have been very helpful. I still have them with me, and they are always assured that I come from Heaven, despite all the discussions which they have had with me. They were the first to announce this wherever I went in the islands, and others went running from house to house, and to neighboring towns, crying loudly "Come! Come! See the men from Heaven!" So all, men and women alike, once their fear was set at rest, came out to welcome us, and they all brought something to eat and drink, which they gave with extraordinary affection and generosity.

In all the islands, they have very many canoes, which are like our rowboats, except they are not so broad, because they are made of a single log of wood. But a rowboat would not be able to keep up with them, since their speed is incredible. In these they navigate among all the islands, and carry their goods and conduct trade. In one of these canoes I have seen with seventy and eighty men, each one with his oar.

In all these islands, I saw no great diversity in the appearance of the people or in their manners and language. On the contrary, they all understand one another . . . and if their Highnesses assent, this will [assist] their conversion to our holy faith of Christ, to which they are very ready and favorably inclined.

I have already said how I went three hundred miles in a straight line from west to east along the seashore of the island of Juana [Cuba], and as a result of this voyage I can say that this island is larger than England and Scotland together. . . . There remains to the westward on this island two provinces to which I have not gone. One of these provinces they call "Avan," and I am told that the people here are born with tails. . . . The other island, Hispana [Hispaniola], has a circumference greater than all Spain. . . . It is a land to be desired and, when seen, never to be left. I have taken possession of this island and all others for their Highnesses so that they may dispose of them as they wish, and all are more richly endowed than I know how or am able to say. Hispana [Hispaniola] is the most conveniently located, and it has the greatest potential for gold mines and all other trade. I have taken possession of a large town, to which I gave the name "Villa de Navidad" [located on the north coast of Haiti], and in it I have made a fort, which by now will be entirely completed. At this fort, I have left enough men as seemed necessary, with arms and artillery and provisions for more than a year, as well as one of our ships and enough skilled men to build others. I also established great friendship with the king of that land, so much so that he was proud to call me "brother" and to treat me as such. And even were the king to change his attitude to one of hostility towards the men left behind, he does not have the power to hurt us. As I have already related, the natives go naked and they are the most timid people in the world, so that the few men whom I have left there alone could destroy them all. The island is without danger if our men follow the regulations and orders that we gave them.

In all these islands, it seems to me that each man is content with one wife, except the chiefs or kings who may have as many as twenty wives. It appears to me that the women work more than the men. I have not been able to learn if they hold private property, but it seemed to me that they all shared what they had, especially of eatable things. In these islands I have so far found no human monstrosities, as many expected . . . on the contrary, the whole population is very well formed. They are not black like the people in Guinea [West Africa], but their hair is flowing. . . .

And so I have found no monsters, nor have I heard of any, except on an island called Charis. . . . This island is inhabited by a people* who are regarded in all the islands as very fierce, and they are cannibals who eat human flesh. They have many canoes with which they range through all the islands of India and pillage and take whatever they can. They are no more malformed than are the others, except that they have the custom of wearing their hair long like women, and they use bows and arrows. . . . They are ferocious towards these other people who are excessively cowardly, but I regard them as no more fearsome than the others. . . . I have also been told of another island, which they assure me is larger than Hispana, where the people have no hair. In this place there is reportedly incalculable amounts of gold. . . .

To conclude this report . . . their Highnesses can see that I can supply them as much gold as they may need if their Highnesses will continue to assist [my voyages]. Moreover, I will provide them spices and cotton, as much as their Highnesses shall command; and mastic and aloe, as much as they shall order to be shipped; and slaves, as many as they shall order to be shipped and who will be from the idolaters. I believe also that I have found rhubarb and cinnamon, and I shall find a thousand other things of value. . . .

Our thanksgiving must be directed the most to the eternal God, Our Lord, Who gives to all those who walk in His way triumph over things which appear to be impossible, and this was one such glorious example. For although men have talked or have written of these distant lands, all was conjectural and without evidence. . . . It is our Redeemer who has given the victory to our most illustrious king and queen, and to their renowned kingdom . . . and all Christendom ought to feel delight and make great feasts and give solemn thanks to our Lord and Savior Jesus Christ, with many solemn prayers for the great exaltation which they shall have in the turning of so many pagan peoples to our Holy Faith, and afterwards for the temporal benefits, because not only Spain but all Christendom will have hence refreshment and gain.

These deeds that have been accomplished are thus briefly recorded while aboard ship, off the Canary Islands, on the fifteenth of February, in the year one thousand four hundred and ninety-three. I remain, at your orders and your service.

The Admiral

NOTES

1. Exploration and expansion have been constants in human history and can be seen in the early evolution of migration patterns, the creation of long-distance trade, and, in many cases, the formation of states and empires.

---

*Columbus is referring to the Caribs, from whom the "Caribbean" gets its name. Scholars believe the Caribs emigrated to the islands of the Caribbean from South America and took advantage of their warrior skills to raid and prey upon the indigenous peoples of the islands, the Arawaks.

2. In some cases, such as the remote interior regions of Africa, these accounts are among the few written sources available for this time period.

3. The *hajj* is the annual pilgrimage to Mecca to worship and visit the holy sites of Islam. It is one of the five "Pillars of Faith," a duty that devout Muslims are expected to undertake once in their lifetimes, if possible. Some scholars have suggested that the ritual and celebration of the *hajj* has created a stimulus for travel that surpasses the rite of Christian pilgrimages during the Middle Ages.

4. In 1279, the Mongols had successfully invaded China and created their own dynasty (Yuan dynasty), the first instance when foreigners ruled over China. But the Mongols were mostly content to impose their rule only in the highest positions of authority, and they actually succeeded in linking China more closely with the outside world via Mongol-controlled overland trade networks in central Asia. Nonetheless, the rule of foreign "barbarians" over the illustrious "Middle Kingdom" proved intolerable to the Chinese, and in 1368, Chinese armies defeated the Mongols and reestablished their authority.

5. Some scholars suggest that the Confucian virtues of cultivating family and ancestral bonds were perceived by later Ming emperors to be in disharmony with the motives and actions inherent in exploration.

6. See the readings in chapter 14 that focus on cultural reactions to disease and bubonic plague.

7. Literally translates as the "Reconquest" and refers to the period of Christian holy war against Muslim control of Spain and Portugal that began as early as the tenth century but that culminated in the expulsion of Muslims (and Jews) from Spain in 1492.

8. The *Columbian Exchange* is a broad term used by historians to refer to the global spread of plants, animals, and diseases following the voyages of Christopher Columbus.

9. Mecca and Medina are both located in the mountainous regions along the Red Sea in the Arabian peninsula. Mecca was the birthplace of Muhammad, and it is the prime site for pilgrimages in Islam (the *hajj*). Medina was the city where Muhammad built a following, and it remains his burial place. Together, they represent two of the most holy sites in Islam.

10. Zhu Di, also known as the Yongle Emperor (1403–1424), was the third Ming emperor, whose great ambition was to rebuild Chinese power following the rule of the Mongols.

11. Scurvy is a painful and life-threatening disease caused by a deficiency in vitamin C (ascorbic acid). It was once a widespread malady among crewmen of sailing ships on long voyages due to the lack of fresh fruits and vegetables.

12. Beginning sometime in the ninth or tenth century, Muslim traders from Arabia moved to coastal towns in east Africa to facilitate their commercial activities. They frequently settled down and married African women, and their future progeny, language, and society became known as Swahili, a mixing of African and Arab bloodlines and cultures. By the time of da Gama's visit, generations of Swahili governed prosperous independent city-states along the coast from present-day Mozambique to Somalia.

CREDITS

❧❧❧

PHOTOS

Page 8: *1.1A top* Simon D. Pollard/Photo Researchers, Inc.; *1.1A bottom* E. R. Degginger/Photo Researchers, Inc.; *1.1B-J* Human Origins Program Dept. of Anthropology National Museum of Natural History Smithsonian Institution. **Page 10:** *1.2* UC Berkeley Department of Anthropology Collection Peter Bostrom/LithicCasting Lab.com; *1.3* © AAAC/Topham/The Image Works; *1.4* UC Berkeley Department of Anthropology Collection Peter Bostrom/LithicCasting Lab.com. **Page 12:** *1.5* © Archivo Iconografico, S.A./Corbis. **Page 13:** *1.6* The Art Archive/Musée des Antiquités St Germain en Laye/Dagli Orti; *1.7* Courtesy of Olga Soffer. **Page 15:** *1.8* © Francis G. Mayer/Corbis. **Page 16:** *1.9* © Jean-Marc Charles/Corbis; *1.10* © The Bridgeman Art Library. **Page 17:** *1.11* © Ali Meyer/Corbis. **Page 18:** *1.12* Courtesy of Randall White, Institute of Ice Age Studies. **Page 19:** *1.13* Courtesy of Randall White, Institute of Ice Age Studies; *1.14* Courtesy of Randall White, Institute of Ice Age Studies. **Page 23:** *1.15* Bildarchiv Preussischer Kulturbesitz/Art Resource, NY; *1.16* Courtesy of Indiana University Archives (2000/061-FPG 15.2). **Page 27:** *1.19* Erich Lessing/Art Resource, NY. **Page 28:** *1.20* © J. M. Kenoyer, Courtesy of Department of Archaeology and Museums, Government of Pakistan and Harappa.com. **Page 29:** *1.21* Werner Forman/Art Resource, NY. **Page 215:** *8.1* © Royalty-Free/Corbis; *8.2* © Burstein Collection/Corbis. **Page 220:** *8.3* © Victoria & Albert Museum, London/Art Resource, NY; *8.4* Indiana University Art Museum. **Page 227:** *8.5* © Scala/Art Resource, NY; *8.6* © Erich Lessing/Art Resource, NY. **Page 234:** *8.7* Courtesy of www.islamcity.com. **Page 403:** *14.1* © Scala/Art Resource, NY. **Page 404:** *14.2* © Scala/Art Resource, NY. **Page 405:** *14.3* © Erich Lessing/Art Resource, NY. **Page 406:** *14.4* © The Bridgeman Art Library; *14.5* © The Bridgeman Art Library. **Page 407:** *14.6* © The Bridgeman Art Library; *14.7* Courtesy of the US National Library of Medicine. **Page 408:** *14.8* From Albert S. Lyons and R. Joseph Petrucelli, *Medicine: An Illustrated History* (New York: Abradale Press, 1987), page 351.

	400	600	800	900	1000
ASIA					
SOUTHWEST ASIA	Justinian (527–565) Hagia Sophia *Corpus iuris civilis* Birth of Muhammad (571)	Sasanid dynasty ends (651) Muhammad's migration to Medina (622) Muslim conquests of Mesopotamia, Persia, and Egypt	Zanj revolt in Mesopotamia (869–883)	Hajj of Jamila bint Nasir al-Dawla (976–977)	Philosophers al Ghazali and Ibn Rushd Saljuq Turk leader Tughril Beg recognized as sultan Battle of Manzikert (1071)
EAST AND CENTRAL ASIA	Sui dynasty (589–618) Yang Jian (589–604)	Sui Yangdi (604–618) Grand Canal Tang dynasty (618–907) Tang Taizong (627–649) Xuanzang's journey to India (629–645) Silla dynasty in Korea (7th century) Nara period in Japan (710–794) An Lushan rebellion (755–757) Heian period in Japan (794–1185)	Huang Chao rebellion (875–884)	Song dynasty (960–1279) Song Taizu (960–976) Invention of magnetic compass	*The Tale of Genji* by Murasaki Shikibu Song movable type and paper money Jurchen overrun northern China (12th century) Kamakura shogunate
SOUTH AND SOUTHEAST ASIA	Invasion of White Huns (451)	Harsha (606–648) Arab forces enter India (mid-7th century) Kingdom of Srivijaya on Sumatra (670–1025) Sind falls to Umayyad conquerors (711)	Hindu philosopher Shau Kara (9th century) Chola kingdom (850–1267) Angkor kingdom of Cambodia (889–1431) *Book of the Wonders of India* by Buzurg ibn Shahriyar		Mahmud of Ghazni invades India (1001–1027) Hindu philosopher Ramanuja (early 11th century) Bhakti movement (early 12th century) Buddhist city of Nalanda overrun by Islamic forces (1196)
AFRICA	Establishment of the Kingdom of Ghana		Revolt of east African slaves in Mesopotamia (869–883)	Kings of Ghana convert to Islam (10th century)	Swahili city-states dominate east African coastal trade
AMERICAS & OCEANIA	Development of Maya calendar and writing High point of Teotihuacan state in Mesoamerica (400–600) Austronesians reach Easter Island Spread of sweet potatoes throughout Pacific islands (400–700)	High point of Maya state of Tikal (600–800) Austronesians reach New Zealand Establishment of Pueblo and Navaho societies in North America	Decline of Maya society	Collapse of Teotihuacan Kingdom of Chimu in South America Cahokia mound in North America (900–1250) Toltecs in Mesoamerica (950–1150)	Owasco tribes in North America Establishment of trade networks in central Pacific Development of complex hierarchical societies in Pacific islands
EUROPE & MEDITERRANEAN BASIN	Germanic general Odoacer deposes last Roman emperor (476) Migration and conquests of Visigoths, Ostrogoths, Franks, Lombards St. Benedict of Nursia (480–547) Conversion of Clovis (481–511) Benedict's Rule St. Scholastica (482–543) Invention of heavy plow (6th century) Pope Gregory I (590–604)	Emperor Leo III (717–741) Charles Martel (700s) Charlemagne (768–814)	Louis the Pious (814–840) Division of Charlemagne's empire (843) Saints Cyril and Methodius (mid-9th century) Vikings raid Russia, Germany, England, Ireland, France, Spain King Otto of Saxony (936–973) Foundation of Holy Roman Empire (962) Conversion of Prince Vladimir of Kiev (989)	Otto of Saxony crowned by Pope John XII (962) Foundation of Holy Roman Empire Hugh Capet (987)	Vikings reach Newfoundland (1000) Leif Ericsson reached Newfoundland (1000) Split between Eastern Orthodox and Roman Catholic churches (1054) William of Normandy conquers England (1066) Battle of Manzikert (1071) Conflict between Pope Gregory VII and Holy Roman Emperor Henry IV (1077) First crusade (1096–1099)